The Vulnerability of Empire

A volume in the series

CORNELL STUDIES IN SECURITY AFFAIRS

edited by Robert J. Art, Robert Jervis,
and Stephen M. Walt

A full list of titles in the series appears at the end of the book.

The Vulnerability of Empire

CHARLES A. KUPCHAN

Cornell University Press

ITHACA AND LONDON

First published 1994 by Cornell University Press.

Printed in the United States of America

♾ The paper in this book meets the minimum requirements of the
American National Standard for Information Sciences—Permanence
of Paper for Printed Library Materials, ANSI Z39.48-1984.

Library of Congress Cataloging-in-Publication Data

Kupchan, Charles.
  The vulnerability of empire / Charles A. Kupchan.
    p.   cm. — (Cornell studies in security affairs)
  Includes bibliographical references and index.
  ISBN 0-8014-2885-8 (cloth : alk. paper)—ISBN 0-8014-8124-4
(pbk. : alk. paper)
    1. National security.   2. Military policy.   3. Balance of power.
4. World politics—20th century.   I. Title.   II. Series.
UA10.5.K85   1993
355'.03—dc20   93-24323

For S. Morris Kupchan and
Nancy Kupchan Sonis

Contents

Acknowledgments

I am indebted to many individuals and institutions for their contributions to this book. For their comments on the manuscript, I thank Robert Art, Michael Barnhart, Guenter Bischof, Michael Brown, Thomas Christensen, Anthony Clayton, Wolfgang Danspeckgruber, George Downs, Matthew Evangelista, David French, John Gaddis, Alexander George, Charlie Glaser, Will Hitchcock, Michael Howard, John Ikenberry, Richard Immerman, Akira Iriye, Harold James, A. S. Kanya-Forstner, Peter Katzenstein, Chaim Kaufmann, Clifford Kupchan, Patricia Lane, Melvyn Leffler, Jack Levy, Ariel Levite, John Mearsheimer, James Miller, Douglas Porch, Tina Rosenberg, Nick Rizopoulos, Scott Sagan, Randy Schweller, Eldar Shafir, Jack Snyder, Peter Trubowitz, Stephen Van Evera, Patrick Weil, Stephen Walt, and William Wohlforth. I would also like to express my gratitude—and my apologies—to those whom I have failed to mention by name, either because of lapsed memory or because their comments were offered at one of the many seminars in which I presented earlier versions of this project.

My students at Princeton University provided a steady source of feedback as the book evolved. I had the luxury of teaching a course that was based on the research carried out for this project, allowing me to try out my ideas before an attentive and challenging audience. Several students also provided invaluable assistance with research: Lisa Arone, Olga Bokman, Cherrie Daniels, Will Gray, Jon Kirshner and Naomi Mobed.

I embarked on this project when I was a Ford Fellow at Harvard's Center for International Affairs. I would like to thank the Center and its former director, Samuel Huntington, for providing a stimulating and inspiring environment. My colleagues at Princeton University and the staff of Princeton's Firestone Library offered welcome encouragement and assistance throughout the project. The staff of Britain's Public Record Office (PRO) was very helpful and eased the burden of archival research. Material from the PRO has been reproduced with the permission of the Controller of Her Britannic Majesty's Stationery Office. During my stay in London, the International Institute for Strategic Studies provided a needed escape from the archives and a host of colleagues with whom to argue about grand strategy, past and present. I also thank the staff of France's military archives for their assistance; material has been reproduced with the permission of the Service Historique de l'Armée de Terre. The *Centre d'Etude et de Recherches Internationales* enriched my time in Paris by serving as a meeting place for scholars and as a beautiful setting in which to transform scribblings from the archives into something resembling prose. A sabbatical year at Columbia University's Institute for War and Peace Studies provided a stimulating and welcoming refuge and allowed me to make significant progress in writing the manuscript.

Working with Cornell University Press has been a pleasure. From the outset, Roger Haydon offered valuable assistance and encouragement. Kim Vivier did an excellent job of editing the manuscript. Just as the book was entering its final stages, I joined the staff of the National Security Council and saw my time for scholarly pursuits virtually disappear; Joanne Hindman was more than patient in dealing with the resultant delays.

Financial support for this book was provided by the Pew Charitable Trusts Program on Integrating Economics and National Security, Princeton's Center of International Studies, and Princeton's University Committee on Research in the Social Sciences and Humanities.

My greatest debt of gratitude is to my parents, to whom this book is dedicated. Through example and encouragement, they instilled in me the curiosity, the discipline, and the creativity that made this work possible.

CHARLES A. KUPCHAN

Washington, D.C.

The Vulnerability of Empire

[1]

Great Powers and International Change: The Challenge of Strategic Adjustment

Soon after embarking on a major naval construction program in 1898, Germany found its bid for European dominance blocked by a powerful coalition of Britain, France, and Russia. Rather than scaling back the scope of their imperial ambition, German leaders stepped up their armaments program and intensified their efforts to intimidate and fragment the Triple Entente. But in doing so, they triggered the outbreak of World War I and the bloody battles that led to their country's defeat.

During the second half of the 1930s France and Britain were faced with a formidable rearmament program in Nazi Germany and successive bouts of German aggression in central Europe. Despite the clear warning signs, French and British elites failed to take adequate steps to prepare their forces for continental war and continued to focus on the defense of their vast overseas empires. As a result, Hitler's troops ran roughshod over much of Europe.

In 1941, Japanese elites realized that extending their empire into Southeast Asia would likely lead to war with the Western powers. But Japanese leaders did not rein in their imperial aspirations. Instead, Japanese troops pushed southward while Japanese aircraft attacked the U.S. fleet at Pearl Harbor, triggering full-scale war against a coalition of vastly superior military and industrial capability.

The United States in 1950 embarked on a new and much more ambitious program to contain Soviet expansionism. The Truman administration formed alliances around the perimeter of the Soviet Union, dramatically increased U.S. conventional and nuclear forces, and made clear its intention to resist the spread of communism throughout the world. Instead of enhancing U.S. security, however, this new course fueled the arms race between East and West, heightened Cold War tensions, and lured the United States into costly and protracted Third World conflicts.

All of these historical episodes share a common, and intriguing, feature: great powers that enjoyed a position at or near the top of the international hierarchy pursued policies that undermined their security. To varying degrees and in different ways, each engaged in self-defeating behavior. Although scholars have frequently studied the decline of empires, they have devoted little attention to explaining why great powers often pursue self-defeating policies.[1] Scholarly research on the rise and fall of empires has focused primarily on why maturing empires tend to experience relative economic decline and why technological prowess and productive capability drift from the center to the periphery of the international system.[2] I focus on a different puzzle posed by the phenomenon of imperial rise and decline: Are great powers aware of shifts in the international distribution of power and the implications of those shifts for their security? If so, why are they frequently unable to adjust their foreign policies accordingly? At critical points of international change, how do states go about adapting to a new strategic landscape and why are they often unable to strike a balance between resources and commitments?

Because the international system has experienced striking changes in recent years, a study of how states react to shifts in the international distribution of wealth and military power is both timely and important. The dismantling of the Warsaw Pact, the retraction of Soviet control from Eastern Europe, and the breakup of the Soviet Union itself have led to a dramatic restructuring of international relations: the Cold War is over. In the economic realm, the Pacific Basin has joined Western Europe and the United States as one of the key centers of productivity and technological innovation. Western Europe, including a unified Germany, moves toward further economic integration. Economic development in countries such as China, India, and Brazil promises to lead to the further diffusion of productive capability. This dispersion of the nodes of economic activity has already been accompanied by the spread of sophisticated military technologies. The bipolarity of the Cold War is gradually giving way to a multipolar international setting.

Policy makers around the globe are now seeking to understand how best to adapt to these changes. Successful adaptation is important to states seeking prosperity and security in an environment in flux. As-

---

[1] The main exception is Jack Snyder, *Myths of Empire: Domestic Politics and International Ambition* (Ithaca: Cornell University Press, 1991).

[2] Robert Gilpin, *War and Change in World Politics* (New York: Cambridge University Press, 1981); and Paul Kennedy, *The Rise and Fall of the Great Powers* (New York: Random House, 1987). For a work focusing more on the political dynamics that affect the cohesion and stability of empires, see Michael Doyle, *Empires* (Ithaca: Cornell University Press, 1986).

[2]

sessing and adjusting to change is also of critical importance because major wars have often resulted from shifts in the international balance of power. Scholars have frequently pointed to a disequilibrium between the international order and the underlying distribution of power in the international system as a major source of hegemonic war.[3] Timely and appropriate adjustment to these structural shifts is therefore essential to effecting peaceful change. The nuclear age, because of the potentially catastrophic consequences of great-power conflict, makes especially urgent the need to examine pathways to facilitate peaceful transition.

THE PUZZLE

Over the last two centuries, great powers have frequently confronted rapidly shifting strategic environments. At times, these powers have readily adapted their foreign and defense policies to changes in the strategic landscape.[4] At other times, they either have failed to adjust or have adjusted inappropriately to these changes, often leaving the state pursuing policies that jeopardize its primary security interests.[5] States fall prey to two main types of adjustment failure. One involves overly cooperative behavior and results in *strategic exposure*. The other involves overly competitive behavior and results in either *self-encirclement* or *overextension*. States are overly cooperative when they fail to take reasonable steps to balance against rising threats to primary secu-

---

[3] See, for example, Gilpin, *War and Change*; A. F. K. Organski and Jacek Kugler, *The War Ledger* (Chicago: University of Chicago Press, 1980); and Geoffrey Blainey, *The Causes of War* (Basingstoke: Macmillan, 1988).

[4] Adaptation to international change can take many forms. I am concerned exclusively with how grand strategy can be adjusted to bring economic and military resources (means) into balance with international commitments (ends). *Grand strategy* refers to a state's overall plan for providing national security by keeping military resources and external commitments in balance. This focus on grand strategy restricts the scope of the inquiry to relatively short-term questions of foreign and defense policy. Adjustments to grand strategy take the form of diplomatic and military initiatives aimed at augmenting or redistributing resources (increased extraction from the domestic polity or colonial territories, reallocation of forces, alliance formation) or decreasing commitments (retrenchment, diplomatic resolution of disputes, alliance formation). Long-term adjustments to international change such as renewal of industrial infrastructure or reorientation of economic base thus lie outside the scope of this book.

[5] Successful adjustment should not be equated simply with a state's ability to cope with external threats. A country may adjust to a new constellation of power to the best of its ability, but nevertheless be defeated by an adversary with preponderant military and economic resources. Successful adjustment must therefore be measured in terms of a state's ability to identify primary strategic interests (ends) and to allocate available resources (means) so as to protect those interests. The process of successful adjustment should take the form of reasonable efforts to bring means and ends into balance.

[3]

rity interests. By repeatedly accommodating the demands of adversaries and failing to prepare adequately for deterrence and defense, states fall prey to strategic exposure. States are overly competitive when they pursue expansionist policies that succeed only in undermining their security. When expansionist behavior provokes confrontation with a robust opposing coalition in the core, the state falls prey to self-encirclement. When the state engages in expansion in the periphery that only weakens the metropole's military and economic strength, it falls prey to overextension.[6] The costs of building empire and engaging in protracted conflict with imperial competitors may simply outstrip the benefits and distract needed resources from the metropole. Whether through self-encirclement or overextension, overly competitive behavior saddles the state with a range of international commitments that it is unable to uphold.

Studying the causes of strategic exposure, self-encirclement, and overextension entails asking not why states choose to cooperate or compete with potential adversaries, but why they sometimes pursue cooperation or competition to excess, to a degree that is self-defeating.[7] It makes sense that states should at times cooperate with potential adversaries, especially when those adversaries are motivated by insecurity. Cooperation can avoid unintended spirals of hostility. It can also lead to the resolution of outstanding disputes and enable a state to disengage from some of its external commitments without fearing exploitation. It does not make sense, however, that states should persistently make concessions to adversaries that exhibit aggressive intent or leave themselves open to exploitation by failing to balance against ex-

---

[6] Even though the costs of building peripheral empire may frequently exceed the benefits, great powers are often able to absorb such costs without jeopardizing primary security interests. I restrict the notion of overextension to refer only to instances in which peripheral expansion occurs at a clear cost to metropolitan security. *Metropole* refers to the homeland of a state that annexes regions, acquires colonial possessions, or makes strategic commitments in areas outside the homeland. *Core* refers to the metropole and regions that, because of either geographic proximity or geostrategic importance, have an immediate and direct bearing on metropolitan security. *Periphery* refers to regions separated by a considerable distance from the metropole that do not have immediate and direct bearing on the security of the homeland. In the case of Great Britain, for example, the metropole consists of the British isles, the core of Britain and Europe, and the periphery of extra-European regions.

[7] Competitive behavior entails standing firm in disputes with other states and maintaining superiority or keeping pace with other states in terms of military capability. Cooperative behavior entails accommodating the demands of other states and making either mutual or unilateral concessions in terms of relative military capability. It is admittedly an oversimplification to assume that states face a dichotomous choice between competition and cooperation in interacting with other states. Obviously, there are many gradations of competitive and cooperative behavior, and states often pursue policies that reflect a mix of both types of behavior. Nevertheless, the notions of competition and cooperation do capture the essential choice that states face in interacting with one another in the international arena.

[4]

ternal threats. Similarly, it stands to reason that states should at times compete with potential adversaries, especially when those adversaries are motivated by aggressive intent. So too do even expansionist policies make sense as long as the resulting expansion contributes to the security of the metropole.[8] But it does not stand to reason that states should pursue competitive policies that lead to self-destructive aggression against an opposing preponderant coalition or to the acquisition of a range of peripheral commitments that undermines metropolitan security. This book addresses the causes of overly cooperative and overly competitive policies. My objective is to understand why great powers engage in self-defeating behavior.

Given this agenda, this book is of necessity about power. Studying international power lies at the center of the research agenda in international relations. This study parts company with the mainstream literature, however, in an important respect: it is concerned not only with the material constituents of power, but also with how elites and masses think about and understand power.[9] In addition to focusing on economic and military capability, the analysis focuses on how elites assess and interpret the distribution of power and how these assessments and interpretations shape grand strategy. In this respect, the book is concerned with the beliefs that inform elite decisions about strategic priorities and how best to protect the state's security. I also focus on mass attitudes and the collective images and conceptions of national security that spread throughout the broader political community. Most studies are concerned with the ability of self-interested governmental or nongovernmental actors to manipulate policy to maximize material gains. Instead, I concentrate on how *strategic culture*—deeply embedded conceptions and notions of national security that take root among elites and the public alike—affects decisions and shapes the policy-making process. Strategic culture, the realm of national identity and national self-image, consists of images and symbols that shape how a polity understands the relationship between metropolitan security and empire, conceives of its position in the international hierarchy, and perceives the nature and scope of the nation's external ambition. These images and symbols at once mold public attitudes and become institutionalized and routinized in the structure and process of decision mak-

---

[8] I use the notion of expansion to refer not only to territorial conquest, but also to efforts to increase the state's relative power position by building up military force or through diplomatic initiatives.

[9] I use the term *elites* and *decision makers* synonymously to refer to those individuals responsible for formulating and implementing foreign and defense policy. To study their motivations and beliefs offers the most direct and accurate means of tracing the key considerations that shape policy.

ing; they affect how political leaders, government bureaucracies, and the military services define their central roles and missions. Inasmuch as strategic culture shapes the boundaries of politically legitimate behavior in the realm of foreign policy and affects how elites conceive of the national interest and set strategic priorities, it plays a crucial role in shaping grand strategy. This focus is meant to suggest not that traditional concern about the self-interested behavior of economic interest groups or military officers is misguided, only that it is too narrow. How the polity as a collective entity conceives of national power and understands the value of empire are central to studying the ways in which elites adjust to international change.

I focus on elite beliefs and strategic culture not only because these concepts are essential to constructing a satisfying explanation of the puzzle I have laid out. In addition, I am explicitly addressing an important gap in existing literature. As mentioned, the vast majority of work on power in international relations focuses on material components of power and on how elites *should* understand power rather than how they *do* understand it.[10] The dominant intellectual paradigm in the field—realism—takes material inducement to be the key motivating force behind state behavior. Elite interests are taken as givens: to maximize wealth and security. This approach is intuitively compelling, inasmuch as most states, like most humans, seek prosperity and security. Furthermore, material indices of power are far easier to measure than nonmaterial variables, and data collection presents less of a problem. In a field that values rigor, it is not surprising that scholars shy away from unwieldy variables such as beliefs and strategic culture. As a result of these disciplinary concerns, however, research on where elite and mass interests come from and how decision makers choose among competing options for securing those interests is poorly developed and needs to receive increased attention.

In addition, most attempts to move beyond the realist paradigm attempt to refute, not to modify or qualify, its basic suppositions about the overriding importance of the distribution of power in shaping state behavior in the international arena. As a result, the research agenda in international relations has been intellectually compartmentalized. Some scholars argue that the international distribution of power is the

---

[10] As Aaron Friedberg has noted, "Virtually all of this work [on measuring power] . . . aims to demonstrate how power *should* be evaluated by detached, rational observers rather than to determine how it has been or is being weighed by residents of the real political world." *The Weary Titan: Britain and the Experience of Relative Decline, 1895–1905* (Princeton: Princeton University Press, 1988), p. 12. Friedberg's study and the literature on perception and the psychology of decision making are clear exceptions.

[6]

most important variable shaping state behavior.[11] Others point to the
primacy of domestic politics in determining foreign policies.[12] And a
third group stresses the central importance of cognitive and ideational
variables in guiding state actions in the international arena.[13] This book
eschews such compartmentalization and explicitly seeks to integrate
these three perspectives in explaining outcomes. It addresses how systemic, domestic, and cognitive variables interact in shaping state behavior.[14]

The nature of this study entails a departure from a traditional focus
on material components of power for two additional reasons. First, the
book focuses on historical episodes of relatively short duration in
which elites must react to rapid shifts in the international distribution
of material power. I am concerned with how elites perceive and assimilate these shifts and with whether and how they adapt policy to a new
constellation of power. Material indices of national strength on their
own may be powerful explanatory variables over the long term, but
when faced with the need to make immediate, discrete policy choices
to respond to changes in the external environment, elites are guided
in their allocation of military and economic resources by strategic beliefs and domestic political forces.

Second, the phenomenon of adjustment failure itself confounds realist analysis that rests on material notions of power alone and on the
assumption that states are rational agents. Adjustment failure is so
curious precisely because it leads to outcomes—strategic exposure,
self-encirclement, and overextension—that stand in stark contrast to
the outcomes expected if military and economic power were the key
determinants of state behavior and if states were rational actors. Realist
analysis indicates that states *should* react readily to international
change in order to maximize their security and prosperity. When they
do not, the realist paradigm cannot explain outcomes.[15] To understand

[11] As a primary example, see Kenneth Waltz, *Theory of International Politics* (Reading, Mass.: Addison-Wesley, 1979).

[12] See, for example, Snyder, *Myths of Empire.*

[13] See, for example, Robert Jervis, *Perception and Misperception in International Politics* (Princeton: Princeton University Press, 1976).

[14] This compartmentalization stems in part from methodological considerations. Many recent works in international relations set out to test competing hypotheses drawn from these three levels of analysis. The explicit goal is to determine whether system, state, or individual is the most important variable shaping outcomes. The discipline has also favored mono-causal explanations, strengthening the appeal of this approach. This study begins from the supposition that forces at all three levels of analysis shape international relations. It explicitly sets out to uncover how system, state, and individual interact, not to determine which level of analysis should be privileged or which single variable best explains outcomes.

[15] The realist paradigm could explain outcomes if uncertainty and imperfect information were the main causes of adjustment failure. As I argue in Chapter 2 and in the

why states fail to behave as rational calculators and why elites pursue policies that prove to undermine, rather than enhance, national security, it is necessary to move away from exclusive focus on material notions of power and relax assumptions of state rationality. In addition to studying the effects of the international system on the behavior of states, it is important to probe both the beliefs that inform how elites think about power and set priorities, and the domestic forces that constrain how elites react to international change.

THE HISTORICAL CASES

This theoretical and empirical agenda entails the examination of historical periods in which major powers face significant shifts in the international distribution of military and economic capability. Moreover, the powers under study must perceive the existence of one or more adversaries in both the core and periphery. Under these conditions elites confront the challenge of adjusting grand strategy to a new strategic landscape and deciding whether to cooperate or compete with adversaries. The analysis must focus on episodes of both successful and unsuccessful adjustment. Studying instances of adjustment failure can point to factors contributing to self-defeating behavior, but only by comparing successful and unsuccessful cases is it possible to isolate the critical variables inducing elites to adopt seemingly irrational policies that jeopardize the state's primary security interests.[16] In addition,

---

case studies, however, uncertainty and poor information do not provide an adequate explanation of extremist behavior.

[16] Given my concern with studying the causes of self-defeating behavior, I have deliberately selected cases in which elites made policy choices that clearly jeopardized the state's primary security interests. Readers might object that it is only with the advantage of hindsight that one can discern that elites made inopportune policy choices. At the time that specific decisions were made, skeptics might charge, elites made the best choices they could given available information. Whereas my coding of the cases is shaped by outcomes, I go to considerable lengths in the historical chapters to provide evidence that these outcomes were not the result of uncertainty and miscalculation. I do so by examining the information that elites had before them and showing that, by standards of reasonable judgment, they should have pursued policies other than those they did. Whenever possible, I buttress my interpretation by examining the assessments and policy choices of elites in other countries, who had access to similar information. I also provide evidence that, in many cases, decision makers actually had grave reservations about their own policy choices. They recognized the fundamental flaws in grand strategy but nevertheless continued to pursue policies that jeopardized primary security interests. Objections to my selection and coding of cases are clearly refuted if the elites responsible for the specific decisions that I characterize as extremist are themselves aware of the self-defeating implications of their policy choices. In short, my coding of the cases relies not only on hindsight, but on the information available to decision makers and on their own evaluation of the costs and benefits of alternative policy choices.

[8]

it is important to select historical examples of adjustment failure resulting from overly cooperative policies as well as those resulting from
overly competitive policies. The case studies must also examine both
the behavior of a single state across different time periods and the
behavior of different states during a single time period. Holding state
structure constant while varying external conditions and holding external conditions constant while varying state structure enhances the analytic power of comparative analysis.[17] Furthermore, the book examines
the behavior of states that are ascending the international hierarchy of
power as well as those experiencing relative decline. The aim is to
isolate behavior that may be related to a state's stage of development
or to whether its position in the international hierarchy is rising or
falling. A final consideration shaping the selection of case studies
stems from the impact of changes in technology on the costs and benefits of empire. Because the Industrial Revolution produced a quantum
leap in the ability of leading states to project power to and secure
communications and trade with imperial territories, it fundamentally
changed the nature of empire. In order to maintain consistency on
this technological dimension, the book examines cases only from the
nineteenth and twentieth centuries.[18]

These considerations lead to the following selection of case studies:
Britain (1904–1914, 1932–1939), France (1870–1904, 1904–1914, 1932–
1939, 1949–1954), Japan (1931–1937, 1937–1941), Germany (1870–1897,
1897–1914), and the United States (1945–1949, 1949–1950). Several
guidelines informed the selection of periods and the identification of
historical breakpoints. All the periods examined correspond to times
of rapid change in the international distribution of power. During the
years 1870–1914, Germany's unification and its subsequent emergence
as a premier industrial and military power radically altered power balances in Europe. The period from 1932 to 1939 corresponds to the rise
of Germany and Japan as world-class powers. Between 1945 and 1955,
all major powers were adjusting to the outcome of World War II and

---

[17] It should also be noted that the case studies focus primarily on peacetime decision
making, not on wartime planning. This characteristic of the research design stems from
the observation that state structures and decision-making procedures often change dramatically during war. The balance of decision-making authority between civilian and
military elites tends to shift after war breaks out, and policy makers are more able both
to act without domestic interference and to extract from society the economic and human
resources needed to cope with external threats. Examining wartime decision making
would not be less interesting, but it would constitute a different study altogether.

[18] The Soviet Union is not included in this study largely because of the inability to
gain access to the necessary source materials. The book's focus on elite perceptions of
the balance of power, strategic beliefs, and strategic culture necessitates access to archival
materials or secondary sources based on primary materials.

the emergence of U.S. and Soviet military and economic dominance. The case studies cover periods that are sufficiently long to allow for time lags between assessment of international change and the corresponding policy adjustment, if any. They are sufficiently short to allow for in-depth study of the particular policy dilemmas and debates that follow recognition of a changing constellation of international power. The specific periods examined in each case study are based on the behavior of the state under consideration. Each period corresponds to a phase of relative consistency in grand strategy. The breakpoints mark key changes in grand strategy.[19]

The chapter on Great Britain compares British grand strategy during the 1904–1914 period with that of 1932–1939. During the first period, Britain reacted to the rise of German power by fundamentally reorienting its grand strategy. British elites prepared their navy and army to defend the metropole and pursued competitive policies to deter German expansion. At the same time, they pursued cooperative policies in the periphery to facilitate the withdrawal of their military forces

[19] For Britain, the years 1904–1914 cover the period that begins with Britain's initial strategic reorientation in response to Germany's naval buildup and ends with the outbreak of World War I. The period from 1932 to 1939 encompasses the beginning of Britain's interwar rearmament to the outbreak of World War II. The first French case (1870–1904) begins with the Franco-Prussian War and covers the period during which France acquired a vast colonial empire and integrated this empire into its grand strategy. The year 1904 serves as a key switching point because from then until 1914, France focused on and prepared for war with Germany. The 1932–1939 period covers French rearmament and strategy during the years leading up to the outbreak of World War II. The years 1949–1954 begin with the French decision to increase force levels dramatically in Indochina and ends with Dien Bien Phu and the French decision to withdraw from the war. Although the French were indeed involved in Indochina between 1945 and 1949, it was between 1949 and 1954 that French elites were forced to make stark choices between metropolitan defense and prosecution of the war in the Far East. Within the 1945–1955 decade, the 1949–1954 period is thus the most interesting in terms of the concerns of this study. The first Japanese case begins with the invasion of Manchuria in 1931 and runs until the outbreak of the China war in 1937. During this period, Japanese elites pursued a policy of selective, paced expansion. The year 1937 was a key switching point because, after the outbreak of the China war, elites embarked on a path of self-defeating aggression, eventually leading to the decision to bomb Pearl Harbor in 1941. The first German case runs from the Franco-Prussian War and unification (1870–1871) until 1897. During this period, German elites pursued a policy of paced expansion, relying primarily on diplomacy to achieve their objectives. The year 1897 was a key switching point because in that year decision makers began to pursue overly competitive policies—including an ambitious military buildup—that provoked the formation of a preponderant opposing coalition and eventually led to the outbreak of World War I in 1914. The first U.S. case runs from the end of World War II (1945) to 1949. During this period, U.S. elites relied primarily on political and economic initiatives to contain the Soviet Union. The year 1949 was a key switching point because political and economic efforts to contain the Soviets were replaced by a militarized and globalized version of containment. The second U.S. case stops in 1950 only because the new policies were in place by the middle of that year. I am more concerned with the causes of this shift in policy than with its long-term consequences.

from the overseas empire. Despite their intention to send only a rela- | key
tively small contingent to fight on the Continent, British decision mak- | argument
ers demonstrated an impressive ability to adjust to significant changes
in the balance of power. During the 1932–1939 period, British elites
were overly cooperative in the core and overly competitive in the periphery; the country fell prey to both strategic exposure and overextension. Although confronted with Nazi Germany's rapid rearmament
and overt aggression in central Europe, Britain chose to concentrate
on the defense of its peripheral possessions while making manifestly
inadequate efforts to prepare for the defense of its primary security
interests in Europe. Britain faced a more threatening environment in
this second period—it confronted a hostile power in virtually every
theater—but its decision to take a firm stand in the periphery while
adopting a policy of appeasement in the core and failing to equip the
army for continental operations is nevertheless puzzling. Comparing
these two episodes of successful and unsuccessful adjustment offers
rich material for studying the causes of both strategic exposure and
overextension.

The French case studies focus on four periods: 1870–1904, 1904–
1914, 1932–1939, and 1949–1954. During the late nineteenth century,
France's overseas empire grew considerably, despite both Germany's
increasing economic and military power on the Continent and the existence of a French public and National Assembly that were hostile to
the notion of peripheral empire. It was an industrious colonial lobby
and an errant colonial army that imposed overseas territories on the
French state during the late 1800s. Thereafter, French elites seemed
unable to decide whether their future lay in continental power or in
overseas empire. During the decade before World War I, they successfully adjusted to the rising German threat, downgrading the importance of overseas possessions and marshaling their resources for war
on the Continent. During the interwar period, however, French decision makers, like their British counterparts, adopted overly cooperative
policies in the core and overly competitive policies in the periphery.
Even after Germany had demonstrated its willingness to occupy neighboring countries by force, French elites left their homeland dangerously unprepared to deal with German aggression, concentrated too
heavily on imperial defense, and vastly exaggerated the potential contribution of the colonies to the defense of the metropole. France fell
prey to both strategic exposure and overextension. During the 1949–
1954 period, French elites were forced to choose between economic
and military reconstruction in Europe and defense of their empire in
Indochina. Understanding their decision to defend Indochina at a clear

cost to domestic recovery and metropolitan security should offer much insight into the central questions addressed by this book.

The chapter on Japan focuses on the 1931–1937 and the 1937–1941 periods. During the first period, Japan expanded its empire at a moderate pace, and the growth of its military establishment was accompanied by impressive economic performance. Japanese elites concentrated on developing overseas territories in order to enhance their contribution to the industrial and financial strength of the metropole. They pursued competitive policies but reined in the scope of their ambition and were careful to avoid both self-encirclement and overextension. During the 1937–1941 period, Japanese elites pursued overly competitive policies; imperial expansion drained the metropole's economy and set Japan on the path to war against an opposing coalition of preponderant strength. By 1941, Japanese decision makers faced a clear choice: they could either scale back their imperial aspirations dramatically or push into Southeast Asia to secure access to the resources needed to sustain expansionist policies. Japanese elites decided to drive southward and initiate war against the United States, despite awareness that they were taking on an enemy of vastly superior war-making capability. Japan fell prey to both self-encirclement and overextension. The chapter addresses why Japanese behavior was so different during these two periods and why elites initiated a conflict, knowing full well that the chances of victory were slim.

The German case studies deal with the 1870–1897 and the 1897–1914 periods. Between 1870 and 1897, Germany pursued a competitive policy of selective expansion in both the core and periphery. Bismarck succeeded in establishing Germany as the pivot of European diplomacy by constructing a network of defensive alliances with other major powers. At the same time, Germany acquired overseas possessions, though peripheral expansion was relatively limited in scope. After 1897, German elites began to pursue overly competitive policies. In contrast to the other cases examined in this book, Germany did not experience overextension through peripheral expansion. It did, however, fall prey to self-encirclement in the core. Germany's aggressive diplomacy and the buildup of its navy and army succeeded only in inducing Europe's other major powers to ally against it. The outbreak of World War I marked a German decision to initiate war against an opposing coalition of preponderant strength. This chapter seeks to explain not only why Germany engaged in self-defeating expansion in the core, but also why, unlike other powers, it did not overextend in the periphery.

The chapter on the United States examines the 1945–1949 and the 1949–1950 periods. During the first five postwar years, the United

States adjusted to a new constellation of international power in which the Soviet Union emerged as the principal adversary. Competitive policies were pursued to contain the Soviet Union, but containment relied primarily on economic and political initiatives. American decision makers sought to avoid policies in the core that would exacerbate Soviet insecurity and U.S.-Soviet rivalry and were careful to limit U.S. military commitments in the periphery. Beginning in late 1949 and early 1950, the Truman administration implemented a far more militarized version of containment and vastly increased the scope of U.S. defense commitments in the periphery. These overly competitive policies intensified the Cold War and led to overextension by miring the United States in intractable Third World conflicts. This chapter explains how and why this consequential shift in U.S. policy came about.

THE ARGUMENT

Adjustment failure results from dysfunction within a state's decision-making apparatus. Hypothetically, this dysfunction could occur at the level of individual decision makers or at the state level, where governmental and nongovernmental actors can intervene in the formulation and implementation of policy. At the individual level, decision makers might lack the information and analytic skills needed to assess accurately international change. The problem may be one of assessment failure; elites may simply be unaware of the need for adjustment. Alternatively, decision makers may recognize that consequential change has taken place but fail to respond accordingly. Psychological distortion, miscalculation, or inappropriate strategic beliefs arising from cognitive constraints might cause elites to pursue self-defeating strategies of adjustment. At the state level, private economic interests, domestic political structure, and the military establishment could all be important factors that skew or constrain the adjustment process. Since defense policy and the management of empire affect the interests of industrialists, bankers, politicians, diplomats, the masses, and the military, each could play an instrumental role in preventing or impairing strategic adjustment.

If decision-making communities are consistently unable to perceive international change when it occurs, the conceptual puzzle is solved. Elites cannot be expected to adjust to changes of which they are unaware. The historical cases examined herein, however, suggest that this explanation is unsatisfying. The measurement of shifts in the international distribution of power and their strategic implications is indeed difficult and the source of much dispute among elites. But the cases

[13]

reveal that decision-making communities have generally been aware of significant change in the international constellation of power and the opportunities and constraints associated with such change. The problem is not one of poor information.

On the contrary, the central argument of this book is that the perception of high metropolitan vulnerability produced by international change is the root cause of self-defeating behavior. The core of my argument is as follows: The perception of high metropolitan vulnerability resulting from rapid and adverse shifts in the international balance of power creates the need for strategic adjustment but also prevents that adjustment from taking place. Perceptions of high vulnerability, rather than inducing caution and moderation, paradoxically lead to both overly cooperative and overly competitive behavior. High vulnerability refers to conditions of strategic deficiency. Decision makers calculate that their own resources, even in combination with the resources of their allies, are insufficient to cope with threats to the homeland; they believe that war, if it breaks out in the core, would likely jeopardize the sovereignty or territorial integrity of the metropole. Perceptions of high vulnerability produce self-defeating behavior through a three-stage process.

At time 1, the perception of high metropolitan vulnerability under conditions of uncertainty about if, when, and where threats will come due leads to strategic beliefs that induce elites to adopt extremist policies. An extraordinary strategic environment produces extraordinary policies. In powers that are declining in relative terms, elites adopt overly cooperative policies in the core and overly competitive policies in the periphery. Elites in rising powers tend to adopt overly competitive policies in both core and periphery.[20] This behavior represents a rational response to conditions of strategic deficiency.[21] At time 2, in order

---

[20] A state is declining if its military and economic position relative to other major powers is decreasing. A state is rising if its military and economic position relative to other major powers is increasing. I am here referring to broader trends over time and not to discrete, short-term changes in the relative power positions of states as they prepare for war. I am assuming that elites are aware of these trends and, consequently, of whether their state is rising or declining. I distinguish between declining and rising states in order to capture the different objectives that inform their grand strategies. A declining state seeks to maintain the status quo in order to protect its position of primacy in the international order. A rising state seeks to challenge the status quo in order to establish a position of primacy. As Robert Gilpin writes, a newly powerful state "will try to expand its political, economic, and territorial control; it will try to change the international system in accordance with its particular set of interests." *War and Change,* pp. 94–95. For a more extensive treatment of how to define and measure rise and decline, see Charles Doran, *Systems in Crisis,* Cambridge Studies in International Relations: 16 (Cambridge: Cambridge University Press, 1991).

[21] I classify overly cooperative and overly competitive policies as those that are more cooperative or more competitive than prudence would dictate under unexceptional cir-

to garner domestic support for these extremist policies, elites propagate throughout the body politic specific images and conceptions of empire. Public attitudes change, as do the central roles and missions of the decision-making bodies, bureaucratic structures, and military organizations responsible for formulating and implementing national strategy. As a result, elite beliefs and strategic culture run on parallel tracks and reinforce each other. At time 3, as the ill effects of extremist policies mount, and uncertainty about the strategic landscape diminishes, elites realize that their policies are coming to jeopardize the security of the metropole by leading to strategic exposure, self-encirclement, and/or overextension. They come to appreciate that their beliefs are inconsistent with incoming information, and although these beliefs tend to adapt only sluggishly to disconfirming evidence, decision makers do become aware of the need to adjust grand strategy. Nevertheless, the shifts in strategic culture brought about by elite lobbying during time 2 prevent the occurrence of adjustment. Strategic culture constrains elites by raising the domestic political costs of reorienting grand strategy to unacceptable levels and/ or by imbuing the elite community with powerful strategic images and conceptions that so orient individuals and bureaucracies toward the attainment of specific goals that desirable policy options are effectively removed from consideration. In sum, great powers pursue self-defeating behavior because vulnerability causes elites to become entrapped in a strategic culture of their own making.

I now spell out this argument in more detail. Whether a state adjusts successfully to international change depends upon elite perceptions of the balance of power. Under conditions of low vulnerability, both declining and rising powers adjust successfully to changes in their international environment. Low vulnerability refers to conditions of strategic sufficiency. Decision makers calculate that their own resources, in combination with those of their allies, are sufficient to cope with threats to the metropole; they believe that their state is likely to prevail should war break out in the core.[22] Elites in declining powers

---

cumstances, but not necessarily those that are nonrational. Under certain circumstances, extremist behavior makes good sense. I am arguing that elites initially pursue overly cooperative and overly competitive policies for sound reasons: because they face resource deficiencies. Extremist behavior leads to self-defeating outcomes only later—when elites realize that their policies are no longer appropriate but find themselves unable to reverse course.

[22] Measures of vulnerability are based on the assessments available to decision makers of relative military capabilities. These assessments include assets already existing, those that can be mobilized in relatively short order, and those of allies expected to commit forces against the identified adversary or adversarial coalition. I thus code level of vulnerability in terms of elite *perceptions* of the relative balance of power, not in terms of objective conditions and the actual balance of power. Accordingly, I measure vulnerability in terms of the information available to elites and their assessment of the likely outcome

adopt competitive policies in the core to marshal resources against rising threats, while adopting cooperative policies in the periphery to facilitate retrenchment. Timely balancing results. Elites in rising powers adopt competitive policies in both the core and periphery to contribute to the metropole's strength, although they pursue expansion selectively to avoid both self-encirclement and overextension. Paced imperial growth results. Under high vulnerability, elites operate under conditions of strategic deficiency; they calculate that war in the core would likely jeopardize the security of the metropole. Different policy choices result. Elites in declining powers adopt overly cooperative policies in the core to appease the adversary and avoid war, and overly competitive policies in the periphery to defend empire and redress material inadequacy in the metropole. Appeasement in the core and indiscriminate defense in the periphery lead to strategic exposure and overextension. Elites in rising powers pursue overly competitive policies in the core and the periphery in order to challenge adversaries seeking to block their state's ascendance. Indiscriminate expansion on both fronts leads to self-encirclement and overextension. These policy choices and the outcomes they produce are shown in Tables 1, 2, and 3.

The causal connection between perceptions of metropolitan vulnerability and policy choice is as follows.[23] Under low vulnerability, elites calculate that they can prevail against the likely adversary should war break out in the core; they operate under conditions of strategic sufficiency. Self-interest impels elites in declining states to balance in a timely fashion against emerging external threats. Balancing usually involves internal mobilization, alliance formation, and the reduction of peripheral commitments. Self-interest impels elites in rising states to take advantage of opportunities to enhance the country's power and influence but also to avoid pursuing policies that could undermine strategic sufficiency. Aware of the potential for expansionist policies to trigger the formation of a preponderant opposing coalition and to drain metropolitan strength, elites expand only selectively and rein in the

---

of war, not on information gathered after the fact and my own assessment of whether a state faced conditions of high or low vulnerability. As I discuss in the following chapter, elites generally have a fairly accurate assessment of the balance of power; that is, elite perceptions of vulnerability usually correspond with actual conditions. My argument rests, however, only on perceptions: adjustment failure should occur when elites *think* that they face conditions of strategic deficiency and, therefore, that war would likely jeopardize the security of the metropole.

[23] I am not making the self-evident argument that elites should have the most difficulty adjusting to international change when the resources at their disposal are constrained. Rather, I am making the counterintuitive argument that under conditions of high vulnerability—when one would expect elites to go to greater lengths to bolster the security of the metropole than under low vulnerability—decision makers do just the opposite. They engage in behavior that only exacerbates the metropole's security predicament. In

Table 1. Policy choices under low vulnerability

Country	Core	Periphery
Declining state Britain 1904–14 France 1870–1904, 1904–14	Competitive [power balancing]	Cooperative [retrenchment]
Rising state Japan 1931–37 Germany 1870–97 United States 1945–49	Competitive [selective expansion]	Competitive [selective expansion]

Table 2. Policy choices under high vulnerability

Country	Core	Periphery
Declining state Britain 1932–39 France 1932–39, 1949–54	Overly cooperative [appeasement]	Overly competitive [indiscriminate defense]
Rising state Japan 1937–41 Germany 1897–1914 United States 1949–50	Overly competitive [indiscriminate expansion]	Overly competitive [indiscriminate expansion]

Table 3. Outcomes

	Low Vulnerability	High Vulnerability
Declining state	Timely balancing	Strategic exposure and overextension
Rising state	Paced imperial growth	Self-encirclement and overextension

scope of imperial ambition. Put differently, conditions of low vulnerability constitute an unexceptional decision-making environment in which elites have at their disposal the resources necessary to attain their objectives in a changing strategic environment. Elites thus behave in an unexceptional manner; conditions of strategic sufficiency enable them to respond readily to the constraints and opportunities arising from shifts in the distribution of material power.

Conditions of high metropolitan vulnerability, on the other hand,

---

other words, my argument focuses not on why states faced with resource deficiencies may often lose wars, but on why elites in these states pursue self-defeating policies that often precipitate the very outcome they are seeking to avoid.

constitute an exceptional strategic environment that gives rise to exceptional policies. Perceptions of high vulnerability lead to overly cooperative and overly competitive behavior by altering the fundamental beliefs that drive elite decisions. Because decision makers facing high vulnerability operate under conditions of strategic deficiency, they base their decisions on a different set of suppositions than they do under low vulnerability. Elite beliefs change as a logical response to the security environment. In contrast to the analysis of other authors, I argue that elites initially pursue extremist policies for sound, considered reasons; such policies lead to self-defeating outcomes only later when elites find themselves unable to reverse course.[24]

The essential logic driving overly cooperative and overly competitive behavior is as follows. In declining powers, elites faced with high metropolitan vulnerability, rather than balancing against emerging threats in the core, see the need to cooperate with the adversary in order to avoid war. Efforts to accommodate the demands of a rising adversary stem directly from the perception of strategic deficiency. Elites calculate that their own resources and those of their allies are insufficient to enable them to prevail against the likely adversary or adversarial coalition. Accordingly, they fear that competitive policies will engage the state in a conflict that it has neither the military nor economic capability to win. Facing a daunting military imbalance and little prospect of redressing this imbalance in the short term, elites seek to avert war or, at the least, to delay it until more favorable circumstances prevail. In short, elites initially feel incapable of balancing against the rising adversary and therefore calculate that cooperative policies are more likely to enhance their state's security. It is a sense of weakness that provides the impetus behind overly cooperative behavior and sets the stage for strategic exposure.[25]

---

[24] Other authors tend to attribute extremist policies to dysfunctions within or distortions of the decision-making process. In *Myths of Empire,* for example, Jack Snyder views overly competitive policies as the result of logrolling among self-interested imperial interest groups. Paul Kennedy in *The Rise and Fall of the Great Powers* and Aaron Friedberg in *The Weary Titan* suggest that adjustment failure results from inadequate and erroneous assessments of power. Richard Ned Lebow views counterproductive policies as the result of cognitive failure. *Between Peace and War: The Nature of International Crisis* (Baltimore: Johns Hopkins University Press, 1981). The views of these and other authors are examined in more depth in the following chapter.

[25] The logic producing cooperative behavior in the core is similar to that described by Stephen Walt in his explanation of why states sometimes bandwagon with rather than balance against external challengers. According to Walt, states tend to bandwagon when they are at a marked strategic disadvantage and therefore view cooperative policies as more likely to preserve their security. In Walt's words, weak states bandwagon because "they can do little to determine their own fates." *The Origins of Alliances* (Ithaca: Cornell University Press, 1987), pp. 173, 28–33.

At the same time that they pursue overly cooperative policies in the core, elites in declining powers initially respond to high vulnerability by adopting overly competitive policies in the periphery. Immediate retrenchment from the periphery is unattractive because it will not succeed in meeting the strategic shortfall in the core. Indeed, this strategic shortfall is the cause of increasing ambition in the periphery. Conditions of strategic deficiency produce peripheral ambition through logical inferences that elites draw about three issues: resolve, resources, and legitimacy. High vulnerability induces elites to believe in the need to demonstrate resolve to potential adversaries by adopting firm, deterrent strategies in the periphery. Demonstrations of resolve are to compensate for material inadequacy by persuading challengers not to attack and by preserving the prestige associated with the external appearance of strength. An adverse shift in the balance of material power is to be offset by a favorable shift in the balance of resolve. Deterrent strategies pursued for reputational reasons tend to be directed toward the periphery as opposed to the core precisely because high metropolitan vulnerability makes elites fearful that demonstrations of resolve in the core could provoke a war that would have disastrous consequences for the homeland. At the same time, even if carried out only in the periphery, demonstrations of resolve may succeed in deterring adversaries in the core. The perception of high vulnerability also leads to a heightened valuation of the material and strategic benefits offered by peripheral empire. This change in beliefs results primarily from the search to redress the material imbalance in the core by extracting resources from imperial possessions. Finally, high metropolitan vulnerability, by threatening the legitimacy of ruling elites, reinforces the impulse among decision makers to adopt ambitious external policies. Elites view the successful pursuit of foreign ambition not only as a means of deterring potential adversaries, but also as a way of rallying popular support behind the government. It is this combination of inferences that induces decision makers to pursue policies that push the state toward overextension.

Elites in rising powers initially respond to high vulnerability by adopting overly competitive policies in both the core and periphery. The difference between the behavior of declining and rising powers in the core is the result of two considerations. First, elites in declining states seek to preserve the vestiges of imperial power, not to develop it. Inasmuch as they are attempting to maintain the status quo, cooperative strategies are a viable and attractive option. Elites in rising states seek to fulfill new imperial aspirations, not to protect the remains of old ones. Inasmuch as they are attempting to challenge and reshape the status quo, cooperative strategies are inadequate to attain

[19]

their objectives; only competitive policies can alter the international order.

Second, elites in a great power at the top of the international hierarchy react to challenges to the status quo; they do not initiate them. Decision makers must therefore be careful to avoid actions that could trigger spirals of hostility and precipitate conflict. Competitive policies risk provoking a war that would likely lead to defeat. Preventive war is not a viable option, and deterrent threats lack credibility.[26] Cooperative policies, on the other hand, would ensure that unintended spirals of hostility do not come about and might succeed in satisfying the demands of the rising state, thus avoiding war altogether. Should accommodation fail to satisfy the challenger, the time bought by the initial pursuit of cooperative policies would enable the defender, through mobilization and alliance, to improve the military imbalance. In contrast, elites in a rising state have much more control over outcomes. They are able to choose when and how to attempt to overturn the status quo. They do not have to initiate such a challenge unless and until they perceive a good chance of prevailing. Should competitive policies prove to exacerbate vulnerability by tightening and strengthening the opposing coalition, elites can moderate their behavior and thereby avoid conflict. Status quo powers will not initiate conflict unless forced to do so. Elites in rising states thus view competitive policies in the core as both necessary to attain their goals and sufficient to preserve the state's security. Elites in declining states view cooperative policies in the core as both sufficient to attain their goals and necessary to preserve the state's security.

The logic through which high vulnerability induces elites in rising powers to pursue overly competitive policies also emerges from inferences that they draw about resolve, resources, and legitimacy. Facing conditions of strategic deficiency, elites turn to competitive policies to demonstrate resolve and bolster reputation. They are less concerned with deterring attack than with intimidating adversaries and splitting the coalition that is potentially emerging to block their state's ascendance. Elites also view imperial growth as a way of gaining access to new resources and of making the best use of available assets by expanding before the opposing coalition gains strength. Finally, high metropolitan vulnerability threatens the legitimacy of ruling elites, inducing decision makers to turn to foreign success to foster domestic stability.

---

[26] This generalization does not apply during the nuclear age. Nuclear weapons give declining powers the ability to deter and resist even challengers of decidedly superior military capability.

Although elites operating under high vulnerability do adopt these beliefs and the extremist policies that follow, this set of logical inferences is not sufficient to produce adjustment failure. Vulnerability affects strategic beliefs in the manner specified above only under conditions of uncertainty, when the strategic implications of a new constellation of power have not yet crystallized. Elites realize they face conditions of strategic deficiency but are uncertain about if, when, and where threats may come due, about what motivates the adversary, and about how the adversary will react to their initiatives. Within the context of this uncertainty, it is reasoned and reasonable for elites in declining, vulnerable states to seek to avert war in the core and to turn to peripheral ambition to demonstrate resolve and bolster reputation, to seek more resources to redress the imbalance in the core, and to be concerned about the potential effect of perceived weakness on domestic legitimacy. So too is it reasonable for elites in rising states to respond initially to high vulnerability by seeking to strengthen resolve, marshal resources, and bolster legitimacy through external ambition. But as uncertainty diminishes, elites gradually become aware that overly cooperative and overly competitive policies are not producing their intended effects; they realize that their behavior has served to erode, not to enhance, the metropole's security. In other words, when the ill effects of extremist policies become apparent, elite beliefs change accordingly. Decision makers in declining powers realize that their state is falling prey to strategic exposure and overextension, and they come to see the urgent need for efforts to balance against threats in the core and to retrench from peripheral empire. Elites in rising powers come to appreciate that overly competitive policies are leading only to self-encirclement and overextension and that they must scale back the scope of imperial ambition. There is often a significant lag between receipt of incoming information and these changes in beliefs. In fact, vulnerability tends to increase this lag time, causing decision makers to cling to outmoded strategic beliefs even in the face of clearly discrepant information. But elites eventually come to realize the need to reorient grand strategy in order to protect an exposed metropole. That they are still often unable to effect a reorientation of grand strategy suggests that forces other than strategic beliefs are contributing to adjustment failure.

This point leads to my claim that adjustment failures ultimately result from the severe constraints placed on elites by strategic culture. This claim is predicated on the assumption that deeply embedded conceptions of security and notions of empire take root among elites and masses alike. I call such notions strategic culture. Strategic culture is distinguishable from elite beliefs in that it is based on images and symbols, not on logic and causal inference. Beliefs consist of causal suppositions about the dynamics of world politics; strategic culture refers to the images that shape how the nation as a collective entity defines its well-being and conceives of its security. These images concern the relationship between metropolitan security and empire, the nation's position in the international hierarchy, and the scope and nature of its external ambition. When elites and the public internalize specific images of empire and its relationship to the nation's well-being, legitimacy becomes contingent on the preservation or realization of that conception of national security. Political leaders and bureaucracies orient their goals and functions accordingly. Under these circumstances, the domestic costs of adjusting policy in ways that challenge prevailing conceptions of security rise markedly; the need to maintain legitimacy constrains elites and can prevent them from pursuing policies consistent with sound, considered strategic decisions. These constraints may emerge from electoral considerations: political survival may conflict with strategic pragmatism. Alternatively, they may manifest themselves in more subtle ways, by removing desirable options from the political agenda. Strategic culture may so infuse the elite community with certain images and so orient the bureaucracy and military services toward specific missions that important policy options become unacceptable and do not even receive serious consideration. In these instances, the strategic images that shape intellectual paradigms, inform elite values, and define organizational interests conflict with and override strategic logic. Even though military and economic assessments might make elites aware of the need to undertake strategic adjustment, they are unable to do so because such policies are inconsistent with the maintenance of ruling coalitions and domestic support and/or may conflict with the fundamental conceptions and central images of national security embedded and institutionalized in the elite community.

These two arguments about the effects of vulnerability on strategic beliefs and the role of strategic culture in constraining adjustment do not operate independently; they are sequentially linked in the following manner. High metropolitan vulnerability under conditions of uncertainty induces elites to pursue overly cooperative and overly competitive policies. Because of the electoral and coalitional dynamics involved in gaining support for extremist policies, elites must propagate strategic conceptions compatible with their policy choices. In declining powers, elites must justify cooperative behavior in the face of rising threats in the core, as well as competitive behavior in the periphery which distracts already scarce resources from the metropole. In rising powers, elites must sell to the polity expansive strategic conceptions in order to justify imperial ambition and the increasing extraction of resources from the populace necessitated by growing military expenditures. The problem is that the successful propagation of these strategic conceptions, although it initially enables elites to achieve their external goals, eventually comes to constrain decision makers when they realize the need to reorient grand strategy in order to protect an exposed metropole. Because it would be politically costly for elites to challenge the commitments for which they had just rallied support, because elites may not have time to spread new strategic images, and because the broader decision-making community may have come to internalize and define its goals in terms of the strategic arguments that were initially crafted for instrumental purposes, policy makers are unable, at least in the short term, to alter the conceptions of empire that had recently been propagated. In this domestic environment, to reorient grand strategy would jeopardize political survival and/or challenge the essential images of security to which the elite community had become committed in cognitive, emotional, and organizational terms. Decision makers find themselves entrapped in a strategic culture of their own making.

A second mechanism contributes to the constraining effects of strategic culture. Exogenous shocks and vivid events such as war or political and economic crisis can independently affect the imperial notions and national self-images that take root within the polity. Conceptions of national security thus change in ways unintended and unforeseen by elites. Although most changes in strategic culture are initiated by elites, these other forces shaping strategic images produce shifts in mass attitudes, the intellectual paradigms and values of decision makers, and the orientation of government bureaucracies on a greater scale of magnitude and in directions not originally intended. Strategic culture can take on a life of its own, thus confounding elites and further constraining the adjustment process.

To summarize, adjustment failures are driven by shifts in the international distribution of power that produce perceptions of high metropolitan vulnerability. Conditions of strategic deficiency induce elites to pursue—for sound, considered reasons—both overly cooperative and overly competitive policies. To rally domestic support for extraordinary policies, decision makers propagate specific strategic conceptions. But by selling powerful strategic images to the polity—molding public opinion and reshaping the roles and missions of the broader decision-making community—elites unwittingly entrap themselves in a strategic culture that later prevents them from reorienting grand strategy and avoiding self-defeating behavior. Irrational outcomes—strategic exposure, self-encirclement, and overextension—are the product not of assessment failure, psychological dysfunction within the elite community, or the instrumentalist behavior of capitalists or military officers, but of the sequential, accumulated impact of vulnerability on strategic beliefs and strategic culture. Taken in isolation and within the context of uncertainty, it is rational for elites, when lacking the resources necessary to cope with threats to the metropole, to seek to avert war in the core or to pursue external ambition in order to demonstrate resolve, to extract increasing resources from empire, and to counter the effects of external weakness on domestic legitimacy. But when these strategic beliefs lead to an accompanying shift in strategic culture, decision makers find themselves facing constraints from which they cannot escape. By the time the need for strategic adjustment becomes glaringly apparent, it is too late; elites are entrapped by domestic political forces and/or by a conception of national security deeply embedded and institutionalized within the decision-making community. Elites are unable to bring commitments and resources into equilibrium, and are left pursuing policies that expose the empire at its very heart.

CAVEATS

The enterprise in which I am engaged is an ambitious one—in terms of the puzzle I address, the breadth of my historical cases, and the complexity and scope of my argument. The phenomenon I seek to explain—self-defeating behavior—is itself elusive and difficult to identify. Adverse outcomes, such as defeat in war, are not necessarily the product of self-destructive behavior. A state may prepare for war to the best of its ability, but still be defeated by a superior adversary. Accordingly, the identification of self-defeating behavior must depend not on real-world outcomes, but on subjective evaluation of policy choice; the burden falls on my shoulders to provide convincing evidence that elites, given the information available to them, should have pursued policies other than those they did. To do so, I apply the following test: Were the policies pursued by elites consistent with those that would be pursued by a group of reasonable, prudent decision makers facing the same conditions and information? It is when the answer to this question is no—when actual decisions diverge from those that an objective third party would consider reasonable and prudent—that I characterize policy choices as self-defeating.

My evaluation of which cases fit this criterion entails making judgments about historical episodes that are still the object of vociferous scholarly debate. Historians have yet to agree, for example, as to whether German elites in 1914 should have foreseen that their country did not have the wherewithal to prevail against the Triple Entente, or as to when during the 1930s British and French elites should have come to recognize the severity of the threat posed by Nazi Germany. I acknowledge that all of the historical periods I examine are complicated, and that interpretations other than those offered are indeed possible. But I do ask the reader to suspend his or her preconceptions about these historical episodes and to remain open to the evidence and interpretations I present.

My theory about the causes of self-defeating behavior provides an explanation of adjustment failure that is at once logically compelling and consistent with the historical record. My claim is that this model identifies the underlying causal mechanisms that lead to self-defeating behavior, not that it captures the full range of decisions and processes that determines outcomes. I have sought to construct an account of adjustment failure that is rich enough to do justice to the historical cases, yet parsimonious enough to constitute a generalizable theory. In addition, each case study is unique and fits this model to varying degrees. My model purports to capture the common thread, the main theme that unites all the historical cases.

Some of the principal variations across the cases are as follows. In the British and French cases, World War I played a key role in shaping the strategic culture that constrained elites during the 1930s. Elite lobbying during the interwar period contributed to the propagation of the strategic conceptions that impaired adjustment, but the experience of the war itself is central to understanding why the British and French fell prey to strategic exposure in the core and overextension in the periphery. The war left both powers preoccupied with imperial defense—to the detriment of metropolitan security. The British were far more concerned about the reputational effects of peripheral empire than the French, who were intent on strengthening their metropolitan army with troops extracted from the periphery. In the Japanese case, overextension in the periphery was driven by the search for raw materials needed to attain economic autarky, not by efforts to bolster reputation or recruit indigenous soldiers. In addition, unlike in the other cases, the domination of decision making by Japan's military establishment played a key role in the formulation of a grand strategy that far outstripped available resources. In the U.S. case, the historical puzzle is more ambiguous; during the period I examine, the United States did not engage in behavior that unequivocally jeopardized primary security interests and diverged from reasonable standards of prudence. Nevertheless, the policies that U.S. elites began to pursue in 1950 were overly competitive; they fueled the Cold War and eventually led to a range of commitments that needlessly strained American resources.

[25]

The U.S. case is also unique in that the advent of nuclear weapons had a profound impact on American thinking about empire and the allocation of resources between core and periphery. The German case, for two important reasons, strays farthest from the model. First, domestic political vulnerability, as opposed to strategic vulnerability, played a key role in shaping German policy and fueling excessive imperial expansion. Second, overly competitive policies led only to self-encirclement in the core; unlike the other powers being studied, Germany did not fall prey to overextension in the periphery. These aberrations, however, can be explained within the context of the theory set forth above; the German case requires a nuanced understanding, but not a reformulation, of my central argument.[27] In sum, the argument presented above captures the essential dynamics that are at work in all the case studies.

Finally, my reliance on the notion of strategic culture to explain outcomes warrants mention of the dangers and opportunities associated with theories that use culture as a key variable. Critics of cultural explanations of political behavior raise three main objections. First, they claim that culture tends to be used as a residual variable; that is, scholars rely on it when other more conventional and concrete variables fail to provide an adequate explanation of outcomes. Scholars turn to culture by default, because the evidence disconfirms competing explanations, not because it convincingly confirms cultural ones. Second, critics charge that culture is an amorphous and malleable concept that is difficult to define and to measure. Furthermore, culture must be measured independently of the behavior that it allegedly explains; otherwise the argument becomes tautological. Such independent measures are, however, difficult to devise and to observe empirically. Constructing cultural explanations therefore entails treacherous methodological dangers—dangers that threaten to mire any cultural argument in intractable dispute over conceptual and evidentiary issues. Third,

---

[27] Other scholars have noted that vulnerability from international threats and domestic vulnerability can have similar effects on decision making. Richard Ned Lebow, for example, argues that brinkmanship crises often result when the initiator is faced with an adverse shift in the balance of international power or "the political vulnerability of a leader of government" or the "instability of the political system as a whole." *Between Peace and War*, pp. 66–70; the quotation is on p. 69. As I argue in Chapter 6, Germany did not fall prey to overextension mainly because German elites, largely for geographic reasons, never sold peripheral empire to the polity. Elites whipped up strong strains of expansionism among the populace, but strategic culture was oriented toward asserting German power in the core, not in the periphery. This outcome in fact bolsters my main argument about the constraining effects of strategic culture, inasmuch as the one case in which elites did not sell overseas empire to the public, the bureaucracy, or the military establishment—even though they did acquire overseas possessions—is the one case in which overextension did not come about.

[26]

inasmuch as culture changes little over time, critics claim that cultural arguments tend to be nonfalsifiable. Because it is difficult to conceive of and test a counterfactual (how would a state's behavior change if it were guided by a different set of cultural forces?), it is difficult to make a convincing case that culture did or did not play a key role in shaping any specific outcome.[28]

These three objections have merit and provide good reason to proceed with caution in constructing and devising tests for cultural arguments. In building my own theory about the importance of strategic culture, I have dealt with these objections in the following manner. What makes the notion of strategic culture problematic and unwieldy—its focus on deeply embedded assumptions and collective self-images—is precisely what makes it appealing. By using the term culture, I am seeking to capture the extent to which widely held conceptions of national security and empire come to shape the parameters within which policy is formed. These conceptions determine the boundaries of politically legitimate behavior, the intellectual paradigms and fundamental values that shape how individual decision makers conceive of and choose among competing options, and the strategic objectives around which governmental institutions, bureaucracies, and the military services define their roles and missions. Strategic culture thus affects outcomes through political, cognitive, emotional, and organizational mechanisms. From this perspective, strategic culture is a residual variable only in that it is ideational in nature and the case for its importance can be considerably strengthened if other explanations can be disconfirmed. Explanations that rely on the balance of power and static notions of the national interest enjoy a privileged position within the discipline not because deductive or empirical examination has proved them superior or more powerful in analytic terms, but largely because they rely on variables that are material in nature and therefore easier to measure. That disconfirming explanations focusing on material variables strengthens the case for cultural explanations is by no means an indictment of cultural theories. Rather, it is integral to the process of theory-building, especially when working with ideational variables.

The methodological problems involved in measuring strategic culture vary with one's definition of the concept. My definition of strategic

---

[28] For general discussion of these issues, see Gabriel Almond, "The Intellectual History of the Civic Culture Concept," in *Comparative Politics in the Post-Behavioral Era*, ed. Louis Cantori and Andrew Ziegler, Jr. (Colorado: Lynne Reinner Publishers, 1988); David Laitin, "Political Culture and Political Preference," *American Political Science Review*, 82 (June 1988), 589–593; Lucian Pye, "Culture and Political Science: Problems in the Evaluation of the Concept of Political Culture," in *The Idea of Culture in the Social Sciences*, ed. Louis Schneider and Charles Bonjean (Cambridge: Cambridge University Press, 1973).

culture is more narrow and concrete than that used by others, and is therefore easier to measure. Jack Snyder, for example, defines strategic culture as "the sum total of ideas, conditioned emotional responses, and patterns of habitual behavior that members of a national strategic community have acquired through instruction or imitation or share with each other with regard to . . . strategy."[29] This definition is so broad that problems of measurement and testing are legion, if not insurmountable. My notion of strategic culture refers only to the images and symbols that shape how a polity conceives of the relationship between empire and national security.[30] I also distinguish between the inference-based suppositions (beliefs) that inform strategy and the image-based conceptions (strategic culture) that shape how the polity— the public, top elites, the bureaucracy, the military—defines national security.[31] In doing so, I enhance the analytic utility of the notion of

[29] Jack Snyder, "The Soviet Strategic Culture: Implications for Limited Nuclear Operations," R-2154-AF (Santa Monica: Rand, 1977), p. 8. Ken Booth adopts a similar definition: "Strategic culture refers to a nation's traditions, values, attitudes, patterns of behaviour, habits, symbols, achievements and particular ways of adapting to the environment and solving problems with respect to the threat or use of force." "The Concept of Strategic Culture Affirmed," in *Strategic Power: USA/USSR,* ed. Carl Jacobsen (London: Macmillan, 1990), p. 121. For further discussion of the concept of strategic culture, see Snyder, "The Concept of Strategic Culture: Caveat Emptor," in *Strategic Power,* ed. Jacobsen, pp. 3–9; Booth, *Strategy and Ethnocentrism* (New York: Holmes and Meier, 1979); and Colin Gray, *Nuclear Strategy and National Style* (Lanham, Md.: Hamilton Press, 1986).

[30] The following example makes more concrete and explicit the notion of strategic culture that I am articulating. In the late nineteenth century, the French polity was ambivalent about, if not hostile toward, overseas empire. The public cared little for foreign escapades, the National Assembly was unwilling to authorize funding for colonial operations, most top-level elites devoted little attention to the overseas empire, and within the bureaucracy and the mainstream military establishment, colonial affairs were of low priority. In terms of public attitudes, the intellectual paradigms and core values of individual decision makers, and the organizational interests of elite institutions, national security was defined in terms of metropolitan security. By the 1930s, a majority of the populace felt that losing any portion of the empire was tantamount to losing a portion of metropolitan territory. Legislators demonstrated unbridled enthusiasm for imperial ambition. Top-level elites devoted considerable attention to imperial matters. And within the bureaucracy and military, overseas empire was elevated to a position of prominence; because of changes in organizational structure and incentives, core and periphery were merging into a single theater. In terms of public attitudes, the intellectual paradigms and core values of individual decision makers, and the organizational interests of elite institutions, imperial security had become an integral component of national security.

[31] An example will serve to illustrate the distinction I am drawing. An inference-based supposition about the value of peripheral empire is grounded in assessments of the ability of colonies to provide to the metropole troops, raw materials, markets, access to main lines of communication, or international influence. An image-based conception of the value of peripheral empire rests on symbols of and widely held attitudes toward the relationship between metropole and periphery. These images may originate in inferential logic, but they come to occupy the realm of identity and emotion. Individuals often engage in religious practices, for example, not because they believe such practices will contribute to their material well-being, but because such practices are consistent with their identity and provide the emotional satisfaction derived from participation in a

strategic culture and facilitate the tasks of measurement and testing, thereby minimizing the tradeoff between rigor and richness.

On an intuitive and deductive level, it makes perfect sense that widely shared popular attitudes, embedded strategic conceptions, and institutionalized national self-images should have a significant impact on state behavior. Marshaling the evidence to demonstrate that this is the case is the methodological and empirical challenge. When possible, I use public opinion data to measure how strategic culture is manifested in popular attitudes and to determine when widely held strategic conceptions change over time. When such data is not available, I rely on other indicators: voting patterns in legislative bodies, membership in imperial lobby groups, and images and representations of empire in newspapers, literature, film, and educational texts. To measure how strategic culture affects thinking within the decision-making community, I examine the nature and content of political discourse among elites, consider how elites handle incoming information that contradicts prevailing strategic conceptions, study how specific policy debates are framed and which options are included as part of the agenda, examine career paths and organizational structures within the military and foreign policy bureaucracy, and investigate how governmental bodies responsible for formulating and implementing policy define their central roles and missions.

My more narrow definition of strategic culture also solves the problem of falsifiability. If strategic culture refers to "the sum total of ideas, conditioned emotional responses, and patterns of habitual behavior," then it persists over time and changes only incrementally and slowly. Strategic culture defined in such broad terms might be useful in explaining a state's behavior over long periods of time—say decades or even centuries. But without greater, measurable variation over the short term, it cannot be used to explain different outcomes separated by only a matter of years. By restricting strategic culture to refer only to the images and symbols that shape how a polity conceives of the relationship between empire and national security, the notion becomes more analytically powerful. If specific conceptions of empire take root within a polity over a period of ten years, reshaping the boundaries of politically legitimate behavior and the missions of the bureaucracy and military, then these images may well explain variations in state behavior over the period in question. Furthermore, if these changes in

---

community of shared values and symbols. Similarly, a polity might acquire or defend empire not because it contributes to the material well-being of the metropole, but because the polity has come to identify its own well-being and security with the attainment of imperial objectives.

strategic culture are caused primarily by elite propaganda campaigns—as I hypothesize—then the argument becomes even easier to test and falsify. Did elites wage a campaign to mold popular attitudes toward empire? If so, was this campaign successful in altering collective images of national security? Were the roles and central missions of the military and foreign policy bureaucracy reoriented? Did these images and the political, cognitive, emotional, and organizational constraints associated with them eventually impair the ability of decision makers to adapt to international change?

One final comment about the value of the concept of strategic culture warrants mention. Skeptics of cultural explanations often claim that behavior attributed to culture can, in most cases, be attributed to material self-interest. If one can construct an explanation of outcomes on the basis of the interests of involved parties, they ask, why complicate matters by introducing the murky concept of culture? If political leaders in Germany prior to World War I, for example, found that they needed to pursue expansionist policies to stay in power, then self-interest is adequate to explain the overly competitive trajectory of German foreign policy. Similarly, if scaling back the scope of imperial ambition would have diminished the Japanese military's political power in the late 1930s and early 1940s, then the self-interest of the military services can explain Japan's self-defeating aggression. Why bother with unwieldy notions of strategic culture?

The problem with this line of argument is that it ignores the fundamental question of interest formation. Why did Germany's political leaders come to equate their self-interest with the pursuit of expansionist policies? Why did the Japanese military find itself in a predicament in which it had to choose between going to war against a far superior adversary and risking its political power by reducing the scope of its imperial ambition? To answer these questions, the concept of strategic culture is vital. As I will show, German elites found it in their self-interest to pursue overly competitive foreign policies because they sold expansionist imperial images to the polity, altering strategic culture and the determinants of legitimacy. Elites were responsible for creating the domestic environment in which their own political interests conflicted with the imperatives of the international environment. Nor was it inevitable that the political power of the Japanese military would come to be associated with its ability to extend Japan's imperial reach from Manchuria to the Dutch East Indies. Only because of the images and the strategic conceptions that the services had sold to the Japanese polity did the self-interest of the military come to be equated with the attainment of unrealistic goals. The military was itself responsible for creating the expectations that it proved unable to meet. Interests may explain outcomes in both the German and Japanese cases, but the more important question concerns where those interests came from to begin with. It is in answering this question that the concept of strategic culture is indispensable.

METHOD AND STRUCTURE

This book deals with a broad and complex question that cuts across the disciplines of political science, psychology, history, and economics. A study of this scope entails methodological trade-offs and selective use of historical materials. Given the number of variables that could plausibly affect grand strategy and the adjustment process, it is impossible, within the context of a small number of case studies, to give full treatment to each. The historical chapters of necessity condense a wealth of source material. Although the case studies rely heavily on the work of historians, additional archival research and new analytic perspectives have led to novel interpretations of the historical record. I have tried not only to provide convincing evidence for these new interpretations, but also to summarize and point to the shortcomings of traditional perspectives. Furthermore, whenever possible, I have substantiated such challenges to existing interpretations by consulting primary materials. Imputing beliefs from behavior alone is too risky an enterprise; strategic assessments, war plans, and cabinet minutes are key sources for probing elite perceptions and the rationale behind specific strategic decisions.

The structure of this book emerges from a research design that provides analytic rigor, historical richness, and relevance to contemporary problems and policy questions. I begin Chapter 2 by reviewing the literature relevant to studying adjustment failure, drawing on five main bodies of literature to lay out competing hypotheses about the causes of self-defeating behavior. I also show why each of these five hypotheses fails to provide an adequate solution to the puzzle. In the second section of Chapter 2, I set forth my own argument in detail by synthesizing and moving beyond the existing literature. In Chapters 3–7, I test my argument as well as competing explanations against the British, French, Japanese, German, and U.S. case studies, respectively. The questions that emerge from Chapter 2 provide a framework for setting up a structured, focused comparison and guide the analysis through an otherwise overwhelming amount of historical material.[32] Although

---

[32] Alexander George, "Case Studies and Theory Development: The Method of Structured, Focused Comparison," in *Diplomacy: New Approaches in History, Theory, and Policy*, ed. Paul Gordon (New York: Free Press, 1979).

each of the case studies focuses on a unique set of empirical puzzles, similar logic and the same conceptual agenda inform the structure and organization of all the historical chapters.

The final chapter of the book draws on the preceding theoretical and empirical analysis to shed light on both the causes and the policy implications of the profound international changes associated with the ending of the Cold War. The analysis undertaken in this book not only deepens understanding of why the Cold War has come to an end, but also suggests steps that the major powers can take to ensure that the far-reaching changes now occurring in the international system are accompanied by successful adjustment and peaceful transition.

[2]

The Causes of
Self-Defeating Behavior

This chapter examines why states engage in self-defeating behavior. I begin by reviewing the literature relevant to studying the causes of adjustment failure. As few authors have addressed this problem directly, I draw on five disparate bodies of theory to generate competing hypotheses about the causes of adjustment failure. I lay out how to test these hypotheses and then demonstrate that each of them, for both deductive and empirical reasons, fails to provide a satisfying solution to the puzzle. One of the main shortcomings of much of the existing literature is its emphasis on explaining outcomes by focusing on a single level of analysis. In the final section of the chapter, I present my own argument, uncovering how systemic, domestic, and cognitive variables interact in producing strategic exposure, self-encirclement, and overextension.

The first two hypotheses that I consider focus on the level of the individual decision maker. The first concerns the assessment process, and the second, the adjustment process:

1. Assessment failure. Because of the nature of incoming information or the analytic difficulties impairing the processing of that information, elites may simply be unaware of change in the international distribution of power and the consequent need for adjustment of grand strategy.
2. Psychological distortion, miscalculation, and cognitive constraints. Elites may be aware of the need for adjustment, but because of psychological dysfunction, miscalculation, or inappropriate strategic beliefs arising from cognitive constraints, they respond by pursuing overly cooperative and overly competitive policies that jeopardize primary security interests.

The second class of explanation examines the relationship between domestic variables and external policy. There are three alternative formulations, all of which focus on the ability of domestic actors to constrain adjustment:

1. The power of economic interest groups. Industrial and financial elites, because they benefit from military expenditure and foreign trade and investment, place political pressure on decision makers to pursue policies that favor narrow sectoral interests as opposed to the interests of the state as a whole. Inopportune strategic choices result.
2. Domestic politics. Domestic political structure may impair timely adjustment to international change. Autocratic government, by centralizing power in the hands of leaders removed from the moderating checks and balances of representative institutions, could give rise to extremist policies. Alternatively, democratic government, by enabling public opinion, electoral pressures, and the maintenance of governing coalitions to interfere with the conduct of foreign policy, could prevent the pursuit of policies consistent with strategic pragmatism. Finally, cartelized polities, because of the logrolling that occurs among imperial interest groups, could be responsible for producing self-defeating behavior.
3. The power of the military. The military establishment may engage in behavior intended to enhance its institutional autonomy, political power, and access to national resources. To achieve these objectives, the military services may pursue policies against the will of, or at least without the sanction of, political elites, or they may propagate self-serving strategic conceptions among elites and the public at large. In either case, the military subordinates the state's broader interests to its own narrow concerns, and pushes forward policies that jeopardize metropolitan security.

ASSESSMENT FAILURE

The process of net assessment is laden with ambiguity. As a result, elites may be unaware that consequential shifts in the strategic landscape are taking place.[1] They may lack sufficient information about the

---

[1] As mentioned in Chapter 1, I am concerned not with the sources of change in the international system, but with whether and how elites react to such change. Shifts in the international distribution of power are the product of several forces. Nodes of economic activity and technological innovation tend to drift from the center to the periphery of the international system. Over time, the productive capability of the most powerful states in the system is surpassed by that of rising states. See Robert Gilpin, *War and Change in World Politics* (New York: Cambridge University Press, 1981), esp. chaps. 2 and 4. Newly powerful states also reap certain benefits from economic backwardness. When they begin to modernize, they are able to rely on relatively advanced technologies developed elsewhere. Their industrial infrastructure may reflect state-of-the-art technology

external environment. Cognitive constraints could also impair assessment; the complexities and uncertainties inherent in the international environment may prevent decision makers from recognizing change. Alternatively, assessment failure could be the result of the structure of the planning community and the lack of communication among the key agencies responsible for formulating grand strategy. At least in the abstract, politicians, diplomats, defense planners, financial authorities, and industrialists should all be involved in the formulation of grand strategy. That elites may simply be unaware of the need to alter policy is, in fact, one argument that other scholars have used to explain isolated cases of adjustment failure. Paul Kennedy argues that the Spanish Habsburgs fell prey to overextension in part because of the "failure to recognize the importance of preserving the economic underpinnings of a powerful military machine."[2] Similarly, Aaron Friedberg writes that British decline at the turn of the century "was by no means uniformly, completely or automatically apparent to contemporary observers."[3]

The key concern in this section is whether such ambiguities in the assessment process prevent elites from recognizing or assimilating consequential shifts in the international distribution of power. Overly cooperative behavior may occur because elites fail to see emerging threats in the core. So too might overly competitive behavior be the result of inaccurate or ambiguous assessments about the strength of an opposing coalition or about the potential for overextension in the periphery. Do adjustment failures occur because elites lack the information, analytic skills, or cognitive capacity necessary to recognize significant

---

and be able to incorporate innovations while that of states that industrialized earlier grows obsolete. Furthermore, late industrializers, because centralized planning is needed to coordinate rapid economic growth, tend to have institutional structures better able to extract resources from the domestic populace and to intervene in industrial management. See Alexander Gerschenkron, *Economic Backwardness in Historical Perspective: A Book of Essays* (Cambridge: Harvard University Press, Belknap Press, 1962). While observers dispute the causes of shifts in the relative distribution of productive and war-making capabilities, most agree that these shifts are the catalyst for long-term change in the international system and the key force driving the rise of one power and the eclipse of another. For a broad application of this thesis to the experiences of great powers since the sixteenth century, see Paul Kennedy, *The Rise and Fall of the Great Powers* (New York: Random House, 1987).

[2] Kennedy, *Rise and Fall of the Great Powers*, p. 55.

[3] Aaron Friedberg, "Britain and the Experience of Relative Decline," *Journal of Strategic Studies*, 10 (September 1987), 352. Friedberg expands on this argument in *The Weary Titan: Britain and the Experience of Relative Decline, 1895–1905* (Princeton: Princeton University Press, 1988). He writes that the policies British elites pursued "fell far short of lasting success" in large part because "some people did not see or refused to acknowledge the extent of erosion in their national position. Others understood what was happening in one area but not elsewhere. Still others had moments of lucidity and concern, followed by a relapse into complacency" (p. 293).

change in the distribution of international power? Testing this proposition is crucial inasmuch as elites can be expected to undertake adjustment only if they are aware that consequential power shifts have taken place. Gathering the evidence necessary to carry out this test is relatively simple. By consulting the planning documents that informed decisions—as I do in the following chapters—it is possible to examine the data that were available to elites and determine whether they were aware of the need to undertake strategic adjustment.

A central contention of this book is that, even though identifying and interpreting power indices are difficult enterprises, elites have been keenly aware of significant shifts in the international distribution of power and have been able to assess the broad implications of those shifts for their state's security. This claim is based on the argument that methods of net assessment, although they do not allow elites to determine military and economic balances with precision, do enable the planning community to measure gross shifts in the international distribution of power. Information about power balances may not be exact, but it is of sufficient accuracy to permit elites to see significant change in the strategic landscape. As the case studies demonstrate, far from being oblivious to consequential power shifts, decision makers are all too aware of growing gaps between their resources and commitments. The core of the problem lies in the realm of adjustment, not in the realm of assessment.

Several caveats are in order. In this study, I am examining discrete historical periods during which relatively gross shifts in the international distribution of power took place. Even rudimentary methods of measuring power would be adequate to capture shifts on this order of magnitude. Put differently, the research design is biased; the book examines only cases in which the scale of international change made it relatively easy for elites to assimilate the shifts occurring in their external environment. The argument is by no means meant to suggest that elites would be similarly able to recognize more subtle shifts in the constellation of power. Furthermore, because of its concern with grand strategy and the scope of international commitments, this study focuses more on relative military capabilities than on relative economic capabilities. The tangible nature of military assets makes them easier to measure than economic assets.[4] Shifts in the balance of military

---

[4] Even before the benefits of high-technology surveillance systems, intelligence services have been able to provide fairly accurate information about the adversary's military capabilities. See Ernest May, *Knowing One's Enemies: Intelligence Assessment before the Two World Wars* (Princeton: Princeton University Press, 1984), pp. 504–505.

power are therefore more recognizable than shifts in relative economic strength.[5]

Despite the assertion that elites, at least during the periods under investigation, were aware of the power shifts occurring in the international arena, it is important to recognize two persistent sources of ambiguity and uncertainty that have consequences for the timing and nature of strategic adjustment. First, the planning community must establish indicators through which to measure power, and standards through which to evaluate what level of capability—as measured by those indicators—constitutes sufficiency. Second, elites must cope with the problem of incorporating intentions into threat assessment and into the drafting of the war plans that serve as the basis for setting requirements.

The broad indicators used to assess power balances tend to be fairly resistant to change. Barring wars or glaring changes in technology that illuminate the obsolescence of certain indicators, planners generally rely on the measures of power handed down to them by their predecessors. Assessments of military capability have focused largely on troop levels and the quality and quantity of weaponry.[6] Indicators of eco-

[5] Consider that during much of the Cold War, the United States possessed a fairly thorough accounting of Soviet military hardware but had much more difficulty assessing Soviet economic strength and Soviet military spending as a percentage of GNP. For discussion of some of the methodological problems involved, see Franklyn Holzman, "Politics and Guesswork: CIA and DIA Estimates of Soviet Military Spending," *Interna-*¹ ᵣₑfₑᵣₑₙₑ *tional Security*, 14 (Fall 1989), 101–131. Similarly, in his study of British assessment between 1895 and 1905, Friedberg finds that the planning community had the most difficulty assessing Britain's economic strength—that is, its relative industrial capability. Elites differed as to what indicators best captured relative industrial strength. Furthermore, there was a dearth of reliable statistics about the performance of the British economy as well as about the economies of foreign powers. Some elites feared that Britain was experiencing a distinct fall from industrial preeminence, but they could not marshal sufficient evidence to convince their colleagues or the electorate of their concerns. Assessment of Britain's changing security environment, though laden with ambiguity, pointed more clearly to the erosion of the country's preeminent position. See Friedberg, *Weary Titan.*

[6] Although recent improvements in data collection and analysis have allowed for more accurate assessment of military capabilities, planners during earlier periods were well aware of the shortcomings inherent in basing strategic assessments on raw numerical comparisons. For example, the British War Office at the turn of the century was already using analytic techniques of impressive sophistication to incorporate logistical constraints and organizational concerns into its assessments. See Public Record Office (PRO), CAB 38/10/84, "Suggestions as to the Basis for the Calculation of the Required Transport of an Army Operating in Afghanistan." (CAB is the PRO classification for cabinet documents.) For discussion of contemporary methods of strategic assessment, see Charles Kupchan, "Setting Conventional Force Requirements: Roughly Right or Precisely Wrong?" *World Politics*, 41 (July 1989), 549–555. In addition, elites frequently took into account social and institutional factors when assessing threats. Before World War I, for example, the British, French, and Germans all adjusted their assessments of Russian war-making capability to take Russia's social and organizational problems into con-

nomic capability have fluctuated somewhat more over time to keep pace with changes in technology.[7] Although reliance on a relatively static set of indicators at times breeds insensitivity to subtle technological changes or to shifts in power resources not covered by these indicators, consistency in measurement enables elites to be aware of major shifts in the strategic landscape. Decision makers may frequently fail to assimilate fully the strategic implications of specific changes in military or industrial technology, but they have been able to assess, albeit in approximate terms, broader shifts in the military and economic balance.

Standards of sufficiency are, however, far less static in nature than numerical measures of relative military and economic capability. At the turn of the century, for example, the British used the Two-Power Standard to determine naval force levels: the Royal Navy had to be at least equal in size to the next two most powerful fleets. As the naval balance worsened, the Admiralty scaled back the standard, arguing that it should apply only to likely adversaries, not to all countries. This allowed planners to exclude the U.S. fleet when calculating force levels.[8]

---

sideration. See William Wohlforth, "The Perception of Power: Russia in the Pre-1914 Balance," *World Politics*, 39 (April 1987), 353–381; and Keith Neilson, "Watching the 'Steamroller': British Observers and the Russian Army before 1914," *Journal of Strategic Studies*, 8, 2 (1985), 199–217.

[7] World War I served as a watershed in terms of elite thinking about the relationship between economic capability and military power. Before the war, elites realized that a world-class military depended on a world-class economy. But they believed that war in Europe would be short—a matter of months—and that military capabilities existing at the outset would be more important than economic durability in determining the outcome. British decision makers, for example, believed that peacetime governmental and institutional arrangements would be adequate to marshal resources for battle. In the words of David French, strategic planning and the demands of war did not entail deviating from "business as usual." During this period, British planners relied primarily on trade data to assess the strength of the manufacturing sector. It was only after the scope and length of the war became apparent that elites realized that industrial mobilization and productive capacity would be key determinants of the outcome. Even for parties that were involved only peripherally, such as Japan, World War I illuminated the vital connection between industrial strength and war-making capacity. During the 1930s, elites in the major powers were accordingly far more sensitive to the importance of economic and financial preparations for war. They also began to rely on more sophisticated indicators, such as steel production and share of manufacturing output, to measure industrial capacity. See French, *British Economic and Strategic Planning 1905–1915* (London: Allen and Unwin, 1982); and Robert Shay, Jr., *British Rearmament in the Thirties: Politics and Profits* (Princeton: Princeton University Press, 1977), esp. chaps. 3 and 7.

[8] Friedberg, *Weary Titan*, pp. 173–174. The determination of force levels for the army went through a similar transition. At the turn of the century, British planners attempted to derive force requirements by assessing threats, determining force levels needed in each section of the empire, and summing the requirements for all regional missions. See PRO, CAB 38/1/6, 10 Aug. 1901, "Military Needs of the Empire in a War with France and Russia." These standards were relaxed after 1904 when the British began to focus on the possibility of conflict with Germany.

During the interwar period, when faced with severe financial constraints and the rapid buildup of potentially hostile fleets in both Europe and the Far East, the Admiralty again scaled back the definition of sufficiency: the Royal Navy had to be large enough to defeat the German fleet while simultaneously maintaining a deterrent force in the Far East. Similar constraints induced the Nixon administration to scale back the yardsticks of sufficiency used to set U.S. conventional force levels.[9]

It is plausible that such shifts in standards of sufficiency prevent elites from recognizing, or at least seeing as consequential, imbalances between resources and commitments; if any given definition of sufficiency is of only transient importance, then the force requirements that devolve from that notion of sufficiency become less meaningful. The ability to alter standards of sufficiency does not, however, mean that elites are unable to generate determinate assessments of force requirements. On the contrary, the case studies show that shifts in standards of sufficiency often result from economic and political pressures. Elites turn to manipulation of these standards as a way of reducing defense expenditure, maintaining commitments for which sufficient resources do not exist, and/or sustaining domestic support for defense policy. The problem is one not of analytic ambiguity or uncertainty, but of conscious manipulation. Standards of sufficiency come to be based on what is economically and politically feasible, not on what is strategically sound.

The difficulties involved in incorporating intentions into threat assessment could also contribute to the recurrence of adjustment failure.[10] It is possible that planners may be aware of a significant shift in the distribution of power but fail to respond accordingly because they do not appreciate the imminence or severity of a specific threat. Alternatively, the planning community may be unable to reach a consensus about what scenarios should serve as the basis for war plans. During the early 1930s, for example, the British army, navy, and air force each based its war plans on confrontation with a different adversary, in part because they could not agree on which adversary posed the most

---

[9] The Kennedy administration adhered to a two-and-a-half war standard: a major war in Europe and Asia, and a small war elsewhere. The Nixon administration, facing political and economic constraints stemming from the Vietnam War, adhered to a one-and-a-half war standard: a major war in either Europe or Asia, and a small war elsewhere. See John Lewis Gaddis, *Strategies of Containment* (New York: Oxford University Press, 1982), p. 297.

[10] As John Prados remarks, "The question of capabilities versus intentions is the thorniest of conceptual problems." *The Soviet Estimate: U.S. Intelligence Analysis and Russian Military Strength* (New York: Dial Press, 1982), p. 296.

[39]

pressing threat to British interests.[11] Such episodes, however, are rare. During the five- to ten-year periods before the outbreak of major wars, elites have generally been aware of their major foreign adversaries and allies and have succeeded in focusing the attention of the planning community accordingly. While planners are not able to predict exactly when or where war will break out, they usually do base war plans on a scenario that turns out to be reasonably accurate.[12] Again, inherent imprecision in forecasting does prevent planners from carrying out net assessment with exactitude, but it does not prevent them from being aware of broad shifts in the international distribution of power and of the consequent need to adjust grand strategy. The assessment process itself does not play an important role in the failure of states to adjust appropriately to international change.

PSYCHOLOGICAL DISTORTION, MISCALCULATION, AND COGNITIVE CONSTRAINTS

How elites react to international change is highly dependent on their beliefs about the strategic landscape. If elites believe the coming war is to be a long one, they are likely to slow rearmament in order to build economic durability. If they believe the war will be short, they will sacrifice economic growth in order to pursue a rapid military buildup. If decision makers predict that the outcome of the war will be determined on land, they will allocate resources to the army. If geography and technology point to the importance of sea control, elites will orchestrate a naval buildup.

These observations are commonsensical. Furthermore, they have very different theoretical consequences depending on how one understands the nature of beliefs. If beliefs are accurate reflections of reality, the medium through which observations are conceptualized and processed into vocabulary, then they play little, if any, independent role in shaping decisions. If, on the other hand, beliefs are the product of experience and learning, the lens through which elites interpret and structure reality rather than a reflection of that reality itself, then they

---

[11] The air force focused on the air defense of Great Britain, the navy on operations in the Far East, and the army on the defense of India.

[12] Studies of surprise attack corroborate this assertion. Surprise attacks have been successful not because the defender failed to identify the potential threat and to plan accordingly, but because he failed to interpret correctly available information about the timing of attack. Planning communities tend to discount indications that attack is imminent because they hold prior beliefs that the adversary is either unwilling or unprepared to attack. See Richard Betts, *Surprise Attack: Lessons for Defense Planning* (Washington, D.C.: Brookings Institution, 1982).

play a far more consequential role in determining behavior. They must be treated as a crucial variable shaping the adjustment process and not simply as the cognitive medium through which observations are conceptualized. From this perspective, elite belief systems consist of causal inferences about the world, "knowledge structures" that are formed about the fundamental interactions that shape outcomes in the international system. These beliefs are used to assimilate and make sense of incoming information. Strategic beliefs can thus be conceived of as inference-based suppositions about the dynamics that drive international relations, suppositions that shape how elites order and understand external reality.

Drawing on this distinction between beliefs as an accurate reflection of reality and beliefs as a cognitive construct for understanding the external world, cognitive psychology and the study of elite belief systems offer three broad explanations of adjustment failure. First, crisis resulting from adverse shifts in the balance of power and the growing likelihood of war may lead to high levels of stress and associated psychological dysfunctions within the decision-making community. Stress can induce motivated biases that lead elites to distort or view selectively incoming information.[13] As a result, they may base strategic decisions on information that they *want* to see rather than on information that they *do* see. Elite beliefs about external reality become distorted. According to this formulation, decision makers operating under high stress experience psychological dysfunction and therefore make inopportune strategic choices.

Second, adjustment failure could be the result of miscalculation. Elite beliefs may accurately reflect incoming information but lead to suboptimal outcomes because of unforeseen and unpredictable events. Responding to rapid international change entails making decisions under conditions of complexity and uncertainty. Complexity emerges from the difficulties inherent in strategic assessment and in choosing among competing values and interests. Uncertainty emerges from the inability of elites to predict with reliability if, when, and where threats may come due, to ascertain the motivations of adversaries, and to judge how adversaries will react to their behavior. Even if elites are able to recognize the need to adjust, they may simply miscalculate the likelihood and/or the costs and benefits of certain outcomes and make judg-

---

[13] An extensive literature exists on stress-induced psychological dysfunction. Common manifestations of this dysfunction include defensive avoidance, selective search of information, and premature cognitive closure. See Irving Janis and Leon Mann, *Decision Making: A Psychological Analysis of Conflict, Choice, and Commitment* (New York: Free Press, 1977); and Richard Ned Lebow, *Between Peace and War: The Nature of International Crisis* (Baltimore: Johns Hopkins University Press, 1981).

ments that, in hindsight, were misguided. They may do a good job of assessing the situation, identifying likely outcomes, and considering fully available options, but nevertheless make choices that prove, as events unfold, to be inappropriate. As Alexander George warns, "We must be careful . . . not to confuse error with irrationality, not to infer from post hoc observations that an error or oversimplification that occurred in policymaking was due to some form of irrational perception or judgment."[14] Even if beliefs are the product of logical inference, they may still lead decision makers to make inopportune strategic choices. Especially under conditions of complexity and uncertainty, miscalculation is always possible.

Third, adjustment failures could be the product of cognitive constraints that cause elites to hold inappropriate strategic beliefs. For this argument to have explanatory power, beliefs must not be viewed as simply the medium through which observations of some objective reality are represented and verbalized. On the contrary, they must be conceived of as cognitive constructs or knowledge structures that individuals use to understand and order reality, that give shape and substance to an otherwise unmanageable mass of perceptions and information. From this perspective, "the mind cannot perform without structuring reality," and it is beliefs that fulfill the structuring function.[15] The way in which the human mind processes information indeed shapes the nature of these beliefs. Cognitive constraints—the need to simplify complex events, the inclination to fit incoming information to preexisting categories, the tendency for knowledge structures to persevere in the face of contradictory information—affect how individuals structure reality. But these unmotivated biases are associated with the normal functioning of the mind, not with stress-induced psychological distortion.[16]

---

[14] Alexander George, *Presidential Decisionmaking in Foreign Policy: The Effective Use of Information and Advice* (Boulder, Colo.: Westview Press, 1980), p. 62.

[15] Ibid., p. 77. This conception of beliefs is standard within the literature on social psychology. The analysis in this section draws on the terminology and conception of beliefs presented in Richard Nisbett and Lee Ross, *Human Inference: Strategies and Shortcomings of Social Judgment* (Englewood Cliffs, N.J.: Prentice-Hall, 1980).

[16] Motivated biases are produced by emotional needs, whereas unmotivated biases are the product of cognitive limitations. Motivated biases can occur under noncrisis as well as crisis conditions. Any decision maker faced with incoming information that produces psychic discomfort could experience a motivated bias. My formulation of the hypothesis on stress-induced psychological distortion and this hypothesis on cognitive constraints is based on three considerations. First, motivated biases are most pronounced during crisis; urgency increases psychic discomfort. If motivated biases are at work, they should manifest themselves most readily in a crisis setting. In the context of day-to-day decision making, biases affecting decisions are far more likely to be unmotivated in nature. Second, setting up the problem in this manner will isolate temporally the sources of the beliefs that lead to adjustment failure. Are the beliefs that impair adjustment the product

Elite beliefs take shape gradually and are the product primarily of personal experiences, learning, and important external stimuli.[17] Efforts to map belief systems by coding records of elite discussions and by circulating questionnaires among elites demonstrate that most decision makers indeed have consistent and logically coherent beliefs. Such studies also suggest that elites usually do behave in ways consistent with their belief systems.[18] Surveys of elites provide further evidence of the importance of belief systems and the extent to which they shape policy choice. In examining the effects of the Vietnam War on the belief systems of American leaders, Ole Holsti and James Rosenau find that deep cleavages among elites "appear to be embedded within and sustained by well-defined clusters of supporting beliefs that extend from conceptions of the international system to the most effective means by which the United States should pursue its foreign policy goals."[19]

———————

of crises, or do they emerge more gradually under normal decision-making conditions? The answer to this question will provide guidance as to the sources of overly cooperative and overly competitive behavior and, consequently, as to how such behavior can be avoided. Third, since the outcomes produced by motivated and unmotivated biases may be similar, and both biases can occur in noncrisis settings, it is difficult in methodological terms to distinguish between them. In noncrisis settings, I begin by assuming that only unmotivated biases are at work for the following reason. Analysis that focuses on motivated biases, inasmuch as it relies on assumptions about emotions and cognition, adds a level of complexity to analysis that focuses on unmotivated biases, which relies on assumptions only about cognition. In the interests of parsimony, explanations should move to higher levels of complexity only if needed to understand observations. Accordingly, in noncrisis settings, motivated biases should be turned to only when unmotivated biases are insufficient to explain outcomes. Furthermore, an explanation that assumes the operation of unmotivated biases is widely applicable; all humans, regardless of the decision-making environment, face cognitive constraints. An explanation that assumes the operation of motivated biases is more restrictive. It would apply only under certain conditions—namely, when the decision makers under examination are in an environment producing psychic discomfort. These considerations shape the hypotheses above. Also for these reasons, in constructing my own argument in the second half of this chapter, I begin by seeking to construct an explanation of outcomes that relies on unmotivated biases. I then examine what analytic insights can be gained by positing that motivated biases are also at work.

[17] Nisbett and Ross, *Human Inference*, p. 30.

[18] Throughout this study, I assume that beliefs do shape behavior. Demonstrating causality between beliefs and policy choices does, however, present thorny methodological problems. On this issue see Ole Holsti, "Foreign Policy Viewed Cognitively," in *Structure of Decision: The Cognitive Maps of Political Elites*, ed. Robert Axelrod (Princeton: Princeton University Press, 1976), pp. 34 ff., 57. See also the relevant sections in Nisbett and Ross, *Human Inference*; and in Susan Fiske and Shelley Taylor, *Social Cognition* (Reading, Mass.: Addison-Wesley, 1984).

[19] Ole Holsti and James Rosenau, "Vietnam, Consensus, and the Belief Systems of American Leaders," *World Politics*, 32 (October 1979), 56. See also James Rosenau and Ole Holsti, "U.S. Leadership in a Shrinking World: The Breakdown of Consensuses and the Emergence of Conflicting Belief Systems," *World Politics*, 35 (April 1983), 368–392; and D. Michael Shafer, *Deadly Paradigms: The Failure of U.S. Counterinsurgency Policy* (Princeton: Princeton University Press, 1988). For discussion of elite beliefs and economic policy, see Peter Hall, ed., *The Political Power of Economic Ideas: Keynesianism across Nations*

From this perspective, adjustment failure occurs when a set of strategic beliefs induces elites to adopt policies that impair adaptation to international change. Even if elites are well aware of a shift in the material distribution of power, different beliefs will lead to different interpretations of the implications of those shifts. If elites believe that threats will deter an opponent, they will challenge and stand firm against a rising adversary. If, on the other hand, they believe that overt threats are more likely to provoke war, they will accommodate the demands of the adversary. If elites believe that peripheral empire contributes to metropolitan security, they will hold on to overseas possessions as the international environment grows more dangerous. If they believe that empire is a net drain on metropolitan resources, they are more likely to retrench as threats to the metropole mount. An eventual outcome that proves to be suboptimal could well be the product of these beliefs, not the product of stress-induced psychological distortion or miscalculation.

Elite behavior is consistent with commonly accepted notions of rationality as long as the beliefs that shape policy are based on logical inference, internally consistent, and grounded in historical experience, and as long as elites calculate that the policies they choose will maximize their central values and interests.[20] Such beliefs may prove to be inappropriate, however, because of inherent constraints on the cognitive capacities of the mind. These constraints may manifest themselves in two ways. First, limitations on the capacity of the human mind to process information may mean that logical and internally consistent beliefs are nevertheless inappropriate—that is, they constitute an inaccurate representation of external reality. Experiments indicate that the inferential shortcomings associated with the need to simplify and order a complex reality often impair the individual's ability to recognize accurately causal relationships. Preexisting theories, for example, can sensitize people to certain types of incoming information. Individuals also tend to rely too heavily on causal inferences that are readily available in memory. Richard Nisbett and Lee Ross summarize the implications of these shortcomings:

> The knowledge structures themselves are not infallible guides to the nature of physical or social reality. Some beliefs, theories, and schemas are

---

(Princeton: Princeton University Press, 1989); and Judith Goldstein, "Ideas, Institutions, and American Trade Policy," *International Organization*, 42 (Winter 1988), 179–217.

[20] My use of the term *rational* falls between what are commonly called procedural and substantive notions of rationality. It is procedural inasmuch as it specifies that elites must engage in behavior that they believe will maximize their interests and values. It is substantive inasmuch as the beliefs that inform policy choice must be logically consistent

relatively poor and inaccurate representations of the external world. More dangerous, objects and events are not always labelled accurately and sometimes are processed through entirely inappropriate knowledge structures. Without these structures stored in memory, life would be a buzzing confusion, but their clarity is helpful only in proportion to their validity and to the accuracy with which they are applied to the data at hand.[21]

As Robert Axelrod describes these cognitive constraints on decision making, inopportune decisions may result from "limitations in the structure of the beliefs he [the decision maker] presents as an image of the policy environment."[22]

Second, beliefs that initially represent accurately external reality may become outmoded because of changing circumstances. Knowledge structures tend to persevere in the face of disconfirming evidence. Experiments provide convincing evidence that "people seem to persist in adhering to their theories to a point that far exceeds any normatively justifiable criterion of 'conservatism.'" Nisbett and Ross contend that "there will be less change [in beliefs] than would be demanded by logical or normative standards" and "that changes will occur more slowly than would result from an unbiased view of the accumulated evidence."[23] Information contradicting existing causal inferences may initially cause individuals to cling tightly to those theories in order to preserve stability in their belief systems. Incoming data that are consistent with existing beliefs may be readily assimilated, while data that are discrepant may be ignored or manipulated to fit prevailing strategic conceptions. If causal inferences about international relations lag behind incoming information, then it stands to reason that elites could often adopt ill-suited policies during periods of rapid international change.

The notion of "bounded rationality" captures these limitations on the information-processing capacities of the mind.[24] According to this hypothesis, adjustment failure is the product not of psychological distortion associated with crises or of miscalculation, but of the content and nature of the ideas and beliefs that propagate within the elite

---

and grounded in experience. The analyst, as objective observer, reserves the right to pass judgment as to whether core beliefs are consistent and based on logical inference.

[21] Nisbett and Ross, *Human Inference*, p. 7. This volume provides a comprehensive discussion of common inferential shortcomings.

[22] Axelrod, *Structure of Decision*, p. 57.

[23] Nisbett and Ross, *Human Inference*, pp. 169, 189.

[24] See Herbert Simon, *Models of Bounded Rationality* (Cambridge: MIT Press, 1982); and Robert Keohane, *After Hegemony* (Princeton: Princeton University Press, 1984), pp. 111–116.

community. Inherent constraints on the ability of the human mind to process information—which lead to the formation of inaccurate knowledge structures and/or the perseverance of outmoded knowledge structures—could lie at the roots of overly cooperative and overly competitive behavior.

Because of the difficulties involved in distinguishing empirically among explanations relying on psychological distortion, miscalculation, and cognitive constraints, it is important to specify the types of evidence used to confirm and disconfirm these three competing propositions. The psychological distortion associated with crisis-induced stress should come about when elites must make crucial policy decisions in a compressed time frame. Such conditions are present when elites believe that war is imminent. Stress-induced dysfunctions include premature closure when choosing among policy options, selective neglect of external events and signals, and subtle manipulation of information in order to make assessments conform to expected or desired outcomes. These dysfunctions should manifest themselves in the form of beliefs and assessments that appear, to the objective observer, to be at odds with incoming information. For example, if decision makers are confronted with intelligence reports that, by standards of reasonable judgment, should lead to pessimism about the chances of victory against a given adversary, but elites distort or selectively assimilate such information and remain optimistic about the likely outcome of war, there is good reason to assume that psychological dysfunction is at work. Elites assimilate information in ways that allow them to see what they want to see. If, on the other hand, decision makers become appropriately pessimistic about the chances of victory but nevertheless pursue policies that are likely to lead to war, there is reason to believe that psychological distortion is not the problem. Elites are processing information in a reasonable manner and are being pressed to adopt extremist policies by other forces.

Attributing adjustment failure to miscalculation rests on showing that elites based their actions on reasoned and reasonable assessments and calculations but that unforeseen developments led to suboptimal outcomes. Evidence that elites processed information efficiently and fully considered available options lends strength to this explanation. Adjustment failure should be the product of unpredictable events that elites could reasonably have failed to foresee. The types of adjustment failure exhibited over time should also be somewhat random in nature inasmuch as complexity and uncertainty can produce misjudgment on any number of dimensions.

To examine the relationship between cognitive constraints and adjustment failure, it is necessary to demonstrate that elites base grand

[46]

strategy on a coherent set of strategic beliefs. These beliefs must be relatively consistent with the recent experiences of the state, the lessons drawn from past wars, and current knowledge about technology and warfare. In short, there should be good reason to conclude that elite beliefs have a firm basis in historical experiences and that the causal claims that constitute a belief system are the product of logical inference. From this perspective, adjustment failures occur when certain fundamental dimensions of elite beliefs—beliefs that are consistent with the notion of bounded rationality—produce policies incompatible with adaptation to international change. These beliefs impair adjustment because of inherent constraints on the cognitive capacities of the mind. These constraints could produce beliefs that inaccurately represent external reality from the outset; elites may process information to the best of their ability but still draw faulty lessons and hold beliefs ill-suited to current circumstances. If so, careful empirical analysis and the advantages of hindsight should reveal specific instances in which elites used inappropriate historical analogies and based policy on inappropriate historical lessons.[25] Alternatively, initially accurate beliefs may become outmoded because they persevere in the face of contradictory incoming information. This explanation would be confirmed by evidence that beliefs were reasonable and accurate at time 1, outmoded at time 2, and then gradually brought into line with incoming information at time 3. The problem is one not of discrete psychological distortions associated with crisis, but of knowledge structures and causal inferences that induce elites to adopt policies that impair adjustment. Furthermore, these strategic beliefs must be fundamental in nature and shape how elites understand international relations, structure interactions with other states, and define strategic interests and priorities. In other words, a causal link must exist between these beliefs and the absence of adjustment. Evidence that adjustment failures are similar in nature across time and country would corroborate explanations focusing on the importance of cognitive constraints and their effect on strategic beliefs. Rather than being the product of random misjudgment, adjustment failure would occur when cognitive constraints that affect all decision makers lead to recurring patterns of behavior.

Examination of the case studies leads to the following conclusions. Explanations of adjustment failure relying on crisis-induced psychological dysfunction are not satisfying for two main reasons. First, the

---

[25] For insightful analysis of how elites use historical analogies and why they may use them inappropriately, see Yuen Foong Khong, *Analogies at War: Korea, Munich, Dien Bien Phu, and the Vietnam Decisions of 1965* (Princeton: Princeton University Press, 1992).

strategic beliefs that lead to adjustment failure emerge well before crises, not during them. The psychological implications of crisis-induced stress cannot therefore serve as a key explanatory variable. Second, the cases show that elites, for the most part, do not assimilate incoming information in a manner inconsistent with reasonable judgment. When confronted with intelligence assessments that indicate an unfavorable military balance, decision makers become appropriately pessimistic about the prospect of going to war. When efforts to intimidate the adversary lead only to increasing hostility, elites become aware of the dangerous effects of their policies. They simply do not distort incoming information to see what they want to see. I am not suggesting that the cases examined below do not contain short periods of crisis in which psychological dysfunction contributed to assessment and adjustment failure. But the analysis does show that such dysfunction only exacerbated dynamics driven by other forces.

Miscalculation also fails to offer a compelling explanation for adjustment failure. The case studies do not provide evidence that elites simply make random errors of judgment and are foiled by the complex and unpredictable nature of interstate relations. The developments that lead to strategic exposure, self-encirclement, and overextension are not those that elites can reasonably fail to foresee. Moreover, decision makers are, for the most part, fairly accurate in their assessments of when and where threats come due. Instances of adjustment failure also prove to be similar in nature, suggesting that they are not the product of random misjudgment.[26]

Focusing on cognitive constraints and strategic beliefs offers an account of adjustment failure that is logically compelling and consistent with the empirical material, although it provides only the first piece of the puzzle. As I argue below, a certain set of beliefs induces elites to pursue both overly cooperative and overly competitive behavior. These beliefs constitute a rational response to the external environment. They are the product of perceptions of high metropolitan vulnerability and the logical inferences that elites draw about how best to cope with conditions of strategic deficiency. I also show that the beliefs that lead to extremist behavior persevere in the face of disconfirming evidence; change in belief lags behind change in the external environment. Elites, at least temporarily, base their policies on obsolete beliefs that are ill-suited to a new strategic landscape.

---

[26] Explanations relying on miscalculation, even if they were consistent with the evidence, would not provide a theoretically satisfying account of the empirical puzzle. This approach would indicate that elites sometimes make good judgments that lead to timely strategic adjustment and sometimes make bad judgments that lead to adjustment failure.

[48]

The persistence of obsolete beliefs fails to provide a satisfying explanation of self-defeating behavior, however, because elites eventually bring their beliefs into line with strategic realities. The beliefs that produce extremist behavior do change when repeatedly exposed to contradictory incoming information. The case studies show that the lag between shifts in the strategic environment and shifts in beliefs does explain some instances of *moderate* adjustment failure. The most acute cases, however, are those in which elites see that their beliefs are outmoded and adapt them to strategic reality but nevertheless do not undertake adjustment. The fact that strategic exposure, self-encirclement, and overextension occur despite elite sensitivity to the obsolescence of prevailing strategic beliefs and to the dangers involved in pursuing extremist policies suggests that focusing on cognitive lags and elite beliefs provides only a piece of the puzzle. In a manner consistent with the original formulation of the hypothesis, beliefs based on logical inference and consistent with the notion of bounded rationality initially lead to extremist behavior. These beliefs then become outmoded because they persevere in the face of disconfirming evidence. But because adjustment failure occurs even after these beliefs have been brought into line with reality, it is clear that other forces must be contributing to extremist behavior and constraining the adaptation of policy.

Cognitive mechanisms and belief systems thus play an important role in producing adjustment failure. In laying out my argument in the final section of this chapter, I draw heavily on this discussion of cognition and beliefs. I also show, however, that focusing on cognitive variables alone does not provide a satisfying explanation of self-defeating behavior. This puzzle can be solved only by examining how cognitive forces interact with variables at other levels of analysis.

PRIVATE ECONOMIC INTERESTS

A considerable body of scholarship views private economic interests as the engine driving imperial expansion. This theoretical tradition is predicated on the supposition that industrialists and financiers benefit from the military expenditure and enhanced trade and investment that accompany empire. Because this body of literature focuses on the link between economic interest and imperial expansion, it is far better suited to explain overly competitive than overly cooperative behavior.

But it would reveal little about the conditions that produce these different outcomes and, hence, about the determinants of dysfunction within the policy-formulation process.

Before discussing the potential relationship between private economic interests and overexpansion, however, I briefly consider one hypothesis linking overly cooperative behavior to the self-seeking behavior of economic interest groups.

Firms heavily reliant on international trade and capital flows, although they are likely to benefit from imperial expansion, would oppose policies that carry a high risk of war. Conflict would disrupt the flow of both trade and capital and thereby decrease profits. Private firms might press decision makers to adopt overly cooperative policies in order to avoid war and protect their economic interests. The case studies in fact show that economic interest groups do often exercise a moderating influence on foreign policy. Not only are they concerned about the potential for conflict to disrupt the international economy, but they also fear that high levels of military spending will divert resources from the civilian sector. In interwar Britain, for example, a significant portion of the economic elite supported appeasement of Germany for these reasons. In interwar Japan, as well, the economic elite sought to moderate Japanese foreign policy in order to preserve good trade relations with Western powers and to protect the civilian economy from the military's unlimited appetite for resources.

The problem with this line of argument is twofold. First, although some sectors of the economic community benefit from cooperative foreign policies, others benefit from the rearmament and expansion that accompany competitive policies. Even in states whose economy depends heavily on trade and the provision of goods and services, manufacturing and industrial interests would support military preparations and thus provide a counterweight to firms calling for accommodation. Second, the cases reveal that political leaders—and not private firms— are primarily responsible for orchestrating the pursuit of overly cooperative policies. Economic interest groups may provide added support for accommodation, but the evidence simply does not support the assertion that such groups impose on the political leadership cooperative policies crafted to further their own narrow interests.

A richer set of propositions must be considered in examining the potential links between private economic interests and overly competitive behavior. Since the publication of J. A. Hobson's *Imperialism: A Study* in 1902, scholarly inquiry into the causes of imperialism frequently points to the importance of economic self-interest among individuals and private firms.[27] According to Hobson, capitalist economies tend to experience declining growth rates over time as a result of insufficient domestic demand. Underconsumption occurs because increases

---

[27] J. A. Hobson, *Imperialism: A Study* (London: Allen and Unwin, 1902).

in wages do not keep pace with increases in productivity stimulated by reinvested profits. When return on investment begins to decline, industrialists and financiers invest their capital abroad. The financial elite enlists the diplomatic and military agents of the state to protect its exported wealth, drawing the state into peripheral commitments and laying the foundation for overseas empire. Lenin drew on this theme, identifying monopolistic banks and industries as the key culprits behind imperial expansion.[28] Central to these economic theories of imperialism is the notion that certain individuals and sectors within society benefit from expansion. Even if empire leads to a net economic loss for the state, it is nevertheless pursued because the benefits associated with imperialism accrue to a select few while the costs of expansion, administration, and defense are more evenly distributed through the population in the form of taxation. The individuals who stand to gain from empire—financiers, industrialists, traders, the military, missionaries—exercise their influence among the political elite in order to secure governmental support for imperial expansion.

More recent efforts to explain imperialism in terms of domestic economic forces focus less on the manipulation of policy by specific sectors and more on the extent to which the structure and requirements of a state's domestic political economy shape its foreign policy. As P. J. Cain and A. G. Hopkins conclude in their analysis of the British empire, "Britain's presence and power abroad were closely connected with the development of the domestic economy, the shifting balance of social and political forces which this development entailed, and the varying intensity of Britain's economic and political rivalry with other powers. . . . Britain's overseas concerns expanded as modernization proceeded until, by the time of the First World War, they were crucial not only to particular powerful financial and industrial groups but also to overall economic growth, to internal stability, and to great-power status."[29] From this perspective, the problem is not the behavior of narrow, self-interested firms, but the efforts of a partnership between public and private elites to create an international environment com-

---

[28] See V. I. Lenin, *Imperialism: The Highest Stage of Capitalism* (New York: International Publishers, 1939). Though Hobson and Lenin share hostility toward imperialism and view the export of capital as the key force driving overseas expansion, they differ as to the cure. Hobson argues that redistribution of wealth can prevent underconsumption and falling rates of return at home, thereby obviating the need for exports of capital. Lenin argues that imperialism is inevitable and that only revolution and the overthrow of capitalism can end it.

[29] P. J. Cain and A. G. Hopkins, "The Political Economy of British Expansion Overseas, 1750–1914," *Economic History Review*, 2d ser., 33 (November 1980), 489.

patible with the state's own political economy and conducive to the expansion of the domestic economy.[30]

This theoretical tradition offers compelling explanations for overly competitive behavior. If the economic self-interest of nongovernmental actors within the state gives rise to empire, then it is plausible that these same narrow interests might be responsible for causing overexpansion. Inasmuch as the concerns of these individuals and firms are narrowly economic, they are likely to be unresponsive to and uninformed about strategic considerations. Oblivious to the effects of empire on metropolitan security, economic interest groups may force decision makers to pursue overly competitive policies. Alternatively, elite concern about building an international environment that will serve the interests of the domestic economy might override strategic considerations. Efforts to fashion lucrative investment and trading opportunities abroad might lure the state into strategic overcommitment.

There are several ways to corroborate explanations of overexpansion that are rooted in classical economic theories of imperialism. First, metropolitan agents must have significant economic interests at stake in the empire or have high expectations of attaining such interests. Second, empirical analysis should show that these agents believe that the protective capacities of the state are needed to guard these interests and that the agents therefore press decision makers to preserve if not expand the scope of the state's international commitments. Moreover, there should be evidence that such pressure has a consequential effect on outcomes—that the electoral and financial support of economic interest groups weighs heavily on the minds of decision makers. It is important to demonstrate not only that metropolitan agents have vested interests in empire, but also that these agents are able to influence policy makers. Third, for any given country, a positive correlation should exist between the amount or expected amount of metropolitan investment in and trade with the empire and the timing and extent of adjustment failure. Overly competitive behavior should occur when metropolitan agents view the preservation and/or expansion of imperial commitments as most important to their economic welfare. Fourth, to confirm the version of the argument that focuses on elite concern about creating an international environment in which the domestic economy can prosper, empirical analysis should indicate that foreign policy is driven primarily by economic considerations. Public and pri-

---

[30] For application of this approach to U.S. expansion after World War II, see Michael Hogan, *The Marshall Plan: America, Britain, and the Reconstruction of Western Europe, 1947–1952* (New York: Cambridge University Press, 1987).

vate elites should see access to international markets and resources as critical to the well-being of the domestic economy. Historical analysis should also reveal that these elites believe that the extension of military commitments is needed to protect such access, and that efforts to further the interests of the domestic economy are consequently driving decision makers to assume a range of international commitments that the state cannot uphold.

On the basis of these tests, this book shows that private economic interests do not contribute substantially to adjustment failures. Like economic explanations of imperialism, economic explanations of over-expansion do not hold up under empirical scrutiny.[31] In many of the case studies, metropolitan agents do have either high expectations of reaping profits in the empire or substantial levels of investment and trade already at stake in the empire. Concerned parties indeed make their interests known to the political elite. But the relationship between the economic elite and empire is by no means uniform across the cases. In Japan, France, and Germany, the business community was, at times, hostile to empire. During key debates about the merits of preserving and/or expanding imperial holdings, economic elites sided with those arguing for moderation and retrenchment. In the U.S. case study, political elites were the key actors behind the extension of American economic and military assistance to Europe; a significant portion of the business community had to be persuaded to back the Truman administration. Britain's economic elite was generally more sympathetic to empire but also realized that healthy rates of return were available in other core states. Because investment could usually be redirected without serious cost, the business community had little reason to stand in the way of retrenchment.

Most important, even when the economic stakes are high, there is little evidence that the business community plays an important role in shaping major strategic decisions. Cabinet-level discussions rarely focus on the narrow concerns of firms. Even though decision makers frequently take the overall economic value of a specific territory into consideration when setting strategic priorities, the interests of specific investors or traders do not have a big effect on outcomes.[32] This finding

[31] Economic theories of imperialism have been undermined by telling critiques. Some of the most important and thorough critiques include D. K. Fieldhouse, "'Imperialism': An Historiographical Revision," *Economic History Review*, 2d Ser. 14 (December 1981), 187–217; Ronald Robinson and John Gallagher, with Alice Denny, *Africa and the Victorians: The Official Mind of Imperialism* (London: Macmillan, 1961); and Kenneth Waltz, *Theory of International Politics* (Reading, Mass.: Addison-Wesley, 1979), pp. 18–37.

[32] One could propose that such matters are simply not discussed openly; politicians do not want to admit that they are bowing to economic pressure. The consistent absence

may explain the absence of a positive correlation between overseas investment and trade levels and adjustment failure. It is simply not the case that high levels of private investment and trade correspond with periods of overly competitive behavior. Similarly, successful adjustment does not correspond with periods of relatively low investment and trade.

Nor is it the case that overexpansion results primarily from elite efforts to build an international environment that will serve the interests of the domestic economy. In most of the historical cases, strategic imperatives consistently take priority over economic opportunities. In those instances in which economic objectives guide defense policy, the main motivation is strategic in nature. Japan, for example, advanced toward Southeast Asia in 1940–1941 to secure oil for its war machine, not to meet the needs of the domestic civilian industry. The United States implemented the Marshall Plan after World War II not to lay the groundwork for the expansion of U.S. business interests, but primarily to stem the spread of communism by fostering economic and political stability in Western Europe. The U.S. economy indeed benefited from the establishment of a liberal, multilateral trading order among revitalized industrial centers, but it was the objective of containing the Soviet Union, more than the need to find markets for the U.S. capitalist economy, that drove the extension of U.S. military and economic assistance to Europe and Asia. Economic explanations for overexpansion simply do not withstand historical scrutiny.

DOMESTIC POLITICS

The domestic political structure of a state might be an important determinant of its ability to adjust to international change. The theoretical tradition asserting that democracies are more peaceful and less prone to extremist policies than nondemocracies suggests that it might be autocratic government that gives rise to adjustment failure.[33] Absent the checks and balances of representative government, autocracies provide few means of correcting the excesses and strategic mistakes of the leadership. Centralized power enables eccentric rulers to pursue inopportune policies, regardless of the effects of those policies on the welfare of the populace. Autocracies might be particularly prone to

---

of discussion of the interests of private firms from even memos and correspondence, however, suggests that political timidity does not explain the lack of more frequent reference to the power of economic interest groups.

[33] See Michael Doyle, "Liberalism and World Politics," *American Political Science Review,* 80 (December 1986), 1151–1169.

overexpansion because elites lack the legitimacy that accompanies representative government and may be tempted to use foreign success to garner domestic support.

This line of argument is problematic for two reasons. First, the historical cases reveal that autocracies and democracies alike fall prey to adjustment failure. Autocratic government cannot therefore be the main cause of extremist behavior. Second, the cases reveal that autocracies often adjust successfully to international change. These instances of successful adjustment discredit claims positing a causal link between autocratic government and self-defeating foreign policies.

Alternatively, it is possible that democracy causes adjustment failure. Many scholars have noted that the unwieldy nature of democratic government can impair the pursuit of pragmatic foreign and defense policies.[34] Public opinion, electoral pressures, and the maintenance of governing coalitions could all interfere in the formulation and implementation of policy and thereby prevent timely adjustment to change. Overly cooperative policies could be the result of the public's unwillingness to allocate the resources needed to keep pace with external adversaries. Overly competitive policies could be driven by nationalism or other popular ideologies that favor expansionism.

That autocracies and democracies alike suffer adjustment failure also poses problems for this line of argument. If autocratic states pursue self-defeating behavior, democracy is clearly not the cause. So too do the case studies demonstrate that democracies often adjust successfully to international change. Theories that focus exclusively on the unwieldy nature of democratic government provide no way of explaining why democratic polities sometimes follow a course of strategic pragmatism but other times fall prey to extremist behavior.

Jack Snyder, in *Myths of Empire*, has constructed an account of the causes of overexpansion which synthesizes explanations relying on economic interests with those focusing on domestic structure. Because Snyder has explicitly addressed the causes of self-encirclement and overextension (he restricts his inquiry to overly competitive behavior and thus does not deal with the causes of strategic exposure), it is worth examining his work in some detail. Snyder's main argument is that cartelized polities produce overexpansion through logrolling among imperial interest groups. The more cartelized a state is, the more "power assets—including material resources, organizational

---

[34] See, for example, Alexander George, "Domestic Constraints on Regime Change in U.S. Foreign Policy: The Need for Policy Legitimacy," in *Change in the International System*, ed. Ole Holsti, Randolph Siverson, and Alexander George (Boulder, Colo.: Westview Press, 1980).

strength, and information—are concentrated in the hands of parochial groups."[35] Snyder contends that coalition building and logrolling among groups with vested interests in imperial expansion—industrialists, traders, the military, colonial bureaucrats—are the key causes of self-defeating expansion.[36] When interest groups engage in logrolling, "each group gets what it wants most in return for tolerating the adverse effects of the policies its coalition partners desire." Explanations relying on the activities of individual interest groups (such as that of Hobson) are unsatisfying, according to Snyder, because such groups lack the political power needed to "hijack" the state. By "pooling their power in a coalition," however, imperial interests are able to penetrate and co-opt the state.[37] Though no single party is interested in self-destructive expansion, the cumulative goals of imperial interest groups as a whole eventually saddle the state with commitments that it is unable to uphold. In Snyder's words, overexpansion is "more extreme than any individual group would have preferred, owing to the compounding of separate imperial programs through the logrolling process." "Each interest group insists on its own program of expansion, so the result is far more overcommitted and provokes far more enemies than any of the individual interests thinks is wise."[38] Excessive ambition is exacerbated by the fact that "by capturing the state, groups in the imperial coalition can harness its propaganda resources." These groups then sell "self-serving strategic arguments" to political leaders and the public.[39] At times, coalition leaders come to believe in these "imperial myths" through a process that Snyder calls "blowback."[40]

Snyder correlates the severity of overexpansion with a state's degree of cartelization and, consequently, with the timing of industrialization. The more cartelized a state is, the more intense the logrolling among

---

[35] Jack Snyder, *Myths of Empire: Domestic Politics and International Ambition* (Ithaca: Cornell University Press, 1991), p. 31.

[36] Snyder builds on the work of Mancur Olson. Olson focuses on the extent to which interest groups and distributional coalitions constrain adaptation to change. Though his argument applies primarily to economic efficiency and adaptation, it can also be applied to questions of grand strategy. As societies mature, Olson argues, interest groups proliferate, securing economic gain for their members at a cost to efficiency and growth in the society as a whole. Distributional coalitions make the decision-making arena more complex and divisive. As a result, they "slow down a society's capacity to adopt new technologies and to reallocate resources in response to changing conditions." See *The Rise and Decline of Nations: Economic Growth, Stagflation, and Social Rigidities* (New Haven: Yale University Press, 1982), p. 74. Since Snyder has directly addressed the causes of self-encirclement and overextension and his work effectively subsumes Olson's, I address in detail only Snyder's work.

[37] Snyder, *Myths of Empire*, pp. 44, 15, 17.

[38] Ibid., pp. 17, 44.

[39] Ibid., p. 17.

[40] Ibid., p. 41.

imperial interests. Late industrializers, such as Germany and Japan, tend to have highly cartelized domestic polities and therefore fall prey to extreme bouts of overexpansion. Democracies (early industrializers) and unitary systems governed by a single leader or a ruling group (late, late industrializers) tend to be less cartelized and to experience more moderate forms of overexpansion.[41]

Snyder's creative and synthetic argument provides the most compelling explanation of overexpansion in the existing literature. By building bridges between classical economic theories of imperialism and coalition theory, he circumvents many of the deductive and empirical problems that limit the explanatory power of theories focused exclusively on economic interest groups or domestic structure. Despite its elegance and ingenuity, however, Snyder's approach falls short of providing a satisfying explanation of adjustment failure. His theory faces five main problems.

First, while it is entirely plausible that coalition building should lead to more expansion than any single interest group wants, it is not self-evident why such groups would support policies that threaten to bring ruin to the state as a whole. Snyder takes two approaches to this problem of motivation. He begins by arguing that the groups that support expansion are concerned only with their own narrow interests, not with the general well-being of society: "Groups with a small stake in the fate of society as a whole should be the ones most strongly swayed by a parochial interest in passing along the costs of ruinous imperial enterprises." In contrast, "a strong state or encompassing ruling class, with diverse interests spread across various economic and bureaucratic sectors, might have some parochial interests in overexpansion and mythmaking." But, Snyder argues, "such groups should have a healthy sense of when to stop . . . lest this behavior kill the goose that lays the golden egg."[42]

Snyder's argument rests on the general supposition that certain individuals or groups within the state put their own interests before the collective interests of society as a whole. Yet there is no sound deductive reason why self-interested behavior harmful to the broader polity should be the exclusive domain of imperial interest groups; outcomes that are damaging to the state do not necessarily bear the mark of narrow sectoral interests. Just as an economic interest group or colonial bureaucracy could stand to gain when the state pursues overly com-

---

[41] Snyder notes that states governed by a single leader or cohesive ruling group, although they do not tend to adopt self-defeating policies, can fall prey to extreme overexpansion because the dictator or ruling group faces no domestic checks. See ibid., p. 54.

[42] Ibid., pp. 40–41.

petitive policies, so might self-serving political elites benefit from over-expansion. Politicians frequently take steps to preserve their rule even if such actions do not further the well-being of society. A unified ruling group might propagate nationalist myths or even initiate wars to disarm domestic opposition and consolidate its own power. Indeed, one could plausibly argue that industrialists and financiers, as the owners of the infrastructure and assets that would be destroyed should the state embark on a self-destructive war, have reason to be far more restrained in urging expansionist policies than political leaders who might view expansion, mythmaking, and even self-defeating war as ways to enhance their ability to stay in power.

Snyder's second approach to the problem of motivation in fact challenges his assertion that parochial imperial groups pursue overexpansion to further their narrow interests. He argues that such groups cause overexpansion not because they deliberately pursue reckless policies out of self-interest, but because they unwittingly drag the state into overcommitment. Snyder contends that the groups responsible for excessive expansion may simply be unaware of the potentially ruinous effects of their behavior. Such myopia may result from "uncertainty about the long-run costs of expansion" or when "long-run social costs remain uncalculated because of the highly parochial perspectives of the groups participating in the logrolled coalition."[43] The problem with this argument is that Snyder explicitly states that imperial coalitions have privileged access to strategic information and are, consequently, more knowledgeable about the costs and benefits of expansion than most other sectors of society. It is this access, after all, that helps interest groups hijack the state. As Snyder writes: "Another cause of endemic overexpansion is that self-interested groups favoring militarism and imperial expansion often enjoy an information monopoly. Those who engage in imperial activities and preparation for war automatically gain special knowledge about key elements in strategic cost-benefit calculations, such as local conditions in the hinterland, the strength of the opponent, and the effectiveness of various techniques of fighting."[44] Within Snyder's own framework, it is thus not plausible that imperial interest groups stumble into overexpansion because of inadequate information.

Snyder also argues that even if imperial groups recognize the need to scale back the scope of external ambition, they are unlikely to be able to do so because of the competitive, divisive nature of coalition politics. Theories of overexpansion that assume a unitary leadership

[43] Ibid., pp. 47, 44.
[44] Ibid., p. 35.

are unsatisfying, according to Snyder, because they cannot explain "how a unified elite that is rational enough to devise a strategy of social imperialism nevertheless loses the ability to pull back when the costs of the strategy outweigh its benefits. Logrolling solves this conundrum: "the [cartelized] state's leadership is not a unitary rational actor, but rather is the manager of a heterogeneous coalition that constrains the leadership's ability to adjust policy."[45] The problem with this line of reasoning is that precisely the same argument that applies to a unitary leadership applies to a ruling group formed through coalitional bargaining. A coalition sufficiently astute and powerful to co-opt the state and instigate imperial expansion should also be able to constrain that expansion when it becomes counterproductive and no longer furthers the interests of coalition members. In dealing with Wilhelmine Germany, for example, Snyder essentially challenges his earlier claims about the inability of logrolled coalitions to retrench:

> The overextended foreign policy that resulted from the logrolling should have been reversed once the elites realized the policy was leading to disaster. That is, at least some of the elite groups should have recalculated their interests and decided that the pursuit of parochialism at the cost of an unpromising war was not even in their own narrow self-interest. Rational choice theory makes it clear that a small number of compact groups should be able to solve this kind of collective goods problem by agreeing on new coalition terms that do not involve such disastrous collective costs.[46]

To be sure, retrenchment may be more difficult than under a unified leadership. But even if making sacrifices to competing interest groups is painful, such sacrifices are certainly preferable to self-defeating expansion.

Snyder's final means of dealing with the problem of motivation is to claim that the myths that interest groups propagate in order to facilitate expansion come to be believed by elites and the masses alike. Expansion is then pushed forward by fallacious strategic arguments. This approach is deductively sound and points to a process of entrapment similar to the one that I lay out in my own theory. It does, however, essentially undercut Snyder's central suppositions linking overexpansion to the "compounding of separate imperial programs through the logrolling process." From this perspective, logrolling is consequential

---

[45] Ibid., pp. 16, 17. Snyder writes that "each logroller has a stronger incentive to pursue its parochial interest in expansion than to promote the collective interest in restraint" (p. 47).

[46] Ibid., p. 100.

primarily because it produces strategic myths. But given the fact that such myths could easily be produced in the absence of bargaining among coalitions, logrolling is no longer a logically necessary component of the argument and becomes tangential to Snyder's theory. Imperial interest groups should sell self-serving strategic myths to the polity regardless of its degree of cartelization.[47] Accordingly, domestic structure and the timing of industrialization can no longer serve as key causal variables. Furthermore, this line of argument faces serious empirical problems. As I argue shortly, political leaders themselves, not imperial interest groups, are responsible for propagating the strategic images that entrap the state in self-destructive behavior.

The second problem with Snyder's argument is that although logrolling could conceivably produce overexpansion for the reasons outlined above, there are also sound logical reasons why it should serve to moderate expansive tendencies. According to Snyder, "Logrolling is inherently more apt to produce overexpansion than underexpansion . . . [because] interests in expansion and militarism are typically more concentrated than the interests opposed to them."[48] Even if this specific attribute of logrolling is accurate, other aspects of bargaining and coalition formation serve to lubricate a political system and make more governable a polity divided by competing interests. Logrolling can break political stalemates that might otherwise leave leaders hamstrung and force them to rule through the propagation of expansionist ideologies. In addition, logrolling checks expansion by making individual interests moderate their imperial objectives. Not only is moderation needed to facilitate deal making and coalition formation, but imperial groups are forced to share available resources. Logrolling thus ensures that resources are spread among competing interests. In Wilhelmine Germany and interwar Japan, for example, competition between the army and navy served to rein in the scope of each service's ambition and to limit the military assets that each had available to carry out expansive policies. In short, in cartelized polities, logrolling may in some cases produce overexpansion, but successful logrolling should in other cases serve to limit self-defeating ambition. There is no compel-

---

[47] Admittedly, logrolling could potentially exacerbate the propagation of myths by allowing imperial interests to monopolize the propaganda apparatus of the state. On the other hand, logrolling could potentially moderate the propagation of myths because the deals struck by competing imperial interest groups make it unnecessary for each group to construct a set of strategic arguments to gain support for its particular program among political elites and the masses. From this perspective, the propagation of imperial myths should be worse in polities in which logrolling does not occur than in polities in which bargaining satisfies the individual interests of competing groups.

[48] Snyder, *Myths of Empire*, p. 18.

ling deductive reason why logrolling should necessarily exacerbate rather than moderate expansive tendencies.

The third main problem with Snyder's argument is that a close reading of the historical cases suggests that ruling elites, and not domestic interest groups, are the key culprits behind overexpansion. The chain of causation is the reverse of what Snyder suggests; political decision makers manipulate domestic coalitions rather than vice versa. In Wilhelmine Germany, for example, the logroll between agriculture and industry was initiated by top political elites seeking to govern an increasingly divided polity, not by the interest groups themselves.[49] Agriculture and industry did not co-opt Germany's political leaders. On the contrary, the kaiser and his closest associates co-opted "iron and rye" in order to resist the rising power of the Social Democrats and to rally the domestic polity around external ambition.[50] Furthermore, the logroll that resulted served to dislodge the domestic stalemate and increase the government's control over policy. It was only when the logroll broke down—mainly because neither industry nor agriculture wanted to pay the price of imperial expansion—that political elites were paralyzed and entrapped in powerful currents of popular nationalism. The following chapters confirm that similar arguments apply to all the historical cases. Top decision makers, not imperial interest groups, are primarily responsible for crafting the strategic concepts and unleashing the domestic political forces that fuel overly competitive policies.

The fourth problem with Snyder's argument stems from his insistence on the instrumental character of strategic ideas: "Beliefs and 'lessons' correlate more strongly with personal and institutional interests than with formative experiences."[51] For Snyder, "the myth of security through expansion originated in each case as a justification for the policies of domestic political coalitions formed among groups having parochial interests in imperial expansion."[52] Whether or not overexpansion occurs depends on domestic structure and the extent to which

---

[49] For Snyder's treatment of the German case study, see ibid., pp. 66–111.

[50] Note how Gordon Craig clearly specifies this chain of causation in describing Admiral Tirpitz's efforts to garner support for the fleet: "By identifying the fleet with the economic development of Germany, he won the support of those interests that had a stake in commercial and industrial expansion, starting with the chambers of commerce of the coastal cities, then enlisting some of the larger banking houses, and finally attracting the eager interest of heavy industry." *Germany, 1866–1945* (New York: Oxford University Press, 1978), p. 307. At times, Snyder's own language confirms this interpretation: "By 1898, the German ruling elite had shifted back to the uneasy marriage of iron and rye, which invoked the vague doctrines of social Darwinism and *Weltpolitik* to justify a heterogeneous mix of assertive foreign policies." *Myths of Empire*, p. 85.

[51] Snyder, *Myths of Empire*, p. 30. I thank Charlie Glaser for suggesting this criticism.

[52] Ibid., p. 1.

concentrated imperial interests are able to co-opt the state through logrolling. This explanation rests on the assumption that self-interest impels imperial interest groups—traders, industry, the military—*always* to pursue expansive policies. It is this assumption that allows Snyder to isolate logrolling as the mechanism through which overexpansion comes about. Otherwise, he would also have to provide an account of why and under what conditions specific groups within the state come to propagate expansive strategic ideologies to begin with.

Several problems emerge. The agents within the state that Snyder identifies as the producers of harmful strategic ideologies do not always support expansive policies. As the cases show, military organizations, industrial and financial concerns, and colonial bureaucracies are not engines of imperial expansion that produce self-defeating behavior whenever the domestic polity becomes cartelized.[53] It is also questionable to assume that the strategic concepts espoused by domestic interest groups, even when those concepts are expansionistic, are necessarily the product of instrumental calculation. In this sense, Snyder's account is strangely absent of consideration of the historical trajectory of ideas. The desire for increased profits, growing military budgets, and enhanced institutional power indeed plays a role in shaping strategic concepts, but formative experiences and the lessons of history do so as well.[54] In a related way, Snyder's claims about the instrumental nature of strategic conceptions lead him to equate expansionism with parochial interests that of necessity run contrary to the welfare of the state as a whole. But it is by no means the case that all actors that advocate ambitious external policies are necessarily motivated by self-interest. Competitive policies and expansion often pay.[55]

[53] In Wilhelmine Germany, for example, neither the navy nor industry agitated for a major naval construction program until the 1890s. The navy was content to focus on protecting trade routes and imperial links. Traders and industrialists initially opposed the building of a major fleet because they feared that the consequent erosion of relations with Britain would impair international trade. It is simply not the case that self-serving strategic concepts existed within the navy and industry from 1871 onward and suddenly bore fruit in the late 1890s because of Bismarck's fall from power and the growing intensity of logrolling.

[54] For example, U.S. insistence on establishing a liberal, multilateral trading order after World War II was more the product of reigning assumptions about the causal connection between economic nationalism and war than of the self-seeking behavior of U.S. corporations. See Chapter 7 for further discussion of this point. On the general issue of when and how elites learn from history, see George Breslauer and Philip Tetlock, eds., *Learning in U.S. and Soviet Foreign Policy* (Boulder, Colo.: Westview Press, 1991); Khong, *Analogies at War*; and Jack Levy, "Learning and Foreign Policy: Sweeping a Conceptual Minefield" (unpublished paper, Rutgers University, June 1992).

[55] Snyder acknowledges that "up to a point, imperial expansion may be a paying proposition for a strong power" (*Myths of Empire*, p. 8). But he does not link this acknowledgment to the possibility that political leaders and interest groups might pursue expansion for other than self-interested reasons.

By assuming that imperial strategic conceptions emerge from the instrumental behavior of interest groups, Snyder precludes the possibility that expansionist policies may initially be adopted for sound reasons. They may become counterproductive only later, because of changes in the external environment or because of the growing intensity of imperial ambition.[56]

The final problem with Snyder's argument is that by defining the puzzle exclusively in terms of overly competitive behavior rather than focusing as well on examples of overly cooperative behavior, Snyder fails to capture the severity of the bouts of adjustment failure experienced by democracies. Granted, the Japanese and German cases are the most severe in that both powers initiated self-defeating war. But Britain and France, by appeasing Nazi Germany, failing to prepare adequately for war against Hitler's forces, and investing scarce resources in the defense of the periphery, pursued policies that jeopardized their core security interests. For Snyder, such behavior was the product of admirable strategic learning and the open evaluation associated with democratic debate: "Britain . . . was relatively successful at calculating the marginal costs and revenues of expansion; it almost always learned to retrench in the face of negative feedback." He further notes, "When the [democracies] . . . met resistance, they typically retrenched, attempting to defuse mounting opposition by offering concessions to their opponents."[57] But Snyder mistakes strategic learning for strategic paralysis and, in so doing, overestimates the extent to which democracy cures the pathologies that lead to inopportune policies and exaggerates the relationship between domestic political structure and adjustment failure.[58]

[56] Had Japan during the interwar period limited its expansion to Manchuria and North China, the adventurous behavior of the army during the early 1930s would take on a different light. Since this early bout of expansion contributed to the economic strength and military security of the metropole, the army's behavior was quite consistent with the interests of the state as a whole.

[57] Snyder, *Myths of Empire*, pp. 9, 305. Snyder does recognize that "some argue that Britain learned the lessons of appeasement and retrenchment too well between the world wars, jeopardizing its security through strategic passivity" (p. 7). He responds that this is a "doubtful" case of "underexpansion," however, because British behavior can be understood in terms of strategic considerations and domestic politics (p. 8).

[58] That the timing of industrialization and domestic structure fail to explain adjustment failure is further demonstrated by the fact that empires have been falling prey to overexpansion since well before the industrial revolution. The Roman, Byzantine, and Ottoman empires, to name a few, all suffered from counterproductive expansion. Snyder suggests that his theory could be applied to these earlier periods by identifying and measuring political cleavages within preindustrial societies (*Myths of Empire*, p. 62). This qualification is somewhat unsatisfying, however, since the process and timing of industrialization are central components of Snyder's theory. A longer historical perspective thus presents difficult challenges for a theory of imperial overexpansion that relies on industrialization as a key causal variable.

[63]

As becomes evident in the final section of this chapter, Snyder heads in the right direction by pointing to strategic ideology and domestic constraints as chief causes of overexpansion. He correctly observes that elites are often pressed to engage in overly competitive behavior by strategic conceptions initially crafted for instrumental reasons. But by focusing exclusively on domestic forces—and, in particular, logrolling among imperial interest groups—he misses the central role played by systemic and cognitive factors in producing self-defeating behavior.

MILITARY SERVICES

Scholars have repeatedly pointed to military organizations as a main source of strategic error.[59] It is possible that adjustment failures occur when the military, as the agent within the state exclusively responsible for implementing defense policy, engages in self-seeking behavior that runs counter to the interests of the state as a whole. Because of the military's monopoly on the use of force and its ability to penetrate the decision-making arena, civilian elites might be left to accept its actions as faits accomplis. Alternatively, the military establishment may co-opt civilian elites by persuading them to buy into its strategic notions. In either case, strategies that are self-serving for the military become self-defeating for the state.

This proposition does not provide a compelling explanation for overly cooperative behavior. Military organizations, like other bureaucratic agencies, generally pursue policies that increase their prestige, political power, and share of government expenditure. Underselling the nature of the external threat and advocating accommodation do not further these goals.[60] This line of inquiry does, however, offer a potential explanation for overly competitive behavior. The military may

[59] See, for example, Stephen Van Evera, "Causes of War" (Ph.D. diss., University of California at Berkeley, 1984); Barry Posen, *The Sources of Military Doctrine: France, Britain, and Germany between the World Wars* (Ithaca: Cornell University Press, 1984); and Jack Snyder, *The Ideology of the Offensive: Military Decision Making and the Disasters of 1914* (Ithaca: Cornell University Press, 1984).

[60] Under certain circumstances, the self-interest of the military could lead to overly cooperative behavior. Individual services may become so wedded to specific types of missions that they resist preparing for other types of missions even if ordered to do so by civilian elites. During 1979–1980, for example, the American military resisted instructions from civilian elites to undertake preparations for operations in Southwest Asia after the Iranian Revolution. The services preferred to focus their attention and resources on major missions in Europe. See Charles Kupchan, *The Persian Gulf and the West: The Dilemmas of Security* (Boston: Allen and Unwin, 1987), pp. 83–98. In general, however, the military services readily take on new missions because additional force requirements justify an increased allocation of resources.

seek to increase its mission requirements—and hence its budget—either through threat inflation or through taking on new commitments. It might unnecessarily advocate the adoption of offensive strategies in order to enhance its control over policy making and to justify increased expenditure. Competition among individual services for resources can also exacerbate bouts of expansionism orchestrated by military organizations. These potential sources of expansionist behavior will result in overly competitive policies only if civilian authorities are unable effectively to control the military establishment. The military may simply ignore instructions from civilian authorities. Alternatively, military officials may penetrate, subordinate, or sell dangerous strategic concepts to the civilian elite, enabling the military to influence, if not determine, the outcome of debate over grand strategy. The narrow interests of the military services come to saddle the state with a range of external commitments that it is unable to uphold.

This hypothesis can be tested by examining the following issues. Are the military services in favor of expansion and opposed to strategic retrenchment during periods of adjustment failure? If so, does the position of the military differ substantially from that of the civilian elite? Do the strategic concepts that fuel self-defeating behavior emerge exclusively within the military and then spread to the civilian leadership? Or does the military serve as a vehicle for the propagation and institutionalization of strategic concepts crafted by civilians or economic interest groups? What is the tenor of civil-military relations, and is the military ignoring civilian instructions and/or dominating the policy formulation process?

The case studies show that, in certain circumstances, military services do contribute substantially to overexpansion. The formulation and implementation of Japanese grand strategy during the 1930s, for example, were crucially affected by the military's subordination of civilian government. Similarly, French expansion in Africa during the 1880s was orchestrated by a colonial army acting surreptitiously and, frequently, in direct violation of orders from civilian elites in Paris.

These examples constitute the exception, however, not the rule. In most cases, belief in the need for expansionary policies is at least as prevalent among civilian elites as among military elites. Although the services often act as a vehicle for the spread of ambitious strategic concepts, these concepts generally do not emerge exclusively within the military. Competition for scarce resources does induce the services to seek new missions and inflate mission requirements. But civilian leaders usually maintain effective control over the military. While military officials indeed have input into grand strategy, civilian elites are the critical actors in most major strategic decisions. In short, the self-seeking behavior of military organizations sometimes contributes to, but is not the major cause of, adjustment failure.

VULNERABILITY, STRATEGIC BELIEFS, AND STRATEGIC CULTURE: THE CAUSES OF SELF-DEFEATING BEHAVIOR

None of the five hypotheses set forth above offers a satisfying account of adjustment failure. The review of the literature just presented does, however, provide an analytic foundation for constructing a theory that is logically compelling and consistent with the historical record. I now build on this analytic foundation and integrate systemic, domestic, and cognitive perspectives to present my own argument about the causes of self-defeating behavior.[61]

Measuring Strategic Beliefs

Characterizing the beliefs that inform collective decisions is a difficult, if not dangerous, enterprise.[62] Unanimity among top elites is the exception, not the rule. The emergence of a consensual position usually reflects political compromise, not the coalescence of competing beliefs through discussion and persuasion; strategic beliefs tend to be fairly stable and insensitive to short-term change.[63] Nevertheless, by consulting cabinet debates and planning papers, it is possible to identify the causal suppositions that inform policy decisions. This approach does not overlook the existence of dissenting opinions or deny that individuals often support the same policy for different reasons. But it does assume that certain beliefs are sufficiently dominant within the policy community to allow a consensual position to emerge. Reliance on closed-door discussions and classified memos and documents, as opposed to public presentations of policy, also minimizes the risk that

[61] I define key terms as follows. *Strategic beliefs* refer to causal suppositions derived from logical inference about the dynamics of state interactions in the international arena. *Strategic logic* refers to a set of interrelated strategic beliefs. *Strategic culture* refers to deeply embedded notions of security that take root within a polity. These notions are based on *strategic images*, not on logical inference. *Strategic assumptions* are the reigning concepts that guide elite behavior. These concepts are shaped by both strategic beliefs and strategic culture—that is, they are produced by both inference-based and image-based sources. The terms *strategic assumption, strategic outlook,* and *strategic conception* are used synonymously.

[62] For discussion of formal cognitive maps of collectivities, see Axelrod, *Structure of Decision,* pp. 239–243.

[63] See George, *Presidential Decisionmaking,* pp. 57–61; Robert Putnam, *The Comparative Study of Political Elites* (Englewood Cliffs, N.J.: Prentice-Hall, 1976), pp. 90–103; and Rosenau and Holsti, "U.S. Leadership," pp. 390–391.

individual representation of strategic suppositions and causal arguments reflects political rhetoric more than actual beliefs.

Although elites hold beliefs at various levels of abstraction and on many different dimensions, several considerations help narrow the analytic task of probing the causal suppositions that inform grand strategy. I am concerned with identifying a class of beliefs that occupies an analytic category between deep philosophical beliefs about human nature and more narrow beliefs about what set of policies will maximize short-term interests. This analytic category consists of causal claims about the dynamics of interstate relations. These claims serve as axioms or norms that guide elites in their formulation of grand strategy.[64]

Rather than seeking to identify and measure the full range of beliefs that occupy this category, a more manageable approach consists of distilling out a small number of fundamental beliefs from which other, second-order suppositions devolve. In other words, it is necessary to identify a few key dimensions of belief that are critical in shaping how elites structure grand strategy and evaluate the costs and benefits of empire. These beliefs serve, in Philip Converse's terminology, "as a sort of glue to bind together many more specific attitudes and beliefs, and these postures are of prime centrality in the belief system as a whole."[65] These dimensions of belief should by no means explain the full range of elite behavior in the international arena, yet they should be adequate to explain the general positions that decision makers take on key issues concerning interstate relations and resource allocation.

Two dimensions of belief fulfill these criteria. The first dimension concerns elite beliefs about how best to deal with potential adversaries. Such beliefs manifest themselves in terms of three basic strategies or types of interaction: compellence, deterrence, and accommodation. Compellence is a coercive strategy aimed at forcing the adversary through punishment or the threat of punishment to acquiesce to specific demands. Deterrence is a strategy of dissuasion aimed at pre-

---

[64] In *Presidential Decisionmaking*, Alexander George distinguishes among three categories of elite beliefs: those concerning the nature of international politics and conflict, those concerning the extent to which history is guided by actions, and those concerning the appropriate strategy and tactics for dealing with allies and adversaries (p. 45). In "'Operational Code,'" he identifies two categories of beliefs: deep philosophic ones about human nature and instrumental ones about how best to pursue objectives. The type of beliefs with which I am concerned corresponds most closely to George's notion of instrumental beliefs. See "The 'Operational Code': A Neglected Approach to the Study of Political Leaders and Decision-Making," *International Studies Quarterly*, 13 (June 1969), 190–222.

[65] Philip Converse, "The Nature of Belief Systems in Mass Publics," in *Ideology and Discontent*, ed. David Apter (New York: Free Press, 1964), p. 211.

venting the adversary through punishment or the threat of punishment from undertaking specific actions. Accommodation is a conciliatory strategy aimed at moderating the adversary's behavior through concession and compromise. Identifying which strategy or strategies decision makers choose and why offers much insight into the causal suppositions that inform elite thinking about the essential dynamics of interstate relations. Probing elite beliefs about how to deal with potential adversaries exposes the fundamental causal claims that guide strategic interactions in the international arena.

The second dimension of belief focuses on how elites conceive of the state's geostrategic priorities. I am concerned with what decision makers believe about the importance of empire to the economic and military welfare of the metropole. Examination of this dimension of beliefs revolves around two specific questions. First, what are the relative weights assigned to military, economic, and reputational considerations in setting geographic priorities? Second, does a clear ordering of strategic priorities guide elite behavior and policy choice, or do decision makers tend to regard external commitments as interdependent and, therefore, of more equal importance? This dimension of beliefs reveals what causal suppositions impel elites to acquire and/or abandon territories beyond the borders of the metropole.

The Effects of Vulnerability on Strategic Beliefs

Having identified these two fundamental dimensions of belief and how to measure them, I proceed with my argument about the effects of vulnerability on the content of these beliefs. As far as interacting with adversaries is concerned, at low levels of metropolitan vulnerability, elites in declining powers respond to simultaneous threats to the core and periphery by believing in the need to practice deterrence in the core and accommodation in the periphery. Elites in rising powers believe in the need to adopt a mixed strategy of deterrence and compellence in both the core and periphery. Perceptions of high metropolitan vulnerability produce a quite different set of beliefs about how to interact with adversaries. Elites in declining powers believe in the need to adopt strategies of accommodation in the core and deterrence in the periphery. Elites in rising powers believe in the need to adopt a strategy of compellence in both the core and periphery (see Table 4).

Perceptions of vulnerability have a related effect on beliefs about strategic priorities. At low levels of vulnerability, elites in both declining and rising powers focus on strategic and economic considerations in setting priorities; concern about reputation and resolve is far less

[68]

Table 4. Beliefs about interacting with adversaries

Conditions of low vulnerability		
	Core	*Periphery*
Declining state	Deter	Accommodate
Rising state	Deter/Compel	Deter/Compel

Conditions of high vulnerability		
	Core	*Periphery*
Declining state	Accommodate	Deter
Rising state	Compel	Compel

prominent.[66] Elites tend to believe that commitments are relatively independent—that is, that events and outcomes in one geographic area have little bearing on developments in another. Accordingly, they hold fairly clear and ordered conceptions of strategic priorities.

Perceptions of high vulnerability produce elite beliefs about strategic priorities that are characterized by quite different attributes. The standards used to assess priorities shift; reputational concerns increase in prominence relative to strategic and economic considerations. Elites tend to believe that commitments are interdependent—that is, that interests and threats in one theater cannot be evaluated independently of those in other theaters. Strategic priorities become less ordered, and elites tend to blur the distinction between primary and secondary interests (see Table 5).

Perceptions of low and high vulnerability, via the beliefs described

Table 5. Beliefs about strategic priorities

Low Vulnerability	*High Vulnerability*
Low reputational concerns	High reputational concerns
Commitments independent	Commitments interdependent
Clear priorities	Blurred priorities

[66] It is important to reiterate that I am dealing only with periods in which states are faced with consequential shifts in the international balance of power as well as with adversaries in both the core and periphery. These propositions do not necessarily apply during other periods, when states perceive a relatively static international environment

above, produce very different policy choices. At low vulnerability, elites hold beliefs that lead to timely adjustment to international change. In declining powers, they engage in power balancing in the core and seek accords and alliances in the periphery in order to facilitate retrenchment. In rising powers, they take advantage of opportunities to pursue expansionist behavior in the core and periphery which increases the state's security, but they engage only in selective expansion and explicitly avoid policies that could lead to self-encirclement and overextension. At high vulnerability, elites hold beliefs that lead to overly cooperative and overly competitive policies. In declining powers, elites appease adversaries in the core while they indiscriminately defend positions in the periphery. In rising powers, elites pursue indiscriminate expansion in both the core and periphery.

Where do the beliefs and extremist policies associated with high vulnerability come from? Are they the result of psychological distortions produced by the stress that accompanies vulnerability? Or are the effects of vulnerability on strategic beliefs the product of rational inference, the output of normal inductive and deductive reasoning associated with the notion of bounded rationality? If so, through what inferences, causal claims, and cognitive mechanisms does vulnerability affect beliefs?

I argue that these beliefs are consistent with the notion of bounded rationality for two principal reasons. First, the effects of vulnerability on beliefs are the product of logical inference, not of stress-induced psychological failure. The beliefs induced by vulnerability are based on causal suppositions and are internally consistent and logically coherent. As discussed below, low vulnerability leads to timely adjustment because conditions of strategic sufficiency enable elites to respond readily to the constraints and opportunities arising from shifts in the distribution of material power. High vulnerability impairs adjustment because conditions of strategic deficiency force elites to adopt overly cooperative and overly competitive policies. Elite beliefs and the policies they produce change as a logical response to the security environment. In contrast to the authors examined above, I am arguing that decision makers adopt extremist policies for sound and considered reasons. Learning and psychological stimuli indeed shape these beliefs, but these processes and stimuli are consistent with the normal functioning of the mind and with rational (in the bounded sense) evaluation of incoming information.

Second, the posited relationship between high vulnerability and strategic beliefs is contingent on uncertainty. When elites are aware of international change and conditions of strategic deficiency, yet still uncertain about if, when, and where threats may come due, about

---

and the absence of adversaries, and therefore do not need to confront the problem of adjusting grand strategy to broad shifts in the distribution of power.

what motivates potential adversaries, and about how these adversaries will react to cooperative and competitive initiatives, high vulnerability creates a propensity for extremist policies, a predisposition toward excessive cooperation or competition. As the strategic landscape solidifies and the ill effects of extremist policies mount, elites gradually adapt their beliefs to incoming information. They become aware of the gaps that are emerging between their beliefs and the nature of the landscape, and they realize that their policy choices are not producing their intended effects. Decision makers come to appreciate that they are leading the state toward strategic exposure, self-encirclement, and/ or overextension. This is not to suggest that there is not a considerable time lag between receipt of disconfirming information and change in beliefs. Vulnerability affects not only the content of elite beliefs, but also the timing of their adaptation to incoming information. While low vulnerability produces vigilance and sensitivity to incoming information, high vulnerability induces decision makers to cling tightly to existing beliefs, lengthening the time lag between receipt of new information and adaptation of beliefs. Elites cling to preexisting beliefs in order to minimize the intensity of threatening information. Initial receipt of disconfirming evidence often leads to a period of resignation and paralysis.[67] As a result, elites, at least temporarily, base policy on a set of outmoded strategic beliefs. But when disconfirming evidence becomes overwhelming, elites do bring their beliefs into line with incoming information. It is under conditions of uncertainty, then, that high vulnerability, via strategic beliefs, leads to overly cooperative and overly competitive behavior. As uncertainty diminishes and the harmful effects of extremist policies become apparent, elites, in accordance with the notion of bounded rationality, tend to show sensitivity to glaring gaps between preexisting beliefs and reality.

---

[67] Motivated biases provide a compelling explanation of why high vulnerability should increase the lag time between receipt of disconfirming information and change in belief system. At low vulnerability, elites believe that they have at their disposal the resources necessary to deal with external threats. Strategic sufficiency enables them to respond relatively promptly to rising external dangers, although the normal tendency to fit incoming information to preexisting beliefs still operates. At high vulnerability, elites perceive that they do not have sufficient resources to defend the metropole. The normal cognitive tendency to fit incoming information to preexisting beliefs is exacerbated by a situation in which adaptation of belief systems exposes individuals to quite unpleasant realities. The need to reduce fear and stress motivates individuals to ignore selectively information indicating a worsening security predicament. When initially confronted with disconfirming information of a particularly threatening or distasteful nature, individuals give greater credence than usual and cling more tightly than usual to evidence that confirms their beliefs and ignore or downplay longer than usual evidence that is discrepant. See Nisbett and Ross, *Human Inference,* pp. 169–192; and Taylor and Fiske, *Social Cognition,* pp. 162–177.

I lay out this argument first by analyzing the beliefs and associated policies that prevail under low vulnerability. I then examine the logic that induces elites in declining powers facing high vulnerability to pursue policies of appeasement in the core and indiscriminate defense in the periphery. Next, I outline the logic that induces elites in rising powers to pursue a policy of indiscriminate expansion in both the core and periphery. Finally, I consider three types of bias within the decision-making community that may also contribute to the link between high vulnerability and these beliefs and the extremist policies they produce.

Under low metropolitan vulnerability, elites operate under conditions of strategic sufficiency. They calculate that a combination of military assets already existing, those that can be mobilized domestically or from imperial possessions in relatively short order, and those that can be secured through alliance arrangements will render their state able to prevail against likely adversaries in the core. Strategic sufficiency enables decision makers in declining powers to take steps to balance in a timely fashion against emerging threats, thereby preserving the status quo and an international order compatible with their interests. Self-interest dictates that elites respond to rising threats in the core by adopting firm, deterrent strategies and marshaling their military resources to defend the metropole.[68] Deterring and, if necessary, stopping the adversary entail withdrawing assets from the periphery to achieve a comfortable margin of superiority in the core.[69] To facilitate such retrenchment, elites in declining powers pursue accommodationist strategies in the periphery. Elites are relatively immune to arguments about the reputational costs of retrenchment. Reputational concerns run low precisely because elites do not need to rely on demonstrations of resolve to affect outcomes; preponderant military and economic capability speaks for itself. As a result, elites tend to set priorities on the basis of strategic and economic considerations, to consider external commitments as independent of one another, and to hold ordered conceptions of strategic priorities.

---

[68] Should elites believe that conflict with the rising state is unavoidable, they may even resort to preventive war in order to defeat the adversary while they still have the capability to do so. For further discussion of preventive war, see note 75 below.

[69] A declining power facing low vulnerability does not necessarily need to withdraw from the periphery in order to marshal preponderant power in the core. Should its material resources in the core be vastly superior to those of the rising challenger, it can pursue a policy of power balancing in the core while continuing to pursue competitive policies in the periphery. I am assuming, however, that a rising state would not challenge the status quo unless it had power resources sufficient to pose a significant threat to the dominant state or states in the international system. Accordingly, I assume that power balancing in the core necessitates retrenchment in the periphery.

In rising powers, elites appreciate that strategic sufficiency and improvements in the military and economic position of their state relative to other major powers enable them to challenge the status quo and to shape an international order more conducive to their state's interests. Self-interest thus impels elites in rising powers to engage in expansionist behavior. Enhancing security, however, also entails avoiding policies that might jeopardize a favorable strategic balance. Accordingly, elites in rising powers pursue a mix of deterrent and compellent strategies in both the core and periphery. They take advantage of opportunities to enhance their power base and increase their security but engage only in selective expansion and are careful to rein in the scope of their external ambition in order to avoid both self-encirclement and overextension. Conditions of strategic sufficiency also mean that elites are able to rely on their military and economic capabilities to deter or compel adversaries; they do not need to turn to demonstrations of resolve. The resulting focus on the strategic and economic—as opposed to reputational—benefits of empire leads to belief in the independence of external commitments and to ordered strategic priorities. A clear sense of strategic priorities reinforces the ability of decision makers to pursue initiatives only if they contribute to the material strength of the metropole. In both declining and rising powers, then, strategic sufficiency enables elites to respond readily to the constraints and opportunities arising from shifts in the distribution of material power.

Under high metropolitan vulnerability, elites operate under conditions of strategic deficiency. They calculate that their own resources and those of their allies are insufficient to enable them to prevail against the likely adversary or adversarial coalition. Extraordinary policies are required to deal with an extraordinary strategic environment. Rather than balancing against emerging threats in the core, elites in declining powers seek to preserve the status quo—even if somewhat modified to make room for the challenger—by appeasing the adversary. An accommodationist stance devolves directly from the perception of strategic deficiency. Immediate retrenchment is not pursued because it will not suffice to meet the shortfall in the core. Facing a daunting military imbalance and an inability to redress that imbalance in the short term, elites seek to avert war through making concessions. It might be possible to avoid conflict altogether by meeting the demands of the adversary. At a minimum, accommodation will postpone conflict and buy time for the defender to seek added resources and improve the military balance. Furthermore, elites in a declining power cannot risk provoking a superior adversary by pursuing competitive policies. An unintended spiral would lead to a war that the defender cannot win. In sum, elites in declining powers, when faced with high vulnerability, adopt accommodationist strategies in the core because they lack the resources necessary to adopt a credible policy of deterrence and defense. They view cooperative policies in the core as both sufficient to attain their goals—preservation of the status quo—and necessary to preserve the state's security.

At the same time that they seek to appease adversaries in the core, elites in declining powers initially respond to high metropolitan vulnerability by adopting policies of indiscriminate defense in the periphery. Three specific patterns of inference affect how high vulnerability shapes thinking about peripheral strategy: decision makers come to believe in the need (1) to demonstrate resolve to potential adversaries to offset strategic deficiency; (2) to extract increasing resources from the empire to marshal them in the metropole; and (3) to bolster the legitimacy of the ruling group by successfully pursuing external ambition. These inferences induce elites to believe in the need to adopt a deterrent stance in the periphery and lead to a blurring of strategic priorities.

Resolve. Elites believe in the need to demonstrate resolve because they reason that they can offset insufficiency of material resources by bolstering reputation and prestige.[70] Elites seek to rely on these intangible components of power to compensate for the relative loss of the material components of power. Demonstrations of resolve are meant to affect the behavior of external actors by bolstering the state's reputation for standing firm and for defending its homeland and imperial commitments against all challengers. Potential adversaries tempted to take advantage of a shift in the balance of material power will be deterred by a shift in the balance of resolve.

---

[70] *Resolve* refers to a state's ability to communicate to potential adversaries its determination to secure a specified outcome. *Reputation* refers to evaluations by other parties of a state's resolve and its willingness to uphold external commitments. Reputation is earned largely through past behavior and previous demonstrations of resolve. *Prestige* refers to a powerful state's ability to affect outcomes simply by virtue of the fact that other states recognize its dominant position within the international hierarchy. With this recognition comes a certain degree of deference, a willingness to acquiesce to the more powerful state even if that state does not threaten to use its preponderance of resources to attain its objectives. Occupying a top rung in the international hierarchy is a source of power in and of itself, inasmuch as elites in secondary states become conditioned by and socialized into their position of subordination. (For a study examining how and when socialization takes place between hegemonic and secondary states, see G. John Ikenberry and Charles A. Kupchan, "Socialization and Hegemonic Power," *International Organization*, 44 [Summer 1990], 284–315.) The notion of *respect* captures the cognitive affect that induces compliant behavior. Resolve and reputation affect the behavior of a potential adversary by increasing his expectation that the opponent will stand firm if challenged.

Elites also reason that communication of a commitment to defend the status quo prevents the loss of prestige associated with a state's dominant position in the international hierarchy. Inasmuch as prestige is an attribute or cognitive affect that emerges gradually over time, behavior consistent with that attribute can preserve external appreciation of a state's status and prestige even if the material configurations of power that gave rise to that attribute have eroded. While reputation can enhance a state's ability to deter attack, prestige can prevent challenges from emerging and affect outcomes by preserving external recognition of a state's dominant position in the international hierarchy. Because the scope of a state's imperial reach and its willingness and ability to secure outcomes favorable to its interests are key sources of prestige, elites perceive the need to defend imperial possessions. Furthermore, because prestige allows a state to influence outcomes without the exercise of military or economic resources, relying on it becomes especially attractive when material resources are strained. In sum, elites come to believe in the importance of the external appearance of strength and the demonstration of resolve precisely because the material resources at their disposal are insufficient to cope with prospective external threats.

This concern about demonstrating resolve is pronounced under high vulnerability because elites simply have fewer options at their disposal than under low vulnerability. Unlike under conditions of strategic sufficiency, elites are unable in the short term to marshal the resources necessary to deal with existing threats to the metropole. It is sensible at least to try to cope with a worsening international situation by bolstering reputation and prestige. Furthermore, the potential payoff is high and the risks manageable. The potential payoff entails the maintenance of the status quo at low cost. The principal risk is that efforts to bolster reputation could provoke adversaries and precipitate a spiral of increasing hostility. If a deterrent strategy backfires in this manner, however, elites can alter their policies and seek to mollify the adversary by pursuing a more accommodationist line. Adopting a deterrent posture may not have achieved its intended goal, but the strategy was worth trying. As an initial response to high vulnerability, demonstrating resolve and bolstering reputation thus make good sense.

Concern about the potential for demonstrations of resolve to backfire also explains why deterrent strategies adopted to bolster reputation and prestige are usually practiced in the periphery, not in the core. Elites in declining powers avoid such strategies in the core precisely

---

Prestige affects a potential adversary by preventing him from even considering challenging the status quo.

because high metropolitan vulnerability makes them fearful of provoking a war that could have disastrous consequences. Ambitious strategies that are viewed as provocative by peripheral adversaries entail fewer risks. If war should prove unavoidable, it would break out in areas far from the metropole. Furthermore, core states usually enjoy marked military advantages over peripheral states, meaning that demonstrations of resolve are likely to be cheap and that the outcome of war is likely to be favorable should it occur. Efforts to bolster reputation by taking actions in the periphery may also succeed in deterring adversaries in the core.

This pattern of inference affects beliefs both about how to deal with potential adversaries and about strategic priorities. With regard to dealing with adversaries, high vulnerability creates a predisposition to adopt deterrent policies in the periphery. Belief in the need to practice deterrence stems less from evaluation of the behavior and motives of individual adversaries than from appreciation of the need to demonstrate resolve and to create the external appearance of strength as a means of coping with insufficiency of material resources. The appearance of power and the preservation of prestige rival material power itself in importance. Elites faced with mounting threats and insufficient resources look to deterrent strategies to bolster reputation and prestige and to mask material weakness.[71]

These inferences about the importance of demonstrations of resolve have a similar effect on elite beliefs about strategic priorities. Reputational concerns come to dominate strategic and economic considerations in determining priorities. The value of a given territory is defined more in terms of the loss of reputation and prestige that would accompany withdrawal than in terms of the material cost or gain associated with its defense. Furthermore, efforts to endow a specific commitment with reputational significance are self-fulfilling. Once decision makers have publicly declared their intention to defend a given territory, reneging on that declaration does entail greater reputational costs than had withdrawal occurred without a prior reaffirmation of commitment. Upholding the commitment itself becomes the objective, meaning that elites are willing to expend far more effort to attain this goal than warranted by the intrinsic strategic and economic assets at stake.

[71] Past scholarship on deterrence theory has noted the causal relationship between perceptions of vulnerability and these strategic beliefs. See Patrick Morgan, "Saving Face for the Sake of Deterrence" in *Psychology and Deterrence*, ed. Robert Jervis, Richard Ned Lebow, and Janice Gross Stein (Baltimore: Johns Hopkins University Press, 1985); Lebow, *Between Peace and War*; Richard Ned Lebow, "The Deterrence Deadlock: Is There a Way Out?" in *Psychology and Deterrence*, ed. Jervis et al.; Jervis, *Perception and Misperception in International Politics* (Princeton: Princeton University Press, 1976), chap. 10; and Robert Jervis, "Deterrence Theory Revisited," *World Politics*, 31 (January 1979), 289–324.

These inferences about strategic interactions and strategic priorities often manifest themselves in the prevalence of three ancillary suppositions about the dynamics of interstate relations. First, increasing reliance on demonstrations of resolve to mask material inadequacy fuels the assumption that reputation and prestige are fungible across theaters. By leading elites to rely more heavily on bolstering reputation and maintaining the external appearance of strength as key instruments of policy, high vulnerability encourages elites to view commitments as interdependent. Inasmuch as reputation is intangible and therefore potentially fungible across theaters, decision makers come to perceive that adversaries will interpret acquiescence in one area as weakness in all areas, regardless of the interests at stake. Similarly, demonstrating resolve in one theater will serve to bolster reputation and prestige vis-à-vis all adversaries. Demonstrating resolve in the periphery can therefore strengthen deterrence in the core. As a result of this logic, strategic priorities become blurred. Not only do peripheral commitments come to be interdependent and of equal importance, but periphery and core begin to merge into a single strategic theater.[72]

Second, elites faced with high vulnerability tend to believe in the predominance of bandwagoning. According to bandwagoning logic, states tend to ally with rather than balance against the strongest states in the international system.[73] External perceptions of weakness will therefore cause one's allies to defect in search of a more robust partner. This belief attribute is a by-product of elite concern about the overriding importance of demonstrating strength and resolve. The appearance of weakness, elites reason, will not only invite attack, but also cause the defection of allies seeking to side with the militarily superior challenger. Once exposed, the same weakness that makes a state an attractive target for attack also makes it a less attractive partner for alliance.

Third, belief in the falling of dominoes—that a single setback will lead to further adverse developments—tends to become entrenched in the elite community. Concern with reputation and prestige and with

---

[72] Reputation, inasmuch as it is intangible, is potentially fungible across theaters. Unlike military force, which can only be in one place at one time, reputation earned in a given encounter could *conceivably* affect later encounters with other adversaries. Whether a state's reputation from its behavior in previous encounters *actually* is an important determinant of how other adversaries evaluate its resolve in later encounters is a topic of ongoing debate. For the position that reputation is fungible and shapes outcomes in encounters other than the one in which it is earned, see Thomas Schelling, *Arms and Influence* (New Haven: Yale University Press, 1966), pp. 124–125. For the position that reputation is not important in strengthening deterrence, see Paul Huth and Bruce Russett, "What Makes Deterrence Work? Cases from 1900–1980," *World Politics*, 36 (July 1984), 496–526.

[73] For more extensive discussion of bandwagoning logic, see Stephen Walt, *The Origins of Alliances* (Ithaca: Cornell University Press, 1987).

[77]

the interdependence of commitments leads decision makers to assume that any setback is likely to have harmful reverberations: the loss of a given territory, regardless of its intrinsic strategic value, will encourage others to challenge the status quo. If reputation is fungible, then events that damage it should have as far-reaching implications as events that strengthen it.

Like belief in the fungibility of reputation, belief in bandwagoning and dominoes follows from elite reasoning about the need to offset an unfavorable shift in the balance of material power with a favorable shift in the balance of resolve. The more elites rely on demonstrations of resolve to affect outcomes, the more deeply they are drawn into a strategic logic in which states bandwagon and dominoes fall. These beliefs reinforce the tendency of elites facing high vulnerability to adopt firm, deterrent strategies in the periphery and to blur strategic priorities. The argument presented here is not that belief in the fungibility of reputation, bandwagoning, or dominoes occurs only under conditions of high vulnerability, but that high vulnerability—via the inferences outlined above—markedly increases the likelihood that elites operate under these three suppositions.

High metropolitan vulnerability produces a similar logic among elites in rising powers. Demonstrations of resolve are viewed as necessary to compensate for material inadequacy. Concern about resolve affects beliefs about both interactions with adversaries and strategic priorities. Yet the nature of the logic that prevails in rising states differs from that in declining states in two respects. First, in rising powers, concern about resolve induces elites to believe in the need to practice compellence rather than deterrence. Second, efforts to bolster reputation lead to competitive policies in the core as well as in the periphery. These differences are the result of the following considerations.

Rising states, as newcomers to the top echelon of the international hierarchy, must build reputation and earn prestige by challenging the existing order. Demonstrations of resolve therefore entail compellent strategies that alter the status quo, not just deterrent strategies that preserve the status quo. In addition, elites in rising powers try to demonstrate resolve and bolster reputation not to deter attacks against their state, but to undermine and fragment the coalition seeking to block their state's ascendance. Demonstrating resolve and bolstering reputation are intended first and foremost to intimidate and cause splits among those states seeking to preserve the status quo. The goal is not to prevent other powers from taking specific actions, but to coerce these powers into acquiescing to the challenger's demands. This objective can be achieved only through compellence.

Elites in rising powers adopt competitive policies in the core as well

[78]

as in the periphery for two main reasons. First, because they seek to fulfill new imperial aspirations, not to protect old ones, to practice compellence only in the periphery is inadequate. Only by challenging the status quo in the core—where the hierarchy among major powers is largely determined—can the old order be overturned. Second, elites in rising powers, as challengers to the status quo, can control the implications of their competitive stance in the core. They do not have to initiate a challenge to the existing order unless and until they perceive a good chance of prevailing. Should compellent policies backfire and only strengthen the cohesion of an opposing coalition, elites in the rising power can back down and avert confrontation. Status quo powers have no reason to attack unless provoked into doing so. Elites in a declining power do not have such latitude; they react to, rather than initiate, challenges to the status quo. They reason that accommodationist strategies are preferable regardless of the rising adversary's motives and intentions. If the challenger does not have aggressive intent, efforts to strengthen resolve through competitive policies in the core risk triggering a spiral with the rising challenger which cannot be interrupted, thus precipitating the onset of a self-destructive war. If the challenger has aggressive intent, accommodationist strategies are still needed to buy time for war preparations. While elites in declining states view accommodationist strategies in the core as both sufficient to attain their goals and necessary to preserve the state's security, elites in rising states view compellent strategies in the core as both necessary to attain their goals and sufficient to preserve the state's security.

Resources. The second set of logical inferences through which high vulnerability alters strategic beliefs concerns assessment of the material contribution of empire to metropolitan security. Faced with a strategic imbalance in the core, elites in both declining and rising powers turn to imperial territories for assistance. Colonial possessions can furnish raw materials, manufactured products, workers, and troops to help meet shortfalls in the metropole. Increased extraction of war-making material from possessions offers a relatively rapid and low-cost means of meeting deficiencies in the core.

Among elites in declining powers, this set of inferences about the empire's potential material contribution to metropolitan defense alters beliefs about strategic priorities. The outlying empire rises in importance precisely because its preservation contributes to the defense of the metropole. Allocating scarce assets to imperial defense becomes justifiable because a short-term sacrifice in metropolitan resources will eventually serve to enhance metropolitan security. Defense of the homeland remains the primary objective in the long term, but as-

[79]

signing top priority to the empire becomes consistent with this objective. This evaluation of strategic priorities provides added impetus for elites in declining powers to practice deterrence in the periphery. Ambitious strategies are needed to deter potential adversaries from attacking overseas possessions and to prepare for the defense of these possessions should deterrence fail.

Concern about resources has a similar effect on the beliefs of elites in rising powers, though these concerns are somewhat different in character. Rising powers need to acquire imperial territories to gain access to additional resources; they cannot, as declining powers can, simply extract more from a preexisting colonial empire. As a result, elites must adopt compellent as opposed to deterrent strategies. In addition, as far as increased extraction of resources is concerned, elites in rising powers see the passage of time as working against them, whereas elites in declining powers see time as working in their favor. For vulnerable defenders of the status quo, the longer a conflict can be averted, the more time the metropole has to seek allies and extract resources in order to prepare for war. Buying time is one of the main reasons elites in declining powers initially accommodate superior adversaries in the core. For challengers of the status quo, the logic is just the reverse. They have a head start over status quo powers in preparing for war, and a window of opportunity exists before an opposing coalition becomes more cohesive and marshals its resources, thereby becoming an even more formidable opponent.[74] Elites in rising powers facing a strategic deficit must adopt compellent strategies to garner added resources, but they also must try to do so before the opposing coalition gains relative strength. This logic leads not only to belief in the need for a compellent stance and the blurring of strategic priorities, but also, because of the sense of urgency associated with a military balance that is growing progressively worse, to incentives for preventive war.[75]

Legitimacy. The third set of logical inferences through which high vulnerability affects strategic beliefs involves elite assessment of the

[74] I am referring here to the period during which both challenger and defender are making military preparations for potential conflict. The challenger is still rising when compared to other individual powers but faces a worsening military situation because of the power balancing (resource mobilization and alliance formation) that its behavior has triggered on behalf of threatened defenders of the status quo.

[75] My analysis challenges conventional wisdom about the sources of preventive war in several respects. First, much of the literature focuses on the tendency for dominant states experiencing a relative decline in power to wage war against rising challengers. In Jack Levy's words, "The temptation is to fight a war under relatively favorable circumstances

impact of external threats on domestic politics. Elites in both declining and rising states fear that popular concern about the hazardous security environment may lead to the loss of domestic legitimacy. They therefore pursue competitive external policies and foreign success as a way of bolstering legitimacy and restoring public confidence in the ruling elite. Imperial ambition is to unite the domestic polity and disarm political opponents. This logic explains why domestic vulnerability—as the German case demonstrates—can have the same effects on decision making as strategic vulnerability. Elites see foreign success as a way of disarming domestic opposition, whether arising from political chaos at home or external threats from abroad.[76] Empire becomes an instrument of domestic politics.[77]

These considerations reinforce the tendency of elites facing high vulnerability to believe in the need to adopt competitive external policies. Declining powers pursue competitive policies only in the periphery, while rising powers do so in the core as well. In both cases, demonstrations of resolve come to have a domestic as well as an international audience. Concern with preserving domestic legitimacy also furthers the reevaluation and blurring of strategic priorities. To ensure that ambitious external policies consolidate domestic legitimacy, elites

---

now in order to block or retard the further rise of an adversary and to avoid both the worsening of the status quo over time and the risk of war under less favorable circumstances later" ("Declining Power and the Preventive Motivation for War," *World Politics*, 40 [October 1987], 87). My findings suggest that rising states also launch preventive wars against dominant states even if they have not yet surpassed the strength of the potential adversary or adversarial coalition. (For a similar interpretation, see A. F. K. Organski and Jacek Kugler, *The War Ledger* [Chicago: University of Chicago Press, 1980], chaps. 1 and 3.) Levy appropriately asks why the rising state does not "wait until existing trends in economic and military power . . . catapult it into the stronger position" (p. 84). The answer, as I lay out below, is that elites in vulnerable, rising states—because of either domestic political forces or expansionist strategic concepts—come to see war as necessary to achieve their objectives and therefore inevitable. They then operate under better-now-than-later logic even if current circumstances are not "relatively favorable." On the basis of the case studies that I examine, elites in declining and rising states facing low vulnerability tend not to launch preventive wars primarily because they do not see war as necessary to achieve their objectives. Elites in declining states are uncertain of the rising challenger's intentions and seek to preserve the status quo without resorting to war. Elites in rising states facing low vulnerability calculate that war may well not be necessary to create an international order more conducive to their state's interests. My research therefore suggests that belief in the inevitability of conflict plays a key role in triggering preventive war.

[76] For discussion of how and why domestic and strategic vulnerability have similar effects on decision making, see Lebow, *Between Peace and War*, pp. 66–70.

[77] See Hannah Arendt, *The Origins of Totalitarianism* (New York: Harcourt, Brace, Jovanovich, 1973), pp. 123–157. For a review of the literature on elite efforts to use external ambition to counter domestic instability, see Jack Levy, "The Diversionary Theory of War: A Critique," in *Handbook of War Studies*, ed. Manus Midlarsky (Boston: Unwin Hyman, 1989), pp. 259–288.

must convince the public that empire is desirable and thus worth the costs of defense and/or acquisition. Strategic and economic arguments are marshaled for this purpose. Among elites and the public, extra-metropolitan territories come to occupy an increasingly prominent position in the now-blurred hierarchy of geographic priorities.

It is important to reiterate that these claims about the effects of high metropolitan vulnerability on strategic beliefs assume conditions of uncertainty about if, when, and where threats may come due. Elites realize that they face a dangerous international environment and conditions of strategic deficiency, but they do not know what motivates adversaries or how their own actions will affect their adversaries' behavior. Taken in isolation and within the context of uncertainty and complexity, it is reasonable for elites in declining powers, when faced with a clear strategic deficit, to accommodate challengers in the core to avoid war, and to believe in the need to pursue deterrent strategies in the periphery in order to demonstrate resolve and bolster reputation, to extract more resources from empire, and to counter the ill effects of perceived weakness on domestic legitimacy. So too is it reasonable for elites in rising powers to pursue compellent strategies in both the core and periphery in order to test or fragment the opposing coalition, to gain access to new resources, and to bolster domestic legitimacy. The nature of my claim is that perceptions of high metropolitan vulnerability privilege these inferences and thereby create a propensity among decision makers to pursue the policies outlined above. This is not to suggest that isolated elements of these beliefs never appear under low vulnerability. Nor is it to argue that elites operating under high vulnerability necessarily adopt beliefs wholly consistent with each of these inferences. Taken together, however, these inferences do capture the essential strategic logic through which high vulnerability induces elites to pursue extremist policies.

Although this pattern of logical inference is sufficient to explain the posited relationship between elite beliefs and vulnerability, it is also quite plausible that three biases within the decision-making community contribute to the propensity of elites to respond initially to high vulnerability by pursuing overly cooperative and overly competitive behavior.[78] The first bias involves the effect of domestic political consid-

---

[78] The following discussion is intended to strengthen the deductive argument linking high vulnerability to the set of beliefs described above. In examining the historical cases, I study the initial effects of vulnerability on beliefs primarily by tracing the logic that induces decision makers to pursue overly cooperative and overly competitive policies. This is not to suggest that the following types of biases are not operating, but only to say that they are difficult to detect in methodological terms when decisions can be adequately explained in terms of rational behavior—that is, in terms of the logical infer-

erations on how elites respond to external threats. High vulnerability strengthens the position of hard-liners within the elite community—and hence consolidates support for competitive and unyielding strategies—for the following reasons. There is among any group of decision makers a bias toward adopting competitive as opposed to cooperative strategies in dealing with potential adversaries.[79] The source of this bias is straightforward. For any individual decision maker facing an uncertain international environment, it is safer, in domestic political terms, to stand firm and potentially engage in excessive defense preparation than to make concessions and risk exposing the state to exploitation. To pursue an overly cooperative strategy and, as a result, suffer setbacks entails unavoidable political costs. Those responsible for the strategy will be charged with leaving the state poorly prepared to deal with external threats. In contrast, the main risk in pursuing an overly competitive strategy is that of provoking an escalating spiral of hostility. Should this unintended spiral come about, the political costs to the ruling elite are lower than if they had pursued a cooperative strategy and been exploited. Even if a deterrent or compellent strategy does provoke increasing hostility, the backers of hard-line policies can defend themselves against both elite and public criticism by arguing that the adversary acted according to its own predisposition: the spiral was the result of the adversary's aggressive intent, not of provocation. Furthermore, political leaders would rather be viewed as tough-minded and strong than lax and weak. A leader's political future is better served by building a reputation for being hard-headed and firm—even if overly so—than for being naive and easily intimidated. Efforts to minimize political risk thus privilege deterrent and compellent as opposed to accommodationist strategies.

As a result of this dynamic, individuals supporting accommodation or the moderation of imperial ambition must buck a preexisting bias within the elite community. At low vulnerability, supporters of cooperative strategies and moderation will face less opposition; conditions

---

ences laid out above. Without using detailed testing methods that go beyond the scope of this study, I can only show that conditions were conducive to the operation of certain biases and that observed outcomes were consistent with the outcomes that one would expect to see if certain biases were operating, not that such biases did in fact shape decisions. For discussion of how to test for psychological biases in specific foreign policy decisions, see Chaim Kaufmann, "Out of the Lab and into the Archives" (unpublished paper, University of Michigan, 1992).

[79] I am assuming that elites realize that they face a threatening international environment but are still uncertain as to the precise nature of external threats and as to what motivates potential adversaries. They are therefore uncertain as to whether a cooperative or competitive strategy is most appropriate for any specific adversary. The argument, then, is that, *ceteris paribus*, a bias exists toward adopting competitive strategies.

of strategic sufficiency mean that there will be little fear of being caught unprepared and accused of leaving the state exposed to external challenges. Put differently, it will be easier for supporters of retrenchment or selective expansion to persuade others to adopt their stance and hence easier to overcome the bias toward the consistent pursuit of competitive and unyielding strategies. High vulnerability strengthens the hard-line position. Those arguing for the need to stand firm against challenges can back up their position by pointing to a hostile and dangerous international environment. Those favoring concessions and the scaling back of external ambition risk being branded naive, if not treasonous. They will face increased difficulties in persuading their colleagues to accommodate adversaries, retrench from specific commitments, or reduce the scope of imperial ambition. In effect, the higher the level of vulnerability, the more pronounced this bias toward adopting competitive and overly ambitious strategies.[80]

The second bias potentially contributing to the link between high vulnerability and extremist policies draws on prospect theory. Prospect theory posits that people are risk-averse with respect to gains and risk-seeking with respect to losses.[81] This means that a given individual will prefer a sure chance of receiving one hundred dollars to an even chance of receiving two hundred dollars or nothing, but will prefer an even chance of losing two hundred dollars or nothing to a sure chance of losing one hundred dollars.

The application to the problem at hand is as follows. Under low vulnerability, elites believe that they will be able to attain their international objectives. Even if war breaks out, elites believe that victory is likely; they are operating in the realm of gains. They will therefore behave in a risk-averse manner and pursue policies that ensure continued strategic sufficiency and the security of the metropole. For elites in declining powers, to accommodate in the core and practice deterrence in the periphery to garner resources or as a means of demonstrating resolve and potentially averting war is unacceptably risky, as it would initially distract resources from the metropole and weaken its

---

[80] This dynamic does not apply to the behavior of declining powers in the core for the reasons outlined above: strategic deficiency makes the adoption of competitive policies in the core too dangerous. Although elites, for domestic reasons, may want to deter challengers in the core, they calculate that they do not have sufficient resources to do so. The risk of provoking a disastrous war is simply too high.

[81] For a summary of prospect theory and several applications in the realm of political choice, see George Quattrone and Amos Tversky, "Contrasting Rational and Psychological Analyses of Political Choice," *American Political Science Review*, 82 (September 1988), 719–736; Daniel Kahneman and Amos Tversky, "Choices, Values, and Frames," *American Psychologist*, 39 (April 1984), 341–350; and Eldar Shafir, "Prospect Theory and Political Analysis," *Political Psychology*, 13, 2 (1992), 311–322.

strategic position. Elites in rising powers will pursue selective expansion to add to the strength of the metropole. But they will not risk undermining strategic sufficiency by adopting extremely expansive policies that could lead to self-encirclement or overextension, even if such policies hold out the possibility of even greater gains.

Under high vulnerability, elites believe that they may not be able to attain their international objectives and they calculate that war, were it to break out, would likely jeopardize the security of the metropole. Operating in the realm of losses, they behave in a risk-seeking manner and adopt extreme policies in order to escape their predicament. Elites in declining powers seek to avert war and avoid losses altogether, or at least to buy time to extract added resources from the periphery, despite the fact that such behavior initially leaves the metropole at an even greater disadvantage. Elites in rising powers are willing to risk that compellent strategies will obviate the need to scale back imperial ambition by forcing the opposition to back down and by gaining access to new resources, even though compellence could also lead to more acute self-encirclement and overextension. Confronted with the prospect of losses from the outset, decision makers are willing to engage in risky behavior that may avoid losses altogether, even though it increases the severity of the loss should the risk not pay off.

One final bias may also be at work: it is much easier in psychological terms for an individual to make concessions from a position of strength than from one of weakness. To back down from external commitments or objectives is to demonstrate a degree of immunity to potential setbacks. Such immunity is derived from a sense of security and confidence; it comes with the appreciation that one's core values, although under threat and in need of protection, are essentially intact. Insecurity, on the other hand, breeds the opposite affect: hypersensitivity and an inability to back away from commitments or challenges of even minor importance. Indeed, an insecure person is likely to overreact to challenges. Consider how two people—one feeling secure and the other vulnerable—would react to a challenge to engage in a game of "chicken." The secure individual might well laugh off the challenge and refuse to participate, without fearing a loss of face. For him, standing firm in a contest of wills would contribute little, if anything, to his central values or sense of well-being. The insecure individual, by virtue of his hypersensitivity and preoccupation with potential loss of face, is far more likely to be enticed into the game. He perceives the contest as central to his self-esteem and sense of well-being. It is the psychological need to disprove and/or hide his essential insecurity that drives his behavior.

This bias could well contribute to overly competitive behavior on the part of elites operating under conditions of strategic deficiency. As argued above, elites faced with high vulnerability reason that they can offset deficiency in material resources by demonstrating resolve and bolstering reputation. I am arguing here that vulnerability also produces an emotional bias that reinforces this inferential logic. Decision makers not only reason that they can compensate for an unfavorable shift in the balance of material power through a favorable shift in the balance of resolve, but also face psychological pressure to behave in ways that contradict or mask their acute sense of vulnerability. This combination of inference and affect helps explain why the case studies contain numerous instances in which decision makers faced with high vulnerability come to place excessive reliance on reputation in interacting with adversaries and setting strategic priorities. As Patrick Morgan describes this phenomenon, vulnerability "converts a concern for reputation from a rational extension of the art of commitment into a pretense used to hide a pervasive insecurity."[82] These psychological considerations strengthen the tendency of elites facing conditions of high vulnerability to adopt overly ambitious policies.

In sum, perceptions of high metropolitan vulnerability under conditions of uncertainty—through the logical inferences and, possibly, the biases just described—induce elites to pursue overly cooperative and overly competitive behavior. An extraordinary strategic environment produces extraordinary policies. As an initial response to high vulnerability, such behavior is reasoned and reasonable and conforms to the notion of bounded rationality.

The effect of vulnerability on beliefs provides, however, only the first piece of the puzzle. When uncertainty diminishes and incoming information indicates that extremist policies are not producing their intended effects, elites continue to behave according to the notion of bounded rationality: they begin to adapt their beliefs and realize that they must reorient grand strategy. Change in beliefs usually occurs slowly; vulnerability tends to impair the adaptation of belief systems. Moreover, the lag between receipt of new information and adaptation of beliefs can have consequential effects on the ability of states to adjust their grand strategies to rapid shifts in the constellation of power. This cognitive dynamic does explain some instances of moderate adjustment failure. Nevertheless, elites eventually do alter their beliefs when the causal suppositions that inform strategy are persistently challenged by discrepant information. Elites in declining powers realize that their policies are not satisfying the adversary or improving the metropole's security; they come to see the need to practice deterrence in the core

[82] Morgan, "Saving Face," p. 134.

[86]

and accommodation in the periphery. Elites in rising powers come to appreciate that compellent strategies are not fragmenting the opposing coalition or adding to national strength; on the contrary, they are eroding metropolitan security by leading to self-encirclement and/or overextension. That elites often fail to orchestrate a much-needed reorientation of grand strategy even after they adapt their beliefs to incoming information reveals that the impact of high vulnerability on elite beliefs is not sufficient to explain gross adjustment failure. The tendency for belief systems to persevere in the face of disconfirming evidence does not cause decision makers to pursue overly cooperative and overly competitive behavior when the imminence and severity of the threat to the metropole become manifest; elites eventually come to see the need for strategic retrenchment even though beliefs may lag considerably behind incoming information. To understand why adjustment does not occur even after elites adapt their beliefs to strategic reality, it is necessary to look at other constraints on the policy-making process.

The effect of vulnerability on strategic beliefs thus explains why elites initially respond to high vulnerability by adopting overly cooperative and overly competitive policies. It also explains why, when first confronted with disconfirming evidence, elites tend to cling tightly to existing knowledge structures; belief change lags behind change in the external environment. But since beliefs are gradually brought into line with strategic realities, the effect of high vulnerability on elite beliefs cannot alone explain adjustment failure. The impact of vulnerability on beliefs does, however, set the stage for the second and final piece of the puzzle. As I argue in the following section, elites, by seeking to gain domestic support for their extremist policies, eventually entrap themselves in a strategic culture that prevents them from adjusting grand strategy even though they come to appreciate the need to do so.

Strategic Culture and the Process of Entrapment

Although the causes of adjustment failure do not lie in domestic structure, domestic politics may nonetheless play a key role in producing self-defeating behavior. It is plausible that adjustment failure is the result of bargaining and gamesmanship among competing political coalitions. In autocracies, democracies, and cartelized polities alike, the need to hold together fragile governing coalitions may paralyze leaders or force them to adopt policies ill-suited to the strategic environment. Alternatively, the populace at large, through its ability to grant or withhold its political support for elites, can place major constraints on decision makers. Elites must maintain the support of the public in order to stay in power. The political power of the masses is likely to be stronger in democratic states than in authoritarian ones, but elites in virtually all systems must seek to preserve their legitimacy by pursuing policies consistent with the material needs and normative orientations of the populace. Coercive rule can last only so long. As Max Weber notes, "Every such system attempts to establish and to cultivate the belief in its legitimacy."[83] From this perspective, the constraints imposed on decision makers by the need to maintain governing coalitions and popular legitimacy—regardless of domestic structure—could lie at the root of adjustment failure. The requirements of staying in power might prevent elites from pursuing policies consistent with strategic pragmatism.

In fact, domestic politics and the dynamics of elite-mass linkages provide the final piece of the puzzle. I use the notion of strategic culture to capture the mechanism through which domestic political forces contribute to self-defeating behavior. Strategic culture is the set of images that shapes a polity's collective disposition toward the behavior of its state in the international arena. It refers to the realm of national identity and consists of the images and conceptions that determine how the polity understands the relationship between metropolitan security and empire, the nation's position in the international hierarchy, and the scope and nature of its external ambition. These images not only shape national identity, but also affect how the polity conceives of the relationship of other territories to its own. As Kenneth Boulding writes, "The images which are important in international systems are those which a nation has of itself and of those other bodies in the system which constitute its international environment."[84] These images may be concrete and easily identified by the individuals who hold them, or they may be more difficult to recognize because they are so embedded in the way that those individuals define their nation and its relationship to external actors. In Herbert Kelman's words, "We are interested not only in the individual's verbalizations about what the object is like, but also in the conceptions of the object that are *implicit* in the ways in which he relates himself to it."[85] The images that constitute strategic culture manifest themselves in and are propagated by nu-

[83] Max Weber, *Economy and Society*, ed. Guenther Roth and Claus Wittich, vol. 1 (Berkeley: University of California Press, 1978), p. 213.

[84] Kenneth Boulding, "National Images and International Systems," *Journal of Conflict Resolution*, 3 (June 1959), 121.

[85] Herbert Kelman, "Social-Psychological Approaches to the Study of International Relations," in *International Behavior: A Social Psychological Analysis*, ed. Herbert Kelman (New York: Holt, Rinehart, and Winston, 1965), p. 25.

merous structures and mechanisms such as speeches, governmental institutions, popular literature, educational curricula, and local organizations. Kelman's conceptualization is again useful: "The nation-state as a system conveys—through its institutional structures, basic documents, and elite communications—a certain definition of its character and functions and of the roles that its nationals must enact if the system is to carry out its functions. Individual nationals in turn adopt, as part of their personal belief systems, certain images of the state and of their own roles in relation to it."[86]

Unlike elite beliefs, strategic culture does not emerge from causal propositions. It is image-based, not inference-based; it provides a deeply embedded notion of what constitutes national security, not a short-term set of suppositions about the nature of international relations. Both strategic beliefs and strategic culture are ideational, but the ideas that give them content fall into quite different realms. The realm of beliefs is restricted largely to the elite community and concerns the following types of issues: whether to deter or accommodate adversaries, whether the defense or the offense has the advantage, whether the next war will be long or short. The realm of strategic culture is the wider body politic and the issues it concerns are very different: whether the nation as a collective entity views the protection of imperial possessions as integral to its well-being; whether the polity views its external influence as being consistent with its position in the international hierarchy; how the polity understands the scope and objectives of external ambition.[87] As mentioned above, strategic beliefs— after a certain time lag—are fairly sensitive to incoming information and disconfirming evidence. Strategic culture, on the contrary, is more resistant to incoming information and to change. Vivid events, such as war and crisis, can alter strategic culture relatively rapidly. Otherwise,

---

[86] Ibid., p. 26.
[87] For example, the key strategic beliefs informing British policy during the 1930s were that the most immediate threats to British interests were in the periphery, that accommodating Hitler's demands was the best way to contain German expansion and prevent war in Europe, and that rearmament needed to proceed slowly in order to foster economic recovery and prepare the country for the long war that might be unavoidable at some point in the future. During this same period, British strategic culture consisted of two central images: that the country's well-being and status as a great power depended upon the integrity of its overseas empire, and that Britain, in the aftermath of the devastation suffered in World War I, had to avoid at all costs involvement in a land war on the European continent. These two images were not the product of careful deliberation about how best to protect the security of the British isles. On the contrary, they represented deeply embedded elements of how the polity—elites and masses alike— conceived of British security. These images thus provided the political imperatives, intellectual paradigms, and institutional orientations in which policy was formed.

shifts in collective self-image and identity take place much more slowly than shifts in elite beliefs.[88]

A key contention of this book is that the particular conceptions of empire embedded in strategic culture can place very severe constraints on the ability of elites to undertake strategic adjustment. Inasmuch as strategic culture represents fundamental and deep-rooted images and normative orientations, it defines the boundaries of politically legitimate behavior for the ruling elite. When political legitimacy becomes wedded to a specific notion of empire, the pursuit of policies that threaten that notion becomes very difficult. Should the external environment make such policies desirable, the exigencies of strategic reality would come into conflict with the exigencies of political survival. Moreover, images of empire may become so integral to how a polity—including the elite community—defines national security that policies that deviate from that image do not even receive consideration. To maintain political power, preserve ruling coalitions, and protect a deeply embedded and institutionalized image of what constitutes national well-being, elites may be forced to abandon the adjustments to grand strategy that would be consistent with strategic pragmatism.

By examining the mechanisms through which shifts in strategic culture come about, I can now complete the argument linking high vulnerability to adjustment failure. Recall that perceptions of high metropolitan vulnerability under conditions of uncertainty induce elites, via strategic beliefs, to adopt both overly cooperative and overly competitive policies. In order to gain domestic support for their extraordinary policies, elites must seek to mold popular images of empire. To build support for overly cooperative policies in the core and overly competitive policies in the periphery, elites in declining powers downplay the imminence of threats in the core and sell peripheral empire to the polity. To build support for overly competitive policies in both the core and periphery, elites in rising powers peddle expansive conceptions of security to the polity. Over time, elite propagation of these images leads to deep-rooted shifts in public attitudes. In Boulding's terms, "The image of the powerful cannot diverge too greatly from the image of the mass without the powerful losing power. On the other

[88] To return to the British example, during the second half of the 1930s, elite beliefs changed in accordance with incoming information. British elites came to appreciate that Germany posed the most pressing threats to British interests, that appeasement was not satisfying Hitler's appetite for expansion, and that rearmament had to take precedence over economic recovery. Strategic culture, however, was far less responsive to incoming information. Despite clear indications that Britain had to concentrate its resources in the core and prepare for a land war in Europe, adjustment was constrained by deeply embedded strategic images that equated British security with the integrity of the empire and the avoidance of a continental commitment.

hand, the powerful also have some ability to manipulate the images of the mass toward those of the powerful."[89]

This conception of the crucial role of elite beliefs in shaping popular attitudes is consistent with past research into the linkages between elite and mass attitudes and belief systems. Robert Putnam writes that elite beliefs are far more structured and detailed than those of non-elites.[90] Elite beliefs also adapt more readily to incoming information, and "elite opinion is most apt to run ahead of mass opinion in periods of rapid change." As a result, Putnam argues, "the elaboration and propagation of new political concepts is largely the province of elites."[91] Milton Rosenberg agrees that beliefs generally emerge among elites and then percolate down to the mass level. Because popular attitudes tend to lag behind and derive from elite beliefs, they are more likely to constrain elite options than to serve as a source of policy innovation.[92] Philip Converse similarly finds that belief systems among mass publics are fragmented and consist of jumbled "idea-elements." Whereas elite beliefs have a profound impact on discrete decisions, mass beliefs are of far less consequence: "The broad contours of elite decisions over time can depend in a vital way upon currents in what is loosely called 'the history of ideas.' These decisions in turn have effects upon the mass of more common citizens. But, of any direct participation in this history of ideas and the behavior it shapes, the mass is remarkably innocent."[93]

The shifts in popular attitudes brought about by elite lobbying do succeed in providing decision makers with domestic support for their policies. The core of the problem is that the same shifts in public opinion that initially empower decision makers eventually come to constrain them. Elites sell strategic conceptions to the polity tailored to gain support for overly cooperative and overly competitive policies but fail to foresee that the consequent shifts in mass attitudes may restrict their freedom of action should pursuit of these policies no longer prove viable or strategically sound.[94] As argued above, it is under conditions

[89] Boulding, "National Images," p. 122. George also notes that leaders often react to domestic constraints by "trying to manipulate and control public opinion." See "Domestic Constraints," p. 234.

[90] Putnam, *Political Elites*, pp. 90–91.

[91] Ibid., pp. 139–140.

[92] Milton Rosenberg, "Images in Relation to the Policy Process," in *International Behavior*, ed. Kelman, pp. 285–286, 330.

[93] Converse, "Nature of Belief Systems," p. 255.

[94] The historical cases reveal that elites, even if not confronted with high vulnerability, sometimes propagate strategic images among the populace to gain support for their policies and legitimate their rule. This finding does not present problems for the sequencing stipulated by my model for two main reasons. First, in these instances, elites begin to lobby the public in order to gain support for policies needed to cope with

of uncertainty that high vulnerability leads to overly cooperative and overly competitive behavior. As uncertainty diminishes, elites become aware of the need to undertake strategic adjustment; their beliefs do adapt to incoming information. But because they previously succeeded in shaping public opinion and altering the determinants of domestic legitimacy, domestic constraints prevent them from implementing the policies that they now deem most appropriate; political survival conflicts with strategic pragmatism. As Kelman describes the decision maker's entrapment, "The victim of his own propaganda, he may be unaware of the extent to which his own communications contributed to the state of public opinion that now ties his hands."[95]

The constraining effects of elite propagation of strategic images also manifest themselves in more subtle ways, by removing certain options from the political agenda and making them, as it were, unthinkable. Even if strategic images are crafted primarily for public consumption, they gradually spread through the top-level elite community, the bureaucracy, and the military services. They become, as it were, organizing principles for the broader decision-making community. Over time, individual members of the elite community come to believe in the strategic conceptions that they repeatedly articulate before the public. Especially when decision makers pursue policies consistent with the images they are propagating, they are likely to internalize these im-

---

prospective threats. Accordingly, it is a sense of anticipated vulnerability that initially induces elites to propagate strategic images among the public. Second, it is only after elites are confronted with conditions of strategic deficiency that lobbying efforts intensify and succeed in embedding in strategic culture the images and conceptions that eventually prevent adjustment.

[95] Kelman, "Social-Psychological Approaches," pp. 583–584. My argument about the constraining effects associated with elite manipulation of popular attitudes draws on an extensive literature on the domestic causes of international conflict. This literature falls into two broad categories. One group of scholars argues that elites deliberately initiate war in order to unite the domestic polity and disarm political opponents. See, for example, Levy, "Diversionary Theory of War"; Quincy Wright, *A Study of War* (Chicago: University of Chicago Press, 1965); Richard Rosecrance, *Action and Reaction in World Politics* (Boston: Little, Brown, 1963); Arno Mayer, "Domestic Causes and Purposes of War in Europe, 1870–1956," in *The Responsibility of Power*, ed. Leonard Krieger and Fritz Stern (New York: Doubleday, 1967); and Lebow, *Between Peace and War*. Others argue that public opinion and domestic political forces are responsible for pushing elites to initiate conflict. See, for example, Ernest May, *Imperial Democracy* (New York: Harper Torchbooks, 1973); and Jack Levy, "The Causes of War: A Review of Theories and Evidence," in *Behavior, Society, and Nuclear War*, vol. 1, ed. Philip Tetlock, Jo Husbands, Robert Jervis, Paul Stern, and Charles Tilly (New York: Oxford University Press, 1989), pp. 209–333. My argument combines these two perspectives. Elites adopt ambitious external policies in part to counter domestic threats and bolster legitimacy. They then find that their success in molding popular attitudes stirs up powerful political forces that constrain their ability to alter policy and avoid self-defeating behavior.

ages.[96] The intellectual paradigms and fundamental values that shape policy choice change accordingly.[97] New members of the elite community and those not in the inner circle will be unaware that prevailing strategic conceptions were originally crafted for instrumental purposes. Individual elites become committed, in both cognitive and emotional terms, to these strategic conceptions. At the same time, as specific strategic notions and conceptions of empire spread throughout the polity, the bureaucracy itself goes through a process of socialization. Governmental bodies come to define their missions and functions in terms of these strategic images, institutionalizing them, changing career paths, and wedding the self-interest of both individuals and organizations to their fulfillment. Within the military services, career incentives, budgetary considerations, procurement programs, war plans, force structures, and command structures all become oriented toward specific missions and objectives.[98] These organizational interests and routines impair adjustment, especially when the organizations in question face a threatening external environment.[99]

In this sense, the strategic arguments and rhetoric intended to rally domestic support come to shape the central assumptions that guide

[96] According to Darly Bem's self-perception theory, individuals shape their attitudes and emotions to conform to their behavior. In Deborah Larson's words, "behavior leads to the development of attitudes by providing evidence of what we *really* believe." *Origins of Containment*, p. 43. This process of attitude change provides one feedback mechanism through which elite beliefs, via elite-mass linkages, come back to shape elite thinking.

[97] I use the term *intellectual paradigm* to capture the notion of mindset or world view. It refers to the set of starting assumptions or template that shapes elite thinking. Intellectual paradigms influence behavior through cognition. I use the term *value* to refer to the intrinsic worth that elites assign to specific outcomes. Values influence behavior through affect and emotion.

[98] For an excellent treatment of how institutional interests, biases, and dogmas affect the behavior of military organizations, see Snyder, *Ideology of the Offensive*, esp. chaps. 1 and 8. Snyder writes that militaries develop an "organizational ideology . . . [that becomes] embodied in field manuals, war plans, and organizational structures, and . . . perpetuated through the socialization of new officers" (p. 210). For more general discussion of organizational interests and behavior, see Herbert Simon and James March, *Organizations* (New York: Wiley, 1958); and Morton Halperin, *Bureaucratic Politics and Foreign Policy* (Washington, D.C.: Brookings, 1974).

[99] The literature on organizational behavior indicates that a threatening external environment induces organizations to cling tightly to existing norms and patterns of behavior. When threatened, organizations hold more tightly to embedded assumptions and routines and are less adaptive than when operating under normal conditions. For calling my attention to this literature, I am indebted to Beth Kier, "The Cultural Roots of Doctrinal Decisions," unpublished manuscript, 1993. See L. J. Bourgeois, Daniel McAllister, and Terrence Mitchell, "The Effects of Different Organizational Environments upon Decisions about Organizational Structure," *Academy of Management Journal*, 21 (1978), 508–514; and Barry Staw, Lance Sandelands, and Jane Dutton, "Threat-Rigidity Effects in Organizational Behavior: A Multilevel Analysis," *Administrative Science Quarterly*, 26 (December 1981), 501–524.

[93]

elite behavior.[100] Elite thinking and elite institutions may be so infused with certain images that important options are effectively removed from consideration. These images affect how elites conceive of the *essence* of national security, regardless of more narrow causal suppositions; an image-based conception of security clashes with one that is inference-based. In these instances, powerful strategic images—and the cognitive, emotional, and organizational imperatives associated with them—contradict and override strategic logic, creating a set of reigning assumptions that may bear little resemblance to those that would be produced by logical inference. Though certain territories may be thousands of miles away from the metropole and, in geopolitical terms, of no strategic importance, their security may be perceived as being inseparable from that of the metropole. To retrench would be to threaten the intellectual paradigms and core values of individual decision makers and to challenge the central missions and organizational interests of the bureaucracy and military. Even if incoming information discredits elite beliefs and points to the urgent need for a reorientation of strategy, prevailing strategic conceptions may make certain policy options inconceivable. These conceptions do not directly prevent elites from carrying out policies that they consciously prefer; it is not fear of falling from power that drives elite behavior. Rather, deeply embedded strategic conceptions shape how elites conceive of the notion of national security and how elite institutions define their primary roles and organizational interests.[101]

[100] As the case studies show, most of the strategic images that come to infuse elite thinking and that impair adjustment initially emerge as packages of ideas that elites use to shape public attitudes. They are the product of elite-mass linkages and the efforts of decision makers to manage domestic politics. It is also possible that the strategic conceptions that impair adjustment could emerge and be propagated exclusively within the decision-making community. Competing coalitions, for example, could concoct and propagate strategic images for use in intra-elite struggles. So too might elites develop and propagate powerful strategic images to galvanize the bureaucracy and military and overcome institutional inertia. In these cases, intra-elite dynamics, as opposed to elite-mass linkages, would be the key source of the strategic assumptions producing self-defeating behavior. In deductive terms, the strategic images that impair adjustment could propagate through either mechanism. My emphasis on the overriding importance of elite-mass linkages is based on examination of the historical cases.

[101] An example will help illustrate my point. Japanese elites in 1941 faced a choice between going to war with the United States and scaling back the scope of imperial ambition because of insufficient resources. The latter option, while it made more strategic sense, was simply unthinkable for most leaders. Withdrawal from China and the abandonment of the Greater East Asia Co-Prosperity Sphere threatened the image of a Japanese empire in Asia to which elites had become deeply committed in both cognitive and emotional terms. So too would withdrawal undercut the political power of a military establishment that had staked its preeminent position within the elite community on its ability to build an empire that would bring Japan economic self-sufficiency. Decision makers were constrained not by party politics or public opinion, but by the strategic conceptions that had become deeply embedded within the elite community.

In sum, I am arguing that elite efforts to garner domestic support for their extremist policies lead to shifts in strategic culture—that is, in the core images that inform public attitudes, the intellectual paradigms and central values of decision makers, and the organizational interests of elite institutions. Strategic culture then entraps elites through two distinct, yet complementary, processes. One is primarily political in nature: elites appreciate the need to reorient grand strategy, but cannot do so because of discrete domestic pressures. Political survival conflicts with, and overrides, strategic pragmatism. The other is primarily cognitive, emotional, and organizational in nature: the images propagated by top elites so infuse the decision-making community and the content of political debate that the policies consistent with strategic pragmatism do not even receive serious consideration. The attainment of specific imperial goals becomes so integral to how top-level elites, the bureaucracy, and the military services define their roles and missions that decision makers are unable to reverse course. The problem is not simply fear of losing power, but of challenging the central images and symbols that constitute national identity and that anchor and define the national security community and the role of specific actors within that community. These actors may well fear the political repercussions of reorienting grand strategy, but at least as important in impairing adjustment are the extent to which individual elites have come to internalize and believe in these strategic conceptions, the extent of their emotional commitment to the fulfillment of these conceptions, and the extent to which these conceptions have shaped how elite institutions define their objectives and interests. For cognitive, emotional, and organizational reasons, strategic images override strategic logic.[102]

It is important to emphasize the sequential nature of the argument. Elites propagate strategic images to gain support for their policies, unaware that their actions may later come to constrain them. Ac-

[102] My argument about the role of strategic culture in causing adjustment failure is similar to Charles Doran's argument about the causal link between systemic change and major war. See *Systems in Crisis*, Cambridge Studies in International Relations, 16 (Cambridge: Cambridge University Press, 1991). According to Doran's "power cycle theory," systemic change triggers conflict during critical points when gaps emerge between the relative power position of one or more great powers and the international role that those great powers seek to play. In Doran's words, "role suggests informally legitimated responsibilities and perquisites associated with position and place" (p. 39). These responsibilities and perquisites are based on a state's own aspirations that devolve from relative national capability as well as on the willingness of other members of the system to allow the state to fulfill such aspirations. When role is challenged by power shifts and new projections of the state's relative power position in the future, uncertainty and stress impair the decision-making process and make conflict more likely. In Doran's words, "When the future role projection of a major state changes abruptly and dramati-

cally, the structural anchors for decision are cut adrift." Psychological and domestic sources of instability become more salient and "the rational decision-making calculus breaks down as anchors of structural certainty disappear" (pp. 21–22).

My notion of strategic culture shares common ground with Doran's notion of role. Both refer to deeply embedded aspirations and assumptions that lag behind the strategic imperatives associated with shifts in the distribution of power. His critical periods correspond in rough terms to the third phase of my causal argument—when incoming information disconfirms prevailing strategic beliefs but fails to induce a shift in national strategy. We both agree that the stress and psychic discomfort that accompanies these periods impairs decision making.

Doran and I part company, however, in two important respects. First, Doran's concept of role connotes embedded strategic conceptions that are a natural outgrowth of national capability. My notion of strategic culture connotes embedded conceptions that are politically and socially constructed. Accordingly, role should constrain adjustment whenever a state undergoes a shift in its power cycle and experiences a change in prevailing projections of its future power position. Strategic culture, on the other hand, should constrain adjustment only when it has been constructed by elites—that is, only when they are confronted with high vulnerability. This causal assertion is the basis of my claim that great powers facing conditions of low vulnerability should be able to adjust successfully to international change.

Second, Doran and I differ over the key dynamics leading to the emergence of critical historical junctures. For Doran, these junctures emerge when statesmen recognize that prevailing assumptions about role are erroneous—that is, when a gap emerges between relative power position and role. Elites in a rising state, for example, might realize that the rate of increase in their state's relative power position has slowed, or that the state has entered a phase of relative decline. From my perspective, it is not assessment of long-term trends and awareness of turning points in these trends, but assessment of power balances in the near term, that determine whether a state adjusts successfully to systemic change. Elites may recognize that their state has entered a phase of relative decline, but will pursue self-defeating strategies only if faced with high vulnerability. Elites may believe that their state is enjoying a steady increase in its relative power position, but nevertheless engage in extremist behavior if changes in alignment and preparations for war lead to perceptions of high vulnerability.

Furthermore, I do not accept Doran's claim that elites are fully aware of discrete shifts in their state's long-term power trajectory as they occur. As Doran admits, "The true significance of the power cycle paradigm for the rise and decline of great powers lies not in the *post-hoc* depiction of the trends of history, but in being able to depict trends—and the inversions in the trends—as they are experienced" (p. 89). The problem is that even contemporary elites with modern analytic techniques at their disposal have considerable difficulty depicting trends and projecting future power trajectories. Doran himself devotes an entire chapter to discussing how to measure national capability and decides to focus (for the 1815–1950 period) on iron and steel production, population, size of armed forces, coal production, and urbanization. Without supporting empirical evidence, it is difficult to accept that elites, especially during earlier historical periods, would be aware of the specific trends and turning points predicted by these indicators. During the pre–World War I years—the period from which Doran draws much of his empirical evidence—elites simply did not have sufficient understanding of the components of national power or sufficient access to statistical data about their own country or about other countries to be able to predict relative power trajectories over the coming decades.

The following example illustrates my point. Doran contends that Germany's relative power position peaked around the years 1905–1907. He bases this assessment on his own relatively sophisticated, post-hoc measures of national capability. Doran then goes on to claim that German elites were aware that the country was "passing through a critical point on its power cycle" (p. 126). But he offers unconvincing evidence to support his claim. The empirical evidence he provides refers exclusively to projected shifts in

cording to my argument, elites repeatedly fail to heed the warning of Irving Janis and M. Brewster Smith that "communications to the public must consider not only the requirements for getting immediate support for a given policy, but also the requirements for maintaining support for future policies, when the world situation may have shifted."[103] The sequential nature of the problem raises two issues. First, why are elites unable to recognize this potentially pernicious feedback mechanism and avert its constraining effects? Second, if elites are able to sell specific conceptions of empire to the polity and shape strategic culture, why are they unable, once the need for strategic adjustment has become apparent, to sell new strategic conceptions to the polity and gain support for a different set of policies?

Politicians fail to avert setting the entrapment process in motion for three reasons. First, they tend to have short time horizons. Because leadership changes hands fairly frequently, ruling elites are preoccupied by the challenges facing them today and tomorrow and rarely consider the future implications of their present behavior. They may also simply ignore the potential for international change and thus neglect the need to preserve the political leeway to respond accordingly. Second, elite belief systems tend to be insensitive to cyclical patterns of causation. Axelrod finds that elites tend to see causation as "flowing outwards, and not turning back to affect some other concept variable that is regarded as causally prior." As a consequence, "even sophisticated decision makers operating in the field of their competence have a very strong tendency to conceptualize causation in a way that prevents them from spontaneously recognizing feedback in their policy environments."[104] In short, cognitive limitations may prevent elites from fully recognizing the cyclical implications of their behavior. Third, even if elites recognize that their current behavior may later come to constrain them, the immediate need to pursue specific policies may override this concern. An eroding security environment and waning domestic legitimacy are likely to have far more influence on elite behav-

---

the military balance over the next few years, not to awareness of a key turning point in Germany's long-term power trajectory. As I argue in Chapter 6, German behavior did change during this period, but the explanation is far simpler than Doran suggests. The formation of the Triple Entente fueled German fears of encirclement, altered German assessments of the military balance, and confronted elites with conditions of strategic deficiency. Shifting alignments, new assessments of the military balance, and perceptions of high vulnerability—not awareness of a turning point in Germany's long-term trajectory as a great power—were driving German behavior.

[103] Irving Janis and M. Brewster Smith, "Effects of Education and Persuasion on National and International Images," in *International Behavior*, ed. Kelman, p. 192.

[104] Axelrod, *Structure of Decision*, p. 238.

ior than the prospect of facing new domestic constraints at some unde-termined point in the future.

There are also three main reasons why elites are unable to reverse course—and effect the necessary changes in strategic culture—once they have recognized the need to adjust policy. First, the time lags involved in molding popular attitudes make it difficult for elites to alter in short order prevailing conceptions of security. Mass images tend to be relatively unsophisticated and somewhat insensitive to regular events and incoming information. It may have taken years to embed specific images in the public mind. Even if elites assimilate information indicating that their policies are leading to strategic exposure, self-encirclement, or overextension—and orchestrate a propaganda cam-paign to that effect—they may be unable to communicate readily their message to the public. Recall that there is a significant time lag between receipt of disconfirming information and change in elite beliefs. It will also take time for elites to organize and then effectively carry out a campaign to sell new strategic images to the public. Rapid changes in the international environment may mean that elites simply do not have sufficient time to reshape public attitudes and gain support for a much-needed reorientation of strategy.

Second, elites may find it costly in political terms to refute precisely those images that they had previously been championing. By seeking to reverse course, decision makers may be discredited and viewed as opportunists by the public. This problem is likely to be alleviated by a change of leadership. New leaders, by criticizing and distancing themselves from the policies pursued by their predecessors, should be better able to challenge prevailing strategic images without incurring high political costs. But even for a new set of elites, informing the polity that it must swallow its imperial ambition and support a radi-cally different external policy entails significant political risks. Elites may fail to undertake efforts to reshape public attitudes because they fear that such efforts would themselves lead to the loss of legitimacy for the ruling group. Especially in democratic systems, elites usually do not run for office or begin their term by adopting stances that are unpopular and likely to fuel opposition.[105]

Third, because strategic culture can affect outcomes not only by cre-ating domestic political constraints but also by infusing the elite com-munity and its institutions with powerful images that override strategic logic, elites may not even accept that they must reverse course despite incoming information pointing to the need to do so. When these im-ages redefine the central missions and roles of elite institutions, only

[105] Consider the following examples from the recent experiences of U.S. presidents. President Bush clearly suffered during the 1992 campaign from breaking his own pledge

the most bold and perspicacious members of the decision-making community would be able to recognize that elites had become entrapped in their own strategic conceptions. Realization of the need to adjust strategy would likely spread slowly through the elite community. Those initially in favor of new policies would be opposed by colleagues who would find such proposals threatening in political, cognitive, and emotional terms. So too would the organizational interests of the foreign policy bureaucracy and the military be threatened by a large-scale change in national strategy. As a result, individuals recognizing the need to undertake strategic adjustment are likely to be excluded from the decision-making arena. If not excluded, they will face the formidable task of reorienting the central roles and missions of the bureaucracy and military. They may well be unable even to disabuse their colleagues of dangerous strategic conceptions, much less to reshape public attitudes.[106]

In addition to the constraints just enumerated, one other factor contributes to the tendency for elites to entrap themselves in strategic culture. Although elites implant within the polity the images that constitute strategic culture, exogenous shocks shape those images in ways unintended and uncontrollable by decision makers. Wars, crises, and

---

that he would not raise taxes. His repeated statements on this issue ("Read my lips") left him little room for maneuver. Bush's reaction to the Iraqi invasion of Kuwait similarly constrained the administration's options. After Bush repeatedly told the American people that this action could not stand, his credibility became associated with ensuring an unconditional Iraqi withdrawal. In this domestic political context, it would have been very difficult for Bush to negotiate a settlement that entailed making concessions to Iraq. A broader look at U.S. foreign policy during the Cold War confirms that a change in personnel facilitates the task of altering course and challenging prevailing strategic conceptions. Upon coming to office, Richard Nixon and Henry Kissinger violated the hard-line paradigm that had been in place since the early years of the Cold War by pursuing detente with the Soviet Union and rapprochement with China. The arrival of a new administration allowed a cleaner break with the past. Interestingly, domestic support for detente dwindled during the course of the 1970s in large part because Nixon and Kissinger failed to articulate to the populace the rationale and conceptual underpinnings for their policies.

[106] Consider the example of Japanese decision making in 1941. During the months preceding the decision to go to war against the United States, bold individuals—both military personnel and civilians—attempted to halt the southern advance, accommodate the concerns of Western powers, and avoid conflict with the United States. Their objections went unheeded, however, and they were effectively silenced by colleagues committed to enlarging the empire and going to war with the West. Retrenchment was unacceptable for those who had come to believe sincerely that Japanese security depended on the establishment of the Greater East Asia Co-Prosperity Sphere. In addition, scaling back the scope of imperial ambition threatened to weaken the political power of the military services, who had staked their preeminent domestic position and their huge allocation of resources on the need to establish economic self-sufficiency through imperial conquest. In sum, a campaign to reshape public attitudes and redefine the central missions and roles of elite institutions was never launched because the few elites willing to face up to Japan's predicament were unable to disabuse even their top-level colleagues of the strategic conceptions fueling self-defeating behavior.

other spectacular events shared by the population as a whole can leave a lasting impression on attitudes and mold collective images and identities independently of elite manipulation.[107] The ways in which war or crisis affects strategic culture are by no means uniform across different countries. The images prevailing before a war and the unique experiences of that country during the war determine the impact of the event on strategic culture. In Britain, for instance, one of the most powerful reactions to World War I was the adoption of a "never again" attitude toward involvement in a continental war. The horrors of the trenches convinced the British—elites and masses alike—that they should seek security and prestige through peripheral empire and avoid continental entanglements. The French had a quite different reaction to the war. Because of the material contribution that the overseas territories made to the defense of the metropole, the emotional link between the French polity and the empire grew dramatically stronger during the interwar period. In the public mind, in elite debate, and in terms of bureaucratic structures, France and its overseas territories began to merge into a single strategic theater. These shifts in strategic culture had an important effect on how British and French elites reacted to the rapid shifts in the balance of power that occurred during the 1930s.

Although initially shaped by elite manipulation, a nation's collective image of empire, as embodied in attitudes and institutions, can take on a trajectory of its own. Moreover, strategic culture is sensitive not only to spectacular events, but also, under certain circumstances, to less dramatic changes in the external environment. Once elite manipulation or exogenous shocks have increased the salience of certain issue areas among the public and in the decision-making community, attentiveness to these issues can remain high.[108] After elites have sold peripheral empire to the populace, for example, the public may react to increasing external threats or foreign setbacks by turning to imperial ambition as a means of reaffirming national power and demonstrating behavior consistent with prevailing images of the state's well-being and international status. Rising vulnerability can thus affect strategic culture directly as well as via elite manipulation.[109] A polity's image of and attachment to peripheral empire may also intensify gradually as a result of repeated and prolonged contact with territories outside the metropole. As an increasing percentage of the population comes into contact with imperial possessions directly through travel or indirectly

[107] Ithiel De Sola Pool, "Effect of Cross-National Contact on National and International Images," in *International Behavior*, ed. Kelman, pp. 134–137, 157–160, 183; and Boulding, "National Images," p. 123.

[108] De Sola Pool, "Effect of Cross-National Contact," pp. 139–140, 157.

[109] See William Scott, "Psychological and Social Correlates of International Images," in *International Behavior*, ed. Kelman, pp. 87–90.

through literature and word of mouth, empire comes to be lodged more firmly in the public mind.[110] As the number of soldiers serving in overseas territories increases, career paths and organizational incentives within the military become oriented toward peripheral empire.

In sum, elite manipulation of prevailing images of empire, in combination with the independent effect of exogenous events on those images, can lead to profound changes in strategic culture. Specific notions of empire may become embedded in the national self-image in a way and to a degree never intended by elites. Although a shift in the determinants of domestic legitimacy and a redefinition of what constitutes national security initially empower decision makers, elites eventually find themselves unable to adjust to shifts in the international environment, entrapped in a strategic culture of their own making. It is this dynamic that explains why elites, even when the need to undertake strategic adjustment becomes apparent, pursue extremist policies and engage in self-defeating behavior.[111]

Using the case studies to corroborate this argument about the constraining effects of strategic culture involves two tasks. First, I show that strategic culture does in fact change over time in the manner suggested above, that these changes in strategic culture are primarily the result of elite campaigns to gain domestic support for the extremist policies adopted to respond to high vulnerability, and that adjustment failure occurs in the wake of these elite campaigns. I measure strategic culture through several indicators. Public opinion and voting data, the number and size of organizations and lobby groups focusing on imperial questions, the treatment of empire in educational texts and literature, and data on resettlement in and travel to imperial territories all shed light on the degree and nature of popular attitudes toward empire. To measure how strategic culture is manifested in elite thinking

---

[110] William Scott writes that public images of other states or territories are molded through direct contact or when "the social environment may provide norms about an object that serve to mold an image of it in the absence of direct contact." These norms are most often communicated by the media, lectures, the arts, and friends. Ibid., pp. 92–95.

[111] I am arguing that a strategic culture wedded to a specific conception of empire, like perceptions of high metropolitan vulnerability, is a necessary, though not sufficient, condition for adjustment failure. During periods of low metropolitan vulnerability, when elite beliefs do not lead to overly cooperative or overly competitive policies, the nature of mass attitudes toward empire and the organizational interests of the bureaucracy and military are not sufficient to alter the behavior of decision makers. Before World War I, for example, peripheral empire was already embedded in British strategic culture—in terms of both public attitudes and the orientation of elite institutions. Nevertheless, in part by obscuring their actions from public view and taking radical steps to redefine the main missions of the military, elites were able to scale back their peripheral commitments and prepare the British army for continental operations against Germany. It is only when high metropolitan vulnerability and the elite beliefs associated with it are combined with a strategic culture infused with powerful strategic images that adjustment failure comes about.

and institutions, I examine the prevailing strategic conceptions that shape political discourse among decision makers, the content of policy debates and the specific policy options included in these debates, and career paths, organizational structure, and patterns of resource allocation within the foreign policy bureaucracy and the military.

Second, I demonstrate causation by showing that it is strategic culture and not some other variable—say, psychological distortion or private economic interests—that prevents elites from adjusting grand strategy even when they have come to realize that their extremist policies are leading the country toward potential disaster. Whenever possible, I use the opinion and voting data available to elites and the statements of decision makers to evaluate the impact of public attitudes and coalition building on policy choices. For obvious reasons, however, elites are loath to say in public or in private meetings that they are adopting unsound policies in order to advance their political fortunes. I also provide evidence that elites actively try to reverse course and wean the public away from the strategic images that constrain policy. Findings showing that public attitudes are unresponsive to new propaganda campaigns or that the political costs of reversing course are extremely high corroborate my argument. Furthermore, I pay as much attention to what is *not* on the political agenda as to what is explicitly discussed by top elites. Strategic culture can have a crucial effect on outcomes by removing certain options from the policy arena, by shaping and institutionalizing the central images that define how elites conceive of national security. If the constraining effect of electoral politics does not appear to be powerful, but elites nevertheless fail to adopt or even to consider the policies that they should given available information, there is good reason to believe that strategic images may be overriding strategic logic. Cabinet-level debates offer good material for assessing the extent to which image-based conceptions of security deeply rooted within the top leadership, the bureaucracy, and the military services clash with incoming strategic information and the associated inference-based suppositions about how best to address external threats. I strengthen the case for the importance of strategic culture by demonstrating the inadequacy of competing explanations of the nature of the agenda and of the failure of elites to adapt policy to incoming information.

CONCLUSIONS

The vulnerability resulting from rapid shifts in the international distribution of power creates the need for strategic adjustment but also sets in motion a sequence of changes in elite beliefs and in strategic culture which prevents that adjustment from taking place. At time 1, perceptions of high metropolitan vulnerability under conditions of uncertainty about if, when, and where threats will come due produce strategic beliefs that induce elites to adopt overly cooperative and overly competitive policies. These beliefs constitute a reasoned and reasonable response to conditions of strategic deficiency. An extraordinary international environment produces extraordinary policies. At time 2, in order to garner domestic support for these extreme policies, extract from the populace the resources necessary to pursue external ambition, and preserve political legitimacy, elites propagate throughout the polity specific images of empire. During this phase, elite beliefs and strategic culture run on parallel tracks and reinforce each other. At time 3, as uncertainty about the strategic implications of international change diminishes, elites realize—albeit with some time lag—that their strategic beliefs and external policies are inconsistent with incoming information. They gradually recognize that their decisions have come to jeopardize primary security interests and that the state is falling prey to strategic exposure, self-encirclement, or overextension. The need to adjust grand strategy becomes apparent. Nevertheless, the shifts in strategic culture that took place during time 2, ironically brought about by elite lobbying and, potentially, by exogenous shocks, prevent adjustment from occurring. Strategic culture affects outcomes by creating domestic political pressures that prevent decision makers from pursuing their preferred policies or by embedding and institutionalizing within the elite community powerful strategic images that override strategic logic. Top decision makers, the bureaucracy, and the military become so oriented toward the attainment of specific goals that important policy options, for cognitive, emotional, and organizational reasons, are effectively removed from consideration. Adjustment failure is the result not of assessment failure, psychological dysfunction, or the self-seeking behavior of capitalists or military officers, but of the sequential, accumulated impact of vulnerability on elite beliefs and strategic culture.

I now turn to the historical cases to test both my own argument about the causes of self-defeating behavior and the alternative explanations set forth in the first half of this chapter. The method of structured, focused comparison entails systematically applying a set of questions to the case studies. These questions, which fall into three categories, are as follows.

Strategic assessments: To what extent were elites aware of changes in the international distribution of military and economic resources? What did available intelligence information indicate about relative military balances? Given this information, did elites perceive low or high metropolitan vulnerability; that is, were they operating under conditions of strategic sufficiency or strategic deficiency?

Dealing with the adversary: What set of beliefs informed grand strategy and decisions about the allocation of resources? Did elites choose to interact with potential adversaries through compellence, deterrence, or accommodation? How did decision makers conceive of strategic priorities and what were the standards used to set these priorities? When elite beliefs changed, did policy change accordingly? Were the central assumptions that informed grand strategy consistent with logical inference, or were they shaped by image-based strategic conceptions?

Domestic considerations: What private economic interests were at stake in empire and to what extent did concerned nongovernmental agents have access to those responsible for determining geographic priorities and setting grand strategy? Was the debate about empire and grand strategy politicized and did elites propagate among the public strategic images and notions of what constitutes national security? If so, did they succeed in molding public opinion and gaining domestic support for their policies? How did the bureaucracy and military define their central roles and missions? To what extent did the self-serving behavior of the military services shape prevailing strategic conceptions and affect grand strategy?

Each case study also addresses my key causal claims about how systemic, cognitive, and domestic variables interact in producing self-defeating behavior. Did shifts in the level of perceived metropolitan vulnerability produce changes in elite beliefs about how to deal with adversaries and about how to set strategic priorities? If so, did these shifts in beliefs lead to extremist policies? Did elite efforts to gain support for their policies lead to shifts in strategic culture that eventually came to entrap decision makers? If so, did strategic culture constrain adjustment by preventing elites from pursuing their preferred policies (because political survival clashed with strategic pragmatism), or by altering and institutionalizing strategic conceptions within the elite community itself (because strategic images overrode strategic logic)? The answers to these questions reveal why great powers, with such striking regularity, fall prey to strategic exposure, self-encirclement, and overextension.

[3]

Britain

The rapid expansion of German military power that occurred after 1897 confronted British elites with a profound dilemma. Since the Congress of Vienna in 1815, three main objectives had informed British grand strategy: maintaining mastery of the seas, protecting peripheral empire, and avoiding entanglement in continental affairs. As the twentieth century began, the prospect of German expansion in Europe and a German High Seas Fleet that could challenge the Royal Navy in home waters called into question the feasibility of a British strategy of "splendid isolation." From 1904 onward, British elites successfully reoriented grand strategy. Ententes were formed with France and Russia to balance against German power, accords were struck with imperial competitors and British battleships and ground troops were withdrawn from the peripheral empire to the European theater, and preparations were made for the commitment of troops to continental operations. Given the previous orientation of British strategy, this instance of strategic adjustment was indeed impressive.

During the 1930s, British elites confronted a similar, though more acute, strategic predicament. Not only did Britain face simultaneous threats in Europe and the Far East, but the German danger was far greater than it had been before World War I both because of German predominance on the ground and because the advent of air power exposed the British Isles to direct attack. Unlike between 1904 and 1914, however, elites failed to adjust strategy to deal adequately with the precipitous rise of German military power. British elites fortified Singapore and built battleships in response to growing Japanese aggressiveness in the Far East while neglecting almost completely preparations for preventing Germany from overrunning continental Europe. Although Adolf Hitler's aggressive intent became increasingly clear from 1936 onward, it was not until the spring of 1939 that British elites began to ready the army to participate in a land war on the Continent. Britain fell prey to both strategic exposure and overextension. Why, between 1932 and 1939, were British decision makers unable to adjust successfully to a changing constellation of power that threatened the empire at its heart when they were able to do so between 1904 and 1914?

1904–1914: STRATEGIC RETRENCHMENT AND THE DEFENSE OF THE METROPOLE

Strategic Assessments

The Boer War forced elites to undertake a fundamental reassessment of the costs and benefits of empire. The war's human and financial toll raised troublesome questions both about the value of an empire consisting of far-flung appendages and about Britain's ability to maintain that empire. Military expenditures ran far beyond original estimates that the conflict would cost approximately £10 million. In reality, the bill for transporting troops to South Africa and suppressing the Boer uprising came to £211,156,000 and added some 25 percent to the national debt.[1] So too was there concern that the war in South Africa drained far too many soldiers from the United Kingdom. In March 1900, when the home army reached its most depleted state, there were some 371,000 armed men in the United Kingdom, only 17,000 of whom were trained and equipped to a relatively high standard. The rest "would have been a mere mob of armed, but imperfectly trained, men lacking all military cohesion, or power of movement."[2] As late as 1902, British planners remarked that in the event of a war with France or Russia, the absence in South Africa of such a large proportion of our trained soldiers and reservists would render our position at home one of grave anxiety."[3]

These concerns about the adequacy of Britain's forces stimulated a rash of planning papers focusing on the military requirements of the empire. One such document, entitled "Military Needs of the Empire in a War with France and Russia," sought to assess the forces needed to defend each of Britain's possessions and arrived at total requirements by summing regional and functional missions.[4] The general con-

[1] Public Record Office (PRO), CAB 38/16/6, 20 April 1910, "Paper on the Finance of War," by Edgar Crammond, read before the Institute of Bankers, pp. 1–2. Unless otherwise stated, the documents cited in this chapter are contained in the PRO collection. The PRO uses the following abbreviations to classify documents: CAB = Cabinet; ADM = Admiralty; WO = War Office; CO = Colonial Office.
[2] CAB 38/5/9, 28 Feb. 1903, "Liability of United Kingdom to French Invasion during the South African War," pp. 1, 4.
[3] CAB 38/1/9, 10 Jan. 1902, "F. M. Roberts' Response to 'The Military Resources of France and Probable Method of Their Employment in a War between England and France,'" p. 1.
[4] CAB 38/1/6, 10 Aug. 1901. The requirements for defended ports, for example, were calculated by classifying each port in one of the following categories: principal naval

[106]

clusion of the study was that "while the force for home defence seems in excess of our requirements, that for expeditionary action and for the reinforcement of our Indian and colonial garrisons is seriously deficient."[5] During the next few years, force planners focused primarily on dealing with the Russian threat to India and Afghanistan.[6] These studies concurred with the assessment that British troops were insufficient to defend India and to protect other imperial possessions. Lord Esher summed up concern about the growing gap between resources and commitments by asking, "Is it not . . . true that, in spite of the expansion of the Empire . . . the Imperial distribution of our military forces is much upon the same plan as it was at the close of the Napoleonic wars?"[7] The key point is that when Britain began to confront the strategic implications of a naval race and escalating antagonism with Germany, elites were fully aware that the military resources of the empire were already under considerable strain.[8]

It is important to assess the extent to which top military officials and decision makers had confidence in and relied on the estimated

---

base, naval base, secondary naval base, coaling station, port of refuge, defended commercial port. The total of 703,675 troops was broken down as follows: U.K., 350,000; ports/colonies, 71,000; Egypt, 8,010; India, 102,159; India reinforcements, 72,518; offensive expeditions, 115,000; deduct native troops in garrison, 15,048.

[5] Ibid., p. 4.

[6] The papers produced were of high quality and sophistication, even when judged by current standards. See, for example, CAB 38/10/84, 20 Nov. 1905, "Suggestions as to the Basis for the Calculation of the Required Transport of an Army Operating in Afghanistan." This paper calculates the number of troops the Russians could maintain in Afghanistan by determining the carrying capacity of the camels that would provide logistical support. Calculations include the twenty-five pounds of hay and the six pounds of grain that each camel would consume per day. This approach (with trucks substituting for camels) is essentially the same one that Joshua Epstein adopts in calculating the logistical constraints that the Soviets would have faced had they invaded Iran. *Strategy and Force Planning* (Washington, D.C.: Brookings Institution, 1987), pp. 112–116.

[7] CAB 38/11/9, 28 Feb. 1906, "Military Requirements of the Empire," p. 2.

[8] For further discussion of elite awareness of deficiencies in ground forces and naval assets, see Aaron Friedberg, *The Weary Titan: Britain and the Experience of Relative Decline, 1895–1905* (Princeton: Princeton University Press, 1988), chaps. 4 and 5. My treatment of the British case differs from Friedberg's in two critical respects. First, I argue that British elites were well aware of the broad changes taking place in Britain's international position, especially in the realm of security affairs. Friedberg agrees that decision makers did recognize the erosion of the country's position in military terms but believes that ambiguity about the economic dimensions of national power prevented them from more fully appreciating the implications of relative decline. Second, I argue that British elites, between 1904 and 1914, in fact adjusted with remarkable success to the rise of German power and the consequent threat that Germany posed to British security. They fundamentally altered their grand strategy to cope with a changing strategic landscape. Friedberg reaches very different conclusions. He argues that elite efforts to adjust to international change "fell far short of lasting success" (p. 293). It should be noted that Friedberg examines an earlier period (1895–1905) and, in contrast to my own exclusive concern with security affairs, focuses on economic as well as strategic adjustment.

requirements produced by the planning staff. There was indeed widespread acknowledgment of the limitations inherent in war games and other mathematical approaches to determining requirements. As one study of the strategic situation in India concluded, "Although the War Game furnishes an interesting study of the problem dealt with, it cannot be regarded as being based on conditions bearing a close resemblance to those which we are justified in supposing would obtain in actual war."[9] As a result of these uncertainties, elites recognized that the force levels derived from war games were only approximate and by no means ensured military sufficiency. Nevertheless, this more rigorous approach to strategic assessment was deemed to be better than any other, and its conclusions were generally accepted despite the acknowledged ambiguities and unknowns. A study of rail logistics in Afghanistan written in 1906 captured this attitude:

> It is not for a moment maintained that the estimates arrived at in this paper are exact. They are, however, distinctly favorable to the Russians, and they do not take account of the whole of the difficulties involved. Absolute figures could not be laid down. . . . The most that can be claimed . . . is that they indicate the way in which the question can be scientifically approached, and that they supply a needed corrective to wild conjectures. . . . Guesswork is futile in dealing with problems of this nature, and clear thinking, based upon proved experience and accepting only reasonable probabilities, is necessary to provide trustworthy guidance for the shaping of national policy.[10]

How did the rapid increase in Germany's naval power and the shifting alignments among Europe's major powers affect calculations of Britain's force requirements? Were British elites aware of the dramatic shifts in the military balance that were taking place? Given the fact that the planning community was, at the turn of the century, already concerned about a gap between resources and commitments, did the German buildup and the accompanying rearmament programs of Germany's partners in the Triple Alliance—Austria-Hungary and Italy—create conditions of high metropolitan vulnerability? According to intelligence estimates, did Britain, France, and Russia—the Triple Entente—have the wherewithal to prevail against the Triple Alliance?

Intelligence assessments of the military balance during the years before the outbreak of war provided a fairly favorable picture of the

[9] CAB 38/5/43, 5 May 1904, "Defence of India: Observations on the Records of a War Game Played at Simla, 1903," p. 10.

[10] CAB 38/11/22, 20 May 1906, "Number of Troops that Can Be Maintained by a Single Line of Railway," pp. 5–6.

security of the British Isles. Assessments of the naval balance in the North Sea showed that the Royal Navy would be able to keep pace with the expansion of the German High Seas Fleet. The Admiralty posited that a safe margin entailed a 60 percent superiority over the German fleet.[11] As Chart 1, prepared in 1912, shows, Britain's building program enabled the Royal Navy to maintain this margin—and in most periods to surpass it—through at least 1920.

The confidence of British elites in their ability to maintain sea supremacy in home waters led to several important strategic assumptions. The Admiralty believed that it would be able both to trap the German fleet in the North Sea and to sink it should it venture out of port. The Royal Navy would therefore be able to blockade Germany's commercial ports, stifling its war-making capability. Confidence in sustaining sea control also led elites to believe that Germany would be unable to mount a successful invasion of the British Isles. If Britain maintained a home army sufficient to defend against an invasion of seventy thousand, Germany would attempt to cross the Channel only if it had assembled an invading force of at least that size. A convoy large enough to transport the invading force would never be able to avoid the Royal Navy and would be sunk before it reached the British coast.[12] British elites were thus quite confident of the Royal Navy's ability to maintain sea supremacy and, consequently, to protect the British Isles against invasion.

The naval situation outside home waters also appeared favorable. Alliance with Japan and entente with Russia assuaged Britain's concern about its possessions in the Far East and South Asia. India, the focal point of the army for decades, fell from the top of the planning agenda after Russia and Britain signed a military convention on 31 August 1907.[13] The situation in the Mediterranean, despite the growing hostility and naval strength of Italy and Austria-Hungary, also appeared to be manageable through naval arrangements made with France. In return for Britain's assumption of responsibility for the Atlantic and North Sea, France devoted virtually all its naval strength to the Mediterranean. Chart 2, prepared by the British Admiralty in 1912, shows that this arrangement gave the French a projected superiority over a combination of Italy and Austria-Hungary through at least 1915.

Elite perceptions of the military balance on land are more problematic, largely because detailed assessments of requirements on the Con-

---

[11] ADM 116/3493, 4 July 1912, 117th Meeting of the Committee of Imperial Defence (C.I.D.).

[12] See, for example, CAB 3/2/42, 20 July 1907, "Invasion."

[13] John Gooch, *The Plans of War: The General Staff and British Military Strategy, c. 1900–1916* (New York: John Wiley and Sons, 1974), p. 231.

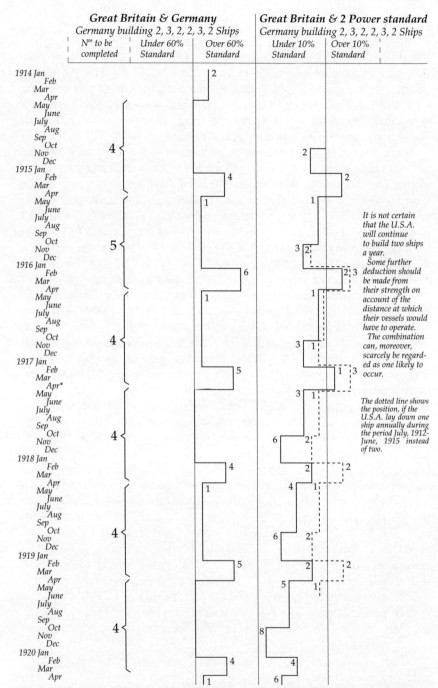

These diagrams are prepared on the assumption that in future programmes, British ships are completed in January of each year, German ships in April, and United States ships in October. Germany and United States are taken as the two next strongest Powers, but it cannot be stated positively that this will be the case as the Building Programmes for Powers other than Germany are not known.

"New Zealand" and "Australia" have been included in the British totals.

*Two "Lord Nelsons" fall out at this date.

Chart 1. Comparative naval strength, Great Britain and Germany. Reproduced by permission of the Controller of Her Britannic Majesty's Stationery Office, doc. ADM 116/3099, p. 75.

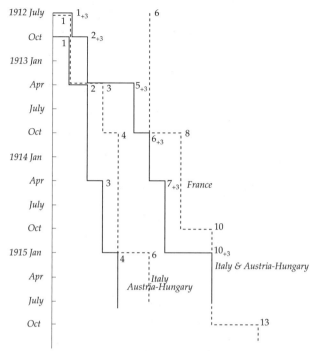

The Naval Attaché has reported that the present intention in
Italy is to lay down two more ships in October next.

The three Austrian "Radetzkys" have never been counted as "Dreadnoughts" nor are they included
in the main figures of the above diagram, but they are ships of approximately equal value to the
"Lord Nelson" class and little inferior to the French "Dantons" which are included.

Chart 2. Comparative naval strength, France, Italy, and Austria-Hungary. Reproduced
by permission of the Controller of Her Britannic Majesty's Stationery Office, doc. ADM
116/3009, p. 75.

tinent simply were not undertaken until the war had already begun.
The size of the British Expeditionary Force (B.E.F.) that Britain planned
to send to the Continent to help France block a German advance clearly
was not determined by mission requirements. The B.E.F. consisted of
six divisions—essentially, the number of troops that were not already
allocated to peripheral missions.[14] But the B.E.F. was not viewed as a

[14] Samuel Williamson, *The Politics of Grand Strategy: Britain and France Prepare for War,
1904–1914* (Cambridge: Harvard University Press, 1939), pp. 93–103. Williamson notes
that during 1906, the year in which the B.E.F. was created, no thorough review of the
requirements of continental war was carried out. He asserts that the size of the B.E.F.
was "a political expedient which bore little correspondence to actual British needs or
obligations" (p. 100).

token "throwaway" force; strategic assessments indicated that even a small British contribution to the Continent could be decisive. British assessments of the overall ground balance showed a steadily improving situation, largely as a result of the increasing military strength of Russia. A Russian offensive was crucial to diverting enough German forces to the eastern front to allow Britain and France to prevail in the west. British planners viewed Russia as "capable only of defense until 1910, regaining the potential for offensive warfare sometime between 1910 and 1912, and by 1913 becoming fully war-ready."[15] In 1913, British planners assumed that the Triple Entente would soon catch and then surpass the Triple Alliance in terms of overall ground forces.[16] Sir Henry Wilson, director of military operations, portrayed the military balance in 1913 as a rough equilibrium.[17] Given this assessment, Britain's six divisions could play an important role in ensuring success on the western front.

Despite these relatively favorable assessments of the balance, British elites did hedge their bets. The small size of the B.E.F. served to limit Britain's continental liability just in case the Triple Alliance prevailed in the ground war. Even if the Germans proved invincible, Britain would lose only the B.E.F.; the navy and the Territorial Army would be intact to defend the homeland. As Sir Edward Grey put it in August 1914, "If we are engaged in war [on the Continent], we shall suffer but little more than we shall suffer even if we stand aside."[18] Although such statements were in part intended to win broad political support for a continental commitment, they did point to a fundamental inconsistency in British thinking. Elites had decided to send the B.E.F. to France because they deemed that German domination of Europe would be inimical to British interests. But they also derived a sense of security from the fact that the small size of the B.E.F. limited Britain's potential losses in a land campaign. On the one hand, elites abided by the

---

[15] William Wohlforth, "The Perception of Power: Russia in the Pre-1914 Balance," *World Politics*, 39 (April 1987), 357.

[16] Ibid., pp. 357–358. By 1914, the Triple Entente in fact enjoyed considerable superiority in force levels. When fully mobilized, France, Britain, Belgium, Russia, and Serbia could field 199 divisions, while Germany and Austria could field 136. See Jack Snyder, *The Ideology of the Offensive: Military Decision Making and the Disaster of 1914* (Ithaca: Cornell University Press, 1984), p. 107. Some analysts also believed that the Germans would stay below the Meuse when attacking France. If so, the roadway would constrict the number of advancing divisions to 51. Given roughly 40 French divisions, the addition of 6 British divisions would be almost sufficient to establish parity. See Williamson, *Politics of Grand Strategy*, p. 169.

[17] Wilson acknowledged that the Triple Alliance enjoyed a numerical advantage in terms of deployable divisions but maintained that many of these were second-class units that would not be involved in the initial German advance. See Williamson, *Politics of Grand Strategy*, pp. 309–310.

[18] Grey quoted in Paul Kennedy, *The Rise and Fall of British Naval Mastery* (London: Macmillan, 1983), p. 236.

prophecies of Halford Mackinder and recognized that a German mono-lith on the Continent would eventually develop sufficient capability to bring harm to the United Kingdom itself. On the other hand, politicians and military planners alike seemed content to revert to Alfred Mahan's teachings about the importance of command of the sea to conclude that Britain could remain invulnerable to developments on the Continent.[19] Either the defense of France and the low countries did matter and Britain should have been prepared to send, if necessary, a much larger force to the Continent, or the defense of France was not of vital strategic importance, in which case even a smaller B.E.F. would have sufficed to strengthen deterrence and assuage French anxieties. Not until the war began were elites forced to choose between these contradictory positions. During the prewar years, however, a limited continental commitment reinforced confidence within the elite community that Britain would fare well should a European conflict break out.

Assessments of material sufficiency in the military realm were bolstered by confidence in the strength of Britain's economic position. In hindsight, it is clear that by the early 1900s Britain's industrial dominance was rapidly waning. Germany had surpassed Britain in a key measure of industrial output: steel production. In fact, Germany's steel production in 1910 was greater than that of Britain, France, and Russia combined.[20] The problem was that data of this sort were simply not available to elites. The planning community relied primarily on trade statistics to assess the health of the British economy.[21] These indicators offered an ambiguous measure of British economic strength and, just before the war, provided cause for optimism. Between 1911 and 1913, Britain's overall current account balance was the largest ever: an average of £206 million per year.[22] Furthermore, elites had little information about overall production and growth rates in other countries and thus could not accurately assess Britain's relative economic performance.[23]

It is also the case that the planning community was understandably unaware of the extent to which the outcome of a European war would depend on economic durability. Elites recognized that the foundation

---

[19] As discussed below, this contradiction was in part a by-product of rivalry between the army and navy as well as of domestic political constraints on the scope of Britain's continental commitment. See Zara Steiner, *Britain and the Origins of the First World War* (New York: St. Martin's Press, 1977), pp. 209–210.

[20] The figures, measured in millions of tons, are 13.6 and 13.4, respectively. Paul Kennedy, "The First World War and the International Power System," *International Security*, 9 (Summer 1984), 13.

[21] Friedberg, *Weary Titan*, pp. 44–45.

[22] Robert Gilpin, *U.S. Power and the Multinational Corporation* (New York: Basic Books, 1975), p. 95.

[23] Friedberg, *Weary Titan*, p. 44.

of Britain's miltitary power was grounded in industrial and financial strength. Lord Overstone in 1859 made this clear: "We have ample means of self-defence, in accumulated wealth, and productive energies sufficient to support all necessary expenditure; in mechanical skill and applicances, and in abundance of mineral products, which, properly applied, must render us predominant in all the scientific machinery of modern warfare." Moreover, decision makers were aware that war with Germany would require economic mobilization and that "the integrity of the Empire mainly depends upon . . . the readiness of its people to undertake the personal and pecuniary obligations incidental to such provision."[24] But belief that the coming war would be a short one focused the attention of planners on existing military assets, not on the ability of the economy to sustain the production of war goods over a number of years. As a result, economic planning for war proceeded under the assumption of, in the words of David French, "business as usual."[25] Elites erroneously assumed that, with only minor changes in the structure and management of the economy, Britain's industrial base would be able to sustain the war effort.

Two other factors contributed to elite insensitivity to the suitability of Britain's industrial infrastructure for involvement in a major war. First, liberal economic principles so pervaded the elite community that direct government intervention in the domestic economy was virtually unthinkable. Second, there was no central bureaucratic authority responsible for managing the economic aspects of strategic planning.[26] This is not altogether surprising, however, since British decision makers before 1914 had never before experienced or even contemplated a war of the scope and magnitude into which they were about to enter. Nevertheless, institutional structures biased the planning community against paying more attention to the economic aspects of war preparation.

Equipping and supplying British troops during the war indeed proved to be a daunting task for British industry. Provisions for even the prewar size of the B.E.F. fell short of requirements. There were insufficient munitions and not even enough munitions producers to make up the shortfall.[27] Because the government placed few peacetime orders with private firms, many munitions factories had been converted to produce consumer items. During the prewar years, however,

---

[24] CAB 38/1/6, "Military Needs," p. 10; CAB 38/16/20, 3 Nov. 1910, "Home Defence," p. 2.

[25] David French, *British Economic and Strategic Planning, 1905–1915* (London: Allen and Unwin, 1982), esp. chap. 4.

[26] These two points are made by French (ibid., pp. 2–3).

[27] Ibid., chap. 3.

these problems went unforeseen. Favorable, but misleading, assessments of Britain's economic strength reinforced perceptions of strategic sufficiency, leading elites to believe that Britain and its allies would prevail in a European conflict and that the British Isles would continue to enjoy relative invulnerability.

Dealing with the Adversary

Despite the relatively small size of the force that Britain planned to send to the Continent, British elites did adjust with remarkable alacrity to the shifts in the international balance of power that occurred between 1904 and 1914. Decision makers successfully managed a reorientation of grand strategy and force dispositions to cope with the rising German threat: they pursued a policy of power balancing in the core and one of retrenchment in the periphery. This reorientation was accomplished through an impressive naval construction program, the withdrawal of naval forces from the periphery, a change in the central role and strategy of the army, and a series of diplomatic initiatives that removed enemies in the imperial periphery and won allies in the core. Elites recognized that interests in the imperial periphery might suffer, but a clear sense of strategic priorities focused attention on the situation at home. As I argue below, elite perceptions of low metropolitan vulnerability and conditions of strategic sufficiency gave rise to the beliefs that led to this clear ordering of strategic priorities and the adoption of a strategy of deterrence in the core and a strategy of accommodation in the periphery.

Britain steamed into the twentieth century under the protection of the Two-Power Standard, which maintained that the Royal Navy was to be equal or superior in strength to a combination of the next two most powerful fleets. The disposition of the British fleet depended on where the potential enemy chose to locate its fleet and how the Royal Navy would best be able to establish sea supremacy in any given theater. As Lord Selborne, first lord of the Admiralty, described this strategy in 1902, "At whatever spot, in whatever sea, these [enemy] ships are found and destroyed, there the whole Empire will be simultaneously defended."[28] As a result of this concern with maintaining sea control and protecting the imperial lines of communication, Britain's battleships were scattered throughout the empire's waters. After the Boer War, the distribution of Britain's battleships was as follows: eight

---

[28] CAB 38/15/8, 30 April 1909, "Precis of Important Events Connected with the Question of Colonial Naval Contributions," p. 5.

ships each in the Home and Channel fleets, twelve ships on station in the Mediterranean, and five dispatched to China.[29]

In 1904–1905, Sir John Fisher, first sea lord, orchestrated the first of several redistributions of the Royal Navy. The most important changes involved the withdrawal to home waters of all five battleships from the Far East and four from the Mediterranean. This shift was motivated primarily by the growth of German naval power and Fisher's recognition of the need to concentrate more of the fleet in home waters.[30] Not only were more battleships stationed in or near the North Sea, but Fisher reorganized personnel to provide crew for some two hundred ships that were in the home reserve fleet.[31] In view of the time that it would take to train new crew for these ships, Fisher chose instead to ready the reserve fleet by bringing home many personnel that had been on foreign stations. This led to a virtual withdrawal from the Western Hemisphere, including the abandonment of bases at Halifax, Esquimalt, and St. Lucia, and the scaling down of the cruiser fleets at Jamaica and in the Far East.

The next significant redistribution occurred in 1906–1907, when Fisher augmented the fleet concentrated in home waters by withdrawing two more battleships from the Mediterranean. Furthermore, war plans drawn up after 1907 posited the recall of the entire battleship fleet from the Mediterranean should war break out with Germany.[32] The Admiralty also stiffened the standards used to set force levels in home waters. No longer was a fully commissioned fleet equal or superior to the German High Seas Fleet sufficient. In addition, there had to be "a second Fleet in partial reserve which is so stationed as to be able to concentrate without being molested before the principal fleet can support it."[33] Fleet redistribution and an ambitious naval construction program were to meet these standards and allow Britain to keep pace with the growing German High Seas Fleet. The construction program not only increased the size of the fleet, but also led to the development of the dreadnought, a new battleship with superior firepower. By 1908, naval war plans for a conflict with Germany had been drafted and Britain's battlefleet was concentrated primarily in home waters.[34]

The objectives of this concentration of naval power in the North Sea

---

[29] Kennedy, *Naval Mastery*, pp. 217.

[30] Some of the changes implemented by Fisher were not directly related to the German threat but were the product of general efforts to improve the quality of the navy. The Admiralty began to express concern about the German naval program in 1901–1902. See Steiner, *Origins of the First World War*, p. 31.

[31] ADM 116/942, Feb. 1907, "Reasons for Constituting the Home Fleet."

[32] Kennedy, *Naval Mastery*, p. 223.

[33] ADM 116/1043B, 1908, p. 24.

[34] Williamson, *Politics of Grand Strategy*, pp. 107–108.

were twofold. First, the Royal Navy would set up a blockade of Germany's ports. Without access to sea transport, the Admiralty contended, the demands of war would quickly ravage the German economy. Second, should the German fleet venture from port, the Royal Navy would have sufficient superiority to rout it. To rely on sea power was to turn to Britain's strength. It was therefore on the sea that Britain would make its principal contribution to a European conflict. Elites recognized that they could accomplish this concentration of naval power in the North Sea only by jeopardizing the country's interests in the periphery. Despite the persistent complaints of the Foreign Office that Fisher's redistribution exposed the periphery and placed the integrity of the empire at risk, the Admiralty insisted that the top priority was naval supremacy in home waters and that the Mediterranean and Far East would, if necessary, be abandoned.[35] In the euphemistic language of a Colonial Defence Committee memorandum, "The rise of German naval power—demanding an increased concentration of our fleets in European waters—has increased the difficulty of making the requisite naval force available to maintain British naval superiority in these [other] waters. . . . Naval action in remote waters might . . . have to be postponed until by the clearing of the situation in home waters adequate naval force could be brought to bear."[36]

The final redistribution of the Royal Navy, completing its concentration in home waters, occurred in 1912, the year after Winston Churchill became first lord. While Churchill was personally committed to focusing virtually all Britain's resources on the German threat, his cause was furthered by Germany's supplementary Naval Law of 1912.[37] Before 1912, Germany had planned to build seventeen battleships, four battle cruisers, and twelve small cruisers. Under the new naval law, the building program called for twenty-five battleships, eight battle cruisers, and eighteen small cruisers, with far less demobilization during winter than in the original program.[38] To respond to this situation, Churchill recommended that the fleet based at Gibraltar be moved to home waters and that the Malta fleet be moved to Gibraltar, changes leading to the effective abandonment of the Mediterranean. Though Churchill, under pressure from his opponents, agreed in principle to leave a battle fleet at Malta equal to a one-power standard, the Mediterranean

---

[35] For the position of the Foreign Office, see, for example, CO 537/348, Feb. 1907, "Foreign Office to Admiralty," No. 4876.

[36] CAB 8/5/405M, undated memo on 1906–1907 redistribution, "Colonial Defence," pp. 3–4.

[37] Kennedy, *Naval Mastery*, p. 223.

[38] CAB 38/21/25, 2 July 1912, "The Strategical Situation in the Mediterranean."

was effectively void of British battleships from 1912 onward.[39] Churchill was not one to mince his words: the Malta squadron "certainly will not operate in the Mediterranean till a decisive and victorious general action has been fought in the North Sea: then, and not till then, can it go to the Mediterranean."[40] This decision effectively meant that the entire battleship fleet of the Royal Navy had been recalled from the imperial periphery and stationed in home waters. Were war to break out, there was no equivocation about the sole strategic mission of this massive fleet: the blockade of Germany and the destruction of the German High Seas Fleet. In comparison with the scattered distribution of the Royal Navy at the turn of the century, the concentration of the battlefleet in home waters by 1912 was indeed striking. As Paul Kennedy put it, "There is no denying that the pace of this withdrawal into the North Sea was remarkably swift."[41]

The story of the British army is not dissimilar. From 1906 onward, the preoccupation of the army with peripheral missions gradually gave way to a focus on the European continent. There was no explicit withdrawal from the imperial periphery as there was with the navy; colonial garrisons were left intact, although reduced to a minimum. An overview of military planning does, however, indicate a clear shift in the primary mission of the army and confirms the argument that British strategy underwent a fundamental reorientation during the decade before World War I.

The army's comprehensive review of the military needs of the empire in 1901 made clear the importance of defending Britain itself: "If the heart of the Empire fall into the enemy's grasp, its existence must cease, and our first care must, therefore, be for the heart. Home defence, therefore is the primary problem to be solved."[42] Invasion of the United Kingdom, however, was deemed to be very unlikely. Any invasion force large enough to pose a serious threat would be unable to avoid the British navy and would be sunk before reaching British shores. Furthermore, Germany was primarily a land power and could not challenge British naval supremacy. An Anglo-German conflict was therefore likely to result in a stalemate: "A war between Germany and Great Britain would in some ways resemble a struggle between an elephant and a whale, in which each, although supreme in its own element, would find difficulty in bringing its strength to bear on its antago-

---

[39] Kennedy, *Naval Mastery*, p. 226. See also Steiner, *Origins of the First World War*, pp. 99–104.
[40] ADM 116/3099, 22 June 1912, memo by Winston Churchill, pp. 2–3.
[41] Kennedy, *Naval Mastery*, p. 237.
[42] CAB 38/1/6, "Military Needs," p. 9.

nist."[43] As a result of this assessment, there was a firm consensus that "the main purpose for which the army exists is not the defence of these shores but the protection of the outlying portions of the Empire, and notably India."[44]

By 1906, however, this consensus on the role of the army was unraveling. The rapid growth of German military and industrial strength raised anxieties about German intentions and about the implications for British security of a successful invasion of France. In response to these concerns, the army created, under the direction of R. B. Haldane, an expeditionary force of six divisions—approximately 158,000 men. Officers and troops from outlying garrisons were recalled to England to increase the number of trained regulars in the home army.[45] While it remained unclear whether the primary mission of this force was on the Continent or in India, these developments prompted Colonel Callwell, an influential member of the General Staff's Directorate of Military Operations, to query in 1906: "What is to be the military policy of the country? For years past that policy appears to have been that the army was not primarily intended for war on the continent. Has this changed?"[46]

Between 1907 and 1909, the answer to Callwell's question became increasingly clear. The notion of a continental commitment—though it was stoutly resisted by the navy—gradually gained acceptance within the Committee of Imperial Defence (C.I.D.), the main governmental body responsible for formulating defense policy. In 1908, a subcommittee of the C.I.D. confirmed that the main mission of the British army was in Europe, not India. Staff talks between the British and French focused on how many forces Britain would send to the Continent and laid out plans to move these troops by rail from port to forward positions.[47] In July 1909, the C.I.D. collectively supported plans to dispatch to France four of the six divisions of the B.E.F. in the event of German aggression.[48] The rationale for this fundamental shift in policy was best summarized in a War Office memorandum of March 1909:

> In past wars the ubiquity conferred by sea power has ever given to a British military expedition a value out of all proportion to its strength. Sea power remains essential, but the improvement in land communica-

[43] CAB 38/4/9, 28 Feb. 1904, "The Military Resources of Germany," p. 7.
[44] CAB 38/8/14, 24 Feb. 1905, "Our Present Minimum Military Requirements," p. 1.
[45] Virtually all white troops were withdrawn from the West Indies, for example. See CAB 38/10/85, 21 Nov. 1905. Minutes of the C.I.D., 81st meeting.
[46] WO 106/44/E1/7, 12 March 1906, memo by Callwell, p. 1.
[47] Williamson, *Politics of Grand Strategy*, pp. 101, 113.
[48] See CAB 38/15/15, 24 July 1909, "Report of the Sub-Committee of the C.I.D. on the Military Needs of the Empire."

tions and the enormous growth of modern European armies have greatly lessened, if they have not as yet completely destroyed, the advantages which this ubiquity once gave. Robbed of this enhancement of her military power, the United Kingdom can no longer hope to maintain the relative importance of her assistance in a land campaign without a substantial increase in the forces available for immediate action oversea.[49]

The final phase in the evolution of Britain's continental commitment began in 1911. Plans were prepared to send all six divisions of the B.E.F. to the Continent, and, in consultation with the French, efforts were begun to lay out detailed mobilization and concentration schemes.[50] The General Staff made arrangements to reinforce the B.E.F. by recalling troops from the imperial periphery to fight on the Continent. A memorandum drafted in August recommended that two divisions of native troops be withdrawn from India, that units of the 7th Division be recalled from Malta, Egypt, and South Africa, and that "other formations . . . from the dominions should be brought to the theatre of operations as rapidly as possible."[51] These plans were not the product of either wishful thinking or mere rhetoric. On 23 August 1911, the C.I.D. effectively approved the army's plans for responding to German aggression against France. In the words of Maurice Hankey, secretary to the C.I.D., "From that time onwards there was never any doubt what would be the Grand Strategy in the event of our being drawn into a continental war in support of France."[52]

It should be noted that the B.E.F. did not enjoy such widespread support within the cabinet itself. In 1912, cabinet members supporting the dispatch of the B.E.F. to the Continent in the event of a German attack on France included H. H. Asquith, Sir Edward Grey, R. B. Haldane, Lord Crewe, Winston Churchill, and David Lloyd George.[53] The opposition of other cabinet members—some of whom were not fully informed about the extent of the changes in strategy taking place—did play a role in limiting the size of the B.E.F. But such opposition did not prevent the army from preparing for continental operations or from undertaking staff talks with the French. It was not until August 1914, however, that the full cabinet—the only body with the authority

---

[49] WO 106/45/E1/1, 8 March 1909, "Value of an Alliance with the United Kingdom," pp. 3–4.

[50] Williamson, *Politics of Grand Strategy,* pp. 172–176.

[51] CAB 38/19/47, 15 Aug. 1911, "The Military Aspect of the Continental Problem," pp. 2–6.

[52] Hankey cited in Kennedy, *Naval Mastery,* p. 235. For further discussion of the C.I.D. meeting of 23 Aug. 1911, see Steiner, *Origins of the First World War,* pp. 200–202.

[53] David French, *British Strategy and War Aims, 1914–1916* (London: Allen and Unwin, 1986), pp. 2–5.

to do so—formally approved the dispatch of British troops to the Continent.

The strategy and geographic orientation of the British army thus underwent a fundamental change between 1906 and 1914. The army's strategic reorientation was based on two key considerations. First, changes in technology and warfare had increased the strategic importance of land power with respect to sea power. The General Staff concluded that "the result of such a war [between France and Germany] would be that Germany would attain to that dominant position which has already been stated to be inimical to the interests of this country." Second, it had become apparent that "having regard to the fact that the resources of the Empire are not unlimited, it is clearly not possible to maintain permanently, in all parts of it, sufficient forces to render each part secure in war."[54] The army, like the navy, when faced with the difficult question of allocating resources between the core and the periphery, realized correctly that the heart of the empire, not its limbs, was the top priority.

The reorientation of military strategy and the successive redistributions of the Royal Navy went hand in hand with diplomatic developments that led to the formation of a coalition—the Triple Entente—intent on stopping German expansion in the core, and that moderated, and in some cases removed, the most serious threats to British interests in the periphery. Even before British elites began to focus on the German threat, they realized that they did not have sufficient resources to defend all quarters of the empire against all potential enemies. Diplomatic efforts were therefore needed to close the gap between resources and peripheral commitments.[55] Increasing requirements in the core then reinforced the need to turn to diplomatic initiatives both to facilitate peripheral retrenchment and to consolidate an opposing coalition powerful enough to resist German expansion.

The withdrawal from the Western Hemisphere was accompanied by improved relations with the United States.[56] In January 1902, Britain entered into an alliance with Japan, moderating the threats to British interests in the Far East and, later, easing the recall of the fleet from the China station. British elites considered extending this alliance to cover India, hoping to enlist Japanese assistance in coping with the Russian threat.[57] Such steps proved unnecessary, however, as a result of the Anglo-Russian entente of 1907. This entente provided crucial

---

[54] CAB 38/19/47, p. 1; CAB 5/2/62C, 28 April 1911, "Principles of Imperial Defence."
[55] See Steiner, *Origins of the First World War*, pp. 28–30.
[56] Kennedy, *Naval Mastery*, pp. 211–212.
[57] Friedberg, *Weary Titan*, pp. 266–268.

momentum to the General Staff's efforts to focus the planning community on war in Europe, not in South Asia. The emergence of the Entente Cordiale (1904) between France and Britain further moderated threats to British interests in the periphery. More important, it set the stage for staff talks between the British and French militaries, for the formation of the Triple Entente in 1907, and for the negotiations of 1912 leading to the withdrawal of Britain's Mediterranean battlefleet to the North Sea in return for French willingness to assume responsibility for sea control in the Mediterranean.

There is no question that this network of accords facilitated the reorientation of the navy and army toward a European conflict. It would be misleading, however, to view Britain's diplomatic successes as preconditions for a recall of assets to the core rather than as key components of a general policy of power balancing in the core and retrenchment in the periphery. Britain effectively withdrew from the Western Hemisphere because elites realized that they could not keep pace with the growth of the U.S. navy and simultaneously defend interests closer to home. Accommodation of the United States emerged from recognition that Britain *had* to withdraw from the region; withdrawal was not the result of successful accommodation.[58] After a meeting with the first sea lord in 1904, Lord Selborne summarized Fisher's thinking on this issue: "He said that under no conceivable circumstances could we escape an overwhelming and humiliating defeat by the United States and therefore he would leave Canada to her fate and no matter what the cause of quarrel or merits of the case he would not spend one man or one pound in the defence of Canada. And he meant it."[59] Similar thinking informed the decision to engage in a formal alliance with Japan. Britain alone could cope with rival fleets in the Far East only by diverting vessels from home waters. But, as Selborne spelled out, Britain could not afford to reduce the strength of the home fleet: "If the British Navy were defeated in the Mediterranean and the Channel the stress of our position would not be alleviated by any amount of superiority in the Chinese seas. If, on the other hand, it were to prove supreme in the Mediterranean and Channel, even serious disasters in Chinese waters would matter little."[60] British elites initially turned to alliance with Japan because they realized that they could not jeopardize security interests in the core to defend the periphery.

It is also the case that Britain was by no means assured of the durabil-

[58] Ibid., pp. 163–165; and Kennedy, *Naval Mastery*, pp. 211–212.
[59] Selborne cited in Friedberg, *Weary Titan*, p. 198.
[60] Selborne cited in ibid., p. 176. See also Steiner, *Origins of the First World War*, p. 28.

ity of these arrangements and was therefore clearly willing to put its peripheral interests at risk in order to defend the metropole. As mentioned above, elites recognized that withdrawal from North American waters would expose Canada to a potential U.S. attack. But they also realized that Britain could do little in a military sense to block such an attack. Japan and France could take advantage of British retrenchment to further their own imperial designs, especially if the diplomatic climate should change. As First Sea Lord Walter Kerr warned, "Our superiority ought to be self-contained and not made up of foreign and possibly very unreliable sources. . . . While the understanding [with Japan] lasts it would be most useful to us in the East and indirectly in European waters, but it would be a very unsafe policy to rely on it."[61] Similarly, many British military officers and politicians were extremely wary of engaging in staff talks with the French. Furthermore, British and French colonial rivalry persisted even after the Anglo-French entente.[62] These accords were thus the result, and not the cause, of imperial retrenchment. The strategic adjustment that took place was motivated primarily by recognition that like-minded powers had to aggregate their resources to cope with the German threat in the core and that the British army and navy could no longer devote the bulk of their resources to the defense of the imperial periphery.

During the decade before World War I, British elites believed that they had to respond to the rise of German military power by adopting a strategy of deterrence in the core. Deterring Germany and preparing for a full-scale military conflict, should it prove unavoidable, were the key considerations behind the program of strategic adjustment implemented between 1904 and 1914. This program of adjustment consisted of two components. First, British elites increased military assets available in the core by building naval vessels, recalling ships from the periphery, and preparing an expeditionary force to fight on the Continent. Second, they ended decades of splendid isolation and formed an entente with France and Russia to help balance against German power.

Britain's approach to the periphery was dramatically different. Elites believed in the need to adopt a strategy of accommodation to reduce threats to British interests and to effect the withdrawal of military resources from the imperial periphery. These accords did succeed in moderating threats to British territories, but it was clear that decision makers were prepared to sacrifice peripheral interests in order to de-

---

[61] Kerr cited in Friedberg, *Weary Titan*, p. 180. For further examples of elite concern about reliance on alliances, see CAB 11/118/12, 7 April 1909, "Colonial Defence."
[62] Steiner, *Origins of the First World War*, pp. 45–46.

fend the metropole. It is not necessary to rely solely on inference to support this argument; elite thinking on this issue was evident in planning and policy papers, even well before war with Germany grew imminent. In 1905, the Admiralty considered the value of attacking and annexing French territories in East Asia in the event of war with France. The Admiralty concluded that annexation "would mean a large extension of our Asiatic territory. This is a very serious matter. . . . To add to our Asiatic possessions would add to our difficulties for all time, and expose us still further to the form of pressure which we are least able to resist. . . . The 'extinction' of the latter [France] as an Asiatic Power is not therefore an event which is likely to be beneficial to Great Britain in the long run, and a far-seeing policy should not aim at encompassing that end, or increasing our Asiatic liabilities." The War Office was similarly convinced in 1908 that there was little point in attacking German colonies in the event of war. "The conclusion is forced upon us that the capture of the German colonies promises no results commensurate with the cost of the expeditions and would do nothing towards the solution of the deadlock which an Anglo-German war seems likely to reach at an early stage."[63] Even Britain's own African possessions would have to be neglected in the event of a war in Europe. The Colonial Defence Committee made clear its priorities: "The fate of our African possessions in a war with a European power will be determined by the ultimate issue of the war, and will therefore depend upon the result of naval and military operations in the main theatre of war and not upon the issue of minor operations in remote regions."[64]

Underlying the adoption of a deterrent strategy in the core and one of accommodation in the periphery was a clear sense of strategic priorities. Defense of the homeland was the key objective. Economic and military resources had to be marshaled exclusively for this purpose. Concern about the reputational importance of preserving empire ran low. Elites did not see imperial commitments as interdependent; on the contrary, core and periphery were distinct, separable theaters. Churchill himself dealt deftly with those who claimed that a strategic withdrawal from the periphery would lead to a loss of prestige and influence that would ultimately destroy the empire. He simply dismissed the argument that Britain had to deploy naval forces around the globe to give an appearance of strength that did not exist. Given

[63] ADM 116/3111, July 1905, "Military Policy—B," pp. 8–9; WO 106/46/E2/2, 2 July 1908, "Military Policy in a War with Germany," p. 26.
[64] CAB 38/17/24, 29 April 1911, "The Position of the East and West African Protectorates in the Event of War with a European Power," p. 2.

the gravity of the situation in home waters, Britain had to disengage from the imperial periphery. To his detractors who insisted on keeping a squadron at Malta to maintain a deterrent posture, Churchill responded: "Bluff and pretence nowadays is no use; besides which it is un-English, and does more harm than good to our prestige."[65] A clear sense of strategic priorities and the objective of confronting Germany with preponderant military power drove British policy.

Beginning in 1904, Britain gradually withdrew its navy from the imperial periphery and reorganized its army for continental operations not because a series of convenient accords emerged, but because British leaders were aware that they did not have sufficient resources to defend all imperial interests and that clear choices therefore had to be made. Through rearmament and the help of allies, elites calculated that they had sufficient resources to defend the metropole but that few, if any, assets could be spared for peripheral defense. Decision makers acted on the recognition that the periphery was of little import when compared to the core and that British security was ultimately immune to events in the periphery. Britain's diplomatic and military arrangements with France, Japan, and Russia and the consequent absence of imminent threats to the peripheral empire indeed facilitated retrenchment and withdrawal. Yet Britain could afford to pull back from and accept damage to its outlying empire precisely because elites saw that such events would have little or no impact on the security of the British Isles. The reorientation of British naval and military strategy between 1904 and 1914 reflected a remarkable ability to adjust to a rapidly changing distribution of military and industrial power and a clear recognition that the limbs of the empire would be meaningless if the heart were destroyed.

Domestic Considerations

Domestic forces indeed had an effect on the formulation of grand strategy during the decade before the outbreak of war. As the following analysis demonstrates, however, domestic considerations did more to constrain strategic adjustment than to facilitate it. It is also important to recognize that, during the years before World War I, discussion of naval distributions and the organization and operational strategy of the British army was, for the most part, confined to the realm of high policy. These issues were primarily the domain of the cabinet, the C.I.D., and the planning staffs of the Admiralty and War Office. The public was largely uninterested in foreign and defense policy. In the

[65] ADM 116/3099, 22 June 1912, memo by Churchill, p. 3.

words of A. P. Thornton, "Until the outbreak of war . . . the public knew and cared nothing of Army quarrels, and nearly as little about foreign policy."[66] The electorate was content to leave the formulation and execution of foreign policy to the experts in the government.[67]

Private Economic Interests. To the extent that they took a position on questions of military strategy, private economic interests resisted, and did not encourage or abet, the retrenchment described above. The withdrawal from the Western Hemisphere, the recall of battleships from the China station, the effective abandonment of the Mediterranean to the French were all clear indicators of a retreat from the periphery. Those individuals and firms trading with or investing in the periphery—the key "culprits" in all economic theories of imperialism—were, if anything, concerned that the reorientation of strategy would jeopardize their economic interests.[68] Nor was there a powerful armaments industry lobbying for a strategic focus on the German threat.[69] As World War I approached, it was the government that was attempting to induce industry to produce more war materiel, not industry that was pushing the government to take on new commitments or add more missions to the planning agenda.[70] In short, strategic adjustment ran contrary to the interests of those groups that might have had sufficient political leverage to influence policy. Furthermore, there is no evidence to support the assertion that economic interest groups played an influential role in shaping policy.

Domestic Politics. The Boer War did lead to a reevaluation of the costs and benefits of empire, a reevaluation that was not restricted to the elite community. The loss of life and the economic burdens of the war dampened mass enthusiasm for future escapades into the far-flung reaches of the empire. This reaction, however, by no means led to support for abandoning the periphery or even for limited imperial retrenchment. Proimperialists in fact used the uprising in South Africa

[66] A. P. Thornton, *The Imperial Idea and Its Enemies: A Study in British Power* (London: Macmillan, 1959), p. 131.

[67] Harold Nicolson, "British Public Opinion and Foreign Policy," *Public Opinion Quarterly*, 1 (January 1937), 56. The press did succeed to some degree in mobilizing the public and impressing on the electorate the severity of the threat posed by Germany. See A. J. A. Morris, *The Scaremongers: The Advocacy of War and Rearmament, 1896–1914* (London: Routledge and Kegan Paul, 1984).

[68] See P. J. Cain and A. G. Hopkins, "The Political Economy of British Expansion Overseas, 1750–1914," *Economic History Review*, 33 (November 1980), esp. 485–489.

[69] Individual legislators did consistently support the naval program in order to provide employment for their constituents, but there was not a powerful "armaments bloc" within Parliament. See Steiner, *Origins of the First World War*, pp. 57–59.

[70] French, *British Economic and Strategic Planning*, chaps. 8–10.

to make the case that Britain could not afford to withdraw troops from the periphery. The British populace remained strongly supportive of the overseas empire.[71] The Liberals, a party more circumspect about empire than the Conservatives, did win the 1906 election. But their platform was far from anti-imperialist; it called for avoidance of wars in the periphery and a restriction of expansion, not a withdrawal from the empire. The partisan debate over defense issues that might have emerged was suppressed by a compromise of sorts between the two main parties. Thornton asserts that "there was a tacit bargain made between the political parties in the pre-1914 era. The Liberals would maintain the Navy—while the Tories would not press for any form of expansion."[72] Nor were the Radicals in favor of a retrenchment from empire. They were concerned primarily that Britain eschew involvement in the continental balance of power. They joined others in contending that pursuit of a confrontational policy with Germany would entangle Britain in alliances and eventually drag the country into war.[73]

It was precisely because of such opposition to the notion of a continental commitment that planning for the B.E.F. proceeded quietly, outside the purview of many politicians. Those elites responsible for shaping the nature of Britain's commitments in Europe made few efforts to apprise their colleagues or the public of their actions and intentions. Cabinet, parliamentary, and public opposition to a continental commitment in fact constrained top British elites in their handling of the July Crisis in 1914. The foreign minister, Sir Edward Grey, had to moderate his warnings to Germany and equivocate on Britain's intention to send troops to the Continent in order to maintain a united front at home.[74]

In view of the considerable political opposition to both imperial retrenchment and a continental commitment, the successive waves of strategic adjustment that took place between 1904 and 1914 cannot be understood as the result of political gamesmanship or coalitional bargaining. Politicians had little to gain, in a narrow political sense, from the difficult decisions that drove forward the process of strategic

[71] Steiner, *Origins of the First World War*, pp. 15–18. For popular reaction to the Boer War, see pp. 19–20.

[72] Thornton, *Imperial Idea*, p. 129. See also Nicolson, "British Public Opinion," p. 55. Not all Tories stuck to this compromise. Some members of the party in fact lobbied for a larger, conscript army.

[73] See Howard Weinroth, "The British Radicals and the Balance of Power, 1902–1914," *Historical Journal*, 13 (December 1970), 653–682.

[74] See Jack Levy, "Preferences, Constraints, and Choices in July 1914," in *Military Strategy and the Origins of the First World War*, ed. Steven Miller, Sean Lynn-Jones, and Stephen Van Evera (Princeton: Princeton University Press, 1991), pp. 243–244. See also Steiner, *Origins of the First World War*, pp. 127, 215–241.

adjustment. On the contrary, the loss of overseas possessions would no doubt have entailed significant political costs. So too did the decision to prepare the B.E.F. for continental operations involve political risks. But, as I have shown, these were costs and risks that elites were prepared to accept. The domestic setting thus reinforces the view that strategic adjustment was driven primarily by the strategic beliefs of elites and their appreciation of the need to counter the rise of German power. If anything, domestic politics constrained strategic adjustment. It was recognition of a new constellation of international power that impelled elites to overcome these constraints and reorient grand strategy.

Military Services. The military services acted as an initial constraint on the process of strategic adjustment. The organizational interests of both the army and navy were tightly wedded to their historic mission—the defense of empire. This focus on peripheral operations was institutionalized in force levels, force structures, war plans, and career incentives. A reorientation of grand strategy thus entailed altering the central mission of the military establishment.

Interservice rivalry also impaired the adjustment process.[75] Squabbling between the services affected the timing and the coordination of shifts in navy and army strategy. But bureaucratic competition acted principally as a constraint on the adjustment process; it was not a source of policy innovation. The navy actively opposed the army's adoption of a continental commitment and succeeded in delaying the garnering of support for the B.E.F. both in the C.I.D. and in the cabinet. Furthermore, the navy took steps to prevent the recall of troops from the periphery by announcing that it would refuse to reinforce colonial outposts during war and that "garrisons of defended ports abroad should be maintained at war strength in time of peace."[76] The Admiralty also balked at the prospect of transporting the army to the Continent and initially agreed to do so only within the context of a diversionary raid on German territory intended to support naval operations.[77]

Despite these impediments, both services did eventually reorient their strategies and redefine their central missions. Although initially opposed to a continental commitment, the navy was the first service to begin withdrawing its assets from the periphery to concentrate them in home waters. This turnabout was driven principally by the perspi-

[75] For discussion of the roles of the army and navy in shaping strategy, see Steiner, *Origins of the First World War*, pp. 189–214.
[76] See, for example, CAB 38/16/13, 8 July 1910, "Principles of Imperial Defence," p. 9.
[77] CAB 38/19/49, 23 Aug. 1911, 114th Meeting of the C.I.D., pp. 2–4.

[128]

cacity and tenacity of individuals like Fisher and Churchill. The army, also through the persistence of key individuals such as Sir Henry Wilson, was eventually able to overcome the navy's efforts to prevent the C.I.D. from supporting a continental commitment. The legacy of the navy's position was not, however, inconsiderable; the Admiralty was partly responsible for the small size of the B.E.F. The navy's misplaced confidence in the effectiveness of a blockade was one factor limiting the size of the expeditionary force. Moreover, by refusing to plan for the transport of troops across the Channel, the Admiralty contributed to the absence of a more thorough assessment of continental requirements.

These considerations do not minimize the importance of the reorientation undertaken by the army before 1914, especially in light of its long-standing focus on the defense of empire. Furthermore, assessments of a roughly equal force balance on the ground, of the efficacy of a naval blockade, and of the likelihood of a short war provided good reason for elites to believe that even a six-division B.E.F. could play a decisive role in the battle. The army's planning for continental war constitutes a striking instance of strategic adjustment when placed within the context of the historical legacies and organizational interests that it successfully challenged.

Conclusions

During the decade before the outbreak of World War I, British elites reacted to the rise of German power by orchestrating an impressive and striking reorientation of grand strategy. Generally favorable assessments of the military balance led decision makers to be confident of their ability to defend the metropole. Strategic sufficiency enabled elites to balance in a timely fashion against German threats in the core. Strategic adjustment was based on the belief that Britain had to adopt a deterrent stance toward Germany by building up its own forces and by seeking allies on the Continent. At the same time, elites recognized the need to accommodate adversaries in the periphery and to retrench from the outlying empire in order to concentrate the resources at their disposal in the imperial core. Reputational concerns ran low. Because of conditions of strategic sufficiency, elites did not need to rely on demonstrations of resolve to offset material inadequacy. On the contrary, to allocate resources to the periphery for reputational reasons would only divert assets needed in the core. Retrenchment reflected a clear sense of strategic priorities and an appreciation that withdrawal was necessary despite the potential setbacks in the periphery that it might entail. This set of strategic beliefs motivated elites to overcome the domestic forces constraining adjustment.

During the 1930s, Britain was unable to respond to rapid shifts in the strategic landscape with the degree of rationality and purpose that characterized planning before World War I. On the contrary, both the navy and the army remained committed to their peripheral missions well into 1939. Elites believed in the need to deter adversaries in the periphery and to accommodate adversaries in the core. They did not base policy on a clear set of strategic priorities, but focused instead on reputational considerations and blurred the distinction between primary and secondary interests. Rather than pursue a policy of retrenchment in the periphery and one of power balancing in the core, decision makers pursued a policy of indiscriminate defense in the periphery and one of appeasement in the core. They concentrated on protecting the outlying empire while failing to make adequate preparations for metropolitan defense. What caused this marked difference in policy between the two time periods?

The impact of vulnerability on elite beliefs and strategic culture provides the key to solving this puzzle. During the first half of the 1930s, British policy was informed by a set of logical inferences that emerged from conditions of strategic deficiency. Well aware that they did not have sufficient resources to wage war in the core as well as in peripheral theaters, elites sought to address only the most immediate threats to British interests. They tried to dampen the potential sources of conflict on the Continent by integrating Germany into a concert of major powers. When Germany began to rearm, British decision makers pursued a policy of appeasement in order to satisfy German demands or, if that proved to be impossible, to buy time for rearmament. In the meantime, they concentrated on protecting imperial commitments that were threatened by nationalism and by Japanese and Italian aggression. Because they lacked the resources necessary to fulfill these missions, elites relied heavily on demonstrations of resolve and reputational posturing to preserve the integrity of the empire. Defense spending was kept to a minimum in order to further the recovery of the economy and, in so doing, better prepare the country for major war should it become unavoidable. Through the mid-1930s, British grand strategy was well suited to the strategic landscape.

The problem was that these suppositions, from the mid-1930s on-

[130]

ward, grew increasingly divorced from strategic realities. German behavior during the second half of the 1930s should have led to a fundamental reorientation of strategy: an end to appeasement, the reduction of peripheral commitments, and more rapid rearmament, including the preparation of the army for continental missions. Instead, elites clung ever more tightly to a set of increasingly obsolete strategic assumptions. The problem was not simply one of change in beliefs lagging behind change in the strategic landscape. Elites were confronted with unambiguous incoming information that should have led far earlier to the abandonment of policies based on accommodation in the core and deterrence in the periphery. In fact, by 1938, British elites openly admitted that they were appeasing Hitler not because they believed that accommodation would satisfy Germany or buy time to rearm, but because they had no choice; they had simply failed to prepare the country for war.

It was strategic culture that was constraining the ability of elites to adjust grand strategy. In the aftermath of the devastation suffered during World War I, elites bought into and propagated among the public two fundamental strategic notions. First, elites committed themselves never again to send British troops to die on the Continent. This aversion to a continental commitment spread widely among the populace. Second, elites turned to peripheral empire and the notion of imperial integrity to reaffirm Britain's status as a great power and to consolidate their domestic rule by appealing to the strong currents of enthusiasm for empire which cut across political cleavages. Accordingly, from World War I onward, British security became increasingly synonymous with the avoidance of a continental commitment and the integrity of the empire. Elites stepped up their efforts to champion these strategic notions during the 1930s in order to gain domestic support for the extremist policies that emerged from conditions of strategic deficiency. They needed to sell appeasement to a public growing wary of Hitler's intentions and to justify the allocation of resources to the periphery despite successive adverse developments in the core. Among elites and masses alike, British security was coming to be defined in terms of the avoidance of continental entanglements and the preservation of imperial integrity. Through the mid-1930s, then, elite beliefs and strategic culture were running on parallel tracks.

The problem during the second half of the 1930s was that incoming information had to discredit not only the logic of appeasement and peripheral defense, but also the images that had become deeply embedded in strategic culture and that shaped both the fundamental conception of security that had taken root in the polity and how elites—top decision makers, the bureaucracy, and the military—defined their central roles and missions. Public opinion initially constrained the process of strategic reorientation. But even after public opposition to rearmament had waned and it had become clear that appeasement was not working, the conviction among elites that Britain had to avoid continental entanglements and the commitment to protecting imperial integrity were virtually impervious to change. These strategic images had come to shape intellectual paradigms, fundamental values, and organizational interests; they served as conceptual anchors within the decision-making community. For cognitive, emotional, and organizational reasons, elites found themselves entrapped in the strategic images that they had earlier propagated. As William Rock observes, "As the policy [of appeasement] proved inadequate, and eventually downright erroneous . . . the more it became a passion, an obsession, which led its proponents to ignore evidence which did not fit their preconceptions."[78] As a result, Britain tolerated successive acts of German aggression and failed to reequip the B.E.F. for continental operations until it was far too late. It took the German invasion of Czechoslovakia in the spring of 1939 to shock elites into facing the appalling military weakness of the country and into undertaking full-scale rearmament.

In the late 1930s, British strategy was the product not of rational calculation, but of strategic images and obsolete strategic assumptions that overrode incoming information and strategic logic. Justifiably, elites found themselves operating in an atmosphere of increasing fear and self-doubt. As Martin Gilbert writes, hanging over British decision makers was "the grey cloud of fear, which covered all acts of appeasement after 1937 with a shadow of doubt, hesitation, and uncertainty."[79] The strategic culture that took shape during the interwar period prevented elites from withdrawing from the periphery and preparing in a timely fashion for continental operations. British grand strategy exposed the empire at its heart and nearly led to the subjugation, if not destruction, of British society. Britain fell prey to both strategic exposure and overextension.

The Legacy of World War I

World War I had a profound effect on the sense of invulnerability that had informed elite thinking during the prewar years. The strategy of continental commitment had proved extremely costly. The British lost hundreds of thousands of troops on the continental battlefield.

---

[78] William Rock, *British Appeasement in the 1930s* (London: Edward Arnold, 1977), p. 95.
[79] Martin Gilbert, *The Roots of Appeasement* (London: Weidenfeld and Nicolson, 1966), p. 181.

The Royal Navy, despite its numerical superiority, proved unable to have a telling effect on the outcome of the land war. Full-scale rearmament strained the domestic economy; the burdens of the war effort were felt and shared by all. Despite these human and economic sacrifices, Britain was still dependent on American intervention to bring the war to a close. In other words, World War I itself shattered whatever illusions British elites had previously held about British hegemony and invulnerability. Britain's economic decline and the military weaknesses that followed had been exposed.

Despite its position as a victor, Britain emerged from World War I physically, psychologically, and financially ravaged by the war. Victory celebrations were characterized more by a sense of mourning than by a feeling of nationalistic pride.[80] Economic hardship was widespread. Domestic discontent was so strong in 1921, the General Staff felt, that the Regular Army should remain in Britain to deal with civil disturbances.[81] The government was committed to redressing the dire economic conditions that had resulted from the war. Taxation and defense spending dropped sharply during the first three postwar years. In 1920, the defense budget fell £604 to 292 million. By 1922, spending on defense had declined to £111 million.[82]

In the domestic political milieu that existed after the war, however, it was not enough to demobilize much of the country's military establishment and drastically cut defense spending. For instrumental political reasons—pacifism was spreading among the public—and due to a sincerely felt aversion to the horrors of the trenches, elites committed themselves never again to allow the country to become involved in a continental war.[83] The phrase "never again" was far more than a planning assumption to guide defense policy; repugnance toward a continental commitment spread throughout the electorate and became a key feature of the political landscape. In Williamson Murray's words, "Britain's elite, as well as the great majority of her population, had concluded that victory in the First World War had gained nothing and that little separated the lot of the losers from that of the victors."[84] Many elites and a not insignificant portion of the electorate had also been convinced that traditional power politics had to be eschewed in

---

[80] Michael Howard, *The Continental Commitment* (London: Temple Smith, 1972), p. 74.
[81] Ibid., p. 77.
[82] Ibid., p. 78.
[83] Ibid., p. 79.
[84] Williamson Murray, *The Change in the European Balance of Power, 1938–1939* (Princeton: Princeton University Press, 1984), p. 50.

favor of collective security and general disarmament.[85] For them, war not only entailed unacceptable costs; it was also immoral. These views created "a powerful anti-war movement dedicated to the proposition that the Great War must never happen again."[86] This change in elite and public attitudes was to play a key role in shaping how decision makers reacted to German rearmament during the 1930s.

The retraction of British commitments in Europe was accompanied by the extension of British commitments in the imperial periphery. Even before the outcome on the central front had been decided, Britain was diverting troops to missions in the periphery. Initial operations in Mesopotamia and the Dardanelles failed miserably and prompted the cabinet late in 1915 to place a moratorium on all missions in the Middle East. By the end of the following year, the moratorium was relaxed, and British troops were authorized in 1917 to undertake several major operations in the eastern Mediterranean area.[87] By 1918, British troops had moved into Palestine, Mesopotamia, the Caucasus, South Persia, and Trans-Caspia, markedly increasing the number of troops committed to operations in the periphery.

Why, after withdrawing forces from the empire to fight Germany, were British elites sending troops back to the periphery even before the European conflict had been decided? War aims indeed played some role. The British military hoped to open another front in southeastern Europe, thereby diverting German troops from both the western and eastern fronts. Furthermore, elites feared that Germany might expand into southern Russia and into the crumbling Ottoman empire, availing itself of the region's many resources and threatening imperial lines of communication. In supporting the extension of British control in the Middle East in 1918, Leo Amery, assistant secretary in the office of the War Cabinet, argued: "All these objects [in the periphery] are desirable in themselves . . . because they increase the general sphere of British influence and afford a strategical security which will enable that Southern British World which runs from Cape Town through Cairo, Baghdad and Calcutta to Sydney and Wellington to go about its peaceful business without constant fear of German aggression."[88]

Yet the pace and extent of British expansion were fueled more di-

[85] See Howard, *Continental Commitment*, pp. 106–110; and Laurence Martin, *Peace without Victory: Woodrow Wilson and the British Liberals* (New Haven: Yale University Press, 1958).

[86] Larry Fuchser, *Neville Chamberlain and Appeasement* (New York: W. W. Norton, 1982), p. 6.

[87] Howard, *Continental Commitment*, p. 65.

[88] Amery cited in Christopher Andrew and A. Kanya-Forstner, *The Climax of French Imperial Expansion, 1914–1924* (Stanford: Stanford University Press, 1981), p. 65.

rectly by two other sources: the need to recover imperial prestige and
to beat France and Russia to the spoils of the Ottoman empire; and by
the British government's efforts to use external success as an instrument of domestic politics. Even early in the war, peripheral areas were
held despite the fact that such operations made little strategic sense.
In late 1915, General Murray, chief of the Imperial General Staff, summarized the case for and against evacuating Gallipoli as follows: "The
arguments in favour of retaining our positions on Gallipoli are based
mainly on conjectures as to the effect on the East of withdrawal, and
questions of Imperial and military sentiment. The arguments on the
other side are based on cold calculations of military strategy."[89] Confronted with setbacks in Europe, elites were returning to empire to
reaffirm Britain's identity as a great power; "imperial sentiment" had
been rekindled. Furthermore, given constraints on resources, elites
would have to rely on reputation and prestige to protect imperial integrity. In 1915, after successive British losses in Mesopotamia, Salonica,
and Gallipoli, Colonel Hankey wrote that "these three misadventures
will destroy the last vestige of our prestige, upon which our Eastern
Empire depends; it will ruin our hopes among the Arabs, in Persia
and probably in China; it will place our position in India and possibly
in Egypt in peril." As David French argues, British elites believed that
"their rule was based on a political conjuring trick," that the viability
of the empire rested on projecting an image of strength and resolve.[90]
Far from showing immunity to reputational concerns, decision makers
were becoming increasingly preoccupied with preserving a façade of
imperial strength. Stymied and weakened by the devastation in Europe, elites returned with relish to the peripheral empire and adopted
competitive policies to demonstrate resolve and protect imperial integrity.[91]

Domestic politics and the politicization of foreign policy also fueled
the return to peripheral empire. The government suffered considerably
during the course of the war for several reasons. Worsening economic
conditions at home eroded electoral support. Setbacks in the prosecution of the war, both in the European theater and in the periphery,
fueled growing opposition to the government. French writes, "It was
not the British administrations in Delhi or Cairo which were brought
crashing down by the defeats at the Dardanelles and Kut but the As-

[89] Cited in Gooch, *Plans of War*, p. 321.
[90] Hankey cited in Andrew and Kanya-Forstner, *French Imperial Expansion*, pp. 60–61;
David French, "The Dardanelles, Mecca and Kut: Prestige as a Factor in British Eastern
Strategy, 1914–1916," *War and Society*, 5 (May 1987), 56.
[91] See Andrew and Kanya-Forstner, *French Imperial Expansion*, chaps. 3–7; and Howard,
Continental Commitment, pp. 59–73.

quith coalition government in London."[92] Toward the end of the war, the Conservatives turned to defense of the empire and peripheral expansion to consolidate the center-right coalition that had emerged to resist the gaining momentum of the left.[93] In Charles Bright's words, "Positions of power at home rested upon imperial foundations. In this way the empire was a crucial asset in the domestic war of position—a 'national' interest above party."[94] Concern about protecting imperial integrity and projecting an image of prestige in order to mask material inadequacy, and efforts to use peripheral expansion as an instrument of domestic politics elevated overseas empire to a new importance within prevailing conceptions of British security.

The events of World War I are thus crucial to understanding the behavior of British elites during the interwar period. The war politicized foreign policy and set in motion two important shifts in strategic culture. First, "the memories of the Great War and its long drawn-out horrors" led to a deep aversion to the notion of a continental commitment.[95] In 1914, British elites deviated from a long-standing policy of "splendid isolation" and paid dearly for it. Never again would they allow British soldiers to be dragged into the battlefields of Europe. The League of Nations and collective security, not balance-of-power politics, were to preserve peace in the future. This visceral rejection of involvement in a continental war imbued public opinion, elite thinking, and the organizational interests of elite institutions. It played a key role in inducing British elites to appease Germany far longer than they should have. Second, overseas empire came to occupy a new position of prominence in British conceptions of security, both among elites and among the public. Although thousands of Indian soldiers and troops from the dominions contributed to the British war effort, the heightened level of attachment to empire was less the result of a reevaluation of the periphery's economic and strategic value than a reaction to setbacks on the Continent and the perceived need to reaffirm national strength through imperial success. Britain was a victor only in nominal terms; the war had made clear the country's fall from preeminence and had exposed its economic and military weakness. If anything, the return to empire was a retreat, an attempt to hold to-

[92] French, "The Dardanelles," p. 58.

[93] By advancing a set of liberal war aims and taking advantage of the political costs associated with military setbacks, the left gained ground during 1917–1918. See Martin, *Peace without Victory,* pp. 132–134, 148–154; and Arno Mayer, *Political Origins of the New Diplomacy, 1917–1918* (New Haven: Yale University Press, 1959), p. 14.

[94] Charles Bright, "Class Interest and State Policy in the British Response to Hitler," in *German Nationalism and the European Response, 1880–1945,* ed. Carole Fink, Isabel Hull, and MacGregor Knox (Norman: University of Oklahoma Press, 1985), p. 239.

[95] Gilbert, *Roots of Appeasement,* p. 116.

gether Britain's remaining claim to great-power status. And because of resource constraints, elites became increasingly concerned about reputational considerations; even less important possessions had to be protected in order to project the image of prestige that would preserve imperial integrity. Imperial ambition also served an important domestic political function. The Conservatives whipped up popular support for imperial expansion and used external success to disarm the left and solidify the center-right coalition. Accordingly, as Britain entered the 1920s, elites and the public alike defined the nation's well-being more than ever before in terms of the security and integrity of the overseas empire. This attitude went hand-in-hand with aversion to a continental commitment; in the future, British security depended on protecting the empire and remaining aloof from European entanglements. In Gilbert's words, "Many politicians felt that Britain's prime responsibility was to her Empire, and that if foreign policy were dominated by European problems, imperial interests would suffer."[96]

Strategic Assessments

Despite Britain's enthusiastic return to empire after World War I, the demobilization of the army occurred quite rapidly.[97] By 1927, the number of troops available for overseas duty was smaller than in the pre-1914 period.[98] Because of the neutralization of the German threat by the Versailles Treaty and the cap on the Japanese navy imposed by the Washington Naval Conference, the liabilities associated with imperial rule may not have been immediately clear. But by the late 1920s, both internal and external threats to the integrity of the empire were mounting. Resistance to colonial rule in India, Egypt, and Palestine placed increasing demands on the British army. The Japanese invasion of Manchuria in 1931 and the emergence of German militarism shortly thereafter meant that Britain was again faced with a growing gap between resources and commitments that threatened to expose the empire at its heart. The new territories taken during World War I only added to the already long list of peripheral liabilities. As Michael Howard writes, "The characteristics which made the British empire seem so strong in 1919 were in almost every respect elements of weakness rather than of strength."[99]

---

[96] Ibid., p. 122.

[97] For a comprehensive treatment of British defense policy during the 1920s, see John Robert Ferris, *Men, Money, and Diplomacy: The Evolution of British Strategic Policy, 1919–26* (Ithaca: Cornell University Press, 1989).

[98] CAB 4/17/847B, Nov. 1927, "The Present Distribution and Strength of the British Army in Relation to Its Duties," p. 1.

[99] Howard, *Continental Commitment*, p. 75.

Assessments of the military balance during the 1930s stand in stark contrast to those of the pre–World War I years. Instead of pointing to the relative invulnerability of the British Isles, intelligence data indicated strategic vulnerability on virtually every front. The naval situation in home waters was the one exception. Despite the severe financial constraints imposèd on the military establishment during the 1920s and the first half of the 1930s, the Royal Navy was able to maintain at least a 60 percent superiority over the German fleet throughout the interwar years. Britain entered the war with an effective naval strength of twelve capital ships while Germany had five.[100] The problem, however, was the Far East. In the event of Japanese aggression, the Admiralty wanted to send to the Pacific a fleet that would be larger than the Japanese fleet by one ship. If Britain had to keep a minimum of eight or nine capital ships in home waters, it could send at best four to the Far East.[101] Yet Japan's fleet was far superior in the late 1930s: Japan entered the war with a fleet of ten battleships, against which Britain's four would be of little utility. The commitment to defend British interests in the Far East thus left the Royal Navy with a mission that it simply did not have the resources to carry out.

A broader look at the naval situation presented an even gloomier picture. While an Anglo-French alliance enjoyed superiority in battleship strength over the opposing coalition of Germany, Italy, and Japan, Britain and France faced serious deficiencies in other vessel classes (Table 6). Although these imbalances did not erode British superiority in the North Sea, they did undermine Britain's ability to guard the sea

Table 6. Naval strength

	Britain and France	Germany, Italy, and Japan
Large destroyers	16	74
Other modern destroyers	119	140
Older destroyers	65	84
Submarines	134	224
Torpedo boats	28	83

Note: The two sides were roughly equivalent in terms of aircraft carriers and eight-inch and six-inch cruisers.
Source: CAB 16/209, 14 March 1939, British Strategical Memorandum, p. 9.

[100] Kennedy, *Naval Mastery*, p. 293.
[101] In 1937, the Admiralty proposed increasing capital ship strength to twenty. This would allow Britain to keep ten in home waters and send ten to the Far East. The Admiralty projected that Japan would have nine battleships by the outbreak of war. CAB 16/182, 29 April 1937, "A New Standard of Naval Strength," pp. 10–12.

lanes needed to transport supplies to the metropole as well as to ensure the integrity of the empire.

Naval defense of the home islands was attainable as long as most of the Royal Navy remained in home waters, but technological developments meant that naval power alone could no longer ensure the physical security of the British Isles. The advent of air power transformed the English Channel from a formidable moat into an incidental feature of geography that German planes could cross in a matter of minutes. Despite the fact that the Royal Air Force received top budgetary priority, Britain was unable, until 1939, to match Germany's output of bombers. A few months before the war began, Britain and France had approximately 2,740 aircraft available for metropolitan service while Germany and Italy had more than 5,000.[102] Because the technical difficulties involved in air defense were not yet solved, elites were obsessed with Britain's vulnerability to air attack throughout the 1930s. Though no careful studies of the feasibility of such a campaign were completed, planners feared that Germany would be able to deliver a "knock-out blow" against London.[103] These concerns fundamentally altered the strategic assumptions shaping defense policy; British naval supremacy was no longer able to protect the heart of the empire against direct attack.

The situation on the ground offered little consolation. During the second half of the 1930s, Germany amassed a formidable army. By 1939, British intelligence estimates showed that Britain and France, with one month of mobilization, could place some 81 divisions in the field while Germany and Italy could mass approximately 182 divisions.[104] While Germany did not enjoy either a quantitative or qualitative edge in tanks, the German army had created armored divisions that would be used for independent attack and breakthrough operations rather than to support infantry.[105] Neither the British army nor the French army demonstrated such flexibility in doctrine. Furthermore, air power meant that the defense of the low countries was of even more strategic importance than during the pre-1914 period. As the Chiefs of Staff (C.O.S.) noted in 1934, "It is not too much to say that the occupation and successful defense of the Low Countries against German invasion would be the most effective means of miti-

[102] CAB 16/209, 14 March 1939, British Strategical Memorandum, p. 12.

[103] Brian Bond, *British Military Policy between the Two World Wars* (Oxford: Clarendon Press, 1980), p. 283.

[104] CAB 16/209, 14 March 1939, British Strategical Memorandum, p. 10.

[105] On the development of Germany's tank units, see Murray, *European Balance of Power*, pp. 33–38, 101–104.

gating the severity of German air attack on London."[106] The C.O.S. estimated that the Luftwaffe, if operating from occupied airfields rather than from Germany, would be able to increase the sortie rate over British territory by 50 percent and the bomb load by 30 percent.[107]

The strategic environment facing British decision makers in the 1930s was thus fundamentally different than that of the pre–World War I period. The Royal Navy, if devoted to home waters, was sufficient in size to cope with the German fleet. But naval supremacy was no longer sufficient to protect the British Isles; London itself was vulnerable to potentially devastating attack by air. The advent of air power enhanced the importance of blocking a German invasion of the low countries. Yet the B.E.F. in 1939 was less well equipped to assist France in this task than it had been in 1914. The periphery was even more vulnerable than the metropole. The Admiralty planned to send a battleship fleet to the Far East despite the fact that it could not spare enough vessels to challenge the Japanese fleet. A potentially hostile Italy raised doubts about whether the Royal Navy could maintain sea control in the Mediterranean.

These perceptions of high metropolitan vulnerability in the military realm were only exacerbated by concern about the fragility of the British economy. In fact, the inadequacy of Britain's military establishment was due in large part to the severe constraints placed on rearmament by anxiety about the domestic economy. The Treasury made this amply clear in 1932: "The fact is that in present circumstances we are no more in a position financially and economically to engage in a major war in the Far East than we are militarily. . . . The Treasury submit that at the present time financial risks are greater than any other we can estimate." The prime minister himself was adamant on this issue in 1933: "It must be clearly understood that there would be no big extension of expenditure because this would be out of the question."[108]

This new level of concern about the economy was the result of several factors. First, World War I had demonstrated the importance of economic durability in determining the outcome of major war. Accordingly, the Treasury played a far more influential role in the formulation of foreign and defense policy during the interwar period than it did before World War I.[109] Second, the planning community had better

---

[106] CAB 16/111/#111, 14 May 1934, note by Chiefs of Staff, p. 12.

[107] CAB 16/110, 31 July 1934, "The Disarmament Conference 1932," p. 35.

[108] CAB 4/21/1087B, 11 March 1932, "Imperial Defence Policy," p. 2; CAB 2/5, 6 April 1933, Minutes of the 258th Meeting of the C.I.D.

[109] For a detailed study of the role of the Treasury during the 1930s, see G. C. Peden, *British Rearmament and the Treasury: 1932–1939* (Edinburgh: Scottish Academic Press, 1979).

economic data on which to base its assessment of relative economic performance. Rather than rely on trade statistics as they did before World War I, analysts had access to information about manufacturing capability and output. And the indicators were not reassuring. Britain appeared to be incapable of matching German output of key war-making materials. Between 1935 and 1939, Britain could produce only 11.8 million metric tons of steel to Germany's 20.4. In 1939, the British were capable of producing only one-fifth the number of machine tools manufactured in Germany.[110] Britain had the option of importing machine tools, but this would only undermine the long-term strength of the economy by worsening the balance of payments and stunting the growth of domestic industrial capacity.

Third, the Great Depression and the economic crisis of 1931 created extreme sensitivity to preserving financial stability. During the first half of the 1900s, the vitality of the British economy came to rely much more heavily on the provision of goods and services than on industrial manufacturing.[111] Sustaining foreign confidence in the health of the British economy was essential to maintaining Britain's position as the dominant international financier. Full-scale rearmament, because of the need to import raw materials, would jeopardize financial stability. Britain's importation of war materiel constituted some 25 to 30 percent of the cost of rearmament. High levels of importation would drain gold reserves and foreign investment and require increased foreign borrowing. A high deficit in the balance of payments would undermine foreign confidence in the British economy, erode London's position as a financial center, and preclude any hope of keeping pace with the growth of German military power.[112] A slower pace of rearmament would allow for the gradual expansion of the industrial infrastructure and mean that the economy would be better able to bear the burdens of war if and when it were to occur.

Anxieties about the fragility of the economy had a direct impact on military expenditures throughout the interwar period. Britain was the only one of the major powers to decrease substantially its level of military spending between 1925 and 1934.[113] Despite awareness of growing threats from Germany and Japan after 1934, the allocation of national resources to defense increased only marginal. Through 1938, the government effectively placed a fixed ceiling on defense expenditure. The services then based force levels and procurement plans on whatever

[110] Ibid., p. 180.

[111] Gilpin, *U.S. Power*, chap 3.

[112] Peden, *British Rearmament and the Treasury*, pp. 63–66; figures on the cost of rearmament are on p. 63.

[113] See CAB 16/109, 28 Feb. 1934, Defence Requirements Sub-Committee Report, p. 30.

share of the budget they were allocated, not on the missions they would likely have to fulfill in the event of war.[114] A comparison of British and German annual defense spending between 1934 and 1940, expressed as a percentage of GNP, reveals the slow pace of British rearmament through 1938 (Table 7).

Table 7. British and German annual defense spending (as % of GNP)

	1934	1935	1936	1937	1938	1939	1940
Britain	3	3	4	6	7	18	46
Germany	6	8	13	13	17	23	38

Source: Peden, *British Rearmament*, p. 8.

To what extent did elites assimilate the implications of these gloomy assessments of relative power capabilities for their strategic predicament? Was the planning community aware that commitments were outstripping resources and that the security of the British Isles was being jeopardized? The archival record indicates that, soon after the close of World War I, military planners were preoccupied with the problem of strategic deficiency. The nub of the dilemma was that imperial commitments were increasing while military resources were dwindling. Henry Wilson, chief of the Imperial General Staff, in a memo drafted in 1920, made clear his concerns to the cabinet: "I would respectfully urge that the earnest attention of His Majesty's Government may be given to this question [of the allocation of troops] with a view to our policy being brought into some relation with military forces available to it. At present this is far from being the case. . . . I cannot too strongly press on the Government the danger, the extreme danger, of his Majesty's Army being spread all over the world, strong nowhere, weak everywhere, and with no reserve to save a dangerous situation or avert a coming danger." In the same year, the General Staff carried out an overall assessment of the liabilities of the empire, concluding, "Wherever we look we find our garrisons beset by potential dangers which may far exceed their strength, and in the sum our liabilities are so vast, and at the same time so indeterminate, that to assess them must be largely a matter of conjecture."[115] As mentioned above, Britain's military capability had shrunk even further by the mid-1920s. In 1926, the C.O.S. made clear its frustration not only with existing force

[114] See Norman Gibbs, *Grand Strategy: Rearmament Policy*, vol. 1 (London: H.M.S.O., 1976), p. 296.
[115] CAB 24/107, 9 June 1920, "British Military Liabilities," pp. 1–2; CAB 4/7/255B, 27 July 1920, "Military Liabilities of the Empire," pp. 8–9.

levels but also with the difficulties involved in shaping defense policy given the fact that the country's external commitments far outstripped available resources: "The size of the forces of the Crown maintained by Great Britain is governed by various conditions peculiar to each service, and is not arrived at by any calculation of the requirements of foreign policy, nor is it possible that they ever should be so calculated." The C.O.S. went on to note the "smallness of our defence forces when compared with the vast extent of our Imperial responsibilities and commitments. We wish to place on record our view that the forces available for Imperial Defence are now reduced to a minimum and are barely capable of dealing with the problems that are liable to arise either singly or simultaneously."[116]

The hypothetical threats that caused these anxieties in the 1920s turned into real threats in the 1930s. In each of the empire's three main theaters, Britain faced increasingly hostile and powerful enemies: Germany in northern Euorope, Italy in the Mediterranean, and Japan in the Far East. These developments induced the C.I.D. to cancel in 1932 the Ten-Year Rule, a planning assumption adopted in 1919 and reaffirmed on a regular basis, which posited that Britain would not be engaged in a major war for at least ten years. And even after the cancellation of the Ten-Year Rule, the cabinet delayed eighteen months before authorizing the services to rebuild the country's military capability.[117] So began the process of rearmament that was to have enabled Britain to keep pace with its chief rivals. Rearmament proceeded slowly and laboriously until 1939, however; the gap between capability and likely military missions widened throughout most of the decade. The first sea lord gave some indication of the inadequacy of rearmament in a memo written in 1935 noting that, if war broke out in the Mediterranean, the navy had roughly a one-week supply of antiaircraft ammunition.[118] The following year, Lord Ernle Chat made clear his concern about the growing gap between resources and commitments: "Our foreign policy had not been in line with our defence policy of the last few years. In former days it had been possible for the Service Departments to determine the likely enemy, or enemies, and then to calculate how long we had to prepare for hostilities, what our needs were and what actions we should take if war broke out. At present he said at any moment, without warning, we were liable to be plunged into war with forces which were not adequate or properly disposed to meet the occasion."[119] By 1938, though the gravity of the threats facing

---

[116] CAB 4/15/701B, 22 June 1926, "Imperial Defence Policy," pp. 11–12.
[117] Gibbs, *Grand Strategy: Rearmament Policy*, p. 80.
[118] CAB 16/138, D.P.R. 15, "Italo-Abyssinian Dispute," p. 5.
[119] CAB 53/6, C.O.S./174, 13 May 1936.

Britain was all too clear, the situation was no better. The C.O.S. plainly admitted that "we cannot foresee the time when our defence forces will be strong enough to safeguard our territory, trade and vital interests against Germany, Italy and Japan simultaneously."[120]

In short, throughout the interwar period, and especially during the 1930s, elites were acutely aware that Britain's military capabilities were insufficient to cope with rising external threats. As during the years before World War I, the rise of German power necessitated a reorientation of strategy and efforts to protect the metropole. I now examine how the planning community responded to this need for strategic adjustment.

Dealing with the Adversary

British grand strategy during the 1930s was based on belief in the need to accommodate German demands in the core while adopting a deterrent stance in the periphery. Well aware that Britain could not simultaneously fight two first-class wars, elites sought to appease Germany and focus attention on the defense of the outlying empire. Appeasement would allow Britain either to avoid continental war altogether or, at the least, to delay conflict with Germany until Britain's economy and military forces were better prepared for full-scale war. A deterrent stance in the periphery was intended to discourage external and internal challenges to imperial possessions and prepare imperial defenses should deterrence fail. It was these calculations that initially induced British elites to accommodate Hitler's appetite for aggression and to focus attention on imperial defense.

This grand strategy did not, however, enjoy uniform support among decision makers. From the early 1930s onward, elites recognized that they had to choose between devoting scarce resources to the defense of empire and preparing the metropole for a potential war with Germany. The debate over Britain's naval posture in the Far East encapsulates the dilemmas facing British elites during the interwar period. The cabinet first approved the construction of a naval base at Singapore in 1921 yet did not approve funding for completion of the first stage until 1932—after the Japanese invasion of Manchuria. Japanese aggression sparked a heated debate within the government about whether Britain could afford to commit resources to the Far East in order to defend the formal empire as well as Australia and New Zealand. The Admiralty insisted that the Far East was "the greatest and most immediate of our

---

[120] 1938 C.O.S. Report cited in CAB 16/209, 1939, Strategical Appreciation Sub-Committee 13, pp. 2–3.

commitments" and should receive top priority in terms of war planning and resource allocation.[121] The Foreign Office was similarly enthusiastic about increasing Britain's presence in the Far East, arguing that a conciliatory approach to the Japanese would only invite further aggression.[122]

The Treasury took the opposite position, arguing that it made little sense to divert scarce military resources from the European theater to the Far East. In 1934, Sir Warren Fisher, secretary to the treasury, warned that Britain's productive capability was limited by its manpower and resources. "It is for this reason," he wrote, "that the selection of, and concentration on, our greatest single risk are of supreme importance. For it negatives, in my view, our ability to fight simultaneously two first-class wars on widely separated fronts." Later that year, the chancellor of the exchequer, Neville Chamberlain, responded similarly to proposed military programs designed to protect British interests in distant quarters of the empire:

> The result of our deliberations is, to put it bluntly, that we are presented with proposals impossible to carry out. Therefore, since we cannot do all we would, we must begin again by considerations of priority and seek to isolate the salient points. The world situation is not static; it is kaleidoscopic. . . . But to-day it can hardly be disputed that the anxieties of the British people are concentrated on Europe rather than on the Far East, and that if we have to make a choice we must prepare our defence against possible hostilities from Germany rather than from Japan. My first proposition then is that during the ensuing five years our efforts must be chiefly concentrated upon measures designed for the defence of these Islands.[123]

The Treasury's position lost out to a "powerful ministerial consensus that it was a vital interest to protect the imperial connection overseas." There was widespread support for the Admiralty's position that withdrawal from the Far East would be "letting go the principal link which holds the Empire together."[124] Even after the scope and pace of German rearmament became apparent during the second half of the 1930s,

---

[121] CAB 16/109/1113B, Oct. 1933, Defence Requirements Sub-Committee Annual Review 1933, p. 3.

[122] Bright, "Class Interest," p. 236. There were dissenting opinions in the Foreign Office. Sir Robert Vansittart, for example, permanent under-secretary of state for foreign affairs, argued that preparation for war with Germany should take clear precedence over preparations for operations in the Far East. CAB 16/109, 4 Dec. 1933, 3d Meeting of the Defence Requirements Sub-Committee, p. 2.

[123] CAB 16/109, 29 Jan. 1934, note by the secretary, p. 2; CAB 16/111/#120, 20 June 1934, "Disarmament Conference 1932," p. 2.

[124] Bright, "Class Interest," p. 239; CAB 16/111/125, 18 July 1934, "Naval Defence Requirements," p. 1.

Britain stood by its commitments in the Far East. In 1937, the Joint Planning Committee (J.P.C.) made the following unequivocal statement: "In the event of Japanese aggression occurring simultaneously with or subsequent to an act of aggression against British interests in Europe, it would be our policy to send to the Far East a fleet which is at least adequate to contain that of the Japanese." In 1938, the C.O.S. maintained that the "security of the United Kingdom and the security of Singapore would be the keystones on which the survival of the British Commonwealth of Nations would depend."[125] The Far East was thus assigned a higher priority than the Mediterranean. As the C.O.S. put it in 1938, "The chief result of Japanese participation would be that our naval forces in the Mediterranean would be reduced to a few submarines and light surface forces."[126]

These priorities led to a particularly acute dilemma for planners because of the decreasing number of battleships in service. After 1930, British capital ship strength decreased from twenty to fifteen.[127] Given the number of vessels out of service for repairs and refitting, Britain in 1939 had only nine capital ships. The distribution of the fleet in February 1939 was as follows: four battleships in home waters, two stationed at Gibraltar, and three in the Mediterranean; cruisers were scattered at these three stations and throughout the Red Sea, China, South Atlantic, North America, West Indies, Persian Gulf, Australia, and New Zealand.[128] The rationale for this disposition of forces was clearly set forth before the Strategical Appreciation Sub-Committee in March, only six months before war began. In a war with Germany and Japan, according to a British Strategic Memorandum, "the despatch of a British Fleet to Singapore would be imperative and the situation in the Mediterranean would rest with France."[129] Elites maintained this commitment despite recognition that Britain could well face three hostile powers simultaneously, that the Mediterranean could be dominated by an adversary, and that dispatch of the fleet to the Far East by the Cape route would take at least three months.[130]

Public declarations of this commitment to defend British interests in the Far East were no doubt intended at least in part to reassure the dominions and to deter the Japanese. That this commitment was more

---

[125] Cited in Neidpath, *The Singapore Naval Base and the Defense of Britain's Eastern Empire, 1919–1941* (Oxford: Oxford University Press, 1981), p. 138; CAB 16/183A, D.P.(P.) 18, 21 Feb. 1938, "Mediterranean, Middle East and North East Africa Appreciation," p. 63.

[126] C.O.S. memorandum cited in Gibbs, *Grand Strategy: Rearmament Policy,* p. 419.

[127] After the London Naval Conference of 1930, four Iron Dukes and the Tiger were scrapped; they were not replaced until the late 1930s.

[128] CAB 16/182, D.P.(P.) 44, 20 Feb. 1939, "European Appreciation," p. 85.

[129] CAB 16/209, 14 March 1939, "Anglo-French Staff Conversations," p. 41.

[130] Neidpath, *Singapore Naval Base,* p. 145.

than rhetorical, however, was made clear both by its repeated affirmation in private meetings and classified planning papers and by the naval construction program of the late 1930s. During 1936–1938, the Admiralty urged the cabinet to switch from a one-power to a two-power standard in order to enable the Royal Navy to cover the German fleet at home while maintaining supremacy over Japan in the Far East. While the cabinet did not approve this recommendation, it did allocate funds to move toward the force levels desired by the Admiralty. As Gibbs describes this compromise, "The Two-Power Standard . . . was not adopted even in principle before war broke out in September 1939, although building programmes from 1936 onwards were to some extent based on its scales."[131] As a result, the naval construction program focused on building battleships so that Britain could improve the balance in the Far East. In doing so, the Admiralty failed to acquire the smaller vessels needed for antiaircraft and antisubmarine operations in the European theater and swallowed up funds that could have been profitably used by the other services. As one commentator on British naval policy remarked in 1938, "The Admiralty . . . seem to have been committing the grave error of preparing for ambitious operations in a far distant theater without first taking steps to ensure the safety of the home base."[132]

After Munich, British decision makers began to question this commitment to send a sizable fleet to the Far East. War plans still called for the navy to send capital ships to Singapore in the event of Japanese aggression. But the size of the fleet sent and the timing of its departure were to be determined by the government of the day. Moreover, it was no longer assured that the Mediterranean would be abandoned in favor of the Far East. Gibbs describes the reorientation that took place during 1939: "The Mediterranean, for the first time, was accorded a place of major importance in planning and, equally for the first time, the possibility or necessity of sacrificing Britain's position in the Far East was openly discussed."[133] This reconsideration by no means settled matters. Constraints on the building program and ongoing uncertainties about when and where available vessels would be used left "unsolved problems of priority and strategic distribution which still remained when war broke out."[134] This naval strategy, the construction program, and the distribution of capital ships stand in stark contrast to the situation following the naval redistribution of 1912, when virtually all Brit-

---

[131] Gibbs, *Grand Strategy: Rearmament Policy*, p. 378.
[132] Russell Grenfell, cited in Murray, *European Balance of Power*, p. 75.
[133] Gibbs, *Grand Strategy: Rearmament Policy*, pp. 430–431.
[134] Ibid., p. 378.

ain's capital ships were concentrated in home waters to focus on the defense of the metropole.

The evolution of army strategy parallels that of the navy. During the 1920s, troop levels were insufficient to meet the demands of imperial garrisons, not to mention to engage in continental operations. The B.E.F. continued to be an amalgamation of whatever troops were not on overseas duty: "The *size* of the Expeditionary Force had no relation whatever to the strategical problem of a Franco-German conflict. This force consisted merely of the spare parts of our oversea military machine, assembled to form a provisional weapon with which to meet the threatening emergency."[135] With the cancellation of the Ten-Year Rule, complacency about the absence of an expeditionary force for continental operations began to wane. The C.I.D. again took up consideration of a continental commitment, driven by appreciation of the fact that Britain had to ensure "that the Low Countries are not overrun again by a great continental Power."[136]

Between 1933 and 1939, the General Staff's successive efforts to reequip the B.E.F. and prepare it for continental operations met with staunch opposition from the Treasury and cabinet. The C.O.S. responded to Hitler's coming to power by affirming that Germany would likely pose a profound threat to British security within three to five years.[137] Nevertheless, the army's requests for funding for the Regular and Territorial armies were repeatedly slashed by the Treasury. Not only were there financial constraints, but it was not at all clear that the cabinet was even willing to support a continental commitment in principle. Discussion in the Cabinet Ministerial Committee in May 1934 illustrates, in a manner that is both humorous and tragic, the confusion that pervaded this issue:

Mr. Chamberlain said he thought it was a little startling saying that an Expeditionary Force had been approved.

Lord Hailsham said, on the contrary, he thought that such a thing had been part of policy since we had had a policy.

Mr. Chamberlain said he thought that no specific discussion or decision to approve an Expeditionary Force had been taken by the present Government.

Sir Maurice Hankey said that, as a matter of fact, the Force was fixed at

[135] WO 33/1004, 10 Jan. 1922, "The Interim Report of the Committee on National Expenditure," Doc. VII, p. 51.

[136] CAB 16/109/113B, Oct. 1933, "Imperial Defence Policy: Annual Review," p. 3.

[137] Robert Shay, Jr., *British Rearmament in the Thirties: Politics and Profits* (Princeton: Princeton University Press, 1977), p. 28.

five divisions, but the Defence Requirements Sub-Committee had suggested four.

Sir Philip Cunliffe-Lister thought the position was, perhaps, that the Government had not accepted the idea of a policy of an Expeditionary Force.[138]

The German remilitarization of the Rhineland in 1936 again focused attention on Britain's inability to intervene on the Continent. A Defence White Paper remarked that Britain now had to redress its gaping military deficiencies or be left in a position of permanent vulnerability.[139] Nevertheless, no changes in the size or readiness of the B.E.F. were forthcoming. By the end of 1936, only two divisions could have been sent to the Continent on short notice, and neither would have been "fit for war."[140] The situation in fact worsened during 1937 and 1938, when support for the B.E.F. reached its lowest point.[141] An interim report on defense requirements prepared in late 1937 urged that the notion of a continental commitment be dropped from official policy. Thomas Inskip, minister for the co-ordination of defence, was primarily responsible for making the case to the cabinet. His own misgivings were apparent and prophetic:

I must . . . warn my colleagues of the possible consequences of this proposal in order that they may share my responsibility for the decision to be taken with their eyes open. Notwithstanding recent developments in mechanised warfare on land and in the air, there is no sign of the displacement of infantry. If France were again to be in danger of being overrun by land armies, a situation might arise when, as in the last war, we had to improvise an army to assist her. Should this happen, the Government of the day would most certainly be criticised for having neglected to provide against so obvious a contingency.[142]

Despite this warning, the cabinet promptly accepted Inskip's recommendation, formally eliminating the army's continental mission.[143] In its "Review of Imperial Defence" for 1937, the C.O.S. stated clearly that the "Regular Army is being maintained at the strength necessary for its duties in garrisoning and policing overseas possessions."[144] At the end of the year, roughly 100,000 of Britain's 200,000 soldiers were serv-

---

[138] CAB 16/110, 3 May 1934.
[139] Shay, *British Rearmament in the Thirties*, p. 83.
[140] CAB 16/141, 16 Nov. 1936, "The Organization, Armament and Equipment of the Army," p. 5.
[141] See Bond, *British Military Policy*, chaps. 10–11.
[142] Cited in Gibbs, *Grand Strategy: Rearmament Policy*, p. 469.
[143] Shay, *British Rearmament in the Thirties*, pp. 170–184.
[144] CAB 21/700, 22 Feb. 1937, "Review of Imperial Defence," p. 12.

ing overseas, with 50,000 in India alone.[145] The fall of Austria on 13 March 1938 led to a temporary reevaluation of this policy; after the Anschluss, Germany incorporated more than 100,000 Austrian soldiers into its army.[146] The cabinet's deliberations, however, led to a reaffirmation of its decision to eliminate the army's continental role.[147] Accordingly, the expeditionary force was outfitted with equipment and supplies for colonial, not continental, missions.[148]

In September 1938, the cabinet did reverse its earlier decision and approve the notion of sending an expeditionary force to the Continent. This decision was of only symbolic importance, however, inasmuch as the cabinet approved *in principle* the continental role of the B.E.F. but failed to provide funds for its reequipment. After repeatedly rebuffing successive French efforts to secure an alliance with Britain, British elites were hoping to stiffen French resolve by at least expressing a willingness to come to France's assistance.[149] In February 1939, Prime Minister Chamberlain, under pressure from his colleagues in the cabinet, did agree to improve the readiness of two divisions of the B.E.F. to enable them to be deployed to the Continent in twenty-one days.[150] But it was not until Germany's invasion of Czechoslovakia in March that the cabinet finally acquiesced to the recommendation of the C.O.S. that the dispatch of the B.E.F. to the Continent "be accepted as a primary commitment."[151] In the spring of 1939, only months before Hitler's armies moved into Poland, the army began belated preparations to transform the B.E.F. from a paper force into a force capable of contributing to the defense of the low countries. Yet it was exceedingly late. Even with conscription and industrial mobilization, the army had to overcome years of neglect and an industrial infrastructure and labor pool limited in its ability to meet demand for armaments. By July, the infantry divisions earmarked to be sent to the Continent had only 72 of their full complement of 240 heavy antiaircraft guns (and only 30 percent of the approved scale of ammunition), 108 of their 226 light antiaircraft guns, and 144 of their 240 antitank guns.[152] Given the tenor of German behavior from 1933 onward, and in light of the timely preparations for continental war made by Britain during the pre–World

[145] Gibbs, *Grand Strategy: Rearmament Policy*, p. 450.
[146] Murray, *European Balance of Power*, p. 152.
[147] Shay, *British Rearmament in the Thirties*, pp. 197–200.
[148] Gibbs, *Grand Strategy: Rearmament Policy*, p. 473. For further discussion of the debate over the army's continental role, see pp. 441–490.
[149] Shay, *British Rearmament in the Thirties*, pp. 235–238.
[150] Murray, *European Balance of Power*, pp. 277–278.
[151] CAB 16/209, Strategical Appreciation Sub-Committee, "European Appreciation," p. 3.
[152] Gibbs, *Grand Strategy: Rearmament Policy*, p. 516.

War I years, the extreme lateness of this decision to equip the B.E.F. for continental operations is indeed striking.

The reluctance of the cabinet to fund the B.E.F. was to some extent a by-product of the assumption that Britain could rely on the Royal Air Force (RAF) to deter German aggression. Planners contended that if the RAF maintained a bomber force adequate to inflict considerable damage on German territory, Britain could deter a German attack on the British Isles by threatening retaliation. The cabinet's decision to assign top budgetary priority to the RAF was based largely on this rationale. Building a sizable bomber force was the best way to deter Germany without incurring the financial and industrial dislocation associated with reequipping the B.E.F.[153]

This approach to coping with the rise of German power was flawed for two main reasons. First, reliance on a deterrent threat to shape German behavior faced problems of credibility and proportionality. Britain might be able to deter attack on the home islands, but it could not credibly threaten to bomb Germany—and suffer retaliation in kind—in response to a German invasion of the low countries or France. In short, the RAF did not pose an effective deterrent to German occupation of continental Europe, an outcome that elites fully recognized would be inimical to British interests.[154] Second, should deterrence fail, the RAF could do little to stop German aggression. And because British industrial centers were more concentrated and vulnerable to attack than those of Germany, Britain's war effort would suffer more than Germany's from an exchange of bombing raids.[155] This problem was exacerbated during the late 1930s, when the number and quality of the RAF's bombers began to fall behind those of the Luftwaffe. The RAF was thus neither an effective deterrent nor the key to blocking a German advance to the west; for this task, Britain needed a continental army.

For these reasons, Britain's interwar air strategy could not be relied on to deter or stop German aggression. The development of the RAF by no means provided a sound rationale for eliminating Britain's continental commitment or assuming that the allocation of scarce resources to the defense of the imperial periphery did not entail extreme risks in the core. Furthermore, the cabinet became increasingly aware of the fundamental flaws in RAF strategy. Early in 1938, the cabinet overturned the RAF's decision to focus on the procurement of bombers.

---

[153] Shay, *British Rearmament in the Thirties,* pp. 78–80.

[154] See Malcolm Smith, *British Air Strategy between the Wars* (Oxford: Oxford University Press, Clarendon Press, 1984), pp. 312–313.

[155] Ibid., p. 317.

Civilians directed the air force to concentrate on the production of fighters and on the technology needed to improve bomber detection and interception.[156] Recognizing that a threat of retaliation was insufficient to deter Germany, elites began to focus on the difficult task of defending the British Isles against air attack.[157]

The approach of British elites to forming alliances during the interwar period also stands in stark contrast to their behavior before World War I. From the mid-1930s onward, French elites made repeated attempts to form a military alliance with Britain. British elites persistently refused and made it quite clear that France could not count on a British contribution to a land war. In late 1938, when war between Germany and Czechoslovakia appeared likely, decision makers decided to avoid staff talks with the French even if hostilities broke out.[158] Not until after the invasion of Czechoslovakia did British elites begin to make earnest preparations to assist France on the ground. Alliance with the Soviet Union was similarly avoided. Even after Germany's invasion of Czechoslovakia—a development that added the equipment of thirty-eight infantry divisions and eight mobile divisions to the Wehrmacht—British decision makers refused to consider allying with the Russians. British elites distrusted the Russians for ideological reasons and believed the Soviet military to be of very low quality.[159] In addition, Chamberlain argued that it was more important to stand behind Poland and resist Soviet requests to deploy troops in Eastern Europe than it was to ensure that Germany had to split its forces between two fronts. As Gibbs remarks, "When Russia's help was discussed there is no evidence to suggest that Mr. Chamberlain ever brought himself to admit that it was essential."[160] British intransigence was soon rewarded with the signing of the Nazi-Soviet Nonaggression Pact.[161]

In 1912, British elites were prepared to withdraw all battleships from distant waters in order to defend the home islands against Germany. The C.I.D., also by 1912, had effectively approved sending the B.E.F. to France, and detailed discussions were taking place with the French military about where along the front British troops would concentrate. Entente with France and Russia created a formidable counterweight to German military power and ensured that Germany had to split its

---

[156] Ibid.

[157] Public concern about air attack also played a role in switching the focus of the RAF from bomber production to fighter production and air defense technology. See Bright, "Class Interest," p. 234.

[158] Murray, *European Balance of Power*, p. 166.

[159] William Rock, *Appeasement on Trial* (Hamden: Archon Books, 1966), p. 219.

[160] Gibbs, *Grand Strategy: Rearmament Policy*, pp. 803–804.

[161] Murray, *European Balance of Power*, pp. 300–305.

forces between two fronts. In the late 1930s, British elites were strengthening the naval base at Singapore and building battleships to be used against the Japanese in the Far East. Until 1939, the B.E.F. was in a state of utter disrepair and probably was incapable of making any significant contribution to a continental war. When support for the B.E.F. reached its low point in 1937–1938, Hitler's troops were incorporating Austria and the Sudetenland into the Reich. What is more, these policies were adopted despite the fact that decision makers, from the early 1930s onward, were fully aware that Britain could not simultaneously fight two first-class wars.[162] The first sea lord himself admitted in 1939 that the contingent of five or six ships Britain could send "against a Japanese Fleet of 10 ships plus her full strength in other classes of ships is not adequate in the proper meaning of that word."[163] Why, then, did decision makers insist on maintaining a commitment to fight in the Far East when they were fully aware of the imminent dangers at home and of the inadequacy of the forces they could send against the Japanese? What motivated British elites to adopt policies that not only scattered their forces around the globe but also left the homeland exposed and woefully unprepared to deal with the German threat?

Before World War I, British elites adopted a strategy of deterrence in the core. They rearmed and sought continental allies to balance against rising threats to the metropole. In the periphery, they adopted a strategy of accommodation and withdrew from missions that they did not have the resources to uphold. Before World War II, British elites pursued a strategy of accommodation in the core. They responded to the rising German threat by explicitly deciding not to build a continental army and by shunning allies in Europe. It was only after Hitler had occupied much of central Europe that elites began to address in earnest how to prevent Germany from overrunning the Continent. In the periphery, they adopted a strategy of deterrence and clung tightly to their commitments in the Far East despite overwhelming inferiority. Planning during the pre-World War I years was characterized by clear strategic priorities and the independence of core and peripheral theaters. During the interwar period, commitments became interdependent and the distinction between core and periphery blurred; elites seemingly lost the clear sense of strategic priorities needed to drive

---

[162] See, for example, CAB 16/109, D.R.C. 16, 12 Feb. 1934.
[163] CAB 16/209, 28 Feb. 1939, "The Despatch of a Fleet to the Far East," p. 2.

forward the adjustment process. As a result, Britain chose to defend the imperial periphery despite the associated costs to metropolitan security.

The high metropolitan vulnerability of the interwar years was the key factor leading to these radical differences in grand strategy. Granted, withdrawal from the periphery was easier before World War I because the threats to imperial possessions were much less severe than during the interwar period. During the 1930s, elites had good reason to believe that reducing Britain's military presence in the overseas empire would lead to the loss of at least some colonial possessions and expose the dominions to attack. But why, unlike during the years before World War I, were British elites so unwilling to countenance imperial retrenchment and focus on home defense, especially when the constraints on defense spending were so severe and the strategic predicament in the core so dire?

Perceptions of high metropolitan vulnerability—working through both elite beliefs and strategic culture—were the main cause of the gross adjustment failure of the 1930s. British policy was initially based on a set of logical inferences that emerged from conditions of strategic deficiency. These policies persisted, however, even after the beliefs on which they were based had been discredited by incoming information. As I argue below, stress-induced psychological distortion, miscalculation, and the cognitive constraints delaying the adaptation of beliefs to new information, though they may have contributed to adjustment failure, are insufficient to explain outcomes. Strategic culture—images tightly wedding the reigning conception of British security to the integrity of the peripheral empire and the avoidance of a continental commitment—best explains the failure of elites to adjust policy to a new strategic landscape. The strategic images that elites propagated after World War I and during the 1930s to gain support for their policies had come to define the intellectual paradigms, fundamental values, and organizational interests that informed national strategy. The problem was that these images conflicted with and, in fact, overrode strategic logic. Even after the domestic political pressures constraining adjustment had dissipated, elites, for cognitive, emotional, and organizational reasons, found themselves entrapped in a strategic culture of their own making.

British strategy during the 1930s, both the focus on defense of empire and the effort to appease Nazi Germany, emerged from the effect of perceived vulnerability on strategic beliefs—that is, on inferences drawn by elites about how to deal with adversaries and set geographic priorities. As far as peripheral strategy is concerned, the strategic logic that emerged from conditions of strategic deficiency ran as follows. As mentioned above, British elites in the aftermath of World War I turned to the preservation of Britain's peripheral empire both to reaffirm the country's status as a great power and to rally domestic support for the government. In the early 1930s, Japan posed the most immediate and formidable threat to British interests either in Europe or in the periphery. Accordingly, elites justifiably focused their attention and their resources on the Far East. The problem was that available resources were severely constrained. Given the state of the British economy in the early 1930s, a full-scale rearmament program was simply not feasible.

Precisely because British elites were acutely aware of the country's military weakness, they reasoned that they had to rely on demonstrations of resolve to offset material inadequacy. They viewed the empire as standing not on British strength per se, but on external perceptions of British strength. Decision makers came to see their military forces not as a coercive instrument of policy, but as a façade needed to project the appearance of imperial power. The task for British elites was to prevent potential adversaries—whether foreign powers or nationalist movements within the empire—from seeing through this façade and finding an overextended and vulnerable network of imperial commitments. Should an adversary call Britain's bluff, the façade was likely to crumble and, with it, the empire would unravel. British thinking became infused with the notion of dominoes; even a single setback in the periphery would lead to a series of reversals that would result in the end of empire. As a result of these inferences, elites believed that Britain could not afford to appear weak in any part of the empire, for weakness would only invite attack. Imperial possessions were valued less in terms of their economic and military significance than in terms of their reputational importance. Decision makers were no longer defending specific interests; they were defending a façade of imperial strength behind which British weakness was hiding. Any development that could damage or tarnish that façade had to be prevented. This set of strategic beliefs transformed immunity to events in the periphery into hypersensitivity.

This strategic logic consisted of two distinct, yet interrelated, strands. First, elites were seeking to rely on demonstrations of resolve to deter Japan from attacking British possessions. There was general agreement that Japan would be unresponsive to conciliation and that the Japanese would view accommodation as an invitation for aggression. While elites hoped to return to "our old terms of cordiality and mutual respect with Japan" through an "ultimate policy of accommodation," it was first necessary to "show a tooth." A deterrent stance was necessary, the Defence Requirements Committee reasoned, because "Japan is more likely . . . to respect and listen to a power that can defend its interests rather than to one that is defenceless."[164] Successive proposals to withdraw from the Far East or to reduce the scope of Britain's commitment were defeated because of fear that such policies would reveal weakness to the Japanese and invite aggression.[165]

Second, elites were seeking to bolster reputation and prestige by preserving the appearance of imperial integrity and strength. Despite, or more accurately because of, awareness that Britain no longer had the material resources necessary to defend empire, elites did not want Britain's weakness to become apparent to external actors. By 1920, elites were already preoccupied with the implications of withdrawal for Britain's prestige. The General Staff responded to a proposal to reduce the size of the garrison in Mesopotamia in the following manner: "The ease with which orientals misinterpret any retrograde movement as a sign of weakness must not be forgotten. Any withdrawal *at present* would have a serious effect on the internal condition of Mesopotamia, and might well involve us in grave internal disorders." Furthermore, the appearance of weakness would not be confined to Mesopotamia itself; troop reductions "could not fail to lower our prestige in the whole of the Middle East."[166] For the most part, the General Staff recognized that areas such as Mesopotamia and Palestine were of marginal strategic significance.[167] Yet, because withdrawal would expose Britain's weakness to indigenous populations and potentially fuel nationalistic movements, it would be unsound to reduce the size of the garrisons.

This strategic logic was reinforced by the growing vulnerability of the 1930s. The façade of imperial strength was becoming increasingly fragile. Because elites were preserving the appearance of strength rather than concrete power resources, maintaining the integrity of the empire was paramount. Withdrawal from any possession would jeopardize British prestige and potentially expose the fundamental weakness of the links holding the empire together. This perspective was reflected in Britain's inability to withdraw from even minor overseas positions. Consider the debate over Hong Kong. In 1937, the C.O.S. evaluated the merits of withdrawing the garrison at Hong Kong in order to concentrate British troops in Singapore. This proposal made little headway; opponents argued that withdrawal would not only invite Japanese aggression, but would also jeopardize Britain's position

[164] CAB 16/109/1147B, 28 Feb. 1934, "Imperial Defence Policy," Part 1.
[165] See CAB 2/5, 6 April 1933, 258th Meeting of the C.I.D.; and CAB 53/4, 28 Feb. 1933, 107th Meeting of the C.O.S.
[166] CAB 24/107, C.P. 707, 20 Feb. 1920, "Possibility of Reducing the Garrison in Mesopotamia," p. 1; CAB 24/99, C.P. 1469, 12 June 1920, "The Situation in Mesopotamia," p. 4.
[167] See, for example, CAB 2/3, 174th Meeting of the C.I.D., 12 July 1923, p. 2.

and prestige everywhere. As one influential member of the C.O.S. put it, "A voluntary abandonment of important Imperial possessions would be the beginning of the end of the British Empire." The C.O.S. argued against moving the garrison for the following reasons: "The evacuation of an important fortress on the outbreak of war would itself entail a very serious loss of prestige, not only in the Far East, but throughout the world; and might influence other potentially hostile Powers to form an exaggerated idea of the weakness of our position, and to throw in their lot against us."[168]

British elites had thus become committed to defending a commitment, not to defending specific strategic positions or assets. By publicly placing their reputation at stake, decision makers only maneuvered the country into the position they were seeking to avoid: the stronger the verbal commitment, the greater the loss of prestige should Britain be forced to withdraw. Furthermore, basing policy on the defense of commitments rather than on the defense of positions of intrinsic military or economic value led to a strategic vision in which geographic regions became interdependent; reputation transcends regional boundaries. Specification of priorities became lost in a preoccupation with prestige.[169] Elite thinking was so infused with falling dominoes and concern about hiding pervasive insecurity that decision makers lost sight of strategic priorities and indiscriminately defended imperial positions.

While the effect of vulnerability on strategic logic provides a compelling explanation for why elites initially adopted a deterrent strategy in the periphery, it does not explain why they failed to adjust policy as the decade progressed. Two developments should have led to the discrediting of this strategic logic and the reorientation of peripheral strategy. First, during the second half of the 1930s, it should have become increasingly apparent that a deterrent strategy aimed at bolstering reputation was not achieving its intended effects. Japan continued to build up its military forces throughout the decade. In 1937, Japanese forces invaded China and began their efforts to destroy the Nationalist regime. Italy as well had embarked on an expansionist policy in the periphery. So too did nationalist movements continue to

---

[168] CAB 53/7, 18 May 1937, Minutes of the 207th Meeting of the C.O.S.; CAB 16/182, D.P.(P.) 5, "Situation in the Far East, 1937," p. 32.

[169] As Patrick Morgan writes, "A concern for image has no natural bounds. It may readily extend to actions other than responses to provocation. The objection to seeing commitments as interdependent is that this invites a loss of perspective and judgment; excessive defense of unimportant obligations is likely to prove debilitating." "Saving Face for the Sake of Deterrence," in *Psychology and Deterrence*, ed. Robert Jervis, Richard Ned Lebow, and Janice Gross Stein (Baltimore: Johns Hopkins University Press, 1985), p. 135.

present pressing internal threats to British possessions. In 1937, one-half of the British army was serving in the periphery to counter these threats. Deterrent strategies in the periphery were not solving Britain's strategic predicament.

Second, and more important, it should have become evident that developments in the core made it impossible for the British to continue devoting resources to the defense of the periphery. After 1935, it was no longer justifiable for elites to assume that Japan posed the most immediate and serious threats to British interests. Even if decision makers continued to believe that a deterrent posture would succeed in protecting Britain's peripheral possessions, the increasingly dire situation in the core should have forced them to abandon their preoccupation with peripheral defense. This analysis is not meant to suggest that decision makers during the second half of the 1930s should have simply withdrawn from the entire overseas empire. On the contrary, Britain was highly dependent on seaborne trade for imports of food and raw materials; war and industrial mobilization would only accentuate that dependency. But British elites surely should have recognized the need to consolidate imperial commitments and set priorities based on the need to marshal resources in the core. They should have focused primarily on protecting shipping routes in the Atlantic. A considerable portion of Britain's oil came from the Caribbean, and North America was a vital source of trade and assistance. The British were less reliant on Middle East oil, but it may well have made sense to protect the area's sea lanes and garrisons, if only to deny the Germans access to the region's oil.[170] Arguments that major portions of the empire—the Far East in particular—had to be defended because of their potential contribution of manpower and materiel to a European war are far less compelling. War-making industry in the dominions and colonies was virtually nonexistent. In addition, "dominion armies in peacetime lacked enough equipment even to train for modern warfare . . . and as a result dominion forces could only be equipped and trained on arrival in Britain or the Middle East by diversion of resources from the British army, itself desperately short of equipment and instructors."[171] In short, Britain did need to keep open key trading routes and to defend select portions of the empire. But the money spent on building up Singapore and procuring battleships to protect Britain's empire in the Far East would have been much better spent on vessels to protect

---

[170] See G. C. Peden, "The Burden of Imperial Defence and the Continental Commitment Reconsidered," *Historical Journal*, 27 (1984), 421–422.

[171] Peden, "Burden of Imperial Defence," pp. 420–421. Peden does argue that troops from the dominions could potentially have been made ready for continental operations if the war had lasted some years.

convoys in the Atlantic or to prepare the army for continental operations.[172] As mentioned above, in 1939 elites finally considered the possibility of sacrificing interests in the Far East in order to concentrate assets in the European theater. But ongoing efforts to preserve the integrity of the empire and the façade of imperial strength continued to distract British decision makers from concentrating on those elements of the imperial system that did contribute to metropolitan security.

Stress-induced psychological distortion does not provide a satisfying explanation for why elites failed to reorient peripheral strategy. Crisis conditions by no means prevailed throughout the second half of the 1930s. Stress-induced dysfunction may well have contributed to decisions taken at critical junctures—say, during Munich or just after Japan's decision to proceed with the southern advance. But successive decisions to defend the eastern empire were, for the most part, made under normal decision-making conditions. Furthermore, elites assimilated available information in a reasonable manner; there is little evidence that they distorted assessments to relieve stress. On the contrary, elites openly discussed both the unfavorable balance in the Far East and the implications of defending the eastern empire for Britain's force posture in the Mediterranean and on the Continent. It was precisely because they confronted their predicament head-on that they considered in 1939 the possibility of sacrificing the Far East to concentrate assets in the European theater. Elites did not defend empire because they distorted information and convinced themselves that the task would be an easy one.

The problem was also not one of miscalculation. Elites were not caught off-guard by peripheral adversaries that suddenly attacked unprepared British positions. By the late 1930s, the empire faced precisely those threats that had caused concern within the elite community for much of the decade. Overextension was not the product of events that elites could have reasonably failed to foresee.

Nor does the time lag involved in adapting beliefs to incoming information solve the puzzle. If successive Japanese, Italian, and German challenges to the status quo before September 1939 did not undermine elite confidence in the ability of demonstrations of resolve to deter war, then the outbreak of war in Europe and, eventually, in the Pacific, certainly did so. War in Europe also made it amply clear that the most pressing threats to British interests were not in the periphery. Nevertheless, decision makers upheld their commitment to defend the east-

[172] On the protection of shipping lanes, see Gibbs, *Grand Strategy: Rearmament Policy,* pp. 433–434.

ern empire. Despite the precarious military situation in Europe and the overwhelming imbalance in the Far East, Britain sent two battleships to confront the Japanese, only to have them sunk by the enemy as soon as they arrived. This behavior cannot be explained as the product of beliefs that persevered too long in the face of discrepant information.

Focusing on elite beliefs thus provides only the first piece of the puzzle. The logic that emerged from conditions of strategic deficiency explains why elites initially blurred strategic priorities and adopted a deterrent strategy in the periphery, but it does not explain why they persisted in defending remote regions of the empire as long as they did. Psychological dysfunction, miscalculation, and cognitive lags may well have played some role in contributing to adjustment failure, but they are insufficient to explain outcomes. As I argue shortly, strategic culture provides the second piece of the puzzle.

The effect of high vulnerability on strategic beliefs also explains the evolution of British strategy in the core during the 1930s. Elite behavior was based on a set of logical inferences that emerged from conditions of strategic deficiency. Given the lessons drawn from World War I and the strategic landscape that emerged during the 1920s, appeasement made sense in three important respects. First, until the Nazis came to power, there was every good reason to assume that Germany was a status quo power that should be accorded the same rights as other European countries. Weimar Germany showed few signs of a return to international aggression. British elites had also come to believe that the terms of the Versailles Treaty were too harsh and that Germany should be reintegrated, in both political and economic terms, into a concert of European powers. Continued punishment of Germany might fuel grievances that could threaten the peace and potentially entail new continental commitments, while reintegration and accommodation would foster a community of like-minded nations.[173]

Second, as the analysis above showed, British elites were well aware that the scope of their international commitments far outstripped available resources. It was therefore necessary to use diplomacy to remove at least some of Britain's potential enemies.[174] During the 1920s and early 1930s, it made good sense to focus attempts at accommodation on Germany as opposed to on other powers. Japan in Manchuria and Italy in Abyssinia demonstrated their capacity for aggression earlier than did Germany. The most likely threats to British interests thus lay

[173] See Gilbert, *Roots of Appeasement*, pp. 64–71.
[174] Paul Kennedy, "The Tradition of Appeasement in British Foreign Policy, 1865–1939," in *Strategy and Diplomacy, 1870–1945*, ed. Paul Kennedy (London: Allen and Unwin, 1983), p. 18.

in the periphery, not in Europe. Japanese expansion in the Far East also meant that the dominions were pressing London to help with defense in the periphery as well as to avoid entanglement in European affairs.[175] In addition, given the fact that elites adopted a strategy of deterrence in large part to demonstrate resolve and enhance reputation and prestige, the risks associated with a deterrent posture were far lower in the periphery than in the core. If British strategy succeeded in provoking, rather than deterring, Japan, Britain stood to lose Singapore and the eastern empire. The potential results of provoking Germany were far more serious: the bombing of central London, if not the invasion of the United Kingdom.

Third, economic recovery *was* essential to building up military strength in the long term. Rapid rearmament in the early 1930s would have placed a huge strain on civilian industries and jeopardized financial stability. And it was not until the second half of the decade that Germany began to rearm in earnest and to pose a credible threat to Europe's other major powers. It therefore made sense—at least until 1935—to forgo reequipping the B.E.F. and to sacrifice short-term military strength for long-term economic strength. If and when war with Germany appeared to be unavoidable, Britain could then undertake full-scale rearmament and draw on a much more robust economic base. Economic strength was particularly important, elites reasoned, because war, if it broke out, was likely to be long in duration. For the time being, Britain simply did not have the resources to keep pace with German rearmament and therefore had to accommodate Germany in order to avoid war.

Although these suppositions were justifiable and grounded in reality during the early 1930s, they grew increasingly obsolete as the decade progressed. The signals that should have led to a dramatic reorientation of policy could hardly have been clearer. Within weeks of Hitler's election as chancellor in 1933, the domestic situation took a turn for the worse: Hitler was granted full dictatorial powers by the Reichstag; he repeatedly denigrated international agreements and scoffed at the need for international understanding; communists, trade unionists, and Jews were arrested and beaten. These developments were reported with alarm in the British press.[176] In 1934–1935, Germany embarked on an ambitious rearmament program; land, sea, and air forces expanded at an impressive rate. Germany's reoccupation of the Rhineland in 1936 was the first in a succession of aggressive acts: the Ansch-

---

[175] On the role of the dominions in supporting appeasement, see Gilbert, *Roots of Appeasement*, pp. 180–181; and Rock, *British Appeasement in the 1930s*, p. 48.
[176] Gilbert, *Roots of Appeasement*, pp. 138–139.

luss in March 1938, the annexation of the Sudetenland the following September, the invasion of Czechoslovakia in March 1939, and the invasion of Poland the following September.

Appeasement was not abandoned nor the B.E.F. reequiped until the spring of 1939, yet German behavior should have led to a far earlier reorientation of strategy. The developments of 1933 themselves warranted a reevaluation of whether it made sense to accommodate Germany. As Austen Chamberlain noted in debate in the House of Commons soon after Hitler came to power, "Germany is afflicted by this narrow, exclusive, aggressive spirit, by which it is a crime to be in favour of peace and a crime to be a Jew. This is not a Germany to which we can afford to make concessions." The Foreign Office expressed similar concerns: "Whereas up till a year ago the difficulty in the way of world appeasement might . . . be declared to be the attitude of France, who seemed determined to maintain her military and political predominance in Europe, the difficulty is now uncontestably the threatening and provocative attitude of Germany."[177] This view was only confirmed by assessments of German rearmament. Under the terms of the Versailles Treaty, the German army was limited to 100,000 men in not more than seven infantry divisions and three cavalry divisions. In late 1934, intelligence reports indicated that the German army had grown to some 300,000 men in twenty-one infantry divisions and three cavalry divisions.[178] If domestic political developments, rearmament, and the unilateral reoccupation of the Rhineland were not enough to convince British elites that appeasement was not working, the annexation of Austria should certainly have done so. As William Rock notes, "The shock of the Anschluss . . . might reasonably have prompted a serious re-appraisal of both policy and strategy. It did not." He continues, "The upshot was no important change in the tempo of defence preparation and an undiminished reliance on diplomacy to protect the nation."[179] Given available information, British elites, by the spring of 1938 at the very latest, should have realized that accommodation was not satisfying Germany's appetite for expansion and that they therefore had to abandon appeasement.

So too did German behavior undercut the second supposition on which appeasement was based: that developments in Europe posed the least likely threats to British interests. During the second half of the 1930s, Britain's strategic predicament indeed worsened considerably as

---

[177] Chamberlain cited in Gilbert, *Roots of Appeasement*, p. 139; Foreign Office memorandum quoted in Gibbs, *Grand Strategy: Rearmament Policy*, p. 74.
[178] Gibbs, *Grand Strategy: Rearmament Policy*, p. 136.
[179] Rock, *British Appeasement in the 1930s*, pp. 6, 8.

the British faced increasingly powerful adversaries in each of three main theaters. The need to use diplomacy to eliminate enemies was more pressing than ever. But, after 1935, British elites could no longer claim that defense of the empire should remain the top priority. On the contrary, German behavior provided more than enough reason for elites to conclude that peripheral commitments had to be radically reduced in order to defend the empire at its heart. From the mid-1930s onward, defense of the British Isles, not imperial security, should have been the top priority.

Finally, the scope and pace of Germany's military buildup and its willingness to use force to challenge the status quo meant that by early 1938, at the latest, British elites could no longer justify delaying rearmament in order to buy time to strengthen the country's economic base. British decision makers were indeed correct in viewing economic strength and financial stability as central to preparing the country for war. Furthermore, throughout the 1930s, elites were uncertain as to whether the United States would involve itself in a European conflict, and thus could not count on massive U.S. aid should the costs of rearmament lead to economic chaos. Nevertheless, at some point during the second half of the 1930s—a point that could only have been determined by judgment—defense preparations should have taken precedence over economic and financial considerations because of the severity of the threat to the metropole. British elites calculated that that point had not been reached until the spring of 1939. Given developments on the Continent and the state of the metropolitan army, however, it is difficult to fathom why they did not decide considerably earlier that more severe economic sacrifices were both warranted and necessary. Appeasement had succeeded in buying time for the British to improve their economy, but they should have begun far sooner to translate economic capability into military power.

Furthermore, it is puzzling, to say the least, that British elites saw the choice as one of all or nothing: either no continental army or conscription and a fifty-division force that did, in fact, lead the country toward bankruptcy. Why, after 1936, did decision makers not build a ten-division force capable of rapid deployment to the Continent? Such a force would have strengthened Britain's diplomatic hand and provided an insurance policy should war have broken out. And ten divisions would not have undermined the economy. There may well have been a ceiling above which further expenditure on defense would have jeopardized the stability of the domestic economy, but that ceiling was far from being reached. As Gibbs comments, "With a different economic philosophy, not 'business as usual' but 'business for war,' no doubt much more could have been done."[180] These points give much credence to the claim that financial considerations alone do not provide a compelling explanation for the absence of timely preparations for war.

This line of argument is strengthened by the fact that, from 1936 onward, voices within the British government warned against the dangers of failing to equip in a timely fashion an expeditionary force for continental operations. In 1936, after the reoccupation of the Rhineland, secretary of state for war, Duff Cooper, warned that the size of the Wehrmacht and the increased mechanization of warfare meant that "we cannot rely on having time [after the outbreak of war] as we had in the last war to build up and equip an army. Our regular forces are considerably smaller and at present far less adequately equipped, if modern developments are taken into account, than they were in 1914." British officials also appreciated that the imbalance of forces on the Continent called into question the prevailing assumption of a long war and expressed concern that the French front "can only be expected to hold for a limited period, and that in the least favourable contingency it may hold for a short time only."[181] Following Germany's incorporation of Austrian forces into the Wehrmacht, the Chiefs of Staff reported that the military balance virtually precluded the option of going to war. General Ironside commented that "the paper on our rearmament . . . is truly the most appalling reading. How we can have come to this state is beyond believing. . . . No foreign nation would believe it."[182] Far from enabling Britain to improve the military balance, appeasement and the delay in rearmament were only allowing Germany to increase its superiority. That not even German annexation of the Sudetenland triggered full-scale rearmament clearly "refuted the theory . . . that appeasement was a policy devised to gain time for rearmament."[183]

In short, from 1936 onward, incoming information that grew increasingly unambiguous challenged the basic suppositions that informed the adoption of a policy of appeasement in the core. That British elites did not alter this policy until the spring of 1939 raises two crucial questions. First, why did it take so long for the cabinet to abandon appeasement? In 1935 and 1936, accommodating Hitler and assuming that a continental commitment could be avoided may have been justifiable. But given the pace of German rearmament and the steady advance of German troops from the initial remilitarization of the

---

[180] Gibbs, *Grand Strategy: Rearmament Policy*, p. 317.
[181] Cooper cited in Fuchser, *Chamberlain and Appeasement*, p. 65; Lord Halifax cited in Gibbs, *Grand Strategy: Rearmament Policy*, p. 501.
[182] Ironside cited in Rock, *British Appeasement in the 1930s*, p. 46.
[183] Rock, *British Appeasement in the 1930s*, pp. 89–90.

Rhineland to the invasion of Czechoslovakia, the cabinet's willingness to accommodate Hitler's demands until after the invasion of Czechoslovakia in 1939 is striking. Between 1936 and 1939, it was simply unreasonable for elites to believe that accommodation was the best strategy for stopping German aggression. Second, even if it did make sense to appease Germany, why did Britain not simultaneously prepare for the possibility that appeasement might fail? Accommodating German demands by no means precluded building up the B.E.F. and preparing for continental war. Again, between 1936 and 1939, it was simply unreasonable for elites to believe that the likelihood of war in Europe was so low that preparations for continental operations were unnecessary.[184]

Stress-induced psychological distortion, miscalculation, and the cognitive tendency for beliefs to persevere in the face of discrepant information do not provide adequate answers to these questions. Crisis conditions did not prevail throughout the second half of the 1930s; stress-induced biases could not have been driving elite behavior. Furthermore, there is little evidence that elites distorted incoming information in order to relieve anxiety. They were well aware of the imbalance on the Continent and the importance of defending the low countries. They openly discussed the eroding strategic environment and did not engage in obfuscation intended to minimize the severity of their predicament. Isolated episodes of psychological distortion may have occurred, especially at the time of Munich and the invasion of Czechoslovakia. But the general problem was not one of assimilating incoming information, but one of deciding how to act on that information.

Miscalculation also does not provide a satisfying account of outcomes. The change in German foreign policy that followed Hitler's rise to power was by no means sudden. From the mid-1930s onward, British elites were well aware of the threat that Germany posed to British security. Decision makers repeatedly alluded to the possibility of facing the precise array of threats that they eventually confronted in 1939. Elites simply did not fall prey to events that they reasonably could have failed to foresee.

Attributing adjustment failure to the cognitive constraints delaying the adaptation of beliefs to new information is unsatisfying because incoming information not only should have disconfirmed prevailing beliefs, but in fact did do so. By 1938, British elites openly admitted that

---

[184] Recall that elites did not deny that German occupation of Western Europe would threaten the security of the metropole. They were simply relying on the assumption that Germany would not attack France or the low countries.

appeasement was failing to achieve its objectives and that the initial ratio-
nales for accommodating Germany were no longer operative. After the
Anschluss, the military chiefs informed the cabinet that virtually nothing could be done to prevent Germany from overrunning Czechoslovakia.[185] Successive intelligence estimates indicated that "Britain could
not face war under any circumstances."[186] As Gibbs concisely notes,
"Britain's inability to act was largely a result of her own weakness."[187]
In September, during debate over how to respond to Hitler's demands
for the Sudetenland, the Joint Planning Committee of the C.O.S. issued
the following stern warning: "To attempt to take offensive action
against Germany until we have had time to bring our military, naval,
and air forces, and also our passive defense services onto a war footing
would be to place ourselves in the position of a man who tries to show
how brave he is by twisting the tail of a tiger which is preparing to
spring before he has loaded his gun." When the Germans invaded
Czechoslovakia, the C.O.S. offered a similarly gloomy assessment: "We
can do nothing to prevent the dog getting the bone, and we have no
means of making him give it up, except by killing him by a slow process
of attrition and starvation."[188] Even Chamberlain recognized the country's military weakness and the associated constraints on Britain's options. After the Anschluss, he wrote, "You have only to look at the
map to see that nothing France or we could do could possibly save
Czechoslovakia from being overrun by the Germans, if they wanted to
do it. . . . I have, therefore, abandoned any idea of giving a guarantee
to Czechoslovakia." In August, Chamberlain pressed the cabinet to
forgo issuing a formal warning to Germany against further agression,
arguing that "no state . . . certainly no democratic state ought to make
a threat of war unless it was both ready to carry it out and prepared
to do so."[189]

In sum, by 1938, many British decision makers had come to realize
that it was a dangerous illusion to assume that Britain could avoid or
delay war through accommodation and thereby gain time to build up
its financial reserves and industrial infrastructure. They found them-

[185] Fuchser, *Chamberlain and Appeasement*, p. 117.

[186] Murray, *European Balance of Power*, p. 210. For further discussion of intelligence estimates during this period, see Robert Beck, "Munich's Lessons Reconsidered," *International Security*, 14 (Fall 1989), 182–187. Interestingly, historians agree that British
assessments were excessively pessimistic. See ibid.

[187] Gibbs, *Grand Strategy: Rearmament Policy*, p. 314.

[188] CAB 53/13, J.P. 315, 23 Sept. 1938, "The Czechoslovak Crisis," cited in Murray,
European Balance of Power, p. 209; CAB 16/183A, 28 March 1938, "Military Implications of
German Aggression against Czechoslovakia," p. 9.

[189] Chamberlain quoted in Rock, *Appeasement on Trial*, p. 63; Chamberlain quoted in
Fuchser, *Chamberlain and Appeasement*, p. 136.

selves avoiding war because a desperate military imbalance left no other choice, not because of a strategy carefully constructed to keep German troops within their borders or to prepare the country for a long war at some point in the future. Elites came to appreciate that the causal suppositions that gave rise to a policy of appeasement had been discredited and that the country was falling prey to strategic exposure. Cognitive mechanisms no doubt delayed the adaptation of beliefs to incoming information, but by 1938, elites were well aware that events had made obsolete the logic of appeasement.

My argument is that strategic culture—images and conceptions of empire deeply embedded in the public mind and the elite community—best explains the absence of strategic adjustment in both the periphery and the core. Elite beliefs alone provide a compelling explanation for why British elites initially adopted a policy of indiscriminate defense in the periphery and one of appeasement in the core. But for the reasons spelled out above, psychological distortion, miscalculation, and the time lag involved in adapting beliefs to a new strategic landscape do not provide a satisfying explanation of outcomes.

As far as the effects of strategic culture on peripheral strategy are concerned, World War I and elite lobbying during the interwar years had tightly wedded the reigning conception of British security to the integrity of the empire. More than ever before, Britain *was* empire. As they had in World War I, troops from the colonies and dominions would likely come to Britain's aid should war with Germany again break out. But this deep attachment to empire was based less on a reevaluation of the economic and strategic value of the periphery than on more visceral forces. This was an emotional tie to empire, an outlook rooted in an image-based notion of security: because of the economic and military decline of the metropole, Britain's self-image as a great power was wholly dependent on its imperial reach. Britain's well-being had become inseparable from the empire's well-being. In the minds of top decision makers, according to Howard, "the need to defend Britain's Eastern Empire bulked at least as large as the need to redress the balance of force in Europe, and at times . . . very much larger."[190] The bureaucracy, the army, and the navy defined their roles and missions accordingly. This conception of security was not confined to the elite community; decision makers had propagated it among the public at the close of the war in order to use external success as an instrument of domestic politics. Elites continued to champion empire through much of the 1930s, in large part because a domestic polity that equated national security with imperial integrity would be

---

[190] Howard, *Continental Commitment*, p. 100.

supportive of the ambitious policies that elites were pursuing in the periphery. Elite beliefs about the importance of demonstrating resolve and preserving prestige and a strategic culture wedded to overseas empire were running on parallel tracks.

The problem during the second half of the 1930s was that elites were confronted with the need to adopt policies that ran contrary to the images that they had been propagating since the end of World War I. To retrench from the periphery was to challenge the notion of imperial integrity that had become so firmly embedded in strategic culture: it was to threaten the very essence of the conception of security that had taken root among the public and within the elite community during the interwar years. The equation of British security with imperial security shaped public attitudes, the intellectual paradigms and values of individual decision makers, and the orientations and objectives of elite institutions. In Charles Bright's words, "The empire was still at the core of Britain's political culture in the 1930s, part of the existing order of things."[191] As I argue below, domestic political pressures did contribute to adjustment failure. But the most important constraint was the set of strategic conceptions prevailing among decision makers themselves. For top elites, the idea that events in the periphery were immaterial to Britain's primary security interests had become, as it were, unthinkable. As members of the Chiefs of Staff Sub-Committee repeatedly stressed in debating whether to defend positions in the Far East, "It was impossible to consider giving up Hong Kong . . . it was unthinkable to abandon the base entirely."[192] The cause of adjustment failure in the periphery was not elite beliefs that lasted too long, but institutionalized strategic images that tied reigning conceptions of Britain's security and well-being to imperial integrity and overrode incoming information indicating that elites needed to sacrifice imperial interests to defend the metropole. That British elites continued to invest in the protection of peripheral interests even after the outbreak of World War II suggests that not even war itself could recast a strategic culture deeply wedded to empire.

As far as strategy in the core is concerned, the experience of World War I and elite reliance on the notion of "never again" to regain the confidence of the electorate meant that aversion to a continental commitment had become embedded in strategic culture. British decision makers reverted to the same assumption that they had held before 1904: metropolitan security could best be ensured by avoiding entanglements in continental rivalries. But like the attachment to peripheral

---

[191] Bright, "Class Interest," p. 237.
[192] Deverell and Chatfield cited in CAB 53/8, COS/217, 11 Oct. 1937.

empire, such aversion to a continental commitment was not based on hard-headed strategic assessments of the potential costs associated with a continental commitment. This was an image-based conception of security: "War . . . had emerged in the British mind as the ultimate evil."[193] This was also a question of national self-image. Among elites and the public alike, Britain's strength and future lay in its overseas empire; to avoid involvement in Europe's rivalries was the best way to ensure the health and well-being of the homeland as well as of the imperial periphery. As Howard writes, "The cabinets which governed Britain in the 1930s were composed of men who believed that almost no price was too high to pay to avoid another war."[194] Although this was an outlook rooted in the experience of World War I, elites continued to propagate it through most of the 1930s in order to justify and rally support for appeasement. The avoidance of a continental commitment became integral to how the elite community defined British security.

In the core, as in the periphery, elites eventually found themselves entrapped in the strategic images that they had propagated to gain support for their policies. An image-based notion of security overrode clear and repeated indications that the security of the metropole depended on making a continental commitment and building an army capable of contributing to the defense of the low countries and France. Even after public opposition to rearmament had waned, elites could not overcome their deep-seated resistance to building a continental army. Those responsible for shaping policy as well as historians of the period have noted the extent to which avoidance of a continental commitment was based more on emotion and instinct than on hard-headed strategic assessment. Chamberlain himself admitted that "opinions will, no doubt, differ as to whether or not this almost *instinctive aversion* from large-scale military preparations corresponds with a sound perception of the principles upon which our foreign policy should be founded."[195] Even after the invasion of Czechoslovakia, it appears that Chamberlain was still unwilling to prepare the army for war against Germany. As Murray notes, "at heart, Chamberlain refused to acknowledge the inevitability of war with Germany."[196] Gibbs agrees that "the desperate unpreparedness of the Army . . . was just

[193] Rock, *British Appeasement in the 1930s*, p. 41.

[194] Howard, *Continental Commitment*, p. 99.

[195] Chamberlain cited in Gibbs, *Grand Strategy: Rearmament Policy*, p. 447. Emphasis added.

[196] Murray, *European Balance of Power*, p. 283. For further evidence of Chamberlain's refusal to accept that Britain might have to go to war to stop German aggression, see Fuchser, *Chamberlain and Appeasement*, pp. 167 ff.; and Gilbert, *Roots of Appeasement*, p. xii.

as much the result of a general reluctance to face again the horrors of trench warfare as to find the money for an army equipped and of a size to fight a major continental campaign."[197] The never-again syndrome is central to understanding the reluctance of British decision makers to approve the reequipment of the B.E.F. and prepare for its deployment on the Continent.

The picture that emerges is one in which a deep-seated aversion to a continental commitment played a key role in preventing elites from undertaking a much-needed reorientation of policy. By the time of the Anschluss, elites had clearly begun to realize that appeasement was not achieving its intended effects. Yet incoming information had to discredit not just the logic on which appeasement had initially been based, but also a strategic culture in which British security was defined in terms of imperial security and the avoidance of a continental commitment. It was for this reason that British elites, by the time of Munich, found themselves supporting appeasement not because they had good reason to believe that it would quench Germany's thirst for expansion or buy time for improving the military balance, but because military weakness precluded the option of standing firm and risking war.

At Munich, Chamberlain may well have been justified in abandoning Czechoslovakia, given the fact that Britain was totally unprepared for war. The key question is not why Chamberlain acquiesced to Hitler's demands, but why British elites allowed themselves to end up in a position in which the absence of a continental army left them with so few options. The answer is that despite increasingly clear indications that appeasement was neither constraining German expansion nor allowing Britain to improve the military balance, strategic culture prevented elites from adjusting policy. For nearly two decades, elites had based grand strategy on the assumption that Britain would never again become involved in a land war on the continent. Through their communications to the public and their directives to the bureaucracy, elites fueled political and organizational resistance to establishing a continental army, factors to which I soon turn. But they also established the avoidance of a continental commitment as an integral component of how the decision-making community defined British security. The problem was that elites found themselves entrapped in the strategic images that they had earlier propagated to gain support for their policies. Strategic culture, through cognitive and emotional mechanisms, caused decision makers to cling stubbornly to an outmoded and self-defeating grand strategy.

It took the invasion of Czechoslovakia to dislodge the strategic im-

---

[197] Gibbs, *Grand Strategy: Rearmament Policy*, pp. 318–319.

ages deeply entrenched within the elite community and to shock decision makers into facing strategic realities. Germany had added Austrian and Czechoslovakian capabilities to its military machine. The vulnerability of the homeland had become so glaring that the cabinet was in revolt and the British public was clamoring for immediate efforts to deal with a strategically exposed metropole. British elites had no choice but to confront the fundamental flaws in grand strategy. Chamberlain reluctantly acquiesced to a continental commitment and began to reequip the B.E.F.

In sum, Britain's approach to both the periphery and the core was shaped more by deeply embedded strategic images that elites had propagated during the interwar period than by a rational assessment of incoming information. These images served as organizing principles for the decision-making community and came to define how elites conceived of British security. From the mid-1930s onward, information readily available to elites should have provided two unambiguous messages: that peripheral commitments needed to be substantially reduced and that Britain had to begin preparing for a potential land war against Germany. Indeed, elites came to appreciate that the strategic logic that initially led to strategies of deterrence in the periphery and accommodation in the core had become outmoded. Nevertheless, incoming information was persistently overridden by a strategic culture infused with images of imperial integrity and with the never-again syndrome. At no point in its history was Britain more in need of radical measures to reduce its imperial commitments and focus on metropolitan security. Yet it was precisely this need and the vulnerability associated with it that led to a set of strategic assumptions remarkably resistant to change, assumptions that prevented elites from taking the necessary steps of abandoning peripheral commitments and defending the core. Only after being confronted with overwhelming contradictory evidence did British elites act on the realization that preparations for continental war were necessary. And even after this realization and the outbreak of war, British elites continued to commit resources to the defense of the periphery, demonstrating the depth of their cognitive and emotional commitment to the preservation of empire.

This interpretation, while it specifies a causal mechanism that has not been identified by other students of Britain's interwar strategy, is indeed consistent with previous historical treatments of the period. Rock agrees that the failure of elites to respond earlier to "overpowering evidence . . . that appeasement simply was not accomplishing its purpose . . . is difficult to fathom and impossible to defend." He also notes: "This was largely a matter of deficient judgement, not of sinister intentions, on the part of responsible leaders, a failure to adjust ideas born of one period to the changing circumstances and requirements of another." The problem was not that information was inadequate or erroneous, but that appeasement had become "a passion prompting its devotees to ignore any evidence which did not suit their purpose." As Britain grew more vulnerable and appeasement increasingly untenable, elites clung ever more tightly to their outmoded strategic assumptions and "imperceptibly converted their tentative hopes to pious convictions, thereby succumbing to self-deception."[198] Gilbert agrees that appeasement in the late 1930s was a policy "dictated by fear and weakness." "Munich," he writes, "was not appeasement's finest hour, but its most perverted."[199]

That British policy was being shaped by strategic conceptions deeply embedded within the elite community—and therefore very resistant to change—was also demonstrated by the extent to which the planning community ended up crafting military assessments to conform to existing strategic notions, rather than adapting strategy to incoming information. Instead of deriving force levels from mission requirements, the military services engaged in deliberate alteration of the measures of military sufficiency to enable them to sustain missions for which they did not have adequate resources. This manipulation of the assessment process was not the result of stress-induced psychological distortion. Alteration of the standards of sufficiency occurred at sporadic intervals throughout the second half of the 1930s, not in the midst of crises. The changes made in planning assumptions were intended not to reduce psychic discomfort, but to enable the planning community to produce coherent plans for upholding strategic commitments for which the military establishment did not have sufficient resources.

For example, planners during the 1930s began to set requirements under assumptions of force fungibility; that is, they assumed that forces structured to deal with European contingencies were interchangeable with those needed to deal with the defense of India.[200] Given the different geographic conditions and the need for mechanized and armored divisions to counter the growing number of German tanks, it made little sense for planners to assume that a B.E.F. structured to fight on the Continent would be of much use in the mountains of Afghanistan. Furthermore, influential members of the General Staff admitted in the C.I.D. that an expeditionary force structured to fight in India would *not* be suitable to fight on the Continent.[201]

---

[198] Rock, *British Appeasement in the 1930s*, pp. 88, 87, 89, 95.
[199] Gilbert, *Roots of Appeasement*, pp. 187, 186.
[200] See, for example, CAB 16/109/1147B, "Imperial Defence Policy," p. 11.
[201] See, for example, the statement of Sir Edward Montgomery-Massingberd in CAB 2/6, 9 Nov. 1933, Minutes of the 261st Meeting of the C.I.D.

In fact, during 1937 and 1938, one of the reasons for restricting the army to colonial missions was to save the money that would have otherwise been spent on buying the armor and equipment needed for continental operations. Leslie Hore-Belisha, the secretary of state for war, in reaffirming in 1938 that the sole role of the army's expeditionary units was in colonial defense, noted that "their equipment and war reserves will not be on the Continental scale."[202] Planning on the basis of force fungibility, although not justified because of the different force structures needed to fulfill different missions, did allow the army to continue to uphold at least rhetorically commitments for which it did not have sufficient resources.

The standards of sufficiency used to set force requirements were also molded by elites to fit available resources, rather than the military resources adjusted to meet predetermined measures of sufficiency. When elites recognized that the navy would be unable to maintain the Two-Power Standard in the Far East, for example, they posited in 1921 that the Far Eastern fleet should be equal in strength to the Japanese fleet plus an additional buffer to offset Britain's geographic disadvantage.[203] By 1936, it was no longer possible to meet this standard; henceforth, Britain would maintain a fleet "fully adequate to act on the defensive and to serve as a strong deterrent against any threat."[204] By 1939, even this standard had become unrealistic. The new standard of sufficiency was set at that level of naval power adequate to keep open the sea lanes of communication in the Indian Ocean.[205] This successive scaling down of measures of sufficiency meant that there was no conceptual guidance as to strategic objectives. The Admiralty remarked, "So long as our ultimate naval strength remains undecided *in principle*, it is difficult to prepare war plans or to consider general strategic dispositions. Such uncertainty prevents the Admiralty from being able to guarantee the navy's ability to implement our foreign policy."[206] Rather than facing the fact that Britain did not have sufficient resources to defend its interests in the Far East, elites altered standards of sufficiency to enable them to uphold a commitment that they could not countenance abandoning.

The Admiralty also introduced unusual planning assumptions to allow the navy to meet established standards of sufficiency, however transient those standards might be. During the late 1930s, given the

---

[202] Hore-Belisha cited in Gibbs, *Grand Strategy: Rearmament Policy*, pp. 476, 512. See also Peden, "Burden of Imperial Defence," p. 411.

[203] CAB 4/7/277B, 5 Oct. 1921, "The Washington Conference," p. 5.

[204] CAB 16/112, D.P.R. 9, 6 Feb. 1936, "Defence Requirements," p. 2.

[205] CAB 16/209, 28 Feb. 1939, "The Despatch of a Fleet to the Far East," p. 2.

[206] CAB 16/182, 29 April 1937, "A New Standard of Naval Strength," p. 4.

need to keep most of the battlefleet near home waters, the Admiralty acknowledged that the Japanese would enjoy marked numerical superiority in the Pacific. The Admiralty posited, however, that the Japanese navy was only 80 percent as efficient as the British navy, and argued that qualitative superiority would offset this numerical inferiority. This assumption was seemingly made without any empirical foundation whatsoever. Given the performance of the Japanese navy against the Russian navy in 1904–1905 and the pace of its building and training program in the 1930s, there was little, if any, reason for disparaging the quality of Japan's naval forces.[207] The Admiralty also argued that the British navy would be able to defend Singapore because Britain's land-based aircraft would offset its naval inferiority. There seems to have been no consideration, however, of the implications of Japanese carrier-based aircraft for the vulnerability of either British airfields or battleships. It is difficult to imagine why British aircraft were to be a decisive factor in the battle while Japanese aircraft would be of no importance. James Neidpath politely comments on the potential source of this inconsistency: "Perhaps . . . anxious to produce some cogent theory of how a numerically inferior Eastern Fleet might succeed, the Chiefs of Staff did not probe too deeply into this question."[208]

The reaction of British elites to the Italo-Abyssinian Crisis in 1935 revealed a similar tendency to bend assessments to fit existing policies. After 1935, it was readily apparent—and recognized as such—that Italy had to be considered a hostile power in the Mediterranean and that the communication lines to the Far East were therefore in jeopardy.[209] In its 1936 review of defense requirements, however, the C.I.D. Sub-Committee on Defence Policy and Requirements made the following illogical recommendation: "In connection with our communications to the Far East . . . our defence requirements are so serious that it would not be possible within the three-year period with which this Report mainly deals, to make provision for the case of a hostile Italy; we feel that the view that it is not urgently necessary nor feasible to make provision for a permanently hostile Italy should be endorsed."[210] Planners chose to ignore this contingency because they knew that a hostile Italy would jeopardize plans to send a fleet to the Far East and cast further doubt on the viability of Britain's commitment to defend the eastern empire. In the words of Gibbs, elites calculated that it was

---

[207] Neidpath, *Singapore Naval Base*, pp. 141–142, 146–147.
[208] Ibid., p. 147.
[209] See, for example, CAB 55/2, 16 June 1936, Minutes of the 101st Meeting of the Joint Planning Committee. Elites actually considered sending British forces to intervene in the crisis.
[210] CAB 16/112, p. 2.

"materially impossible" to cope with a hostile Italy and then acted on the assumption that "what was not practicable was not necessary."[211] The images linking British security to the defense of the eastern empire were so deeply embedded and resistant to change that elites, rather than adapting policy to fit a changing strategic landscape, repeatedly altered planning assumptions to make assessments conform to existing strategic commitments.

My central argument is that high metropolitan vulnerability—acting through both strategic beliefs and strategic culture—played a key role in shaping the set of reigning assumptions that proved to be so resistant to change. Extremist policies were initially a rational response to conditions of strategic deficiency. But the strategic images propagated by elites to justify and gain support for their policies proved to constrain the adjustment of strategy when it became so needed during the second half of the 1930s. Imperial integrity and the avoidance of a continental commitment had become so integral to how elites defined British security that incoming information could not alter preexisting strategic notions and conceptions. As a result, an increasingly dire strategic imbalance in the core led only to paralysis and illusion, not to the ready adaptation of policy. Decision makers undertook a much-needed reorientation of strategy in 1939, but only after being confronted with overwhelming evidence that the course they had been pursuing was fundamentally flawed.

Domestic Considerations

Because elites during the interwar years propagated powerful strategic images among the populace to garner domestic support, it makes sense that domestic political pressures would play a role in constraining strategic adjustment. Indeed, private economic interests, public opinion, and the organizational interests of the military all contributed to the adjustment failure of the 1930s. The following evidence demonstrates, however, that each of these domestic forces had an indirect and ancillary effect on policy choice. Investment patterns, public attitudes, and the orientation of the military mirrored the images propagated by elites; they were reflective of the strategic culture that took shape during the interwar period. But the key variable constraining adjustment was the set of strategic assumptions that had taken root among decision makers, not the discrete political pressures brought to bear by the public or powerful interest groups.

---

[211] Gibbs, *Grand Strategy: Rearmament Policy*, p. 386.

Private Economic Interests. Economic interest groups resisted two key components of strategic adjustment: withdrawal from overseas possessions and the adoption of a continental commitment. Individuals and firms that traded with and invested in the formal empire were justifiably concerned that retrenchment would jeopardize their economic interests. During the 1930s, they consistently lobbied for the maintenance of Britain's military presence in the Far East and against rapprochement with Japan.[212] Their protestations did not go unnoticed. There was concern in the cabinet, for example, that businesses with trading or financial interests in China would react with "great agitation" to a reduction of garrisons in the Far East.[213]

Some sectors of the economic elite were also opposed to a continental commitment. As mentioned above, the British economy had shifted its focus from manufacturing to financial services. Britain's position as premier financier in Europe depended on good relations with European powers; appeasement was preferable to an arms race and the reemergence of Anglo-German antagonism. Paradoxically, many industrialists were also reluctant to see the country undertake full-scale rearmament and reequip the B.E.F. for continental operations. British industry was focused on the production of consumer goods; conversion to the production of munitions involved a costly modification of physical plant. In addition, there was a dearth of skilled labor, and firms were reluctant to invest in training a new labor force that was likely to be conscripted as soon as war began.[214] Financiers and industrialists also shared the Treasury's concern that rapid rearmament would lead to financial instability and therefore jeopardize economic recovery.

Although these considerations indicate that private economic interests did play a role in shaping policy, the evidence suggests that they were not crucial in constraining the adjustment process. Governmental debate about defense policy in the periphery was dominated by concern about imperial integrity and the preservation of prestige. References to the protection of private economic interests were extremely rare. Lobbying appears only to have provided impetus to a set of policies being pursued for other reasons. It is also the case that the heyday of British investment in the imperial periphery was long past. By the turn of the century, return on investments in the empire had already

---

[212] Bright, "Class Interest," pp. 235–237.

[213] CAB 2/6, 14 Oct. 1935, Minutes of the 271st Meeting of the C.I.D.

[214] See, for example, the concerns of Sir Ian Fraser, director of a firm that produced solder, in CAB 16/141, D.P.R. 175, Nov. 1936, "Recruitment for the Auxiliary Forces," pp. 2–3.

fallen below returns available in Europe and in domestic markets.[215] Furthermore, even when rates of return in the empire were higher than elsewhere, over 90 percent of British investment went to Europe, the dominions, and the colonies with extensive white settlement. The amount invested in Asia was small and could easily have been shifted to other areas. As Lance Davis and Robert Huttenback argue, "In aggregate terms, it appears that the dependent Empire received such a small share of the capital flows that, under any reasonable set of assumptions, a redirection of those resources to other parts of the world would have only trivially affected the realized rate of return."[216] Many domestic interest groups could therefore have adjusted to strategic retrenchment without incurring serious financial losses.

Private economic interests appear to have played a similarly ancillary role in delaying the adoption of a continental commitment. While some industries stood to suffer from the economy's concentration on the production of defense goods, others benefited enormously.[217] Cabinet debate about the B.E.F. also reflected little concern about opposition within the business community. Decision makers cared far more about the overall health of the economy and about the depth of *public* opposition to a continental commitment, the issue to which I now turn.

Domestic Politics. Public opinion and coalition maintenance had considerable effect on British strategy during the interwar years. The Conservatives maintained power after World War I by attracting moderate Liberals and others near the center of the politcal spectrum. The Conservative-Liberal coalition combined with naval and business interests to form a strong constituency in favor of empire.[218] The electorate was also more concerned about defense policy than before World War I. And throughout most of the interwar period, elites—in both public and private—continued to define British security in terms of imperial security and to use to their political advantage the proimperial sentiment that they had stirred up among the populace. Among elites and masses alike, support for empire ran strong; overseas empire was deeply embeddded in strategic culture.

This is not to suggest, however, that political opportunism best explains the behavior of decision makers. Elites were not defending empire simply because they feared the political implications of setbacks in

---

[215] Lance Davis and Robert Huttenback, *Mammon and the Pursuit of Empire* (Cambridge: Cambridge University Press, 1986), p. 309.

[216] Ibid., p. 72.

[217] Industries involved in the production of aircraft, for example, made huge profits. See Shay, *British Rearmament in the Thirties*, pp. 249–257.

[218] Bright, "Class Interest," pp. 219–237.

the periphery. The archival record provides no evidence that decision makers preferred to pursue a policy of retrenchment but failed to do so because of the potential political costs involved. As argued above, reigning strategic conceptions themselves impelled elites to cling tightly to empire. Their behavior was less the product of instrumental political concerns than of their intellectual and emotional attachment to the notion of imperial integrity; British security had become equated with the well-being of empire. This association between empire and British security in the minds of elites was no doubt linked to national self-images embedded within the broader polity. During the early post–World War I years, elites used the notion of imperial integrity and the preservation of imperial prestige to consolidate their rule. During the 1930s, they continued to propagate proimperial strategic notions. The strategic images that shaped policy thus emerged in large part as a tool for managing coalitional dynamics and elite-mass linkages. But these images came to infuse elite thinking and did not affect outcomes primarily through domestic political constraints. Elites clung to empire because of a sincerely held conviction that British security depended on doing so, not because they feared the political repercussions of retrenchment.

Electoral politics played a more direct and instrumental role in the formulation of British strategy in the core. After World War I, aversion to a continental commitment quickly spread among elites and the public. Public interest groups such as the Union of Democratic Control, the National Peace Council, and the League of Nations Union emerged to lobby for disarmament. During the 1930s, elites continued to communicate to the public that Britain did not need an army capable of fighting on the Continent. Especially after Germany and Italy had demonstrated expansionist tendencies, decision makers needed to justify their policies before a public growing increasingly concerned about the security of the metropole. While limited support for a continental commitment emerged in the cabinet during the early 1930s, elites favoring the reequipment of the B.E.F. usually hid their intentions from public scrutiny.[219] Those favoring a more ambitious rearmament program had few political incentives to broadcast their views. As Sally Marks notes, "Having just convinced the citizenry that disarmament was a sure and swift route to peace, and economical besides, they could hardly sound the tocsin . . . and demand expensive rearma-

---

[219] See, for example, CAB 16/111, #113, 20 April 1934, "Imperial Defence Policy," and #120, 20 June 1934, "Disarmament Conference 1932," p. 2.

ments."[220] By-elections held in the early 1930s, such as those in Clay Cross and East Fulham, were won by candidates running on a platform opposing rearmament. As Paul Kennedy observes, "the voting public preferred pacifist candidates in favour of pro-armaments Conservatives."[221] At least until the second half of the decade, these trends within the electorate clearly reinforced hesitation within the cabinet to accept reequipping the B.E.F. for a continental mission.[222] Furthermore, public concern about London's vulnerability to air attack gave impetus to the government's decision to favor the air force in its budgetary allocations.[223]

Claims that public opinion and electoral concerns played a significant role in shaping strategy throughout the interwar period are undermined, however, by the fact that after 1935, public opinion and British military strategy diverged widely. The pace of Hitler's rearmament program, which began in earnest in 1935, was widely publicized, as was Benito Mussolini's aggressive behavior during the Abyssinian Crisis. These events reduced public opposition to rearmament.[224] Labour, staunchly against rearmament in 1932–1933, was forced to revise its stance. In the spring of 1935, the party acknowledged that some degree of rearmament was necessary. This shift led to an unlikely alliance of Tories and Labourites critical of the slow pace of rearmament and the lack of preparation for dealing with Hitler.[225] Public opinion continued to turn against appeasement in response to the occupation of the Rhineland, the Anschluss, and Munich. In February 1938, Anthony Eden, Chamberlain's foreign secretary, resigned from the cabinet to protest the government's soft stand on Italian fascism. This development sparked a vociferous public debate over appeasement and strengthened the opponents of accommodation.[226] Opinion polls conducted in the spring of 1938—well before Munich—showed that 58 percent of the electorate disapproved of Chamberlain's foreign policy while only 26 percent approved.[227] An assessment of public opinion in April pointed to "a great suspicion of the Chamberlain policy of

---

[220] Sally Marks, *The Illusion of Peace* (London: Macmillan, 1976), pp. 142–143.

[221] Paul Kennedy, *The Realities behind Diplomacy* (London: Fontana Paperbacks, 1981), p. 242.

[222] Howard, *Continental Commitment*, pp. 106–110.

[223] Ibid., p. 109.

[224] Elizabeth Monroe, *Britain's Moment in the Middle East, 1914–1971*, 2d ed. (London: Chatto and Windus, 1981), pp. 144–145.

[225] Shay, *British Rearmament in the Thirties*, pp. 217–219.

[226] Rock, *Appeasement on Trial*, p. 45.

[227] "Public Opinion Survey," *Public Opinion Quarterly*, 4 (March 1940), 77–79.

appeasement."[228] In 1938, 72 percent of the electorate favored increased defense spending.[229]

Chamberlain was indeed aware of public sentiment. While meeting with Hitler in Godesberg to discuss the fate of the Sudetenland, Chamberlain received a telegram from his colleagues in the cabinet indicating that the "great mass of public opinion seems to be hardening the sense of feeling that we have gone the limit of concession and that it is up to the Chancellor [Hitler] to make some contribution."[230] Chamberlain proceeded to acquiesce to Hitler's demands for the Sudetenland. In by-elections held during the first months of 1939, "there was a trend opposing Chamberlain." The Conservatives lost several seats, and their margins of victory in successful contests were, in most cases, considerably reduced.[231] After the German invasion of Czechoslovakia in March 1939, it became politically unfeasible for the government to continue neglecting the B.E.F. and accommodating Germany. Public opposition to appeasement was overwhelming.[232]

Despite these radical shifts in public opinion, support within the government for sending the B.E.F. to France reached its lowest point during 1937–1938, suggesting, if anything, an inverse relationship between strategy and electoral pressure. Rearmament lagged far behind the willingness of the public to support it. The public appears to have adapted to incoming information much more readily than the elite community. Electoral pressures thus did contribute to the cabinet's reluctance to approve a continental commitment during the early 1930s. But the key cause of the dangerous delay in the adoption of a continental commitment and reequipping of the B.E.F. was the set of strategic conceptions that had taken root in the elite community and its resistance to change, not domestic political pressures. Strategic culture indeed played an important role in producing adjustment failure. But it did so not by entrapping elites in domestic political pressures, but by infusing the elite community with powerful strategic images that overrode strategic logic.

Military Services. The military served as one of the main vehicles through which prevailing strategic images became institutionalized

---

[228] Salter group memorandum cited in Beck, "Munich's Lessons Reconsidered," p. 181. For a concise summary of the debate over public attitudes and their impact on policy, see pp. 178–182.

[229] "Public Opinion Survey," *Public Opinion Quarterly*, 4 (March 1940), 77–79.

[230] Cited in Murray, *European Balance of Power*, pp. 202–203.

[231] Rock, *Appeasement on Trial*, pp. 200–202.

[232] Shay, *British Rearmament in the Thirties*, pp. 231–232. See also Rock, *Appeasement on Trial*, pp. 207–209.

and routinized. Throughout the interwar period, the army's mission was defined almost exclusively in terms of colonial defense. Its manpower needs, force structure, and procurement programs were shaped accordingly. Although the navy's top priority remained in Europe, the Admiralty's war plans and procurement programs were shaped by taxing responsibilities in overseas theaters. Indeed, the Admiralty was one of the strongest proponents of upholding Britain's commitments in the Far East, of fortifying Singapore, and of sending a fleet to the region should Japanese forces proceed into Southeast Asia. Accordingly, both the army and navy had powerful organizational interests at stake in the periphery, interests that played a role in impairing adjustment.

It would be inappropriate, however, to view the military's imperial orientation as the cause of adjustment failure, rather than as a symptom or manifestation of a strategic culture wedded to peripheral empire. The army and navy were acting out of self-interest only in that both had been instructed to focus on overseas operations by political elites; roles and missions came to be defined accordingly. The army did not need India, nor the navy the Far East, to justify its requests for an increased budget. The European mission alone was sufficient for that. Furthermore, in terms of enhancing its budget and input into policy, the army had good reason to argue in favor of a continental commitment. A continental mission would have drastically increased the army's personnel needs and required the modernization of weaponry. Indeed, throughout the 1930s, there was significant support within the General Staff for a B.E.F. equipped for continental missions.

In short, the services were by no means the instigators of British unwillingness to abandon portions of the outlying empire and make a firm continental commitment. On the contrary, politicians were as, if not more, committed to maintaining Britain's position in the periphery. Similarly, responsibility for delaying the development of the B.E.F. until a few months before the outbreak of war rests primarily with civilian decision makers, not with the military. The services were simply not dragging the government into unwanted and unintended commitments or preventing politicians from preparing for continental war.

Conclusions

Britain's failure to adjust to a changing constellation of international power during the 1930s emerged principally from the effect of vulnerability on strategic beliefs and strategic culture. As far as peripheral strategy is concerned, World War I had a profound impact on elite and mass attitudes toward empire. Since well before the war, overseas empire loomed large in elite conceptions of British security and in the public mind. But the periphery took on new meaning after World War I. In the wake of the devastation suffered on the Continent, elites turned to the notion of imperial integrity to consolidate their rule. Furthermore, the war had exposed Britain's fall from economic and military predominance. Even before the war was over, decision makers had looked to the imperial periphery to serve as the substance and symbol of the nation's great-power status. Led by elites, the polity retreated into empire during the interwar years to preserve its self-image as a great power; more than ever before, national well-being was equated with the integrity of the empire.

Until the mid-1930s, the image equating British security with imperial integrity was reinforced by a strategic logic that emerged from conditions of strategic deficiency. During the early 1930s, the most pressing threats to British interests were in the periphery. Lacking the resources needed to deal with these threats, elites adopted deterrent strategies in the periphery both as a means of demonstrating resolve to adversaries and as a means of preserving the façade of imperial strength on which British prestige rested. The clear sense of geographic priorities exhibited before World War I was lost in a strategic dialogue of pervasive weakness and falling dominoes. Elites became preoccupied with demonstrating resolve and bolstering prestige precisely because the material resources at their disposal were so woefully inadequate. To gain support for these policies and legitimate their rule, they stepped up efforts to champion overseas empire. Both in public and in private, elites continued to define British security in terms of imperial security. Elite beliefs and strategic culture were running on parallel tracks.

The problem was that the strategic culture that elites initially molded to gain support for their policies eventually came to constrain adjustment. During the late 1930s, elites found themselves entrapped in the images of imperial integrity that they had propagated, unable to pursue peripheral retrenchment despite growing awareness of the need to focus on metropolitan security. The interaction between elite beliefs and strategic culture led to a set of strategic assumptions so deeply embedded in the intellectual paradigms and values of top decision makers and in the organizational interests of elite institutions that they were impervious to contradictory incoming information. Because of cognitive, emotional, and organizational resistance to challenging the fundamental strategic conceptions that informed policy, assessments were crafted to conform to reigning assumptions rather than reigning assumptions altered to reflect strategic realities. Abandoning major portions of the overseas empire, though consistent with strategic pragmatism, was incompatible with the fundamental conception of security that had taken root within the polity during the interwar years. The problem was not that elites feared falling from power, but that they had sincerely come to equate British security with the security and well-being of the overseas empire. As a result, Britain fell prey to overextension.

Strategic exposure in the core was also the product of the interaction of vulnerability, elite beliefs, and strategic culture. In response to the tragedy of World War I and to rally support among the electorate, elites bought into and propagated among the public the notion that British soldiers would never again fight on the Continent. This strong aversion to a renewed continental commitment was reinforced during the first half of the 1930s by a strategic logic that emerged from conditions of strategic deficiency. Accommodation of German demands was to enable Britain to avoid war in the core and focus on threats in the periphery. Even if appeasement failed and war with Germany proved to be inevitable, decision makers reasoned, rearmament had to proceed slowly in order to build up the financial reserves and industrial infrastructure needed to support a long war. To gain support for these policies, elites continued to propagate images linking British security to the avoidance of a continental commitment; strategic beliefs and strategic culture ran on parallel tracks.

During the second half of the 1930s, the scope and pace of German rearmament and successive acts of blatant aggression made appeasement increasingly obsolete. The problem was that elites found themselves entrapped in the strategic images that they had earlier used to manage domestic politics and rally support for their policies. Long after the logic of appeasement had been discredited and public opposition to rearmament had waned, the image equating British security with the avoidance of a continental commitment remained intact. For cognitive and emotional reasons, elites still refused to equip the B.E.F. for continental operations. In 1938, decision makers found themselves appeasing Hitler not because they believed that accommodation would satisfy Hitler's appetite for expansion or buy time for war preparations, but because they faced a desperate military imbalance and were simply unprepared to go to war. Despite awareness that the metropole was falling prey to strategic exposure, the conviction that Britain had to avoid a continental commitment prevented elites from undertaking strategic adjustment. By the time of Munich, elites were clinging to outmoded strategic assumptions in an atmosphere of increasing fear and illusion. It was only after Germany had conquered much of central

Europe and after appeasement had become politically unviable that the cabinet reluctantly approved funding for the B.E.F. and began to prepare for a ground war. Elites finally adapted policy to strategic realities, overcoming the powerful constraints of strategic culture and their visceral aversion to a continental commitment. But the lateness of this adaptation almost cost Britain its sovereignty.

[4]

France

From the Franco-Prussian War until the end of World War II, French elites were understandably preoccupied with the military and industrial strength of Germany. After 1870, the loss of Alsace and Lorraine, Otto von Bismarck's transformation of Prussia into a unified German state, and the rapid growth of Germany's population and industrial infrastructure left French decision makers no choice but to focus their attention on defense of the northeast border. The existence of an increasingly threatening neighbor did not, however, prevent France's overseas empire from growing markedly in Africa, the Middle East, and the Far East. In fact, French interest in the imperial periphery appears to have intensified in step with Germany's military power.

Despite the imperial expansion of the late 1800s, French elites during the decade before World War I adjusted successfully to growing German ambition on the Continent and pursued a viable diplomatic and military strategy for thwarting German aggression. They retrenched from empire and, through rearmament and alliance, concentrated preponderant opposing force in the core. During the 1930s, however, France fell prey to both strategic exposure and overextension. Despite the overt hostility and growing military power of Germany under Hitler's rule, French elites pursued imperial ambition at a cost to metropolitan security and failed to make adequate preparations for continental defense. The prospect of extracting from the periphery the soldiers and materiel needed to offset the imbalance in the core was one of the main motivations behind French colonial ambition. Indeed, a sizable contingent of indigenous troops was deployed in the metropole by the time German forces attacked in 1940. Nevertheless, France's vast empire was able to do little to avert disaster for the metropole; the French army collapsed within weeks of the initial German offensive into the low countries. Similarly, after World War II, French elites pursued empire despite clear costs to metropolitan defense. Between 1949 and 1954, they waged a futile war in Indochina that impaired the country's economic recovery and devastated the quality of the metropolitan army.

How and why did French elites fail so thoroughly to make adequate preparations for metropolitan defense before World War II? Especially during the second half of the 1930s, when German military strength grew rapidly, did it make sense for decision makers to devote scarce resources to building and protecting the overseas empire? Did the empire realistically hold promise of enabling the metropole to prevail against the Germans? After World War II, why did French elites jeopardize their commitment to NATO in order to fight a distant war in Indochina? It is more understandable that Britain, isolated from the Continent by the Channel, might orient its grand strategy toward empire and avoid continental entanglements. But for France, faced with land threats on all but its western frontier, building overseas empire at an expense to metropolitan security is far more puzzling.

Despite clear differences between the British and French experiences, the two countries fell prey to strategic exposure and overextension for quite similar reasons. Before World War I, French elites believed that the Triple Entente had sufficient capability to prevail against the Triple Alliance. Conditions of strategic sufficiency enabled them to pursue a policy of power balancing in the core and one of retrenchment in the periphery. During the interwar period, intelligence assessments led to perceptions of high metropolitan vulnerability. Changes in strategic beliefs and strategic culture followed. Conditions of strategic deficiency induced elites to adopt a strategy of accommodation in the core and one of deterrence in the periphery. Appeasement of Germany was to prevent war or, at a minimum, delay it until more favorable circumstances prevailed. Imperial ambition was to preserve France's status as a great power and enable the French to redress their glaring military inferiority on the Continent. A vast overseas empire was to provide the troops and war-making capability needed to offset Germany's military superiority. It was these arguments that lured elites into the periphery, that led to a blurring of strategic priorities, and that prompted decision makers to sell overseas empire to the French polity.

The problem was that French grand strategy, though relatively well suited to the strategic environment in the early 1930s, grew increasingly divorced from strategic realities as the decade progressed. The construction of the Maginot Line, the army's limited mobility and offensive capability, the appeasement of Hitler, and the elaborate plans to ferry troops from the periphery to the metropole might have made sense in 1935. But the strategic beliefs on which those policies were based soon became outmoded. Available information should have discredited the suppositions that informed grand strategy, but elites *policy choices not rational* nevertheless failed to update prevailing strategic beliefs. Policy choices were not based on rational calculation. On the contrary, acute vulnera-bility and the absence of politically attractive options for redressing German preponderance produced a period of effective paralysis and resignation, causing decision makers to cling to obsolete military and diplomatic strategies far longer than they should have. This paralysis was exacerbated by a host of domestic factors. The instability of succes-sive governments and splits between left and right were obstacles to forging a military alliance with the Soviet Union. Suggestions that France move toward a professional military in order to build a more capable, modern army were shot down by civilian leaders fearful that a professional military would pose a threat to the republican regime. Within the military itself, reliance on infantry and static defense so imbued organizational doctrine, strategy, and mobilization schemes that the high command was unable and unwilling to revamp the army's outmoded plans for metropolitan defense. These domestic considera-tions were partly responsible for making highly unattractive the op-tions available for coping with strategic deficiency.

Strategic exposure in the core was integrally wedded to overexten-sion in the periphery. French elites had entrapped themselves in a *exaggeration!* strategic culture that led to a vast exaggeration of the value of empire. After years of elite campaigns to sell empire to the populace, elites and the public alike assimilated powerful strategic images that equated metropolitan security with imperial security. In terms of popular atti-tudes, the intellectual paradigms and values of top decision makers, and the central roles and missions of elite institutions, France and its overseas empire were merging into a single theater. France's military establishment became oriented toward imperial defense, and scarce metropolitan resources were allocated to peripheral missions. As An-thony Clayton notes, "The French Army became as much an African army as a European one."[1] The quality and morale of the metropolitan army suffered accordingly. Furthermore, the widespread conviction that the war-making capability of the overseas empire would eventually play a key role in continental defense was one of the main reasons that elites remained dangerously complacent about the state of the metropolitan army. As in Britain, overwhelming contradictory informa-tion eventually induced French elites to begin adapting prevailing as-sumptions to strategic reality. But it was far too late to deal adequately with the Nazi military machine.

[1] Anthony Clayton, *France, Soldiers, and Africa* (London: Brassey's Defence Publishers, 1988), p. 20.

[187]

Similar dynamics plagued France during the early post–World War II years. The effect of vulnerability on strategic beliefs and strategic culture mired the French in Indochina despite the war's ill effects on the recovery and security of the metropole. Although these arguments must be interpreted within the unique context of French geography, politics, and nationalism, the causes of adjustment failure are remarkably similar to those that almost cost Britain its sovereignty.

This chapter is divided into four sections. The first examines the growth of the French empire from the Franco-Prussian War until the turn of the century and the beginning of Germany's ambitious naval buildup. I investigate why the number and scope of France's overseas possessions grew rapidly during this period and how this expansion was related to French continental strategy. The second section examines French planning and strategy between 1904 and 1914. Like Britain, France was able to subordinate protection of the periphery to the demands of continental defense. Sections three and four study French planning before World War II and during the Indochina War (1949–1954), respectively. It was during these two periods that French elites pursued overly competitive policies in the periphery while failing to take adequate steps to ensure the security of the metropole.

1870–1904: War, Recovery, and Empire as Fait Accompli

France's vast overseas empire had been virtually dismantled by the end of the Napoleonic Wars. The French emerged from the Congress of Vienna in 1815 with only a smattering of colonial holdings: Réunion, Guadeloupe, Martinique, Saint Pierre and Miquelon (located off the coast of Newfoundland), and some small trading posts in India and Africa. Between 1815 and the outbreak of the Franco-Prussian War in 1870, French troops did expand into peripheral areas, incorporating Algeria, Senegal, and parts of Cochin China into the empire. Yet these bouts of expansion were more the product of historical accident than of a deliberate decision to rebuild France's peripheral empire. The Algerian operation in 1830, for example, was undertaken by Charles X to reassert his control over the Bey through a temporary show of force. French troops were to have withdrawn after six weeks, but they remained until they were forced out more than a century later.[2]

The public, parliament, and the business community were largely ill-disposed toward imperial expansion during these decades. The French

---

[2] Christopher Andrew and A. S. Kanya-Forstner, *The Climax of French Imperial Expansion, 1914–1924* (Stanford: Stanford University Press, 1981), p. 8.

populace, unlike that of Britain, had little interest in seeking new colonies.[3] Politicians were preoccupied with continental diplomacy, and industrialists and financiers had quite limited investments in the periphery. In 1829, M. Bessières, a member of parliament, made the following evaluation: "Considering the value to us of our colonies and what they cost us, we should be much better off without them. A profitable colonial system is no longer practicable. I do not see how it can be denied that it has ceased to be necessary."[4] So too were bureaucratic organs oriented toward continental affairs. Responsibility for colonial policy had oscillated for decades between the Ministry of Marine and the Ministry of Commerce, confounding efforts to formulate a coherent policy. The Ministry of Marine maintained continuous hold over colonial affairs between 1831 and 1883 but was concerned largely with the naval imbalance with Britain and protecting trading routes, not with colonial operations or administration.[5] In addition, there was considerable opposition to the spending of public funds on the protection of external trade. General Foy expressed in 1822 an opinion shared by many French elites: "Work out what we are spending on the navy so as to protect our overseas trade. Would not this be better spent on improving our agriculture, increasing our internal trade and developing our industry?"[6]

These fundamental sources of opposition to overseas empire did not, however, prevent peripheral expansion during the closing decades of the 1800s. On the contrary, France's colonial empire grew markedly during the 1880s. Given France's devastating defeat at the hands of Prussia in 1870–1871 and the loss of the population and industrial resources of Alsace and Lorraine, this period of imperial expansion is especially puzzling. One would expect French elites to have been more preoccupied than ever before with their military position on the Continent; a unified Germany of growing military and economic strength should have focused the attention of decision makers exclusively on their northeast border. Nevertheless, by the onset of World War I, the French had acquired a vast overseas empire. In Africa alone, the French empire covered some ten million square kilometers.

I now consider in more detail this anomalous episode of imperial growth. I argue that most French elites were opposed to imperial

---

[3] "Introduction," by Ronald Robinson, in Henri Brunschwig, *French Colonialism, 1871–1914: Myths and Realities* (London: Pall Mall Press, 1964), p. viii.

[4] Cited in Brunschwig, *French Colonialism*, p. 16.

[5] See Service Historique de l'Armée de Terre (SHAT), 7-N-68, Oct. 1883, "La Défense des colonies," p. 2. Unless otherwise noted, all archival citations refer to the SHAT collection in Vincennes, France. Translations are my own.

[6] Cited in Brunschwig, *French Colonialism*, p. 16.

expansion during this period, largely because they recognized the need to devote their resources to metropolitan defense. Elites operated under conditions of strategic sufficiency but realized that few, if any, assets could be spared for peripheral missions. The empire expanded largely because of the persistent efforts of a powerful colonial lobby working in conjunction with an errant colonial army.

Strategic Assessments

The 1870s were a decade of *recueillement* (recovery and repose) for the French. A consensus existed within the public at large, the government, and the military services that "colonial expansion was a luxury and was nothing but a completely futile expenditure of effort."[7] The military was concerned mainly with the loss of Alsace and Lorraine and the implications of German unification and military prowess for French security. The poor performance of the French army during the war led to a revision of the conscription system in 1872 and an expansion of the number of men under arms. Conscripts served for either five years or one year, the shorter term obtained through a lucky draw in the lottery system or the influence of personal contacts. These changes set the number of trained soldiers at approximately five hundred thousand, a level roughly equivalent to that maintained by Germany.[8] A military convention between France and Russia that took shape between 1891 and 1893 helped the French cope with Germany's rising population and economic strength. German military superiority would be more than offset should Germany have to split its forces between a western and eastern front.

This emphasis on the army was accompanied by a neglect of the navy, which had played an insignificant role in the Franco-Prussian War. French sailors actually had contributed to the defense of Paris, but only after they were removed from their ships and deployed on land. Gaston Moch in 1874 concisely summarized the reasons behind substantial cuts in the naval budget: "We do not have the means (and who does?) to be a first-class power at the same time on land and at sea. But it is indispensable that our army be strong enough to fight

---

[7] Jean Ganiage, *L'Expansion coloniale de la France sous la Troisième République (1871–1914)* (Paris: Payot, 1968), p. 21. Translations of quotations from this book, and from other books published in French, are my own.

[8] On French force levels, see Jean Doise and Maurice Vaïsse, *Diplomatie et outil militaire, 1871–1969* (Paris: Imprimerie Nationale, 1987), pp. 32–34. See also Richard Challener, *The French Theory of the Nation in Arms, 1866–1939* (New York: Russell and Russell, 1955). German force levels climbed from about 400,000 in the early 1870s to 485,000 by 1890. The army expanded to 555,000 in 1893 and then grew only gradually until the major increases of 1912. See Gordon Craig, *The Politics of the Prussian Army, 1640–1945* (New York: Oxford University Press, 1955), chaps. 6 and 7.

that of Germany. . . . To think that with the twenty-five million francs a battleship costs, we could buy and maintain the horses we need in order to have as much cavalry as the Germans, and that a division of cavalry will weigh more in the balance than the most formidable battleship."[9] Even the minister of marine, Admiral Louis-Pierre-Alexis Pothuau, admitted in 1872 that "all our efforts must be concentrated on land. Indeed, what good will a navy be to us now"[10] As a result of these attitudes, there was a distinct decline throughout the 1870s in both the number of operational vessels and the size and quality of materiel stockpiles. Naval strategists abandoned hope of developing a competitive high-seas fleet and focused instead on commerce raiding and protection of France's overseas stations.[11]

With this exclusive focus on its continental army, France managed to keep pace with German military power. But demographic trends did not augur well for the future. At the time of unification, Germany's population was already greater than that of France. Because the birth rate in France was substantially behind that in Germany, the population gap between the two countries increased steadily during the last decades of the century.[12] By 1915, Germany had seventy million inhabitants, compared to forty million in France. Coupled with Germany's rapid economic and industrial growth, these demographic trends made it clear to French elites that Germany could potentially present a formidable threat to the security of the metropole. Matters were made no better by the fact that France's other principal antagonist, Britain, was amassing a fleet that vastly overshadowed the deteriorating French navy. The French thus had sufficient resources to match German power—especially with the help of Russia—but they could little afford to devote assets to other missions.

Given appreciation of the growing demographic imbalance on the Continent, why did French eliltes divert scarce military and economic resources to pursue peripheral empire? How could decision makers rationalize expansion when they fully recognized the need to guard against a potential German threat to metropolitan security?

Dealing with the Adversary

France's defeat in the Napoleonic Wars consolidated Britain's position as the world's premier naval power. The Franco-Prussian War confirmed that France had also lost its position as the dominant land

---

[9] Cited in Theodore Ropp, *The Development of a Modern Navy: French Naval Policy, 1871–1904* (Annapolis: Naval Institute Press, 1987), pp. 30–31.

[10] Cited in ibid., p. 31.

[11] Ibid., pp. 33–34.

[12] Ganiage, *L'Expansion coloniale*, p. 18.

power in Europe. War plans drafted after 1870 attempted to address threats from both potential adversaries: the navy, until 1903, focused its attention on Britain, while the army concentrated on the German threat. As mentioned above, alliance with Russia in 1893 helped the French cope with Germany's rising military power.

Despite the preoccupation of the central military bureaucracy with continental developments, colonial expansion proceeded at a rapid pace, especially in Africa. The implications of the growth of France's peripheral empire for metropolitan security were less severe than one might think, given the scope of expansion. The adverse impact on force dispositions and the allocation of resources was buffered by two factors. First, most colonial expeditions were carried out by relatively small contingents. French forces were able to overcome local resistance in the periphery by relying on superior tactics as opposed to advantages in firepower or force size.[13] The prosecution of colonial wars thus did not require a large diversion of soldiers, equipment, or armaments from the metropole. Second, responsibility for overseas operations rested with the navy; it was primarily the *infanterie de marine* and the *artillerie de marine* that carried out colonial expeditions. This division of labor limited the extent to which peripheral expansion degraded the *armée de terre*.

Assigning the Ministry of Marine responsibility for colonial missions, however, incurred certain costs. Partly in response to the growing colonialist movement and their role in it, naval strategists during the 1880s focused on defense of coasts and overseas ports. Procurement policies were oriented toward these missions, not toward continental security and resuscitation of France's ailing high-seas fleet. The preoccupation of the Ministry of Marine with colonial operations thus took its toll on metropolitan defenses: "The ultimate effects of the navy's colonial activities on its readiness for European conflict were little short of disastrous. The large fleet maintained for operations on overseas stations was perfectly useless for combat against a European opponent, while vast sums disappeared in the navy's murky administration as part of France's new colonial effort."[14] Metropolitan garrisons manned by the infanterie de marine were reduced by 50 to 75 percent to support colonial operations. The quality of naval artillery and other materiel also suffered because the navy's best engineers had been posted overseas.[15]

---

[13] See Jean Gottmann, "Bugeaud, Galliéni, Lyautey: The Development of French Colonial Warfare," in *Makers of Modern Strategy*, ed. Edward Mead Earle (Princeton: Princeton University Press, 1971).

[14] Ropp, *French Naval Policy*, p. 142.

[15] Ibid., p. 143.

what
why to expanded
after 1870
defeat

Why did French elites deliberately divert resources from the Continent to pursue peripheral empire? What strategic beliefs informed such actions? Paradoxically, France's defeat in the Franco-Prussian War and its inability to recover the territories or prestige lost to Germany were the key factors leading to the acquisition of new peripheral territories. France had been dislodged from its position of continental pre-eminence and, because of insufficient manpower, could not redress this wound within the confines of continental affairs. After the fundamental blow dealt to the nation by Prussia, peripheral expansion was to be the panacea, the path that would allow France to recover its prestige and international status. The goal was as much to reaffirm the French people's own image of France as a great power as to project this image to other states. In addition, overseas possessions could compensate France in more concrete terms. As one deputy put it during a parliamentary debate over colonial policy, the overseas territories constitute "an immense reservoir of devoted soldiers, an immense reservoir of men whom the motherland at time of danger can call upon to resist the invader."[16] While pursuit of empire could not guarantee the return of Alsace and Lorraine, it could begin to replace the population and industrial resources that had been lost to Germany.

It was this logic that provided the impetus behind efforts to reconstruct a large-scale overseas empire. Jules Ferry and other procolonialists rested their case for empire on the claim that *la politique de revanche* (the politics of revenge) was bankrupt and that France therefore needed to look outside Europe to reaffirm its position as a great power. The procolonialists—organized through lobby groups that came during the 1890s to be known as the *parti colonial*—succeeded in expanding French territory in Indochina, the Sudan, and Tunis during the 1880s. In justifying his policies before the National Assembly, Jules Ferry, prime minister during the early 1880s and a chief proponent of imperial expansion, warned that France had to protect its "stature" and that "to regard any expansion towards Africa and the Far East as a snare and a rash adventure . . . would mean that we should cease to be a first-rate power and become a third- or fourth-rate power instead." "The politics of recovery and abstention," he maintained, "is quite simply the road to decadence." On the establishment of the Tunisian Protectorate in 1881, Léon Gambetta, Ferry's confidant and successor as prime minister, remarked that "France is becoming a Great Power again."[17] To those who claimed that overseas territory would constitute

[16] 7-N-75, 28 Oct. 1902, Chambre des députés, No. 388, Procès-verbal, p. 8.
[17] Ferry cited in Brunschwig, *French Colonialism*, p. 80, and in Ganiage, *L'Expansion coloniale*, p. 49; Gambetta cited in Brunschwig, *French Colonialism*, p. 57.

a drain on the metropole's economic resources, the procolonialists argued that empire could not be evaluated in simple cost/benefit terms; the colonies were not "branch offices that the metropole could liquidate at whim after taking an account of profits and losses." On the contrary, the nation's colonies were part of an inseparable unit that was essential "to assuring the reign of greater France." The costs of colonial defense had to be seen as "part of a vast program of defense spanning the globe, adopted by the metropole; they [such expenditures] are intended less to assure protection of our overseas domain than to maintain our global strategy *(politique mondiale)*."[18]

The procolonialists were aided in building their case for empire by the fact that the 1880s were a decade of growing European rivalry in the periphery. Britain, France, Belgium, Germany, and Portugal all participated in the Scramble for Africa. After the loss of France's foothold in Egypt following Britain's intervention in 1881, French decision makers repeatedly sought to recover some influence over colonial affairs in Africa. Elites believed that successive challenges to British interests would bring Britain to the negotiating table and demonstrate that France too was to be a key actor in deciding the fate of Africa; French elites were looking for status and diplomatic leverage more than territory itself. Britain and France also jostled for position in the Far East, their attention focused largely on Siam because it was nestled between the French in Indochina and the British in Burma. The extension of continental rivalry to the periphery both fueled and provided justification for Ferry's attempt to recover French stature through imperial expansion. In his own words, "France must put itself in a position where it can do what others are doing. A policy of colonial expansion is being engaged in by all the European powers. We must do likewise."[19] Since France had been denied its preeminent position on the Continent, French elites turned to the periphery to reaffirm national power. They believed that the enhanced reputation and prestige that would accompany empire could offset the relative loss of material power on the Continent itself.

The colonialist movement did not rely solely on the notion of *la grandeur* to justify its program; Ferry did provide economic reasons for pursuing empire. He maintained that colonies would provide both an essential market for French manufactured goods and an outlet for capital that could not be profitably invested in the metropole. Many historians agree, however, that Ferry's economic arguments were little more than an ex post facto justification of policies that he was pursuing for

---

[18] 7-N-75, 28 Oct. 1902, No. 388, Procès-verbal, pp. 10, 69, 40.
[19] Cited in Brunschwig, *French Colonialism*, p. 80.

other reasons.[20] The data also suggest that, throughout the last quarter of the nineteenth century, France's trade with and investment in its colonies reached, at their peak, only 10 percent of total foreign trade and investment.[21] French manufacturing output simply did not require a vast colonial market. Nor did the underdeveloped colonies have the purchasing power to increase substantially the demand for goods manufactured in the metropole. On the contrary, France generally ran a trade deficit with its colonies, with imports of raw materials outstripping export of finished products. Similarly, industrialists and financiers questioned the reliability of investing in the periphery and showed little interest in exporting large quantities of capital to the colonies. In short, the evidence casts serious doubt on the sincerity of Ferry's economic justification for expansion.

Between 1870 and 1904, the French military establishment focused primarily on continental affairs. Though the French did not attempt to keep pace with British seapower, they did seek to offset Germany's demographic advantage by maintaining a metropolitan army roughly equal to that of Germany and by entering into diplomatic arrangements with Russia that would ensure that German forces would be split between two fronts should war break out. France was thus strong enough to adopt a deterrent stance toward Germany but not sufficiently powerful to recover the territory—and hence the prestige—lost in 1870–1871. To accomplish this objective, a small group of French elites turned to the periphery. The search for status and the reaffirmation of the nation's identity as a great power were the primary factors motivating these elites to pursue empire. Peripheral expansion was to enhance France's international influence and maintain the country's position as a major power. It was also to compensate the domestic populace for the loss of Alsace and Lorraine to Germany. Christopher Andrew and A. S. Kanya-Forstner succinctly capture the essence of Ferry's brand of imperialism: "France cannot be France without greatness."[22]

Curiously, peripheral expansion went forward despite the fact that enthusiasm for empire was not widespread among the French elite.

[20] See, for example, Brunschwig, *French Colonialism*, pp. 85–104; and Ganiage, *L'Expansion coloniale*, p. 22. Ferry did discuss the economic implications of expansion in speeches before the National Assembly and at the Berlin Congress (1885). It was not until 1890, however, that these speeches were published in a collection of documents entitled *Le Tonkin et la mère patrie*.

[21] Jacques Marseille, *Empire colonial et capitalisme français: Histoire d'un divorce* (Paris: Albin Michel, 1984), pp. 37, 96–100; and Andrew and Kanya-Forstner, *French Imperial Expansion*, pp. 14–18.

[22] Andrew and Kanya-Forstner, *French Imperial Expansion*, p. 26.

Most decision makers appreciated that the military situation on the Continent made it impractical to divert resources to colonial expansion. The National Assembly and the central bureaucracy sought, with mixed results, to rein in the procolonialists during the 1890s. Paris slashed funding for expeditions, tried to constrain further expansion, ordered European troops to return to the Continent, and pulled the nation away from the brink of war by backing down at Fashoda.[23] Had such restraint not been imposed on the colonialist movement, the French navy might well have found itself waging war against a far superior British fleet. Given the fact that the National Assembly and the central bureaucracy seemed well aware of the costs of empire and wanted to focus the nation's resources on bolstering metropolitan security, it is puzzling that Ferry and his colleagues in the colonialist movement were able to expand France's overseas possessions to the extent that they did. To understand how the procolonialists circumvented a populace and parliament ill-disposed toward empire, it is necessary to look more closely at domestic politics.

Domestic Considerations

Private Economic Interests. The historical record suggests that economic interest groups played little, if any, role in orchestrating the imperial expansion of the late nineteenth century. As mentioned above, France's trade with and investment in its overseas empire during the pre–World War I decades never exceeded 10 percent of total external trade and investment. Moreover, parliamentary debate over colonial policy demonstrated that there was widespread agreement in the Chamber that France's colonies simply were not a paying proposition. Deputies frequently referred to the "enormous costs imposed on the metropole by colonial policy."[24] Spending on colonial administration, development, and defense climbed steadily. Public expenditure in Algeria, which often comprised close to 50 percent of annual expenditure on the overseas territories during the second half of the nineteenth century, far exceeded revenues. Between 1850 and 1900, the deficit in Algeria fluctuated between 63 and 138 million francs.[25] Similar, though much smaller, deficits were incurred in colonies outside North Africa, deficits that were not made up by trade and investment. In 1900, for example, the metropole did enjoy a positive balance of trade with the

---

[23] British and French expeditions raced each other to Fashoda, the area in which the Nile begins, almost precipitating war in 1898.

[24] 7-N-75, 28 Oct. 1902, No. 388, Procès-verbal, p. 66.

[25] François Bobrie, "Finances publiques et conquête coloniale: Le Cout budgetaire de l'expansion française entre 1850 et 1913," *Annales* (1976), 1228.

colonies of 50 million francs (200 million francs of exports and 150 million francs of imports).[26] But parliament approved a colonial budget for 1901 of 110 million francs, more than offsetting the positive balance of trade.[27] Indochina was the only territory that showed promise of being able to absorb the costs of its defense and administration and contribute to the metropolitan economy.[28] Furthermore, French territories continued to trade more heavily with foreign countries than within the empire itself. Between 1890 and 1899, annual trade between the metropole and the colonies or among the colonies themselves averaged 230 million francs, while trade between the colonies and other countries averaged 265 million francs.

The Chamber was similarly unimpressed by the return on and the opportunities for direct investment in the empire. Before World War I, investment in the colonies never exceeded more than 10 percent of all capital exported from the metropole. Despite the fact that rates of return were considerably higher in the periphery, the lower risks associated with continental investment restricted the flow of capital to the colonies.[29] As one deputy put it, "Capitalists who can invest in Russian or Spanish railroads are not going to buy colonial bonds. Let's not deceive ourselves on this point. No colonies are bringing profit to the metropole."[30] In 1900, Frenchmen invested roughly 50 million francs in the colonies, a figure that was relatively high for the pre–World War I years.[31] Even under the optimistic assumption of a return of 20 percent, these investments would have added only 10 million francs to the metropolitan economy.

A further critique of economic explanations for expansion emerges from the fact that only a small portion of the membership of the parti colonial had business interests in the periphery. In fact, though some businessmen did join the various organizations that constituted the parti, membership consisted primarily of geographers, intellectuals, and politicians. The Comité de l'Afrique Française, the group responsible for initially suggesting and then funding the Fashoda expedition,

---

[26] 7-N-75, 28 Oct. 1902, "Annexe—Tableaux," pp. 96–97. Algeria and Tunisia are not included in these data. In 1899, total commerce in Algeria and Tunisia stood at roughly 665 and 105 million francs, respectively. Trade data in this paragraph are from ibid., pp. 96–111.

[27] 7-N-75, 28 Oct. 1902, No. 388, Procès-verbal, p. 13.

[28] Between 1890 and 1899, Indochina's economy expanded enormously, with imports rising from 60 to 115 million francs and exports rising from 56 to 137 million francs. These figures represented roughly one-third of all colonial trade.

[29] Shares in mining interests in Tonkin, for example, paid dividends of over 30 percent, while dividends from mining stocks on the Continent were closer to 10 percent. See Marseille, *Empire colonial*, p. 110.

[30] Lucien Hubert cited in 7-N-75, 28 Oct. 1902, No. 388, Procès-verbal, p. 43.

[31] Marseille, *Empire colonial*, p. 112.

received less than 5 percent of its subscriptions from the financial, industrial, or transport sectors. Most donors had no economic interests at stake in the periphery but shared enthusiasm in an expansionist strain of French nationalism.[32] Since the parti colonial was an obvious instrument through which economic interest groups could channel imperial enthusiasm, the small representation of such groups in the parti casts serious doubt on their role in the expansion of the empire. There is general agreement among historians that the financial and industrial community had a minor impact on the expansionary policies of the late 1800s.

Domestic Politics. Weak governmental structures and the central bureaucracy's disinterest in colonial affairs paradoxically contributed to colonial expansion during the late 1800s. It was precisely because the French state was weak and its bureaucracy ill-prepared to handle imperial policy that a powerful domestic lobby was able to circumvent the National Assembly's substantial opposition to expansion. The Assembly repeatedly made clear its reluctance to bear the costs of overseas expansion. In 1881, partly because he had ordered the occupation of Tunis without parliamentary approval, Ferry was removed from office following a vote of no confidence. The next year, Charles Desquies de Freycinet's fall from power was related to the National Assembly's decision, by a vote of 416 to 75, to deny his request for credits to send French troops to Egypt to intervene jointly with the British.[33] In 1885, Ferry again fell from the helm after French forces suffered defeat while attempting to expand their control in Indochina. Not only did he lose a vote of confidence by 306 to 149, but some deputies also accused him of treason.[34]

Parliamentary debate over colonial policy revealed the sources of this substantial opposition to peripheral expansion. During discussion of the proposed Egyptian operation in 1882, M. Déroulède told those who argued that France should take territory in the periphery to compensate for the loss of Alsace and Lorraine, "I have lost two sisters and you offer me twenty chamber-maids." Albert Decrais, shortly before being appointed minister of colonies, remarked: "Happily, France is a great colonial power. But she is above all, and she must remain above all, a great European power. We have in Europe interests which outweigh all others, and to them our general policy must be subordi-

---

[32] C. M. Andrew and A. S. Kanya-Forstner, "The French 'Colonial Party': Its Composition, Aims, and Influence, 1885–1914," *Historical Journal,* 14, 1 (1971), 104, 110–113.
[33] Ganiage, *L'Expansion coloniale,* p. 99.
[34] Ibid., p. 57.

nate." Georges Périn rebutted as follows the argument that France had to keep pace with British expansion: "What the English can do with impunity, we cannot undertake without peril. To those who say: "'You are timorous,' I respond: "'You are blind and deaf. Blind because you do not see the open frontier on the Vosges; deaf because you do not hear the great noise of armament in Germany.'" Georges Clemenceau, one of the most outspoken critics of imperial expansion, warned the Assembly, "We must not thoughtlessly put the army at risk . . . in adventures in which no one can foresee the end and which may lead us to disaster, and the ruin of the homeland."[35] Similar statements can be found in virtually all the debates on empire that took place after 1880. Despite Ferry's seductive plan to restore French stature through peripheral expansion, neither the French public nor its elected representatives were persuaded that empire was the answer to the nation's woes. The German threat simply loomed too large.

Given this persistent resistance to empire and the consequent political costs borne by those who pursued it, how and why did the French periphery expand so dramatically between the Franco-Prussian War and the turn of the century? The answer lies in the ability of procolonialist politicians and military officers to take advantage of the weak institutional structures and instability of successive governments. Between 1870 and 1914, the average lifespan of a government was only nine months. Ministers were preoccupied with domestic issues and were rarely in office sufficiently long to become knowledgeable about colonial affairs. As the newspaper L'Autorité commented in covering a debate on the question of colonial troops, "There are very few ministers who care to know about the issue, and even fewer who care to defend before the Chamber a project which is likely to lead to passionate discussions which they feel incapable of sustaining."[36] Ministers were, therefore, largely at the whim of those politicians who had developed expertise in imperial policy and administration.

The bureaucracy was unable to provide the coherence lacking in the legislature. From 1881 to 1894, responsibility for colonial administration shifted constantly between the navy and the Ministry of Commerce. In 1881, the navy passed the baton to Commerce; in 1882 it came back. It returned to Commerce in 1889 and back to the navy in 1892. Commerce again took control in 1893 until a separate Ministry of Colo-

---

[35] Déroulède cited in Andrew and Kanya-Forstner, French Imperial Expansion, p. 13; Decrais cited in A. S. Kanya-Forstner, The Conquest of the Western Sudan: A Study in French Military Imperialism (Cambridge: Cambridge University Press, 1969), p. 2; Périn cited in ibid., p. 1; Clemenceau cited in ibid., p. 107.

[36] 28 Oct. 1896, in 7-N-68 (my translation).

nies was formed in 1894.[37] The establishment of a new ministry only added to the bureaucratic chaos. The Ministry of Colonies took charge of general colonial policy, but the administration of certain territories was lodged in other offices. The Ministry of the Interior was responsible for Algeria, the Foreign Ministry for the Tunisian and Moroccan protectorates, and the Ministry of War for certain territories outside North Africa.[38] Furthermore, because a posting to the Ministry of Colonies was one of the least prestigious assignments, the quality of the ministry's staff was well below average. As a result of these factors, French colonial policy during the last quarter of the nineteenth century lacked coherence and coordination.

The absence of an identifiable locus of decision making on imperial policy allowed the colonial lobby to influence significantly the course of French expansion. The colonialist movement, by the mid-1880s, had effectively organized and pushed forward a program of imperial growth based on nationalist and expansionist ideology. Through publications and meetings, it disseminated its message that France needed to compensate for its losses on the Continent through peripheral expansion. Through lobbying in the National Assembly and providing funds for operations in the periphery, it furthered its goal of increasing the size of French holdings overseas. With its independent sources of funding and its ability to focus its resources on a single political cause, the colonialist movement was able to manipulate a parliament and a state bureaucracy that was essentially incapable of coordinating colonial policy. The lobby initially sought to influence policy within the National Assembly itself. Failing that, it could simply advocate and fund operations in the periphery, expeditions that would later be presented to parliament as faits accomplis.[39] Furthermore, deputies were often led to believe that credits voted for the navy were earmarked for Channel and Mediterranean defenses when they were actually used to support colonial expeditions.[40]

Military Services. The manipulation of imperial policy by the colonial lobby obviously depended on the cooperation of French agents in the periphery. The proimperialists could hardly have hoped for more willing collaborators than the colonial army. Responsibility for their administration and budget oscillated between the Ministries of Marine and

---

[37] Ropp, *French Naval Policy*, p. 141.
[38] Andrew and Kanya-Forstner, *French Imperial Expansion*, pp. 18–20.
[39] See C. M. Andrew, "The French Colonialist Movement during the Third Republic: The Unofficial Mind of Imperialism," *Transactions of the Royal Historical Society*, 5th ser., 26 (1976), 158.
[40] Ropp, *French Naval Policy*, p. 143.

War.[41] Both ministries had primary missions with which they were preoccupied; the administration and control of colonial troops received little bureaucratic attention. Unfettered by centralized command, the colonial army in the 1870s began to undertake operations without the approval, and in some cases against the wishes, of befuddled political and military elites in Paris. Those responsible for pushing forward the borders of the empire were driven not only by personal ambition. These officers also viewed their own behavior as an expression of national vitality, as an effort to sustain a certain dynamism within national life. As Douglas Porch describes this attitude, "Colonial soldiers sought to transport the unity of purpose felt in the colonies back to the fatherland, uniting Frenchmen in a common bond of fraternity and national purpose."[42]

The history of French expansion in the Western Sudan is one of the most conspicuous cases of military imperialism on record. Commanders in the field chose when and where the French empire was to expand. When they received telegrams from Paris ordering them to stop further expansion, they plunged deeper into the African interior, later informing Paris that the telegram had arrived too late.[43] In Kanya-Forstner's words, "The Military formulated their own policies and generated their own expansive force which often carried them far beyond the limits envisaged by their metropolitan employers."[44] The greater the territory under military control, the tighter the grip local officers had on policy and daily administration. The colonial army came to be a proving ground for officers, and service in Africa became important to career advancement. The cult of the colonial army had a deleterious effect on the continental army by diverting officers and damaging morale. Furthermore, commanders such as Thomas-Robert Bugeaud, Joseph Galliéni, and Louis Hubert Gonzalve Lyautey developed a brand of colonial warfare that challenged existing views on continental strategy and tactics.[45]

Faced with a colonial army that was virtually out of control and the prospect of the continuing diversion of continental resources to peripheral expansion, Paris by 1890 began efforts to reassert authority over its agents in Africa. An initial order to end all expansion in the

[41] See 7-N-68, Oct. 1883, "La Défense des colonies," for a history of the colonial army.
[42] Douglas Porch, "Bugeaud, Galliéni, Lyautey: The Development of French Colonial Warfare," in *Makers of Modern Strategy: From Machiavelli to the Nuclear Age*, ed. Peter Paret (Princeton: Princeton University Press, 1986), p. 406. See also Douglas Porch, *The March to the Marne: The French Army, 1871–1914* (Cambridge: Cambridge University Press, 1981), pp. 134–168; and Clayton, *France, Soldiers, and Africa*, pp. 9–12.
[43] Kanya-Forstner, *Western Sudan*, p. 8.
[44] Ibid., p. 266.
[45] See Gottmann, "French Colonial Warfare."

Sudan and return European troops to the Continent was completely ignored: "No forts were abandoned; no troops were withdrawn; and the era of military expansion did not come to an end."[46] In succeeding years, Paris did manage to gain control of affairs in the Sudan by removing errant commanders and building a new administrative structure. Gaining control, however, by no means meant withdrawing from previously claimed territory or reducing the mounting costs of defense and administration. More through unintended consequences than deliberate decision, France found itself with a massive empire in Africa in which most of the electorate and National Assembly had little interest. Collusion between the colonial lobby and the colonial army allowed a small group of proimperialists to push forward the frontiers of the French empire despite substantial domestic opposition.

Conclusions

The 1890s were a decade of consolidation of the French empire. Opposition to voting credits to maintain the new possessions began to wane. With growing European rivalry in the periphery and the spread of nationalism to the right, the National Assembly and the French public came, however reluctantly, to accept their new colonial appendages.[47] Administrative control was gradually established over acquired territories. The Ministry of Colonies created in 1894 gave greater bureaucratic weight to colonial affairs. Ministers and bureaucrats in Paris also monitored their peripheral agents much more carefully and succeeded in preventing commanders and local officials from whimsical and surreptitious forays into unclaimed territories.[48]

The realization that the colonies were becoming a more permanent component of France's defense responsibilities led to a reconsideration of the organization and administration of colonial troops. Some deputies argued that, because of the increasing importance and permanence of the colonies, the troupes coloniales should be attached to the Ministry of War; metropolitan and colonial defense should be coordinated by a single ministry. Others argued that "the mission of the Ministry of War is already so heavy that one should not add the crushing charge

---

[46] Kanya-Forstner, *Western Sudan*, p. 173.

[47] When the government in 1896 asked for credits so that Jean Baptiste Marchand could lead an expedition to Fashoda to "reclaim our rights on the Nile," the Assembly acquiesced by a vote of 471 to 18 (Andrew, "French Colonialist Movement," p. 153). Deputies rallied behind the idea that it was time for France to force Britain to the negotiating table to reassert its political influence in Egypt.

[48] Paul Doumer, governor-general of Indochina from 1896 to 1902, tried to mount several expeditions into Yunnan but was prevented from doing so by the Foreign Ministry. Andrew and Kanya-Forstner, *French Imperial Expansion*, p. 22.

of defense of the colonies." Furthermore, it would be folly to commit more metropolitan resources to colonial defense: "In matters of colonial defense, one consideration must always weigh against our temptation to augment troops. This consideration is that, in the event of an international conflict, the fate of our armies on the continent will to a large extent determine the fate of our colonies. Victorious on the continent, we will not lose our colonies."[49] The solution was to preserve the exclusive focus of the Ministry of War on the Continent but to augment the size of the *force mobile*, a special contingent stationed in the metropole that could be used for either continental or colonial defense. This reserve corps had a "double mission and a hybrid character. It would assure the relief of colonial garrisons but, organized with more troops than needed for this mission, it would also prepare for continental action."[50]

The navy also benefited from this growing interest in overseas empire. The Chamber approved naval bills in 1900 and 1901 that allocated funds for augmenting the size of the fleet and improving the defenses of overseas ports. In part stimulated by the Fashoda crisis and an ambitious naval program in Germany, the revival of the French navy strengthened the momentum behind the movement to enhance France's global role. Overseas ports also figured prominently in existing war plans. Until 1903, the navy continued to base its war plans on conflict with England. Given the overwhelming superiority of the British battlefleet, France was going to rely heavily on torpedo boats and smaller vessels for sporadic attacks on the British fleet and its lines of communication. Because of their limited range, at least some of these smaller vessels had to be stationed at overseas ports.[51]

The French state was going through the process of adjusting to an overseas empire that it did not want. Expansion had been sustained by a unique mix of weak government structures and a powerful colonial lobby. This lobby was driven not by economic interest groups, but by a group of individuals who believed that France had to reclaim the international status that it had lost through setbacks on the Continent. The broader elite community thought otherwise. In a manner consistent with my central argument, mainstream elites responded to conditions of strategic sufficiency by focusing their attention and resources on metropolitan security and limiting peripheral liabilities. But a select group of elites, reacting to the Franco-Prussian War and France's inability to seek compensation on the Continent, turned to empire as a way

---

[49] 7-N-75, 28 Oct. 1902, No. 388, Procès-verbal, pp. 49, 68.
[50] Ibid., p. 51.
[51] For discussion of French naval strategy, see Ropp, *French Naval Policy*.

of restoring the nation's reputation, influence, and great-power status. Despite the fact that most elites were aware that expansion would make the metropole less, not more, secure and that the National Assembly was opposed to the acquisition of new overseas possessions, the colonial lobby collaborated with an errant colonial army to circumvent its opponents.

Had the state not imposed control over colonial affairs, overseas expansion would likely have been much more extensive and, perhaps, costly to metropolitan security. Such restraint on imperial ambition pulled France back from the brink of war with England in the Fashoda incident. Imposing such control, however, also meant de facto acceptance of new overseas responsibilities. By the 1890s, overseas empire had won greater acceptance among mainstream elites. Although many deputies remained skeptical of the economic and strategic benefits of empire, the National Assembly was more willing to shoulder the financial burdens of colonial administration and defense. The bureaucracy and military establishment were becoming more oriented toward overseas responsibilities; organizational incentives were changing accordingly. So, too, was popular hostility toward the overseas territories waning. In short, empire was taking root in the nation's political consciousness; supporters of expansion had begun to effect a change in strategic culture. It was not until after World War I, however, that the French polity was to show great enthusiasm for empire. In the meantime, the French were preoccupied with a rapid and perilous rise in the continental threat.

1904–1914: The German Threat and Successful Adjustment

France's tightening embrace with its overseas empire was interrupted by continental developments. From 1904 onward, an increasingly aggressive and militarily powerful Germany turned the attention of French elites from the peripheral empire to defense of the northeast frontier. France adjusted to the rapid rise of German power with impressive alacrity. During the decade before the outbreak of war, elites pursued a policy of power balancing in the core. They rearmed and sought allies to help ensure that Germany would be confronted with a preponderant opposing coalition. At the same time, French decisionmakers pursued a policy of retrenchment in the periphery. They signed a series of agreements to moderate the threats to the overseas possessions and gradually withdrew forces from imperial outposts to concentrate them in the metropole.

Strategic Assessments

Under what set of assumptions about the military balance did French elites succeed in implementing this process of adjustment? Did they perceive high metropolitan vulnerability and conditions of strategic deficiency, or were they confident that the metropole had the where-withal to cope with a German attack? Assessments of the military balance during the years before the outbreak of war reveal that elites were relatively confident about France's ability to prevail against the Triple Alliance as long as the assistance of Britain and Russia could be ensured. Military arrangements with Britain were crucial mainly because they allowed France to concentrate its naval forces in the Mediterranean, achieving superiority over the combined Italian and Austrian fleets, while Britain assumed responsibility for naval operations in the Atlantic and North Sea.[52] Maintaining sea control in the Mediterranean was essential to ensuring the transport of troops from North Africa; the navy insisted that it would not risk transport operations until it had secured "mastery in the western basin of the Mediterranean."[53] Without British assistance in the Atlantic, the French would have had to split their fleet between two main theaters. This was simply untenable: "Weakness in the Mediterranean and weakness in the North, and, as a consequence, the impossibility of taking any useful action in one sea or the other—this would be the result of the dispersion of our naval forces."[54] While French elites indeed welcomed a British contribution to the land campaign, they viewed the six divisions of the B.E.F. likely to cross the Channel as a less than vital result of entente with England. This view was based on the assumption that "the Triple Entente has sufficient means to dominate, on the land frontiers, the forces of the Triple Alliance and that, even in the event of the defection of England, Russia and France would still be able to engage in the battle without disadvantage."[55]

The guarded confidence of the planning community about the outcome of the land campaign emerged from a comparison of forces avail-

---

[52] For assessments of the naval balance in the Mediterranean, see Chap. 3, Chart 2.
[53] 2-N-1, #45, May–June 1913, p. 3.
[54] 2-N-1, #52, 23 June 1913.
[55] 2-N-1, #36, 9 Jan. 1912, p. 6.

Table 8. Forces on the Franco-German Border

	France	Germany	France and Britain
Battalions	899	841	975
Squadrons	380	420	427
Field batteries (pieces)	3,200	4,728	3,668
Heavy artillery (pieces)	84	400	108

Note: Austrian and Italian forces are not included. French elites assumed that the Austrians would devote all their forces to fighting Russia. The Italians could hypothetically send four to six corps to the Franco-German front, but they would likely be unable to arrive at the front soon enough to affect the outcome of the initial decisive battles. Under optimum circumstances, Italian troops would begin to arrive at the front on the eighteenth day.
Source: 2-N-1, #36, 9 Jan. 1912, Annexe Nos. 3 and 4.

able on the Franco-German border after full mobilization (Table 8). These figures were based on the assumption that Germany would have to divert a significant portion of its manpower to deal with Russian forces. According to French estimates, Russia would be able to mobilize 1,500 battalions, 1,000 squadrons, and 5,200 pieces of field artillery in the European theater. While French elites were well aware that the Russian army was not up to German standards, they believed that Russia's military was improving steadily from 1912 onward. This assessment was based on the marked expansion of Russia's strategic railroad network as well as the Russian army's adoption of offensive strategies.[56] As long as the Russians mobilized quickly and took the offensive by the fifteenth day of mobilization, planners calculated, Germany would have to devote a minimum of 212 battalions and 11 divisions of cavalry to the eastern front.[57] These assessments led French elites to believe that the Triple Entente had the wherewithal to defeat the Triple Alliance. Decision makers were operating under conditions of strategic sufficiency.

Dealing with the Adversary

Defense planning between 1904 and 1914 focused on the task of deterring and, if necessary, defeating Germany, while accommodating

---

[56] William Wohlforth, "The Perception of Power: Russia in the Pre-1914 Balance," *World Politics*, 39 (April 1987), 359.

[57] The French enjoyed an advantage in terms of manpower but were at a distinct disadvantage in terms of artillery (Table 8). Furthermore, the figures in the table include reserve forces. Counting only active forces, the French advantage disappears: Germany had eight divisions of cavalry and twenty-one to twenty-three corps of active infantry to France's eight divisions of cavalry and twenty-two corps of infantry. As one planning

peripheral adversaries in order to facilitate retrenchment. Efforts to fulfill this task revolved around three initiatives: strengthening the metropolitan army and navy, concentrating in or near the metropole troops and vessels previously devoted to overseas service, and forming accords that served both to aggregate the military capability needed to resist German aggression and to moderate threats to peripheral territories. As far as domestic mobilization was concerned, France embarked on a naval construction program to enable it to maintain sea control in the Mediterranean. The French army also grew in size and readiness as war looked increasingly likely. When Germany moved to increase its force levels in 1912, France followed suit. The introduction of three-year military service increased the number of active-duty soldiers to 736,000.[58] Despite important tactical and operational errors that allowed the Germans to penetrate deeply into French territory, the French succeeded in building an army sufficiently strong and mobile to stop the Germans at the Marne.[59]

French elites also put limitations on expenditure on colonial defense and began to recall vessels, equipment, and troops from the imperial periphery. Discussions within the Conseil Supérieur de Défense Nationale (CSDN), the main body responsible for formulating defense policy, clearly reveal a shift in thinking about strategic priorities. In 1908, for example, the CSDN was told that garrisons in Indochina, the most prized and economically developed overseas territory apart from French North Africa, faced a considerable shortfall of manpower. Deficits were listed as twenty-one battalions of infantry and twelve batteries

---

paper described the balance, "Our active forces would be equal, to within a few units, to the corresponding German force" (2-N-1, 19 Oct. 1912, "Comparaison des forces," p. 3).

[58] Jack Snyder, *The Ideology of the Offensive: Military Decision Making and the Disasters of 1914* (Ithaca: Cornell University Press, 1984), p. 43.

[59] French prosecution of the war suffered from three main shortcomings. First, the army was committed to undertaking a major offensive despite the existence of weaponry (such as the machine gun) that favored the defense and despite having insufficient manpower both to defend French territory and to counterattack the enemy. Second, the French concentrated their forces on the Franco-German border and in fact engaged in a costly advance into German territory at the outset of the war, thus wasting personnel and resources and leaving Belgium and France's norther border open to a rapid German advance. French intelligence failed to predict that the Germans would sweep through Belgium north of the Meuse. Third, the French underused their reserve forces by assigning them to secondary functions. These failings were, however, primarily tactical and operational in nature. Unlike during the interwar years, French elites suffered not from paralysis and the effective disintegration of grand strategy, but from miscalculation about the advantages of offense and about where the Germans would concentrate their attack. Furthermore, there was considerable debate over French doctrine and strategy during the years preceding war, and war plans were revised and updated several times between 1909 and 1914. See Samuel Williamson, *The Politics of Grand Strategy: Britain and France Prepare for War, 1904–1914* (Cambridge: Harvard University Press, 1939), chaps. 5 and 8; and Snyder, *Ideology of the Offensive*, pp. 41–106.

of artillery.[60] Despite these shortfalls, the minister of colonies himself justified a substantial reduction of troops in terms of "the need to concentrate in the metropole the financial and material assets necessary for national defense."[61] The governor-general of Indochina remarked that because the loss of sea control could well cut the link between the metropole and the Far East, force levels had to be sufficient to ensure self-defense. But he also recognized the "urgent need to reserve all military and naval forces to protect primary interests in Europe and north Africa."[62] The prime minister (Clemenceau) and the minister of foreign affairs agreed that the Japanese and the Chinese posed a considerable threat to French interests but argued that it made little sense to fortify a French contingent that would likely be quickly overrun by a vastly superior opponent. "It would in all circumstances be folly," Clemenceau stated, "to try to defend Indochina and to spend millions without profit." Clemenceau went on to say that "under all circumstances, the vital questions will be settled for us on the frontier of the Vosges; the rest is nothing but accessory."[63] Convinced that France could do little to defend Indochina and that events in the Far East were of small import given the situation in Europe, the CSDN in its meeting of 23 April 1908 approved a significant cut in troop levels and in defense expenditures for Indochina.[64]

French elites also began to transfer troops and vessels stationed in overseas territories to the metropole and drafted elaborate plans to transport the 19th Corps of the French army and thousands of indigenous troops from North Africa to the metropole should war break out on the Continent. With simultaneous departures from Algiers, Oran, Philippeville, and Bizerte, the French prepared to send thirty-four loaded transport ships to the metropole by the seventh day of general mobilization. The troops were to arrive at Marseille forty-eight hours later and depart immediately for the front.[65] Furthermore, the CSDN decided to abandon battery placements in the colonies and along the metropolitan coast in order to supplement the number of trained artillery personnel in the northeast.[66] Plans were also drawn up to transfer the units stationed along the Italian and Spanish borders to the frontier with Germany. These redeployments were motivated by a single objec-

---

[60] 2-N-1, #2, CSDN meeting of 6 Dec. 1906, Note Annexe No. 3, p. 3.
[61] 2-N-1, #20, 3 Feb. 1908, p. 1.
[62] 2-N-1, #23, 22 April 1908, p. 7.
[63] 2-N-1, #26, CSDN meeting of 23 April 1908, pp. 14, 15.
[64] Ibid., pp. 17–19.
[65] 2-N-1, #36, CSDN meeting of 9 Jan. 1912, Annexe No. 8, p. 2.
[66] 2-N-1, #36, CSDN meeting of 9 Jan. 1912, pp. 7–11.

tive: "This concise and simple goal consists of crushing Germany. . . . All other tasks must be considered as secondary."[67]

Ongoing efforts to counter indigenous resistance in Morocco posed problems for plans to repatriate troops stationed in North Africa should war break out on the Continent. Twenty-six battalions, fifteen squadrons, and ten batteries of artillery were involved in the Moroccan campaign.[68] This diversion reduced considerably the number of forces earmarked for immediate transport to Marseille. The CSDN appreciated, however, the need to ensure that as many troops as possible be available for transport to the metropole.[69] As the situation on the Continent grew more precarious, the resident general of Morocco was in fact ordered to prepare to call an end to military operations in the country. The telegram that he received from the minister of foreign affairs was unequivocal: "In the event of a continental war all your efforts must lead to maintaining in Morocco only a minimum of indispensable forces. The destiny of Morocco will be decided in Lorraine. All secondary ports and advanced positions must be temporarily abandoned." The minister requested a return telegram specifying a schedule for the departure of the expeditionary force from Morocco to the metropole.[70] Even though the French had by no means consolidated their position in Morocco, the CSDN was unwilling to entertain a diversion of resources from the main theater of battle; the timely arrival of the 19th Corps was deemed essential to coping with the German threat.

While reductions in the number of troops stationed in the colonies faced little opposition, deciding what to do with the navy's main overseas ports (points d'appuis) was more problematic. These ports were vital to maintaining lines of communication among the French colonies and to allowing the navy to sustain operations in distant waters; they provided, in short, the skeleton of the overseas empire. Nevertheless, as requirements on the Continent grew more urgent, the CSDN gradually reduced expenditure on overseas ports. The growth of the German, Italian, and Austrian fleets made it increasingly clear that the main French fleet would not be able to undertake operations distant from the metropole's Mediterranean and Atlantic coasts. In 1908, Noumea and Fort Courbet/Hongay were both dropped from the list of points d'appuis, leaving Saigon/Cap-St. Jacques, Diego-Suarez, Dakar, and Fort de France.[71] In 1913, the CSDN found it impossible to rationalize

[67] Ibid., p. 3.
[68] 2-N-1, #36, 9 Jan. 1912, Annexe No. 9, p. 2.
[69] See, for example, 2-N-1, #46, CSDN meeting of 17 May 1913, p. 15.
[70] 5-N-8, 27 July 1914.
[71] 2-N-1, #69, Commission d'Etudes, March 1914, "Rapport," p. 4.

new expenditures on even these four ports. In a meeting of 26 November, Vice-Admiral Le Bris, representing the navy, put forth the following remarkably blunt argument: "The conditions have changed; entente with England as well as the development of the German, Austrian, and Italian navies have modified the ideas informing the employment of our naval forces; these are concentrated in the Mediterranean, except for a few cruisers charged with protecting our coasts septentrionales, or on station in the Far East. The Fleet's *points d'appuis* in the colonies have thus lost their raison d'être, and the Minister of Marine requests for them no new expenditures."[72] By 1914, Dakar remained the only overseas port receiving funds for improvements, largely because of its proximity to North Africa and its potential use as a point of embarkation for transport ships headed to the metropole.[73] France had not abandoned its overseas possessions, but it had clearly retrenched from all portions other than the one major port that showed promise of contributing to metropolitan defense.

As in Britain, diplomatic initiatives accompanied these dramatic changes in France's defense posture. The Entente Cordiale of 1904 ended centuries of overt and latent hostility between France and Britain. The most important implication of the Entente was that French elites would no longer have to worry about war with England and could focus their attention on Germany. Joint military planning emerged between the British and French, and by 1906 there was a strong conviction within the CSDN that, in the event of war with Germany, France would be fighting with the support of Britain.[74] The naval accord reached in 1912 was crucial to allowing France to assume responsibility for sea control in the Mediterranean while the British fleet concentrated in the North Sea. Successive accords with Russia were also of critical importance in improving the military balance on the Continent. As discussed above, the opening of an eastern front was essential to distracting at least some of the German army from the French border. The formation of the Triple Entente was thus a central feature of France's deterrent strategy in the core.

Diplomatic initiatives served not only to address the strategic situation on the Continent, but also to reduce rivalry and moderate threats to French interests in the periphery. The 1904 accord between France and Britain established fixed spheres of influence in the Far East, preventing a clash over Siam. The French also signed accords with Japan in 1902 and with Siam in 1907. These arrangements were part of a

[72] 2-N-1, CSDN meeting of 26 Nov. 1913, p. 2.
[73] 2-N-1, #70, CSDN meeting of 7 March 1914, p. 12.
[74] 2-N-1, #9, CSDN meeting of 31 Dec. 1906, p. 2.

broader effort to reduce the likelihood of conflict in the Far East and to facilitate the withdrawal of French forces from the region. As the minister of colonies put it in February 1908, the reduction of troops in Indochina was facilitated by "the new international situation resulting from the accords and conventions recently concluded with diverse powers, notably England, Siam, and Japan."[75] A similar reconciliation of French and British interests took place in Africa. These accords moderated, but by no means eliminated, threats to French imperial possessions. There was concern that the Japanese might take advantage of a European withdrawal to attack French possessions in Indochina. Indigenous threats to French rule were also mounting, especially in North Africa. Nevertheless, as demonstrated above, the CSDN recognized the overriding importance of concentrating troops in Europe to deal with the German threat and thus resisted the urge to reinforce the colonies.

French elites thus succeeded in adjusting to rapid shifts in the continental balance of power by recalling assets from the empire and devoting their military and diplomatic resources to confronting the German threat. Conditions of strategic sufficiency enabled them to adopt a strategy of deterrence in the core and one of accommodation in the periphery. Decision makers increased the size of the metropolitan army and signed accords with Russia and Britain to offset the growing military power of Germany. They embarked on a naval construction program and coordinated operations with the British navy to maintain sea superiority over the Triple Alliance. Keeping pace in the core was facilitated by retrenchment from the periphery. Accords formed with imperial rivals lowered the potential costs of withdrawal, but assets were recalled to the metropole because of the German threat, not because they were not needed in the periphery. These policies reflected a clear sense of strategic priorities and an appreciation of the fact that the limbs of the empire would be meaningless if the heart were destroyed. Reputational concerns ran low; threats to French interests would be dealt with through the marshaling of preponderant military power, not through demonstrations of resolve. Rather than seeking overseas territories to compensate for France's losses on the Continent, elites became immunized to setbacks in the periphery as they redressed more pressing matters in the core. By the outbreak of war, Dakar was effectively the only overseas port still viewed as a *point d'appuis*, a decision based on its importance as a port of embarkation for colonial troops headed for the metropole. Other than serving this

[75] 2-N-1, #20, 3 Feb. 1908, p. 1.

purpose, as Vice-Admiral Le Bris put it, empire had lost its raison d'être.

Domestic Considerations

Domestic forces presented few obstacles to elite efforts to pursue a policy of power balancing in the core and one of retrenchment in the periphery. Although the French empire had expanded considerably after 1880, colonial affairs had not yet become a prominent feature of the political landscape. Economic interest groups, because of the relatively small amount of trade and investment at stake, did not stand in the way of retrenchment in the periphery. As during the first decades of the Third Republic, financiers continued to doubt the reliability of imperial investments. Nor were there high political costs associated with downgrading the strategic importance of the colonies. While the National Assembly was warming to empire, domestic legitimacy was by no means wedded to the preservation of imperial commitments; empire did not yet loom large in the public mind. There was some public opposition to entente with Britain because of lingering Anglophobia, but historical memory was insufficient to block the formation of the Entente Cordiale. Finally, there was little bureaucratic resistance to imperial retrenchment. The organizational interests of elite institutions were not tightly wedded to overseas missions. Especially because such a small portion of the military establishment had been involved in peripheral operations, the military services had few problems with the decisions of the CSDN to focus almost exclusively on continental defense. Even the navy, the service with the most vested interests in overseas missions, recognized the need to concentrate on metropolitan defense.

Conclusions

French elites adjusted with speed and purpose to the rapid shifts in the international balance of power that took place after the turn of the century. The military and diplomatic components of grand strategy were well integrated. France rearmed and recalled its troops and its naval forces from the periphery. On the diplomatic front, French elites signed a series of accords with Japan, Russia, and Britain both to reduce threats to the overseas territories and to offset German military might. They realized that there was only one primary security concern: the defense of the metropole. The empire may have offered the opportunity to recover the status lost in 1871, but such status was of little use in dealing with the Triple Alliance. Military force, not reputation, was needed to stop German aggression. Strategic sufficiency enabled French elites to cope with rapid shifts in the continental balance of power in a seemingly rational and sensible manner: they prepared for continental war by rearming, seeking allies, and recalling forces from the periphery to protect the heart of the empire.

1932–1939: Adjustment Failure and
the Apotheosis of Empire

World War I rekindled the imperial impulse among the French elite. The postwar years were characterized by unprecedented enthusiasm for the expansion and development of the overseas territories. During the 1930s, however, elites again had to rein in imperial ambition; France faced rapid and adverse shifts in the continental balance of power which threatened the security of the metropole and necessitated a reorientation of grand strategy. French elites indeed recognized the severity of the German threat and the pressing need to marshal resources against it. But, unlike during the years before World War I, they were unable to reorient strategy and find a viable diplomatic and military plan for the defense of the metropole. Instead of adopting a strategy of deterrence in the core and one of accommodation in the periphery, French elites pursued policies of appeasement in the core and indiscriminate defense in the periphery. By the end of the 1930s, the French found themselves diplomatically isolated and protected by an army ill-suited, in both qualitative and quantitative terms, to cope with the Wehrmacht. As Germany rearmed and demonstrated increasingly aggressive intentions, the French did increase the size of their metropolitan army and devoted considerable financial resources to improving metropolitan defenses. But throughout the decade, the quality and doctrine of the metropolitan army stagnated as the French military devoted far too much attention as well as some of its best equipment and personnel to peripheral missions. Despite the fact that French elites had sufficient time to transport their finest troops from Africa to the metropole before the German attack, the metropolitan army lasted only a matter of weeks against Hitler's forces. France fell prey to both strategic exposure and overextension. How did French elites find themselves with a grand strategy that demonstrated little sensitivity to the gross shifts in diplomatic alignments and in the balance of power that occurred in the 1930s? Especially in light of the strategic reorientation undertaken between 1904 and 1914, this adjustment failure is striking and begs deeper inquiry.

The Legacy of World War I

The overseas territories made a significant contribution to the defense of the metropole during the course of World War I. The demand for colonial contributions became especially acute late in 1917 when the predicted collapse of the eastern front pointed to a shortfall in manpower in the west that exceeded 300,000 men.[76] The colonies indeed rose to the occasion. By November, some 333,000 recruits had arrived in the metropole, most of them from Algeria and West Africa.[77] In addition, almost 200,000 workers from all corners of the empire were transported to France to further the war effort.[78] This tangible contribution of the periphery to metropolitan security was to alter fundamentally the way in which elites and the French public conceived of their overseas possessions. As becomes evident below, the image of masses of indigenous troops arriving on the Continent to defend the metropole was to create an indelible link between core and periphery that colored French policy throughout the interwar period.

Imperial objectives became of increasing importance even before the outcome of the continental struggle was clear. As during the decades after the Franco-Prussian War, the parti colonial took advantage of the government's preoccupation with metropolitan affairs to press for the expansion of French possessions in the Middle East. The British decided in 1916 to fortify their forces along the Mediterranean littoral both to support an eastern flank against the Germans and to incorporate into their sphere of influence chunks of the crumbling Ottoman empire. Driven principally by concern about preventing British domination of South Asia and the Middle East, the colonial lobby—mainly the Comité de l'Asie Française—began to press the government to divert troops from the central front to Lebanon and Syria. The cabinet initially scoffed at these proposals, arguing that, with the battle raging in France, "nothing appears less desirable than intervention in Syria." To the suggestion of the minister of foreign affairs late in 1917 that troops be sent from North Africa to the Middle East, the minister of war responded negatively, arguing that this was precisely the time at which "we are taking from North Africa the most vigorous elements of the infantry to place them in the French theater of operations."[79]

---

[76] Andrew and Kanya-Forstner, *French Imperial Expansion*, p. 138.
[77] Ibid., p. 134.
[78] Ibid., p. 140.
[79] Ibid., p. 69; 4-N-61, 24 Dec. 1917, p. 2.

Again emulating the 1880s, the procolonialists circumvented this resistance by acting without governmental approval: the minister of the navy agreed to a joint British-French operation in the Dardanelles without informing the cabinet.[80] He justified his furtive behavior by arguing that "not to take part in the operation would have been . . . for us French, who are deeply involved in the Orient, a very painful renunciation of our national pride and perilous for our interests."[81]

This theme was to resonate within the cabinet during 1918, when the government finally ceded to pressure to send an expeditionary corps to the Middle East and authorized the dispatch of an initial contingent of 3,000 troops. By the middle of the year, the French were maintaining roughly 6,500 troops in the Levant.[82] The small size of the force testifies to its largely symbolic objectives; Britain, by January 1918, had well over 100,000 combatants in Egypt and Palestine. The French contingent was to serve primarily as a signal that France was unwilling to accept British hegemony throughout the Middle East. Cabinet-level communications confirm the extent to which rivalry with Britain motivated French behavior. An influential document drafted by the Comité de l'Asie Française and discussed by ministers lays bare French concerns:

> The establishment in the Levant of a domination other than that of France would inflict upon us a *considerable loss of prestige throughout the Orient*, in all of the Moslem world and particularly in North Africa.
>
> It would be *perilous for the maintenance*, after the war, of *our alliance with England*, if that power were to take in the Levant advantages which would not be shared by us, despite the sacrifices that we have made for the common cause. This peril would be especially great if these advantages spread to Syria, which we consider to be the traditional domain of our influence.[83]

To prevent this outcome France needed to have an expeditionary force in the region that could both engage in joint operations with the British against the Turks and act independently to provide internal security in Lebanon and Syria. In either case, the presence of troops would enable the French government to play a greater role in the postwar partition of territories and "to enhance the prestige of France."[84] Though allies on the Continent, Britain and France had, by late 1917,

---

[80] Andrew and Kanya-Forstner, *French Imperial Expansion*, p. 71.
[81] Cited in ibid., p. 72.
[82] 4-N-61, 6 Oct. 1918. Figures include both French and indigenous troops.
[83] 4-N-61, 7 Feb. 1918, "Analyse d'une note."
[84] 4-N-61, 17 Jan. 1918, Picot to Ministry of Foreign Affairs.

rekindled their rivalry in the periphery and begun to disperse into the empire the troops that had been recalled only a few years earlier to prevent German domination of the Continent.

The pressing need for manpower in the metropole severely restricted the number of French troops serving in the periphery during the war. The Versailles Treaty then released the French army from its responsibilities in the core. French troops during the early postwar years rushed to reclaim positions in the imperial periphery that had been abandoned before and during the war. The empire in 1921 reached its largest size since the Napoleonic era, expanding into new territories in the Middle East. Many indigenous troops were returned to their places of origin, although a significant number continued to serve on the Continent. Tens of thousands of French career soldiers also departed for the empire. In 1923 alone, some 70,000 French troops left for the Levant and North Africa.[85] This outward flow of troops was accompanied by a reduction in the size of the standing army from roughly 900,000 to 500,000 during the 1920s.[86] Colonial service became a popular route for career advancement, contributing to the strategic reorientation of the military services toward the imperial periphery. As Clayton writes, "The day to day business of active soldiering was in Africa, or on occasions Indochina or the Levant."[87] Given the limitations imposed on the size of the German army at Versailles and the guarantees of collective security embodied in the Treaty of Locarno, this resurgence of imperial fervor posed no immediate threat to the security of the metropole. During the 1930s, however, the implications for metropolitan security of this return to empire were to take on a different complexion.

Strategic Assessments

From the early 1920s onward, French elites were all too aware that military missions were rapidly outstripping military resources. The French empire was expanding at the same time that the size of the French army and its budget were undergoing drastic cuts. In September 1920, Marshall Lyautey remarked that the military "has taken on more missions than it is materially possible for this country to support."[88] The situation worsened in the mid-1920s because of indigenous uprisings throughout the empire. In 1925, the French put down

---

[85] Doise and Vaïsse, *Diplomatie*, p. 281.
[86] Ibid., p. 283.
[87] Clayton, *France, Soldiers, and Africa*, p. 20.
[88] Cited in Doise and Vaïsse, *Diplomatie*, p. 268.

a Druze rebellion in Syria. During the 1920s and 1930s, some 300,000 troops participated in a series of pacification campaigns in Morocco. French troops were also repeatedly used in Indochina during these years to cope with sporadic revolts. Though the French made extensive use of recruits raised in their overseas territories, increasing numbers of career soldiers were drawn from the metropole to train and command indigenous units. The occupation force in Germany shrank from 100,000 to 60,000 by 1927 and was entirely withdrawn by 1930. The growing need for troops in the periphery was one of the main reasons for the withdrawal of the occupation force. As Doise and Vaïsse describe this process, "The need for troops in Morocco and the Levant led to the dismantling of the army of the Rhine."[89]

The impact on metropolitan security of this steady outward flow of troops was exacerbated by a precipitous drop in the quality of the units remaining in France. This qualitative decline came about for three main reasons. First, because conscripts were legally ineligible for overseas service, colonial missions had to be fulfilled by career troops and officers. This law left the home army with few experienced personnel, turning it into more of a training institution than an effective fighting force. In the early 1930s, well over half of France's career soldiers were serving overseas; those remaining in the metropole were preoccupied with training one-year conscripts.[90] Second, financial constraints severely limited the modernization of equipment. After the Great Depression, the financial crisis of 1931, and the devaluation of the franc that followed, military spending dropped sharply, falling by 32 percent between 1931 and 1935.[91] A significant portion of the remaining funds were poured into fixed defenses on the northeast border: the infamous Maginot Line. Hit hardest by the cuts were the main units of the territorial army. Throughout the 1930s, many of these units were still using firearms and ordnance made before or during World War I. Third, because of both the devastation suffered during the war and the priority consistently assigned to colonial defense, efforts to improve metropolitan forces were met with a pervasive sense of lethargy. During the early 1930s, many officers left the military because of low pay, few opportunities for advancement, and lagging morale.[92] These factors and the qualitative decline that they produced led General Maxime Weygand to write in a report on the general state of the military sub-

---

[89] Ibid., p. 274.

[90] William Shirer, *The Collapse of the Third Republic: An Inquiry into the Fall of France in 1940* (New York: Simon and Schuster, 1969), p. 174; and Doise and Vaïsse, *Diplomatie*, p. 284.

[91] Doise and Vaïsse, *Diplomatie*, p. 305.

[92] Challener, *Nation in Arms*, pp. 138–139; and Shirer, *Collapse of the Third Republic*, p. 173.

mitted in April 1930 that "the French army threatened to become nothing but a costly façade unsuitable for waging war."[93]

After fifteen years of the virtual neglect, if not outright dismantling, of the home army, the French faced a striking military imbalance with Nazi Germany during the second half of the 1930s. Even before Hitler's rearmament programs were under way, French elites saw their military inferiority looming on the horizon. They "realized that because of her greater manpower and industrial strength Germany would be, as soon as she rearmed, militarily superior to France alone."[94] These predictions proved all too accurate. In 1935, Hitler decreed the establishment of a conscript army of thirty-six divisions, roughly twice the size of the French army serving in the metropole. During the same year, the French increased the length of military service from one to two years. But the Germans had roughly twice the number of men of military age, leading to vast German superiority in terms of active and reserve ground divisions. From 1936 onward, the military produced increasingly unfavorable assessments of the Franco-German military balance. By the end of the decade, Germany's rearmament program and the incorporation of Austrian and Czech assets into its military machine produced a daunting imbalance. The General Staff in 1939 calculated that, *including* the troops stationed in North Africa, France could field roughly 100 divisions in comparison to Germany's 200. The balance looked even worse when potential coalitions were taken into consideration. Planners estimated that a Franco-British coalition would be able to field 120 divisions while the Germans and Italians could mobilize more than 250. The General Staff concluded that unless the British undertook a massive rearmament program, "the numerical balance could be reestablished only by the constitution of a [new] coalition." Poland, Romania, and Yugoslavia were listed as potential candidates.[95]

The situation in the air was even worse. Before the mid-1930s, the French had focused their attention on civilian aviation and, in particular, on using planes to facilitate links between the metropole and its overseas possessions. To the extent that airpower was developed as a

[93] Cited in Doise and Vaïsse, *Diplomatie,* p. 279.
[94] Shirer, *Collapse of the Third Republic,* p. 183. On French assessments of the military balance, see Anthony Adamthwaite, *France and the Coming of the Second World War, 1936–1939* (Totowa, N.J.: Frank Cass, 1977), esp. chaps. 11–13; and Robert Young, *In Command of France: French Foreign Policy and Military Planning, 1933–1940* (Cambridge: Harvard University Press, 1978), esp. chaps. 7 and 8.
[95] 7-N-3439, 28 March 1939, "Conversations d'Etat-Major France-Britanniques," pp. 5–7. For French assessments of the German strength in 1938, see Williamson Murray, *The Change in the European Balance of Power, 1938–1939* (Princeton: Princeton University Press, 1984), pp. 164–165.

military instrument, planners assumed that aircraft would be used exclusively to support army and navy operations.[96] In 1938, while considering the possibility of going to war with Germany after the Anschluss, General Joseph Vuillemin, the chief of staff for the air force, estimated that French air power would be totally destroyed by the fifteenth day of combat.[97] Despite a new building program begun in 1938 to develop an independent air arm and construct more than 4,700 aircraft, the French found themselves in mid-1939 with 1,735 planes (only 500 of which were modern) while Germany and Italy combined had more than 5,000.[98] Although Britain had some 1,660 (most of which were antiquated), they were not of great consolation to the French inasmuch as it was unlikely that they would be used to defend French territory.[99]

The balance at sea was also cause for concern. While French elites hoped that the Atlantic coast and North Sea would be covered by the British navy, allied sea control in the Mediterranean was by no means ensured, especially since Britain had decided to give priority to the Far East and had repeatedly shunned formal alliance with France. The French fleet had five battleships and battlecruisers while the Italian fleet had six battleships. The French had 59 submarines while the Italians had 105.[100] The French navy was also going to be preoccupied with transporting troops, not attacking enemy fleets. According to the 1939 version of the war plans, the primary mission of the navy was "to assure at any cost . . . during the first weeks of the war the transport of troops to the metropole."[101] Unsure of its ability to traverse a body of water potentially patrolled by hostile ships and submarines, the navy, from the early 1930s onward, was unable to guarantee the minister of war that it would be able to carry out successfully the transport mission without considerable delay.[102] As becomes evident shortly, this uncertainty about the navy's ability to secure a timely link with Africa raised serious problems for French war plans. In summary, elites during the 1930s were well aware of the extreme vulnerability of the metropole;

---

[96] Doise and Vaïsse, *Diplomatie*, pp. 291–292.

[97] Cited in ibid., p. 317.

[98] Ibid., p. 314.

[99] CAB 16/209, 14 March 1939, British Strategic Memorandum, p. 9; and Paul Kennedy, *The Rise and Fall of British Naval Mastery* (London: Macmillan, 1938), p. 294.

[100] Kennedy, *British Naval Mastery*, p. 294. These are 1940 figures.

[101] 7-N-3884, 1 Jan. 1939, "Plan de défense de la IVème Région maritime," p. 27.

[102] See, for example, 7-N-4193, Dossier 10, Feb./March 1933 (undated), "Observations sur le rapport du General Rinck."

on land, in the air, and at sea, the imbalances were, to say the least, daunting.

Dealing with the Adversary

French grand strategy was initially well suited to the strategic environment of the interwar period. French elites devised a coherent set of war plans for coping with conditions of strategic deficiency. They accommodated German demands in the core in order to avoid war, while adopting a deterrent stance in the periphery in order to extract from the colonies the troops needed to offset the material shortfall in the metropole. The problem was that this grand strategy grew increasingly divorced from strategic realities during the second half of the 1930s. Despite the availability of incoming information that contradicted the basic tenets of French strategy, elites did not undertake a much-needed reorientation of policy until it was far too late. Growing metropolitan vulnerability produced a period of virtual paralysis in the core and the adoption of increasingly ambitious strategies in the periphery.

French grand strategy during the interwar period was predicated on three key suppositions. First, because of both the huge losses incurred in the offensives of World War I and France's manpower deficit, planners posited that France could best cope with the German threat by preparing its forces for defensive operations and building formidable fortifications. After withdrawing from the Rhineland in 1930, France started construction on the Maginot Line, an elaborate network of fixed fortifications running along the Franco-German border. French elites assumed that the Maginot Line would force the Germans to attack through the low countries. The Franco-Belgian military alliance signed in 1920 would allow French forces to take up prepared defensive positions in Belgium and blunt the German attack well before the Wehrmacht reached French territory.[103] A substantial portion of French defense spending was allocated to the construction of the Maginot Line and defensive weaponry, especially antitank and antiaircraft guns. As a result, the French were developing an army that was extremely limited in terms of both mobility and offensive capability.

Second, the military based war plans on the supposition that French forces would be fighting alongside a host of allies. Of primary importance was Great Britain. French elites deemed the Royal Navy essential to maintaining sea control in the European theater and to protecting

---

[103] For a concise summary of these plans, see Barry Posen, *The Sources of Military Doctrine: France, Britain, and Germany between the World Wars* (Ithaca: Cornell University Press, 1984), pp. 105–140.

imperial lines of communication.[104] Such an alliance was natural given the overlap between British and French imperial interests. The British would, out of self-interest, protect the main sea lanes of communication; the French, enjoying the benefits of British efforts, would offer in return access to overseas bases and facilities.[105] French elites were also hoping to secure the participation of the British army in the ground battle as well as the participation of the Royal Air Force in air operations. In addition, as before World War I, the French sought alliances with countries to Germany's east to ensure that the Wehrmacht would be forced to split its forces between two fronts. During the 1920s, France formed defensive alliances with Czechoslovakia, Poland, Romania, and Yugoslavia. French elites also sought to retain cordial relations with Italy to ensure both that Italian naval forces did not threaten French territories or shipping in the Mediterranean and that French forces would not have to be redeployed from the northeast to the Franco-Italian border. Until the mid-1930s, the lack of robust offensive capability did not undercut the credibility of France's alliance network. Germany's military strength remained limited. The Rhineland was demilitarized. Should Germany have attacked one of France's allies in central Europe, the French could have retaliated and advanced into Germany's industrial heartland without great difficulty. The diplomatic and strategic components of French grand strategy were in synch.

Third, French elites based grand strategy on the supposition that a continental war would be long in duration and that the outcome would rely heavily on the ability of the combatants to marshal troops and resources over the long term.[106] The supposition of a lengthy war was crucial to French grand strategy. Even if the adversary enjoyed considerable superiority on the ground, French defenses would delay, if not halt, the initial German offensive. The allies, in the meantime, would steadily be gaining strength because of an increase in the pace of rearmament and the arrival of resources from their colonial empires. Like their British counterparts, French elites deliberately slowed the pace of rearmament during the 1930s in order to protect the domestic economy. After the outbreak of hostilities, they reasoned, the pace of rearmament could be quickened and the economy would be better prepared to support a long war.[107] Increasing stocks of materiel and

[104] On French thinking about Franco-British military cooperation, see 7-N-3439, Dossier 1.

[105] See, for example, 7-N-4196, Dossier 1, 13 Oct. 1938, "Note," and 7-N-3439, Dossier 1, 16 May 1939, "Note."

[106] Young, *In Command of France*, pp. 27–28.

[107] Adamthwaite, *Coming of the Second World War*, p. 27; and Young, *In Command of France*, p. 41.

the steady influx of troops from the periphery would allow Britain and France to redress German ground superiority both by increasing troop levels on the western front and by opening a second front in the east.

French war plans were thus predicated on a two-stage battle.[108] During the first stage, French and allied forces deployed on the Continent would block the initial German advance. The allies would have the capability to stalemate Germany but not to take the offensive or defeat German forces. In the meantime, war-making capability in the imperial periphery would be transported to the metropole. During the second phase of the war, France and its allies, fortified by the resources of the empire, would take the offensive and destroy German forces. French elites thus believed that success in a war against Germany and its potential allies depended critically on France's ability to extract from the colonies military resources lacking in the metropole itself. French decision makers assumed during the second half of the 1930s that the overseas territories, not including North Africa, would furnish more than 300,000 soldiers and close to 200,000 workers to the metropole

Table 9. Troops to be transported to the metropole and Mediterranean basin

Overseas Territory	Trained Soldiers	Untrained Soldiers	Workers
Indochina	2,000	65,000	60,000
Black Africa	77,000	100,000	73,000
Indian Ocean	20,000	25,000	51,000
Antilles/Pacific	15,000	—	5,000
Total	114,000	190,000	189,000

Source: 7-N-3927, Dossier 6, 23 Feb. 1939.

during the first year of the war (Table 9). So too would thousands of metropolitan Frenchmen and North African soldiers converge on the metropole.

The assumption that metropolitan security rested on the assistance of the empire was clearly reflected in force levels and deployments during the 1930s. Intensified recruitment efforts in the colonies led to steadily increasing numbers of indigenous troops. Military leaders also engaged in the difficult process of ranking the overseas territories in order of their strategic importance. Troops were then withdrawn from territories of secondary importance and concentrated in North Africa and important colonial garrisons. There was little disagreement within the planning community over the standards that should be used to judge the importance of overseas possessions. Three considerations

[108] See Young, *In Command of France*, pp. 41–42.

[222]

were most prominent in assessing the value of a given territory: its capacity to send soldiers and workers to the metropole, its potential contribution to war industry and materiel stockpiles, and its utility as a base for protecting sea lanes of communication to facilitate the transport of troops and materiel.[109] General Jules-Antoine Bührer, chief of the General Staff for the Colonies, strongly supported a policy of selective retrenchment based on these standards. An examination of current force dispositions, Bührer argued, reveals that 'there is such an outmoded dispersion of personnel and materiel that one cannot expect any results in the case of external aggression.'[110] Before a gathering of the Chiefs of the General Staff in late September 1938, Bührer reiterated that "the budgetary effort is divided among all the colonies; this dispersion is harmful to national defense. . . . One consideration dominates all others: What do we intend to defend? This determines how we deduce what means to allocate to the defense effort."[111]

After a heated debate about whether to rank the overseas territories in terms of their strategic importance, the General Staff did distinguish between territories worth defending at all cost and those to be held by police forces only.[112] In their meeting of 25 November 1938, the chiefs identified the following territories as those to be defended only by police: in West Africa—Guineau (except Conkary), Ivory Coast (except Abidjan), Togo, and Dahomey; in Central Africa—Cameroon (except Douala), Gabon, Oubanghi-Chari, Middle Congo (except Pointe-Noire); French East Africa (except Diego Suarez); the Antilles (except Fort de France); all outposts in India; all Pacific islands; Saint Pierre and Miquelon.[113] The chiefs also decided that garrisons in French conces-

---

[109] See, for example, 7-N-4196, Dossier 2, 10 Nov. 1938, "Note," General Staff, Overseas Section, p. 2; 7-N-3927, Dossier 4, 1938 (undated), "Plan d'ensemble de défense des colonies," p. 1; and 7-N-3927, Dossier 4, 12 Oct. 1938, "Note," pp. 1–2.

[110] 7-N-3927, Dossier 4, 31 March 1938, Bührer to the Vice-President of the Conseil Supérieur de la Guerre, pp. 5–6.

[111] 2-N-246, Dossier 2, 28 Sept. 1938, Procès-verbal, p. 3.

[112] Opponents of this view argued that it was impossible to make such distinctions in the abstract; priorities could be assigned to different portions of the empire only after the outbreak of war and clarification of the enemies' intentions and capabilities. In other words, they wanted to define priorities in terms of the severity of the threat, not in terms of intrinsic strategic value. The minister of colonies maintained that "it is not possible to decide a priori which important fractions of the Empire will not be defended except by police." Such matters would be addressed by the proper committee only when and if the need were to arise (2-N-246, Dossier 2, Sept. 1938, Note, p. 1). Similarly, Admiral Jean Darlan, chief of the General Staff for the Navy, doubted whether it would be possible to draw up a list of possessions of so-called secondary importance: "I think that the list of these territories—after taking into consideration the diverse aspects of the needs of national defense—will be ultimately reduced to a very few places" (2-N-246, Dossier 2, 1 Sept. 1938, Darlan to the Chief of the General Staff for National Defense, p. 1).

[113] 2-N-246, Dossier 2, Procès-verbal, Annexe II.

sions in China were to be reduced to a minimum. The rationale is particularly interesting in light of Britain's decision that it could not reduce its garrison in Shanghai because such a move would only invite Japanese aggression; for the British, it was better to fight and lose than not to fight at all. Bührer's thinking was just the opposite: "The corps of occupation [in China] has nothing more than a symbolic value; its reduction, if pushed to the extreme in peacetime, will allow its total withdrawal without injury and without delay in case of tension."[114] A general review of imperial defense plans concurred: reducing the China garrison would allow France to concentrate in Indochina "the totality of our military effort in the Far East." And, in any case, French positions in China could not be defended "without consenting to a permanent budgetary effort out of proportion with the real importance of the interests at stake." If the concession areas are attacked, the report concluded, all European soldiers and civilians should be evacuated.[115]

In part as a result of this ordering of priorities, units from distant parts of the empire were transferred to North Africa to ease their transport to the metropole and to release French and North African soldiers for metropolitan service should war break out.[116] Planners drafted elaborate mobilization and transport schedules to ensure the timely arrival of these troops in France. The first major wave of reinforcements was to arrive three to four months after the outbreak of war, and the remaining units would follow during months five through twelve.[117]

Until the mid-1930s, the three critical assumptions on which French grand strategy was predicated were quite consistent with the strategic landscape. Construction of the Maginot Line had proceeded apace, and the military alliance with Belgium stood firm. The French enjoyed good relations with their allies in the east and had little reason to doubt Britain's willingness to help prevent German aggression. And the German army was small enough, the prospect of a German attack sufficiently remote, and the German frontier sufficiently susceptible to penetration by French forces to warrant sacrificing metropolitan readiness to defend empire and to raise indigenous troop levels. Moreover, the war-making capacity of the empire was growing, and good rela-

---

[114] 7-N-4196, Dossier 3, 23 Nov. 1938, Note, p. 4.

[115] 7-N-3927, Dossier 4, 1938 (no date), "Plans d'ensemble de défense des colonies," Annexe 5, pp. 2, 5.

[116] The process of amassing troops in North Africa began in the early 1930s. See, for example, 2-N-243, Dossier 2, 31 July 1935, Rapport, p. 4.

[117] See, for example, 7-N-3927, Dossier 5, 19 July 1937, Instructions.

tions with Italy suggested that France would have little problem transporting troops and materiel to the metropole should they be needed.

The problem, however, is that the strategic landscape changed rapidly from 1936 onward, making these critical assumptions dangerously obsolete. Not only was German rearmament well under way by 1936, but Belgium renounced its 1920 alliance with France and declared a return to its traditional policy of neutrality. As Jeffrey Gunsburg notes, "The loss of Belgium was not only a disaster for France in 1936, it disrupted the foundations of French strategy against Germany."[118] France could no longer count on taking up fortified positions in Belgium and stalemating the Germans before they could reach French territory. In effect, France's northern border began to look very much like its northeastern border; the Maginot Line, or an equivalent network of defensive fortifications, needed to be extended along the Franco-Belgian border.[119] Some fortifications were built in response to Belgian neutrality, but they were far inferior to those constructed on the frontier with Germany. The French built not a continuous line of robust defensive positions, but sporadically placed fortified areas.[120] Furthermore, the German decision to move toward more armored and mechanized ground forces and the success of armored offensives and of air attacks in the Spanish Civil War (1936–1939) should have made French elites increasingly concerned about the army's defensive doctrine, its lack of armor and mobility, and the consequent difficulties French troops might encounter in blocking a German advance. Indeed, beginning in 1935, French intelligence warned that German armor threatened to render obsolete the army's defensive war plans. Isolated members of the elite community—both civilians and military officers—warned of the need to modernize and mechanize the metropolitan

---

[118] Jeffrey Gunsburg, *Divided and Conquered: The French High Command and the Defeat of the West, 1940* (Westport, Conn.: Greenwood Press, 1979), p. 30. See also Posen, *Sources of Military Doctrine*, pp. 109–124.

[119] Some military leaders, doubtful of France's ability to block the German advance in Belgium, urged the construction of such fortifications even before the Belgian declaration of neutrality. See, for example, the views of General Weygand, in Young, *In Command of France*, pp. 37–38; and the views of General Joffre in Shirer, *Collapse of the Third Republic*, p. 172.

[120] There were clear financial and political obstacles to extending the Maginot Line. Some opponents argued that the country simply did not have sufficient economic resources to build major fortifications on the northern border. See Adamthwaite, *Coming of the Second World War*, pp. 161–162. Others argued that the construction of such fortifications would indicate that France had written off the defense of Belgium. Such a move might undermine the confidence of France's other allies and lower Germany's expected costs of advancing into the low countries. See Gunsburg, *Divided and Conquered*, p. 21. Despite these reservations, the Belgian declaration of neutrality should have stimulated a far more ambitious effort to fortify France's northern border.

army.[121] Nevertheless, the French army clung to its traditional focus on infantry and artillery. Tanks were to be used primarily to support infantry. As Robert Young notes, "The infantry remained the queen of battle; artillery remained her consort. In contrast, the role of aviation and armored units, the most dramatic innovations of the war, won scant recognition."[122] In addition, the potential need both to move rapidly into Belgium to meet advancing German troops and to make use of thinly spread fortified areas meant that French forces needed increased mobility. But in this respect as well, adjustment did not take place; little was done to bring more mobility to French forces or to focus training more on maneuver as opposed to firepower. In 1937, cavalry regiments that were to have been mechanized were still relying on horses for mobility.

Reflecting on the situation in 1936, the French Commission of Enquiry convened after the end of World War II was "highly critical of the state of the French Army and of the armaments industry at the time. . . . The French High Command had failed to produce new plans for reorganisation in accordance with technical advances, or any plans with new ideas, modern doctrines or original thought." Furthermore, the problem was not a financial one. In 1935, the army used only 40 percent of the funds allocated to it.[123] In 1936 and again in 1938, despite weaknesses in the domestic economy, the government approved major increases in defense spending and the expansion of rearmament programs. The credits approved in late 1938 for defense expenditure in the coming year represented 85 percent of expected government receipts for 1939. But the money was not spent where it was most needed. At the beginning of 1939, the French were producing their heavy tanks at a rate of only eight per month.[124] Unlike in Britain, the problem was not that elites were unwilling to expend resources on rearmament. Rather, they were devoting their resources to a rearmament program predicated on outmoded strategic suppositions. As Young writes, "By the end of 1936 the practicability of France's entire defensive strategy was open to question." Anthony Adamthwaite

[121] See Robert Young, "Preparations for Defeat: French War Doctrine in the Inter-War Period," *Journal of European Studies*, 2, 2 (1972), 166, 171. See also Martin Alexander, "Did the Deuxieme Bureau Work? The Role of Intelligence in French Defence Policy and Strategy, 1919–1939," *Intelligence and National Security*, 6, 2 (1991), 325.

[122] Young, "Preparations for Defeat," p. 160. Paul Reynaud and Charles de Gaulle were two of the most outspoken proponents of the need to adapt French strategy to technological change.

[123] The report of the commission as summarized in Norman Gibbs, *Grand Strategy: Rearmament Policy*, vol. 1 (London: H.M.S.O., 1976), p. 244.

[124] Shirer, *Collapse of the Third Republic*, pp. 418, 178. In 1938, France was producing forty aircraft per month while Germany was producing 250 per month (pp. 333–334).

agrees that "a radical revision of strategy and tactics was needed" after 1936.[125] Such a revision, however, was simply not forthcoming.

The assumption that France would be fighting alongside a host of allies also grew increasingly obsolete from 1936 onward. Virtually all of France's alliances were either formally broken or called into question during the second half of the 1930s. French elites did little other than watch their alliance network unravel. The alliance with Belgium was not France's only diplomatic setback in 1936. The absence of a French response to Germany's reoccupation of the Rhineland left France's eastern allies somewhat skeptical of France's willingness and ability to defend its autonomy and territorial integrity. As one historian of the period put it, "Neither in doctrine nor in force preparations were the French prepared for that immediate offensive response which could almost certainly have denied Germany the fruits of her initial surprise and that probably without a major conflict."[126] Part of the problem was that French war plans prevented offensive action until full mobilization of the defensive covering force (*couverture*). Given the fact that such mobilization took at least two weeks, this scheme effectively meant that French forces were incapable of taking spontaneous action to reverse Germany's move or to come to the rapid assistance of allies.[127] Furthermore, having reoccupied the Rhineland, the Germans soon began to construct defensive fortifications. Fixed defenses made punitive French action in response to German aggression in the east even more unlikely. The lack of French offensive capability now took on a different complexion. In the face of growing German military strength and ambition, French inaction and the army's limited ability to mount offensive operations began to undermine the credibility of France's alliance network. The diplomatic and strategic components of French grand strategy were drifting apart.

At roughly the same time, the Abyssinian Crisis threw Franco-British relations into turmoil. In response to Mussolini's invasion of Abyssinia in October 1935, British elites wanted to work through the League of Nations to impose an oil embargo on Italy. French elites, fearful of alienating Mussolini and then having to cope with a hostile Italy potentially allied with Germany, refused to support the British. The consequent estrangement between London and Paris only reinforced British unwillingness to form a military alliance with France and to make a continental commitment. From 1936 to 1939, the British repeatedly

---

[125] Young, "Preparations for Defeat," p. 168; Adamthwaite, *Coming of the Second World War*, p. 248. For further discussion of the shortcomings in French doctrine and their sources, see Robert Doughty, *The Seeds of Disaster: The Development of French Army Doctrine, 1919–1939* (Hamden, Conn.: Archor Books, 1985).

[126] Gibbs, *Grand Strategy: Rearmament Policy*, p. 243.

[127] Young, *In Command of France*, pp. 39–40.

rebuffed French efforts to form closer ties and engage in joint military planning. Sporadic staff talks led only to a cursory exchange of information. The dilapidated state of the B.E.F. made it clear to French elites that the British were sincere in their stated intent to remain aloof from continental affairs. British elites made it equally clear that in the event of war with Japan, they intended to send a fleet to the Far East, effectively abandoning the Mediterranean. Far from being able to count on British assistance in the event of war with Germany, French decision makers were receiving clear signals that a western front might well be devoid of British soldiers and that they could not rely on the Royal Navy to maintain sea control in the Mediterranean and Atlantic.

The Spanish Civil War made French relations with Italy the next casualty. France's Popular Front government, though supportive of Spain's republican regime, decided to take a stance of nonintervention in the conflict between forces loyal to the regime and General Francisco Franco's forces. Mussolini, not surprisingly, chose to support the fascist cause, leading to closer relations with Hitler's Germany and eroding ties with France. The changing constellation of diplomatic alignments had inauspicious strategic implications for France. French elites now had to worry not only about Italy's absence from an anti-German coalition, but also about a potential Italian invasion through the Alps, a hostile Italian fleet in the Mediterranean, and the possibility that a victory for Franco would mean the emergence of a new threat on France's southeast border.

What remained of France's alliance system collapsed in 1938. The Anschluss effectively incorporated Austria and its 100,000 regular soldiers into the Reich. A military response by France was essentially ruled out; the air force was wholly unprepared for war, and the time needed for mobilization of the couverture meant that offensive action would have been possible only after the annexation of Austria had been completed.[128] In September, the alliance with Czechoslovakia was abandoned when France signed off on Hitler's annexation of the Sudetenland. Little stood in the way of Hitler's invasion of the rest of Czechoslovakia the following March. As if France did not already face a decidedly unfavorable military balance, the loss of Czech military capability from the allied camp and its incorporation into the Wehrmacht tipped the scales even further in Germany's favor. At this point, only the Soviet Union could open a militarily meaningful eastern front. But for strategic and political reasons, French elites continued to be

---

[128] Ibid., pp. 198–201. The army recommended only that leave be cancelled for border troops and that new funds be allocated to strengthen the Maginot Line. See Shirer, *Collapse of the Third Republic*, pp. 328–329.

extremely skeptical of alliance with the Soviets and never made it past initial staff talks before announcement of the Nazi-Soviet Nonaggression Pact brought such contacts to a sudden halt.[129]

By March 1939, profound changes in the strategic landscape meant that the French were diplomatically isolated and confronted with a superior enemy that was, by all indications, intent on overrunning Europe. Granted, French elites should not be blamed for the disintegration of the country's alliance network. They clearly wanted to maintain as many allies as possible; it was primarily the international environment and German behavior that caused the network to unravel.[130] But French elites could have done much more to sustain a coalition against Germany. They could have acquired more offense to bolster the credibility of alliance commitments. They could have taken a harder line in response to successive acts of German aggression. And they could have

---

[129] Throughout the second half of the 1930s, Soviet elites pressed French elites to engage in staff talks and conclude a formal military convention. Although successive French governments were tantalized by the prospect of securing Soviet participation in a war against Germany, they avoided formal alliance with the Soviet Union for several reasons. First, French elites feared that alliance with the Soviets might provoke Hitler and precipitate a continent-wide war. Appeasing Germany, on the other hand, left open the possibility that Hitler would direct his territorial ambition eastward, sparing France from having to engage in a conflict for which it was poorly prepared. See Shirer, *Collapse of the Third Republic*, pp. 240–246, 315, 348–350. Second, the Soviets insisted that a meaningful alliance with France necessitated securing the right of Soviet troops to enter countries in Eastern Europe—Poland and Romania, in particular—in the event of German aggression. The East Europeans resisted, fearful that the Soviets would use such arrangements as an excuse to occupy their territory. The French were unwilling to press their allies in the east on this issue until it was too late. Third, as discussed above, Britain was reluctant to form an alliance with France, not to mention with the Soviet Union. British hesitancy reinforced France's tentative approach to the Soviets and heightened concern in Paris that France might find itself drawn into a war with Germany allied only with an unreliable partner in the east. Fourth, domestic politics and divisive splits between left and right made it very difficult for even those politicians enthusiastic about alliance with the Soviets to proceed with staff talks and formal military arrangements. The right, inherently hostile toward Bolshevism and convinced that the Comintern sought to subvert French society, suspected the Kremlin's intentions and staunchly opposed a military convention. The left, far more sympathetic to formal alliance with the Soviets, was hamstrung by its own internal divisions. Of the three parties comprising the Popular Front government—the Radical-Socialists, Socialists, and Communists—only the latter had close ties to the Soviet Communist Party. See ibid., pp. 192–193. Finally, French intelligence tended to denigrate the capability of Soviet armed forces, arguing that they would not play a key role in the outcome of a continental war. Even though the Soviet military indeed had its problems during the 1930s, this argument appears to have been largely a rationalization for avoiding alliance with the Soviets for the reasons just enumerated. The conservative political orientation of the officer corps clearly contributed to the army's reluctance to forge close ties with the Soviet military. See Adamthwaite, *France and the Coming of the Second World War*, pp. 236–237; and Young, *In Command of France*, pp. 234–240.

[130] On this point, see Douglas Porch, "Arms and Alliances: French Grand Strategy and Policy in 1914 and 1940," in *Grand Strategies in War and Peace*, ed. Paul Kennedy (New Haven: Yale University Press, 1991), pp. 136–137.

made far earlier and much more vigorous efforts to secure an alliance with the Soviets. Instead, French decision makers were clinging tenaciously to essentially the same set of strategic assumptions that had prevailed in the mid-1930s, assumptions that now bore little resemblance to strategic reality.

Within the context of growing diplomatic isolation and an increasingly unfavorable military balance on the Continent, the third key component of French strategy—reliance on the resources of the empire to enable the metropole to prevail against its adversaries—appears to make good sense. In fact, the absence of French efforts to adjust strategy to the changes in the strategic landscape that occurred after 1935 can be at least partially understood as a function of the French conviction that imperial resources would come to the rescue of the metropole. In justifying to the minister of war his request for a significant increase in indigenous troop levels in the colonies, the minister of colonies in October 1938 pointed to "the necessity to reinforce the metropolitan and North African military forces in proportion to the augmentation of the German army—especially since this augmentation is accompanied by the disappearance of an ally in central Europe."[131] It stands to reason that French planners would divert crucial resources to the periphery if this temporary diversion promised to provide the answer to the metropole's military inferiority. The French decision to devote so much effort to imperial defense during the 1930s would then constitute a striking instance of successful, not unsuccessful, adaptation to international change.

Did French planners have good reason to believe that imperial resources would be a determining factor in the eventual outcome of the continental struggle? Or did available information suggest that the empire was likely to contribute little to metropolitan defense? Can French strategy in the periphery be viewed as the product of a calculated risk that did not pay off, or was it the product of dysfunction within the planning process?

Three main arguments cast doubt on the assertion that French belief in the ability of empire to provide the metropole the wherewithal to defeat Germany was simply the product of uncertainty and reasonable miscalculation. Rather, the historical evidence points to a glaring gap between the information available to elites and their assessment of the strategic importance of empire. First, the assistance that the territories could potentially offer to the metropole was vastly exaggerated. In terms neither of personnel nor of war materiel did empire hold promise of significantly offsetting the military imbalance on the Continent.

[131] 7-N-4196, Dossier 3, 11 Oct. 1938, pp. 2–3.

Second, the timing of the redeployment of troops from Africa to the metropole raises serious questions about the coherence of war plans. From 1935 until mid-1939, many of France's best units were devoted to colonial operations. It was only during the second half of 1939 and early 1940 that the bulk of the Armée d'Afrique and the Infanterie Coloniale was moved to the metropole. This distribution of forces and the consequent state of the metropolitan army contributed to France's weak diplomatic hand in dealing with Germany between 1935 and 1940. Furthermore, assessments indicating that France might not be able to maintain sea control in the Mediterranean after the outbreak of hostilities should have induced French elites to transport colonial troops to the metropole far earlier than they did. Third, while tactical and operational errors indeed played a role in the rapid defeat of French forces in 1940, France's strategic orientation toward empire—in particular, the impact of this orientation on the metropolitan army's quality and doctrine—also bears a significant degree of responsibility for the inadequacy of French preparations for war. I now examine these three points in more detail.

It was simply illusory for elites to assume that the overseas territories could provide the metropole with a strategic reserve on the order of magnitude envisaged in the planning documents. The following points suggest that the strategic value of the empire was being grossly exaggerated. By May 1940, roughly eighteen divisions of the Armée d'Afrique and the Infanterie Coloniale had been deployed in the metropole to cope with the expected German attack. Because many of these divisions contained a mix of metropolitan Frenchmen and indigenous soldiers, it is difficult to pinpoint the exact number of men that the empire contributed to the metropole. A regimental breakdown suggests that these eighteen divisions contained roughly equal numbers of indigenous soldiers and Frenchmen. Accordingly, the overseas territories, in addition to returning many of the Frenchmen serving abroad, contributed the equivalent of roughly nine divisions of indigenous troops to metropolitan defense. If the number of Frenchmen still serving abroad in May 1940 is taken into consideration, the net contribution of the empire to metropolitan defense was in the range of five to six divisions.[132] This constitutes a significant, though by no means

[132] A regimental breakdown can be found in Clayton, *France, Soldiers, and Africa*, pp. 120–126. As of May 1940, the following regiments, consisting primarily of metropolitan soldiers, were still serving abroad: six regiments of the Infanterie Coloniale in Indochina; six regiments of the Legion in North Africa, Syria, and Indochina; and thirteen regiments of Zouaves and Chasseurs d'Afrique, primarily in North Africa. The Infanterie Coloniale and Legion regiments consisted primarily of Europeans, while the Zouaves and Chasseurs regiments were more mixed. See Clayton, *France, Soldiers, and Africa*, pp. 125–126.

decisive, contribution, considering the fact that the French army consisted of roughly one hundred divisions and that it faced a German army approximately twice that size. Furthermore, the redeployment that took place virtually gutted North Africa of its well-trained and well-equipped forces.[133] Had France not fallen so quickly, new troops could have been recruited and more contingents sent to the metropole, but they would have been, for the most part, of low quality. Mobilization schedules showing the arrival of hundreds of thousands of indigenous troops included many fresh recruits who would have been of little value in continental warfare.[134] Furthermore, members of the General Staff acknowledged that many indigenous troops would likely have been virtually worthless during the winter months.[135] To say the least, it appears to have been overly optimistic to assume that the arrival of largely untrained indigenous units was going to give France the wherewithal to turn back Germany's troops. In sum, the empire's contribution to the metropolitan army was significant, but hardly decisive. Even had the war been more protracted, elites appear to have vastly exaggerated the extent to which empire would solve France's strategic predicament.[136] As Douglas Porch writes, "Colonial manpower could offer only a minor palliative" to France's strategic deficit.[137]

So too was the assumption that empire was needed to resupply the metropole with war-making capabilities grossly exaggerated. France was indeed reliant on imports of raw materials to supply its war-making industry. But it was illusory to assume that the colonies constituted the only sources for replenishing the metropole's depleted war stocks.[138] To be sure, it made good sense to defend certain overseas ports. Fort de France, for example, played a key role in supplying oil to the metropole. But many of the minerals and metals imported from France's colonies could have been found elsewhere. In addition, since

[133] Clayton, *France, Soldiers, and Africa*, pp. 124–126.
[134] Though figures vary, it appears that roughly 450,000 soldiers from the empire (340,000 of them from North Africa) were stationed in the metropole/North Africa bloc—most of them in North Africa—by the spring of 1940. See Marc Michel, "La Puissance par l'empire: Note sur la perception du facteur imperial dans l'elaboration de la défense nationale (1936–1938)," *Revue Française d'Histoire d'Outre-Mer*, 69, 254 (1982), 38. Many of these troops were not, however, poised to be sent to the metropole. They had been gathered in North Africa to enable the trained contingents of the Armée d'Afrique and the Infanterie Coloniale to converge on the metropole.
[135] For a succinct review of these objections, see 7-N-4193, Dossier 11, 23 Feb. 1933 meeting of the Comité Consultatif de Défense des Colonies.
[136] For further discussion of this point, see Michel, "La Puissance par l'empire"; and Charles-Robert Ageron, "La Perception de la puissance française en 1938–1939: Le Mythe imperial," *Revue Française d'Histoire d'Outre-Mer*, 69, 254 (1982), 7–22.
[137] Porch, "Arms and Alliances," p. 135.
[138] For percentages of key war-making materials that had to be imported from overseas, see Young, *In Command of France*, p. 19.

the French were heavily reliant on the British merchant marine to transport goods and the British navy to guard the sea lanes, it made little sense for the French to sustain a global network of ports for protecting their own limited shipping network. During the second half of the 1930s, France depended on foreign merchant ships to carry roughly 75 percent of its import-export tonnage.[139]

French assumptions that the colonies would provide finished munitions and weaponry to the metropole were equally unrealistic. The stocks of munitions that existed in the territories had been supplied largely from the metropole; regional commanders would be loath to return them because of the demands of local defense. More important, repeated references to the construction of thriving armaments industries in Algeria and Indochina were simply not based in fact. "The Economic Role of Overseas France in National Defense," a comprehensive study prepared for the General Staff during the second half of the 1930s, asserted that the construction of arms-producing industries in the colonies "presented difficulties of many kinds" and that "none of the present projects are in the realm of being realized." A separate review of industrial conditions in Indochina, the territory that held the most promise of supporting war industries, reached similar conclusions: "The organization of an autonomous munitions industry in Indochina is unrealizable." This situation will not change, the report concluded, without "a complete transformation of the conditions of economic life."[140] In short, the assumption that the territories could meet the metropole's desperate need for munitions was simply illusory and diverged considerably from information readily available to elites.[141]

The second argument casting doubt on the consistency and coherence of French strategy in the periphery has to do with the timing of the redeployment of troops from Africa to the metropole. France's troops for colonial operations—the Infanterie Coloniale and the Armée d'Afrique—were, for the most part, "markedly superior" to the largely conscript metropolitan army.[142] Except for a few contingents stationed in the metropole, the Armée d'Afrique served exclusively in the overseas territories. Most regiments of the Infanterie Coloniale were also posted overseas, though some units were stationed in the metropole and dispatched as needed to colonial destinations. Furthermore, ef-

---

[139] Young, *In Command of France*, pp. 20–23.

[140] 7-N-4196, Dossier 3, date: "between 1934 and 1939," p. 1; 7-N-4194, Dossier 3, 25 June 1937, Rapport, p. 49.

[141] For further discussion of this point, see Ageron, "La Perception de la puissance française," pp. 10–11.

[142] Clayton, *France, Soldiers, and Africa*, pp. 20, 126.

forts to recruit and train new indigenous forces in fact meant that increasing numbers of French officers and career soldiers had to be stationed in the periphery. It was necessary to maintain a fixed proportion of French to indigenous troops to ensure the quality of instruction. The presence of French troops would also serve to deter or quell local insurgency that might result from resentment about the increased recruitment burden or from political organizing that could easily be carried out among newly gathered recruits. In Indochina, for example, the ratio of European to indigenous troops was to be maintained at three to five.[143]

These considerations ensured that through much of the 1930s, a significant proportion of the standing French army was stationed in the overseas territories. A conservative estimate suggests that at least 150,000 officers and troops were serving in North Africa and the overseas colonies throughout the 1930s—that is, until the large-scale transport of troops from North Africa to the metropole which began in 1939.[144] Estimates of the size of the standing French army during this period range from 400,000 to 500,000.[145] It is striking that such a large proportion of France's best soldiers was in the periphery when the force imbalance in Europe was as precarious as it was and when Germany had made amply clear its aggressive intentions.[146] The numbers also fail to capture the full extent of the impact of this disposition of forces on the metropolitan army. The fact that only career personnel could serve overseas and the priority assigned to overseas troops in allocating new equipment meant that the state of the metropolitan forces was more dire than troop levels indicate. The air force engaged in a similarly marked diversion of scarce resources to the periphery. In August 1938, Commandant Cornillon complained that "the situation of the Air Force is presently so critical in the metropole because important funds have been distracted to the benefit of overseas territories."[147] So too was the navy expending resources to build up overseas ports rather than concentrating on the metropole and arguing, as it did before World War I, that the *points d'appuis* had lost their raison d'être.

It is thus the case that through 1938, while Germany rearmed and

---

[143] 7-N-3927, Dossier 3, 11 March 1937, Etude, pp. 6, 8.

[144] It is difficult to pinpoint the number of officers and soldiers serving overseas. Units of the colonial army rotated among the metropole, North Africa, and the colonies. Furthermore, the historical record—both archival documents and secondary sources—is incomplete and contains contradictory information. For figures on the number of French troops stationed in North Africa, see 2-N-243, Dossier 2, June 1939 (undated), "Répartition des effectifs." For figures on the colonies, see 7-N-3927, Dossier 1, 3 Aug. 1938, Commission, Annexe 1, p. 12; and 7-N-3927, Dossier 3, 1938–1939, Tableaux.

[145] Doise and Vaïsse, *Diplomatie,* pp. 304, 335.

[146] Clayton, *France, Soldiers, and Africa,* pp. 8–10, 27–28.

[147] 7-9-3927, Dossier 1, 3 Aug. 1938, Commission, Annexe 1, p. 11.

demonstrated increasingly hostile intent, a substantial portion of France's best units was serving in the overseas territories.[148] This disposition of forces is especially striking given the fact that French elites seriously considered going to war in 1938 to deny Germany its claim to the Sudetenland. This dispersion of the French army no doubt contributed to the military's repeated warnings to political elites (discussed below) that the country was unprepared to go to war and that they should therefore acquiesce to Hitler's demands.

Furthermore, the evidence suggests that French elites should have been—and indeed were—concerned about the navy's ability to transport troops to the theater of war in a timely fashion. War plans called for troops to arrive from the periphery throughout the year *after* the outbreak of hostilities. But two points call into question the timing of the planned redeployment. First, the absence of fortifications on the northern border, the metropolitan army's lack of armor and mobility, and the success of armored offensives in the Spanish Civil War should have raised doubts about the prevailing assumption of a long war. Should the initial battles turn out to be decisive—as they did—France's superior troops in North Africa would have been able to do little more than cheer on their metropolitan compatriots.

Second, and more important, it became increasingly clear throughout the late 1930s that metropolitan France might well be severed from its empire after the outbreak of war. Even with the assistance of Britain (which was by no means ensured), the navy could not guarantee sea control and thus the safe passage of transports in the Indian Ocean, Pacific, or Mediterranean. Even the vital link between North Africa and France was called into question, especially in view of the British decision to give the Far Eastern theater priority over the Mediterranean.[149] British elites in fact made very clear to their French counterparts that, in the event of Japanese aggression, they intended to abandon the Mediterranean in order to send a battlefleet to the Far East. The minister of war was also dubious that France could maintain sea control and transport troops and materiel even along the Atlantic coast of Africa, arguing that land and air routes might have to be relied on to enable black Africans to reach North Africa.[150] The poorly

---

[148] The major redeployment of troops from Africa to the metropole occurred during 1939–1940. By August 1939, four divisions and other assorted units of the Armée d'Afrique and five divisions of the Infanterie Coloniale had been deployed in the metropole. Clayton, *France, Soldiers, and Africa,* pp. 121–122.

[149] Planners were quite uncertain of France's ability to maintain sea control even in the Mediterranean basin itself. See 7-N-3927, Dossier 4, 31 March 1938, General Bührer to the Vice-President of the Conseil Supérieur de la Guerre, pp. 5–6.

[150] 7-N-3927, Dossier 3, 28 April 1937, Minister of War to General Staff of the Army.

developed transport system in Africa thus left planners uncertain as to whether troops and materiel would reach ports in North Africa, not to mention whether they would reach the metropole.[151] A lengthy planning paper drafted in February 1939, entitled "The French Colonies in National Defense," reaffirmed the central assumption that "an intact and strong empire is necessary for carrying out strong French action in Europe [and is] an essential condition for maintaining the balance on the continent." But it also asserted that, given the difficulty and dangers involved in transporting troops in waters patrolled by enemy ships, troops from the overseas territories might well arrive too late, if at all.[152] French elites were not the only ones worried about the French navy's ability to prevail against the Italian navy. In February 1938, Britain's Chiefs of Staff, looking at estimated force balances through 1940, doubted whether France, if unassisted, could cope with the Italian fleet in the Mediterranean.[153]

That planners took seriously these warnings about the loss of sea control after the outbreak of hostilities was reflected in growing support for the notion that large numbers of indigenous troops should be transported to the metropole during peacetime. This concern, however, led only to largely symbolic initiatives. In April 1938, orders were given to recruit an additional 44,500 troops in the overseas territories. Of these, only 8,800 (8,000 from Senegal and 800 from Madagascar) were immediately sent to the metropole.[154] More ambitious efforts to station large contingents from the overseas territories in the metropole were not pursued for two main reasons. First, to remove major units from the colonies in peacetime would impair the training of new recruits. Few trained soldiers would be available to organize mobilization should it be necessary; this would jeopardize France's goal of eventually sending 500,000 soldiers and workers to the metropole.[155] Second, there was growing concern that preparations for colonial defense were woefully inadequate and that, in the event of war, the overseas territories simply could not afford to release their troops for service elsewhere. On the contrary, since the loss of sea control might well deprive the overseas possessions of assistance from the metropole, force levels and fortifications in the territories had to be increased in order to prepare them for self-defense. In 1937, General Gaston-Henri-Gustave Billotte,

[151] See Ageron, "La Perception de la puissance française," p. 10; and Michel, "La Puissance par l'empire," p. 39.

[152] 7-N-3927, Dossier 6, 21 Feb. 1939, pp. 15, 19.

[153] See Gibbs, *Grand Strategy: Rearmament Policy*, p. 309.

[154] 2-N-246, Dossier 2, 10 Jan. 1939, Minister of Colonies to Minister of War.

[155] 7-N-4194, Dossier 4, 23 Nov. 1937, Meeting of the Comité Consultatif de Défense des Colonies.

president of the Consultative Committee for Defense of the Colonies, warned that Indochina would likely be cut off from France throughout the war.[156] Preparations for its defense therefore had to be made during peacetime. In 1938, the decision was made to strengthen fortifications and troop levels in the Levant, assuming that it too would be severed from the metropole for at least six months.[157] Even as troops were being ferried to the metropole during 1939–1940, regiments of the Infanterie Coloniale and the Armée d'Afrique were being sent to reinforce garrisons in Indochina and the Levant.[158]

A fundamental and seemingly irresolvable contradiction thus cut to the heart of French strategy. The empire, because of its vast supply of manpower, was to provide France the wherewithal to outlast and eventually defeat Germany. Yet, as late as 1940, efforts were under way to strengthen colonial defenses and render imperial possessions self-sufficient because the links between metropole and periphery would likely be severed from the start of the war. The value of the overseas territories supposedly lay in their potential contribution to metropolitan defense. Yet without sea control and protected lines of communication, the empire, far from serving as the ultimate savior of metropolitan security, would constitute a precipitous drain on the already scarce resources needed to cope with the German threat. As it turned out, because of the time lag between the declaration of war in September 1939 and the beginning of full-scale hostilities the following May, France was able to transport its troops to the metropole without encountering enemy resistance. But given German behavior from 1935 onward and French concern about maintaining sea control after the outbreak of war, the lateness of this redeployment is indeed quite striking.

The third argument casting doubt on the coherence of French grand strategy concerns the qualitative impact on metropolitan forces of the army's preoccupation with imperial defense during the interwar years. The costs to the metropole's military establishment of this imperial strategic orientation took several forms. The morale and fighting capability of the metropolitan army suffered considerably. Because many officers and professional soldiers were serving abroad, metropolitan units consisted primarily of poorly trained conscripts. Funding priorities and the allocation of modern equipment also frequently favored troops serving in the overseas territories. So too was service in the periphery considered by many to be more alluring and prestigious

---

[156] 7-N-3927, Dossier 3, 11 March 1937, Etude, pp. 4–5.
[157] 7-N-3926, Dossier 5, March 1939 (undated), p. 2.
[158] Clayton, *France, Soldiers, and Africa*, pp. 120–126.

than life in the metropolitan garrisons.[159] The strategic orientation toward empire also slowed the process of modernizing and mechanizing the French army. Although there were strong advocates of moving toward an armored force, many of them believed that only a professional army could effectively operate modern armor.[160] To professionalize the metropolitan army, however, was politically unacceptable. A citizen army symbolized the ideals of the republic, and a professional army might pose a threat to the regime. The colonial troops were the closest the French came to a professional army, but they did not need armor to prosecute colonial wars. Furthermore, metropolitan officers doubted whether indigenous troops could be trained to use the equipment and, if so, whether such capabilities might one day be used to resist French rule.[161] The army's focus on operations in the periphery similarly contributed to the stagnation of doctrine and tactics in the metropole.[162] Many of the commanders serving in the metropole had little or no training in the type of warfare they encountered in 1940. General André-Georges Corap, the commander of the Ninth Army deployed in the Ardennes—where the Germans focused their main attack—had made his reputation in Algeria and Morocco. He had virtually no experience in armored warfare or the use of air power. General Charles Huntzinger, commander of the adjoining Second Army, was in the same position. As Clayton aptly notes, "The tactics of Morocco in the 1920s could not be a proper preparation for new-style West European mechanized warfare. . . . Colonial campaigning, in sum, had played a part, significant though not major, in the intellectual sterilization of the French Army."[163]

What caused these fundamental inconsistencies that plagued French strategic planning? Why did the planning elite fail to prepare more adequately for war with Germany? Given available information, how could elites continue to base grand strategy on the assumption that imperial resources were the answer to metropolitan vulnerability? It may well be that France would have been defeated by Germany regard-

---

[159] Ibid., pp. 8–10.

[160] Young, "Preparations for Defeat," p. 169.

[161] Clayton, *France, Soldiers, and Africa*, p. 27.

[162] My argument is that the army's imperial orientation was one of several factors that led to doctrinal stagnation, not that it was the main cause of such stagnation. The French army would likely have failed to modernize its doctrine and equipment even in the absence of this focus on overseas missions. Those responsible for formulating French strategy in the core were not distracted by the burden of colonial campaigns. Yet had some of the country's best officers not been preoccupied with peripheral strategy, they may have contributed to the formulation of a more vital and appropriate strategy in the core.

[163] Clayton, *France, Soldiers, and Africa*, p. 28.

less of the steps taken to prepare for war. But the adjustment failure of the 1930s is nonetheless glaring. The implications of tolerating the inconsistencies between strategic assumptions and strategic reality were, to say the least, consequential.

In the mid-1930s, French grand strategy was well suited to the strategic and diplomatic landscape. The French intended to hold the Germans on their northeastern border, stalemate the enemy in Belgium, and await the mobilization of the domestic armaments industry and the arrival of resources from both the empire and allies before beginning the counterattack. From 1936 onward, French strategy unraveled and became increasingly divorced from strategic reality. The Belgian declaration of neutrality undercut the rationale for restricting the Maginot Line to the Franco-German border. Changing military technology, Germany's procurement of armored divisions, and the success of armored offensives and air power in the Spanish Civil War raised questions about France's ability to stalemate the initial German advance. One by one, France's allies either made it clear that they were not interested in alliance or were incorporated into Germany's military machine. France's ability to maintain sea control and transport troops and supplies from the colonies to the metropole looked increasingly uncertain.

Rather than seeking to adjust to these changes, however, French elites entered a period of virtual paralysis. They clung to outmoded strategic beliefs despite the availability of incoming information that should have discredited the logical inferences on which those beliefs were based. By 1938, elites were tolerating successive bouts of German expansion mainly because they had no choice. The couverture and its mobilization scheme meant that spontaneous offensive action was virtually precluded. Nor was the country ready for full-scale war. A significant portion of France's best troops were overseas, far from the European battlefield. The army and the air force were in a low state of readiness, and materiel was in dangerously short supply. During 1938, the military elite repeatedly warned decision makers that the country was simply too weak to go to war.[164] Yet French decision makers were all too aware of the implications of delay. With each act of German aggression that went unanswered, Germany's military superiority grew more pronounced. It was for this reason that French elites were initially prepared to take a firm stand on the Sudetenland—they ordered the military to mobilize for war in early September—only to be

---

[164] See Adamthwaite, *Coming of the Second World War*, pp. 226–227.

persuaded by Britain to acquiesce to Hitler's demand.[165] It was also for this reason that French troops plunged into German territory after Hitler's invasion of Poland, only to be withdrawn soon thereafter because of Poland's rapid collapse and because elites feared a German counterattack.[166]

If and when France should have initiated war before May 1940 is the critical counterfactual—and one that is difficult to answer. The Czech crisis of 1938 appears to have been a window of opportunity. The bulk of Germany's divisions were deployed in the east against a formidable Czech army, and Germany's fixed defenses in the west were not yet complete. But even by 1938, the balance had shifted decidedly in Germany's favor. French troops would likely have been able to advance into German territory with little resistance, but would then have had to engage Germany's main units as they turned their attention from Czechoslovakia to the western frontier. The French military was, in fact, quite pessimistic about the balance and staunchly opposed going to war over the Sudetenland.[167]

Even if one assumes, however, that France was justified in not initiating war during the 1930s, French strategy was still fundamentally flawed. French elites seemingly ignored developments that cut to the very core of existing plans for metropolitan defense. Little was done to fortify the northern border. Despite the considerable funds applied to rearmament, the army did not adapt its doctrine and strategy to technological change and therefore lacked sufficient armor and mobility, the infantry was not well trained in the use of modern weaponry, and munitions stockpiles lagged far behind what was needed to engage Germany in the prolonged battle that was envisaged. Until 1939, a major portion of France's best-trained personnel remained in the overseas territories. And French decision makers—civilians and military elites alike—shunned what was perhaps France's best hope for dealing with its strategic predicament: alliance with the Soviet Union.

It was not until the invasion of Czechoslovakia that elites undertook earnest efforts to reorient grand strategy. The army redoubled efforts to modernize equipment and acted on the need to move toward increased armor and mobility. A decision was taken to supplement the two existing heavily armored divisions with one or possibly two more.

---

[165] Young, *In Command of France*, pp. 201–216. Young maintains that the French cabinet was deeply split over the question of whether to go to war over Czechoslovakia. He argues that France would have stood firm and backed Czechoslovakia's rejection of Hitler's demands had Britain been willing to follow suit. For a similar interpretation, see Shirer, *Collapse of the Third Republic*, pp. 339–413.

[166] Shirer, *Collapse of the Third Republic*, pp. 520–524.

[167] Adamthwaite, *Coming of the Second World War*, pp. 226–227.

Elites speeded up aircraft production and recognized the need to procure aircraft to support independent armored movements on the ground.[168] They made an earnest effort to secure a military alliance with the Soviet Union. And elites finally began to transport to the metropole large numbers of troops that had been stationed overseas. But it was simply too late. The armaments industry did not have sufficient infrastructure to produce the equipment and armor that were called for.[169] It was not possible to revamp in short order the doctrine, strategy, and tactics that contributed to the rapid defeat of French forces in May 1940. And by the time French elites were ready to consider seriously alliance with the Soviets, Hitler had already beaten them to it. Despite the fact that much of the Armée d'Afrique and the Infanterie Coloniale were deployed in France without enemy interference, they could do little to salvage a fundamentally flawed grand strategy.

The causes of France's adjustment failure are complex. Indeed, the outcome is overdetermined: many different variables played a role and it is difficult to isolate the most important ones. I will argue that French perceptions of high vulnerability were the root cause of adjustment failure during the 1930s. Vulnerability affected strategy through two key mechanisms. First, because French decision makers saw no attractive options for coping with Germany's superior manpower and industrial might, they entered a period of effective paralysis. Germany's perceived military superiority convinced French elites to avoid all actions that could provoke war. It was the strategic imbalance, more than any other factor, that induced French inaction in response to successive bouts of German aggression and French reluctance to secure alliance with the Soviets. As this imbalance worsened, elites operated in an atmosphere of increasing fear and resignation. This resignation manifested itself in a cognitive lag that left elites clinging to a set of strategic suppositions that grew increasingly obsolete. To admit the obsolescence of the fundamental assumptions upon which grand strategy was based would have exposed the elite community to quite threatening realities. Second, metropolitan vulnerability induced elites to sell overseas empire to the French polity—both to reaffirm French stature and to extract resources needed in the metropole. A strategic culture wedded to empire in turn explains why the French concentrated on peripheral defense and so exaggerated the potential contribution of empire to metropolitan security. I begin laying out this argument by examining the effect of vulnerability on the content of elite beliefs and on the

---

[168] Gunsburg, *Divided and Conquered,* pp. 70–72.
[169] Ibid., p. 104.

timing of their adaptation to incoming information. In the following section, I examine the role of strategic culture as well as a host of other domestic factors that affected French strategy.

France's adjustment failure in the core cannot be viewed as the result of stress-induced psychological distortion. The French indeed faced successive crises during the second half of the 1930s: the reoccupation of the Rhineland, the Anschluss, Munich. These discrete periods during which the likelihood of war increased dramatically may well have given rise to episodes of psychological dysfunction and distortion of incoming information. But such dysfunction does not explain why French elites clung to outmoded strategic beliefs over a period of several years. Furthermore, it is clear that decision makers assimilated incoming information fairly accurately and did not delude themselves about the severity of their strategic predicament. The military repeatedly informed political elites of the country's weakness; intelligence assessments, if anything, exaggerated German superiority. Elites were by no means oblivious to developments that challenged prevailing strategy and doctrine. They openly discussed the need to fortify the northern border and to increase the mobility and armor of French forces. They recognized the importance of finding new allies. So too did decision makers confront the possibility that the empire might well be cut off from the metropole in the event of war. In short, elites did not manipulate information to convince themselves that the strategic challenges facing the country were not serious ones. On the contrary, they clearly recognized the nature of the predicament but nevertheless failed to adapt policy to incoming information.

Nor can adjustment failure be viewed as the result of miscalculation under uncertainty. Elites were not caught off-guard by events that they could reasonably have failed to foresee. Unpredictable operational considerations no doubt contributed to the rapid defeat of French forces in the spring of 1940, but the shortcomings in French strategy went well beyond a failure to predict a German offensive through the Ardennes. On the contrary, the analysis above suggests that elites clung to existing strategic beliefs despite the ready availability of information that should have disconfirmed the logical inferences that gave rise to those beliefs. A glaring gap existed between prevailing strategic conceptions and strategic reality, but elites simply failed to update these conceptions.

My argument is that France's adjustment failure during the 1930s was caused by two principal forces, both of which were the product of perceptions of high vulnerability: (1) paralysis caused by the absence of attractive options for redressing strategic deficiency and manifested in inaction and a cognitive lag in the adaptation of beliefs to incoming information; and (2) a strategic culture wedded to overseas empire. Acute metropolitan vulnerability, rather than triggering the timely adaptation of policy, virtually paralyzed decision makers and left them clinging to outmoded strategic beliefs. Elites did realize that the strategic imbalance was only worsening over time, but they saw no attractive options for dealing with their predicament. Moreover, they began to recognize that some of the discrete suppositions upon which grand strategy was based had been discredited. For cognitive and emotional reasons, however, they were incapable of bringing prevailing strategic conceptions into line with the strategic landscape. To admit that the northern border was inadequately fortified, that French forces lacked the armor and mobility to counter German capability, that France was losing its ability to advance into German territory to defend its allies in the east, and that the country might not have time to await the arrival of resources from allies and colonial possessions would have confronted the elite community with unpleasant realities. These realities would have forced elites to pursue alliance with the Soviets, to revamp their plans for metropolitan defense, and, possibly, to wage preventive war against Germany—options that in both political and emotional terms were highly unattractive. The cognitive tendency for beliefs to persevere in the face of incoming information was exacerbated by high vulnerability and the sense of fear and resignation it produced.[170]

As I argue below, this paralysis, resignation, and cognitive resistance to adaptation were reinforced by domestic political instability and by a military establishment whose organizational interests were tightly wedded to a strategy, war plan, and force structure predicated upon a specific set of strategic suppositions. To admit the obsolescence of these suppositions was to threaten severely the organizational essence of the military. Organizations, like individuals, tend to grasp tightly to existing norms and routines when facing a threatening external environment. As a result of these combination of factors, the thorough reevaluation of French strategy that was desperately needed after 1936 was not forthcoming. Instead, precisely because they were faced with high vulnerability and the absence of attractive options for redressing marked strategic deficiency, elites continued to rely on suppositions that were no longer grounded in strategic reality and based on incoming information.

---

[170] As discussed in Chapter 2, I am arguing that motivated biases exacerbated the normal cognitive tendency for preexisting conceptions to persist in the face of discrepant information. Were elites to have updated their strategic beliefs, they would have been confronted with the need to pursue policies that they did not want to adopt.

This interpretation is not only consistent with the characterization of French thinking and behavior presented above, but is also corroborated by two further pieces of evidence. First, decision makers were quite self-conscious about the extent to which their behavior was shaped by perceptions of the country's weakness. From the reoccupation of the Rhineland through the German invasion of Poland, elites justified their successive decisions to forego resort to military force in terms of France's military inferiority and the consequent need to avoid war. Even in 1936, when France was capable of driving from the Rhineland the German forces that had just reoccupied it, elites opted to accommodate German behavior because of the prospect of facing Germany in a protracted war. As General Gamelin described the situation, "At the beginning, under present conditions, we would have the preponderance, but in a long war the superiority of our adversaries in numbers and industrial capacity would play a strong part."[171] So too did France's strategic deficit play an important role in convincing elites to maintain an army capable of undertaking primarily defensive operations. Military leaders reasoned that France simply did not have sufficient manpower both to defend French territory and to attack Germany, especially in light of the high casualties they assumed would accompany offensive operations. Reliance on a defensive strategy in turn was used to justify the high command's complacency about the army's lack of armor and mobility. Finally, perceptions of weakness played a key role in convincing elites to avoid alliance with the Soviets. Although certain quarters of the elite community resisted alliance with the Soviets for political and ideological reasons, all shared a common concern: that an overt military convention with the Kremlin might provoke Hitler and draw France into a war for which it was ill-prepared. In the words of Robert Coulondre, French ambassador to Moscow and a strong proponent of a Franco-Soviet alliance, it was the "winds of fear" that prevented his government from entering into a military convention with the Soviet Union.[172] In sum, the content of elite debate itself makes clear the extent to which decision makers felt paralyzed by the strategic imbalance. The absence of attractive options in turn created strong cognitive pressures for elites to cling to existing strategic suppositions.

The second piece of evidence lending support to this interpretation stems from the collective nature of the paralysis that gripped the deci-

---

[171] Gamelin cited in Shirer, *Collapse of the Third Republic*, p. 263. For similar statements during the Anschluss, Czech crises, and invasion of Poland, see pp. 328–329, 333–335, 355–359, 388, 410, and 524.

[172] Coulondre cited in ibid., p. 350. In Shirer's words, French elites feared "being pushed into a war with Hitler in which the Russians would give little aid" (p. 315).

sion-making community. If it were only the military that counseled inaction and tolerated the maintenance of an obsolete grand strategy, bureaucratic inertia and organizational routine would suffice to explain French behavior. If it were only civilian elites who resisted a reorientation of strategy, domestic instability and political opportunism would be likely sources of France's adjustment failure. If it were parliament that refused to vote credits for rearmament or back the cabinet's resolve to stand firm, public attitudes and pacifism would emerge as key factors shaping strategy. But the sources of paralysis were not isolated to specific sectors of the decision-making community. Top civilian elites, military commanders, members of parliament, and the public were acutely aware of France's strategic predicament and recoiled from the prospect of going to war against Germany. In William Shirer's words, "If . . . the military High Command was found wanting, so was the government, the Parliament, the press, the people. It was a collective failure that paralyzed France's will to act."[173] That resignation and paralysis affected all quarters of the French polity strengthens the argument that the causes of adjustment failure were systemic in nature: the strategic imbalance and the fear it produced.[174]

[173] Ibid., p. 283.

[174] Readers may note that I offer somewhat different explanations of French and British adjustment failure in the core. In the British case, I argue that incoming information did in fact disconfirm prevailing beliefs; it was strategic culture—the visceral aversion to a continental commitment—rather than effective paralysis and outmoded strategic suppositions, that prevented elites from building a continental army until 1939. In the French case, I am arguing that resignation and the tendency for beliefs to persevere in the face of disconfirming information—a tendency exacerbated by high vulnerability—played a more important role. This difference in interpretation stems from two considerations. First, the nature of adjustment failure was not identical in the two cases. In the French case, elites did increase the size of the army and devote considerable resources to rearmament in their efforts to develop a force capable of blocking a German advance. But the force they built was predicated upon outmoded assumptions about the likely length of the war, the utility of air power, the offense-defense balance, the need for mobility and armor, the likely role of allies, and the strategic value of empire. The nature of the problem resonates with an interpretation that focuses on the paralysis and resignation caused by German preponderance and manifested in inaction and the failure of elites to update beliefs about strategy, doctrine, and tactics. In the British case, the problem was quite different. At the beginning of 1939, British elites found themselves with no continental army, not simply with an army hampered by outmoded strategies and doctrines. The gross nature of the adjustment failure points to causes other than resignation and cognitive lags; on an intuitive level, strategic culture and the visceral aversion to a continental commitment offer a far more satisfying account of why British elites delayed so long in building a force capable of fighting on the continent. Second, in the French case there was no powerful strategic image or reigning strategic conception—similar to the "never again" syndrome—that infused public and elite debate about core strategy. The French indeed suffered dearly during World War I and pacifism gained strength among elites and masses alike. But France's main reaction to the war was to guard against the reemergence of German power, not to opt out of continental affairs. As I argue shortly, strategic culture—the French polity's tightening embrace with its overseas colo-

The interpretation I have offered enjoys considerable support among historians of the period. Jean Doise and Maurice Vaïsse argue that French elites responded to successive adverse shifts in the military balance by oscillating between exasperation and resignation, watching with increasing apprehension as Germany grew more powerful and more threatening.[175] As Judith Hughes writes, "The sluggishness of France's traditional leaders, their increasing reluctance to assume responsibility for their nation's defense, brings into clear focus the undercurrent of depression and hopelessness that pervaded the late 1930s." Richard Challener agrees that "a listless reluctance" and "partial paralysis of the will to resist" played a key role in producing "the stagnation in French military thought and achievement in the thirties."[176] According to John Young, "That the high command failed to modify its strategic and tactical concepts in accordance with France's diplomatic commitments and the new dimensions of warfare is unmistakably true; and it is this bureaucratic lethargy and intellectual stultification where one must look to find the origins of the military disaster of 1940."[177] William Shirer agrees that "this fear of being left alone to face the Fascist dictators was to haunt the French leaders, military and civilian . . . and to paralyze any initiative in foreign policy that might have strengthened France in Europe, wrought an anti-Axis coalition, and discouraged Hitler and Mussolini from further aggression."[178]

In addition to the effect of high vulnerability on the content of elite beliefs and the timing of their adaptation to incoming information, a second key factor was driving France's adjustment failure in the core: a strategic culture wedded to overseas empire. The belief that imperial resources would eventually enable France to prevail played a key role in slowing the pace of metropolitan rearmament and leaving the homeland poorly prepared for war. It was the supposition that the overseas territories would come to the metropole's rescue that also allowed elites to allocate substantial defense resources to the periphery despite the imbalance in Europe. So too did the army's focus on colonial operations for much of the interwar period contribute to the low quality of the

---

nies—did have an important effect on French strategy in the core. But even in the absence of a strategic culture wedded to overseas empire, France's strategy for metropolitan defense would likely have lagged behind changes in the strategic landscape. The imperial orientation of elites, the bureaucracy, the military, and the public contributed to, but does not fully explain, adjustment failure in the core.

[175] Doise and Vaïsse, *Diplomatie*, pp. 297–298.

[176] Judith Hughes, *To the Maginot Line: The Politics of French Military Preparation in the 1920s* (Cambridge: Harvard University Press, 1971), pp. 230–231; Challener, *Nation in Arms*, pp. 218–220.

[177] Young, "Preparations for Defeat," p. 172.

[178] Shirer, *Collapse of the Third Republic*, p. 335.

metropolitan army and to the stagnation of its doctrine and tactics. To be sure, the empire did repay some of its debt to the metropole; indigenous troops fought valiantly against the Germans in 1940. Unlike their British counterparts, French elites did not fear that pulling troops out of the overseas possessions would expose the façade of imperial strength and lead to the unraveling of empire. On the contrary, debate about peripheral strategy revolved around a single issue: the marshaling of resources for metropolitan defense.[179]

Why, then, did French elites so exaggerate the potential role of empire in contributing to the defense of the metropole? Why did they not transport colonial troops to France far earlier, given the precarious situation on the Continent and information suggesting that the link between metropole and periphery might be severed after the outbreak of the war? Why did elites tolerate the qualitative impact on metropolitan forces of the army's colonial orientation when the threat in the core was so severe? Why did they forgo fortifying the northern border while they were fortifying the overseas colonies likely to be cut off from the metropole after the outbreak of war?

Two answers emerge. First, it makes good sense that the same acute vulnerability that led to a core strategy characterized by resignation, paralysis and outmoded beliefs should produce a peripheral strategy exhibiting similar traits. The strategic suppositions that made good sense in the mid-1930s persisted far too long in the face of discrepant information. Given the overwhelming military imbalance between France and Germany, as well as the poor prospects for securing allies, there were indeed strong emotional and cognitive incentives for elites to continue believing that the marshaling of imperial resources would avert disaster for the metropole, even if incoming information and logical inference should have indicated otherwise. As argued above, it was in large part belief in the empire's potential contribution to metropolitan defense that allowed elites to posit a two-phase war and to be complacent about the low state of readiness of metropolitan forces. To face the fact that the empire might not live up to expectations would have been to admit that the country's grand strategy was fundamentally flawed.

---

[179] This is not to suggest that reputational concerns had no impact on French thinking. As in the British case, adopting a deterrent strategy in the periphery was intended, at least in part, to bolster reputation and to demonstrate that France would tolerate neither external nor internal threats to the integrity of the empire. The General Staff believed that conditions in the Middle East were integrally tied to developments in Africa. Especially after the uprising in Abyssinia in 1935 and the Franco-Syrian Treaty of 1936, elites believed that "in North Africa, it is now more than ever necessary to affirm that our three possessions are definitely part of the French Empire." See 7-N-3926, Dossier 2, 19

This cognitive dynamic was no doubt at work. But the argument is incomplete in that it still does not explain key components of French behavior. If concern about bolstering metropolitan security had been the only force driving imperial strategy, then France should have abandoned more territories and concentrated many more troops in the metropole during peacetime. Elites should not have countenanced the qualitative decline in the metropolitan army that resulted from imperial ambition. Moreover, it made little sense for French elites to prepare the colonies for being cut off from the metropole when the value of those colonies was supposedly to rest entirely in their ability to furnish war-making capability to the metropole. Nevertheless, decision makers did just that even as a European war looked more and more likely. In fact, after the setback at Munich, the government openly pursued a more ambitious and hard-line policy in the periphery. So too was there a more widespread outpouring of colonial sentiment among the public.[180] Such behavior cannot simply be understood as a newfound appreciation of the importance of the empire to metropolitan defense. Rather, as they did after the Franco-Prussian War, the French appear to have been escaping from setbacks in the core by turning to the empire. As Anthony Adamthwaite put it, many argued that "France should redeploy her energies and resources, withdrawing from the East and consolidating her position in the Mediterranean and overseas. . . . [They] nursed the hope that the new imperial vision would in time soothe the trauma of Munich."[181] This behavior suggests that a strategic culture deeply wedded to empire may well have been playing a role in shaping both core and peripheral strategy. A domestic polity infused with powerful images linking metropolitan well-being to imperial security would help explain French behavior. The analysis therefore moves beyond the realm of elite beliefs and turns to domestic politics, elite-mass linkages, and the changing nature of French strategic culture during the interwar period.

Domestic Considerations

In this section, I consider domestic explanations for the adjustment failure that France experienced during the 1930s. I argue that domestic factors had an important impact on French strategy in both the core

---

Sept. 1936, "Le Traité Franco Syrien," p. 12. Reputational concerns, however, clearly played a secondary role in shaping French strategy in the periphery.

[180] Adamthwaite, *Coming of the Second World War*, p. 256; and Young, *In Command of France*, p. 216.

[181] Adamthwaite, *Coming of the Second World War*, pp. 296–297. See also notes 219 and 220 below.

and the periphery. As far as core strategy is concerned, political divisions between left and right contributed to effective paralysis and the inability of elites to update prevailing strategic conceptions. So too did the military's organizational commitment to a defensive strategy and the primacy of infantry impair the adjustment process. As far as peripheral strategy is concerned, I show that the relationship between the French polity and its overseas empire went through a fundamental transformation during the interwar period. The role played by indigenous troops in the European battles of World War I led to an increasingly intense bond between the French public and *la France d'Outre-Mer.* The level of metropolitan investment in the empire rose dramatically, tightening the link between core and periphery. The images linking the fate of the metropole to the overseas empire similarly infused the elite community. The intellectual paradigms of individual decision makers and the structure and organizational interests of bureaucratic actors became oriented toward the periphery. Indeed, the distinction between metropole and periphery blurred; the French came to see the empire as a unified political and strategic entity. After decades of trying to do so, elites finally succeeded during the interwar period in embedding overseas empire in French strategic culture. France's interwar strategy must be understood within the context of the changing nature of national identity and national self-image among elites and the public alike.

Private Economic Interest. Private economic interests did serve as a constraint—though not a major one—on the reorientation of strategy in the core. Industrialists initially resisted full-scale rearmament for two main reasons. First, they were hesitant to invest large sums to expand and modernize their factories because they were uncertain that future orders would be sufficient to enable them to recover their outlays. Second, the left-leaning Popular Front government in power from 1936 to 1938 introduced social legislation designed to benefit the working class. Some of these measures cut into corporate profits and exacerbated concern among industrialists that large-scale investment would be a risky proposition. In part because of these considerations, the armaments industry did not have sufficient capacity to meet demand in the late 1930s.[182]

This predicament was, however, more a symptom than a cause of France's under-preparation for war in the core. The interests of the business community would clearly have been better served by faster-paced rearmament and a move toward increased armor and mechani-

---

[182] Shirer, *Collapse of the Third Republic,* pp. 306–307.

zation. The problem was that political and military leaders did not decide to redress the shortfall in tanks, aircraft, armored transports, and modern munitions until it was too late. Recall that in the mid-1930s the army was not even spending the resources that it had been allocated. In 1937, the army was content to have cavalry regiments rely on horses for mobility. Had decision makers and the military elite earlier on placed larger orders for modern armaments, capacity would have expanded and industry would have been better prepared to meet demand in the late 1930s.

Private economic interests had a greater impact on strategy in the periphery. Metropolitan trade with and capital investment in the overseas territories rose dramatically during the interwar years. As a portion of all external trade, French commerce with the territories rose from 10 percent before World War I to 27 percent by the late 1930s.[183] Between 1919 and 1927, French exports to the colonies grew by an annual rate of 13.3 percent.[184] The figures for investment are even more striking. Before World War I, capital investment in the empire represented only 10 percent of all foreign investment; by the end of the 1930s, this figure had risen to roughly 45 percent.[185] In absolute terms, close to 5 billion francs (in 1914 francs) were invested in the empire between 1930 and 1939, while only 6.5 billion francs (in 1914 francs) were invested in the empire during the decades between the establishment of the Third Republic and the outbreak of World War I.[186]

These data certainly provide evidence of a tightening economic embrace between the metropole and the imperial periphery. Given both the absolute volume of imperial trade and investment and the percentages of external commercial activity they represented, the government as well as private firms had a clear interest in protecting the overseas territories as international tensions mounted during the 1930s. But for two reasons, it would be misleading to view economic considerations as a primary cause, rather than as a symptom, of a changing relationship between the French polity and its overseas territories.

First, imperial investment increased during a period in which the profitability of empire was in fact declining. The gap between rates of return in the empire and those in foreign countries was higher before World War I than it was during the interwar years. In fact, rates of

---

[183] C. M. Andrew and A. S. Kanya-Forstner, "French Business and the French Colonialists," *Historical Journal*, 19, 4 (1976), 987; and Marseille, *Empire colonial*, p. 37.

[184] Marseille, *Empire colonial*, p. 44.

[185] Estimates and accounting procedures vary. Marseille, in *Empire colonial*, estimates that imperial investment represented roughly 40 to 50% of foreign investment (p. 103). Andrew and Kanya-Forstner, in "French Business," specify 45% (p. 987).

[186] Marseille, *Empire colonial*, p. 105.

return from imperial investments dropped dramatically during the 1920s from their prewar levels.[187] Similar trends within the British empire led to dropping rates of imperial investment and a reorientation of Britain's portfolio toward foreign countries.[188] The opposite trend within France suggests that profit-seeking was not the only source of a shift in investment patterns. This interpretation is borne out by evidence that the business community in the early 1920s, as it was before World War I, continued to be skeptical of the long-term economic value of overseas empire. A group of business elites that gathered at the close of the war to discuss the future of the French empire expressed deep reservations about the periphery's economic promise and even suggested that the government should consider abandoning major portions of France's overseas possessions.[189] The new interest of investors in the periphery appears to have been driven more by popular enthusiasm for empire than by recognition of new economic opportunities.

Second, the economic data presented above indeed appear less impressive when interpreted within the context of international economic trends. Investment in the empire was driven, at least in part, by the absence of attractive alternatives. As Christopher Andrew put it, investors turned to the empire as "a way of taking refuge from the appalling economic realities of post-war France."[190] After the economic crisis of 1929, the value of the franc declined and the French government placed tight restrictions on the export of capital. These constraints contributed substantially to the rise in imperial investment during the 1930s.[191] The figures on trade must also be placed in this historical context. Exports to overseas possessions did grow rapidly during the early 1920s. But the reason that imperial trade came to represent some 30 percent of external trade by the 1930s was that the volume of foreign trade declined precipitously after the crisis of the late 1920s, not because trade with the empire was growing so rapidly. Between 1927 and 1936, the value of French exports to foreign countries fell 65.8 percent, while the value of exports to the empire fell only 1.7 percent.[192] Furthermore, the trade figures are somewhat deceptive in that imports from the territories far exceeded exports to the empire. Not only was France running an unfavorable balance of trade with the empire during

---

[187] Ibid., pp. 109–111.
[188] See Lance Davis and Robert Huttenback, *Mammon and the Pursuit of Empire* (Cambridge: Cambridge University Press, 1986).
[189] Andrew and Kanya-Forstner, *French Imperial Expansion*, p. 147.
[190] Andrew, "French Colonialist Movement," p. 164.
[191] Andrew and Kanya-Forstner, *French Imperial Expansion*, p. 248.
[192] Marseille, *Empire colonial*, p. 44.

the late 1930s, but the real value of exports to the empire for 1936, 1937, and 1938 was below the level of 1913.[193]

My analysis is not meant to suggest that the empire was not of growing economic importance to traders and investors; it clearly was. But it seems clear that rising rates of imperial investment and trade during the early interwar years were not driven principally by a radical change in the profitability of empire. Other forces were responsible for solidifying the economic tie between metropole and periphery. My argument is that these economic trends were part of a broader shift in strategic culture—a change in the way that the French polity viewed empire and defined national well-being. It was this shift in strategic culture—and not discrete economic considerations—that explains France's failure to undertake a much-needed reorientation of grand strategy. From this perspective, elites, after attempting to do so since the 1880s, had finally succeeded in persuading the French polity to buy into overseas empire. But they also unwittingly entrapped themselves in a strategic culture that played a significant role in the adjustment failure of the 1930s.

Domestic Politics. The 1930s were a decade of political turmoil for the Third Republic. The political landscape was deeply divided between left and right. The economic impact of the depression made it difficult for successive governments to sustain popular support; most cabinets were short-lived. This divided and unstable domestic environment contributed to adjustment failure in three important respects. First, the political vulnerability of successive cabinets militated against the adoption of foreign and defense policies that would threaten tenuous coalitions, mobilize the opposition, or alienate the public. Decisive shifts in French strategy—say, to stand firm against German demands or to enter into an alliance with the Soviet Union—were difficult to orchestrate given the unstable and fragmented political environment and the pressing domestic agenda. The domestic setting thus favored maintenance of the status quo.[194]

Second, because of the perceived threat posed to republican government by the growing strength of the right and by the triumph of fascism in Germany, Italy, and Spain, civilian leaders on the left—who were in power during most of the decade—staunchly opposed moving from a conscript army toward a professional army. Although professionalization offered a pathway to modernize and strengthen France's

---

[193] Charles-Robert Ageron, "Les Colonies devant l'opinion publique française (1919–1939)," *Revue Française d'Histoire d'Outre-Mer*, 77, 286 (1990), 58.
[194] Hughes, *To the Maginot Line*, pp. 259–264.

military forces, the rightist leanings of the officer corps fueled concern that a professional army might pose a threat to civilian rule. A conscript army, although it lacked the training needed to take advantage of developments in weaponry, was far safer in political terms. These considerations reinforced the army's reliance on infantry and its failure to adapt strategy to technological change.[195]

Third, the domestic environment was a powerful obstacle to forging a formal alliance with the Soviet Union. Right-wing politicians and the military were, for ideological reasons, staunchly opposed to a military convention with the Soviets. Even the left was inherently suspicious of the Kremlin's intentions. Of the three parties comprising the Popular Front—the Radical-Socialists, Socialists, and Communists—only the Communists strongly supported alliance with the Soviets. Accordingly, entering into formal arrangements with the Soviet Union would not only have invoked the ire of the right and the army, but also would have precipitated potentially debilitating splits within the governing leftist coalition.[196] Domestic political pressures were thus partly responsible for making highly unattractive the options available for coping with German superiority.

Although these domestic considerations affected French strategy in the core, they are insufficient to explain outcomes; they contributed to, but were not the main causes of, adjustment failure. Political instability indeed impaired the ability of successive cabinets to govern effectively during the 1930s. But the pitched political battles of the decade focused almost exclusively on domestic issues, not on foreign policy. Cabinets rose and fell on the basis of their economic and social policies, not on their approach to military strategy, the scope of rearmament, and their dealings with Germany. On most key dimensions of foreign and defense policy, there was remarkable continuity through successive governments. Political resistance to the professionalization of the army no doubt impaired the move toward more capable, modern forces. But even without a professional army, much more could have been done to modernize the conscript force, to train it more adequately, and to adapt doctrine and strategy to technological change. As far as alliance with the Soviets is concerned, domestic political pressure was only one of many impediments. As mentioned above, fear of provoking war with Germany, an unwillingness to press East European countries to allow Soviet troops access to their territory, and skepticism about the quality of Soviet forces all contributed to French reluctance to ally with

---

[195] Young, "Preparations for Defeat," p. 169.
[196] Adamthwaite, *Coming of the Second World War*, p. 273; and Shirer, *Collapse of the Third Republic*, pp. 240–242, 313–318, 410.

the Soviets. Indeed, there was little pulling and hauling between left and right over this issue. It is by no means clear that French elites would have more readily moved toward a military convention with the Soviet Union had their domestic position been more secure. In sum, domestic political considerations played an important role in shaping strategy in the core. But they did so primarily by reinforcing the most important factor constraining adjustment: paralysis caused by the absence of attractive options for dealing with German preponderance and manifested in inaction and the perseverance of outmoded strategic beliefs due to the fear and resignation produced by high vulnerability.

Domestic politics played a more direct role in shaping peripheral strategy. Furthermore, overextension in the periphery was integrally related to strategic exposure in the core; the imperial orientation of the army and excessive reliance on the potential colonial contribution to home defense contributed significantly to the poor state of the metropolitan army. This imperial orientation was not restricted to the military establishment. During the two decades before the outbreak of World War I, the French polity as a whole grew increasingly receptive to the notion of overseas empire. The parti colonial succeeded in diluting opposition to colonial expenditures within the National Assembly and in gradually winning over public opinion. The empire began to enjoy nonpartisan support among a broad cross-section of political parties. The Radical and Conservative parties, long-standing bastions of anticolonial sentiment, reformulated their platforms and demonstrated guarded acceptance of France's overseas ambitions. In short, by the early 1900s, the pervasive hostility toward empire that had persisted throughout the first thirty years of the Third Republic was beginning to wane.[197]

Although the main sources of opposition to empire had been neutralized by the eve of World War I, it would be inaccurate to suggest that the majority of elites or the public had actually become enthusiastic about overseas expansion. Several factors constrained the extent to which dying opposition could be transformed into active support. First, the socialists remained skeptical of peripheral empire on ideological grounds. Although they were not strongly represented in the Assembly, their position dampened the uniform support that might otherwise have emerged.[198] Second, politicians who were in principle favorably disposed toward empire argued that rising international tensions made the pursuit of ambitious strategies in the periphery increasingly dangerous. Imperial expansion was not worth the risk of inciting

---

[197] Girardet, *L'Idée coloniale en France 1871–1962* (Paris: La Table Ronde, 1972), pp. 94–98.
[198] Ibid., p. 104.

rivalry among the European powers.[199] Third, empire had not yet captured the imagination of the French public; it had not yet become embedded in the *conscience collective*.[200] The average French citizen had little, if any, personal experience with empire. The territories remained distant entities, both figuratively and literally.

It was not until after World War I that overseas empire became deeply rooted in France's strategic culture. A process of national redefinition took place during the interwar period. The overseas territories were incorporated into an expansive notion of the national interest; the continental and imperial strands of French nationalism were finally merged. While the parti colonial grew increasingly active after the end of fighting and during the early 1920s, the experience of war itself helped increase elite and public receptivity to empire. Hundreds of thousands of workers and soldiers had converged on the metropole from the periphery; many had given their lives to defend metropolitan territory. The war thus settled a debate that had been raging since Ferry's proimperial monologues before the National Assembly: the empire *was* of clear economic and strategic value to the metropole. The overseas territories were now much more than a means of preserving France's status as a great power. They were integral to preserving the security of the metropole.

During the 1880s, a small group of elites pursued empire as a way of escaping continental humiliation and reclaiming France's prestige as a first-class power. After World War I, and especially during the 1930s, a much broader cross-section of elites and masses alike viewed France's well-being as linked to the well-being of the overseas empire. Before World War I, French nationalism and the need to reaffirm French power after the Franco-Prussian War indeed contributed to the growth of empire. Yet a different brand of nationalism—one that defined French power solely in terms of metropolitan security—also slowed the imperial process. After the experience of World War I and the participation of the colonies in metropolitan defense, these two strands of nationalism began to merge. Metropolitan security could not be separated from imperial security; the way in which the French conceived of national strength was coming to be redefined. As a source of offsetting France's demographic disadvantages and as a measure of national power in and of itself, peripheral empire was being incorporated into an expanded notion of metropolitan security.

Elite lobbying played an important role in changing popular attitudes toward empire during the interwar period. The experience of

[199] Ibid., pp. 108–109.
[200] Ibid., pp. 112–114.

World War I indeed raised the standing of empire among the public. But much of the National Assembly and the French populace remained somewhat diffident toward the overseas territories through the 1920s. It was not until the parti colonial embarked on an ambitious propaganda campagin between 1927 and 1931 that public enthusiasm for empire was mobilized.[201] The depression and the consequent increase in the economic importance of the colonies provided added fuel for the propaganda campaign. Claims that the empire could contribute to the metropole's economic welfare were finally justifiable. After 1935, the colonial lobby joined political and military elites in concentrating more narrowly on strategic arguments. With German rearmament and the successive disappearance of France's allies in central and eastern Europe, decision makers and the colonial lobby together portrayed the empire as "a decisive factor in national power and national security."[202] These arguments resonated powerfully, building a strong colonial consensus among top decision makers, the National Assembly, and the public.[203]

The dramatic change in the way that the French polity perceived empire can be measured through several indicators. First, a clear shift in thinking took place within the National Assembly: across the political spectrum, empire was not only tolerated but supported enthusiastically. Even the opposition of the extreme right and the socialists began to dissipate.[204] Maurice Barrès, soon after the close of World War I, expressed a fervor for empire common among his fellow deputies: "One is tempted to thank the Germans for opening the eyes of the whole world to the importance of colonial questions. . . . Everything has changed. Colonial policy has become part of our general policy, and the question of the Rhine is now clearly linked with that of the Congo."[205] One could hardly imagine a more revealing statement about changing French perspectives on empire, given the fact that French diplomats had just spent several years trying to ensure that the British saw their security frontier on the banks of the Rhine, not at the cliffs of Dover. Parliamentary support for empire only grew stronger during the 1930s. By the end of the decade, there was unanimity among deputies that the empire was indivisible and that no territorial concessions would be made to either Italy or Germany. The French tolerated Germany's seizure of the Rhineland, Austria, and the Sudetenland but

---

[201] Ageron, "Les Colonies devant l'opinion publique française," pp. 37–50. For details of the propaganda campaign, see pp. 45–53.
[202] Michel, "La Puissance par l'empire," p. 35.
[203] Ageron, "Les Colonies devant l'opinion publique française," pp. 60–73.
[204] Girardet, *L'Idée coloniale*, p. 133.
[205] Cited in Andrew and Kanya-Forstner, *French Imperial Expansion*, p. 209.

could not countenance returning to Germany the colonies it had lost in World War I. Some deputies even put forward proposals to transform the empire into a federal structure.[206]

Second, immigration to the overseas territories proceeded at an unprecedented pace. Long considered unattractive for resettlement, the empire was now viewed as offering unique economic opportunities as well as the chance to contribute to the cause of French nationalism. During the first fifteen years after the war, more than 120,000 Frenchmen moved to Morocco alone.[207] Thousands of others took advantage of increasingly convenient air and sea links to travel to Africa, for both business and holiday. Accordingly, a much larger percentage of the French public had personal contact with the territories, increasing the extent to which the empire became a prominent feature of the political landscape.

Third, there was a virtual explosion of literature dealing with the empire. Fictional accounts of life in the colonies presented glorified tales of military conquest and adventure. Imperial affairs were no longer covered only by the colonial press; mass-circulation newspapers and magazines began to run regular news and feature stories on the empire.[208] Adventure films portraying the excitement and allure of life in the colonies grew increasingly popular.[209] Even the standard textbooks used in primary schools were revised to represent empire in a new light. A popular edition during the interwar period stressed that "colonial empire is necessary to ensure the grandeur and prosperity of France."[210] The vocabulary used in the media and in official documents changed accordingly: *l'empire* gave way to *la plus grande France, France de cent millions d'habitants,* and *la France d'Outre-mer.* The colonies were being transformed from distant appendages into France overseas—extensions of the metropole itself. Awareness of and attachment to the empire was developing among even those Frenchmen who had no direct link to the overseas territories. "The colonial act," according to Raoul Girardet, "ceased to be a vague entity to become a familiar reality. The colonial presence was becoming more and more felt in the interior of the national conscience."[211]

[206] Ageron, "Les Colonies devant l'opinion publique française," p. 70; and Ageron, "La Perception de la puissance française," pp. 16–17.

[207] Girardet, *L'Idée coloniale,* p. 119.

[208] Ageron, "Les Colonies devant l'opinion publique française," pp. 48–49.

[209] Pascal Ory, "Introduction to an Era of Doubt: Cultural Reflections of 'French Power,' around the Year 1948," in *Power in Europe? Great Britain, France, Italy, and Germany in a Postwar World, 1945–1950,* ed. Joseph Becker and Franz Knipping (Berlin: Walter de Gruyter, 1986), p. 399.

[210] Girardet, *L'Idée coloniale,* p. 123.

[211] Ibid., p. 125.

Fourth, opinion polls confirm that a profound shift took place in public perceptions of the relationship between metropole and periphery. In the 1880s, procolonialist politicians battled a National Assembly and an electorate hostile to empire. In February 1939, over 50 percent of the population felt that losing *any* portion of the overseas possessions was tantamount to losing a piece of metropolitan territory itself. Sixty-seven percent of those polled opposed accommodating Germany's claims in the periphery while 89 percent opposed accommodating Italian claims.[212] Girardet describes the sentiment that spread among the public during the interwar period: "France and its external dependencies must be considered as an indivisible whole, an indissoluble unit for which all the portions are mutually and jointly liable."[213]

Fifth, while the timing and extent of imperial investment suggest a newfound emotional as well as economic link between the business community and the empire, investment patterns indicate that popular enthusiasm for *la France d'Outre-Mer* saddled the state with unexpected economic burdens—that a process of entrapment was in fact occurring. During the 1920s, private direct investment constituted some 65 percent of the capital invested in the empire.[214] During this period, 208 private societies were established to channel funds to the overseas territories. This is almost equivalent to the number of similar organizations (212) established between 1849 and 1918.[215] Recall that this vast expansion in the private infrastructure for imperial investment occured while rates of return in the empire were dropping. Private direct investment in the empire fell sharply after 1929, constituting only 17 percent of imperial investment between 1930 and 1939.[216] The government consequently found itself having to pick up the slack left by private investors; public funds were channeled to the territories both through the budget of the Ministry of Colonies and through the issue of government bonds. Communications and transportation projects funded by public sources were to allow the government to realize its plans for development *(mise en valeur)* of the overseas territories. Yet the state intervened in the process of seeking to turn the colonies into profitable enterprises only after the process had already been begun by the French public through private investment. Elites found themselves saddled with an overseas empire in which private investors and traders had already accumulated large-scale interests. It was incumbent on the state to carry forward the baton. As Jacques Marseille describes this

---

[212] Ageron, "Les Colonies devant l'opinion publique française," pp. 70–71.
[213] Girardet, *L'Idée coloniale*, p. 125.
[214] Marseille, *Empire colonial*, p. 105.
[215] Ibid., 108.
[216] Ibid., p. 105.

predicament, "Public investment substituted for private investment, for which [the state] was to wait in vain for relief."²¹⁷ Whether the empire contributed to the economic and strategic welfare of the metropole was of decreasing relevance; elites had to assume responsibility for maintaining and protecting a vast set of imperial commitments in which the French public had deeply invested both economically and psychologically. These were commitments that had become integral to the public's notion of *la plus grande France*.

In sum, World War I and the interwar period brought about a fundamental change in French strategic culture. For elites and masses alike, the distinction between metropole and periphery blurred because of the empire's contribution to continental defense and because of the persistent lobbying efforts of procolonialists. Empire had become the litmus test of national power and its resources were to enable the metropole to prevail against the Axis powers. Among top decision makers within the National Assembly, and among the public at large, the security of the metropole had become inseparable from the security and integrity of the empire. Tony Smith concisely captures this collective shift in national attitudes: "Domestic vitality came to be identified with international greatness which in turn was indissociable from imperial rule. The competition with other powers for the possession of territory, the celebration of bold explorers and military heroes, the evocation of French colonial greatness in classroom texts, parades and fairs became part of the collective conscience of the nation. . . . Nationalism and imperialism were twins."²¹⁸

The key role of perceptions of metropolitan vulnerability and elite lobbying of the public in shaping strategic culture was confirmed by oscillations in public enthusiasm for *la France d'Outre-Mer*. Support for imperial expansion and development waned in the mid-1920s when French elites felt confident about being able to maintain the continental status quo. This was followed during the 1930s by increased elite lobbying and a resurgence of colonial spirit that paralleled German rearmament and the worsening continental balance.²¹⁹ Enthusiasm for empire in fact peaked just as France's main allies on the Continent were disappearing: "The corollary of disengagement from central and eastern Europe was a new emphasis on the empire." In a pattern not unfamiliar with the past, the government turned to empire "as a kind of counterbalance to the strategic losses which had been incurred with

²¹⁷ Ibid., p. 117.

²¹⁸ Tony Smith, "The French Colonial Consensus and People's War, 1946–58," *Journal of Contemporary History*, 9 (October 1974), 242.

²¹⁹ Miles Kahler, *Decolonization in Britain and France: The Domestic Consequences of International Relations* (Princeton: Princeton University Press, 1984), p. 75.

the sale of Czechoslovakia." Charles-Robert Ageron agrees: the outpouring of imperial sentiment in France was "above all a direct reaction
to the threat posed by the Axis powers."[220]

That this shift in strategic culture played a critical part in shaping
French grand strategy during the 1930s is both logical and consistent
with the historical record. Until the mid-1930s, elite beliefs and strategic culture ran on parallel tracks. The Maginot Line and alliances with
Belgium and a host of other countries would likely prevent German
aggression. Furthermore, if a European war did break out, the French
would be able to delay the German attack long enough for the resources of their numerous continental allies and their empire to come
to the assistance of the metropole. After 1936, however, when incoming
information pointed to the need to reorient grand strategy and concentrate on metropolitan defense, elites were stymied by a strategic culture
wedded to overseas empire, by a conception of national security that
erroneously induced elites and the public to look to the overseas territories to solve their strategic predicament. This transformation in the
way that the polity understood the relationship between metropole
and periphery helps explain why elites so exaggerated the strategic
importance of empire. It sheds light on why the best of the French
army was serving abroad while Germany grew more powerful and
more hostile and while France's ability to maintain sea control during
war became increasingly questionable. The conviction that French security depended upon the metropole's link with its overseas appendages also deepens understanding of why elites tolerated the empire's
deleterious effect on the quality of the metropolitan army and why
France entered World War II better prepared to fight colonial campaigns in North Africa than armored battles in northern Europe. The
strategic images that had been manipulated by elites and that empowered them until the mid-1930s came to constrain them as the threat to
the metropole mounted. Elites had finally succeeded in selling empire
to the French polity, but the new degree of attachment to *la France
d'Outre-Mer* contributed to France's inability to prepare adequately for
war with Germany.

Without access to the decision makers themselves, it is difficult to
determine whether strategic culture shaped outcomes by preventing
elites from implementing their preferred policies or through the more
subtle mechanism of infusing elite thinking and causing institutionalized strategic images to override strategic logic. The evidence strongly
suggests, however, that strategic culture affected outcomes primarily

---

[220] Adamthwaite, *Coming of the Second World War*, p. 256; Young, *In Command of France*,
p. 216; Ageron, "Les Colonies devant l'opinion publique française," pp. 71–72.

by overriding strategic logic. The image equating metropolitan security with imperial security and the arrival of troops from the empire was deeply embedded within the elite community. Elites clearly appreciated the need to disengage from at least some portions of the empire and began to do so. They did not intend to defend possessions in which the chances of military success were minimal. They continued to champion publicly the strategic value of empire even during the late 1930s, when the need to concentrate on metropolitan security had become glaringly apparent. And, during 1939–1940, they did gut the overseas territories of much of their military capability. These are not the actions of a leadership motivated primarily by the desire to avoid the political consequences of setbacks in the periphery. On the contrary, it was a shift in the mindset of elites and the public alike— not the discrete pressures of domestic politics—that best explains why French decision makers so exaggerated the potential contribution of empire to metropolitan defense and found themselves with a strategy ill-suited to dealing with the German threat. Powerful strategic images equating metropolitan security with the arrival of troops from secure and thriving overseas territories overrode unambiguous information indicating that empire was not the answer to France's strategic predicament. Strategic culture impaired a much-needed reorientation of strategy and is key to understanding why French elites pursued policies that grew increasingly divorced from strategic reality during the 1930s.

Military Services. Considerable responsibility for the absence of strategic adjustment lies with the military establishment. From 1936 onward, top military leaders consistently claimed that France simply was not strong enough to go to war against Germany. During successive diplomatic confrontations with Germany, the military almost always argued for accommodating Hitler and not risking hostilities.[221] The military was also one of the main vehicles through which outmoded strategic suppositions became institutionalized and routinized—and therefore resistant to adaptation. Especially because it was threatened by changing technology, by steadily growing German power, and by shifts in Europe's strategic and diplomatic landscape, the military clung tightly to existing organizational norms—reliance on the Maginot Line, defensive doctrine and strategy, a mobilization scheme that virtually precluded spontaneous action, and infantry units that had relatively little armor or mobility. Despite sporadic reassessments of war plans

---

[221] Shirer chronicles the assessments and recommendations of General Gamelin and his main colleagues from initial German rearmament through the German attack in 1940. See *Collapse of the Third Republic*, pp. 199–560.

after 1935, the high command failed to call for a major revision of strategy. As Robert Young writes, "There was a review. There were questions, but the old ones. There were answers, but the old ones."[222] Finally, the military's political conservatism contributed to the paralysis that gripped the decision-making community. Had the officer corps been less right-wing in its orientation, civilian elites might have been more receptive to the professionalization of the military and might have pursued with greater vigor alliance with the Soviet Union.

It would be inaccurate, however, to blame the military services alone for the stagnation that characterized core strategy. Paralysis was by no means restricted to the military establishment. Unwillingness and inability to challenge reigning strategic assumptions were as prevalent among civilians as among military elites. Moreover, organizational self-interest should have led to initiatives that were not forthcoming: more rapid rearmament, the development of at least limited offensive capabilities, and more serious efforts to incorporate new technology and doctrine into war plans. More rapid rearmament would have increased the military's share of the national budget. Limited offensive capabilities would have given the military more control over policy and would have allowed the army at least to consider moving preventively against Germany during the successive crises of the 1930s.[223] The incorporation of new technologies into doctrine would have increased the military's prestige and its autonomy. The organizational interests and behavior of the military thus appear to have been more a symptom than a cause of France's adjustment failure in the core.

Turning to the periphery, developments within the military establishment corroborate my argument about the importance of strategic culture in shaping grand strategy. Shifts in the central missions and organizational structure of the military reflected the tightening embrace between metropole and periphery during the interwar years. As mentioned above, overseas operations preoccupied much of the military establishment. This imperial orientation had a profound effect on career paths, training, the disposition of forces, and the morale and quality of the metropolitan army. It also affected command structure. Legislation passed in 1927 noted that "the French army is *one* and one should not make a distinction between the forces stationed in the metropole and north Africa and the forces stationed in the Colonies." Accordingly, the minister of war was to gain control over the mobilization in wartime of all troops serving in greater France, whether in the

---

[222] Young, "Preparations for Defeat," p. 171.
[223] On the relationship between service self-interest and offensive strategies, see Snyder, *Ideology of the Offensive*.

metropole, Algeria, the protectorates, or the colonies.[224] This shift in the command structure was not fully implemented, and an effort to bring it about began anew in 1937. The rationale put forward by the Overseas Section of the General Staff was based on the "unity of the French Domain"—the metropole, North Africa, and the colonies had to be seen as a unified strategic theater.[225] "More and more, questions relative to colonial defense are intimately linked to those concerning the metropole."[226] As a result of these pressures, a Chief of Staff for the Colonies was created in 1938.[227] Colonial affairs were now permanently represented in the highest military council. While the command structure for overseas forces remained a matter of dispute through 1939, it was clear that colonial issues were becoming increasingly important within the military bureaucracy. As General Gaston-Henri-Gustave Billotte summarized the situation, "The defense of our overseas domain cannot be conceived of, at the present time, except within the framework of the total defense of the French Empire; national defense is one."[228] The expansive concept of *la France d'Outre-Mer* that had taken root in strategic culture during the interwar years was manifested not only in popular attitudes and the reigning conceptions that informed grand strategy, but also in the very structure of the decision-making community.

The scope of France's imperial commitments and the centrality of empire in grand strategy were also furthered by bureaucratic squabbling over how to set priorities among the overseas possessions. Views diverged mainly because of differing opinions about how the empire could most effectively contribute to metropolitan defense. North Africa was unquestionably the top priority, but that was the extent of agreement. General Bührer, representing colonial affairs, ranked defense priorities in the following order of importance: Indochina, Black Africa, Somalia, East Africa, and the Antilles. His main concern was the number of troops and the amount of war materiel that could be sent to the metropole. The navy's priorities were Black Africa, the Antilles, and Indochina. The navy was concerned chiefly with protecting troops and supplies being transported in the Atlantic. Oil coming from the Americas was of chief importance, highlighting the value of the Antilles and

---

[224] 7-N-4196, Dossier 1, 25 Jan. 1937, Etude, pp. 8–9. The 1927 law is paraphrased in this document. A copy of the law can be found in 7-N-4196, Dossier 2, 23 July 1927, "Loi sur l'Organization de l'Armée."

[225] 7-N-4196, Dossier 2, 5 Feb. 1937, Note.

[226] 7-N-4196, Dossier 1, 25 Jan. 1937, Etude, p. 13.

[227] For a good summary of organizational changes in colonial defense, see 7-N-3927, Dossier 6, 21 Feb. 1939, "Les Colonies françaises dans la défense nationale."

[228] 7-N-4196, Dossier 1, 23 April 1937, Note, p. 1.

the Atlantic coast of Africa. Admiral Jean Darlan was quite explicit on this point: "It is toward Dakar and Fort de France that the Navy is now directing its principal effort. If the other colonies, especially Indo-China, attract its attention, it is only of secondary importance, for objectives that are local and not directly vital."[229] The air force's ranking was Black Africa, the Levant, Diego Suarez, and Indochina. West Africa, and especially Dakar, was essential to providing aviation fuel. The Levant and Diego Suarez were critical because they were needed as refueling bases if aircraft were to be used in either the Middle East or Indochina.[230] Finally, the army's priorities were Black Africa, Indochina, and Madagascar. The army was mainly concerned with the recruitment of indigenous troops for metropolitan service.[231]

This array of priorities meant that different branches of the military had vested interests in developing and protecting different portions of the overseas empire.[232] There were thus bureaucratic obstacles to the paring down of imperial commitments and the timely transport of colonial troops to the metropole. As mentioned above, however, the behavior of the services was more a symptom than a cause of France's interwar predicament. Unlike during the early decades of the Third Republic, the central bureaucracy had firm control of military operations in the territories; the days of empire by fait accompli were largely over. During the 1930s, the services did not drag the state into unwanted commitments or cling to positions that elites wanted to abandon. Rather, the dispersion of France's military assets, the priority assigned to peripheral missions, and the consequent deterioration of the metropolitan army were the product of a strategic design created and supported by military and civilian elites alike. It was a change in how the French polity understood the relationship between the metropole and its overseas territories, not service rivalry or bureau-

---

[229] 2-N-246, Dossier 2, 1 Sept. 1938, Admiral Darlan to Chief of the General Staff for National Defense, p. 4.

[230] 2-N-246, Dossier 2, 24 Sept. 1938, General Vuillemin to Chief of the General Staff for National Defense, pp. 6–7.

[231] For a concise review of the positions of the Chiefs of Staff, see 7-N-4196, Dossier 3, 23 Nov. 1938, Reunion of the Chiefs of Staff, Note. For further discussion of the views of the individual services, see Michel, "La Puissance par l'empire," pp. 41–44.

[232] The absence of a consensus on regional priorities meant that local commanders were often forced to compete with one another for scarce resources. In the late 1930s, for example, African units were frequently passed from one regional assignment to another, as the General Staff attempted to respond to competing demands from the territories and from the metropole for reinforcements. 7-N-3926, Dossier 4, contains a series of cables and notes concerning the shuttling of Senegalese units among the metropole, North Africa, and the Levant.

cratic self-interest, that led to a redefinition of how the military conceived of its principal roles and missions.

Conclusions

The gross adjustment failure that plagued French strategy during the 1930s was the result primarily of the effect of perceived metropolitan vulnerability on elite beliefs and on strategic culture. Conditions of strategic deficiency initially led to a set of strategic beliefs based on sound inference. In 1935, it made good sense for the French to rely on blocking German forces in Belgium and waiting for the resources of allies and the overseas empire to converge on the metropole before beginning the counterattack. But the suppositions that informed policy should soon have been discredited by international events that challenged the underpinnings of French war plans and that left France diplomatically isolated and facing an increasingly dire military imbalance. The absence of adjustment was the product of two main factors. First, high vulnerability, rather than producing vigilance, led to resignation and paralysis manifested in inaction and a cognitive lag in the adaptation of beliefs to incoming information. Political instability, divisive splits between left and right, and bureaucratic inertia within the military clearly contributed to this paralysis. But the main problem was that military and civilian elites alike saw no attractive options for dealing with conditions of strategic deficiency. They therefore clung to preexisting strategic beliefs rather than undertaking a much-needed reassessment and bringing policy into line with strategic reality. The cognitive tendency for prevailing beliefs to persevere in the face of incoming information was exacerbated by high vulnerability and the sense of fear it produced. French strategy in the core during the late 1930s was more the product of resignation and illusion than of rational calculation. As in Britain, the loss of Czechoslovakia so glaringly revealed the fundamental flaws in strategy that efforts to undertake a major strategic reorientation finally began. But adjustment occurred far too haltingly and far too late to enable the allies to cope adequately with a Germany fortified by successive years of rapid rearmament and military success.

The second factor producing adjustment failure was a strategic culture wedded to empire. Metropolitan vulnerability caused elites to retreat ever more deeply into empire during the interwar period—both to reaffirm national stature at home and abroad and to garner war-making capabilities with which to redress the imbalance in the core. Plans to rely on the empire's troops and materiel to defend the homeland played a key role in allowing inaction in the core. Given the eroding security predicament on the Continent and the absence of more urgent measures to redress it, elites virtually *had* to believe that empire would come to the metropole's rescue. The centrality of the empire in grand strategy was thus partly a result of resignation: the situation in the core induced elites to cling to the notion that imperial resources would avert the fall of France even in the face of disconfirming information.

But the perseverance of outmoded strategic beliefs due to resignation and paralysis are by no means the full story. Metropolitan vulnerability, via elite beliefs and elite lobbying, also led to a shift in strategic culture that reoriented how the domestic polity—top decision makers, the military, and the public—conceived of the relationship between metropole and periphery. It was defeat in the Franco-Prussian War that had initially created the movement to build an overseas empire; beginning in the 1880s, procolonial elites sought to convince the public of the benefits of empire in order to gain support for their policies aimed at recovering international stature through empire. Though they succeeded in substantially reducing domestic opposition to imperial aims, it was the colonial contribution to the war effort between 1914 and 1918, the economic implications of the depression, and the propaganda campaigns of the interwar period that transformed the colonies from distant appendages into *la France d'Outre-Mer* and that merged the continental and imperial strains of French nationalism. Elites were initially empowered by this transformation in how the French polity as a collective entity understood the relationship between metropole and periphery, but they eventually found themselves entrapped in the strategic images that they had propagated. In terms of the public mind, the interests of investors and traders, the intellectual paradigms and values of decision makers, and the organizational structure and interests of the military, empire had become deeply embedded in strategic culture. A strategic culture wedded to empire fueled inflated projections of the potential contribution of overseas territories to metropolitan security. This reformulation of how the polity defined national security explains why elites prepared the colonies for being severed from the metropole when the value of those colonies supposedly lay in their ability to reinforce the metropole. It explains why elites and masses alike reacted to successive setbacks in Europe by expressing increased enthusiasm for empire. The merging of the continental and imperial strains of French nationalism similarly sheds light on the lateness of the decision to transfer the colonial army to the metropole. And strategic culture helps explain why, throughout much of the interwar period, the services concentrated their attention and their best personnel and equipment on overseas operations despite clear costs to the

[266]

quality of the metropolitan army. A strategic culture deeply wedded to overseas empire thus played a key role in producing both strategic exposure and strategic overextension during the interwar period.

1949–1954: Metropolitan Security Versus Indochina

World War II again forced French elites to reassess both defense strategy in the core and the relationship between metropolitan security and overseas empire. After the defeat of Hitler's forces, as after the Franco-Prussian War, French decision makers were faced with two impulses. On the one hand, there was a pressing need to adjust to a new constellation of power on the European continent, both to ensure that Germany did not yet again rearm and to cope with an increasingly hostile Soviet Union whose armed forces were considerably larger than those of the West European allies combined. On the other hand, the devastation suffered during the war as well as the role played by the overseas territories in eventually defeating the Germans rekindled imperial ambition and the French impulse to recover international stature through peripheral empire.[233] The rise of Ho Chi Minh and the threat that he posed to French territory in the Far East made Indochina the focal point of this effort to reaffirm French power through external ambition.

The problem was that these two impulses were incompatible; imperial ambition and the war in Indochina could not be pursued without reneging on French commitments to NATO and placing at risk plans for the economic and industrial recovery of the metropole. Nevertheless, between 1949 and the defeat of French forces at Dien Bien Phu in 1954, French elites decided to prosecute the war in Indochina despite clear awareness of the trade-offs involved. Why did French decision makers choose yet again to jeopardize metropolitan security in order to pursue overseas empire? Did not the experience of the 1930s provide adequate reason to focus France's resources on metropolitan defense?

Strategic Assessments

During the early post–World War II years, French elites saw two main threats to metropolitan security. Germany, though defeated and occupied by the victorious powers, could quickly come to pose a threat to France if allowed to rearm. Accordingly, French decision makers

---

[233] See Charles-Robert Ageron, "La Survivance d'un mythe: La Puissance par l'empire colonial (1944–1947)," *Revue Française d'Histoire d'Outre-Mer*, 72, 269 (1985), 387–403.

were adamant that Germany not be permitted to rebuild its military forces. These efforts to protect against a revival of German militarism, however, only exacerbated the second threat facing the metropole: that posed by the Soviet army. So superior were Soviet forces to the combined forces of the western allies that French elites had little confidence that the Red Army could be prevented from overrunning France should it attempt to do so. In late 1947, after meeting with French leaders, Admiral Richard Conolly, the commander-in-chief of American naval forces in the eastern Atlantic and Mediterranean, summarized French concerns: "What is worrying French officials is SECURITY. They are scared of the colossal ground forces to the eastward. They are afraid that, if Germany is resuscitated, her resources and technical proficiency would be used by the U.S.S.R. against France. They want some concrete assurance that would provide some adequate hope that, in case of attack, they could preserve part of Metropolitan France from invasion and another occupation."[234] In response to the war scare of 1948 resulting primarily from the coup in Czechoslovakia, the French military came close to adopting war plans that called for an immediate retreat to North Africa in the event of a Soviet attack.[235] The problem was not simply that U.S. war plans called for the evacuation of Western Europe if war with the Soviets broke out.[236] "Not even is there an emergency plan for the supply of arms," noted a senior French official. "France is therefore strictly reduced to her own means, since the Brussels Pact unites only *the powerless*. In other words, she is totally exposed."[237]

Matters improved somewhat in 1949 with the signing of the North Atlantic Treaty. French elites committed themselves to contribute ten divisions to NATO by 1950–1951 and an additional five divisions by 1952–1953. By increasing their own force levels, French decision makers were attempting not only to reduce Soviet superiority, but also to convince their NATO allies that German rearmament was unnecessary for coping with the Soviet threat.[238] But, in the short term, the emergence

[234] Conolly to Forrestal, 19 Dec. 1947, cited in Melvyn Leffler, *A Preponderance of Power: National Security, the Truman Administration, and the Cold War, 1945–52* (Stanford: Stanford University Press, 1992), p. 202.
[235] John Young, *France, the Cold War, and the Western Alliance, 1944–49: French Foreign Policy and Post-War Europe* (New York: St. Martin's Press, 1990), pp. 214–215.
[236] For discussion of U.S. war plans, see Chapter 7.
[237] Maurice Couve de Murville memo of 10 May 1948, quoted in René Girault, "The French Decision-Makers and Their Perception of French Power in 1948," in Becker and Knipping, *Power in Europe?* p. 60.
[238] See Service Historique de l'Armée de l'Air (SHAA), Assorted Letters, 25 Aug. 1951, "Avis du Comité des Chefs d'Etat Major"; and SHAA, E/2751, 10 Feb. 1950, Meeting of the Comité de Défense Nationale (CDN), p. 13. Unless otherwise noted, all the documents cited in this section are contained in the SHAA collection (translations are my

of a formal alliance did little to assuage French concerns. Germany, far from being decentralized and controlled by foreign powers as French elites had hoped, was reemerging as an independent European power. At the insistence of the United States, Germany was effectively becoming a divided country, the resources and industrial strength of the western portion being pulled into the emerging Atlantic alliance. At the same time, the division of Germany and the formation of NATO posed a threat to the Soviets, heightening East-West tensions, and, from France's perspective, raising the likelihood of conflict between the two emerging blocs.[239] Despite these French concerns, "the NAT did nothing directly to improve military defenses on the ground."[240] The United States did not significantly augment its ground forces in Europe until 1951, as part of the major buildup of forces sparked by the Korean War. Furthermore, the Soviets successfully tested an atomic weapon in August 1949, ending the U.S. nuclear monopoly and heightening concern about the military imbalance on the Continent and the potential for war with the Soviet Union.[241] Even after the deployment of U.S. forces in Europe after the outbreak of the Korean War, Soviet forces remained numerically superior to those of NATO. In 1952, French planners assumed that if war broke out in Europe, the Soviets, after full mobilization, would be able to send as many as 180 divisions against an Atlantic coalition consisting of roughly 30 divisions. Taking into consideration the relatively small size of Soviet divisions, the army calculated that the Soviets would enjoy a superiority of approximately three to one.[242] Because French elites opposed German rearmament and because of uncertainty about when allied, and especially Ameri-

---

own). The minutes of the CDN meetings can be found in E/2751. The 145/K documents are contained in the SHAT collection.

[239] Pierre Melandri and Maurice Vaïsse, "France: From Powerlessness to the Search for Influence," in Becker and Knipping, *Power in Europe?* pp. 462–467.

[240] Young, *France, the Cold War, and the Western Alliance*, p. 220.

[241] The American nuclear deterrent was not integrated into French strategy during the early postwar years, and it does not appear to have significantly moderated French perceptions of the Soviet threat. Jean Delmas summarizes French thinking, "It was the extreme imbalance between U.S. and Soviet conventional forces which posed so serious a threat to Europe in 1948. The atom bomb was not included in estimates of the distribution of power." "Reflections on the Notion of Military Power through the French Example (1945–1948)," in Becker and Knipping, *Power in Europe?* p. 351. In addition, French elites, unlike their American counterparts, did not view war with the Soviets as a remote possibility. Nor would France be able to fight such a war without having its territorial integrity compromised. U.S. planners believed that the allies could prevail in a war against the Soviets, but only by evacuating Western Europe in the earlier stages of the war and retaliating against the Soviets with atomic weapons from bases on the European rimland. On French perceptions of the likelihood of war, see Young, *France, the Cold War, and the Western Alliance*, pp. 180, 214–215. On U.S. perceptions of the Soviet threat, see Chapter 7.

[242] 24 April 1952, Meeting of the CDN, Report of General Juin, pp. 8–11.

can, reinforcements would arrive at the front, the burden of conventional defense would fall heavily on French shoulders.

While strategic considerations left France quite vulnerable to a Soviet attack and much in need of substantial increases in force levels, financial considerations illuminated the need for severe constraints on the defense budget. General Charles de Gaulle resigned from the government early in 1946 in part because of mounting pressure to cut defense spending to what he deemed were unacceptable levels. The Gouin government that followed considerably reduced military expenditures.[243] Throughout the late 1940s, the Comité de Défense Nationale (CDN), the governmental body ultimately responsible for formulating foreign and defense policy, appreciated that precarious shortfalls existed in munitions and supplies yet also realized that high levels of defense expenditure only weakened France's already tenuous financial situation and slowed the pace of economic and industrial recovery. As President Vincent Auriol said in a meeting of the CDN convened in January 1949 to discuss defense priorities, "The financial problem at this moment takes precedence over all others."[244] Auriol was not alone in holding this view; there was a consensus among French elites that the lack of financial resources was the most serious problem facing the defense community.[245] As defense expenditures continued to rise in the early 1950s, the ministry of finance became increasingly concerned that efforts to deal with the country's security needs would soon lead to economic ruin. Between 1952 and 1954, defense expenditures represented over one-third of total government spending.[246] In 1953, with requests for increased force levels pending before the CDN, the minister of finance warned the committee that "it is not possible to follow a sane economic and financial plan. . . . We must not hide from the fact that [because of our military policy] we are heading . . . toward an economic, financial, and social crisis."[247]

French elites were thus well aware that military responsibilities were straining available economic resources. In Europe, the need for increasing defense expenditures was readily apparent: more conventional forces were required to counter the Soviet threat, to protect against a

---

[243] Robert Frank, "The French Dilemma: Modernization with Dependence or Independence and Decline," in Becker and Knipping, *Power in Europe?* pp. 265–266.

[244] 20 Jan. 1949, Meeting of the CDN, p. 2.

[245] Doise and Vaïsse, *Diplomatie*, p. 388. In April 1951, the minister of finance complained that the CDN could not continue to make decisions about force levels without looking at the economic impact of such decisions. He remarked that "this method is very problematic; it jeopardizes the arrangements agreed upon in the financial plan." 24 April 1951, Meeting of the CDN, p. 25.

[246] Doise and Vaïsse, *Diplomatie*, p. 404.

[247] 24 July 1953, Meeting of the CDN, pp. 26, 30.

revival of German militarism, and to give diplomats bargaining leverage in their negotiations with NATO allies. In the face of severe economic constraints and the task of postwar reconstruction, the European mission itself constituted a heavy defense burden. It is therefore all the more puzzling that French decision makers exacerbated this gap between resources and commitments by undertaking a costly war in Indochina. Given these constraints on military resources, how did elites rationalize a war in the Far East that could be fought only at a clear expense to European security? Having been rapidly defeated by the Germans in 1940 at least in part because of their neglect of continental defenses, why did elites yet again expose the metropole to pursue peripheral empire?

Dealing with the Adversary

French strategy in Europe was based on the supposition that the United States would assist in the economic reconstruction of France while contributing its conventional and nuclear capabilities to deterring the Soviets and, if necessary, defeating them in war. To a large extent, then, French elites, as during the interwar years, assumed that they could rely on alliances to meet their security needs on the Continent. Furthermore, the presence of British and American troops on the Continent ensured that the French would not, as they did in 1939, find themselves standing essentially alone against a markedly superior adversary. A continental strategy heavily reliant on the help of allies was thus much more realistic than it had been in the late 1930s.

The existence of a formal alliance network did not, however, mean that French elites saw no need to maintain a capable conventional army. As mentioned above, Soviet ground superiority and increasing East-West tensions necessitated concerted efforts to build up conventional forces in Western Europe. By augmenting their own forces the French increased the likelihood that the United States would respond to Soviet aggression by defending Western Europe, rather than by retreating to the European rimland. Furthermore, one of the key disagreements between the United States and France focused on the question of German rearmament. In fact, a principal motivation for the formation of NATO was to reassure the French and, in so doing, to persuade them to acquiesce to Germany's integration into the West. Nevertheless, the signing of the North Atlantic Treaty did not placate French concerns. Still fearful of a resurgence of German militarism, French elites wanted to make a sizable contribution to NATO in order to enhance their bargaining leverage and persuade the United States to forgo substantial German rearmament. They welcomed a German contribution to NATO in terms of nonmilitary industrial production, but not in terms of military manpower.[248] Finally, French elites wanted to maintain a robust military capability in the European theater because of growing resistance to French rule in North Africa. Having succeeded with difficulty in persuading its allies to include Algeria within the boundaries of the North Atlantic Treaty, France was not about to neglect the security of its overseas *departement*.

As far as the periphery was concerned, French elites during the late 1940s and early 1950s were preoccupied with Indochina. They adopted an ambitious deterrent strategy vis-à-vis the Vietminh and were willing to incur high costs to preserve France's position in the Far East. Paralleling the early post–World War I years, the French army in 1945 and 1946 poured into the overseas territories at a remarkable pace. During the months after the end of the war, troop levels dropped from 1,300,000 to 460,000. By 1946, only 110,000 troops were serving in the metropole, the rest having been dispersed throughout the territories. The defense budget was also cut dramatically. These reductions were felt most acutely by troops serving in the metropole because priority for equipment modernization was given to overseas forces. Professional incentives quickly shifted away from the Continent, and overseas service again became the pathway to promotion and career advancement. As during the 1920s, these trends had a devastating impact on the morale and quality of metropolitan troops.[249]

The steady flow of French troops to the periphery was stimulated, at least in part, by the emergence of nationalist movements in many portions of the empire. While local resistance to colonial rule was, in some areas, only beginning to gather momentum, by 1946 it was already clear to French elites that the defense of Indochina would entail high costs. They responded to the massacre of civilians in Haiphong in December 1946 by increasing force levels by some 46,000 soldiers, bringing the number of indigenous and European troops stationed in Indochina to roughly 115,000. Troop levels remained fairly steady until the communist victory in China in 1949. After that point, force levels climbed to roughly 150,000 because of fear that Mao Tse-tung might intervene on behalf of Ho Chi Minh.[250]

After Mao's victory and the consequent increase in the size of French forces in Indochina, the General Staff warned that any further effort in the Far East could be made only by degrading continental defenses

---

[248] Young, *France, the Cold War, and the Western Alliance*, p. 229.

[249] Doise and Vaïsse, *Diplomatie*, pp. 392–399.

[250] 145/K/3, 24 Jan. 1951, "L'Effort français en Indochine depuis la liberation," p. 5. By the end of 1949, roughly 50,000 Frenchmen were serving in Indochina (p. 6).

and severely taxing the metropolitan economy. The General Staff insisted that the war in Indochina had already taken its toll on the number and quality of troops in Europe; requirements in Indochina for 1951 had to be calculated without "entertaining a new impoverishment of units in the Europe-North Africa bloc." This view was made clear in a memo to the minister of national defense: "It is not an exaggeration to assert that the ground forces stationed in Europe and North Africa, and principally the combatant units, have been placed in a critical situation which, if further aggravated, will inevitably force us to revise and restrict the scope of their missions."[251] The air force asserted that the diversion of pilots and other personnel to Indochina meant that force levels were inadequate to fulfill designated missions in the Europe-North Africa bloc.[252]

Throughout most of 1950, these concerns restricted the willingness of the CDN to approve the requests of the Far East Command to raise reinforcements. The minister of national defense characterized such requests as "inordinate" and "excessive" and concisely stated the dilemma before the committee: "We must choose between our obligations in Indochina and those on the metropole's northeast frontier."[253] Both the army and the navy stated that they were simply incapable of meeting the specified demands.[254] The minister of finance expressed his strong reservations and warned the committee that it had to choose between ambitious defense policies and economic and social reconstruction.[255] In order to bring resources and strategy more into line, both the minister for overseas territories and the minister of national defense urged that the Far East Command abandon offensive operations in the north and focus its efforts on pacification in Cochin China. This would allow France to maintain its position in the Far East without jeopardizing European defenses.[256]

The consensus within the CDN against committing more forces to Indochina broke down in November 1950, as a result of the rout of French forces retreating from Cao Bang. The Vietminh offensive in the north undercut those who argued for the withdrawal of French forces to Cochin China; the consensus swung toward taking the fight to the enemy. As the prime minister put it, "The defense must be backed up

[251] 145/K/3, Fiche, undated, Review of Decisions, 18 Aug. 1950, "Effectifs français"; 145/K/22, 24 July 1950.
[252] 10 Feb. 1950, Meeting of the CDN, p. 6.
[253] 21 Oct. 1950, Meeting of the CDN, p. 24; and 17 Feb. 1950, Meeting of the CDN, p. 21.
[254] 21 Oct. 1950, Meeting of the CDN, pp. 25–26.
[255] 18 Aug. 1950, Meeting of the CDN, p. 7.
[256] 22 June 1950, Meeting of the CDN, p. 18; and 18 Aug. 1950, Meeting of the CDN, p. 3.

by an offensive spirit. The principle of zones of priority must be admitted. The pacification mission [in Cochin China] must be subordinated to the defense of Tonkin." The CDN approved an increase in force levels, and President Auriol instructed the prime minister to look into "a solution permitting the defense of Tonkin until the arrival of reinforcements."[257] Between the middle of 1950 and early 1951, French force levels climbed from roughly 150,000 to 165,000 troops.

Despite the relatively small increase in force levels in the Far East, the effect on French forces in Europe was significant. Main battle tanks and other equipment were withdrawn from French occupation forces in Germany even though no replacements were available.[258] The parallel with withdrawal from the Rhineland during the interwar period is striking; French troops were again being taken from the occupation force for overseas service. Because only career soldiers could serve overseas, metropolitan units were virtually gutted of officers and experienced soldiers; the quality of the conscript units responsible for continental operations suffered accordingly. By early 1951, the number of infantry fighting in Indochina under French command constituted about 45 percent of those stationed in the metropole. The General Staff estimated that the war in Indochina was using approximately one-third of the country's military resources. It reported that the war effort in the Far East "has resulted in putting the metropolitan army in critical condition in terms of its equipment, top priority having always been given to requirements in the Far East. [These efforts] seriously compromise the arming of our forces earmarked for the defense of Europe. . . . France alone cannot confront this situation and continue on its present course without jeopardizing her defense in Europe."[259] The report went on to say that any further increase in force levels in Indochina would necessitate a thorough review of France's defense policy and its commitment to NATO.

Only a few months after the decision to send more troops to Indochina in response to the Cao Bang incident, the CDN was again faced with requests from General de Lattre, the commander of French forces in Indochina. He now wanted to augment force levels by roughly twelve battalions, an increase of about 25,000 troops for 1951. The General Staff warned that complying with these requests would entail dissolving some twenty-nine units at the battalion or group level. Although most of the troops sent to Indochina would be taken from North Africa, the dissolution of these units would have an immediate

[257] 17 Nov. 1950, Meeting of the CDN, pp. 9, 31, 33.
[258] Ibid., p. 12.
[259] 145/K/3, 24 Jan. 1951, "L'Effort français," p. 14.

impact on the readiness and logistical capabilities of both active and reserve divisions in the metropole.[260] The real problem was not the number of troops per se, but that de Lattre's requests would drain from the metropole the officers, mechanics, and support personnel that were crucial to making the continental army more than a disorganized mass of conscripts.[261] Despite the implications for French forces in the European theater, the CDN, after extended discussion of the proposals during March and April, decided to approve de Lattre's requests.

Members of the General Staff did not fail to express their dismay with the CDN's decision.[262] In August 1951, the Chiefs of the General Staff drafted a review of French policy toward Indochina in which they were strongly critical of the CDN's decisions and urged that troop levels be significantly reduced in the Far East to allow the French to make a serious contribution to European defense. To continue on the present course could have dangerous consequences: "Any other policy would jeopardize irremediably . . . the stability of the rest of the *Union Française*, [and] national rearmament; that is to say, this is the *last chance* that we have to assure the success of our allied defense plans, as well as to avert the menace of a resurrection of the German army." The air force complied with the orders to send aircraft from the metropole to the Far East but made it clear that this redistribution of forces could not be carried out "without compromising the realization of the plan for western defense."[263] The CDN did not heed these calls to reduce French force levels in Indochina and chose instead to tolerate the consequent degradation of metropolitan troops. While the French, at least on paper, were able to fulfill their commitment to provide ten divisions to NATO, they simply did not have the resources to keep force levels in Indochina at roughly 175,000 men and raise the additional five divisions for Europe promised to the allies. To uphold France's commitments in Europe and sustain a viable plan for metropolitan defense, the General Staff urged decision makers to consider extending military service to two years, mobilizing reserves, and securing legislation allowing conscripts to serve overseas.[264] The civilian elite did not accept

---

[260] 145/K/3, 19 March 1951, Fiche 4, pp. 1–2.

[261] De Lattre's requests, for example, included some 1,200 transmission specialists. According to the army's planners, the loss of these specialists would cause "complete disorganization" among units stationed in the metropole-North Africa. See 145/K/22, 7 Feb. 1951, Fiche, p. 2.

[262] See, for example, the remarks of General Juin, 24 April 1951, Meeting of the CDN, p. 18.

[263] Assorted Letters, 25 Aug. 1951, "Avis du Comité des Chefs d'Etat Major sur la politique militaire à suivre à l'Egard du problème indochinois," p. 9; Assorted Letters, 17 Aug. 1951, Fiche, p. 7.

[264] 145/K/3, Notes and Studies of 11, 12, and 13 Oct. 1951.

these recommendations, fearful that they would be extremely unpopular and have potentially disastrous political consequences.[265]

During 1952 and early 1953, the government was given a temporary respite from confronting this trade-off between European defense and the French empire in the Far East; no new requests for major increases in troop levels came before the CDN. But the situation changed dramatically in July 1953 after the defeat of French forces at Langson. Like the Cao Bang incident about two years earlier, the defeat at Langson created new pressure within the Far East Command to take the offensive. General Henri Navarre, the new commander of French forces in Indochina (de Lattre died in early 1952), requested an increase of ten to twelve battalions. This time, however, the CDN was far more reluctant to approve new reinforcements for Indochina and put off the decision on how to deal with the worsening situation in Tonkin. The key problem was that fulfilling Navarre's requests meant not just degrading further what was already essentially a paper force in Europe, but actually dismantling a significant number of units stationed in the metropole.

The General Staff calculated that increasing forces in Indochina to the level specified by Navarre would mean that roughly forty battalions stationed in Europe would lose their fighting capability because of the removal of officers and equipment. This included dismantling about half the infantry units serving in the occupation force in Germany.[266] The commander of French forces in Germany warned that significant portions of the occupation zone would have to be abandoned to German forces and that France's mission within the NATO alliance would have to be completely revised.[267] If this redistribution of forces took place, the entire French army in the metropole would have to be reorganized. During the reorganization period (about six months), the army would be incapable of mobilizing for war.[268]

Faced with these dramatic consequences, the CDN in November decided not to approve Navarre's requests. Members of the CDN expressed doubts about the ability of twelve additional battalions to improve the military situation on the ground. Measures that would likely have little impact in Indochina were simply not worth the cost of dismantling French forces in Europe. At its meetings of 13 November 1953 and 6 February 1954, the CDN not only refused to increase force levels

---

[265] See 15 Oct. 1951, Meeting of the CDN, p. 44; and 22 Nov. 1951, Meeting of the CDN, pp. 22–31.

[266] 145/K/22, 8 July 1953, Note; and 20 July 1953, Mémoire.

[267] 145/K/22, 23 July 1953, Note, p. 2.

[268] 145/K/22, 23 July 1953, "Les Demandes nouvelles de l'Indochine et leurs conséquences," p. 6.

but finally began to consider the possibility that France's war in Indochina was doomed to failure and that the government should begin to think about extricating the country from the conflict. The minister of interior, Léon Martinaud-Deplat, summed up the CDN's debate of 13 November: "At root, the question before us is to know whether we should continue or abandon the battle."[269] While this option was at least discussed in late 1953 and early 1954, it was the French defeat at Dien Bien Phu that ensured France's withdrawal from Indochina. Given the fact that reinforcements could not even keep pace with battle casualties and that the government fell as a result of the stunning blow dealt to French forces at Dien Bien Phu, even maintenance of the status quo became untenable.[270]

Why did French elites commit themselves to the defense of Indochina and continue to prosecute the war despite the clear costs to metropolitan defense? Unlike during the interwar years, decision makers could not rely on the assumption that holding on to empire was crucial to continental defense when they were receiving regular memos from the General Staff warning that the war in Indochina was ravaging the metropolitan army. There was no equivocation about this issue within the CDN. Jules Moch, minister of national defense in 1951, concisely summarized the situation in a way, that in hindsight, seems self-evident: "If we accept the possibility of a conflict in Europe, the problem of priority is resolved without debate. . . . The defense of Indochina appears very secondary: we cannot sacrifice assets indispensable to the defense of Europe to carry out operations in this theater."[271] What set of strategic assumptions impelled elites yet again to expose the metropole to defend the periphery? Were not the lessons of World War II sufficiently clear?

I argue that top decision makers were lured more deeply into the quagmire of Indochina by a set of strategic beliefs and a strategic culture rooted in the vulnerability associated with the postwar military balance and with the experience of World War II itself. I begin by describing the strategic logic that informed French strategy. This logic reveals a good deal about the motivations behind French behavior, but it is insufficient to explain outcomes. Only by bringing strategic culture into the equation can France's war in Indochina be fully understood.

Successive decisions to jeopardize metropolitan security in order to prosecute the war in Indochina were shaped by a set of suppositions

---

[269] 13 Nov. 1953, Meeting of the CDN, pp. 13–14.
[270] 145/K/22, 21 May 1954, General Blanc to the Secretary of State for War, p. 2.
[271] 19 Jan. 1951, Meeting of the CDN, p. 11.

that emerged from perceptions of high vulnerability. To sort out the beliefs on which French strategy in Indochina was based, it is useful to distinguish among three separate, yet interrelated, strategic interactions: (1) with the Vietminh and Vietnamese over the destiny of the French empire in the Far East, (2) with the United States over control of the postwar order in the periphery, and (3) with the communist bloc over the trajectory of the East-West struggle.

In terms of strategic interactions with local actors in Indochina, successive decisions to escalate the war were based on three main suppositions. First, belief in dominoes played a key role in inducing elites to stand firm. General de Lattre was one of many who argued that "the loss of Tonkin would lead . . . to the loss of Indochina." Others saw much broader implications. Moch feared that "the loss of Indochina risks exposing Burma, Malaysia, and India."[272] Most important, many believed that a failure to defend Indochina would lead to the loss of other portions of the French empire. As Jean Letourneau, minister of the associated states, argued, "To refuse General de Lattre the limited assets that he has requested is tantamount to admitting our retreat from Tonkin and, consequently, our retreat from Indochina with all its consequences—not only in Indochina, but . . . new difficulties will not fail to emerge throughout our overseas territories, especially in North Africa."[273] The battle for Indochina was the battle for *la France d'Outre-Mer*. Strategic logic was thus infused by belief in dominoes and the interdependence of commitments, belief attributes commonly associated with high vulnerability and elite efforts to rely on demonstrations of resolve to offset material inadequacy. Like the British during the 1930s, French elites feared that the loss of a single territory would lead to the unraveling of the empire.

Second, elites believed that if France did not demonstrate its resolve to escalate, its local allies in Indochina would defect and join the adversary—that is, any indication of French weakness would lead to bandwagoning with the Vietminh. Military leaders feared that a reduction in French troops would precipitate widespread defections among the Vietnamese in Cochin China.[274] Civilian leaders were similarly convinced of bandwagoning logic. President Auriol warned that any territorial withdrawal or troop reduction would mean that "those who are

---

[272] 145/K/22, de Lattre as paraphrased in 10 Jan. 1951, Memo from the General Staff, p. 3; Jules Moch, Minister of National Defense, in 19 Jan. 1951, Meeting of the CDN, p. 9.
[273] 20 Feb. 1951, Meeting of the CDN, p. 20.
[274] See, for example, the remarks of General Carpentier, 17 Feb. 1950, Meeting of the CDN, pp. 8–9.

with us will pass to the other side and we will have no hope of guarding Cap St-Jacques."[275]

Belief in the importance of the offensive was the third rationale for sustaining the battle for Tonkin and incurring the associated costs. Offensive strategies would demonstrate the resolve needed to prevent bandwagoning and the falling of dominoes. It is important to recall that military setbacks were key events driving forward the scope of France's military commitment in Indochina. Haiphong, the communist victory in China, Cao Bang—these were all turning points in the willingness of elites to escalate the war and to focus on liberating Tonkin as opposed to concentrating on the defense of Cochin China. In the face of these setbacks, only a successful offensive would indicate French willingness to stand firm. Furthermore, to bolster reputation and regain prestige, it was not sufficient to hold Cochin China; victory came to mean crushing the enemy, expelling him from Tonkin. To do this, the French had to take the fight to the Vietminh.[276] Until 1953, members of the CDN believed that France could attain military victory in Tonkin by pursuing offensive strategies and destroying the enemy's war-making capability. By March 1953, however, even before Langson, both military and civilian elites became much more pessimistic about obtaining military victory.[277] Nevertheless, more troops and offensive strategies were still necessary. As General Navarre put it, "It is only through the offensive that it is possible to beat the enemy or, at the least, to realize a military outcome that is favorable enough to convince him that he will not win and that he has an interest in negotiating."[278] In other words, offensive strategies were now needed to secure a favorable bargaining position with the Vietminh should France decide to seek a negotiated settlement.[279] Holding strong in Tonkin would also buy sufficient time to expand the Vietnamese army, another key element in gaining the upper hand in negotiations. Despite a change in military objectives, belief in the need for offensive strategies continued to shape the Far East Command's repeated requests for increases in French force levels.

French decisions about the war in Indochina were also based on considerations at another level of strategic interaction: that between France and the United States. America's strategic entry into the Far

---

[275] 22 June 1950, Meeting of the CDN, p. 15.

[276] For examples of these arguments, see 17 Nov. 1950, Meeting of the CDN, pp. 31–33.

[277] See, for example, the remarks of General Juin after a trip to Indochina, 17 March 1953, Meeting of the CDN, pp. 14–16.

[278] 24 July 1953, Meeting of the CDN, Annex, p. 6.

[279] See R. E. M. Irving, *The First Indochina War: French and American Policy, 1945–54* (London: Croom Helm, 1975), p. 114.

East after the outbreak of the Korean War was, for paradoxical reasons, a key element luring the French more deeply into the war in Indochina. While French elites were content to rely on U.S. troops and economic assistance to promote stability in Europe, the presence of U.S. forces in the Far East made elites hypersensitive to maintaining full control over the prosecution of the war against Ho Chi Minh. French decision makers were more than willing to accept American money and arms, but they resisted direct U.S. interference in the war. Control of the situation in Southeast Asia became an emblem of France's ability to take the fate of its empire into its own hands.

These concerns contributed to the willingness of elites to carry a heavy burden in Indochina. Fears of U.S. encroachment in French affairs conditioned French behavior in several important respects. First, elites believed that if France was not forthcoming in providing sufficient military resources to counter the Vietminh threat, local parties would turn to the United States for assistance. Recognition of the need to preempt such requests by augmenting French military assistance contributed to the CDN's willingness to approve troop increases.[280] Second, though French elites were most receptive to American aid, they demanded that all assistance be funneled through French forces and administrative offices: "All aid in Indochina must pass through us; in particular, the distribution of grants and their use must be held tightly by France."[281] Furthermore, American advisers were not to be involved in operations or in training local forces.[282] President Auriol reaffirmed that "we must not permit the Americans to intervene too visibly or directly in our relations with the Associated States."[283] The objective was both to prevent de facto U.S. encroachment on French affairs and to ensure that local parties recognized the French as the authoritative external actor. Léon Pignon, the high commissioner for Indochina, warned that France had to prevent the local population from believing that American assistance lay behind the war effort. "To this end," he continued, "we must erase among the local population and even among some Frenchmen any doubt about France's commitment to pursue the war in Indochina."[284] Increasing military efforts in Indochina were thus seen as a means of competing with the United States for influence in the Far East.

One final point about the ambivalent reaction of French elites to their material dependence on the United States warrants mention. U.S.

---

[280] See, for example, 17 Feb. 1950, Meeting of the CDN, pp. 8–9.
[281] 17 Feb. 1950, Meeting of the CDN, p. 14.
[282] 17 March 1953, Meeting of the CDN, p. 20.
[283] 10 Feb. 1950, Meeting of the CDN, p. 12.
[284] 17 Feb. 1950, Meeting of the CDN, p. 15.

assistance was central to the fulfillment of French defense policies both in Europe and in Indochina. As far as the Americans were concerned, however, U.S. aid devoted to the reconstruction of Europe was not fungible; that is, it was intended to further military and economic reconstruction in Europe, not to enable the French to defend their empire in the Far East. French elites knew that the United States would look with disfavor on the CDN's repeated decisions to sacrifice metropolitan rearmament and renege on its commitment to NATO in order to prosecute the war in Indochina. This was especially true in 1949, when the Truman administration put pressure on the French government to grant increased political autonomy to its local allies in Vietnam.[285] As a result, French elites went to great lengths to ensure that American officials were unaware of the share of U.S. aid that was being spent in Indochina. The Chiefs of the General Staff stipulated that French representatives, before they negotiate assistance arrangements with U.S. officials, had to be instructed "to avoid all discussion of the apportioning of aid between Europe and Asia."[286] Similarly, before his meetings with U.S. representatives to discuss the war in Indochina, General de Lattre "should be precisely informed about France's commitments to NATO, so as not to say anything that will give the Americans the impression that their efforts on behalf of Indochina might work to the detriment of the defense of Europe."[287] Since increasing force requirements in Indochina entailed degrading, but not actually dismantling, units stationed in Europe, it was not readily apparent to U.S. officials that the French were pursuing the war in the Far East at a high cost to the quality of France's metropolitan army. The willingness of French elites to engage in such deliberate obfuscation and to place at risk their relationship with the United States speaks to the intensity of their commitment to retain their Far East empire. It also reveals, if only suggestively, French pique at being in a subordinate relationship with the United States.

Finally, the set of elite beliefs informing French policy in Indochina must be examined from the perspective of the Cold War. To what extent was the strength of the French commitment to prosecute the war a function of elite concern about stemming the tide of communism? Some studies of the French war in Indochina argue that the aim of

---

[285] The Truman administration feared that anti-Western sentiment and nationalism provoked by French rule would provide inroads for communism. See, for example, Memorandum by the Department of State to the French Foreign Office, May–June 1949 (undated), *Foreign Relations of the United States* (FRUS), 1949, vol. 7, part 1 (Washington, D.C.: U.S. GPO, 1975), pp. 39–45.
[286] Assorted Letters, 25 Aug. 1951, Avis du Comité des Chefs d'Etat Major, p. 7.
[287] 27 Aug. 1951, Meeting of the CDN, p. 18.

defending the "free world" from communism was an important factor shaping decision making.[288] The battle for Tonkin, according to this perspective, was France's contribution to stemming Soviet ideology and influence. Although it is indeed difficult to distinguish rhetoric from belief, the archival record suggests that these studies have exaggerated the extent to which the Cold War shaped French policy in Indochina and that elite references to the threats posed by the spread of global communism were aimed primarily at portraying the conflict in ways that would ensure continued U.S. aid. This assessment is based on two main arguments.

First, before 1951, there was virtually no discussion within the CDN about the links between France's war in Indochina and the battle against global communism. In January 1951, however, debate about French policy began to contain frequent references to "a global strategy in the fight against communism" and the need to defend Tonkin as "the keystone of the defense of Southeast Asia, which now constitutes one of the fronts of the free world."[289] The sudden appearance of this concern could be explained as the result of communist successes in China and the Korean War; external events may have convinced French elites that their colonial war was really better understood as part of a broader struggle against the spread of communism. Yet this is not a satisfactory explanation, given the fact that a communist victory in China looked increasingly likely from early 1949 onward and that the Korean War had been raging for more than six months before elites began to discuss the Indochina conflict in terms of the East-West struggle. If these had been watershed events in terms of French thinking, elite debate should have more readily incorporated the language of the Cold War.

The second argument suggesting that French elites did not view the country's involvement in the Far East as part of a global struggle against communism is that, even after 1951, only a limited number of individuals invoked Cold War ideology in debating Indochina policy: General de Lattre and a few others strongly in favor of increasing the pace of the war. The implication is that these advocates were using Cold War ideology for instrumental reasons—to gain support in the CDN and, more important, to secure increased U.S. aid. This interpretation is consistent with that of R. E. M. Irving, who calls French portrayal of the war as a battle against communism "a veiled request for American aid."[290] Peter Calvocoressi agrees that the changing nature of the

[288] See, for example, Girardet, *L'Idée colonial*, pp. 204, 239.
[289] See 19 Jan. 1951, Meeting of the CDN, p. 9; and 15 Oct. 1951, Meeting of the CDN, p. 19.
[290] Irving, *First Indochina War*, p. 84; see also pp. 133–137.

[282]

policy debate was informed by the realization that "the only way to continue the fight was to call it a fight against communism and invoke the aid of anti-communist friends."[291] This view is corroborated by the fact that individual ministers began to speak about the war as an East-West struggle when they realized the extent to which Cold War ideology imbued U.S. thinking. On return from a visit to the United States, Robert Schuman, minister of foreign affairs, had new enthusiasm both for the Indochina War and for perceiving it as part of an international struggle. Schuman openly admitted that his views had been changed by his visit and his consequent recognition that tapping the powerful currents of anticommunism in the United States was essential to sustaining France's war effort in the Far East.[292]

In sum, elite references linking the war in Indochina to the need to fight international communism appear to have been the product more of instrumental rhetoric than of deep-seated belief in the threat posed by communist ideology. Of far more importance in shaping decisions were elite beliefs about the nature of France's strategic interactions both with local actors in Indochina and with the United States. Working within a strategic logic informed by notions of bandwagoning and falling dominoes, elites adopted firm, deterrent strategies to demonstrate resolve and wear down the adversary, thereby preserving empire in the Far East. Victory in Indochina would in turn send a clear message to other colonial territories, thereby dampening resistance to French rule and preserving the integrity of the empire. Policy was also driven by the supposition that the recovery of France's international status entailed preventing the United States from replacing the French as the key external actor in Indochina.

As for assessment of strategic priorities, reputational concerns were clearly paramount in shaping French thinking about the relative importance of competing geographic missions. Elites were willing to incur the burdens associated with the war because of their conviction that outcomes in Indochina would affect the disposition of other overseas possessions. Belief in the interdependence of commitments, however, could not readily be used to justify the explicit degradation of the metropole's defense capability caused by the war in Indochina. The geopolitical realities were simply too stark; metropolitan France and Indochina were *not* a single strategic theater. Because of both the distance between France and Indochina and the fact that the empire's resources did little to prevent the collapse of the metropole in 1940,

---

[291] Peter Calvocoressi, *World Politics since 1945*, 4th ed. (London: Longman, 1982), pp. 300–301.

[292] 15 Oct. 1951, Meeting of the CDN, p. 28.

elites could not credibly maintain that Indochina had to be held because of its potential contribution to metropolitan security. Other arguments would have to be marshaled to make the case that the periphery should be given priority over the metropole in allocating resources. Three such arguments emerged.

First, proponents of escalation in Indochina maintained that the threat in Europe was not sufficiently imminent to place restraints on French efforts in other theaters. They contended that metropolitan rearmament was, after all, moving forward, even if at a very slow pace.[293] This view was, however, not in the majority; most ministers recognized that shifting resources from continental defense to peripheral defense involved grave risks for the metropole.[294] But, obviously, these were risks that they were willing to accept. Second, some elites invoked dominoes and Cold War rhetoric to argue that the defense of the metropole and the defense of Tonkin were synonymous: "Our action in Tonkin preserves [our position] on the Rhine."[295] This argument also met with little receptivity. While elites seem to have agreed that failure in Indochina would do harm to France's reputation and jeopardize the country's position in other overseas territories, linking the defense of the northeast border to the defense of Tonkin was a bit too far-fetched for most ministers. Few seem to have bought into the argument that defeat in Indochina would encourage France's adversaries on the Continent to challenge the status quo in Europe. Third, staunch defenders of France's stake in Indochina argued that the dispersion of the country's military resources between two widely separated theaters made little sense and led to inadequacy in both theaters. It made much more sense, they argued, to send temporarily to the Far East whatever was needed to attain victory. The sooner the defeat of the Vietminh, the sooner French forces in Indochina could return to the metropole. In other words, they argued that a short-term sacrifice of the metropole's resources would eventually redound to the metropole's benefit.[296] This argument actually carried some weight— as long as the CDN believed that victory was possible. After 1952, when elites began to doubt that defeat of the Vietminh was attainable, this rationale for assigning Indochina top priority also fell by the wayside.

The problem was that the distances were simply too great, the links between the Rhine and Tonkin too tenuous, and the trade-offs between

---

[293] See, for example, 19 Jan. 1951, Meeting of the CDN, Questions.
[294] See, for example, 19 Jan. 1951, Meeting of the CDN, p. 11.
[295] George Bidault, cited in 17 March 1951, Meeting of the CDN, p. 44.
[296] See, for example, 13 Nov. 1953, Meeting of the CDN, p. 6.

metropolitan and peripheral defense too stark to allow these arguments about strategic priorities to take root within the elite community. They were, and were treated as, rhetoric and rationalization for policies being pursued for other reasons. Unlike during the interwar period, elites remained rather sober about the severe trade-offs that existed between metropolitan and peripheral defense. That the CDN nevertheless subordinated metropolitan security to the war in Indochina demonstrates the crucial role that the strategic logic outlined above played in shaping policy.

Focusing on strategic logic alone, however, does not provide a sufficient explanation of outcomes for two main reasons. First, this logic spells out how and why French elites managed the war in Indochina in the manner they did. But it does not explain what drove them to defend empire to begin with, especially when the costs to metropolitan security were so high. Even if elites sincerely believed that the loss of Indochina would jeopardize other portions of the empire, why they placed paramount value on the defense of the imperial periphery remains unanswered. What impelled elites yet again to gut the metropolitan army to protect the overseas territories? Unlike during the 1930s, they were not being driven by the assumption that resources extracted from the periphery would bolster metropolitan security. Second, strategic logic does not explain why French elites sustained the battle for Indochina for a full decade. From 1945 until 1954, despite successive decisions to channel resources to Indochina at a clear cost to metropolitan security, elites received little indication that French forces were either destroying the enemy or eroding the Vietminh's willingness to fight. Discussions within the CDN reveal that top elites, from 1952 onward, grew increasingly skeptical that victory could be attained and began to face the possibility that the battle for Indochina might well be futile. Repeated decisions to increase force levels, far from defeating the adversary and allowing French troops to return to the metropole, only continued to degrade metropolitan security and impair economic recovery. Despite the fact that incoming information disconfirmed the inferences on which strategy was based, elites continued to devote scarce resources to the prosecution of the war. It took the shock of Dien Bien Phu to persuade French elites to reorient strategy and withdraw from Indochina. Forces other than strategic logic were shaping elite behavior.

These two puzzles—why French elites placed such high value on the defense of empire and why they sustained the battle for so long and at such a high cost even when they became aware that their efforts were failing—can be answered only by focusing on strategic culture. In keeping with previous French behavior in the periphery, the recovery of *grandeur* and the reaffirmation of the country's identity as a great power were the key motivations behind the decision to defend France's empire in Indochina at the end of the World War II. As Irving writes, "Many Frenchmen who had followed de Gaulle or fought in the home Resistance saw the building of the French Union, one hundred million strong, as the sole means by which France could recover her national greatness."[297] As during the 1880s and the post–World War I years, France's excessive ambition in the periphery was a function of the perceived weakness of the metropole, the symbolic equation of national well-being with imperial success, and the consequent impulse to recover the nation's honor and self-respect through peripheral empire.

This impulse was particularly pronounced because of the experience of World War II. The French polity was going through the process of recovering from defeat at the hands of the Germans and from the humiliation surrounding the Vichy government and its collaboration with the Nazis. As one French politician put it in 1945, "The military catastrophe of 1940, and particularly the betrayal of the Vichy regime, its surrender to the enemy, its unconditional acceptance of defeat and bondage, have weakened terribly our reputation in the world."[298] Though liberation meant the end of Nazi occupation of French territory, in many respects the nation had been dealt a much deeper psychological blow than during the Franco-Prussian War. The loss of Alsace and Lorraine exposed military weakness. The experience of Vichy exposed a moral weakness that was much more difficult for the French to assimilate. Girardet eloquently describes this postwar atmosphere: "The crushing memory of the defeat of 1940 was tragically present. The liberation of the country, the act of finally joining the victory camp did not suffice to erase the dominant tone of humiliation and anguish. It was as if the collective conscience was conserving, in a profound way, the infinitely painful memory of a certain grief not yet dulled, of a certain wound not yet healed, of a certain shame not yet abolished."[299] In the context of the pervasive sense of vulnerability and humiliation that emerged from the experience of World War II, the military balance in Europe, and the fragility of the metropole's postwar economic and political structures, external ambition was the pathway to national recovery and the relegitimation of the state.[300] France's war in Indochina was driven, first and foremost, by a powerful

---

[297] Irving, *First Indochina War*, p. 144.

[298] Jacques Kayser, addressing the Congress of the Radical Party in Aug. 1945, quoted in Serge Berstein, "French Power as Seen by the Political Parties after World War II," in Becker and Knipping, *Power in Europe?* p. 166.

[299] Girardet, *L'Idée coloniale*, p. 248.

[300] See Kahler, *Decolonization*, pp. 77–91; and Girardet, *L'Idée colonial*, pp. 242–248.

strategic image equating the autonomy and sovereignty of the metropole with the preservation of imperial commitments.

As the overseas territory most threatened by nationalist resistance, Indochina emerged as the litmus test of French power in the postwar era. French elites—Gaullists in particular—saw in Indochina the opportunity to rebuild the domestic legitimacy of the state. Imperial success would restore public confidence in the discredited institutions of governance. The defense of Indochina thus became associated with the autonomy and independence of France itself. It became almost meaningless to talk of the material trade-offs between metropolitan security and the war in Indochina; political elites had come to define the well-being of the metropole more in terms of the security and integrity of the empire than in terms of military preparedness and economic stability in the French state itself. As Girardet puts it, "Not only the political initiative but also the seat and the principle of national sovereignty passed from the metropole to the empire, from continental France to France overseas."[301]

These were the themes that dominated virtually every debate over French policy in Indochina. In a speech delivered on 15 May 1946, de Gaulle claimed that "to lose the French Union would be a humiliation which could cost us our independence. To guard it and make it prosper is to remain great and, consequently, free." As the prime minister expressed it in a meeting of the CDN convened to discuss potential troop reductions in Indochina, "France cannot consent to abandon even a piece of her heritage; without that piece, her entire heritage risks being lost." In supporting his request for increased force levels, General de Lattre posed the dilemma in even more dramatic terms: "The campaign in Indochina . . . is a test of the capacity of France to transform her empire and to create the *Union Française,* that is to say, a political and economic unit adapted to the conditions of modern life."[302] Parliamentary debate was infused with the same concern. At the 1952 party congress of the Christian Democratic Mouvement Républicain Populaire (MRP), the centrist party that played a prominent role in shaping Indochina policy between 1947 and 1954, Pierre-Henri Teitgen declared, "There can be no choice between Indochina and the Metropole: the security and greatness of France and of the French Union are indivisible."[303] In the strategic culture that emerged after World War II, elites had come to see the preservation of empire as

---

[301] Girardet, *L'Idée colonial,* p. 196.

[302] De Gaulle cited in ibid., p. 200; 10 Feb. 1950, Meeting of the CDN, p. 11; 17 March 1951, Meeting of the CDN, p. 17.

[303] Irving, *First Indochina War,* p. 145.

synonymous with domestic legitimacy and the well-being of the metropole. It was this conception of national identity and national self-image—one equating metropolitan recovery with the defense of empire—that lured elites into Indochina and that induced them to pour scarce resources into its defense despite awareness that their policies were eroding the quality of the metropolitan army and jeopardizing economic reconstruction.

Before examining the effects of domestic politics on decision making, it is worth quoting extensively from General de Lattre's speech before the CDN on 17 March 1951 to provide an indication of the extent to which the strategic logic and the strategic culture identified above imbued debate about Indochina:

> The campaign in Indochina is most often considered in political circles and in public opinion an exhausting and painful burden. France reaps nothing but responsibilities and mourning, with no hope for the future other than being evicted from the Far East by a foreign power.
>
> It is similarly believed that Europe, the defense of which appears to all French as the key to everything, suffers because of our distant battles. The priority that the European theater deserves and the weakness of the forces [stationed there] impels us to consider closing this distant and eccentric theater of operations.
>
> These two points of view do not withstand careful examination. As always, reality is infinitely more complex. It is indispensable, to assess the situation judiciously, to get to the bottom of things. The conclusions appear considerably different from conventional wisdom.
>
> The campaign in Indochina is not a distant foreign adventure, such as that in Mexico. It is a test of the capacity of France to transform its empire and to create the French Union, a political and economic unit adapted to the conditions of modern life.
>
> If this is true, as soon as [the situation in] Indochina erodes, Madagascar, Dakar, Tunis, and Rabat will be shaken.
>
> As long as we hold in Indochina, we remain a great power. If we win the match, we will truly be one of the "greats." If, on the other hand, we lose, we will be the "sick man" of the second half of the twentieth century.
>
> In addition, because we are fighting the communist enemy in Indochina, the campaign in the Far East has become one of the episodes of the war between the two blocs. This has been acknowledged by our allies who appreciate our effort. . . .
>
> Tonkin is one of the frontiers of liberty. This truth is now recognized by all foreign publics. The aid given to us devolves from American and British

interests [in this global struggle]. The action of France has thus become a test of the capacity of France to combat communism and the U.S.S.R. . . .

It is in Indochina that we revitalize ourselves (*nous nous reclassons*) for the defense of Europe. The effort demanded is only temporary in nature. The participation in the battle of the armies from the Associated States will grow in size. It is therefore necessary to hold until this happens, at the same time gaining a necessary delay in rearmament in Europe. For 1951, the top priority is Indochina.[304]

Domestic Considerations

To what extent were the arguments eloquently put forward by de Lattre and other supporters of the war influenced by domestic pressures? Was French policy in Indochina the product of a set of strategic assumptions sincerely held by elites, or is it more appropriate to understand the strategic arguments outlined above as window-dressing for policies that were being adopted for reasons of domestic politics? The following analysis shows that economic concerns and the organizational interests of the military services had relatively little impact on policy toward Indochina between 1949 and 1954. Elite-mass linkages and elite efforts to relegitimate the state through imperial success did play a key role in creating a strategic culture wedded to empire and in embedding among decision makers images equating metropolitan securing with imperial security. Yet the evidence suggests that strategic culture influenced outcomes primarily through infusing the decision-making community with these images and affecting how elites conceived of national security, not through the more discrete political forces associated with coalition management and public opinion.

Private Economic Interests. In the aftermath of the Pacific war and the Japanese advance through and occupation of much of Southeast Asia, concern about investment and trade did not have a big impact on French policy toward Indochina. With internal and international rivalries threatening the political cohesion of the region, discussion of the unlimited potential for industrialization and of the renewal of a policy of *mise en valeur* seemed, at best, moot. In 1950, French trade with Indochina was 10 percent of its 1940 level.[305] It is also the case that economic motivations were virtually absent from the original decision

---

[304] 17 March 1951, Meeting of the CDN, pp. 17–19.
[305] Irving, *First Indochina War*, pp. 143–144.

to reoccupy Indochina after the Japanese surrender in August 1945.[306] The archival record similarly indicates that private economic interests did not influence the CDN's repeated decisions to escalate the war. Some politicians did publicly resurrect the economic arguments of Jules Ferry to gain support for the war, but such arguments were not well received.[307] Economic rationalizations for empire had lost not only their justification, but also their credibility.

Domestic Politics. It is clear that France's tightening embrace with its empire during the interwar period and the experience of World War II itself set the stage for France's debacle in Indochina. The way in which elites responded to the country's potential expulsion from the Far East was shaped by a polity receptive to the notion that France could recover from the devastation and humiliation of war through imperial success. Politicians indeed sought to fuel public enthusiasm for empire, but they were operating in a strategic culture in which overseas empire was already deeply embedded. Secondary school textbooks, newspapers, intellectuals, and politicians all spread the message that the sovereignty and well-being of the metropole were inextricably linked to the well-being of the imperial periphery. Whether holding on to Indochina contributed to the metropole's material strength was irrelevant; the defense of the empire in the Far East had become a national emblem for recovery of the nation's self-respect, grandeur, and rank in the world. Virtually every public speech and cabinet debate on Indochina contained references to the vital link between the preservation of the French empire in the Far East and the destiny of the French nation. In a fundamental sense, then, the strategic culture that emerged after World War II both shaped and was shaped by elite thinking about the essence of national power. During the interwar years, empire was glorified because of its potential material contribution to the metropole; during the postwar years, a new brand of imperial ideology glorified the symbolic importance of empire and equated its preservation with the sovereignty and autonomy of the French state.

Did strategic culture affect policy primarily by shaping the intellectual paradigms and values of elites—that is, by leading elites to assume that victory in Indochina was critical to the relegitimation of the state—or did it lead to discrete domestic pressures that prevented elites from

---

[306] For a concise chronology of the events of 1945 and 1946, see D. Bruce Marshall, *The French Colonial Myth and Constitution-Making in the Fourth Republic* (New Haven: Yale University Press, 1973), pp. 189–207.
[307] For examples, see Irving, *First Indochina War*, pp. 143–144.

implementing their preferred policies? Is it accurate to view French policy as the result of sincerely held strategic assumptions that took root in the elite community, or did decision makers pursue the war in Indochina—and marshal the necessary strategic arguments—in order to manage domestic coalitions and preserve political power? Several considerations give credence to a more instrumentalist interpretation. Most governments during the early years of the Fourth Republic were in constant danger of falling. This endemic governmental weakness made politicians particularly sensitive to potentially destabilizing events, such as setbacks in the empire. Furthermore, because preservation of the empire enjoyed widespread support and cut across party cleavages, politicians looked to ambitious external policies as a means of disarming the opposition and preempting interparty struggles.[308] While the Communist party was opposed to the war in Indochina, there was no organized group that was opposed to French imperialism per se. The right and left parted company as to the nature of the tie between metropole and periphery (the left arguing for more local autonomy), but deputies at neither end of the political spectrum actually advocated abandonment of empire altogether.[309] Supporting empire thus offered at least some hope of sustaining political solvency in a domestic milieu otherwise characterized by divisiveness and crisis.

Despite the presence of domestic conditions that made it attractive for politicians to adopt ambitious external policies for opportunistic reasons, several points indicate that public opinion, coalition building, and political gamesmanship were not at the root of the key decisions about Indochina taken during the 1950s. To begin, the level of public interest in the Indochina War remained low throughout most of the conflict.[310] Not only was the French populace primarily concerned with European security and economic reconstruction, but the physical distance between the metropole and Indochina limited public awareness of the war. By 1953, public opinion had been mobilized by elite appeals to nationalism and by events in Indochina.[311] But this mobilization did not necessarily provide increased momentum for the war effort. On the contrary, growing awareness of French involvement in the Far East led to an increasingly vocal antiwar movement. Large public protests

---

[308] See Irving, *First Indochina War*; Kahler, *Decolonization*, p. 32; and Marshall, *The French Colonial Myth*, pp. 195–196. Marshall writes that de Gaulle was concerned about his declining influence in 1945 and that "one means of forestalling such a shift of influence was to make Indochina a rallying point around which all factions could be united by patriotic appeals, at least for a time" (p. 196).

[309] Marshall, *French Colonial Myth*, pp. 271–272.

[310] Kahler, *Decolonization*, p. 81. See also Marshall, *French Colonial Myth*, p. 152.

[311] Kahler, *Decolonization*, p. 86.

condemning France's battle against the Vietminh were commonplace.[312] By late 1953, the cabinet was concerned that the war itself—and not its abandonment—would undermine the government's legitimacy. The minister of the interior warned that "opinion will not support the effort of the Government in this domain and the voices calling for peace 'at any price' are getting louder and louder and encouraging the resistance of the Vietminh, making more uncertain the possibilities for negotiation."[313] After the defeat of French forces at Dien Bien Phu and withdrawal from Indochina, the public did grow far more sensitive to the preservation of the nation's overseas commitments. Domestic political constraints were to play a major role in conditioning France's intransigent response to nationalist resistance to French rule in North Africa. Through the war in Indochina, elites did eventually entrap themselves in discrete political forces at home that constrained adjustment to the forces of decolonization. But during the Indochina conflict itself, France's self-destructive policies came more from within the top decision-making community than from the wider domestic polity.

Even though public interest in the Far East remained at a low level during much of the war, it is reasonable to hypothesize that French policies in Indochina were the result of logrolling and coalition building within a fragile constellation of domestic political power. Indeed, it is clear that the ruling elite faced two sources of coalitional pressure inducing them to adopt ambitious policies in the Far East. First, though not in power between 1949 and 1954, de Gaulle and his Rassemblement du Peuple Français (RPF) did put pressure on the government to take a hard line in Indochina. Fear of losing RPF support was one factor motivating decision makers to bear the costs of war as long as they did.[314] Second, Socialist support for the war was, at least to some extent, the result of efforts among the moderate left to use the Communists' antiwar platform to isolate them. Kahler argues that this strategy was a legacy of the interwar period: "The need to distinguish themselves from the Communists as the 'national' party on the Left pushed the Socialists into the arms of the Third Republic's colonial consensus."[315]

The evidence suggests, however, that coalitional dynamics were not a direct cause of the government's policies and that interparty competition only provided added incentives for the Socialists to pursue proimperial policies to which they were already committed for other

---

[312] Girardet, *L'Idée colonial,* p. 276.
[313] 13 Nov. 1953, Meeting of the CDN, pp. 13–14.
[314] Kahler, *Decolonization,* pp. 82, 84–86; and Irving, *First Indochina War,* pp. 140–143.
[315] Kahler, *Decolonization,* p. 166.

reasons. The RPF during late 1953 and 1954 grew more intransigent and unwilling to countenance compromise on French sovereignty in the periphery.[316] Nevertheless, it was during this period that the CDN turned down Navarre's request for more troops and began to consider in earnest the option of abandoning the struggle for Indochina. Moreover, while coalitional dynamics may have affected the timing and presentation of policy, they did not have a big impact on central decisions about whether to defend France's empire in the Far East. In his study of the views of different parties toward colonial issues, Serge Berstein concludes that "basically all groups agreed on preserving the *Empire* in its integrity. The only notable divergences were about the ways and means of maintaining" it. The mainstream Socialist position on empire was almost as uncompromising as that of the Gaullists: "The French Socialists were almost unthinking nationalists after the experience of the Resistance, which marked the postwar leadership; many became as willing as the Gaullists to see concessions to change as defeat and treason."[317] After Cao Bang, the Socialists stood firmly behind the right in its conviction that France had to increase its effort in Indochina and could not countenance backing down.[318] It is simply inaccurate to view the government's policies toward Indochina as the result of the Socialists' efforts to distance themselves from the Communists or the MRP's attempts to placate the Gaullists. The Socialists, the MRP, and the Gaullists all stood firmly behind the war. As Tony Smith aptly remarks, what mired the French in Indochina "was not so much the fatal logic of a political system as the fatal logic of a colonial perspective."[319]

Military Services. Despite the return of French troops to the periphery during the early postwar years, much of the top echelon of the military establishment was decidedly opposed to the successive decisions of the CDN to subordinate rearmament and the quality of French troops in the metropole to the war in Indochina. Unlike during the 1930s, the military establishment did not labor under the illusion that devoting resources to the periphery would eventually serve to strengthen metropolitan security. Simply put, the battle for Indochina was not being waged in order to marshal resources that could be used in the metropole. Top members of the General Staff were some of the most outspoken critics of General de Lattre's and General Navarre's

---

[316] Ibid., pp. 86–87. Kahler attributes this shift to the absence of de Gaulle's leadership. The RPF responded to potential fragmentation by rallying around maximalist positions.

[317] Berstein, "French Power," p. 178; Kahler, *Decolonization,* p. 259.

[318] Irving, *First Indochina War,* p. 83.

[319] Smith, "French Colonial Consensus," p. 220. On the commitment of the Socialists to the preservation of empire, see pp. 222–233.

prosecution of the war.[320] Civilians repeatedly had to overcome the resistance of the country's top military officials to extract more personnel and resources for operations in the Far East. The Far East Command was the only military organ that consistently lobbied for giving top priority to the battle for Tonkin. Furthermore, unlike during the 1880s, French forces in the periphery were under the control of central authorities. Commanders in Indochina were, for the most part, carrying out orders from Paris, not acting at their own whim. These points suggest that the military acting as a self-interested bureaucracy had little to do with the key decisions affecting the prosecution of the war. As suggested above, the set of strategic assumptions that had taken hold among civilian elites was the most important factor driving policy in Indochina and leading to decisions that yet again severely jeopardized metropolitan security to pursue empire.

Conclusions

I have argued that French policy in Indochina was generated principally by a set of strategic beliefs and a strategic culture conditioned by the experience of World War II, the postwar military balance, and France's subordinate position in the postwar order. French policy in Indochina was in part the product of a strategic logic born of vulnerability. The perceived need to demonstrate resolve and bolster reputation fueled belief in dominoes, bandwagoning, and the supposition that the loss of Indochina would lead to the loss of the entire empire. To thwart Ho Chi Minh was to preempt the emergence of nationalist movements that might threaten the existence of *la France d'Outre-Mer*. French elites also believed that they could use imperial ambition to restore France's international position vis-à-vis other major powers. Successive decisions to escalate the war were motivated at least in part by the need to resist the expansion of U.S. control over the postwar order and to prevent U.S. dominance over events in Southeast Asia. Strategic logic alone, however, is insufficient to explain outcomes. It does not explain why elites deemed the empire sufficiently important to justify its defense at a cost to metropolitan security. In addition, the policies produced by these suppositions persisted long after the suppositions themselves had been disconfirmed by incoming information. Despite repeated indications that French sacrifices were neither destroying the enemy nor wearing down his resolve, French elites continued to prosecute the war until the defeat of French forces at Dien

---

[320] For a wealth of material on thinking within the General Staff, see the private papers *(fonds privées)* of General Clement Blanc, SHAT, especially boxes 145/K/3 and 145/K/22.

Bien Phu led to the fall of the government and withdrawal from Indochina.

It was a strategic culture deeply wedded to overseas empire that both lured elites into Indochina and induced them to sustain the battle even after they realized that the chances of victory were remote. Peripheral empire had been sold to the French polity during the interwar period. The experience of World War II and the vulnerability of the early postwar years only lodged overseas empire more deeply in the national self-image and prevailing conceptions of security. This strategic culture induced elites to turn to the periphery as a way of restoring domestic legitimacy; the autonomy and sovereignty of the state were equated with the successful defence of *la France d'Outre-Mer*. Decision makers gutted metropolitan defenses to pursue the war in Indochina precisely because of their conviction that the recovery of the French state was contingent on the preservation of empire. In terms of the intellectual paradigms and values embedded in the elite community, the defense of Indochina was more integral to the well-being of France than economic and military conditions in the metropole itself. Metropolitan security and imperial security *were* indivisible. This fundamental assumption was sincerely held by decision makers. It was a manifestation of national identity and of how elites conceived of the essence of national security, not a product of political rhetoric or an instrumental response to discrete domestic pressures.

The problem was that elites had become entrapped in their own strategic conceptions. As during the 1930s, elites grossly exaggerated the extent to which empire, by contributing either resources or legitimacy, could alleviate the metropole's strategic and political deficits. Far from relegitimating the state, the battle for Indochina only impaired the recovery of the metropole and led to the fall of the government.

Strategic exposure and overextension during the post–World War II era were in many respects driven by the same dynamics that produced adjustment failure during the 1930s. Both episodes had their roots in the metropolitan vulnerability that resulted from France's fall from continental dominance during the nineteenth century. The fundamental shifts in the balance of power that occurred during the late 1800s implanted within the elite community the notion that France could recover its international position only through peripheral empire. France could be a great power, elites argued, only by acquiring and maintaining major imperial possessions. To rally support for their ambitious policies in the periphery, elites, beginning in the late nineteenth century, peddled imperialist ideologies among the populace. Not only did they succeed in weaning the French electorate from its hostility to empire, but shifts in strategic culture—driven forward by the experience of World War I and the lobbying campaigns of the interwar period—occurred on an order of magnitude not intended by elites. Deep attachment to empire spread steadily throughout the elite community as well as the public and, during the 1930s and post–World War II period, served as the basis for a consensus on colonial policy that cut across party cleavages. Empire had become embedded in strategic culture. Strategic culture then constrained decision makers by infusing the elite community with powerful strategic images that, although initially consistent with elite beliefs, eventually came to override strategic logic. In the 1930s, as during the 1949–1954 period, elites initially propagated a set of strategic images and symbols for instrumental purposes: to respond to vulnerability and gain support for their policies. But these images then came to define how elites conceived of the nation's security and well-being, constraining their capacity for adjustment. As in Britain, a set of strategic assumptions sincerely held by the elite community, not the instrumental concerns associated with domestic politics, was the driving force behind self-defeating behavior.

In sum, the French case suggests that adjustment failure occurs when vulnerability affects strategic beliefs and strategic culture in a sequential manner. Elites justifiably adopt extremist policies to cope with conditions of strategic deficiency but later find themselves entrapped in the strategic images they propagated to gain support for their policies. The sequence is initially generated by systemic change; paradoxically, but crucially for the explanatory power of my theory, adverse shifts in the balance of power both necessitate adjustment and prevent that adjustment from occurring. Vulnerability creates a need for a reorientation of grand strategy but also sets in motion the interaction between elite behavior and strategic culture which impairs the adjustment process.

[5]

Japan

On 18 September 1931, a small contingent of Japanese troops blew up a section of the South Manchurian Railway. The Kwantung Army then used the incident as a pretext to begin its military occupation of Manchuria. So began a decade of preoccupation with the expansion of empire, a preoccupation that was to culminate in Japan's attack on Pearl Harbor in 1941. Even though Japan sought to expand its empire in order to attain economic self-sufficiency and enhance its strategic position in East Asia, the pursuit of these objectives left the country by the late 1930s in a position of extreme economic vulnerability. To continue to prosecute a costly war in China, Japan needed to advance southward to secure access to the oil and minerals of a Greater East Asia Co-Prosperity Sphere that would stretch from Manchuria to the Dutch East Indies. The problem was that to advance southward would precipitate a direct confrontation with the United States and a U.S. embargo on the oil and steel that Japan's industry and military establishment so badly needed. Japanese elites had to choose between imperial retrenchment and going to war with a power that had a vastly superior resource base. By attacking the U.S. fleet at Pearl Harbor, decision makers were able to keep their hegemonial aspirations alive. But they also started a war that they knew they had little chance of winning.

Why did policies intended to enhance national power and produce paced imperial growth eventually lead Japan into a self-defeating war? How did the scope of imperial ambition come to outstrip so dramatically the country's resources? I argue that Japanese grand strategy during the 1930s cannot be seen as a continuum. On the contrary, 1937—the year in which Japan embarked on its futile effort to destroy the Nationalists in China—was a key turning point. From the occupation of Manchuria in 1931 until the outbreak of the China war in 1937, Japanese elites expanded selectively; their behavior was characterized by restraint and caution. The military gradually subverted civilian rule during these years, and there was no shortage of field commanders on the continent and junior officers in Tokyo intent on pushing forward the borders of the empire. Nevertheless, the cabinet and central military authorities constrained expansion, mindful of the need to preserve good relations with Britain and the United States. Japanese decision makers concentrated on developing the economic potential of overseas territories but explicitly avoided expansion that would put excessive strain on the military and economic resources of the metropole. Increasing military spending and industrial development in Manchuria contributed to impressive rates of economic growth. Elites took steps to enhance the country's power and security but were careful to avoid both self-encirclement and overextension.

The situation after 1937 was dramatically different. An unintended clash between Japanese and Chinese troops gradually escalated into general war. Japanese elites initially believed that war with China would be short and absorb only limited military resources. They grossly miscalculated; the conflict turned into a costly quagmire. Well over one million troops poured into China during the late 1930s, despite the lack of progress made in destroying the Nationalist regime. The campaign in China placed a huge strain on resources and forced planners to scuttle Japan's five-year economic plan. Steep increases in military spending induced inflation and starved the civilian economy of the resources needed to fuel growth. Despite the drain on resources, Japanese elites not only continued to prosecute the war in China, but also decided to advance into Southeast Asia and initiate war against the United States. Paced imperial growth gave way to self-defeating aggression. Japan embarked on the path to war with the United States despite clear indications that the consequences of such a war would likely be disastrous.

I argue that perceptions of vulnerability played a key role in inducing this dramatic shift in Japanese strategy. Furthermore, I show that elite beliefs and strategic culture served as the vehicles transforming policies that produced measured expansion into policies that produced self-defeating aggression. During 1931–1937, relatively low metropolitan vulnerability and conditions of strategic sufficiency gave rise to a restrained and cautious imperial policy. Elites took advantage of opportunities to enhance Japan's strategic position in Northeast Asia. A clear sense of strategic priorities led to imperial growth that contributed to the material strength of the metropole. A mixed strategy of deterrence and compellence did produce some expansion, but Japanese elites reined in the scope of their external ambition before it provoked an opposing coalition or led to costly commitments that drained the metropole's economic strength. Two key developments during this period did, however, set the stage for the excessive ambition of the late

1930s. First, the rising power of the military effectively brought an end to parliamentary government. After 1932, the military had essentially a free hand in the formulation and implementation of foreign policy. Second, Japan's forays on the continent—and the army's efforts to justify them to the elite community and to the public—did succeed in setting in motion a shift in strategic culture. Expansive images of empire were becoming embedded among elites and masses alike.

After 1937, elite behavior was driven by steadily increasing concern about the country's economic vulnerability. Decision makers continued to believe that expansion would ultimately lead to economic autarky. Yet efforts to subdue China only increased Japan's dependence on foreign imports of oil, steel, and other war-making materials. A southward advance became necessary to sustain the viability of the empire. But such an advance precipitated a U.S. embargo of the very items that Japan so sorely needed. Conditions of strategic deficiency led to marked changes in elite thinking about how to interact with adversaries and about strategic priorities. Sensitivity to European and American interests in East Asia gave way to a strategy of compellence and confrontation. Compellent strategies were needed both to fragment the opposing coalition and to gain access to new resources through territorial acquisition. Japan now had to expand well beyond Northeast Asia to gain access to the resources needed to fuel its war machine. More competitive policies required increasing sacrifices on behalf of the populace. Although the business community and civilian elites came to support the expansion of empire, they resisted the military's efforts to gain absolute control over domestic politics and the metropole's economy. The concepts of a New Order in East Asia and the Greater East Asia Co-Prosperity Sphere were thus propagated by the government both to lay claim to Japanese hegemony in East Asia and to persuade the domestic populace to make the sacrifices necessary to sustain such hegemony.

The problem was that these images of empire soon came to override strategic logic; empire became an end in itself, not a means to achieving autarky. Although decision makers came to see that their policies were not forcing the United States to back down or redressing the country's resource deficiencies, they were unable to reverse course. Elites appreciated that Japan was falling prey to self-encirclement and overextension, but they found themselves entrapped in the strategic images that they had earlier propagated. Individual decision makers, for both cognitive and emotional reasons, could not countenance giving up the Greater East Asia Co-Prosperity Sphere. Nor could the military, which had defined its organizational interests in terms of imperial expansion and staked its domestic political power on the fulfillment of imperial aspirations, abandon its grandiose strategic objectives. By 1941, Japanese decision makers were in principle forced to choose between war with the West and the scaling back of their imperial aims. In reality, one alternative had been virtually precluded; Japanese hegemony in East Asia had become such an integral and institutionalized component of the strategic vision prevailing in the elite community that withdrawal from empire was out of the question. Measured strategic planning fell by the wayside as decision makers led the country into a self-defeating war.

1931–1937: PACED IMPERIAL GROWTH AND THE SEARCH FOR AUTARKY

Strategic Assessments

Imperial ambition took root among Japanese elites during the last quarter of the nineteenth century. The reforms introduced by the Meiji Restoration were meant to model Japan after the West; the acquisition of overseas empire became part of this imitative impulse.[1] In staking its claim to be a great power in East Asia, Japan colonized Taiwan and Korea before World War I and, during the war, took control of several Pacific islands that had been previously held by Germany. Although elites were affronted by the U.S. annexation of Hawaii and the Philippines and the intense competition among foreign powers for access to the China market, Japan was, in military terms, in no position to challenge the colonial advances of the United States and the European powers.[2] Efforts were made, however, to ameliorate this inferiority: in 1907, the navy set forth plans to achieve parity with the U.S. fleet by building two new battlefleets.[3]

The Washington Naval Conference of 1922 constrained naval construction by placing a limit on the number of capital ships maintained by the United States, Great Britain, France, and Japan. Because the combatants in World War I turned to notions of collective security and arms control both to foster economic recovery and to prevent the recurrence of major conflict, Japan faced no strategic threats on which to base a program of rearmament. Accordingly, spending on military

---

[1] See Marius Jansen, "Japanese Imperialism: Late Meiji Perspectives," in *The Japanese Colonial Empire, 1895–1945*, ed. Ramon Myers and Mark Peattie (Princeton: Princeton University Press, 1984).

[2] See Mark Peattie, "The Nan'yo: Japan in the South Pacific, 1885–1945," in Myers and Peattie, *Japanese Colonial Empire*, esp. p. 180.

[3] James Crowley, *Japan's Quest for Autonomy: National Security and Foreign Policy, 1930–1938* (Princeton: Princeton University Press, 1966), p. 6.

programs fell dramatically during the 1920s, from 39 percent of national budget in 1919 to roughly 16 percent of national budget for the 1923–1931 period.[4]

The Great Depression was the single most important factor precipitating a dramatic change in Japanese foreign and defense policy during the 1930s. The financial hardships of the late 1920s and early 1930s discredited the ruling elite and hastened the demise of parliamentary government. As a result, the military was able to increase substantially its control over the formulation of both foreign and domestic policy. The depression also set in motion a movement toward national renewal that manifested itself in a shift of elite and mass attitudes toward the reaffirmation of national power and the reassertion of Japan's claim to regional hegemony. The principal features of foreign policy during the 1920s—accommodation, arms control, low military spending—increasingly came under attack.

The policies of continental expansion and military buildup that elites pursued during the early 1930s were the result primarily of these domestic changes, not of shifts in the external threats facing Japan. Indeed, assessments of the military balance during the first half of the decade provided a favorable picture of Japan's strategic situation. The army was preoccupied with the Soviet Union; during the first half of the decade, the General Staff focused almost exclusively on planning for war with the Soviets.[5] Improving Japan's ability to cope with the Soviet threat to the Korean peninsula—and, by implication, to the homeland—and to Japan's economic interests in North China was in fact one of the principal motivations for expanding into Manchuria. Paradoxically, the establishment of Manchukuo and the increase in the number of Japanese troops stationed there led to a *less* favorable balance from Japan's perspective. The Soviets responded to Japanese actions by substantially augmenting their forces in the Far East. Soviet personnel stationed east of the Urals rose from 100,000 men in 1931 to 240,000 by 1935. The Japanese did not respond in kind, maintaining force levels at roughly 60,000 throughout the period. The force ratio dropped from about two to one in 1931 to about four to one in 1935.[6]

Japanese complacency in the face of these unfavorable trends in the numerical balance was the product of several considerations. First, the

[4] Peter Duus, *The Rise of Modern Japan* (Boston: Houghton Mifflin, 1976), p. 201.

[5] Shimada Toshihiko, "Designs on North China, 1933–1937," in *The China Quagmire: Japan's Expansion on the Asian Continent, 1933–1941*, ed. James Morley (New York: Columbia University Press, 1983), pp. 197–199.

[6] Hata Ikuhiko, "The Japanese-Soviet Confrontation, 1935–1939," in *Deterrent Diplomacy: Japan, Germany, and the USSR, 1935–1940*, ed. James Morley (New York: Columbia University Press, 1976), pp. 131–132.

occupation of Manchuria enabled the Kwantung Army to adopt a forward force posture that offset existing numerical inferiority. Forward deployment would allow Japan to take the offensive against the Soviet Union should war become imminent. Planners calculated that Japanese force levels needed to be 70 to 80 percent of Soviet force levels for such an offensive to be successful.[7] Should such an operation have become desirable, Japanese troops in Manchuria could have been readily reinforced by the two infantry divisions stationed in Korea or by contingents transported from Japan. The Japanese planning community also assessed the likelihood of a Soviet attack to be quite low. Intelligence operatives were able to inform decision makers that the Soviets maintained a one-front posture until 1936, when they began to prepare for simultaneous operations in the east and the west.[8] Furthermore, the Kwantung Army extended hostilities in Manchuria and North China under the assumption that the Soviets would not retaliate as long as their territory was not violated.[9] In sum, Japanese elites believed that war would break out with the Soviet Union at some distant point in the future. But, for the time being, the likelihood of conflict was low and Japan could afford to be complacent about numerical inferiority in the border areas.

Assessments of the naval balance led to a similar outlook: complacency in the near term, with growing anxiety about the potential for Japan's naval superiority in the Pacific to erode in the coming decade. The Washington Naval Treaty effectively guaranteed Japan naval supremacy in the western Pacific. Although both the United States and Britain were allowed to maintain a greater number of battleships than Japan—the treaty specified a ratio of five to three—requirements in other waters and force levels in other vessel categories left the Japanese in a strong position in the Far East. By the late 1920s Japan had twelve heavy cruisers while the United States had only one.[10] An American decision to build twenty-three heavy cruisers jeopardized Japan's supremacy, however, and led to efforts to place a cap on cruisers at the London Naval Conference of 1930.

The navy General Staff identified a ten-to-seven cruiser ratio as the minimum consistent with Japan's defense requirements. Though the technical rationale for equating sufficiency with this ratio remains ambiguous, the navy insisted that the Japanese government not sign a

[7] Ibid., p. 132.
[8] Ibid.
[9] Shimada, "The Extension of Hostilities, 1931–1932," in *Japan Erupts: The London Naval Conference and the Manchurian Incident, 1928–1932,* ed. James Morley (New York: Columbia University Press, 1984), p. 262.
[10] Crowley, *Japan's Quest for Autonomy,* p. 43.

treaty at London unless this ratio could be agreed on. The United States was equally insistent that the cruiser ratio, like the battleship ratio, be set at ten to six. The Japanese government eventually acquiesced to the U.S. position in order to salvage the negotiations, but the domestic costs were high.[11] The navy claimed that its authority had been undermined and the security of the country jeopardized. Dissatisfaction with the treaty also spread among the public. In large part because of these domestic pressures, elites decided to abrogate the treaty in 1934, despite the fact that the pace of building programs left Japan with a ten-to-seven ratio through 1936.[12] By 1935, Japan had exceeded the quotas set by the Washington and London treaties. Although neither the United States nor Britain showed any intention of posing a threat to Japanese security, the expansionary impulse that emerged after the depression and the prospect of a substantial building program in the United States rallied support for a naval buildup.

The performance of the Japanese economy during the first half of the 1930s contributed to favorable assessments of Japan's security environment and to the willingness and ability of elites to enhance the country's military and political position in the Far East. Japan's industrial capacity expanded markedly; growth in the manufacturing sector averaged 8.2 percent between 1930 and 1935.[13] Heavy industry and sectors producing war-making materials, such as chemicals, machine tools, and steel, experienced particularly pronounced growth. Under Finance Minister Takahashi Korekiyo's expansionary program, steady increases in military spending, by increasing demand, were used to contribute to the boom.[14] Because the economy was growing at a healthy rate, military spending remained at roughly 6 percent of net domestic product through 1936, despite the fact that defense expenditures represented well over one-half of total government expenditure by that year.[15] Capital investment in and resource extraction from Manchuria, though not as profitable as originally hoped for, also contrib-

[11] For detailed discussion of the Japanese position, see Kobayashi Tatsuo, "The London Naval Treaty, 1930," in *Japan Erupts*, ed. Morley.

[12] Another naval conference was scheduled for 1936. Although the London Treaty allowed the United States to build to a 10:6 ratio, Japan would have maintained a de facto 10:7 ratio through 1936. See Crowley, *Japan's Quest for Autonomy*, pp. 54–64.

[13] Hugh Patrick, "The Economic Muddle of the 1920s," in *Dilemmas of Growth in Prewar Japan*, ed. James Morley (Princeton: Princeton University Press, 1971), p. 220.

[14] See Charles Kupchan, "Empire, Military Power, and Economic Decline," *International Security*, 13 (Spring 1989), 44.

[15] Annual growth rates averaged 5.5% between 1928 and 1938, compared to 3.2% during the 1920s. See Patrick, "Economic Muddle," p. 215. For data on military spending, see ibid., p. 251, and Takafusa Nakamura, *Economic Growth in Prewar Japan* (New Haven: Yale University Press, 1983), p. 163.

uted to the strength of the metropolitan economy.[16] Between 1931 and 1936, Japanese investment in Manchuria doubled. New industrial plant also led to a doubling of the region's output of iron ore and pig iron.[17]

The resurgence of Japanese imperialism that occurred during the first half of the 1930s was more the product of opportunity and domestic political developments than a response to increasing international threats. The Japanese did not perceive a hostile international environment. On the contrary, external ambition followed from conditions of strategic sufficiency and from appreciation of Japan's increasing resources and its consequent ability to shape a regional environment more conducive to its economic and strategic interests. I now look in more detail at how this expansion was carried out and at what strategic suppositions informed Japan's grand strategy.

expansion from strategic sufficiency

Dealing with the Adversary

The Japanese military was in large part responsible for the resurgence of imperialism during the 1930s. The Kwantung Army expanded the borders of the empire in Manchuria and North China, often in direct violation of orders from Tokyo. After the fever of expansion had spread to officers in the General Staff and War Ministry, the military gradually wrested control of foreign policy from civilian authorities, effectively undermining parliamentary government. Nevertheless, even after subverting civilian rule, the military did not embark on a self-destructive course of overexpansion. On the contrary, Japanese behavior emerged from a set of logical strategic suppositions, and planners were mindful of the need both to undertake expansion only if it contributed to the metropole's material strength and to avoid actions that would provoke a preponderant opposing coalition. The military pursued policies that were expansionistic and opportunistic but not overly ambitious.

During the late 1920s and early 1930s, two contending schools of thought divided the foreign policy community. Foreign Minister Shidehara Kijuro was the most outspoken proponent of those who believed that Japan had to accommodate the interests of regional and foreign powers and avoid the adoption of expansionary policies that might

---

[16] Cho Yukio, "An Inquiry into the Problem of Importing American Capital into Manchuria: A Note on Japanese-American Relations," in *Pearl Harbor as History: Japanese-American Relations, 1931–1941*, ed. Dorothy Borg and Shumpei Okamoto (New York: Columbia University Press, 1973), pp. 384–385. See also W. G. Beasley, *Japanese Imperialism* (Oxford: Clarendon Press, 1987), p. 216.

[17] Beasley, *Japanese Imperialism*, pp. 215–216.

bring war to the Far East.[18] Foreign Minister Tanaka Gi'ichi represented a school that advocated a more ambitious course for Japan, one that would eventually bring Manchuria and China into Japan's sphere of influence.[19] As Richard Storry has commented, "If Shidehara's name is associated with a respect for China's rights, Tanaka's is linked with a much more aggressive stance."[20] The question of whether to move into Manchuria and China—and, consequently, to risk confrontation with the West—was to lie at the core of debate about Japanese defense policy throughout the 1930s.

Conflict between these competing conceptions of Japan's role in Asia came to a head in 1930 as a result of the London Naval Conference. Despite the opposition of the navy, the Hamaguchi cabinet approved a treaty that set forth a ten-to-six rather than a ten-to-seven ratio. The prime minister and Foreign Office saw acquiescence to the U.S. position as preferable to a naval arms race and the erosion of relations with the United States.[21] Although a victory for the Shidehara school in the short term, in the long term the outcome of the debate over the London Treaty strengthened the position of the hard-line school in three important respects.

First, the navy made no effort to hide its dissatisfaction with the treaty and publicly claimed that the government had jeopardized the country's security. In a statement to the press, Admiral Kato affirmed that "as one who was responsible for national defense and naval tactics, he was still unalterably opposed to the naval tonnage allotted to Japan under the American proposal."[22] The navy's position provided momentum for those advocating a military buildup and a less accommodating position toward foreign powers. Second, the dispute between the Foreign Ministry and the navy sparked a debate about the autonomy of the military in the formulation of defense policy. The navy claimed that the cabinet had violated the military's "right of supreme command" as stipulated in the Meiji constitution. The government responded that the military's right of command applied only to questions of operations and strategy; negotiations on arms control and the setting of force levels remained in the domain of civilian authorities.[23]

---

[18] Shidehara was foreign minister in the Wakatsuki cabinet (1924–1927) and again in the Hamaguchi/Wakatsuki cabinets (1929–1931).

[19] Tanaka was premier and foreign minister from 1927 to 1929.

[20] Richard Storry, *Japan and the Decline of the West in Asia, 1894–1943* (London: Macmillan, 1979), p. 132.

[21] See Kobayashi, "The London Naval Treaty, 1930"; Crowley, *Japan's Quest for Autonomy*, pp. 62–64; and Tatsuji Takeuchi, *War and Diplomacy in the Japanese Empire* (New York: Doubleday, 1935), pp. 284–301.

[22] Kato paraphrased in Takeuchi, *Japanese Empire*, pp. 301–302.

[23] See Kobayashi, "London Naval Treaty," pp. 63–64.

Although the government won this round of the debate, the dispute about "the right of supreme command" became so politically volatile that, after 1930, civilians were increasingly reluctant to challenge the military on questions of defense policy. The government had unwittingly strengthened the hand of the General Staff.[24]

Third, the debate about the London Treaty received a great deal of public attention and mobilized mass interest in defense issues. Mainstream public opinion was generally supportive of the treaty.[25] But the navy devoted considerable effort to spreading its message among the public, seeking to convince the Japanese people that the government was betraying the national interest.[26] Such lobbying succeeded not only in undermining public confidence in the government, but also in setting in motion a process that was, during the course of the 1930s, to lead to a shift in strategic culture; the elite community and public alike began to buy into the notion of an expanded Japanese empire in East Asia.

The political turmoil surrounding the London Naval Conference thus set the stage for the Mukden Incident. Elements within the military, affronted by the navy's defeat in the treaty dispute, were looking for a way to assert their autonomy and push forward a more aggressive foreign policy. Civilian authorities had become more timid and less willing to challenge the military after the debate about the "right of supreme command." And the public was growing more supportive of a bolder foreign policy and a change in the status quo.

While the Kwantung Army's plans for orchestrating a military occupation of Manchuria took shape gradually, the decision to blow up the South Manchuria Railway and use the incident as an excuse for invasion was precipitated by several developments. Closer political and economic ties between Manchuria and China proper threatened Japan's privileged position in Manchuria. Anti-Japanese sentiment in China and in Manchuria was on the rise, leading to several outbreaks of violence between Chinese and Japanese residents in Manchuria. In March 1931, plans for a coup within the Japanese military were uncovered. Although the putsch was abandoned by its organizers, the development fueled pressure for change within the military.[27] In July of the same year, a Japanese army officer serving in Manchuria was allegedly murdered by Chinese or Manchurian soldiers, providing added support to those arguing that it was time for Japan to take action.

[24] Crowley, *Japan's Quest for Autonomy*, p. 80.
[25] Kobayashi, "London Naval Treaty," pp. 58–59.
[26] Takeuchi, *Japanese Empire*, pp. 303–304.
[27] Seki Hiroharu, "The Manchurian Incident, 1931," in *Japan Erupts*, ed. Morley, p. 164.

Egged on by these events, the Kwantung Army drew up plans for and executed the Mukden Incident without notifying the General Staff or the cabinet.[28] Shidehara did hear rumors that the Kwantung Army was planning unauthorized actions in Manchuria and cabled the consul-general in Mukden to "make further arrangements to control these adventurers."[29] On hearing word of the bombing, Shidehara ordered that operations be confined to the narrowest area possible.[30] His cable and his further efforts to confine the conflict were of little use; the Kwantung Army extended hostilities, hoping to bring all Manchuria under its control. Not even the General Staff was able to prevent its units in Manchuria from taking matters into their own hands. The General Staff went so far as to request from the emperor permission to control operations from Tokyo in an effort to wrest authority from field commanders. Though such permission was granted, units continued to disobey orders from central headquarters.[31] Furthermore, central army authorities, though indignant about having their orders violated, soon came to rally behind the Kwantung Army's successes in Manchuria.[32] As a result, the locus of decision making quickly shifted from the cabinet to the Army Ministry and General Staff. Army Minister Minami described the dynamics of a cabinet meeting on 21 September 1931, called to discuss the need to increase troop levels in Manchuria: "He pointed out that the decision had already been made by the conference of the three heads of the army [the army minister, chief of the General Staff, and inspector general of the military education] in the forenoon, upon incessant requests for instructions from the commander-in-chief of the Kwantung army, and said that the war authorities could carry out this decision without consulting the cabinet. He added, however, that he was seeking the approval of the cabinet as a matter of form."[33]

On what suppositions did Kwantung Army leaders base their decision to orchestrate the occupation of Manchuria? Was this simply an instance of errant officers seeking glory, or was the operation related to a set of sound, calculated strategic goals? The Manchurian Incident was planned and executed by Lieutenant-Colonel Ishiwara Kanji and Colonel Itagaki Seishiro, two senior officers in the Kwantung Army. Their planning documents for Manchuria point to one overriding objective: Manchuria's resources and its potential for industrial develop-

---

[28] Ibid., p. 186.
[29] Telegram cited in ibid., p. 201.
[30] Takeuchi, *Japanese Empire*, p. 351.
[31] Shimada, "Extension of Hostilities," p. 272.
[32] Ibid., p. 279.
[33] Quoted in Takeuchi, *Japanese Empire*, p. 353.

[307]

ment were to contribute to Japanese self-sufficiency and economic autarky.[34] Both Ishiwara and Itagaki believed that Japan, at some point in the future, would be at war with the Soviet Union and, possibly, with Britain and the United States. As an island nation, however, Japan had insufficient resources to engage in conflict with the major powers. It therefore had "to prepare for war by making war."[35] Capital investment, industrialization, and extraction of raw materials were to follow military occupation of Manchuria. The principal goal behind operations on the continent was to strengthen the Japanese economy and, in so doing, to prepare for the possibility that Japan might one day find itself in a protracted war with major powers.

Ishiwara and Itagaki were not alone in holding these views. The Japanese military drew the same lessons from World War I as did other military organizations: future wars would likely be protracted conflicts in which industrial mobilization and economic strength would be key determinants of the outcome. Many Japanese officers studied and trained in Germany, where they were inculcated with notions of economic centralization and "total war" planning.[36] By the 1930s, there was growing support within the military for a planned economy that would be better suited to the demands of wartime mobilization.[37] The development of Manchuria and its incorporation into the Japanese economy were, even before the Mukden Incident, becoming an integral part of this plan. As Army Minister Ugaki Kazunari stated several months before the beginning of operations in Manchuria, "It is essential that we work out a solution to the Manchurian and Mongolian problem because Japan cannot exist alone as a self-sufficient economic unit."[38] Given its proximity, its abundance of raw materials, and its potential for industrial development, Manchuria emerged as the answer to Japan's growing preoccupation with economic autarky.[39]

While these economic concerns dominated thinking about Manchuria, strategic considerations helped to gain widespread support within the General Staff for the Kwantung Army's actions. For the Operations Division, the task of planning for a conflict with the Soviet Union was simplified; the occupation of Manchuria made both defensive and offensive operations easier to mount. The Intelligence Division focused

---

[34] For a thorough review of planning for Manchuria, see Seki, "The Manchurian Incident," pp. 143–170.

[35] Ibid., p. 159.

[36] Crowley, *Japan's Quest for Autonomy*, pp. 88–89.

[37] Ibid., p. 113.

[38] Quoted in Seki, "Manchurian Incident," p. 172.

[39] On capital investment and industrial development in Manchuria, see Cho, "Importing American Capital," pp. 383–391.

its attention on North China. With Manchuria effectively under Japanese control, Japan could more easily weaken the Kuomintang's position in the northern provinces.[40] For both economic and strategic reasons, then, Manchuria (known as the independent state of Manchukuo after 1 March 1932) had come to be seen as Japan's "lifeline" on the continent by 1932–1933.[41]

From 1932 to 1937, Japanese elites successfully sought to consolidate Japan's position on the continent and to bring to fruition their hopes of rapid industrial development and economic growth. During this period, three important developments in strategic thinking took place. First, the belief that military security and economic planning were inextricably linked became widespread in elite circles. In 1934, the Army Ministry published a pamphlet entitled *Basic Theory of National Defense and Suggestions for Its Realization,* which emphasized the need for centralized economic planning and for preparing the country for full industrial mobilization and protracted war.[42] Concepts of "general mobilization," "national defense," and "economic planning" came to imbue planning documents and debate about defense policy.[43] In 1937, the Cabinet Planning Board, a body with considerable control over the domestic economy, was established to coordinate strategic and economic planning. In short, the notions of economic autarky, self-sufficiency, and total war which gradually took root among the General Staff during the 1920s were becoming deeply ensconced within the wider elite community.

Second, the consolidation of Japan's position in Manchuria allowed the army to begin focusing its attention on North China. In 1933, the Kwantung Army initiated efforts to establish a military presence in China. Acting against the wishes of the General Staff, the Kwantung Army repeatedly engaged Chinese troops in Jehol province in Manchuria. In return for a cease-fire negotiated in May, Chinese officials agreed to allow Japan to garrison its forces inside the Great Wall and to assume responsibility for patrolling some of the wall's main passes. This agreement provided the Kwantung Army its desired foothold in Hopei province. In the following months, negotiations on rail and air links, trade relations, and postal arrangements provided the Japanese further access into North China. Not surprisingly, these negotiations were conducted exclusively by the Kwantung Army, not by the Foreign Ministry.

---

[40] Crowley, *Japan's Quest for Autonomy,* p. 202.
[41] Takeuchi, *Japanese Empire,* p. 339.
[42] Crowley, *Japan's Quest for Autonomy,* pp. 208–209.
[43] Ibid., p. 256.

The army was gradually assuming full responsibility for Japan's military and political position on the continent.[44]

In 1935, the Kwantung Army furthered its penetration of North China, again using the cease-fire negotiations following border clashes to extract concessions from Chinese elites. The Ho-Umezu Agreement effectively expelled the Chinese Central Army from Hopei. Reforms were introduced to enhance Japanese control over the economy of North China. By the end of 1935, these measures coalesced into the so-called North China autonomy movement: a program aimed at separating the five northern provinces from China proper and incorporating them into Japan's sphere of influence on the continent.[45] Again, economic considerations were paramount; like Manchuria, North China held promise as a valuable source of raw materials, a marketplace for Japanese goods, and a potential site for industrial development. And, as in Manchuria, Japan's position in North China was staked out by ambitious field commanders acting without orders from Tokyo, but central authorities at first tolerated, and then came to welcome, these actions. In Shimada's words, "The North China autonomy movement was now becoming part of Japan's national policy."[46] By 1936, the cabinet had formally approved separating from China its five northern provinces and incorporating them into a Manchuria-North China bloc.[47]

The third important development in strategic thinking involved a shift in the army's orientation: its traditional focus on operations against the Soviet Union gave way to increasing concern with a "southern advance." During the early 1930s, debate about the geographic focus of army planning served as a source of factional struggle. Until the mid-1930s, the Kodo faction, which favored concentration on northern operations against the Soviets, prevailed over the Tosei faction, which argued for a focus on Manchuria and China. After 1935, in part because of the successes of the Kwantung Army in Manchuria and North China, the Tosei faction gained the upper hand. Its position was strengthened even further in February 1936, when junior officers associated with the Kodo faction assassinated two former premiers and a senior general. The purge of northern school officers that followed consolidated the predominance of the southern advance school.[48]

This shift in the orientation of army planning had several important implications. The navy had traditionally rested its case for fleet expan-

[44] For details of these events, see Shimada, "Designs on North China," pp. 11–74.
[45] Ibid., pp. 102–152.
[46] Ibid., p. 152.
[47] Ibid., p. 195.
[48] Storry, *Japan and the Decline of the West*, p. 151.

sion on the need for maritime supremacy in the western Pacific and the potential for imperial expansion to the south. The predominance of the northern advance school in the army therefore left the army and navy pulling in opposite directions, each service checking the other's plans for expansion. The rising influence of the southern advance school, however, meant that bureaucratic competition was no longer a major obstacle to southern expansion. This emerging consensus on the direction of imperial ambition was to play a key role in eroding opposition to deeper Japanese involvement in China. Gathering momentum for a southern advance also forced elites to reconsider the nature of Japan's relationship with foreign powers. An expanded role in China and Southeast Asia would increase tensions between Japan and Western powers. Diverting military assets from the Soviet border also entailed resort to diplomatic initiatives to reduce the threat from the north. Japan turned to Germany to achieve this goal; the two powers signed the Anti-Comintern Pact in 1936.[49]

This southward turn in the focus of Japan's imperial aspirations and the implications of this new orientation for Japan's relations with foreign powers raises several crucial questions. By the mid-1930s, had Japanese elites embarked on the pathway to war, prepared both to engage in a major conflict for the control of China and to accept the risk that such action might bring economic, if not military, reprisals by Western powers? Or were elites cognizant of the dangers involved in a southern advance and mindful of the need to preserve good relations with the West? Put differently, was Japanese behavior the product of a rash and irresponsible military machine that had run amuck, or was it the result of cautious and measured consideration of the opportunities and constraints facing Japan?

The historical record provides ample evidence that central authorities, both civilian and military, resorted to careful strategic planning and exercised considerable caution in executing their plans for imperial expansion. The overriding concern of both the General Staff and the cabinet was to avoid war. During the mid-1930s, war plans did not even include consideration of major operations in China.[50] The avoidance of major war was crucial to the realization of Japan's first and second five-year economic plans and its goal of building up the army and navy. Japan's economy needed time to mature, as did the industrial development of Manchuria and North China. Only after a peaceful period of economic development would the country be prepared for protracted war. These considerations led to a consensus among the army, navy,

[49] Crowley, *Japan's Quest for Autonomy*, pp. 304–306.
[50] Barnhart, *Japan Prepares for Total War*, pp. 77–78.

and cabinet that no actions could be taken that might precipitate Japan's involvement in a major conflict in China.[51]

The General Staff went to considerable lengths to ensure that its units in the field abide by a policy of moderation in China. Officers reputed to be in favor of further advances into China were removed from their posts. Army officials in Tokyo created a North China Army—an organization distinct from the Kwantung Army—to enhance their control over operations on the continent and create a buffer between the unruly units of the Kwantung Army and Chinese territory.[52] In the spring of 1937, growing intransigence on the part of the Kuomintang led to an increasingly conciliatory stance from Japan. Both the General Staff and the cabinet agreed that Japan should drop plans to separate the five northern provinces from the rest of China.[53] As long as economic access to North China was maintained, the Japanese were willing to leave political control to the Kuomintang.[54]

Similar attitudes imbued Japanese thinking about relations with foreign powers. Japanese elites realized that they had to preserve cordial relations with major powers. Japan's involvement in a war with the great powers would destroy any hope of realizing paced economic growth. More important, while planners thought that Japan might be able to prevail in a conflict against a single power, they saw quite clearly that Japan did not have the military means or resource base to take on Britain, the United States, and the Soviet Union simultaneously.[55] A naval arms race likewise had to be avoided; only a measured, planned buildup would enable Japan to achieve its economic goals.[56] Furthermore, because of Japanese reliance on imports of steel and oil from Britain and the United States, even a breakdown of trade relations would jeopardize the country's economic objectives.

These considerations induced Japanese elites to avoid taking actions that would implacably alienate foreign powers. Friendly relations with Britain were deemed of particular importance, as reflected in a joint Army-Foreign Ministry memorandum of July 1935: "One of the keynotes of our foreign policy must be to improve our relations with Britain, which has substantial influence with other world powers, and we must at the very least avoid a face-to-face confrontation with it at all costs."[57] Concern about the American reaction should Japan violate

[51] Crowley, *Japan's Quest for Autonomy*, pp. 284–288.
[52] Barnhart, *Japan Prepares for Total War*, p. 77.
[53] Shimada, "Designs on North China," pp. 226–227.
[54] Barnhart, *Japan Prepares for Total War*, pp. 82–84.
[55] Crowley, *Japan's Quest for Autonomy*, p. 288.
[56] Ibid., pp. 284–285.
[57] Cited in Ohata Tokushiro, "The Anti-Comintern Pact, 1935–1939," in *Deterrent Diplomacy*, ed. Morley, p. 39.

the U.S. open-door policy in China also played a key role constraining Japanese ambition on the continent.[58] In a similar vein, Japanese elites wanted to restrain the Soviets but not to provoke them. Japanese decision makers avoided entering into a formal military alliance with Germany, fearful that it might induce the Soviets to attack. They were even anxious about the wording of the preamble to the Anti-Comintern Pact because they thought it would "anger and alarm the Soviet Union unnecessarily."[59]

Elite concern about limiting the scope of Japanese commitments on the continent and avoiding actions that might precipitate conflict was clearly reflected in force deployments. The number of troops stationed in Manchuria and North China was strikingly small. In 1936, the Soviets had more than sixteen infantry divisions deployed in the Far East; Japan had only three divisions in Manchuria.[60] During the same year, the General Staff decided to increase the number of troops stationed in North China from 2,000 to 5,600.[61] In the naval realm, despite the cabinet's decision in 1934 to abrogate international naval limitations, fleet construction proceeded at a moderate pace. Avoiding a naval arms race and protecting the growth of the economy clearly took precedence over fleet construction.

Japanese grand strategy between 1931 and 1937 was based on several key suppositions. First, elites viewed the development of the economy as absolutely vital to preparing Japan for involvement in a great-power war should it prove to be unavoidable. The ultimate objective was economic self-sufficiency. Second, because the home islands were lacking in natural resources, the incorporation of Manchuria and North China into the Japanese economy became essential to sustaining industrial growth on the scale envisaged by elites. It was this supposition that gave rise to the notion of "preparing for war by making war." Third, because Japan was neither militarily nor economically prepared to go to war, elites were acutely aware of the need to avoid military conflict. Only peaceful conditions would allow the economy to thrive and enable the country to achieve autarky.

When translated into interactions with potential adversaries, these suppositions led Japanese elites to adopt an opportunistic mix of deterrence and compellence in both the core and periphery.[62] They pushed

---

[58] Barnhart, *Japan Prepares for Total War*, p. 80.
[59] Ohata, "The Anti-Comintern Pact," p. 32.
[60] Hata, "Japanese-Soviet Confrontation," p. 131.
[61] Shimada, "Designs on North China," p. 174.
[62] In the Japanese case, it is difficult to identify which geographic areas constitute the core and which the periphery. Because of the strategic importance of Korea and

hard to attain their economic objectives in Manchuria and North China. They abrogated naval agreements and sought to enhance maritime supremacy in the western Pacific. But central authorities also placed strict limits on the scope of Japan's ambition and its continental commitment; they were not about to stray across the line that would mire the country in a war in China or align the Western powers against Japan. Elites were by no means cowed by the West; they undertook actions fully aware that Western powers would disapprove of them. But decision makers would not pursue policies that threatened to jeopardize conditions of strategic sufficiency. They were careful to pull back and to moderate their actions before Western disapproval and suspicion turned into overt hostility.

Elite behavior was also informed by a clear sense of strategic priorities. Although the expansion of the early 1930s was carried out by zealous army units acting without the approval of central authorities, elites in Tokyo did succeed in gaining control over developments on the continent and ensuring that errant officers did not drag Japan into deeper commitments on the mainland. Furthermore, the Kwantung Army did not expand into vast tracts of useless territory, as the French army did in Africa. On the contrary, Japanese expansion was guided by strategic and economic exigencies. The cost of occupying Manchuria was to be more than offset by the region's contribution to the metropole's economy. Japanese elites were far more insistent than their counterparts in either the United States or Europe that empire pay for itself. Indeed, they were exploitative, even ruthless, in their efforts to extract resources from their growing empire. But far from being foolhardy or overly ambitious in their imperial reach, Japanese decision makers directed imperial expansion while keeping careful watch over the balance between resources and commitments.

In short, caution and reasoned judgment characterized how Japanese elites adjusted to the relative increase in power resources that their country enjoyed in the early 1930s. Conditions of strategic sufficiency enabled them to pursue a policy of selective expansion that enhanced Japan's military and economic position in North Asia. In the midst of opportunistic, expansive behavior, Japanese decision makers

---

Manchuria—both in economic terms and in terms of their role in defending the home islands against the Soviet Union—I consider them part of the core. Whether China should be considered core or periphery is more ambiguous. Despite the country's geographic proximity to Japan, developments in China had no immediate impact on Japanese security, in large part because the country lacked sufficient military and industrial capability. I therefore view China as a pivot between Japan's core and its periphery. Southeast Asia, the Pacific islands, and points beyond constitute the periphery.

exhibited moderation and were careful to avoid both self-encirclement and overextension. The result was paced imperial growth.

Domestic Considerations

My analysis has already indicated the overriding importance of domestic politics in shaping the nature of Japanese expansion during the early 1930s. The army was able to pursue continental expansion at least in part because it succeeded in usurping power from civilian authorities and undermining the stability of parliamentary government. Although the military did come to dominate the decision-making arena, it would be inaccurate to suggest that the services were constantly battling against civilian elites and a public that were increasingly disgruntled with repeated encroachments on their political rights. On the contrary, the services capitalized on the wave of popular discontent that emerged during the depression and, through a concerted lobbying effort, co-opted the public and gained its support for a more ambitious foreign policy. Dramatic changes in the public's image of Japan's role in East Asia created a domestic milieu conducive to the military's subversion of parliamentary government as well as its efforts to expand the empire. The business community was one of the few sectors that remained unconvinced of the need for empire.

Private Economic Interests. Several considerations undermine the proposition that industrialists and financiers orchestrated the expansion of the Japanese empire in the early 1930s. First, the Great Depression pushed business leaders and, most notably, the zaibatsu, to the periphery of the political arena.[63] Many blamed the zaibatsu for the depression, arguing that financiers and industrialists had pursued profits for themselves at the expense of the national economy.[64] This perception severely limited the business elite's influence over government policy. Second, because the zaibatsu had been discredited by the depression, the government prevented them from investing in Manchuria.[65] It would therefore make no sense to argue that the business community orchestrated expansion into a region in which it was banned from pursuing economic gain. Third, it is clear that responsibility for events in Manchuria lies exclusively with the Kwantung Army.

[63] *Zaibatsu* literally means "money cliques." During the 1920s, these cartels of industrialists exercised considerable influence over government policy.

[64] Nakamura Hideichiro, "The Activities of the Japan Economic Federation," in *Pearl Harbor as History*, ed. Borg and Okamoto, p. 420.

[65] This policy was reversed in 1934, largely because of the need to attract more capital for industrial development. See Cho, "Importing American Capital," p. 385.

Central military authorities, not to mention the business community, were ignorant of the Kwantung Army's plans for continental expansion. As William Fletcher writes, "Daring officers of the imperial army presented a fait accompli to which the business community had to adjust."[66] Furthermore, the traditional economic elite was generally opposed to an ambitious policy toward the continent. The business community feared that economic development in Manchuria would come to present unwanted competition for domestic industries. Worsening relations with foreign powers would also impair trade. Within the business community, there was "a basic ambivalence about the benefits of empire."[67] Industrialists and financiers were some of the most consistent supporters of Shidehara diplomacy throughout the 1930s.[68] In sum, the business community did not have the opportunity, the incentive, or the will to orchestrate Japanese expansion.

Domestic Politics. The Great Depression of the late 1920s and its impact on the Japanese economy had a profound effect on domestic political trends. The country's experiment with parliamentary democracy came to an abrupt halt; party government gave way to an oligarchic form of rule through which the military gradually increased its control.[69] These changes, sparked by the financial hardships associated with the depression, were precipitated by a "groundswell of discontent, directed against those who upheld . . . the existing order."[70] Many small businesses went bankrupt, leading to high levels of unemployment and labor unrest in urban centers. The recession also spread to agricultural areas, depressing prices and leaving many farmers in dire economic straits.[71]

---

[66] William Fletcher, *The Japanese Business Community and National Trade Policy, 1920–1942* (Chapel Hill: University of North Carolina Press, 1989), p. 65.
[67] Ibid., pp. 107–108.
[68] Nakamura, "Japan Economic Federation," p. 420; and Crowley, *Japan's Quest for Autonomy*, p. 110.
[69] My characterization of the nature of the Japanese polity differs from that of Jack Snyder. Snyder contends that Japan became increasingly cartelized during the 1930s and fell prey to overexpansion because of logrolling among imperialist interest groups. For Snyder's interpretation of Japanese overexpansion, see *Myths of Empire: Domestic Politics and International Ambition* (Ithaca: Cornell University Press, 1991), pp. 112–152. I argue that Japan, from 1933 onward, was effectively governed as a military oligarchy. The military all but dissolved an emasculated Diet. The business elite was discredited by the depression and banished to the periphery of the political arena. Furthermore, the business community opposed a rapid military buildup because of its devastating effect on the domestic economy. As it proceeded down the path to war, Japan increasingly became a strong, centralized, and tightly controlled state, not one buffeted by competing domestic interest groups.
[70] Storry, *Japan and the Decline of the West in Asia*, p. 138.
[71] Duus, *Rise of Modern Japan*, pp. 178–183.

These conditions discredited the party system and the ruling elite, fueling movements calling for radical political change. The liberal principles embodied in the Meiji constitution were coming under attack in universities and newspapers.[72] Many believed that more order and conformity would better serve the interests of the nation. As Gordon Berger writes, "The parties suffered from growing skepticism about their ability to make meaningful contributions to the integration and implementation of national policy."[73] During the early 1930s, membership in right-wing lobby groups doubled in size. Many of these groups rallied around the same cause: to return to traditional values, to restore a sense of national order, to sacrifice the self for national renewal.[74] Accompanying this dissatisfaction with the status quo was growing disaffection with Shidehara diplomacy. An increasing portion of the public came to see the conciliatory stance of the government as "weak-kneed diplomacy."[75] An editorial in the 8 September 1931 edition of the *Tokyo Asahi Shimbun* took note of these shifts in public attitudes: "The people are not able to give unconditional support either to Shidehara's low-key diplomacy or to the army's advocacy of a strong line, a consensus on national policy is acutely needed."[76]

The military both benefited from and capitalized on this change in public attitudes. A core of activists within the army, most of whom were junior officers, sought to establish the army as the vanguard of national renewal. The military was to provide national security not only in a literal sense, but also by embodying the values of duty, sacrifice, and strength that would restore national well-being. Officers committed to traditional values and order could be relied on to replace the corrupt bureaucrats and politicians who had led the country into disarray.[77] Inasmuch as this movement within the military supported an expansionist continental policy, domestic reform came to be associated with imperial growth. Having won the confidence of the public by establishing itself as the leader of national renewal, the military had little trouble selling to the Japanese people its expansionist strategic conceptions. The services published and widely distributed pamphlets calling for a resurrection of Japan's martial spirit and a reassertion of

[72] For a discussion of attacks on liberalism in the press, see Olavi K. Falt, *Fascism, Militarism, or Japanism? The Interpretation of the Crisis Years of 1930–1941 in the Japanese English-Language Press* (Rovaniemi, Finland: Pohjois-Suomen Historiallinene Yhdistys, Societas Historica Finlandiae Septentrionalis, 1985), pp. 44–45.

[73] Gordon Berger, *Parties out of Power in Japan, 1931–1941* (Princeton: Princeton University Press, 1977), p. 60.

[74] Duus, *Rise of Modern Japan*, pp. 206–213.

[75] Seki, "Manchurian Incident," p. 178.

[76] Cited in ibid., p. 198.

[77] Storry, *Japan and the Decline of the West in Asia*, pp. 145–146.

the country's position in East Asia.[78] An alliance between bureaucrats seeking domestic reform and officers seeking continental expansion fueled the process through which national well-being came to be associated with imperial growth.[79]

The impact on domestic politics of the London Naval Treaty and the Manchurian Incident bears out these generalizations about shifts in public attitudes and the role of the military in effecting these shifts. During the confrontation between the navy and the cabinet over the limitations proposed in London, the navy undertook a concerted effort to win public approval for its position. Working through their own publications as well as press statements, naval personnel attempted to convince the public of the importance both of the ten-to-seven ratio and of the military's "right of supreme command." As far as force levels were concerned, the navy's education campaign achieved its goals: "There seems to be little room to doubt that the systematic and organized efforts made during the conference by the naval authorities and navy reservists' associations to 'educate' the public to the idea that the 70% ratio contended for represented the minimum limits for national defense were a complete success."[80] The navy was, however, less successful in persuading the public to accept its position on the scope of the military's constitutional authority. Most newspapers, for example, stood firmly behind the cabinet's position that the government be able to negotiate force levels without the approval of the General Staff.[81]

While public support for a 70 percent ratio was not sufficiently strong to prevent the Hamaguchi government from signing the London Treaty, the navy's lobbying effort did mean that the treaty was viewed by many civilians as compromising the country's security. This perception played a key role in undermining support for the government and, more generally, for Shidehara diplomacy. Civilian authorities became more sensitive to maintaining the support of the services. The military capitalized on this situation to increase its clout within successive cabinets.[82] Shifts in public attitudes were reflected in the Diet. After the treaty debate, the more hard-line Seiyukai party, charging that the government had jeopardized national security, made substantial gains against the majority Minseito party.[83] Although Shidehara diplomacy had not yet been repudiated, the domestic stage

---

[78] Ibid., p. 149.
[79] Barnhart, *Japan Prepares for Total War*, p. 65.
[80] Takeuchi, *Japanese Empire*, p. 303.
[81] Ibid, pp. 311–312.
[82] Crowley, *Japan's Quest for Autonomy*, pp. 80–82.
[83] Takeuchi, *Japanese Empire*, pp. 306–309.

was set for the adoption of a more ambitious foreign policy and for the military's increasing subordination of parliamentary government.

The Manchurian Incident reinforced the domestic political trends set in motion by the depression and the London Treaty dispute. Even before the Kwantung Army began its operations in Manchuria, efforts were being made to rally the public behind a stronger Japanese position on the continent. The Manchurian Youth League, whose members were drawn from among the two hundred thousand Japanese residents of Manchuria, distributed pamphlets and organized meetings throughout Japan. This group attempted to convince the public of the need to protect Japan's political and economic rights in Manchuria. The Youth League was quite successful in communicating its message; numerous elite organizations in Tokyo came out in favor of a harder line in Manchuria after the league's campaign.[84]

Despite these lobbying efforts, the public, like the government, reacted to the Mukden Incident with surprise and was generally opposed to the Kwantung Army's incremental expansion in Manchuria.[85] Such opposition, however, was short-lived; in the weeks following the initiation of hostilities on the continent, the public demonstrated increasing support for a more ambitious policy in Manchuria, buying into the army's assertions that such actions were needed to defend the Japanese homeland.[86] This shift in opinion was reflected in the weakening position of the Minseito government. Criticism in the press, attacks from the Seiyukai party, and the defection of Minseito members from those supporting Shidehara diplomacy led to the fall of the government on 11 December 1931. The new Inukai cabinet showed far more support for a hard-line policy in Manchuria and was much less willing to challenge the military on key issues of foreign policy.

Public attitudes had, by 1932, undergone substantial change. In parliamentary elections held on 20 February, the Seiyukai party soundly defeated the Minseito. The Inukai cabinet, largely because of international criticism of Japan's actions in Manchuria, was reluctant to recognize the new state of Manchukuo when it was founded on 1 March. But, within six months, domestic pressures forced the government to change its policy; by the middle of the year, "an overwhelming majority of the Japanese people had already come to support the founding of Manchukuo."[87] While international criticism did delay Japan's recognition of Manchukuo, foreign pressure also strengthened public re-

---

[84] Seki, "Manchurian Incident," pp. 180–184.

[85] Takeuchi, *Japanese Empire*, pp. 362–363.

[86] Ibid., pp. 364–366.

[87] Murakami Hyoe, *Japan: The Years of Trial, 1919–1952* (Tokyo: Japan Culture Institute, 1982), p. 52.

solve. In the blustery atmosphere of 1932, the Japanese people resented foreign powers attempting to intervene in what was rapidly coming to be seen as Japan's sphere of influence. In the end, criticism from the League of Nations and Japan's eventual withdrawal from the League served only to consolidate public support for an ambitious continental policy.[88]

The public's reaction to the assassination of Prime Minister Inukai on 15 May 1932 provides much insight into the domestic milieu taking shape in Japan. A group of army regulars carried out the murder not because they disapproved of Inukai, but because they hoped that the resulting political chaos would bring party government to an end and allow the military to take effective control.[89] The public reaction was unequivocal: "The assassins . . . attracted a remarkable measure of public support. Indeed, they were seen as heroes."[90] The English-language *Japan Times* wrote that the assassination would find a warm spot in the heart of every Japanese. The *Osaka Mainichi* criticized the resort to violence but expressed sympathy with the assassins' motives.[91] Although the incident did not succeed in enabling the military to establish martial law, it did bring party government to an end. With the selection of a military man, Admiral Saito Makoto, as prime minister, the services attained an unprecedented degree of political power. As James Crowley describes this transition, "The Saito cabinet, in effect, marked the appearance of a new form of political oligarchy in which the authority and influence of the political parties, the Emperor's advisors, and the premier would be appreciably altered—in some instances, almost eradicated."[92] At the same time, the parties eroded from within. Internal disputes about how to respond to the military's increasing political power further undermined popular confidence in party government.[93]

By 1932, the domestic political environment within Japan had changed in two fundamental respects. First, the public had bought into continental expansion and soured on Shidehara diplomacy. Manchukuo was becoming an integral part of the Japanese empire. As Berger writes, "By 1932, the Minseito had followed the Seiyukai lead in abandoning Shidehara Diplomacy, and thereafter, both parties repeatedly endorsed Japan's expansion into China and throughout

[88] Crowley, *Japan's Quest for Autonomy*, pp. 182–184.
[89] Murakami, *Japan: The Years of Trial*, p. 47.
[90] Storry, *Japan and the Decline of the West in Asia*, p. 145.
[91] Falt, *Fascism, Militarism, or Japanism?* p. 38.
[92] Crowley, *Japan's Quest for Autonomy*, pp. 179–180.
[93] Berger, *Parties out of Power*, pp. 74–75.

Asia."[94] Second, the public's commitment to parliamentary government had been superseded by a commitment to national recovery and
traditional order. The military had emerged as the vanguard of this
search for social and spiritual renewal. The services thus did not impose their wishes on a reluctant public. On the contrary, in the wake
of the depression and the lobbying efforts carried out by the military,
the Japanese people were ripe for a change both in Japan's role in East
Asia and in the domestic order.

Military Services. An ambitious and increasingly unfettered military
establishment was quite clearly the principal agent responsible for the
imperial expansion of the early 1930s. The Kwantung Army occupied
Manchuria without the approval of central authorities. More important
in the long term, imperial ambition—and the strategic conceptions
needed to justify it—emerged within select quarters of the officer
corps, spread to the wider military establishment, to the broader elite
community, and eventually to the Diet and the public at large. In this
sense, the military was responsible for setting in motion a profound
shift in strategic culture.

The behavior of the military, however, contributed not only to the
adoption of an expansionist foreign policy and the propagation of expansionist strategic concepts, but also to the pursuit of policies that
were moderate and restrained in scope. Competition for resources between rival agencies within the military establishment did lead to
threat inflation and efforts to base force requirements on new and
more demanding missions. But such rivalry also checked expansionist
tendencies and contributed to the suppression of extremist views. Four
sets of intramilitary bureaucratic competition were of most importance:
the army versus the navy, the General Staff versus the Army Ministry,
the Kwantung Army versus the General Staff, and the Kodo faction
versus the Tosei faction (within the General Staff).

The strategic orientations of the army and navy had been on divergent paths since the nineteenth century. The army focused on northern
operations against the Soviets, the navy on southern operations
against the United States.[95] During the 1920s, the absence of external
threats, the antimilitarist mood of the Versailles era, and the negotiated
caps on naval building limited interservice competition. The military
buildup that followed the London Naval Treaty and the Manchurian
Incident then heightened competition between the army and navy. But
the expansionary tendencies present in both services were kept in

[94] Ibid., p. 354.
[95] See Peattie, "The Nan'yo," p. 180.

check by their divergent strategic foci. The army's efforts to secure resources for continental operations both constrained and were constrained by the navy's persistent requests for a fleet capable of coping with the United States.[96]

The General Staff and the Army Ministry were, in principle, charged with distinct and separable tasks. The General Staff was responsible for war planning and was concerned primarily with the strategic and tactical components of operations against the Soviet Union. The Army Ministry was responsible for personnel and general organization and management. The ministry was concerned more with political and economic, rather than strategic, considerations.[97] As a result, the General Staff tended to view continental expansion in terms of coping with the Soviet threat, while the ministry focused on economic development in Manchuria and North China. Again, these divergent foci served to offset each other. When the Army Ministry pushed for major military operations in China during the mid-1930s, the General Staff—principally because of its concern about the Soviets—played a key role in preventing a major southern advance from taking place.[98]

The Kwantung Army and the General Staff were also engaged in a constant struggle for control over operations in Manchuria and North China. The unauthorized actions of the Kwantung Army had an important impact on thinking within the General Staff; when faced with empire as a fait accompli, central army authorities came to accept and support Japan's new commitments. Nevertheless, the General Staff could not countenance total disregard of its orders and went to great lengths to gain control over continental operations.[99] If only to preserve the command structure, the General Staff consistently acted as a brake on further expansion of the empire's borders.

Finally, the scope of Japanese imperialism was constrained by splits within the General Staff between the northern advance (Kodo faction) and southern advance (Tosei faction) schools. When one of the two factions dominated the General Staff, the other served as an important counterweight. Until roughly 1935, the Kodo faction had the upper hand, but the Tosei faction placed constraints on the scope of the northern advance and Japan's confrontation with the Soviets. After

---

[96] During the mid-1930s, there was a consensus among the services that the army would be built up first, followed by the navy. Nevertheless, the effort to make simultaneous preparations for continental and maritime operations placed a constraint on the building programs of both services. See Crowley, *Japan's Quest for Autonomy*, pp. 284–285.

[97] Crowley, *Japan's Quest for Autonomy*, p. 85.

[98] Storry, *Japan and the Decline of the West in Asia*, p. 153.

[99] For concrete examples of these struggles between the General Staff and the Kwantung Army, see Shimada, "Designs on North China"; and Seki, "Manchurian Incident."

1935, the Tosei faction gained increasing control, but those concerned about the Soviets acted as a restraint on Japan's advance into China.

My analysis is not meant to indicate that without these countervailing bureaucratic pressures, Japan would have dashed headlong into China or precipitated a war against one or more major powers. On the contrary, the evidence presented above shows that there was near unanimity among elites that Japan had to avoid full-scale war in China and could not afford to jeopardize its relations with Great Britain or the United States. Nevertheless, competing organizational interests and institutional perspectives within the military did serve to dampen expansionist tendencies and check the spread of strategic conceptions designed to further the narrow interests of specific factions within the military establishment. These political dynamics within the military also lay the groundwork for understanding how and why Japanese grand strategy began to move in new directions after 1937.

Conclusions

Between 1931 and 1937, Japan engaged in paced, measured expansion on the Asian continent. In both absolute and relative terms, Japan's military and economic power was growing considerably. Conditions of strategic sufficiency enabled elites to adjust in a reasonable manner to a shifting international constellation of power. They took advantage of the increasing resources at their disposal to enhance Japan's political and strategic position in East Asia. At the same time, however, elites were acutely aware of the need to preserve strategic sufficiency. They deliberately avoided both costly commitments on the Asian mainland and actions that would lead to a rift with Britain and the United States. Expansion into Manchuria was undertaken mainly because it would contribute to the economic strength of the metropole and better enable Japan to deal with the Soviet threat. The seeds of overly competitive policies were indeed being sown: the military establishment subverted parliamentary government and helped create a public increasingly supportive of imperial ambition and increasingly hostile to a liberal domestic order. Changes in the intellectual paradigms and values of top elites, in the central roles and missions of the bureaucracy and military, and in public attitudes were leading to a fundamental shift in strategic culture. Nevertheless, the strategic images spreading within the elite community and among the populace were restrained and moderate in their scope. Japanese grand strategy was guided by a clear sense of strategic priorities and by appreciation of the need to constrain expansion in order to avoid conflicts that would drain metropolitan resources or trigger the formation of an opposing coalition of major powers.

1937–1941: RESOURCE VULNERABILITY AND THE PATH TO WAR

On 7 July 1937, Japanese and Chinese troops exchanged fire at the Marco Polo Bridge near Beijing. After repeated efforts to prevent the incident from turning into full-scale war, Japanese elites eventually chose to escalate, calculating that victory against Nationalist forces could be achieved quickly and cheaply. This decision was a fateful one. Essentially by accident, Japanese elites found themselves in a prolonged struggle for China that proved to be a crucial turning point in Japan's interwar grand strategy. Because the United States and Britain supported Chiang Kai-shek, the China war cast an adversarial shadow over Japan's relations with the Western powers. More important, full-scale war on the continent jeopardized Japan's quest for autarky and ravaged plans for economic growth in the metropole. In the mid-1930s, Japanese forces stationed in North China numbered roughly 5,000. By the end of the decade, Japan was sustaining more than 1.6 million soldiers in Manchuria and China. The burden on the metropolitan economy was staggering. In addition, Japan became more economically dependent on foreign powers as the prosecution of the war in China increased demand for imports of oil, steel, and other war-making materials.

By the beginning of the 1940s, Japanese elites had essentially two options. They could extricate the country from the conflict in China and pursue the more moderate imperial goals of the early 1930s. Or they could thrust southward, expanding the Japanese empire into Southeast Asia in order to tap the rich oil and mineral reserves of the East Indies. While the Japanese had the military capability necessary to execute such an advance, this option would bring Japan into direct conflict with the United States, a power of vastly superior war-making capability. Nevertheless, Japanese elites chose to pursue a southward advance, fully aware that the chances of winning a war against the United States were slim.

I argue that it was the acute economic vulnerability that emerged from the China war, working through both strategic beliefs and strategic culture, that induced elites to pursue overly competitive policies and to initiate a self-destructive war. Rather than pursuing a mixed strategy of deterrence and compellence that produced selective expansion, elites began to pursue a compellent strategy intended both to intimidate those powers seeking to block Japan's ascendance and to gain access to new resources. They pursued policies of indiscriminate expansion in both the core and the periphery. Conditions of strategic deficiency also led to a change in geographic priorities in which the objective of a confined, self-sustaining continental empire gave way to the notion of a Greater East Asia Co-Prosperity Sphere stretching from Manchuria to the Dutch East Indies. Elites were propagating expanded imperial concepts not just to guide strategic planners, but also to prepare the domestic populace for the sacrifices entailed in acquiring and sustaining empire.

The problem was that the geopolitical considerations that informed policy during the first half of the 1930s soon fell prey to the image of a Japanese empire spanning the Far East. Decision makers came to realize that compellent strategies were neither forcing the opposition to back down nor alleviating the country's resource deficiencies—they were leading only to self-encirclement and overextension. But Japanese strategy was no longer based on hard-headed strategic calculations. On the contrary, the strategic conceptions that decision makers propagated to respond to vulnerability and gain support for their extremist policies had led to a shift in the mindset of elites and masses alike: a reshaping of strategic culture had taken place. Empire became an end in itself, a component of national identity, not a pathway to autarky. Elites adopted an image-based notion of security, one that identified Japanese hegemony throughout East Asia as "an article of faith," not just a goal of national policy.[100] Because of the depth of their cognitive and emotional commitment to the extension of empire, top decision makers could not tolerate scaling back their imperial aspirations. Because the military had come to define its organizational interests—its claim to domestic political power and its large allocation of national resources—in terms of a southern advance, the services could not tolerate retrenchment. The general public (even though it had little impact on policy by the late 1930s) had come to share in this widespread enthusiasm for imperial expansion. Operating within this strategic culture, elites were unable to abandon their objectives even when strategic calculations suggested that they were unattainable; risking the destruction of the nation became preferable to giving up the Greater East Asia Co-Prosperity Sphere. Decision makers were unable to rein in the scope of their imperial ambition because the powerful strategic images that they had concocted conflicted with and overrode strategic logic.

Strategic Assessments

During the late 1930s, Japan faced no rising military threats from foreign powers. The Soviets continued to pose the most direct military

---

[100] Crowley, *Japan's Quest for Autonomy*, p. xvi.

threat, but planners considered a Soviet attack unlikely, especially following the Anti-Comintern Pact concluded by Germany and Japan in 1936. The United States was building up its naval forces but gave no indication of offensive intentions in the Far East. British elites were preoccupied with the rapid rise of German power and, because of economic constraints, were rearming very slowly. They debated whether to maintain Britain's existing commitments in the Far East, not whether to challenge Japanese security. The China war itself did not threaten Japan's military security. Even though Nationalist forces proved much harder to defeat than originally expected, the Kuomintang was not capable of driving Japanese forces from China or threatening the security of Manchukuo or Japan itself.

The dramatic shift in elite perceptions of vulnerability after 1937 occurred because of the change in economic conditions wrought by the China war, not because of rising external threats and an adverse shift in the military balance of power. The heart of the problem was that the level of Japan's military commitment in China had a devastating effect on the metropolitan economy. In 1936, Japan sustained roughly three divisions in Manchuria and 5,600 troops in North China. By 1940, eleven divisions were stationed in northern border areas to cope with the Soviets while twenty-eight divisions had been deployed in China.[101] Defense spending rose accordingly, from about 6 percent of net domestic product in 1936, to 15.4 percent, 23.0 percent, and 19.3 percent, respectively, for 1937, 1938, and 1939.[102]

Elites were all too aware of the damaging effect of rising military expenditures on national economic performance. Michael Barnhart has summarized an influential study of Japan's economic situation that was drafted in May 1938:

Japan had run an import surplus of 112 million yen in the first four months of 1938. Japan's exports were declining at an alarming pace and were certain to continue falling as the war made increased demands. Import controls bred higher costs for goods produced for export. The huge shipping requisitions for the China Incident deprived Japan of much exchange earned by the shipping sector in the past. Indeed, the balance-of-payments deficit for early 1938 actually exceeded the import surplus, a most ominous sign for a nation that had always run a surplus in invisibles. Unless a radical restructuring of the economy could realize startling improvements in efficiency or peace be effected with China, the 1938 materi-

---

[101] Tsunoda Jun, "The Navy's Role in the Southern Strategy," in *The Fateful Choice: Japan's Advance into Southeast Asia, 1939–1941*, ed. James Morley (New York: Columbia University Press, 1980), p. 287.
[102] Patrick, "Economic Muddle," p. 251.

als mobilization plan could not be executed. Substantial shortages were inevitable.[103]

A balance-of-payments deficit was coupled with declining reserves of foreign exchange. This problem was particularly worrisome because Japan relied so heavily on imports of war-making material. Japanese hopes of extracting needed resources from China quickly dissipated. The war ravaged the Chinese economy; industrial development became all but impossible, and one-fourth of the country's cultivated land was destroyed.[104] As demand for steel and oil increased, Japan was forced to rely more heavily on imports from the West. By the end of the decade, Japan depended on Britain and the United States (including their overseas possessions) for two-thirds of its imports of iron and steel. The United States supplied roughly 80 percent of Japan's fuel needs.[105] The quest for economic autarky was, ironically, leading to greater economic dependence.

The impact of high rates of military spending on national economic performance was exacerbated by the fact that the Japanese economy reached full capacity in 1937.[106] As a result, military expenditures created inflationary pressures and could no longer be used to stimulate demand-led growth. What is more, military allocations almost always took priority over demand in the civilian sector; the domestic economy suffered accordingly. Barnhart describes the effect of a revised economic plan for 1938:

> The civilian sector would bear the brunt of reductions. Even in steel, where the Planning Board limited cuts by imposing more Draconian reductions on other commodities, the civilian allotment would fall over 30 percent, from five million tons to 3.45 million. The original quota for imports of fuels, 566 million yen, fell to 510 million in the revised plan, which would drastically curtail storage and use of oil, especially in civilian industries. Factories were to reduce their consumption of fuel by 37 percent, shipping by 10 to 15 percent. Automobiles were to absorb a 65 percent reduction. Fishing boats, which furnished an appreciable amount of Japan's food, were forced to revert entirely to wind-power.[107]

The primary motivation behind Japanese expansion on the continent was the attainment of economic self-sufficiency. The empire was to

---

[103] Barnhart, *Japan Prepares for Total War*, pp. 109–110.
[104] Usui Katsumi, "The Politics of War, 1937–1941," in *China Quagmire*, ed. Morley, p. 422.
[105] Barnhart, *Japan Prepares for Total War*, pp. 149, 146.
[106] Nakamura, *Economic Growth in Prewar Japan*, pp. 38, 236.
[107] Barnhart, *Japan Prepares for Total War*, p. 110.

stimulate economic growth in the metropole and reduce Japan's dependence on imports. The China war, however, led only to acute economic vulnerability: it wreaked havoc with Japan's domestic economy, raised import levels, and threatened to erode diplomatic relations with precisely those Western countries on which the Japanese economy was becoming more reliant. I now examine the effects of this vulnerability on Japanese grand strategy.

Dealing with the Adversary

Japan's involvement in a major war in China was the product of a haphazard series of events, not of a deliberate decision to expand the empire. Unlike the Mukden Incident, which initiated Japan's advance into Manchuria, the clash at the Marco Polo Bridge was not orchestrated by Japanese troops. After the initial exchange of fire on 7 July 1937, Japanese elites hoped to settle the matter through negotiations. Nevertheless, "a series of blunders and misjudgments was responsible for the extension of the conflict into a full-scale war."[108] While the navy and Army Ministry were more supportive of taking advantage of this opportunity to extend Japanese control into North China, the General Staff argued that escalation would constitute an unnecessary drain on resources. In the weeks following the clash, the order for general mobilization was given and then canceled three times. By the end of August, however, military clashes had become more frequent, hostilities had spread to Shanghai, and the steady flow of Japanese troops into China had begun. High-ranking officers such as Ishiwara Kanji who continued to voice opposition to the extension of hostilities were removed from their posts.[109]

Though an isolated clash had rapidly escalated into general war, Japanese elites initially saw the China Incident as yet another minor confrontation between China and Japan that would soon be over.[110] By the end of 1937, Japanese troops had control of China's five northern provinces. A series of easy victories in the north bolstered initial assessments indicating that Japan would be able to defeat the Kuomintang quickly and inexpensively. Such optimism, however, was short-lived. The Nationalists offered much stiffer resistance than expected. They withdrew into the interior of the country, abandoning the coast and most industrial areas to their adversary but also forcing the Japa-

---

[108] David Lu, "Introduction," in *China Quagmire*, ed. Morley, p. 236.
[109] Hata Ikuhiko, "The Marco Polo Bridge Incident, 1937," in *China Quagmire*, ed. Morley, p. 275.
[110] Ibid., pp. 254–268.

nese to maintain long and more costly lines of communication and support. Furthermore, foreign powers came to the assistance of the Nationalists; supply lines were opened through Burma and French Indochina in the south and through the Soviet Union in the north. The consequent strain on Japan's military resources was exacerbated by the outbreak of border clashes between Japanese and Soviet troops. During the summer of 1938, the Changkufeng Incident led to major engagements along the border. Increasing requirements in Manchuria raised troubling questions about the escalating burden of the China war.[111]

The most serious problem, however, was the economic impact of the war. During 1938, the government instituted successive reforms to increase its control over the domestic economy. The five-year plan had to be scuttled, and major shortages began to wreak havoc with the civilian economy. War materials were in such short supply that American officials assumed that Japan had hidden reserves. No sensible leadership, they reasoned, would prosecute the war in China without far greater stockpiles.[112] Japanese behavior seemed particularly puzzling because the China war not only raised Japan's reliance on imports, but also jeopardized Japan's relations with the very countries on which it was becoming more reliant. The American decision in mid-1938 to place an embargo on the sale of aircraft to Japan and the abrogation of the Japanese-American Commercial Treaty in July 1939 drove home this point to Japanese elites. They were forced to confront the specter of a widespread economic boycott and the stark reality that a cessation of oil imports from the United States would cripple Japan's economy and its military machine.[113]

It was with the realization that their military and economic objectives were incompatible that Japanese elites became preoccupied with the country's acute economic vulnerability. Conditions of strategic deficiency led to three important shifts in strategic thinking. First, voices calling for moderation and restraint in China were lost in the din created by those calling for an uncompromising, compellent posture. By early 1938, a consensus had emerged among decision makers that Japan had only two options in China: the military destruction of the Nationalists or their unconditional surrender.[114] Individuals favoring a negotiated settlement were either removed from their positions or shunted to the periphery of the decision-making arena.[115] This shift

[111] Hata, "Japanese-Soviet Confrontation," pp. 140–142.
[112] Barnhart, *Japan Prepares for Total War*, p. 122.
[113] Ibid., pp. 101–102.
[114] Ibid., pp. 104–105. See also Murakami, *Japan: The Years of Trial*, pp. 70–72.
[115] Barnhart, *Japan Prepares for Total War*, p. 107.

from an opportunistic strategy of deterrence and compellence to an uncompromising strategy of compellence also carried over to Japan's relations with foreign powers. Although Japanese elites, by 1938, were by no means committed to going to war with Britain and the United States, they were willing to risk alienating the Western powers in order to prosecute the China war. Rather than moderating their policies to avoid the formation of an opposing coalition, Japanese decision makers would now intimidate adversaries and compel them to acquiesce to Japan's imperial designs.

Second, elites no longer based geographic priorities on careful consideration of the strategic and economic value of expansion. Unlike during the early 1930s, the General Staff seems to have abandoned efforts to define clear military objectives and bound strategic requirements accordingly. Expansion no longer had to pay in material terms. In Manchuria and North China, strict limitations on the scope of operations and detailed consideration of whether expansion would contribute to metropolitan strength had been crucial to constraining imperial expansion. In China, efforts to limit Japan's commitment quickly fell by the wayside. Almost unwittingly, the General Staff found itself deeply mired in China's vast territory. Because it had been staunchly opposed to advances into China proper, the General Staff was unprepared for the chain of events that led to full-scale war; there simply was no overall plan of operations. In Crowley's words, Japan's foray into China "was not circumscribed by careful or even credible strategic calculations."[116]

Third, elites not only failed to undertake rigorous evaluation of the costs and benefits of expansion, but also adopted more ambitious imperial objectives. The army was becoming increasingly receptive to the navy's position on the importance of focusing on a southern advance. During 1938–1939, the concept of a New Order in East Asia emerged to describe the changing political landscape on the continent. The New Order entailed Japanese control over Manchuria and North China, with China proper to be brought into this sphere on a looser, more informal basis.[117] By 1940, it was clear that even realization of the New Order would not suffice to meet the country's need for raw materials. The only long-term solution to Japan's growing resource deficiency, elites argued, was to gain access to the oil and mineral reserves of Southeast Asia. Through establishing a Greater East Asia Co-Prosperity Sphere reaching from the Soviet border to the Dutch East Indies,

---

[116] Crowley, *Japan's Quest for Autonomy*, p. 378. For further evidence of the deterioration of strategic planning, see Usui, "Politics of War."

[117] Beasley, *Japanese Imperialism*, pp. 206–207.

decision makers hoped that Japan could end its dependence on foreign imports and achieve economic autarky.[118] The concept of a Japanese empire restricted to Northeast Asia was giving way to a much more ambitious imperial conception. As I discuss shortly, the notions of a New Order and a Co-Prosperity Sphere were also crafted for domestic political purposes. A new political order at home—one that was more mobilized and centralized—was needed to support the military's increasingly ambitious external goals.

How did decision makers intend to construct this Co-Prosperity Sphere when Japanese forces were sparring with the Soviets in the north, bogged down in China, and confronted with the prospect of British, Dutch, French, and American opposition to a southern advance? How did the changing strategic and political landscape in Europe affect decision makers' calculations about how to further their imperial goals in East Asia? During late 1938 and 1939, the services and the Foreign Ministry agreed that it was time to choose sides in the burgeoning conflict in Europe, though there was disagreement as to which way Japan should lean. Not surprisingly, the army pressed for an alliance with Germany, hoping to contain the Soviets by keeping their forces split between two distant fronts. The navy opposed a formal military alliance with Germany, arguing that it would alienate Britain and the United States, lead to a potential economic boycott, and therefore jeopardize plans for an expansion of the fleet. In January 1939, the two services reached a compromise: the army would approve the navy's plans for fleet expansion, and the navy would accept a distant and conditional military alliance with Germany, to be publicly presented as a mere extension of the 1936 Anti-Comintern Pact.[119] This position was not, however, acceptable to the Nazis. The Germans wanted a more formal assurance of Japanese military assistance and demanded that the alliance be directed against Britain and France as well as the Soviet Union.[120] Japan and Germany were not able to find a middle ground, and the signing of the Nazi-Soviet Nonaggression Pact on 23 August 1939 brought the negotiations to an abrupt halt.

With the outbreak of war in Europe, Japanese elites, already af-

---

[118] W. G. Beasley states that the term *Greater East Asia Co-Prosperity Sphere* was first used in an official press release on 1 August 1940. Foreign Minister Matsuoka stated that the Co-Prosperity Sphere was "the same as the New Order in East Asia," but was larger in scope, including "areas such as the Netherlands East Indies and French Indo-China." See Beasley, *Japanese Imperialism*, p. 227. Planning documents, especially those drafted after 1939, do not appear to have made a clear geographic distinction between the New Order and the Greater East Asia Co-Prosperity Sphere. I therefore use the two terms interchangeably.

[119] Barnhart, *Japan Prepares for Total War*, p. 141.

[120] Ohata, "Anti-Comintern Pact," pp. 76, 95–111.

fronted by what they interpreted as German duplicity in signing the Nazi-Soviet Pact, tentatively sought to improve relations with France, Britain, and the United States. A cool U.S. response and Germany's stunning victories in Western Europe, however, quickly brought to an end Japan's drift toward the West.[121] Germany's successes in the West provided the window of opportunity for which Japanese elites had been waiting. With France, the Netherlands, and Britain either occupied by the Germans or preoccupied by the war, the door appeared to be open for the southern advance and the establishment of the Greater East Asia Co-Prosperity Sphere. In the months following the German occupation of France, the army drafted a new set of war plans entitled "Outline of the Main Principles for Coping with the Changing World Situation." This document asserted that it was time for Japan to end its dependence on the United States and Britain by building a "self-sufficient economic sphere centering upon Japan, Manchuria, and China" and extending southward to the waters north of Australia and New Zealand. "Never in our history," the document continued, "has there been a time like the present, when it is so urgent to plan for the development of our national power. . . . We should grasp the favorable opportunity that now presents itself."[122] Two problems remained: the Soviet threat prevented Japan from being able to concentrate on the south, and the United States posed a potential obstacle to a southern advance.

Alliance with Germany, inasmuch as it would help to address both obstacles, became more attractive. The Germans would act as a mediator between the Soviet Union and Japan, leading to an improvement in relations with the Soviets which would allow concentration on the south.[123] During 1940, Japan and the Soviet Union were in fact in the process of negotiating a nonaggression pact (the Japanese-Soviet Neutrality Pact was signed on 13 April 1941). Moving closer to Germany was also seen as the best way to cope with American opposition to Japanese expansion. A consensus was emerging that the southern advance had to proceed despite its implications for relations with the United States. Alliance with Germany would send a clear message to the Americans that Japan was willing to sacrifice its relations with the United States in order to attain its imperial goals. A coalition between Italy, Germany, and Japan might also deter the United States from entering the war once Japan had begun to move south. Accommoda-

---

[121] Hosoya Chihiro, "The Tripartite Pact, 1939–1940," in *Deterrent Diplomacy,* ed. Morley, pp. 194–206.

[122] Cited in Tsunoda, "Navy's Role in the Southern Strategy," pp. 247–248.

[123] Hosoya Chihiro, "The Japanese-Soviet Neutrality Pact," in *Fateful Choice,* ed. Morley, p. 48.

tion of U.S. concerns was simply not possible. A memo that apparently served as the basis for a key policy conference held on 19 July 1940 succinctly stated Japan's position: "While Japan will try to avoid unnecessary conflict with the United States, Japan is firmly resolved to resist armed intervention by the United States related to the establishment of the New Order in East Asia."[124]

Planning for the southern advance took shape gradually during 1940 and 1941. Both the army and navy agreed that the ultimate objective had to be the Dutch East Indies, but the services differed as to how to proceed. The army favored quick, small-scale operations against Dutch and British territories. The navy advocated a much slower advance, one that would allow Japan to calibrate the scope and pace of expansion with the U.S. reaction. The navy argued that it simply was not prepared for a major, protracted war with the United States.[125] The navy's position prevailed, at least temporarily. The services agreed that Japan should first seek to secure access to the resources of Southeast Asia through diplomatic, not military, means. Shortly after the outbreak of war in Europe, the Japanese initiated negotiations with the Dutch to purchase fixed quantities of oil and minerals.[126] Force was to be used only if these negotiations broke down.[127] War with the United States was to be avoided if at all possible, though planning for such a contingency had to be undertaken. Largely because of the navy's fears that an overt military alliance with Germany would markedly raise the risk of confrontation with the United States, Japanese elites repeatedly resisted German efforts to conclude formal alliance arrangements.[128]

From mid-1940 until the attack on Pearl Harbor, several developments edged decision makers closer to proceeding with the southern advance and gradually persuaded them to take a far more confrontational stance toward the United States; military conflict became a necessity, not something to be avoided if at all possible. First, negotiations with the Dutch failed to provide Japan with the oil and mineral supplies that it had hoped for.[129] In May 1941, the Dutch even reduced the amount of tin and rubber they were selling to Japan as relations between the countries deteriorated. Foreign Minister Matsuoka Yosuke, in a Liaison Conference convened on 22 May, expressed the frustration

---

[124] Cited in Hosoya, "Tripartite Pact," p. 219.

[125] Barnhart, *Japan Prepares for Total War*, pp. 162, 175.

[126] For details of these negotiations, see Nagaoka Shinjiro, "Economic Demands and the Dutch East Indies," in *Fateful Choice*, ed. Morely.

[127] Hosoya, "Tripartite Pact," pp. 208–209.

[128] Ibid., p. 229. The Germans assumed that the Tripartite Pact would deter the United States from entering the war.

[129] Nagaoka, "Economic Demands," pp. 151–153.

growing within the elite community: "It seems that they are taking advantage of Japan's plight and treating us as a minor power. . . . We can no longer put up with it under present circumstances."[130] The alternative was to extract resources from the Dutch East Indies by force. Elites were not oblivious to the implications. As a participant in the Liaison Conference noted, "If we take this final step against the East Indies, it will eventually be necessary to expand our military operations to the Philippines and Malaya. This is of life-and-death importance to the nation, and the timing and means should be considered with utmost care." Matsuoka spelled out the key issue: "It is possible that . . . the United States may begin a war with Japan."[131]

Second, developments in Europe made the southern advance more attractive and reduced the navy's opposition to the Tripartite Pact, which was concluded on 27 September 1940.[132] Germany's invasion of northern Europe had a major impact on attitudes within the Japanese General Staff. It was during the spring of 1940, just after the Germans had moved into Norway and Denmark, that planning for the occupation of the Dutch East Indies began in earnest.[133] German successes convinced Japanese elites that European dominance in Southeast Asia was finished. More important, the military became confident—overly so—that Germany would soon invade and overrun the British Isles. The General Staff assumed that the fall of Britain and the neutralization of British seapower would force the United States to withdraw from the Pacific in order to concentrate its fleet in the North Atlantic.[134] With the European empires dissolving and the United States unable to devote resources to the Far East because of the German threat in the Atlantic, Japan would be able to move without obstruction into Southeast Asia.

Germany's decision to open an eastern front against the Soviets in June 1941 also provided momentum for the southern advance, but

---

[130] 25th Liaison Conference, 22 May 1941, in Nobutaka Ike, *Japan's Decision for War: Records of the 1941 Policy Conferences* (Stanford: Stanford University Press, 1967), p. 38. Unless otherwise noted, all citations to Liaison and Imperial conferences are drawn from the Ike volume.

[131] Ibid., p. 39.

[132] Several factors appear to have influenced this shift in the navy's position. Barnhart argues that the navy received a higher allocation of military resources in return for its support for the pact. See *Japan Prepares for Total War*, p. 168. Hosoya Chihiro maintains that the navy did not want to be seen as the party responsible for preventing the pact, especially when public opinion favored an alliance with Germany. Naval officials feared their intransigence might lead to domestic turmoil. Hosoya also notes that the revised version of the pact that the navy supported provided Japan more leeway in deciding whether to enter the war than the original version. "Tripartite Pact," pp. 237, 240–241.

[133] Tsunoda, "Navy's Role in the Southern Strategy," pp. 243–244.

[134] Ibid., pp. 270–271, 286.

through circuitous means. Because of both Japan's obligations under the Tripartite Pact and the concentration of Soviet military capabilities on the western front, the Japanese army enthusiastically shifted its focus from southern operations to northern operations against the Soviet Union. The navy, in order to preserve the consensus behind the southern advance, shed its previous reluctance to beginning the advance and started backing initial moves to the south.[135] Navy Minister Oikawa Koshiro made his case before a meeting of the Liaison Conference on 25 June: "The Navy is . . . not confident about a war against the United States, Britain, and the Soviet Union. Suppose the Soviets and Americans get together. . . . This would make it very difficult for naval operations. In order to avoid a situation of this kind, don't tell us to strike at Soviet Russia and also tell us to go south. The Navy doesn't want the Soviet Union stirred up."[136] Mobilization for war against the Soviets also increased the urgency of beginning operations in the south. During July, the General Staff increased force levels in Manchuria from 400,000 to 700,000 and increased war stocks accordingly.[137] Between the war in China and the mobilization in Manchuria, each day of delay in proceeding south only reduced the supplies that Japan would have at its disposal for carrying out the southern advance and, potentially, fighting the United States.[138] This consideration further convinced the navy of the importance of proceeding with the southern advance.

The third development pushing Japanese elites to risk the southern advance and its consequences was the deterioration of economic relations with the United States. During 1940, the U.S. embargo list steadily grew longer. In July, the United States stopped supplying aviation fuel to Japan. In the following months, iron, steel, nickel, copper, zinc, and a host of other war-making materials were added to the list of restricted goods.[139] Given the level of Japan's economic dependence on U.S. imports, the Greater East Asia Co-Prosperity Sphere was becoming far more than a pathway to achieving self-sufficiency: it was becoming essential to the very survival of the Japanese empire. This steadily tightening economic noose also indicated to Japanese elites that the United States did in fact intend to stand in the way of the southern advance. By the beginning of 1941, the severity of Japan's predicament

---

[135] Barnhart, *Japan Prepares for Total War*, pp. 209–214; and Hosoya, "Japanese-Soviet Neutrality Pact," pp. 92–94, 113–114.

[136] 32d Liaison Conference, 24 June 1941, p. 59.

[137] Ike, *Japan's Decision for War*, p. 76. See also Hosoya, "Japanese-Soviet Neutrality Pact," pp. 101–104.

[138] Barnhart, *Japan Prepares for Total War*, p. 249.

[139] Ibid., pp. 195–196.

was becoming increasingly clear: gaining access to the resources of Southeast Asia would entail direct economic and, quite possibly, military confrontation with the United States.

Accompanying growing support for a southern advance was a hardening of attitudes about how to deal with the United States. During debate over whether to conclude the Tripartite Pact, some officials still voiced concern about alienating the United States and precipitating a confrontation. In an Imperial Conference convened on 19 September 1940, Privy Council President Hara Yoshimichi remarked, "I am afraid that a firm attitude on our part may produce an adverse result."[140] Hara was, however, in the minority. A consensus was emerging that it was time to compel the United States to acquiesce to Japanese demands. In the course of arguing for alliance with Germany, Matsuoka spelled out the logic for adopting a compellent stance as follows:

> Only a firm attitude on our part can prevent war with the United States. . . . Japanese-American relations have now deteriorated to the point where no improvement can be expected through courtesy or a desire for friendship. I rather fear such a weak attitude on Japan's part may only aggravate things. All we can do to improve the situation even a little, or to prevent its further aggravation, is to stand firm. If this is so, then we must confront the United States, strengthening our position by allying firmly with as many countries as possible and making our determination known at home and abroad as quickly as possible. This, I believe, is an urgent diplomatic move.[141]

The foreign minister's other main argument for allying with Germany was that an attempt to improve relations with the United States was unacceptable because of the sacrifices that it would entail. Matsuoka's logic reveals a clear commitment to obtain Japan's imperial objectives in East Asia, regardless of the costs:

> If . . . we become involved in a war with the United States, our national economy will suffer severely. In order to avoid these difficulties, it would not be totally impossible to ally with Britain and the United States as well as with Germany and Italy. However, to do so we should have to settle the China Incident as the United States tells us, give up our hope for a New Order in East Asia, and obey Anglo-American dictates for at least half a century to come. Would our people accept this? Would the hundred thousand spirits of our dead soldiers be satisfied with this? . . . In short,

---

[140] Cited in Hosoya, "Tripartite Pact," p. 247.
[141] Ibid., pp. 246–247.

[336]

an alliance with the United States is unthinkable. The only way left is to ally with Germany and Italy.[142]

What was essentially a wait-and-see policy during 1940 and early 1941 was transformed into a clearer set of strategic goals and war plans by mid-1941. Japan was openly allied with Germany and Italy and was ready to confront militarily the United States and Britain should they stand in Japan's way in East Asia. The establishment of the Greater East Asia Co-Prosperity Sphere had become an immutable foreign policy objective and, as the list of embargoed goods lengthened, was also becoming essential to the survival of the empire. The Americans had to be persuaded not to block Japan's path. Otherwise, Japan would resort to the use of force against the United States. "If we make concessions on this point," a joint Government/Supreme Command communiqué noted, "it is evident that we will soon fall prey to the United States."[143] Furthermore, it was urgent that the southern advance begin. The China war and mobilization in Manchuria were draining war stocks at the same time that the United States was building up its war-making capabilities. As Navy Chief of Staff Nagano Osami put it in a Liaison Conference of 21 July, "As for war with the United States, although there is now a chance of achieving victory, the chances will diminish as time goes on. . . . If we could settle things without war, there would be nothing better. But if we conclude that conflict cannot ultimately be avoided, then I would like you to understand that as time goes by we will be in a disadvantageous position."[144] The incentives for preventive war were mounting. These considerations were clearly reflected in a key policy document approved in an Imperial Conference held on 2 July. The key articles of this document, "Outline of National Policies in View of Changing Situation," are as follows:

1. Our Empire is determined to follow a policy that will result in the establishment of the Greater East Asia Co-Prosperity Sphere and will thereby contribute to world peace, no matter what changes may occur in the world situation.

2. Our Empire will continue its efforts to effect a settlement of the China Incident, and will seek to establish a solid basis for the security and preservation of the nation. This will involve taking steps to advance south, and, depending on changes in the situation, will involve a settlement of the Northern Question as well.

---

[142] Liaison Conference, 14 Sept. 1940, cited in ibid., p. 239.
[143] This document was prepared for the Imperial Conference of 6 Sept. 1941. Cited in Ike, *Japan's Decision for War*, p. 161.
[144] 40th Liaison Conference, 21 July 1941, p. 106.

3. Our Empire is determined to remove all obstacles in order to achieve the above-mentioned objectives.

. . . In order to achieve the above objectives, preparations for war with Great Britain and the United States will be made. First of all . . . various measures relating to French Indochina and Thailand will be taken, with the purpose of strengthening our advance into the southern regions. In carrying out the plans outlined above, our Empire will not be deterred by the possibility of being involved in a war with Great Britain and the United States.[145]

By July 1941, the die was cast. Japanese elites were proceeding with the southern advance, ready to accept the consequences, even if that meant war with the United States. On 21 July, the Vichy regime, under duress from Tokyo, signed an agreement providing the Japanese access to bases in southern Indochina. Within days, Japanese troops were deployed in the region. The United States, having broken Japan's diplomatic code, was set to respond. The Roosevelt administration froze Japanese assets and placed restrictions on the export of petroleum to Japan. It was only a matter of weeks before Japan had set in motion preparations to go to war. On 6 September, the Imperial Conference approved plans to "complete preparations for war, with the last ten days of October as a tentative deadline, resolved to go to war with the United States, Great Britain, and the Netherlands if necessary." Negotiations would continue, but "in the event that there is no prospect of our demands being met . . . we will immediately decide to commence hostilities."[146]

During the following weeks, Japanese elites rapidly moved closer to a decision to attack the United States. Military leaders begrudgingly granted the Foreign Ministry another month, allowing negotiations to proceed until the end of November. Pressure for a decision in favor of commencing hostilities mounted because of appreciation that Japan's war-making capabilities were steadily eroding. Each day of delay drained Japan's stockpiles and added to those of the United States. Liaison Conferences held during October and November were characterized by a growing sense of urgency. On 23 October, General Sugiyama Gen warned that "things have already been delayed one month. We can't devote four or five days to study. Hurry up and go ahead." In a seventeen-hour meeting held on 1 November, Nagano interrupted a heated discussion of when to end negotiations by shouting, "Now! The time for war will not come later!"[147] It was at this meeting that

---

[145] Cited in Ike, *Japan's Decision for War*, p. 78.
[146] "The Essentials for Carrying Out the Empire's Policies," cited in ibid., p. 135.
[147] 59th Liaison Conference, 23 Oct. 1941, p. 186; 66th Liaison Conference, 1 Nov. 1941, p. 202.

elites firmly decided that diplomacy could continue only until midnight of 30 November. If no agreement had been reached with the United States by that time, Japan would immediately go to war.

Was this decision the product of considered evaluation of options and of strategic assumptions that were based on logical inference and consistent with incoming information? Did available intelligence estimates suggest that Japan had a good chance of prevailing against the United States and of succeeding in establishing the Greater East Asia Co-Prosperity Sphere? Would this course of action allow Japan to attain national autarky? The following evidence reveals that strategic assessments unequivocally indicated to elites that Japan did not have the economic or military capability to defeat the United States in a protracted war. Japanese strategy made sense only if elites had good reason to believe either that the United States would decide not to respond to Japanese aggression or that the war would be of short duration. That neither assumption prevailed within the elite community raises troubling questions about the coherence of Japan's decision to go to war.

Virtually every quarter of the elite community was faced with strategic assessments that indicated that war with the United States was likely to have disastrous consequences for Japan. In May 1940, the navy carried out a major map exercise to help plan for operations against the United States. This was to be the only full-scale war game undertaken before the outbreak of the Pacific war. This comprehensive game was based on "the most accurate data available and concerned the adequacy of the mobilization plan, the timing of the opening of war, basic strategies, and the construction plan of warships and other vessels during a war."[148] The conclusions were clear:

1. If U.S. exports of petroleum are totally banned, it will be impossible to continue the war unless within four months we are able to secure oil in the Dutch East Indies and acquire the capacity to transport it to Japan.

2. Even then, Japan would be able to continue the war for a year at most. *Should the war continue beyond a year, our chances of winning would be nil.*[149]

Other, less ambitious assessments corroborated these conclusions. In August 1940, the Navy Ministry's Munitions Bureau estimated that stocks of aviation fuel would last only one year from the outbreak of the war. Supplies of other strategic goods were also strained; stocks of nickel, copper, zinc, aluminum, and crude rubber would last about

---

[148] Tsunoda, "Navy's Role in the Southern Strategy," p. 245.
[149] Cited in ibid., p. 246. Emphasis added.

one and a half years. "Such a situation would finish us," according to the chief of Ship Procurement Headquarters. "The navy could barely fight for one year."[150]

Studies carried out by the army provided a similarly sobering outlook. The Army Ministry's War Preparations Section drafted an assessment of Japan's material strength in March 1941. The report stated that "it cannot be denied that the empire's material strength would be insufficient for a long war. While we have munitions sufficient to defeat the enemy within a period of two years, by the end of the second year liquid fuels will become short at least temporarily, and should war be further prolonged, our economic capabilities might be strained."[151] The chief of the War Preparations Section was particularly concerned about marine transport. It was not clear that the oil of the East Indies could be safely transported where it was needed.[152] Furthermore, Japan was likely to lose a substantial number of its transport ships during the course of the war. According to the section chief, "We must pay attention to the situation with respect to marine transport, which is the foundation of the economy. If we lose too many ships or if we cannot maintain a balance between transportation for war operations and transportation for general materials mobilization, we will be unable to continue the war." "In the end," he concluded, "we are no match for the United States and Britain in the event of war."[153]

Officials concerned with management of the domestic economy were no less pessimistic. During the summer of 1940, the Planning Board, a body created in 1937 to oversee economic policy and coordinate industrial production in the military and civilian sectors, made it clear to the military services that the Japanese economy would virtually grind to a halt if deprived of imports from the West. The military capability needed to carry out the southern advance would divert so many resources from the civilian sector that maintaining current production levels would be difficult, and any hope of growth in the industrial sector would be illusory. Top army officials dealt with this news by dismissing a host of analysts from the Planning Board and replacing them with military officers during the spring of 1941.[154]

Efforts to stifle these warnings did not succeed in completely silencing those arguing that the Japanese economy simply could not sustain a war with the United States. This perspective was repeatedly

[150] Ibid., p. 256.
[151] Ibid., p. 292.
[152] Ibid., p. 254.
[153] Ibid., p. 293.
[154] Barnhart, *Japan Prepares for Total War*, p. 171.

represented during the crucial Liaison Conference of mid-1941. On 1 July, in a discussion of whether Japan should strike to the north or south, Minister of Commerce and Industry Kobayashi Ichizo warned: "I do not think we have sufficient strength, so far as resources are concerned, to support war. Both the Army and Navy can resort to force, but we do not have materials for war on both land and sea. . . . What we should do at this point is consider how to make sure we will not be defeated and decide how to settle the China Incident." Eleven days later, Minister of Home Affairs Hiranuma Kiichiro reiterated this point: "It would seem that we must avoid a break with the United States from the standpoint of the Empire's survival."[155] At the Imperial Conference convened on 6 September, Director of the Planning Board Suzuki Teiichi stressed that it would take time to extract resources from southern areas and channel them into the domestic economy: "I believe that if important areas in the South were to fall into our hands without fail in a period of three or four months, we could obtain such items as oil, bauxite, nickel, crude rubber, and tin in about six months, and we would be able to make full use of them after two years or so." The problem was that current stocks might not last that long: "Our liquid fuel stockpile, which is the most important, will reach bottom by June or July of next year, even if we impose strict wartime control on civilian demand."[156] Even foreign officials were trying to force Japanese elites to face up to their predicament. On 2 April 1941, Winston Churchill sent the following message to Foreign Minister Matsuoka: "Is it true that the production of steel in the United States of America during 1941 will be nearly 75 million tons and in Great Britain about 12½ million tons, making a total of nearly 90 million tons? If Germany should happen to be defeated as she was last time, would not the 7 million tons of steel production of Japan be inadequate for a single-handed war?"[157]

Given such overwhelming evidence that Japan simply did not have sufficient resources to take on the West, why did Japanese elites during 1940 and 1941 deliberately and knowingly lead the nation to war with the United States? The decision to initiate hostilities itself undermines the argument that elites believed that war could be avoided. Furthermore, many military and civilian leaders believed that a Japanese invasion of Southeast Asia would in all likelihood lead to military conflict

---

[155] 37th Liaison Conference, 1 July 1941, pp. 76–77; 39th Liaison Conference, 12 July 1941, p. 101.
[156] Imperial Conference, 6 Sept. 1941, p. 148.
[157] Cited in Tsunoda, "Navy's Role in the Southern Strategy," p. 294.

with the United States.[158] From this perspective, the decision to go to war makes sense only if decision makers believed that the United States would pull out of the Pacific when attacked or if they believed that the war would be short.

There was widespread agreement, however, that the United States was not likely to drop out of the war, even if faced with early setbacks. A document jointly drafted by the military and the government was unequivocal on this point: "It is very difficult to predict the termination of the war, and it would be well-nigh impossible to expect the surrender of the United States."[159] Nor is it credible to argue that elites believed in a short war. After World War I, a—if not *the*—central tenet of the Japanese military establishment was that the nation had to prepare for protracted war and that economic strength would be a critical determinant of Japan's fate. Thinking had not changed by 1941. In the Liaison Conference of 8 May, Matsuoka warned that "if the United States participates in the war, it will last a long time." A few days later, he reaffirmed that "the war will be long and develop into a big world war" if the United States decides to be involved.[160] This view was widespread in both military and civilian quarters. At the Imperial Conference of 6 September, the participants agreed that "a war with the United States and Great Britain will be long, and will become a war of endurance."[161] In early September, Chief of the Navy General Staff Nagano gave his assessment of how the war was likely to proceed: "I think it will probably be a long war. Hence we must be prepared for a long war. We hope that the enemy will come out for a quick showdown; in that event there will be a decisive battle in waters near us, and I anticipate that our chances of victory would be quite good. But I do not believe that the war would end with that." He further stated, "We can anticipate that America will attempt to prolong the war, utilizing her impregnable position, her superior industrial power, and her abundant resources."[162]

How, then, can Japan's decision to go to war be understood? Why did elites knowingly pursue what appears to be a set of suicidal policies? The answer lies in the effect of acute economic vulnerability on strategic beliefs and strategic culture.

---

[158] See, for example, the remarks of Matsuoka in the 35th Liaison Conference, 28 June 1941, p. 68; and discussion in the Imperial Conference of 2 July 1941 in Ike, *Japan's Decision for War*, p. 88.

[159] Document prepared for the Imperial Conference of 6 Sept. 1941, p. 153.

[160] 22d Liaison Conference, 8 May 1941, p. 30; 23d Liaison Conference, 13 May 1941, p. 33.

[161] Document prepared for the Imperial Conference of 6 Sept. 1941, p. 153.

[162] 50th Liaison Conference, 3 Sept. 1941, p. 131; Imperial Conference, 6 Sept. 1941, p. 139.

Japan's march to war after 1937 was fueled primarily by a shift in strategic beliefs precipitated by the China Incident. The economic vulnerability that emerged as a result of the war led to a change in elite beliefs both about how to deal with adversaries and about strategic priorities. Awareness of the need to limit expansion and avert confrontation with major powers was replaced by belief in the need to adopt uncompromising, compellent strategies. Rather than avoiding war in China, the Japanese insisted on the defeat or surrender of the Nationalists. Rather than avoiding confrontation with the United States and Britain, Japan allied itself with the West's principal enemy and pursued policies that were clearly at odds with American and British interests. Belief in the need for compellent strategies was based on two suppositions. First, compellence was needed to gain access to raw materials. Given the fact that the China war had drained stockpiles and caused the United States to place increasingly tight restrictions on exports to Japan, access to the resources of Southeast Asia was critical to fueling Japan's war machine. The geographic scope of imperial ambition had broadened considerably. Second, compellent strategies were needed to intimidate and fragment the coalition seeking to stand in the way of Japan's imperial goals. Japanese resolve was to make up for material inadequacy. The operative assumption was that in the core as well as in the periphery Japan had to force its adversaries to acquiesce to its demands. Conciliation and restraint would indicate weakness, strengthen American resolve, and fortify the opposing coalition.

These attitudes increasingly imbued high-level debate during the critical decisions of 1940 and 1941. Matsuoka won support for the Tripartite Pact by arguing that "the only thing that can prevent an American encirclement policy is a firm stand on our part at this time."[163] In making his case for the occupation of southern Indochina and the initiation of the southern advance, Army Chief of Staff Sugiyama insisted that "there is no need to take moderate measures." "If we are strong, I believe the other side will refrain from action."[164] Navy Chief of Staff Nagano was of the same mind: "We must resolutely attack anyone who tries to stop us. We must resort to force if we have to."[165] Even if Japan decides to pursue a negotiated settlement, it must begin by making clear its resolve. As Tojo Hideki put it after becoming prime minister, "If they recognize that Japan is determined, then that is the time we should resort to diplomatic measures."[166] The notion that Ja-

[163] Imperial Conference, 19 Sept. 1940, p. 12.
[164] 30th Liaison Conference, 12 June 1941, p. 52; 29th Liaison Conference, 11 June 1941, p. 50.
[165] 29th Liaison Conference, 11 June 1941, pp. 50–51.
[166] Imperial Conference, 5 Nov. 1941, p. 238.

pan would be better able to meet its security needs through cooperation and compromise was virtually absent from consideration. Only a
strong, compellent posture was appropriate for dealing with powers
that stood in the way of Japan's search for economic self-sufficiency.

This strategic logic led to the initial decision to proceed with the
southern advance. The suppositions that informed strategy were based
on logical inference. Confronted with conditions of strategic deficiency,
elites adopted extraordinary policies to cope with an extraordinary
strategic environment. This strategic logic does not, however, explain
Japan's eventual decision to go to war. By the second half of 1941,
the suppositions that informed grand strategy since 1937 had been
discredited. Elites proceeded with the southern advance despite the
availability of information indicating that compellent strategies were
backfiring and that efforts to create the Greater East Asia Co-Prosperity
Sphere would likely lead to disaster.

Psychological distortion, miscalculation, and cognitive lags do not
provide an adequate explanation for the behavior of Japanese elites.
Decision makers were under conditions of high stress throughout
much of 1941, if not earlier. But the historical record does not indicate
that elites manipulated incoming information and held a distorted
view of their strategic environment. They had a clear sense of the
strategic predicament that they faced and were appropriately pessimistic about Japan's chances of victory. Nor did they delude themselves
by assuming that the United States would drop out of the war if attacked. Elites did not see what they wanted to see. They went to war
despite awareness of a daunting strategic imbalance. Miscalculation
also fails to explain elite behavior. Decision makers were not caught off-
guard by unpredictable events; their adversaries behaved in a manner
consistent with Japanese projections. Nor does the time lag involved
in adapting beliefs to incoming information explain the decision for
war. Incoming information not only should have disconfirmed prevailing beliefs, but in fact did do so. By 1941, decision makers admitted
that Japan's compellent strategy was not producing its intended effects.
The Dutch East Indies indeed had large reserves of oil and strategic
goods that could reduce Japan's dependence on imports from the West.
But elites appreciated that each step southward only tightened the
noose around the Japanese economy. Even with access to the oil and
mineral reserves of Southeast Asia, planners were extremely skeptical
that Japan would be able to survive a protracted war with the United
States. Nor did decision makers operate under the illusion that Japan's
uncompromising stance was forcing the United States to back down.
On the contrary, Japanese elites were coming to the conclusion that
the United States was prepared to go to war to stop Japan's southern

advance and that a war between Japan and the United States was likely to be long in duration. The initial reasons for adopting a compellent strategy had both been discredited.

Japan's decision for war in 1941 can be understood only within the context of the shift in strategic culture that occurred during the 1930s, and especially after 1937. Beginning with the China war, elite beliefs about strategic priorities changed significantly. Concentration on Manchuria and North China gave way to preoccupation with the Greater East Asia Co-Prosperity Sphere, an area of Japanese economic, political, and military dominance stretching along the Pacific littoral from Manchuria to the Dutch East Indies. To be sure, dire resource deficiencies made it imperative for the Japanese to tap the raw materials of Southeast Asia if they were to continue the China war. And justifications were needed for the tightening economic and political conditions at home. But careful assessment of the feasibility of a southern advance was pushed aside by a growing conviction that Japan had no choice but to strike south.

By 1940, the empire was far more than a potential pathway for achieving economic autarky; the Co-Prosperity Sphere had become an unquestioned goal, an integral part of how the decision-making community—top elites, the bureaucracy, the military services—defined national security. As Crowley put it, the notion of Japanese hegemony in East Asia became "an article of faith."[167] Imperial expansion was no longer a means to an end—economic self-sufficiency—but had become an end in itself. An image-based notion of security, one that equated Japan's well-being with the establishment of the Greater East Asia Co-Prosperity Sphere, had replaced hard-headed assessment of how best to augment economic and military power. The image equating Japanese security with the establishment of the Co-Prosperity Sphere so imbued the mindset and values of elites that it overrode logic indicating that efforts to realize this notion of security would likely bring ruin to the metropole. Furthermore, the notion of empire became infused with a sense of moralism and justice: Japan was not simply seeking resources; it was carrying out a spiritual mission. This almost mystical aspect of the Greater East Asia Co-Prosperity Sphere intensified elite aversion to the thought of giving up the southern advance.[168] As I argue below, decision makers did fear the political repercussions of failing to achieve their proclaimed objectives. But the statements of individual decision makers also reveal the depth of their cognitive and emotional commitment to realizing their imperial aspira-

---

[167] Crowley, *Japan's Quest for Autonomy*, p. xvi.
[168] Beasley, *Japanese Imperialism*, pp. 204–205, 243.

[345]

tions. For War Minister Tojo, it was "intolerable if we cannot establish the Greater East Asia Co-Prosperity Sphere." For Prime Minister Konoe Fumimaro, "the ultimate development of the Greater East Asia Co-Prosperity Sphere was the path to Japan's destiny." To abandon this goal was "unthinkable."[169] For Suzuki, giving up the southern advance entailed suffering "unspeakable hardships and privations."[170] An immutable conception of the Japanese empire in East Asia had become deeply entrenched within the elite community; giving up this objective was no longer a viable option. What appears in hindsight to have been a choice between abandoning the greater East Asia Co-Prosperity Sphere and going to war with the United States was really no choice at all.

The heart of the problem was that Japan initially pursued the Co-Prosperity Sphere in order to cope with its economic vulnerability but, in doing so, only exacerbated that vulnerability. By 1941, it was clear to elites that their decisions were leading to both self-encirclement and overextension, not autarky. Turning back, however, was impossible "because we carried out the Manchurian Incident and the China Incident in order to get rid of the yoke" of economic dependence.[171] That a southern advance would provide autarky was an illusion, but elites had become so wedded to the notion of the Greater East Asia Co-Prosperity Sphere that they preferred to perpetuate this illusion and incur the associated costs rather than to adapt their goals to strategic realities. The notion of the Co-Prosperity Sphere was originally crafted for instrumental reasons: to guide Japan's search for economic autarky and rally domestic support for this search. But by 1941, the Co-Prosperity Sphere had become so central to how elites defined Japanese security that, for political, cognitive, and emotional reasons, they could not tolerate abandoning it. An image-based notion of security overrode incoming information that should have led to a much-needed revision of strategy. Elites became trapped in their own strategic conceptions, seeking economic self-sufficiency and finding only increased vulnerability. It was this self-perpetuating cycle that lay at the core of Japan's overly competitive behavior and that ultimately triggered the decision to attack Pearl Harbor.

In addition to the historical material presented above, several other considerations lend support to this argument. To begin with, it is important to note that the military establishment failed to draft careful

---

[169] 39th Liaison Conference, 12 July 1941, p. 102; Konoe cited in Berger, *Parties out of Power*, p. 254, and Hosoya, "Tripartite Pact," p. 239. See also Imperial Conference, 2 July 1941, p. 80.

[170] Imperial Conference, 5 Nov. 1941, p. 220.

[171] Ibid., p. 229.

and comprehensive plans for the Pacific war. Students of the archival record have concluded that "there existed nowhere in Japan a master plan for the conduct of war based on an overall estimate of national power." Tsunoda Jun agrees that "no careful study was ever made of Japan's material ability to carry out a comprehensive policy of southern expansion." Nobutake Ike, translator of the Liaison Conferences of 1941, remarks that "there is no evidence that the crucial question of Japan's chances of winning a war against the United States and Britain was ever seriously studied and discussed in any of these meetings."[172] Even elites involved in the crucial decisions of 1941 remarked on the absence of reliable assessments. Togo Shigenori, foreign minister in the cabinet formed in October, later reflected on the deliberations leading to war: "I was astonished at our lack of the statistical data required for a study of this sort; but even more, I keenly felt the absurdity of our having to base our deliberations on assumptions, since the high command refused to divulge figures on the numbers of our forces, or any facts relating to operations."[173]

This evidence is consistent with the picture of an elite community so wedded in political, cognitive, and emotional terms to certain strategic conceptions that it was unwilling to entertain information that contradicted those conceptions. Elites did not engage in stress-induced psychological distortion and delude themselves with favorable assessments of the military balance. On the contrary, decision makers failed to carry out comprehensive studies because they knew all too well that such studies would point to the extreme dangers involved in proceeding with the plans to which they were already deeply committed. As Asada Sadao comments, "One is almost led to wonder whether the Navy General Staff tended to slight these problems [of transporting oil] because more careful consideration would have made any viable plan of operations impossible."[174] There is considerable evidence that the navy, throughout 1941, was skeptical about the outcome of a war with the United States but simply did not express its opinion or divulge the data that were the source of its pessimism.[175] In some cases, strategic assessments were manipulated so that they would conform to pre-

---

[172] Asada Sadao, "The Japanese Navy and the United States," in *Pearl Harbor as History*, ed. Borg and Okamoto, p. 256; Tsunoda, "The Navy's Role in the Southern Strategy," p. 249; Ike, *Japan's Decision for War*, p. 130.

[173] Cited in ibid., p. 188.

[174] Asada, "Japanese Navy and the United States," p. 257.

[175] It appears that the navy wanted to avoid a split with the army and did not want to admit that it could not cope with the American fleet after spending years preparing for just that contingency. Naval officials feared that such an admission would undermine the service's political influence. See Asada, "Japanese Navy and the United States," p. 255; and Ike, *Japan's Decision for War*, pp. 69, 184–185.

determined policies.[176] The elite community was resigned to the southern advance regardless of the consequences. As Robert Scalapino notes, "Rational dialogue almost ceased just at the time when Japan was moving step by step toward one fateful decision after another. A helplessness swept over the top elite—a paralysis of nerve and will."[177]

The fact that select members of the elite community attempted to reverse the course on which Japan had embarked also lends credence to my general argument. If incoming information was glaringly at odds with a set of strategic conceptions deeply entrenched in the intellectual paradigms and values of decision makers, one would expect bold individuals to raise objections in order to bring policy into line with strategic realities. Evidence should indicate that at least some elites were aware of the dangers arising from Japan's grand strategy and that they therefore sought to reverse course. Indeed, throughout 1940 and 1941, analysts in both services and on the Planning Board repeatedly called to the attention of their superiors the widening gap between Japan's resources and its strategic objectives. For the most part, these individuals were demoted and their analyses quietly buried.[178]

Even among top-level elites, isolated individuals attempted to expose Japan's predicament and slow, if not halt, the rush to war. The new cabinet formed in late July 1941 considered seeking a rapprochement with the United States. War Minister Tojo, however, blocked any movement in this direction by insisting that the government had stated that "it would not change national policies that had already been decided. . . . Moreover, both the War Minister and Navy Minister have demanded in Cabinet meetings that there be no relaxation in national policies."[179] A few weeks later, after the U.S. decision to freeze Japanese assets and place an embargo on exports of petroleum, Foreign Minister Toyoda Teijiro proposed that Japan guarantee Thai neutrality in return for certain concessions from Britain. Tojo again brought to an abrupt halt consideration of moderating Japan's aims: "The acquisition of military bases in Thailand has already been approved. . . . It is not possible to change that at this point." Toyoda tried again at the end of August: "During Matsuoka's time, we tried to deter America with strong language. This aroused the Americans' hostility, and in the end they severed communications with Japan. According, we have to think carefully about the pros and cons of getting the United States even more excited. . . . [Japan] cannot help but give some thought to the

---

[176] See Asada, "Japanese Navy and the United States," pp. 256–258.
[177] Scalapino, "Introduction," in *Fateful Choice*, ed. Morley, p. 121.
[178] Barnhart, *Japan Prepares for Total War*, p. 171.
[179] 40th Liaison Conference, 21 July 1941, p. 105.

question of whether it is better to watch quietly . . . or to go on a rampage. Wouldn't it be better for Japan to be patient and restrained, to calm American public opinion and not irritate the United States?"[180] His words fell on deaf ears. In October, Prime Minister Konoe resigned, in large part because his desire for continued negotiations with the United States was effectively overruled by the military.[181] Realistic glimpses of the strategic landscape indeed entered the decision-making arena. But their impact was negligible in the face of an elite community unwilling to countenance accommodation or to contemplate the possibility that the Greater East Asia Co-Prosperity Sphere might have to be abandoned.

Finally, there is explicit evidence that even those elites who stood most solidly behind the southern advance had deep reservations about the likely consequences of Japan's strategy. Many realized that the chances of military defeat were high but preferred risking the destruction of Japan to acquiescing to retrenchment and the scaling back of their imperial aims. The few indications of optimism that can be found appear to be based on resignation, not on sound assessment. Hara, president of the Privy Council, recognized that "it is inevitable that we must decide to start a war against the United States. I will put my trust in what I have been told: Namely, that things will go well in the early part of the war; and that although we will experience increasing difficulties as the war progresses, there is some prospect of success." Sugiyama acknowledged serious deficiencies in resources but asserted that "we think we can frustrate the enemy's plans by one means or another."[182]

Many others were more straightforward. War Minister Tojo, in responding to his colleagues' fears that Japan might not survive a war with the United States, said that "even if there is no hope, I would like to persist to the very end. I know it is difficult." On 1 November, Army Vice Chief of Staff Tsukada remarked, "In general, the prospects if we go to war are not bright."[183] In the critical Imperial Conference of 6 September, Navy Chief of Staff Nagano admitted that Japan could by no means be assured of victory. But he insisted that it was better

---

[180] 46th Liaison Conference, 14 Aug. 1941, p. 120; 49th Liaison Conference, 30 Aug. 1941, p. 127.

[181] The emperor appointed General Tojo to head the new government and asked him to reevaluate all major policy issues—the so-called clean slate debate. Although such a review did take place, it produced little change in the general direction of policy. See Scott Sagan, "The Origins of the Pacific War," *Journal of Interdisciplinary History*, 18 (Spring 1988), 910–914.

[182] Imperial Conference, 5 Nov. 1941, pp. 236, 226.

[183] 39th Liaison Conference, 12 July 1941, pp. 101–102; 66th Liaison Conference, 1 Nov. 1941, p. 207.

to be defeated in battle than to acquiesce to America's demands; backing down would entail "spiritual as well as physical destruction for the nation." Admiral Yamamoto, commander-in-chief of the combined fleet, made a similarly revealing statement when he realized that Japan was headed for war with the United States: "It's out of the question! To fight the United States is like fighting the whole world. But it has been decided. So I will fight my best. Doubtless I will die on board the *Nagato* [his flagship]."[184] It was preferable to die fighting for the Co-Prosperity Sphere than to live with the knowledge of having bowed to American pressure and abandoned the conception of empire that had become so integral to how elites conceived of Japan's security.

These points confirm that Japanese elites had sufficient information to conclude that their policies would lead to disaster for Japan. But the economic vulnerability that emerged with the China war created a strategic culture and an associated set of strategic imperatives from which the elite community found it impossible to escape. As Barnhart writes, "The essential element that led to war was Japan's terrible economic vulnerability." The China war started "a perverted search for self-sufficiency which would lead ultimately to war with the West and to ruin for Japan."[185] By mid-1941, it was becoming apparent to elites that Japan's grand strategy was a recipe for national disaster, not for national autarky; they realized the country was falling prey to self-encirclement and overextension. Nevertheless, the majority of decision makers clung desperately to their outmoded strategic conceptions, allowing powerful strategic images to override strategic logic. Pursuing a course that would likely lead to military defeat was preferable to admitting that Japan would have to swallow its imperial ambition and abandon the Greater East Asia Co-Prosperity Sphere.

Domestic Considerations

Between 1937 and 1941, the domestic environment grew increasingly conducive to the pursuit of ambitious strategic objectives. Japan's political parties disbanded themselves in the name of national unity. The public enthusiastically supported continued imperial expansion. And the competing factions within the military that had checked expansionist tendencies in the early 1930s coalesced behind the southern advance. The strategic culture that took root after 1937 permeated all

---

[184] Nagano cited in Asada, "Japanese Navy and the United States," p. 254; Yamamoto cited in Tsunoda, "Navy's Role in the Southern Strategy," p. 274.
[185] Barnhart, *Japan Prepares for Total War*, pp. 267, 76.

components of the polity—with the exception of the business community.

Private Economic Interests. As during the 1931–1937 period, economic interest groups between 1937 and 1941 exercised, if anything, a restraining influence on Japan's imperial policy. Domestic producers came to see China as a potentially fruitful market, but they saw no need for Japan to seek political or military hegemony throughout the region. They feared that high levels of military spending would undermine the domestic economy.[186] Business elites also vociferously opposed the draconian cuts in resources allocated to the civilian sector. The military's ever-increasing demand for steel and petroleum had a devastating effect on domestic industries. During the late 1930s and early 1940s, the business community struggled to resist the centralization of the economy consistently advocated by the military. Though economic elites did succeed in delaying the military's efforts to gain control over the economy, they were unable to constrain the services' demand for resources or limit the scope of their imperial goals.[187] The business community was also opposed, for obvious reasons, to confrontational policies that would lead to an erosion of trade relations with the West. On this score as well, economic interest groups were left unsatisfied. As Fletcher writes, "While willing to exploit opportunities in China, the business community did not display much enthusiasm toward autarky. The growth of the nation's industries mandated trade with the West. Moreover, a larger empire might lead to unwanted competition for domestic producers. The business community adjusted to the government's foreign policy rather than act forcefully to affect it."[188]

Domestic Politics. After the military had virtually dismantled parliamentary government during the early 1930s, public opinion and political jockeying in the Diet came to play a fairly insignificant role in the formulation of foreign policy. During the second half of the decade, the services spent far less time lobbying the populace; the Japanese people had already been weaned from Shidehara diplomacy and convinced of the benefits of empire. Elites and masses alike had bought into the imperial conceptions propagated by the military during the early 1930s. The China Incident met with widespread support among

---

[186] Fletcher, *Japanese Business Community*, p. 79.

[187] In late 1940, the business community blocked a move by the Planning Board to transfer management of all enterprises to the state. Barnhart, *Japan Prepares for Total War*, pp. 173–174.

[188] Fletcher, *Japanese Business Community*, pp. 108–109.

the public. In fact, the war in China stimulated a "spiritual mobilization movement" in which "a surge of renewed national confidence and a sense of national purpose gripped all but an insignificant handful of people." By 1938, "victory over China became a national goal no longer questioned in public," and a Diet member was actually expelled from his seat in 1940 for suggesting that Japan might not have the resources necessary to attain military victory over the Nationalists.[189] In general terms, the Diet during the late 1930s increasingly came to support the military in its imperial aims.[190]

Although the remnants of party government did not stand in the way of the military's external goals, they did resist the military's increasing efforts to intervene in domestic economic affairs. As mentioned above, the China war ravaged the domestic economy. The more burdensome Japan's external commitments became, the greater the government's need to centralize and mobilize the domestic polity. The concepts of the New Order in East Asia and the Greater East Asia Co-Prosperity Sphere played a role in this mobilization campaign. A new international order had its analogue at the domestic level: "The new political order and 'high-degree national defense state' concepts were, above all, expressions of the desire of Japan's wartime leaders to intensify the process of national integration, to elevate citizen attitudes toward the state from passive compliance with orders from above to active support for the state."[191] The establishment of the Co-Prosperity Sphere thus went hand-in-hand with a new domestic order. The parties, rather than serving as a means of channeling public opinion, came to serve as conduits for the spread of imperial zeal among the populace.[192]

The government's efforts to mobilize the domestic polity were largely successful. In 1940, all political parties dissolved themselves amid calls for national unity. The military imposed increasing control over the domestic channels of political expression. Government supervision of the press tightened.[193] Though there was some popular resistance to these developments, the public was generally quiescent, despite deteriorating economic conditions. At the end of July 1941, even after the Japanese occupation of southern Indochina and the Roosevelt administration's consequent decision to freeze Japan's assets, the home affairs minister reported that "the general public has shown increasing

[189] Duus, *Rise of Modern Japan*, pp. 218, 224.
[190] Misawa Shigeo and Ninomiya Saburo, "The Role of the Diet and the Political Parties," in *Pearl Harbor as History*, ed. Borg and Okamoto, p. 339.
[191] Berger, *Parties out of Power*, pp. 234–235.
[192] Ibid., pp. 227–228.
[193] Falt, *Fascism, Militarism, or Japanism?* p. 104.

confidence in the Government."[194] Those civilians less comfortable with government policy were simply unwilling to speak out against the military.[195] In fact, elites were far more concerned about ultranationalists who were critical of the government for being too conciliatory than they were about those who feared that Japan's behavior was too competitive.[196] The populace was by no means responsible for Japan's excessive ambition. But a large portion of the public had clearly bought into the strategic notions that had taken root within the elite community and was willing to make the sacrifices necessary to allow the military to pursue the establishment of the Greater East Asia Co-Prosperity Sphere.

This analysis is not meant to suggest that Japanese behavior in 1941 can best be understood as the result of elite manipulation of public attitudes. Decision makers were not entrapped in the currents of popular nationalism they succeeded in stirring up. On the contrary, elites and masses alike had bought into the notion of a vast Japanese empire in the Far East. By 1940, it was the images embedded in the elite community, not domestic political pressure, that were pushing Japan toward war. Nevertheless, elite lobbying of the public in the early 1930s and again after 1937 played a key role in shaping the strategic conceptions that had come to infuse the decision-making community. Efforts to establish a new order at home were integrally related to efforts to build a new order in East Asia. Elite-mass linkages thus help explain both the content and the intensity of the strategic images that impelled Japanese elites to embark on a self-destructive war.

Military Services. The military was clearly the institutional engine driving Japanese expansion. Many of the top decision makers were military officials. The strategic beliefs and accompanying strategic conceptions that fueled the southern advance emerged primarily from within the military establishment. These conceptions then became institutionalized and routinized within the military: the services acted as a key vehicle through which the Co-Prosperity Sphere was transformed from rhetoric into an immutable strategic objective. Procurement programs, budgets, career paths, and organizational self-image all revolved around proceeding with the southern advance. This institutional orientation played an important role in silencing those who questioned the coherence of Japan's grand strategy. Furthermore, had it chosen to pursue retrenchment, the military would likely have had

---

[194] 42d Liaison Conference, 29 July 1941, p. 111.
[195] Barnhart, *Japan Prepares for Total War*, pp. 268–269.
[196] See Hara's comments in the Imperial Conference of 6 Sept. 1941, p. 151.

to give up its virtual monopoly of power on the domestic front. In this sense, the narrow self-interest of the services did contribute to the adoption of self-defeating policies. But why the political interests of the services came to depend on their ability to proceed with the southern advance must be placed in the proper context. The moderation of imperial objectives would have diminished the military's political power only because the services had staked their preeminent domestic position on their ability to achieve specific imperial goals. The military was itself responsible for molding a domestic environment in which retrenchment entailed political costs and for creating expectations and strategic objectives that it was incapable of fulfilling. How the military defined its political interests was simply one more manifestation of the strategic culture that was driving self-defeating behavior. Strategic culture was thus entrapping elites through a host of complementary mechanisms: the cognitive and emotional commitment of individual decision makers to the Co-Prosperity Sphere; the organizational interests of a military establishment that had come to define its principal roles and missions in terms of the southern advance; and the political interests of both individuals and organizations that had staked their domestic power on the fulfillment of specific imperial objectives.

I have argued that it was vulnerability that gave rise to extremist policies, drove the military to propagate grandiose strategic conceptions, and hence set in motion the process of entrapment that led to self-defeating behavior. Others have argued that it was interservice rivalry that drove the military's excessive ambition and led to Japan's eventual decision for war. Because the army and navy were competing for scarce resources, the argument runs, they based their force requirements on particularly ambitious missions. In order to secure its material needs, each service had to win the approval of the other. A logrolling dynamic emerged in which the services saddled the nation with a range of strategic commitments that went far beyond what either the army or navy independently viewed as being consistent with sound policy.[197]

This argument indeed has some validity. Interservice rivalry was rampant between 1937 and 1941; competition for steel allocations was particularly acute.[198] The following examples also demonstrate that these bureaucratic struggles had an impact on the orientation of strategic planning and on the timing of shifts in strategy. Consider the evolution of planning for the southern advance. The army favored quick, small-scale operations focused exclusively on Dutch and, if necessary,

---

[197] Snyder develops this argument in *Myths of Empire*, pp. 112–152.
[198] See, for example, Barnhart, *Japan Prepares for Total War*, p. 202.

British territories. These objectives left no mission for the navy, however, which insisted that war plans—and, consequently, procurement programs—also focus on maritime operations against the United States. The navy initially did not advocate going to war with the United States but did succeed in expanding the scope of the proposed southern advance to ensure its budgetary position vis-à-vis the army.[199] The timing of the navy's decision to proceed with the southern advance was also significantly affected by competition with the army. It was only after the German attack on the Soviet Union focused the army on northern operations that the navy was ready to proceed south. Preparations for a southern advance, naval officials reasoned, would direct the army's attention back to the south, away from its renewed preoccupation with northern operations.[200] Similarly, logrolling played a role in finally convincing the navy to agree to alliance with Germany. The navy dropped its opposition to the Tripartite Pact in return for the army's approval of a higher allocation of resources for naval procurement.[201]

On the other side of the ledger, several considerations suggest that interservice rivalry does not offer a satisfying explanation of Japan's excessive ambition. To begin, while logrolling could conceivably produce more extensive expansion than any single service considered strategically sound, it is by no means clear why bureaucratic rivalry should push either service to pursue policies that it deems likely to lead to self-destructive war. Jack Snyder's explanation for why the Japanese navy agreed to proceed with the southern advance is as follows: "Though fearing this would get Japan into a hopeless war with America, the navy leaders recognized that their budgetary and political position would evaporate the instant they admitted war with America would be unthinkable no matter what resources the navy was given."[202] But it is difficult to accept that the navy's concern about losing a share of its budget to the army was the chief impetus behind Japan's decision to go to war with the United States. Neither collective action theory nor organizational theory would predict that a military service would prefer embarking on a self-destructive war to sacrificing some of its institutional influence and resources.

It is also the case that in many instances, the army and navy checked, more than fueled, each other's expansionary tendencies. In the sum-

---

[199] Ibid., pp. 162–163. The navy was in the awkward position of wanting to prepare for war with the United States but also wanting to avoid actions that would precipitate hostilities. See also Asada, "Japanese Navy and the United States," pp. 249, 258.
[200] Barnhart, *Japan Prepares for Total War*, p. 209.
[201] Ibid., p. 168.
[202] Snyder, *Myths of Empire*, p. 45.

mer of 1941, the army was on the brink of attacking the Soviet Union. Had the navy not played a role in restraining the army, Japan could well have ended up fighting the United States in the Pacific and the Soviet Union in the north. The roles were reversed when the navy wanted the southern advance to begin with operations against the Philippines, a plan that the army initially opposed with success.[203]

The most powerful argument against viewing service rivalry as the main cause of overexpansion is that the army and navy were generally in agreement about the central features of Japan's grand strategy. Both services were committed to economic self-sufficiency and to the Greater East Asia Co-Prosperity Sphere. They were both prepared to go to war with any power that stood in the way of these objectives. Army and navy leaders alike had bought into the strategic conceptions that induced them to move forward with the southern advance despite awareness of the likely outcome of war with the United States. Service rivalry indeed affected these conceptions at the margins and influenced the timing of important diplomatic and strategic initiatives. But it was the effect of vulnerability on the content and intensity of the strategic images that shaped policy, not service rivalry, which is essential to understanding how both services came to define their central roles and missions and how and why Japan's search for economic self-sufficiency went awry.

Two other issues related to the military establishment warrant mention. First, as during the early 1930s, field commanders serving in the China war and in Indochina continued to act without authorization from Tokyo.[204] These episodes were not, however, critical determinants of the predicament in which Japan found itself in 1941. The major decisions that led to the southern advance and the move into Indochina were deliberated extensively in central councils.

Second, between 1937 and 1941, the military only increased its control over the policy-formulation process. The military attained the ability to scuttle cabinets by refusing to appoint service ministers.[205] This political power contributed to the timidity of civilian elites. During 1941, the military wanted decisions taken in the Liaison Conferences to be definitive, even without cabinet approval. When Foreign Minister Toyoda objected to this practice, he was told that the cabinet leaks too much information and that "except for those matters that because of their particularly grave nature should be presented to the Cabinet, in

[203] Barnhart, *Japan Prepares for Total War*, p. 162.

[204] For examples, see Hata, "Japanese-Soviet Confrontation," pp. 140-166; and Hata, "The Army's Move into Northern Indochina," in *Fateful Choice*, ed. Morley.

[205] Crowley, *Japan's Quest for Autonomy*, pp. 313–314.

general the Cabinet should not be consulted."[206] The military's preeminent position in the decision-making arena enabled the services to marginalize or simply ignore the isolated calls for moderation and caution that occasionally emerged from other quarters. Had prevailing strategic conceptions not been so insulated from wider debate, they may have been exposed and moderated before leading to the fateful decisions of 1941.

Conclusions

From 1931 to 1937, Japan succeeded in building a limited empire on the Asian mainland which contributed to the metropole's economic well-being and enhanced Japan's strategic position in Northeast Asia. Between 1937 and 1941, Japan's imperial ambition led to dramatically different results. Elites adopted overly competitive policies and failed to respond to clear information indicating that their behavior was producing a dangerous gap between resources and strategic objectives. They proceeded to initiate a war that left the metropole economically and militarily devastated.

Japan's adjustment failure during the years before World War II was produced by the effect of high vulnerability on strategic beliefs and strategic culture. Conditions of strategic deficiency induced elites to adopt overly competitive policies in order to gain access to new resources and intimidate those powers preparing to block Japanese expansion. These policies constituted a reasonable response to an extraordinary strategic environment. In order to gain support for their extremist policies, elites sought to mold a domestic polity willing to bear the costs of imperial expansion. Ambitious strategic conceptions—principally, the Greater East Asia Co-Prosperity Sphere—were formulated both to guide policy and to shape public attitudes. Although the public was largely cordoned off from the decision-making arena, the strategic notions driving policy were affected by elite-mass linkages and the government's need to mobilize the domestic polity. A new domestic order was required if the military was to realize its goals of creating a new international order in East Asia.

The problem was that imperial expansion exacerbated, rather than ameliorated, vulnerability. The China war drained already scarce resources from the metropole. Efforts to force Western powers to accept Japanese hegemony in East Asia strengthened, rather than weakened, the determination of the major powers to resist Japanese expansion. Elites came to realize that they were leading the country toward disas-

---

[206] 47th Liaison Conference, 6 Aug. 1941, p. 123.

ter and that their policies were resulting in overextension and self-encirclement, not autarky. But this realization did not lead to the adaptation of prevailing strategic conceptions to incoming information. On the contrary, strategic plans were riddled with logical inconsistencies, and important information was either ignored or manipulated to conform to existing war plans; powerful strategic images overrode strategic logic. By 1941, the notion of the Greater East Asia Co-Prosperity Sphere had become so deeply embedded in strategic culture that abandoning imperial aspirations and withdrawing from China were virtually unthinkable. The cognitive and emotional commitment of individual decision makers to empire, the military's organizational interests in proceeding with the southern advance, and the political interests of those individuals and organizations that had staked their rise to power on imperial ambition were all components of a strategic culture that prevented elites from undertaking a much-needed reorientation of grand strategy. Those individuals willing to look more soberly at the strategic landscape were effectively silenced or removed from the policy community. Elites, entrapped in their own strategic conceptions, tried desperately to escape from vulnerability but succeeded only in intensifying the nation's predicament.

It is not only declining powers that fall prey to the self-destructive tendencies that can be induced by vulnerability. Adjustment failures are not restricted to nations seeking to cling to an imperial past. On the contrary, elites in rising states aspiring to acquire empire also entrap themselves in strategic conceptions that produce self-defeating behavior.

[6]

Germany

"This war represents the German Revolution, a greater political event than the French Revolution of the last century. . . . There is not a diplomatic tradition which has not been swept away. . . . We used to have discussions in this House about the balance of power . . . but what has really come to pass in Europe? The balance of power has been entirely destroyed."[1] With these words, Benjamin Disraeli accurately foresaw that Prussia's victory in the Franco-Prussian War and the consequent unification of Germany were to alter fundamentally the European balance of power. Propelled by rapid industrialization and population growth, Germany became, by 1914, the dominant economic and military power on the Continent. When combined with the aggressive strains of nationalism that took root among German elites and masses during this period, the rise of German power was to have disastrous consequences for Europe.

The path of German ascendance after 1871 cannot be seen as a continuum. On the contrary, 1897—the year in which German decision makers formulated plans to build a world-class navy—marks a critical turning point. From 1871 to 1897, German leaders took advantage of the country's rising economic power to enlarge Germany's political influence on the Continent. Bismarck succeeded in establishing Germany as the key player in a network of European alliances. These diplomatic efforts to enhance Germany's position in Europe were accompanied by only a limited increase in military capability. Bismarck, in order to avoid the formation of a coalition intent on blocking German ascendance, was careful not to pose a serious military threat to other European powers. Germany also acquired formal colonies in West Africa, East Africa, and the western Pacific during this period. In comparison with the imperial possessions of France and Britain, however,

---

[1] Benjamin Disraeli in the House of Commons, 9 Feb. 1871, cited in J. C. G. Rohl, *From Bismarck to Hitler: The Problem of Continuity in Germany History* (New York: Barnes and Noble, 1970), p. 23.

Germany's overseas empire was relatively limited in scope. Both the German public and the ruling elite remained ambivalent about the value of overseas colonies. More often than not, German decision makers were prepared to negotiate colonial differences with rival powers and to accept settlements that did not favor Germany's position in the periphery. In both the core and periphery, Bismarck pursued competitive, but not overly ambitious, policies.

After 1897, German elites relied primarily on a military buildup to enhance their country's international position. They assumed that the construction of a world-class navy would compel Europe's other major powers to acquiesce to Germany's rise to continental predominance. But by rapidly increasing the size of their navy and, later, their army, German elites succeeded only in surrounding the country with a militarily preponderant coalition of France, Russia, and Britain. Unlike the other powers examined in this book, Germany did not fall prey to excessive ambition in the periphery. Even after elites perceived high levels of metropolitan vulnerability as a result of the formation of the Triple Entente, German policy toward colonial empire continued to be informed by attitudes of compromise and, at times, disinterest. Germany did, however, fall prey to self-encirclement. German elites reacted to the formation of the Triple Entente by adopting overly competitive policies aimed at fragmenting the opposing coalition. The blocking coalition, however, responded to German threats by increasing its cohesion and military strength. Rather than reversing course, German leaders continued to pursue expansionist policies; they instigated a self-defeating war against the Triple Entente despite information indicating that the chances of victory were slim.

Two important questions emerge. First, what were the causes of Germany's self-destructive behavior? Why did German elites pursue policies that succeeded only in pitting the country against a superior coalition of adversaries? Second, why did Germany fall prey only to self-encirclement in the core and not to overextension in the periphery as well? Why was German behavior toward overseas empire so restrained?

These questions can be answered by examining the relationship between vulnerability—caused by both international and domestic threats—and shifts in elite beliefs and strategic culture. Between 1870 and 1897, German decision makers perceived relatively low levels of metropolitan vulnerability and ruled over a domestic polity that, though divisive, allowed effective governance through logrolling between the traditional agricultural aristocracy and the emerging industrial elite. Conditions of strategic sufficiency led to policies of selective expansion. Bismarck succeeded in establishing Germany as the pivotal actor in Europe by serving as the diplomatic broker among the major powers. He also acquired a limited overseas empire. Bismarck pursued peripheral expansion not because he believed in the intrinsic strategic or economic value of colonies, but because they played an instrumental role in his international and domestic strategies. Bismarck appreciated that geographic considerations—Germany was sandwiched between two major land powers—prevented the allocation of significant resources to peripheral missions. But he used colonies at once to manipulate Germany's relationship with France and Britain and to facilitate the domestic alliance among industrialists, traders, and Junkers. Elites did not attempt to sell peripheral expansion to the German polity. As a result, the public, the bureaucracy, and the military showed little interest in overseas expansion. Peripheral empire remained in the realm of high politics as a tool of statecraft. Despite the acquisition of colonies, overseas empire did not become embedded in strategic culture.

After 1897, an ambitious naval program replaced Bismarck's astute diplomacy as the main means of enhancing German influence in Europe. The naval buildup was to play a critical role in countering political vulnerability at home as well as in extending German influence abroad. At the same time that they began building a battlefleet, decision makers sought to stimulate nationalist sentiment among the German public. The traditional aristocracy found itself increasingly threatened by the rise of the Social Democrats. Nationalism was to transcend factional strife, win the support of the middle classes for the government, and encourage the populace to make the sacrifices necessary to pursue a policy of weltpolitik. Resort to nationalism initially succeeded as a means of maintaining domestic unity and garnering support for external ambition. At the core of the government's domestic strategy was the alliance between iron and rye. This alliance was consolidated at the turn of the century through logrolling *(Sammlungspolitik):* industry received the battlefleet while agriculture secured protective tariffs.

But the logroll was, by 1908, to fall prey to divisive debates over economic policy. Fragmented conservative forces, the rising power of the Social Democrats, and an uncooperative Reichstag effectively paralyzed the government. By this time, as well, Germany's naval program and increasingly intransigent behavior, rather than improving the country's position on the Continent, had stimulated Anglo-German antagonism and produced the balancing behavior that united Britain, France, and Russia in the Triple Entente. From 1906 onward, German decision makers perceived high levels of metropolitan vulnerability. Successive German efforts to use compellent strategies to fragment the Triple Entente only produced the opposite effect. By the end of the decade, elites thus faced simultaneously acute domestic threats and a robust international coalition committed to blocking German ascendance.

It was at this point that elites found themselves entrapped in the expansionist strategic conceptions that they had earlier propagated. Many German elites in the years preceding the outbreak of war came to realize that they could well be leading the country toward disaster. The naval buildup, far from enhancing Germany's position on the Continent, had left the country diplomatically isolated and surrounded by a coalition of preponderant military strength. Nevertheless, German elites were unable to reverse course. They found themselves swept along by the strengthening currents of nationalism that they had stirred up. External ambition had temporarily succeeded in defusing domestic opposition and strengthening Germany's international position. But the costs were extremely high. The nationalist sentiment that German elites cultivated for instrumental reasons turned into a rabid chauvinism that the government could not control. Political survival came to conflict with strategic pragmatism. Furthermore, the military became convinced that conflict could not be avoided and favored launching a preventive war; its central roles, missions, and organizational interests were structured accordingly. Although some top decision makers did attempt to resist the strong currents of nationalism stirred up among the populace, others bought into and sincerely believed the grandiose strategic conceptions originally crafted for public consumption. Overseas empire had never been sold to the German polity; elites were not pressed by domestic forces to pursue indiscriminate expansion in the periphery. But weltpolitik had become embedded in strategic culture; breaking the country's encirclement by the Triple Entente and establishing continental hegemony became irreversible political imperatives for German leaders. Decision makers were pushed toward war by the forces of nationalism and images of continental dominance that they had themselves concocted. Elites were entrapped in a strategic culture of their own making.

1870–1897: Bismarck's Continental Diplomacy and the Acquisition of Peripheral Empire

Strategic Assessments

The newly unified German state emerged into a relatively benign international environment. Germany's confidence in its military prowess was running high after three successive victories: against Denmark in 1864, against Austria in 1866, and against France in 1870–1871.[2] Furthermore, elites saw no pressing threats on the horizon. France's defeat and its loss of Alsace and Lorraine indeed left a legacy of ill will toward Germany. But the French army was not capable of waging an offensive war to recover lost territory. Although Germany and France maintained ground forces of roughly equivalent size, Prussia had demonstrated its military superiority in 1870–1871. The rapid growth of the German population only drove home to the French the futility of seeking to recover by force their lost territories. In 1871, Germany's population was already greater than that of France. During the second half of the nineteenth century, the German population grew by over 50 percent while the French grew by only 10 percent.[3] By 1915, the German population stood at 70 million, the French at 40 million.

Through the 1870s, German elites showed little concern about threats from the east, largely because Germany enjoyed cordial relations with Russia. After the deterioration of Russo-German relations during the 1880s, the General Staff did begin to worry about the possibility of having to fight France and Russia simultaneously. Forces levels climbed steadily from roughly 400,000 in the early 1870s to roughly 485,000 by 1890. Even though these troop levels left German forces considerably outnumbered, the military remained confident of its ability to counter the Russian threat by undertaking limited, offensive strikes into Poland and holding a forward line of defense. The General Staff assumed that the adversary's organizational weaknesses would offset its numerical superiority.[4] In 1887, in response to information that France and Russia were exploring the possibility of alliance, the military urged that Germany and Austria wage a preventive war against Russia. Bismarck, however, restrained the General Staff and ensured that Germany made no threatening gestures toward the Russians.[5] In response to a rapprochement and eventual military convention between France and Russia (1891–1893), the Germans increased force levels by some 70,000, to approximately 555,000. But to secure the bill's passage through the Reichstag in 1893, the military was also forced to decrease the length of service from three years to two.[6] After 1893, German force levels increased only gradually until 1912.

[2] Gordon Craig, *The Politics of the Prussian Army, 1640–1945* (New York: Oxford University Press, 1955), p. 217.

[3] Hajo Holborn, *A History of Modern Germany, 1840–1945* (Princeton: Princeton University Press, 1969), p. 233.

[4] Craig, *Politics of the Prussian Army*, pp. 275–276.

[5] Ibid., p. 268.

[6] Ibid., pp. 243–244; Gordon Craig, *Germany, 1866–1945* (New York: Oxford University Press, 1978), pp. 237–239; and Holborn, *Modern Germany*, p. 320.

The absence of sharp increases in the size of the army between 1893 and 1912 stemmed in part from the military's desire to preserve the social homogeneity of the officer corp.[7] Yet it was also an indication that German elites simply did not sense the need for more ambitious war preparations. Despite the prospect of fighting a ground war on two fronts, the General Staff developed war plans that left elites confident of Germany's ability to cope with simultaneous threats from the east and west. During the 1870s, Helmuth Count von Moltke (the elder) drew up war plans that called for massive offensives against the French at the outbreak of war. After achieving a rapid, decisive victory in the west, the bulk of Germany's forces would be shifted to the eastern front to face the Russians. These plans were based on the assumption that the French military was still disorganized and weak as a result of its defeat in 1871; a quick victory against French forces would be possible.[8] Furthermore, because Germany and Russia remained on good terms throughout the 1870s, elites saw little chance of conflict between the two countries. The German military also calculated that Russia, because of its poor administrative capabilities and disorganized army, would never risk initiating a war against Germany "unless it found an ally in western Europe," a development that was quite remote.[9]

Improvements in French military capability and the deterioration of Russo-German relations after 1878 led to a reorientation of war planning. Moltke by 1879 had decided that German success in a two-front war would now depend on holding in the west and sending the bulk of the army to the east to engage in operations against the Russians. After occupying Poland and stopping a Russian advance, the Germans would then be able to concentrate almost exclusively on operations against the French. These plans were essentially defensive in orientation; German forces were to block the French in the west and undertake a limited offensive in the east in order to halt the Russians. Moltke's strategy served as the basis for Germany's war plans until Alfred Count von Schlieffen, who became chief of the General Staff in 1891, reoriented planning toward the need for initial offensives in the west.[10]

The German navy evolved slowly during Bismarck's leadership. The French and British maintained far superior fleets, but neither posed a threat to German security or trading interests. In 1883, seven armored

---

[7] Hans-Ulrich Wehler, *The German Empire, 1871–1918*, trans. Kim Traynor (Leamington Spa: Berg, 1985), p. 159; and Craig, *Politics of the Prussian Army*, pp. 234–238.
[8] Craig, *Politics of the Prussian Army*, p. 274.
[9] Ibid.
[10] Ibid., p. 279.

frigates and four armored corvettes formed Germany's first tactically unified group of warships. Concentration on the military balance on land dampened enthusiasm for a naval buildup. Operational planning focused primarily on coastal defense.[11] Increased attention and resources were focused on the navy after 1888, when Wilhelm II became emperor. In 1888–1889, the Reichstag approved funds for Germany's first four battleships. In 1895, funds were appropriated for five additional capital ships. The kaiser had a keen interest in seeing Germany acquire a high-seas fleet; he played a key role in the decision to build capital ships.[12] But, during the first half of the 1890s, Germany was not attempting to challenge British naval supremacy in European waters or to counter immediate threats to the nation's security. Rather, the kaiser was seeking to put Germany on the map in naval terms and to stake Germany's new place in the international hierarchy.

Awareness of the pace and scope of the country's economic development bolstered favorable assessments of the strategic environment. German industry during the second half of the nineteenth century experienced explosive growth of unprecedented proportions. The spread of a rail network facilitated both access to raw materials and the distribution of finished product. Technological innovations, especially in the production of steel, gave dramatic boosts to heavy industry. In the space of only a few decades, Germany caught up with and then surpassed Britain in key areas of industrial production. By 1910, German factories produced twice as much steel as British firms and 50 percent more pig iron.[13]

At the time, German elites did not fully appreciate the potential impact of such rapid and extensive economic development on their country's international position. As discussed in earlier chapters, it was not until World War I that the elites of major powers began to understand the integral links between industrial capability and military might. Nevertheless, German elites were aware that the economic changes the country was experiencing had profound implications. The rise of a working class and of a wealthy industrial elite challenged the traditional predominance of the landed aristocracy. Diplomats and traders alike also recognized that new opportunities were opening up and that Germany's position in the international order was not commensurate with its capabilities. It was within this milieu that notions of weltpolitik and German expansionism took root. Some particularly

[11] Holger Herwig, *"Luxury" Fleet: The Imperial German Navy, 1888–1918* (London: Allen and Unwin, 1980), pp. 14–15.
[12] Ibid., pp. 17–32.
[13] Holborn, *Modern Germany*, p. 376.

astute observers sensed the building momentum quite early on. Edmund Jorg wrote in 1871 that "it was no exaggeration but the truth when, months ago, it was proclaimed in Berlin that the new German Reich must be a *Weltreich*, strong enough to defeat, without alliances or treaties, not only any other power but a coalition of all foreign powers."[14]

Dealing with the Adversary

Between 1871 and 1897, German elites pursued a mixed strategy of deterrence and compellence in both the core and periphery. In Europe, Bismarck sought to establish Germany as the key diplomatic actor. His goal was to broker the European balance of power. Bismarck also acquired a limited empire in the periphery. Colonial expansion was intended in large part to enhance Germany's diplomatic leverage in Europe. Bismarck used colonial rivalries to manipulate relations among European powers. But he was careful to moderate imperial expansion and avoid overseas commitments that would drain metropolitan strength or irreversibly alienate imperial competitors.

During the 1870s and 1880s, Bismarck wove an elaborate network of European alliances that is far too intricate to describe in any detail. David Calleo has concisely summarized the fundamentals of Bismarck's alliance system:

> Essentially, Bismarck's celebrated foreign policy consisted of a complex set of agreements meant to keep all the other powers perpetually off balance. Austria, Italy, and Russia were embraced in German alliances, thus denying their support to French plans for revenge and containing their own rivalries with each other. The rivalry of Russia and Austria-Hungary was to be contained by their mutual alliance with Germany, the Dreikaiserbund, while the tensions between Italy and Austria-Hungary were to be controlled by Germany within the Triple Alliance. Meanwhile, the French were encouraged in those colonial ambitions that guaranteed friction with Britain and Italy. Finally, Bismarck sought to maneuver the British into a certain dependence by encouraging them to guarantee Turkey against Russia and France. Russia, thus restrained in Eastern Europe by Germany's diplomatic embrace, and in the Near East by Britain's Turkish guarantee, was supposed to expand further in Asia, where conflict with Britain and its later ally, Japan, became probable. Britain, thus menaced by the extra-European ambitions of both France and Russia, was expected to look to Germany for support. As a result of all these complex constructions, Germany was to be Europe's diplomatic arbiter. Conflict

---

[14] Jorg cited in Rohl, *From Bismarck to Hitler,* p. 24.

would be directed away from Europe so as not to disturb its local equilibrium and force Germany into dangerous choices.[15]

The principal end of Bismarck's alliance strategy was to establish Germany as the pivot of European diplomacy. He sought to do so by playing off existing rivalries and using German leverage as a tool to exacerbate and selectively assuage the vulnerabilities of other European powers. Because of Bismarck's tact and uncanny ability to desist from intrigue just before leverage became provocative threat, he was largely successful in establishing Germany as Europe's diplomatic arbiter during the 1880s. By constructing and carefully monitoring a system of *defensive* alliances, he was able to maintain a stable balance of power in Europe. To be sure, Bismarck deliberately enhanced his country's influence in Europe. But he did so through diplomatic, not military, means. While the military at times favored the use of force, Bismarck had no apparent intention of going to war to alter Germany's position in Europe. On the contrary, after unification, Bismarck seemed adamantly opposed to involving Germany in a European war. In Gordon Craig's words, "His policy was guided by the desire to avoid war, or, if that was impossible, to delay its coming as long as possible."[16] Much of Bismarck's intellectual and diplomatic energy was in fact devoted to ensuring that German behavior not appear too threatening and that increases in German power not incite the formation of an opposing coalition of superior strength.

Bismarck's successors sought to perpetuate this alliance network, but they lacked the tact necessary to sustain a careful balance between threat and reassurance. In 1890, the new chancellor, General Leo Count von Caprivi, allowed the Russian Reinsurance Treaty to lapse, paving the way for the Franco-Russian alliance of 1893. This outcome greatly constrained Germany's room for maneuver. Alliance with Britain was an obvious way of balancing against France and Russia, but this option was soon precluded by the naval program on which German elites embarked in 1897–1898. Germany was left to rely on the Triple Alliance, a coalition with Austria-Hungary and Italy which had been established in 1882 and renewed in 1887. These developments set the stage for the bloc system that was to emerge after the turn of the century, a system that allied Germany with two second-class military powers.

It was in large part because Bismarck was aware of the dangers involved in diplomatic maneuvering on the Continent—and the potential

---

[15] David Calleo, *The German Problem Reconsidered: Germany and the World Order, 1870 to the Present* (Cambridge: Cambridge University Press, 1978), p. 10.
[16] Craig, *Politics of the Prussian Army*, p. 268.

for fixed, competing blocs to emerge—that he relied heavily on Germany's participation in colonial affairs as a means of managing his alliance system in Europe. Existing literature on Germany's acquisition of colonial empire during the 1880s falls into two main camps. One group of historians argues that Bismarck's pursuit of colonial empire was intended only as a lever for calibrating the European alliance system.[17] Another group explains Bismarck's behavior as the product of domestic political pressures.[18] I argue that both international and domestic motives colored Bismarck's behavior in the periphery. He pursued empire in order to manipulate relations with France and Britain. At the same time, he was using colonial expansion as a tool for managing domestic politics. In both the international and domestic realms, Bismarck pursued empire for largely instrumental reasons; he had little interest in overseas possessions per se and thought they would only drain the resources of the state. He therefore made few efforts to sell overseas empire to the German people and did not instruct the bureaucracy and the military to focus more attention and resources on the periphery. Accordingly, the wider elite community and the public at large generally shared Bismarck's skepticism about the value of peripheral empire. As becomes evident below, the absence of efforts to manipulate public attitudes and reshape the roles and missions of elite institutions helps explain why Germany, after 1897, did not fall prey to overextension in the periphery. I present this argument by first examining the international motives for colonial expansion and then considering domestic forces in the following section.

The German government began formal annexation of territory in Africa in 1884 and 1885, but these bouts of colonial expansion were the product more of serendipitous events than of premeditation. In 1883, the German trader Adolph Luderitz obtained economic control of much of Southwest Africa's coast by signing a treaty with a local chief. Britain challenged Luderitz's position, claiming that it infringed on British rights in the area between Angola and the Cape Colony. The German government intervened on Luderitz's behalf, but only to resist the British claim, not to extend a German one. It was only after Bismarck had been affronted by Britain's failure to respond promptly to his protestations that he decided to claim Southwest Africa as a

---

[17] The best example of this approach is A. J. P. Taylor, *Germany's First Bid for Colonies, 1884–1885: A Move in Bismarck's European Policy* (Archon Books, 1967).
[18] See Woodruff Smith, *The German Colonial Empire* (Chapel Hill: University of North Carolina Press, 1978); Craig, *Germany*, p. 117; and Holborn, *Modern Germany*, p. 244.

German protectorate.[19] Bismarck also extended protection to other areas in West Africa where German traders had already established themselves; Togoland and Cameroon were the next additions to the empire. Existing trading posts also led to a handful of colonial acquisitions in the Pacific.

A German colony in East Africa was virtually forced on Bismarck by Karl Peters, a particularly adventuresome and aggressive trader. Peters presented German East Africa as a fait accompli to Bismarck, who was initially reluctant to extend state protection to the territory. Peters forced Bismarck's hand by threatening to offer the territory to Belgium if the German government proved unwilling to act. Though Bismarck finally acquiesced to Peters's claims near the coast, he publicly disavowed any official sanction of the trader's forays into the African interior. The German government explicitly refused to recognize treaties that Peters had negotiated in Uganda, Somaliland, and Madagascar.[20] Herbert Bismarck, the chancellor's son, explained why his father was hesitant to honor Peters's claims: "Salisbury's friendship is worth more to us than the whole of East Africa; my father is of the same opinion."[21]

Bismarck was clearly mindful of the need to limit the scope of Germany's colonial claims in order to avoid direct confrontation with Britain. On the other hand, it was competition with the British over Southwest Africa that initially induced Bismarck to extend formal state protection to German traders in Africa. It therefore appears that one of Bismarck's main motivations for seeking peripheral empire was to regulate Germany's relations with Britain and Europe's other imperial powers. This assessment is in fact consistent with the trajectory of Germany's colonial policy after 1884. Because documentary sources on the motivations behind Bismarck's policies are not available, it is necessary to infer motivations from behavior. The following points support the assertion that the goal of manipulating the European alliance system played a key role in shaping Germany's colonial policy.

First, in the years following Germany's initial annexations, Bismarck extensively used his foothold in the periphery to manage relations with Britain. Inasmuch as Germany's colonies bordered on important British territories, negotiations on border and territorial swaps were ongoing throughout the 1880s. Germany's presence in Africa also allowed Bismarck to play a more central role in the colonial rivalry be-

[19] Mary Evelyn Townsend, *The Rise and Fall of Germany's Colonial Empire, 1884–1918* (New York: Howard Fertig, 1966), pp. 89–91; and Taylor, *Germany's First Bid for Colonies*, pp. 39–44.
[20] Townsend, *Rise and Fall of Germany's Colonial Empire*, pp. 133–141.
[21] Cited in ibid, p. 115.

tween Britain and France, a rivalry piqued by France's exclusion from dual control in Egypt in 1881–1882. From 1884 until his fall from power in 1890, Bismarck oscillated between supporting British and French colonial claims, hoping to influence one power through friendship and the other through threat. He appears to have had little interest in the substantive territorial issues at stake; rather, he wanted to enhance Germany's role as the pivot of the alliance system by serving as the arbiter of Franco-British colonial competition.[22] Bismarck's hosting of the 1884 Berlin Conference convened to settle colonial disputes lends further support to this argument.

Second, the location of German colonies and Bismarck's readiness to make territorial concessions are indicative of an imperial strategy motivated by instrumental concerns. The areas colonized by Germany did not hold much economic promise. Their unprofitability was one reason why they had not yet been claimed by other European powers. Bismarck appears to have been looking for a foothold in Africa, not a thriving overseas empire. Furthermore, Bismarck was careful not to make claims that Britain or France would have found particularly irksome or threatening. As Holborn observes, Bismarck avoided behavior that would threaten "truly vital British interests" in Africa.[23] He publicly disavowed the claims of German traders if he thought they would bring Germany into direct conflict with French or British interests. Bismarck adopted a generally conciliatory stance in settling colonial disputes with Britain. He recognized that because of its location, Germany could not afford to allocate significant resources to the periphery or allow colonial rivalries to sour Germany's relations with the major European powers. To those who claimed that Germany had to adopt a more competitive stance in the periphery, Bismarck retorted, "Your map of Africa is very fine, but my map of Africa is here in Europe. Here is Russia and here is France and here we are in the middle. That is my map of Africa."[24] One of his principal objectives in negotiations during the late 1880s was to trade territory in Africa for Heligoland, an island off the coast of Germany held by Britain. In this instance, Bismarck was explicitly attempting to parlay Germany's position in the periphery into a gain on the Continent. Overall, Bismarck's behavior was suggestive not of a statesman in search of a colonial empire, but of one seeking to use peripheral empire as a source of leverage to further his continental designs.

---

[22] For details of this diplomatic maneuvering, see Townsend, *Rise and Fall of Germany's Colonial Empire*, pp. 101–108; Taylor, *Germany's First Bid for Colonies*; and P. Gifford and W. Louis, *Britain and Germany in Africa* (New Haven: Yale University Press, 1967).

[23] Holborn, *Modern Germany*, p. 245.

[24] Cited in Craig, *Germany*, pp. 116–117.

Third, Bismarck's ambivalence toward overseas empire was demonstrated by his insistence that the costs of colonial acquisition be absorbed by the companies operating in the periphery, not by the state. For the chancellor, overseas colonies, far from being a source of national strength, represented a drain on national resources. To those who argued that a peripheral empire was needed for economic reasons, Bismarck retorted that "for Germany to acquire colonies would be like a poverty-stricken Polish nobleman providing himself with silks and sables when he needed shirts."[25] From the outset, he assumed that the costs of colonial administration and defense would be the responsibility of German trading companies, not the German people.[26] As Bismarck told the Reichstag, he wanted to avoid the familiar trappings of European colonialism: "I repeat that I am opposed to colonies, that is, to the kind of colonies where officials must be placed and garrisons established." Bismarck argued that the Reichstag was also unwilling to allow the state to shoulder the burden of imperialism: "The Imperial Government . . . cannot assume . . . the support of a [colonial] bureaucracy and a military, so long as it is opposed by an antagonistic Reichstag."[27] Because the trading companies proved unable to support the costs of colonial administration, the state was gradually forced to assume financial responsibility for the colonies. But Bismarck succeeded in relegating the colonies to the periphery of governmental affairs. The military remained largely uninterested in the colonies. While Britain had a major portion of its ground and naval forces deployed in the periphery, Germany had only a handful of soldiers in the colonies. The colonial bureaucracy also remained small and staffed by poorly qualified personnel.[28]

After Bismarck's fall from power in 1890, the new chancellor, Caprivi, and his chief councillor in the Foreign Ministry, Friedrich von Holstein, continued to pursue a cautious and restrained colonial policy, one that was oriented more toward adjusting the European alliance system than toward peripheral expansion. Caprivi consummated the deal for Heligoland that Bismarck had been pursuing. The Germans granted Britain major tracts of land in East Africa, leaving themselves only a small claim along the coast. But, in return, they received Heligoland—and soon developed a base for German U-boats on the island. Craig explains that "Caprivi and Holstein had no enthusiasm for colonial acqui-

[25] Bismarck cited in Townsend, *Rise and Fall of Germany's Colonial Empire*, p. 60.

[26] Townsend, *Rise and Fall of Germany's Colonial Empire*, p. 119.

[27] Cited in ibid., pp. 157, 156.

[28] Smith, *German Colonial Empire*, pp. 133–134. The Foreign Office assumed responsibility for colonial affairs until 1906, when a separate office of state was created to handle colonial administration.

sition. To them, the lopsidedness of the bargain was inconsequential as long as it laid the basis for agreements with the British in Europe."[29] Kaiser Wilhelm agreed, noting that Zanzibar's only importance "lay in its being an asset for swapping."[30]

During the second half of the 1890s, the German government—with Wilhelm himself at the helm—began to adopt a more ambitious colonial policy. Germany acquired few new territories but became less willing to compromise in disputes in the periphery; the kaiser sought to exacerbate colonial rivalries, not to moderate them. The causes of this shift in policy are embedded in the domestic political chaos of the 1890s. Further analysis therefore awaits discussion of domestic politics in the following section.

Establishing Germany as the diplomatic pivot of Europe was the primary aim of German grand strategy between 1871 and the middle of the 1890s. Elites were aware that political unification, rapid economic growth, and conditions of strategic sufficiency opened new opportunities for them to shape a political and strategic landscape more conducive to Germany's interests. They sought to attain their objectives through diplomacy and a system of defensive alliances, not through force or territorial expansion on the Continent. Germany's war plans were essentially defensive in orientation, and elites, for the most part, did not see war as the path to security. In the periphery as well, German elites pursued a cautious policy of selective expansion, aimed principally at enhancing German leverage in continental affairs. Decision makers during this period were quite successful in establishing Germany as the pivotal player on the European continent. This achievement was in large part due to Bismarck's ability to use threats and guarantees to manipulate foreign powers. Bismarck drove hard bargains but was remarkably astute about the need to rein in German ambition before it provoked a preponderant opposing coalition. In both the core and periphery, German ambition was kept in check and Bismarck resorted to a careful mix of deterrence and compellence to regulate European affairs.

As far as strategic priorities are concerned, German elites devoted virtually exclusive attention to continental affairs and the protection of the homeland. This preoccupation with developments in the core was largely a function of geography: with major powers on the east and west, Germany could little afford to devote resources to peripheral missions. Yet, especially when compared to the French, who also faced

[29] Craig, *Germany*, pp. 235–236.
[30] Cited in Townsend, *Rise and Fall of Germany's Colonial Empire*, p. 162.

pressing continental requirements, it is striking that German decision makers and the military showed such disinterest in colonial issues. Unlike their French counterparts, German elites were relatively immune to arguments about the reputational importance of peripheral empire. Coming off successive military victories on the Continent and operating under conditions of strategic sufficiency, elites did not perceive a need to rely on demonstrations of resolve to affect outcomes or to turn to overseas empire to affirm great-power status. They focused on accumulating material power and diplomatic leverage in the core and treated empire as a burden, not as a source of national strength or prestige. The colonies served largely an instrumental role in strategy: they were tools for adjusting the European alliance system. German grand strategy was informed by a clear sense of strategic priorities and by appreciation that Germany's future lay in continental affairs, not in the pursuit of overseas empire.

Domestic Considerations

To what extent did domestic forces shape German strategy toward both the core and the periphery? Domestic political developments and German foreign policy were integrally linked from the 1870s onward. Bismarck's ability to integrate the domestic and international components of his strategy is key to understanding his success in establishing Germany as the pivotal actor in Europe. The inability of his successors to keep domestic and international policy in synch is similarly essential to understanding why Germany eventually embarked on a self-destructive path of excessive ambition after 1897.

Private Economic Interests. Private economic interests had little reason to challenge Bismarck's strategy in the core during the first decade after unification. Farmers, merchants, and industrialists were primarily concerned about preserving good trading relationships with Europe's major powers. Heavy industry was still relatively undeveloped, and there was therefore little domestic pressure for a major military buildup. For the most part, the economic interests of the business community were compatible with the diplomatic objectives of the government.

Private economic interests played a more direct role in shaping peripheral strategy. Before unification, the fragmentation of the political and economic system kept segregated those interests that might have otherwise coalesced around imperial expansion.[31] The trading commu-

---

[31] Townsend, *Rise and Fall of Germany's Colonial Empire,* pp. 32–36.

nity was in fact opposed to German imperialism for fear that it would alienate Britain and thereby impair the increasing flow of goods both within and outside Europe.[32] Initial support for colonialism came mainly from the agrarian community, which argued that colonies were needed to resettle the increasing number of Germans searching for arable land. As overseas trade increased during the second half of the 1800s, manufacturers and shippers gradually took interest in peripheral expansion and added an economic dimension to the colonial movement. Legislators were, however, still unconvinced of the value of colonies. A bill to subsidize German traders in Samoa, for example, was soundly defeated in the Reichstag in 1880. In part to overcome such opposition, the numerous societies that sprouted to represent both emigrationist and economic interests in colonialism joined forces in 1882 to found the Kolonialverein. Its mandate was "to extend to a larger circle the realization of the necessity of applying national energy to the field of colonization."[33]

During the late 1870s and early 1880s, the government responded to these growing pressures by encouraging and facilitating overseas trade. In 1876, several treaties protecting German traders were negotiated. Coaling stations were established in the Ellice and Gilbert Islands, the Duke of York Islands, and on the northern coast of New Britain. German firms also clearly contributed to the eventual decision to acquire formal empire. The extent to which private interests influenced Bismarck's peripheral strategy is, however, difficult to judge. On the one hand, traders were responsible for establishing the initial outposts on which the German government's colonial claims were based. From the mid-1870s onward, trading interests put increasing pressure on Bismarck to stake Germany's claim in the periphery or, at the very least, to extend official protection to German firms operating abroad.[34] Individuals with business interests overseas also represented a significant portion of those who formally joined the various colonial societies. On the other hand, membership in these societies remained low, and the economic interests at stake were quite limited. The Kolonialverein had roughly 10,000 members by 1885.[35] The German Colonial Society was founded in 1887 to serve as an umbrella organization for several new groups that had sprouted. Membership rose quite slowly: by 1893, the colonial lobby had about 17,500 members.[36] This lack of enthusiasm was in large part a function of the economic setbacks

[32] Smith, *German Colonial Empire*, p. 5.
[33] Townsend, *Rise and Fall of Germany's Colonial Empire*, p. 82.
[34] Ibid., pp. 62–63.
[35] Ibid., p. 83.
[36] Smith, *German Colonial Empire*, p. 42.

encountered by many firms operating in the colonies. Trading companies closed regularly during the late 1880s, forcing the state to assume the costs of colonial administration. Many individuals who invested in colonial enterprise saw their money disappear.[37] Furthermore, Germany's trade with its overseas empire remained negligible. By the turn of the century, the metropole's trade with its colonies represented only 0.5 percent of total foreign trade.[38]

Industry and finance, well aware that colonial expansion showed little economic promise, remained unexcited about devoting resources to the development of overseas empire. Given the pace of economic growth in the metropole itself, there was little incentive to invest in the colonies, especially in light of the evident risks involved. As Bismarck noted, "The national significance of colonies is not appreciated or supported by capital or business." Caprivi agreed: "Germans have so little confidence in the oversea policy that they prefer government securities which are considered safer."[39] Paradoxically, these attitudes did not mean that big business actively opposed the colonial movement. On the contrary, industry and capital offered guarded support for imperial expansion. They did not value the colonies themselves, but calculated that colonialism would induce the government to adopt a range of economic policies more compatible with their interests. For industry, imperial expansion was to foster a more proindustry, market-oriented outlook among elites. Finance hoped that colonialism would encourage the government to take a more active role in protecting overseas investment and German enterprise more generally.[40] In short, even though industry and capital had little interest in colonies per se, they hoped to use imperialism to further their own ends.

Colonialism thus appealed to several influential sectors of German society. Its immediate economic attraction was restricted to traders and a small number of farmers in search of arable land. But the country's emerging economic elite of industrialists and financiers also supported colonialism as an indirect means of inducing a broad shift in the government's economic policy. The cross-cutting appeal of colonialism opened opportunities for Bismarck to use imperialism to his domestic political advantage.

Domestic Politics. Between 1871 and 1914, a political system dominated by the preindustrial, aristocratic elite clashed head-on with the

---

[37] Townsend, *Rise and Fall of Germany's Colonial Empire*, p. 155.
[38] Ibid., p. 238.
[39] Cited in ibid, pp. 156, 161.
[40] Smith, *German Colonial Empire*, pp. 120–126.

forces of modernization unleashed by industrialization. The emergence of an industrial elite, the empowerment of the working class, and mounting pressure for political reform posed a direct challenge to the ruling aristocracy. The political institutions erected after unification were to strike a balance between traditional monarchy and parliamentary democracy. Yet the traditional elite proved unwilling to part with political privilege. Instead, the landed aristocracy allied with the new industrial elite to resist the forces of political modernization and to counter the rising power of the Social Democrats. The struggle of traditional elites to preserve their political dominance in the face of profound social change exercised a pervasive influence on both the process and substance of German politics. I now show that Germany's acquisition of empire was, at least to some extent, a manifestation of Bismarck's effort to use foreign success as a foil to deal with domestic threats and as a means of uniting a domestic polity fragmented by deep social and political cleavages.

Even before unification, Bismarck used foreign policy as a domestic political tool. One of Bismarck's own maxims was, "As long as we gain respect abroad, we can get away with a great deal at home."[41] On his appointment as chancellor, one newspaper predicted that Bismarck would attempt to "overcome domestic difficulties by a bold foreign policy."[42] Many historians agree that Bismarck's decision to initiate three successive wars against Denmark, Austria, and France must be understood within the context of his domestic political objectives. Military victory was to disarm the liberals and consolidate popular support for the monarchy.[43]

Unification indeed strengthened Bismarck's hand and enhanced the legitimacy of the traditional elite. A severe economic depression that lasted from 1873 to 1879, however, complicated the task of preserving domestic stability. The business community suffered from bank failures and the collapse of stock prices. The agricultural sector faced declining prices and increased competition from abroad. Widespread economic dislocation also contributed to the power of the Social Democrats. As a result, Bismarck found it increasingly difficult to maneuver the government's bills through the Reichstag.[44]

With the Junkers growing more and more isolated and outnumbered in the Reichstag, Bismarck in 1879 moved to ally the landed aristocracy with the industrial elite. The so-called Kartell, an alliance between the

---

[41] Cited in Wehler, *German Empire,* p. 24.
[42] *Kreuzzeitung,* cited in ibid.
[43] Wehler, *German Empire,* pp. 24–31.
[44] Ibid., p. 37.

National Liberals and the conservative parties, was formed around a policy of protective tariffs. Heavy industry, still in its formative stages, benefited from protection against foreign manufactured goods. Agriculture needed tariffs to bolster grain prices in the face of international competition from Russia and the United States. This alliance between "iron and rye" constituted a victory of the conservative elite over liberal forces and allowed Bismarck to maneuver around his political opponents.

The Kartell, however, was only a stop-gap measure. It allowed Bismarck temporarily to frustrate the opposition, but the composition of the Reichstag itself was outside his control. The elections of 1881 constituted a setback for the conservatives. The elections of 1884 threatened to erode further the chancellor's ability to pass legislation through the Reichstag.[45] It was within this context of growing political fragmentation that Bismarck launched his colonial policy. My argument is not that Bismarck explicitly bowed to domestic political pressure; as mentioned above, the colonial lobby was small and not that influential. But, in a manner consistent with his earlier behavior, it appears that the chancellor was seeking to use foreign success to achieve domestic political unity. Colonialism channeled disparate interests to a point of intersection: the Junkers linked colonies to emigration, traders saw economic gain, industrialists saw a move toward a market economy, and the financial community hoped for government protection of German enterprise. Bismarck was hoping to capitalize on these intersecting interests and to use colonialism as a rallying point. As Woodruff Smith explains, "Since the actual economic involvement of most German groups in the overseas empire was very small, the domestic political function of colonialism was the most important feature of colonial politics in Germany. . . . In general, colonial politics were not themselves matters of overriding concern to the parties requiring the enforcement of a consistent line but rather something to be used for varying ends in the domestic political arena."[46]

Bismarck's political strategy had limited payoffs. The initial acquisition of colonies was followed by a surge of proimperial sentiment. But this enthusiasm and the political unity it engendered did not last beyond 1885.[47] The considerations that made colonialism attractive as a domestic tool were also the undoing of this political gambit. The colonies served a largely instrumental purpose for most parties. The government and the business community were generally suspicious of the

---

[45] Craig, *Germany*, pp. 156, 168.
[46] Smith, *German Colonial Empire*, pp. 121, 145.
[47] Ibid., p. 40.

intrinsic value of colonies and made virtually no effort to sell empire to the public. As a result, the Reichstag remained fundamentally hostile to the colonial enterprise. Corruption in colonial administration, the bankruptcy of trading companies, and tales of brutality and exploitation only stiffened parliamentary and public opposition to overseas empire. By the late 1880s, as trading companies failed and were unable to absorb the costs of colonial administration, Bismarck found himself in the awkward position of having to coax a reluctant Reichstag into voting funds to sustain an overseas empire toward which he was decidedly ambivalent.[48] This was not to be the last time that foreign policies intended to unite the domestic polity would come to haunt German elites.

Bismarck's struggle to preserve the traditional political order came to a head in 1890. Two key developments precipitated his fall from power. First, the alliance between agriculture and industry unraveled in 1890 when the consensus on tariffs broke down. Manufacturing output and efficiency had improved steadily since the 1870s. As a result, industry no longer needed or wanted protection; tariffs restricted foreign trade and pushed up wages. Agriculture, on the other hand, continued to face stiff foreign competition and therefore needed tariffs to support the price of domestic grain. Second, relations between Bismarck and the kaiser grew progressively worse during the late 1880s. The core of the dispute was over how to deal with the socialists. Bismarck supported a hard line; he wanted to introduce an antisocialist bill that would effectively neutralize the left. Wilhelm was more sympathetic toward the Social Democrats and preferred some measure of political reform to Bismarck's intransigence. The antisocialist issue had further political implications: it led to a deep rift between the conservatives and the National Liberals. This break, in combination with conservative losses in the elections of February 1890, effectively meant that Bismarck could no longer maneuver legislation through the Reichstag. With the government and the Reichstag in a stalemate and dissension within the government peaking, Wilhelm decided to dismiss Bismarck.[49]

The 1890s were characterized by increasing political chaos and more direct confrontation between the traditional order and the forces of political change. Caprivi attempted to make concessions to the Centre and Radical parties in order to break the stalemate between the govern-

---

[48] Townsend, *Rise and Fall of Germany's Colonial Empire*, pp. 165–173.
[49] On the downfall of Bismarck, see Craig, *Germany*, pp. 170–179; and J. C. G. Rohl, *Germany without Bismarck: The Crisis of Government in the Second Reich, 1890–1900* (London: Batsford, 1967), pp. 27–52.

ment and the Reichstag. He also reduced the power of the chancellor to placate those calling for political reform.[50] This conciliatory approach, however, backfired. The government failed to gain the confidence of the Reichstag. In addition, Caprivi's overture to the center alienated many conservatives, leading to increased dissension within the government itself. Under attack from his colleagues, the army, and the kaiser himself, Caprivi resigned in 1894.[51] The kaiser selected Chlodwig Hohenlohe as the next chancellor, assuming that the Social Democrats would find him a more formidable adversary. Hohenlohe, however, was unable to repair the fissures that had emerged among the ruling elite; from 1894 to 1896, the government lurched from one crisis to the next. The kaiser and his ministers were frequently at odds on central policy issues.[52] The German government was in a state of effective paralysis.[53]

By 1896, the kaiser had achieved the upper hand in this intragovernmental struggle and succeeded in moderating the political chaos. Wilhelm's strategy was to move to the right and to use nationalism as a way of uniting the conservative parties and disarming the Social Democrats. The right and center were to rally behind the kaiser and his effort to expand German power. The Social Democrats would either join the cause or be branded as unpatriotic and banished to the periphery of the political arena. As Bismarck did in 1864, 1866, 1870, and 1884, the kaiser was attempting to use foreign policy as a tool of domestic politics.

---

[50] Rohl, *Germany without Bismarck*, pp. 75, 85.

[51] Craig, *Germany*, p. 261.

[52] Rohl, *Germany without Bismarck*, pp. 118–155.

[53] The fact that German elites continued to pursue moderate foreign policies despite Bismarck's fall from power and growing political chaos poses problems for Jack Snyder's focus on the importance of logrolling in producing overexpansion. The alliance between iron and rye did not suddenly appear at the turn of the century. Not long after unification in 1871, Germany's leaders turned to the coalition between industry and agriculture to consolidate their rule. Snyder argues that the moderate policies of the 1870–1890 period were the result of Bismarck's astute ability to manage domestic coalitions. In Snyder's words, Bismarck "enjoyed a stronger position as a unitary broker for coalition arrangements" than later German leaders (*Myths of Empire: Domestic Politics and International Ambition* [Ithaca: Cornell University Press, 1991], p. 99). But, from this perspective, the domestic logroll should have been particularly pernicious between 1890 and 1897, a period of relative political chaos. Nevertheless, as Snyder acknowledges, "Bismarck's successor, General Leo von Caprivi, pursued a moderately liberal policy at home and abroad" (ibid., p. 84), as did Hohenlohe. Despite two successive leaders who were particularly unsuccessful at managing domestic coalitions, Germany continued to pursue a moderate foreign policy until 1897, when the kaiser and his chief advisers—Alfred Tirpitz, Bernard von Bulow, and Johannes von Miquel—decided to proceed with a major naval buildup. This evidence casts doubt on the argument that logrolling fueled German overexpansion and was held in check only because of Bismarck's ability to manage domestic coalitions.

Wilhelm was not alone in seeing the domestic payoffs of external ambition; the military was pushing him to adopt a more ambitious foreign policy and was explicit about its domestic implications. In 1895, the state secretary of the Reich Naval Office urged the kaiser to undertake an expansive foreign policy to establish Germany's status as a great power and "to no small degree also because the great patriotic task and the economic benefits to be derived from it will offer a strong palliative against educated and uneducated Social Democrats."[54] The kaiser in 1896 was prepared to initiate a major naval building program. He agreed to postpone his plans only after his chancellor and ministers convinced him that a naval bill would precipitate a major confrontation between the government and the Reichstag and lead only to increased political chaos. The navy did not fail to express its disapproval. The head of the navy cabinet wrote that "the entire country is ignorant about the purpose and function of the Navy. We must rouse support in the Reichstag and the country as a whole."[55] Even the army, which was not looking to increase its force levels, appreciated that something had to be done to consolidate the traditional political order. In January 1897, General Alfred Count von Waldersee, chief of the General Staff from 1888 to 1891, warned the kaiser that "in view of the tremendous growth of the Social Democratic organisation, it seems . . . certain that the time is approaching when the power of the State will have to do battle with that of the working masses."[56]

The kaiser's efforts to transcend domestic strife through foreign success focused largely on the realm of colonial policy. After 1893, Wilhelm adopted a more confrontational approach toward Anglo-German relations in the periphery. He was more interested in stirring up trouble than in resolving outstanding disputes. When British and Boer troops clashed in December 1895—the so-called Jameson Raid—the kaiser wanted to send German troops to the Transvaal and urged that Germany formally annex the area. Again, he was constrained by his advisers.[57] The kaiser could not be prevented, however, from sending the Kruger Telegram, an expression of support for the Boers which enraged the British. Moreover, it is of no small importance that German military planners, in the wake of this increase in Anglo-German tensions, drafted for the first time war plans for operations against Brit-

---

[54] Cited in V. R. Berghahn, *Germany and the Approach of War in 1914* (New York: St. Martin's Press, 1973), p. 29.
[55] Rohl, *Germany without Bismarck*, pp. 167–169.
[56] Cited in ibid., pp. 217–218.
[57] Townsend, *Rise and Fall of Germany's Colonial Empire*, pp. 183–186.

ain.[58] In addition, the kaiser did succeed in pushing forward the naval building program, though in a limited way. In 1895, funds were appropriated for five battleships to be completed by 1902.[59]

The kaiser and his inner circle of military advisers were not alone in perceiving the need for a more ambitious foreign policy. The notion of Weltpolitik was beginning to permeate the military services.[60] The political parties were similarly affected. Both the National Liberals and the Centre began to move to the right and incorporated new strains of nationalism and expansionism into their party platforms.[61] Nationalistic values also began to infuse the intellectual community; universities served as a forum for the spread of new thinking about Germany's role in the world. Faculty sympathetic to the left found themselves isolated and their career paths threatened.[62] In Geoff Eley's words, nationalism "had entered the universal currency of political debate. The parties increasingly clothed themselves in the modern legitimacy of the 'national interest.'"[63] In 1896, Admiral Georg Alexander von Muller noted that a distinct shift in public attitudes was taking place: "Caprivi's policy, which is now so widely ridiculed, would have been brilliantly vindicated by history if the German people were not coming to accept an entirely different opinion of their ability and indeed their duty to expand than that expressed in our naval and colonial policy so far."[64]

The kaiser was not the first German leader to use nationalism and external ambition to deal with domestic threats; Bismarck had done so only a decade earlier. And like Bismarck, the kaiser pursued a more ambitious foreign policy not only for domestic reasons, but also because he wanted to enhance Germany's stature in the world, to make it commensurate with the nation's increasing resource base. There was, however, a crucial difference between the domestic strategies employed by the two leaders. Bismarck sought to use colonialism to unite the country, but he did not attempt to sell overseas empire to the German polity by lobbying the public and redefining the central roles and missions of elite institutions. Wilhelm, however, enlisted state institutions—the military services, the universities, the government bureaucracy—to alter public attitudes and to whip up support for a

---

[58] Paul Kennedy, *The Rise of Anglo-German Antagonism, 1860–1914* (London: Allen and Unwin, 1980), p. 221.

[59] Herwig, *"Luxury" Fleet*, p. 26.

[60] Kennedy, *Anglo-German Antagonism*, p. 221.

[61] Geoff Eley, *From Unification to Nazism: Reinterpreting the German Past* (Boston: Allen and Unwin, 1986), p. 75.

[62] Craig, *Germany*, pp. 200–206.

[63] Eley, *From Unification to Nazism*, p. 75.

[64] Cited in Rohl, *Germany without Bismarck*, p. 162.

more expansionist foreign policy. He sought to embed support for foreign ambition far more deeply among the German people and within the elite community. As a result, he was setting in motion powerful domestic forces and institutionalized strategic conceptions that would come to constrain elites when the pursuit of external ambition no longer proved desirable.

By 1897, the kaiser was ready to implement his plans for a far more ambitious foreign policy. To do so, he needed to surround himself with colleagues more sympathetic with his designs. He installed Bernard von Bulow as head of the Foreign Ministry (and as chancellor in 1900) and Alfred Tirpitz as head of the Navy Office. These appointments marked a fateful change of course. The kaiser's strategy of exporting Germany's domestic turmoil directly threatened the interests of Britain, France, and Russia and triggered the establishment of the Triple Entente. By the time elites realized that their new course was leading to the formation of an opposing coalition of superior military strength, it was too late. They had orchestrated a shift in strategic culture from which they could not escape, one that set Germany on a self-destructive path to war.

Military Services. During the 1870s and 1880s, Bismarck succeeded in keeping the political power of the military in check. After his fall from power and in the midst of the political chaos that prevailed during the 1890s, the military came to play a more important role in the formulation of German foreign policy. The services, especially the navy, encouraged the kaiser to adopt a more expansionistic policy and served as vehicles for the propagation of nationalism among the populace. Moreover, the army was one of the bastions of the conservative order and was as threatened as any sector of society by the rising power of the Social Democrats. Even though the officer corps began to accept more middle-class candidates during the 1870s, many officers still came from aristocratic backgrounds.[65] The desire to prevent the adulteration of the social composition of the corps was one of the reasons the army did not seek major increases in force levels during the years of expanding military budgets associated with the kaiser's new policies.

The military's increasing clout was to some extent the result of institutional changes that occurred slowly during the decades after unification. Although the constitution granted the war minister considerable authority in military affairs, the General Staff gradually stripped the office of its input into decision making. The constitution also gave the

---

[65] Craig, *Germany*, p. 159. Nobility comprised roughly 65% of the officer corps in 1865 and about 30% by 1913. See Wehler, *German Empire*, p. 159.

Reichstag influence in the military realm, largely through its control over the budget. The administrative reforms of 1883 somewhat reduced the scope of the Reichstag's authority over the General Staff.[66] But the most important shift in relations between the military and the Reichstag occurred during the 1890s as a result of changing attitudes within the legislature, not as a result of administrative reforms. Between 1870 and the mid-1890s, passing the military budget through the Reichstag was always a formidable task for the government. The legislature was not infrequently dissolved by the chancellor because of its unwillingness to approve funds for the services. By the 1890s, this antimilitary sentiment had dissipated. In its place was a new concern with the efficiency and quality of the country's military forces.[67] By implication, the services enjoyed a new degree of autonomy.

It would be erroneous, however, to claim that the military was primarily responsible for propagating the new strategic concepts and orchestrating the shifts in foreign policy and in public attitudes that occurred during the 1890s. The key actor behind the new course was the kaiser himself. His decision to use nationalism to counter domestic threats required the acquiescence of the military, and he found the services to be willing partners in his scheme. But the military was only one component of a ruling elite—consisting, in addition, of the Junkers, the bureaucracy, and the industrialists—struggling to preserve the traditional order. The crux of the problem after 1897 was not that the military forced decisions on the government, but that civilian and military elites, working in unison, unleashed rampant nationalism and embedded notions of weltpolitik and continental dominance in Germany's strategic culture.

Conclusions

Between 1871 and 1897, Germany's economic and military resources increased significantly in absolute and relative terms. Conditions of strategic sufficiency enabled elites to construct a European order more conducive to German interests. By pursuing a policy of selective expansion in the core and periphery, Bismarck established Germany as the pivot of an elaborate European alliance system. Germany maintained its dominant position in this system through adept diplomatic maneuvering that succeeded in playing off rivalries among the other European powers. Bismarck was careful to avoid overly competitive policies that might cause other states to balance against German power. One

---

[66] Craig, *Germany*, p. 163.
[67] Eley, *From Unification to Nazism*, p. 90.

of his main motivations for acquiring an overseas empire was to use colonial disputes as a tool for managing his alliance system. This strategy for preserving a balance of power in Europe began to unravel after 1890 because of the lapse of Germany's Reinsurance Treaty with Russia and the eventual alliance between Russia and France.

While Bismarck and his immediate successors enjoyed considerable success in attaining their goals in the international arena, they were decidedly less successful in managing domestic affairs. Bismarck relied on the alliance between industry and agriculture to preserve the traditional order and the political privilege of the aristocracy. This alliance, however, was a tenuous one and did not enable the government, except on a temporary basis, to resist the rising power of the Social Democrats or to placate an increasingly hostile Reichstag. The ruling elite put in place the institutions that would allow political modernization to follow social change, but they then prevented that modernization from occurring. The result was, in Hans-Ulrich Wehler's words, "a semi-absolutist, pseudo-constitutional military monarchy."[68]

In part to deal with these domestic tensions, Bismarck pursued a policy of colonial expansion in the mid-1880s. In this respect, imperialism served an instrumental function in both the domestic and international realms. In the midst of the political chaos of the 1890s, the kaiser again resorted to external ambition to deal with domestic threats. But fundamental differences separated Bismarck's strategy from that of Wilhelm. Whereas Bismarck sought to enhance Germany's leverage primarily through diplomatic means, Wilhelm resorted to a massive naval buildup. Bismarck was also careful to integrate the domestic and international components of his strategy. He did not combine pursuit of an ambitious foreign policy with vigorous domestic lobbying. He was therefore able to make the concessions and adjustments necessary to preserve the European balance of power without suffering on the domestic front. Wilhelm, on the other hand, pursued a more ambitious foreign policy while seeking to change public attitudes and reorient the roles and missions of elite institutions—in short, to manipulate strategic culture. In doing so, the kaiser left himself far less room for maneuver on the domestic front. Bismarck pursued policies that stimulated moderate currents of nationalism and that enhanced his influence over foreign powers, not ones that threatened their vital interests. The kaiser's policies whipped up rabid nationalism among the public and wed political and organizational interests within the elite community to a naval program that threatened to overturn the European balance of power, not just regulate it. As a result, between 1897 and 1914,

[68] Wehler, *German Empire*, p. 60.

German elites increasingly found themselves entrapped internally by a domestic polity running on the fuel of aggressive nationalism and rearmament and encircled externally by a preponderant coalition of powers seeking to resist German expansion.

1897–1914: Encirclement, Entrapment, and the Path to War

Between 1897 and 1914, the forces set in motion by the kaiser's ambitious foreign policy brought about profound changes in the political setting within Germany as well as in the European balance of power. Nationalism spread among the German populace while industrialists and naval officers rallied behind the burgeoning high seas fleet. At the same time, construction of this formidable battlefleet altered power balances and political alignments in Europe. Rather than pursuing a policy of selective expansion, German elites began to pursue external ambition in an indiscriminate fashion. The engine initially driving Germany's new expansionism was the political vulnerability of the traditional order; nationalism was being used to unite a fragmented right and to neutralize the mounting threat from the Social Democrats. Military vulnerability was, however, soon added to the equation. Britain and France formed the Entente Cordiale in 1904, and Germany's initial reaction was to seek to split the coalition. In 1906, German elites attempted to drive a wedge between France and Britain by precipitating a crisis over the status of Morocco. But Britain reacted by moving into even closer alignment with France and by continuing efforts, through fleet redistribution and construction, to offset Germany's naval program. In 1907, Britain and Russia resolved their outstanding disputes, leading to the formation of the Triple Entente. The German military now confronted the prospect of facing the combined forces of Britain, France, and Russia should war break out in Europe. Assessments began to indicate conditions of strategic deficiency, not sufficiency. German elites reacted by adopting increasingly ambitious external policies. Repeated attempts to compel adversaries to acquiesce to German demands, however, led only to increases in the cohesion and military strength of the opposing coalition. The naval race between Britain and Germany was accompanied, after 1911, by successive increases in the number of ground troops sustained by the Triple Alliance and the Triple Entente. Far from enhancing German security, Weltpolitik was leading to self-encirclement.

As in the other cases examined in this book, elites eventually recognized the fundamental flaws in their strategic design. By 1910, both civilian and military leaders were coming to appreciate that compellent policies had not produced their intended effects. Germany was diplomatically isolated and confronted with an opposing coalition of superior military strength. Elites found themselves unable, however, to divert the forces of rabid nationalism that they had set in motion to preserve the traditional order and to support the costs of an expanding military establishment. Parties across the political spectrum rallied behind expansionist foreign policies. The interests of the industrialists were wedded to the continued expansion of the fleet. Within the navy and army, organizational interests were oriented toward preparing for the preventive war that the General Staff deemed would offer Germany its best chance of victory. And many top elites had bought into the grandiose strategic conceptions originally crafted for instrumental purposes. Weltpolitik and German hegemony on the Continent had become embedded in strategic culture. The German polity could not allow the Triple Entente to stand in the way of the country's ascendance as a world power. Furthermore, the German government during the years before the outbreak of war was in a state of virtual paralysis. Not only were the Social Democrats steadily gaining ground, but the alliance between iron and rye that had been renewed in 1897 again broke down. The domestic stalemate exacerbated the government's susceptibility to the rising tide of aggressive nationalism. Scaling back Germany's external ambition and moderating the country's continental aims—the only way out of the precarious predicament in which Germany found itself by 1912—virtually disappeared from the political agenda. Fear of falling from power, the organizational interests of the military, and the cognitive and emotional commitment of elites to weltpolitik combined to prevent top decision makers from reversing course. German elites found themselves entrapped in the political forces and strategic images that they had created to deal with both domestic and international vulnerability.

Strategic Assessments

After the turn of the century, Germany continued to enjoy relatively rapid growth in its economic base and its population. Appreciation of the country's advantageous endowment of resources contributed to the growing sentiment among elites that the nation's position in the international arena was incommensurate with its power. So too did strategic assessments indicate that Germany was in good shape from a military perspective. The French army was in no position to wage an offensive war against Germany. Although the Royal Navy retained clear superiority over the German fleet throughout the prewar years, Germany did not perceive maritime inferiority as posing a direct threat to its well-being. German security depended primarily on the balance of ground forces, and Britain's ability to wage continental war was extremely limited. Russia's ground forces were numerically superior to those of Germany, but this numerical edge was more than offset by the lower quality of Russian troops, organizational and administrative weaknesses, and the absence of a rail network capable of transporting Russian divisions toward Germany's eastern border.[69]

Given Germany's preponderance of resources, there was just one path that could turn conditions of strategic sufficiency into high vulnerability. Only a coalition of Europe's major powers could offset German military strength, and it was precisely such a coalition that German behavior succeeded in bringing about. German perceptions of vulnerability were, accordingly, closely related to assessments of the cohesiveness of the Entente Cordiale and, later, of the Triple Entente. Although the Entente Cordiale was formed in 1904, it was not until 1906 that German elites became preoccupied with fear of military encirclement.[70] These fears were precipitated by the Morocco crisis of 1905–1906, in which a German attempt to split the Entente succeeded in drawing the British and French closer. British and French military staffs engaged in formal consultations, sending an inauspicious but accurate signal to German elites that Britain's years of splendid isolation were coming to an end.[71]

After 1906, elites no longer operated under the assumption of strategic sufficiency; metropolitan vulnerability was high and rising steadily. Five factors contributed to this assessment. First, in 1907, the establishment of the Triple Entente solidified an anti-German coalition of Britain, France, and Russia. Should war break out, Germany was now likely to face the combined forces of three major powers. Furthermore, Britain had decided to equip its army for continental operations. Second, Britain did not react to Germany's naval building program as German elites expected. Rather than acting as a source of leverage, the Risk Fleet *(Risikoflotte)* provoked Britain to withdraw its battlefleet from peripheral waters and to embark on an ambitious building program that would allow the Royal Navy to retain a decisive edge in the North Sea. Furthermore, the naval race fueled Anglo-German antagonism and drove Britain closer to France. Third, a German attempt to split

---

[69] A general description of the European military balance during the decade before the outbreak of World War I has already been presented in the chapters on Britain and France. More detailed discussion of German assessments of the balance after 1910 are presented in the following section. For German assessments of Russian capability, see William Wohlforth, "The Perception of Power: Russia in the Pre-1914 Balance," *World Politics*, 39 (April 1987), 353–381.

[70] Craig, *Germany*, p. 321.

[71] Holborn, *Modern Germany*, p. 328.

the adversarial coalition again backfired in 1911. This second effort to challenge France's position in Morocco furthered Franco-British military cooperation, leaving German elites increasingly isolated diplomatically and threatened militarily. Fourth, in 1912, France and Britain entered into formal naval arrangements whereby France would cover the Mediterranean while Britain concentrated its entire battlefleet in the North Sea and Atlantic. It was looking increasingly likely that Germany could not go to war against France without simultaneously taking on the British. Finally, the military balance on the ground began to shift to Germany's disadvantage after 1912. New conscription laws in France and Russia and improvements in the quality and mobility of the Russian army promised to more than offset the increases in the size of the German army undertaken in 1912 and 1913. Furthermore, changing borders in the Balkans raised the number of Serbian divisions that would face a German-Austrian coalition in the east.

In short, from 1906 onward, shifts in the military capabilities of the European powers and Germany's increasing diplomatic isolation led to elite perceptions of high metropolitan vulnerability. As is documented below, the effects of high vulnerability on elite beliefs parallel those laid out in Chapter 2 and in the other case studies. Initially, high vulnerability induced elites to adopt a firm, compellent stance in their dealings with adversaries. Efforts were made to galvanize the public further and persuade them to bear the costs of a more ambitious external policy. As the strategic situation crystallized, however, elites realized that efforts to fragment the opposing coalition were backfiring and they came to appreciate the need for a reorientation of strategy and a scaling back of external ambition. Retrenchment was impossible, however, given the domestic stalemate and the cognitive, organizational, and political constraints associated with the strategic culture that elites had molded. Decision makers proceeded down the path to war despite incoming information indicating that the chances of victory were slim. For good reason, they reached a decision for war in an atmosphere of increasing pessimism and fear. As the chancellor, Bethmann Hollweg, put it, Germany's decision for war was "a leap in the dark."[72]

Dealing with the Adversary

German grand strategy between 1897 and 1914 can be broken down into four components: naval strategy, army strategy, peripheral strat-

---

[72] Fritz Fischer, *World Power or Decline: The Controversy over Germany's Aims in the First World War*, trans. Lancelot Farrar, Robert Kimber, and Rita Kimber (New York: W. W. Norton, 1974), p. 26.

egy, and alliance strategy. The fundamental problem for German elites was that these four components were not well integrated. Indeed, the disjunctures among them grew increasingly acute between the turn of the century and the outbreak of war. Naval strategy and peripheral strategy reflected the strong expansionist momentum that gathered in the second half of the 1890s. The navy embarked on an ambitious building program while the government pursued a much bolder colonial policy. The problem was that Germany's battlefleet and its renewed efforts to build an overseas empire stimulated Anglo-German antagonism and drove Britain and France into closer alignment. This shift in Europe's alliance network left Germany increasingly reliant on alliance with Austria, whose designs in the Balkans fueled tensions between Russia and Germany. The Germany army, however, simply did not have the capability to cope with the British and French in the west and the Russians in the east. Germany's disadvantage on the ground was exacerbated by the General Staff's insistence on undertaking offensive operations in the west before concentrating on the eastern front. I now look in more detail at how these disjunctures within German grand strategy came about.

When the Reichstag passed the first naval law in 1898, Germany faced no immediate seaborne threats. Britain enjoyed unchallenged maritime supremacy, but the Royal Navy posed no danger to German territory nor did it obstruct Germany's overseas trade. This evidence lends support to the argument that the naval program was rooted in domestic political developments and in the ideology of expansionism that emerged from the political chaos of the 1890s (the domestic objectives of the naval program are discussed shortly). The specific foreign objectives sought through the buildup of the navy can be detected through the composition of the fleet. The first naval law authorized the building of nineteen battleships. The second naval law, passed by the Reichstag in 1900, called for thirty battleships, eight heavy cruisers, and twenty-four light cruisers. In addition, eight heavy cruisers and twenty-four light cruisers were to be procured for overseas service.[73] The chief aim of the German fleet was clearly not protecting overseas trade, but challenging Britain's naval supremacy in the North Sea.[74]

Responsibility for formulating a naval program and orchestrating its passage through the Reichstag fell primarily on the shoulders of Admiral Tirpitz. For Tirpitz, a high-seas fleet was the pathway to Germany's ascendance as a great power. Establishing German dominance in Eu-

---

[73] Holborn, *Modern Germany*, p. 308.
[74] Fritz Fischer, *War of Illusions: German Policies from 1911 to 1914*, trans. Marian Jackson (New York: W. W. Norton, 1975), p. 50.

rope did not entail building a fleet that was numerically superior to the world's most powerful navy—that of the British. On the contrary, according to Tirpitz's notion of the Risikoflotte, it was necessary to build only enough battleships to pose a credible threat to Britain's home fleet. Because of its far-flung commitments and consequent need to deploy a considerable portion of its battlefleet in overseas waters, Britain would be forced to respond to a sizable German presence in the North Sea by accommodating German demands.[75] Tirpitz did consider the possibility that Britain might react with hostility to Germany's naval program and attack the German fleet. He believed that a defending fleet operating near its own coasts would be able to defeat an attack as long as it maintained a force ratio of two to three.[76] Tirpitz calculated that Britain would not be able to undertake a building program capable of surpassing this ratio.[77] Thus even if the Risikoflotte failed to attain the political objectives for which it was intended, it would not endanger German security. The principal goal of the naval program, however, was not to alienate the British, but to induce them to accept Germany's emergence as a world power.

Germany's peripheral strategy reflected a similar expansionist urge, a yearning for recognition as a first-class power. Beginning in the late 1890s, the kaiser made clear his desire to enlarge Germany's network of overseas naval bases. Kiaochow was annexed in 1897. The following year, Germany obtained a string of islands in the Caroline chain and some other cable landings and naval stations in the Pacific.[78] The kaiser also stepped up efforts to expand German influence in the Near East and in South America.[79] Like the bout of imperial expansion orchestrated by Bismarck, however, the spurt of colonial activity that began in 1897 was decidedly restrained in its scope and intensity. The kaiser relied on traders and businessmen, not government officials, as his primary agents in the periphery. In the Near East, Germany focused primarily on extending a railway line into Mesopotamia. In South America, the government's main concern was protecting the lucrative trade that had been developed by German merchants. In neither case is there evidence that the kaiser sought formal territorial annexations.[80]

German elites attempted to use colonial rivalry to regulate the Euro-

---

[75] For an excellent summary and critique of Tirpitz's strategy, see Paul Kennedy, "Strategic Aspects of the Anglo-German Naval Race," in *Strategy and Diplomacy, 1870–1945* (London: Fontana Paperbacks, 1983). See also Craig, *Germany*, pp. 309–310.

[76] Kennedy, "Anglo-German Naval Race," p. 134.

[77] Berghahn, *Germany and the Approach of War*, p. 37.

[78] Townsend, *Rise and Fall of Germany's Colonial Empire*, pp. 195–196.

[79] On German involvement in South America, see Holger Herwig, *Germany's Vision of Empire in Venezuela, 1871–1914* (Princeton: Princeton University Press, 1986).

[80] Townsend, *Rise and Fall of Germany's Colonial Empire*, pp. 201–219.

pean alliance system and, in particular, Germany's relationship with Britain. They oscillated between a provocative and a conciliatory stance toward the British. The antagonism that was sparked by the Kruger Telegram was followed in 1898 by a rapprochement embodied in a British-German treaty on Mozambique and Angola.[81] Relations took a turn for the worse as a result of disputes over the Samoan islands. More cordial ties resumed during 1902–1903, when Germany and Britain cooperated in bombarding Venezuela in an attempt to defend their mutual economic interests.[82]

German efforts to alter continental alignments through colonial disputes came to a head in 1905–1906. In March 1905, the kaiser landed in Tangiers to demonstrate Germany's willingness to defend its economic interests in Morocco. Behind this ploy was the desire to split the Entente Cordiale by driving a wedge between Britain and France.[83] The kaiser hoped that the British would back German claims, thereby alienating the French. At the Algeciras Conference of 1906, however, Britain backed France, and German elites returned to Berlin empty-handed. Far from splitting the Entente, German behavior only strengthened relations between France and Britain. In addition to causing a public outcry, the outcome of the first Moroccan crisis led civilian and military elites to begin to show sincere concern about Germany's military vulnerability in the face of a coalition among Britain, France, and Russia. As Craig notes, "It was after the set-back in Morocco that the fear of encirclement began to be a potent factor in German politics."[84]

Perceptions of high vulnerability led to a hardening of elite attitudes. Not only did Germany have to continue to pursue ambitious policies on the Continent and overseas; it had to take a more intransigent stance in its dealings with the European powers. Germany could break encirclement only by standing firm; conciliation would simply strengthen the Entente and convince Britain and France that German expansion could be contained. This attitude was reflected in the initial reaction to the Morocco crisis: German elites were on the brink of launching a preventive war against France. Holstein argued that the timing was right: Britain was recovering from the Boer War and Russia was preoccupied with its disastrous conflict with Japan.[85] The kaiser and Bulow were more level-headed; they had been skeptical of the Morocco enterprise to begin with and took steps to ensure that the

[81] Ibid., p. 190.
[82] See Herwig, *Germany's Vision of Empire in Venezuela*, pp. 80–109.
[83] Craig, *Germany*, pp. 318–321.
[84] Ibid., p. 321.
[85] Ibid., pp. 318–319.

colonial dispute did not develop into continental war.[86] Nevertheless, the incident did exacerbate tensions between Germany and France, pushing the French toward the British and augmenting Germany's sense of isolation. Germany drifted into closer alignment with Austria. German elites increasingly supported Austrian ambition in the Balkans in order to reaffirm Austria's status as a major European power. Given Russian concern about the Balkans, this stance soured relations between Germany and Russia. So too did Germany's overtures to Turkey alienate the Russians and drive them closer to Britain. Intensified German efforts to extend the Baghdad Railway only made matters worse after 1906.[87]

Germany's relations with Britain fared no better. They deteriorated not only because of the Morocco incident, but also because of heightened naval competition. In 1905, the German government introduced a supplement to the 1900 bill, increasing the tonnage of its battleships and ordering more cruisers and destroyers. Britain responded in 1906 by ordering construction of the *Dreadnought*. In 1907, British elites offered to negotiate an end to the naval race, only to be rebuffed by their German counterparts. In 1908, the Reichstag passed a new bill approving the eventual replacement of Germany's battlefleet with dreadnought-class vessels. Britain responded with its own increase in naval estimates.[88] This escalation of the naval race could have been avoided had German elites been willing to make concessions and scale down their building program. But such concessions were out of the question in the blustery atmosphere that pervaded both the public and the elite community after the Morocco crisis.

By 1909–1910, voices of caution were beginning to emerge within the elite community. It had become apparent that compellent strategies and German intransigence were not paying off. Expansionist behavior and an unwillingness to make concessions had eroded, not bolstered, Germany's strategic position on the Continent. More important, Tirpitz's assumptions about how British elites would respond to the Risikoflotte proved to be mistaken in three critical respects. First, British decision makers did not leave their fleet dispersed throughout the periphery but progressively recalled their battleships to home waters. Second, rather than avoiding entangling alliances, British elites actively sought to develop an extensive network of accords to facilitate withdrawal from the periphery and offset growing German strength in

[86] Townsend, *Rise and Fall of Germany's Colonial Empire*, pp. 311–320.
[87] Holborn, *Modern Germany*, pp. 315–316; and Townsend, *Rise and Fall of Germany's Colonial Empire*, pp. 330–331.
[88] For a summary of these events, see Holborn, *Modern Germany*, p. 326.

Europe. Third, Britain embarked on a naval program whose scope and pace surpassed Tirpitz's expectations and left Germany scrambling to keep up. In short, the German fleet, far from enhancing Germany's leverage over Britain, only served to incite Anglo-German antagonism and was arguably the most important factor leading to the formation of the Triple Entente.

As it became more and more evident that Tirpitz's strategy had back-fired, opposition to the government's foreign policy mounted. Members of the business community argued that Germany should now seek to compromise with Britain, as did elites who had originally backed the buildup of the fleet as a means of inducing the British to acquiesce to Germany's rise to continental hegemony. British cooperation, they argued, was essential to the realization of Weltpolitik.[89] Bethmann Hollweg, who replaced Bulow as chancellor in 1909, agreed that Germany could no longer afford to adopt compellent strategies and alienate Britain. He argued that a more moderate and conciliatory approach would be far more effective in furthering German aims: "We must drive forward quietly and patiently in order to regain that trust and confidence without which we cannot consolidate politically and economically."[90] His efforts to constrain German naval building and accommodate British demands brought him into open conflict with Tirpitz.[91]

attempt at accommodation

Growing support for a more conciliatory approach had a clear effect on policy. During 1909–1910, Bethmann sought to reach a naval accord with Britain and was willing to make concessions in Germany's building program. Negotiators were unable, however, to find a ratio acceptable to both sides, and Britain shied away from Germany's request that an agreement on naval matters be linked to a British pledge of neutrality in the event of war between Germany and a coalition of France and Russia.[92] In 1909, efforts to repair relations with France led to an agreement in which Germany recognized French political dominance in Morocco.[93] German elites simultaneously opened a new dialogue with Russia, hoping to moderate tensions and wean the Russians away from the Entente.[94] Those in favor of accommodation were gaining the upper hand and initially succeeded in easing Germany's diplomatic isolation.

This move toward a more conciliatory foreign policy was short-lived. In 1911, German elites again precipitated a crisis over Morocco, bring-

---

[89] Smith, *German Colonial Empire*, pp. 177–179.
[90] Craig, *Germany*, p. 325.
[91] Wehler, *German Empire*, p. 169.
[92] Fischer, *War of Illusions*, pp. 63–68.
[93] Townsend, *Rise and Fall of Germany's Colonial Empire*, pp. 321–322.
[94] Fischer, *War of Illusions*, pp. 67–68.

ing the domestic struggle between hard-liners and accommodationists to a head. In April 1911, French troops landed in Fez, the capital of Morocco, ostensibly to protect foreign residents from native uprisings. This action violated the terms of the Algeciras Treaty, and Alfred von Kiderlen-Wachter, Bethmann's foreign secretary, responded by anchoring a gunboat off the coast of Agadir. He had several aims in mind. He wanted to demonstrate Germany's willingness to protect economic interests in West Morocco, hoped to press French elites to cede part of the Congo to Germany, and saw another opportunity to drive a wedge between France and Britain. The kaiser, however, was opposed to German intervention and fearful of its consequences. Kiderlen-Wachter in fact offered his resignation in response to Wilhelm's open disapproval of his actions.[95] Bethmann, too, cautioned restraint and feared that a colonial crisis would only exacerbate Germany's predicament on the Continent: "Germany can only pursue a strong policy in the sense of a world policy if it remains strong on the continent. . . . If we acquire outposts for the protection of which we must dissipate and weaken our continental resources we cut away the ground from under our feet."[96]

The kaiser and Bethmann could not prevent a crisis from developing between France and Germany, but they did succeed in pressing Kiderlen-Wachter to scale back his demands in the ensuing negotiations. Germany skulked away from Agadir having received from France only a small corridor of land linking the German Cameroons to the Congo. More important, German efforts to split the Entente again succeeded only in driving France and Britain into closer cooperation. Germany consequently became even more reliant on its alliance with Austria. The tightening relationship between Berlin and Vienna and German backing for Austria in the Austro-Serb struggle for mastery in the Balkans set the stage for the chain of events that would soon lead to the outbreak of World War I.

The results of the Agadir crisis also caused a widespread public backlash in Germany which, through a somewhat circuitous route, effectively silenced accommodationist voices. Tirpitz wanted to take advantage of this charged atmosphere to push a major naval bill through the Reichstag. Bethmann, however, tried to block the bill because he feared that it would lead to further deterioration in Anglo-German relations. Bethmann, in conjunction with army leaders, decided to request a major increase in army personnel, thereby forcing Tirpitz to reduce the size of his naval bill to ensure its passage through the Reichstag. Bethmann's scheme worked. The army received a major

---

[95] Ibid., p. 77; and Townsend, *Rise and Fall of Germany's Colonial Empire*, pp. 322–324.
[96] Cited in Fischer, *War of Illusions*, p. 90.

increase in personnel, and Tirpitz had to slash his naval bill accord-ingly.[97] But the costs were also very high. Both France and Russia responded in kind to the increase in the size of the German army. The Triple Alliance and Triple Entente were now engaged in an arms race on land as well as at sea.[98]

Fritz Fischer has argued that German elites in 1912 did more than fuel an arms race and set in motion a series of escalatory moves that culminated in the outbreak of hostilities in 1914. He contends that at a meeting on 8 December 1912, top decision makers in fact decided that they would go to war and that it was time to focus on the question of when, not if, Germany should initiate hostilities. Though historians continue to dispute how critical this meeting was to the events leading to the outbreak of World War I, it is clear that among the kaiser and his chief military advisers, there was considerable support for launching a preventive war. This meeting was precipitated by a crisis in the Balkans, during which the British made it clear that they would not stand idly by should Austria invade Serbia. Helmuth J. L. Count von Moltke (the younger), chief of the General Staff, asserted that Germany should go to war immediately; the military balance would only deteriorate as the French and Russian armies continued to grow in size. Tirpitz argued that a delay of eighteen months was needed before the navy would be ready for war. During this period, the navy would widen the Kiel Canal to accommodate dreadnought-class battleships and prepare the harbor on Heligoland for U-boat operations. Tirpitz succeeded in persuading the kaiser and Moltke to postpone the decision to go to war.[99] Bethmann, who did not attend the December meeting, continued to seek to defuse tensions with Britain.[100] But he soon came to accept the view that Germany would have to go to war in the near future. Bethmann supported Tirpitz's desire for a delay, both to prepare the country militarily and psychologically and to try to weaken the Entente.[101]

Beneath the divergent perspectives of the army and navy as to when

---

[97] For details of this jockeying between Tirpitz and Bethmann, see Fischer, *War of Illusions*, pp. 112–121.

[98] See Eckart Kehr, *Economic Interest, Militarism, and Foreign Policy: Essays on German History*, trans. Grete Heinz (Berkeley: University of California Press, 1977), p. 71.

[99] Fischer, *War of Illusions*, pp. 154–164. See also John Moses, *The Politics of Illusion: The Fischer Controversy in German Historiography* (London: George Prior, 1975), pp. 82–85. For the view that the December 1912 meeting was of less importance, see Wolfgang Mommsen, "The Debate on German War Aims," *Journal of Contemporary History*, 1, 3 (1966), 47–72; and Mommsen, "Domestic Factors in German Foreign Policy before 1914," *Central European History*, 6 (March 1973), 3–43.

[100] Craig, *Germany*, pp. 332–333.

[101] Fischer, *War of Illusions*, pp. 164–169.

to initiate hostilities lay a fundamental disjuncture between the army's operational plans for continental war and the strategic position in which Germany found itself by 1912. The crux of the problem was that the German army simply did not have sufficient manpower to cope with the opposing coalition that had emerged to resist German expansion. This problem was exacerbated by the General Staff's decision to open hostilities with a massive offensive against France. As mentioned above, the elder Moltke's plans for dealing with a two-front war involved blocking a French advance in the west and advancing and holding forward positions in the east. Under Schlieffen's leadership, the General Staff, between 1897 and 1905, undertook a dramatic reorientation of German strategy.[102] Instead of blocking a French advance, Schlieffen decided to attack France from the north, hoping that a massive sweep through Belgium would allow German forces to envelop and defeat French forces in a matter of weeks. Germany would then be able to devote all its resources to the eastern front. The Schlieffen Plan was formally drafted and incorporated into Germany's war plans between December 1905 and January 1906.[103] The younger Moltke became chief of staff in 1906 but did not fundamentally alter Schlieffen's design. He did, however, reduce the size of the attacking right wing of the forces deployed in the west in order to avoid violating Dutch territory and to bolster Germany's defensive line in Lorraine.[104]

The rationale behind the Schlieffen Plan remains extremely obscure. Schlieffen may have been concerned about new Russian fortifications in the areas in which Moltke had planned his main offensives.[105] Jack Snyder argues that a mix of organizational and cognitive factors induced the General Staff to adopt plans for an offensive against France.[106] Whatever the reasons for this reorientation of German strategy, it is clear that the army adopted a set of plans that made little sense, given the strategic landscape in Europe. As I show below, Germany simply did not have sufficient manpower to carry out the Schlieffen Plan. Furthermore, these plans played a key role in ensuring that a conflict over the Balkans would turn into a continent-wide war. As an ally of Austria, Germany supported Austria's declaration of war against Serbia in 1914. The Germans then responded to Austrian and Russian mobilization by implementing the Schlieffen Plan and attacking Belgium and France, drawing Britain into the conflict and leav-

---

[102] Craig, *Politics of the Prussian Army*, p. 279.

[103] Wehler, *German Empire*, p. 152.

[104] Jack Snyder, *The Ideology of the Offensive: Military Decision Making and the Disasters of 1914* (Ithaca: Cornell University Press, 1984), p. 111.

[105] Craig, *Politics of the Prussian Army*, p. 278.

[106] Snyder, *Ideology of the Offensive*, pp. 107–156.

ing German forces divided between two fronts. Moreover, the following evidence suggests that military planners were fully aware of the fundamental flaws plaguing the Schlieffen Plan, flaws that were to play a key role in Germany's defeat in World War I.

Information available to German planners indicated that, after full mobilization, Britain, France, Belgium, Serbia, and Russia could field 199 divisions while Germany and Austria could field 136 divisions.[107] The Germans planned to deal with this numerical inferiority by keeping Britain from entering the war, deploying four-fifths of their army along the western front, and orchestrating a lightning offensive against France. The younger Moltke calculated that after three to six weeks, Germany would be able to turn to the east and fight what was essentially a one-front war.[108]

Yet to assume that the war would progress in this manner directly contradicted several key pieces of information that were readily available to the General Staff. To begin, the forces that Germany deployed on the western front were in numerical terms roughly equal, if not marginally superior, to the French forces they faced. Were six Belgian divisions and three to four British divisions to fight alongside France, however, German forces would be clearly outnumbered on the battlefield.[109] German elites were aware of this problem and expended considerable effort between 1912 and 1914 to ensure that neither Britain nor Belgium would side with France. The kaiser worked on Belgium, trying to persuade elites to offer German troops safe passage through their territory. King Albert unequivocally refused.[110] Bethmann, meanwhile, was working on Britain, repeatedly seeking to ensure British neutrality in the event of war on the Continent. He, too, was unequivocally rebuffed. British elites explicitly indicated to their German counterparts that they intended to send troops to the Continent if France were attacked.[111] The German ambassador to London, Karl Max Furst von Lichnowsky, confirmed the sincerity of Britain's declared intentions, repeatedly warning that the British Expeditionary Force (B.E.F.) would be sent to the Continent if Germany moved west. In 1913, Lichnowsky responded to rising tensions on the Continent by sending

---

[107] Ibid., p. 107.

[108] Moltke's assessments of how long it would take to defeat France range from several weeks to several months. See Snyder, *Ideology of the Offensive*, pp. 114–115; and Fritz Fischer, *Germany's Aims in the First World War* (New York: W. W. Norton, 1967), p. 37.

[109] Snyder, *Ideology of the Offensive*, p. 112. For comparisons of German, French, and Russian force levels, see Fischer, *Germany's Aims in the First World War*, p. 36; and Holborn, *Modern Germany*, pp. 342–345.

[110] Fischer, *Germany's Aims in the First World War*, p. 37; and Fischer, *War of Illusions*, pp. 226–229.

[111] Fischer, *Germany's Aims in the First World War*, pp. 29–32.

a memo to Bethmann indicating that "everything will be lost the moment we become involved in a war with France."[112] During the critical period between the assassination of Austrian Archduke Franz Ferdinand and his wife in Sarajevo and the outbreak of war, Lichnowsky repeatedly informed Berlin of Britain's unqualified intention to enter the war should Germany attack France.[113] Moltke himself expressed deep concern about reports indicating that Britain would intervene as soon as Germany violated Belgian territory.[114] Successive British decisions to recall forces from the periphery, to prepare the B.E.F. for continental operations, and to engage in joint military planning with the French provided independent and concrete confirmation of these intentions.

Despite overwhelming information to the contrary, German elites persisted in their assumption that they could count on British neutrality. They had some reason to be uncertain of British intentions and to hold out hope of British neutrality, but they had no reason to be confident that Britain would refrain from entering the war.[115] As Richard Ned Lebow writes, "Nowhere was German delusion greater than with

[112] Fischer, *War of Illusions*, p. 175.

[113] Richard Ned Lebow, *Between Peace and War: The Nature of International Crisis* (Baltimore: Johns Hopkins University Press, 1981), pp. 131–132.

[114] Holborn, *Modern Germany*, p. 348.

[115] Some analysts maintain that German elites were justified in assuming that Britain would not enter the war. Scott Sagan, for example, correctly asserts that during the summer of 1914 British elites—Sir Edward Grey in particular—were not as clear about Russian intentions as they could have been. See "1914 Revisited: Allies, Offense, and Instability," in *Military Strategy and the Origins of the First World War*, ed. Steven Miller, Sean Lynn-Jones, and Stephen Van Evera (Princeton: Princeton University Press, 1991), p. 126. See also my discussion of the domestic considerations constraining British decision makers, in Chapter 3. It is also the case that elites in Russia and France were somewhat uncertain about British intentions. See Jack Levy, "Preferences, Constraints, and Choices in July 1914," in ibid., p. 242. As the crisis proceeded, however, British elites did clarify their position. Grey by late July made unequivocal Britain's intention to intervene should Germany attack France (Levy, "Preference, Constraints, and Choices," p. 240). Furthermore, there appears to have been only one instance in which British elites indicated to the Germans that Britain in fact intended to remain neutral. On 29 July, the king of England reportedly told Prince Henry that "England will remain neutral in the event of war" (cited in Zara Steiner, *Britain and the Origins of the First World War* [New York: St. Martin's Press, 1977], p. 226). Virtually all other communications and assessments indicated either that Britain would enter the war or that its intentions were uncertain. It is therefore reasonable for top German decision makers to have been *uncertain* about British intentions, but unreasonable for them to have been *confident* of British neutrality. Levy argues that some German elites, especially Bethmann and military officials, thought that Britain would intervene but that British forces would arrive too late to block Germany's lightning strike into France (Levy, "Preference, Constraints, and Choices," pp. 239–240). This view was much more consistent with the information available to decision makers. Furthermore, as the following paragraph indicates, the Germans had good reason to be skeptical of their ability to carry out the Schlieffen Plan *even if* Britain remained neutral.

respect to the expectation of British neutrality."[116] Even as German troops marched across the Belgian border, those who had made the decision to go to war were assuming that Britain would not intervene.[117] Yet this assumption was based more on wishful thinking and on the manipulation of assessments to fit war plans than on careful analysis of incoming information. Elites simply avoided assimilating information that threatened the viability of the Schlieffen Plan and clung tenaciously to erroneous strategic assumptions.

The coherence of Germany's steadfast march toward war is further challenged by the fact that German elites, even if Britain were to refrain from entering the war, had good reason to be quite guarded about the ability of the German army to crush French forces in a matter of weeks. The main problem was France's rail network. Even though the bulk of French forces were deployed along the border with Germany, they could be rapidly redeployed by rail. While German troops would be fighting their way through Belgium on foot, rested French troops, moved to a new front by rail, would be erecting a stalwart line of defense for the main battle. Redeployment by rail in fact proved to be a decisive factor in the early stages of the war. Even though French forces initially took the offensive in Lorraine, they were quickly redeployed when the threat posed by Germany's right wing became apparent. It was in large part because of the French railroad system that Germany's twenty and one-half divisions were stopped at the Marne by an opposing force of thirty-five divisions.[118]

Two pieces of evidence undercut the argument that German elites could have reasonably failed to foresee the advantages that would accrue to French forces because of the greater mobility afforded by rail deployment. First, in exercises undertaken to plan for a war against France, the General Staff assumed that French forces would in fact redeploy by rail to prevent envelopment by German forces.[119] Clearly, German planners knew that the rail network existed and understood its implications for French mobility. Second, one of the considerations affecting the timing of Germany's decision for war was the expected completion of the extension of the Russian railway toward Germany's eastern border. The General Staff wanted hostilities to begin before Russian troops would be able to benefit from the new rail network.[120] Planners fully understood the strategic implications of deployment by rail but seem to have ignored these implications in drafting operations

---

[116] Lebow, *Between Peace and War*, p. 129.
[117] Moses, *Politics of Illusion*, p. 95.
[118] Snyder, *Ideology of the Offensive*, pp. 112–114, 120.
[119] Ibid., p. 114.
[120] Fischer, *War of Illusions*, p. 173.

in the west. In a manner consistent with their thinking about British neutrality, elites had before them information that called the feasibility of their strategic plans into question; nevertheless, they proceeded to go to war. Again, planners allowed assessments to be shaped by a commitment to specific strategic assumptions, rather than allowing those assumptions to be shaped by incoming information. Prevailing strategic conceptions proved impervious to disconfirming evidence.

The bottom line is that German elites could not be confident of their ability to achieve victory even in a war confined to only one front. Despite having deployed four-fifths of their forces on the western front, decision makers had every reason to be dubious of the army's ability to defeat French forces rapidly and decisively. For the Germans to have initiated war against France and Russia, having before them information that Britain and Belgium would likely join the opposing coalition, provides good reason to be quite suspicious of the assumptions and political forces that shaped Germany's decision for war.

There is in fact considerable evidence that, between 1912 and 1914, elites grew increasingly skeptical of Germany's ability to prevail in a continental war. A sense of pessimism, not cautious optimism, pervaded the elite community. The diplomatic corps never apprised top decision makers of its growing doubts about Germany's strategic predicament; "its members failed to criticize policy even when they knew it to fly in the face of reality, and limited their role to carrying out the instructions given them by Berlin."[121] Accompanying such resignation was a sense of desperation, an urgency about going to war that resulted from a military balance that was growing progressively worse. The incentives for launching a preventive war mounted as time passed. Intelligence estimates suggested that Germany's slight edge over France would last only until 1915 and that Russia would attain outright superiority by 1916 or 1917.[122] The problem was exacerbated by the fact that the Reichstag would not approve increases in force levels on the scale requested by the General Staff. In 1912, Moltke asked for 300,000 additional troops but received only 126,000.[123] Serbia's expanding borders, which resulted from successive crises in the Balkans, further tipped the balance against Germany. By 1914, Moltke was insisting that Germany could not afford to postpone war any further: "Any delay reduces our chances, for we cannot compete with Russia when it is a question of masses."[124] The foreign minister's summary of

[121] Lebow, *Between Peace and War*, p. 125.
[122] Wehler, *German Empire*, pp. 198–199.
[123] Fischer, *War of Illusions*, pp. 180–181.
[124] Fischer, *Germany's Aims in the First World War*, p. 49.

Moltke's thinking in March 1914 is also quite revealing: "The prospects of the future seriously worried him. Russia will have completed her armaments in 2 to 3 years. The military superiority of our enemies would be so great then that he did not know how he might cope with them. In his view there was no alternative to waging a preventive war in order to defeat the enemy as long as we could still more or less pass the test. The Chief of the General Staff left it at my discretion to gear our policy to an early unleashing of a war."[125]

Moltke was far from optimistic about Germany's chance of victory even if war began in 1914. When asked what would happen if Germany's initial offensive against France failed, Moltke responded, "I will do what I can. We are not superior to the French." Schlieffen himself recognized the problems facing his strategy, once noting that it is "an enterprise for which we are too weak."[126] Bethmann shared this deep concern about Germany's potential involvement in a war. In 1913, he warned a Reichstag charged with war fever, "Woe be to him whose retreat is not well-prepared."[127]

It is clear that German strategy was plagued by several fundamental flaws. It is also clear that awareness of these flaws within the elite community led to serious doubts about Germany's ability to prevail in a way against the Entente. Despite those doubts, German decision makers proceeded down the path to war. The resultant atmosphere in the elite community understandably bordered on panic. As Berghahn explains, "Cold-blooded planning for war appears to square poorly with the atmosphere of anxiety and pessimism prevailing in conservative circles before 1914. Their actions rather bear the mark of panic. Both at home and abroad they found themselves on the defensive— cornered and desperate."[128] Lebow presents a similar picture: "Both Kaiser and chancellor ultimately lapsed into passive acceptance of the inevitability of war although they continued to clutch at the hope of British neutrality the way a drowning man grasps a life preserver."[129]

From the late 1890s onward, the elite community was infused with notions of expansionism and of Germany's need and right to be a power equal in status and influence to Britain. These notions emerged primarily from the domestic political chaos of the 1890s and the efforts of top elites to use weltpolitik to rally support for the government and disarm political opponents. Exactly what weltpolitik meant and how it

---

[125] Cited in Snyder, *Ideology of the Offensive*, p. 148.
[126] Cited in ibid., pp. 115, 112.
[127] Cited in Berghahn, *Germany and the Approach of War*, p. 174.
[128] Berghahn, *Germany and the Approach of War*, p. 167.
[129] Lebow, *Between Peace and War*, p. 147.

was to be implemented were unclear. As General Waldersee described the kaiser's new policy, "We are supposed to pursue *Weltpolitik*. If one only knew what that is supposed to be."[130] Even though elites were not certain how Germany's ascendance was to manifest itself, they began to pursue more competitive policies in both the core and the periphery. The battlefleet and renewed colonial activities were the main manifestations of these new policies. The battlefleet was to establish Germany as a great European power. Overseas colonies offered some financial reward and could be used to regulate the European alliance system. But elites continued to believe that formal empire would sap, not contribute to, metropolitan strength. That Germany in 1914 had only 6,500 troops in overseas colonies speaks for itself.[131]

At least until 1905, elites operated under the assumption that they could attain their new objectives without the use of force. The main objective of German policy was to convince Europe's major powers to acquiesce peacefully to German ascendance, not to overwhelm them with absolute intransigence or superior force. Elite attitudes hardened after the Morocco crisis of 1905–1906. Perceptions of encirclement and conditions of strategic deficiency induced decision makers to adopt intransigent, compellent policies. Concessions would simply strengthen the Entente; only by standing firm could elites fragment the opposing coalition, break out of encirclement, and establish Germany as a first-class power. The Anglo-German naval race intensified, and Germany rebuffed British attempts to negotiate a compromise. Relations with France and Russia similarly eroded.

As the strategic landscape crystallized, elites realized that their intransigence was backfiring, that compellent policies were increasing, not decreasing, the nation's vulnerability. Efforts to split the Triple Entente had only strengthened the opposing coalition. The Risikoflotte had won Germany suspicion, not political influence. The strategic logic that fueled Germany's overly competitive policies had been repudiated. Accommodationist voices emerged, cautioning that Germany had to scale back its external ambition and cooperate with potential adversaries. This attitude was reflected in a new willingness to make naval concessions and an appreciation of the need to reassure, rather than threaten, the members of the Triple Entente. Strategic assumptions were, however temporarily, being brought into line with incoming information.

This period of accommodationist thinking was brought to a close by the 1911 Morocco crisis. Intense fears of encirclement were rekindled,

---

[130] Cited in Herwig, *"Luxury" Fleet*, p. 20.
[131] Smith, *German Colonial Empire*, p. 138.

and, by the end of 1912, elites were coming to view war as the only way through which the country could solve its predicament. Germany was diplomatically isolated and faced a military balance that was growing progressively worse. Despite awareness that their military forces might well not be able to defeat the Entente, elites clung to the Schlieffen Plan, an offensive strategy that only exacerbated the implications of strategic deficiency. Elites justifiably headed toward war in an atmosphere of increasing fear.

The behavior of German elites cannot be explained as the product of psychological distortion, miscalculation, or beliefs that lasted too long because of cognitive lags. Psychological distortion does appear to have played some role in shaping decisions during the summer crisis of 1914. The confidence of German elites that Britain would remain neutral is indicative of stress-induced psychological dysfunction. Despite evidence that, by standards of reasonable judgment, should have made it clear to German decision makers that Britain intended to intervene should France be attacked, elites in Berlin fell prey to motivated biases and selectively ignored incoming information, leaving them unjustifiably confident that Britain would remain neutral.[132] This was, however, only one discrete and isolated episode of psychological distortion. On balance, German elites recognized that Germany faced a strategic imbalance that was growing progressively worse, and they were appropriately pessimistic about the prospect of going to war. Crisis conditions by no means prevailed throughout the 1912–1914 period. Nevertheless, elites continued to proceed down the path to war. Decision makers initiated hostilities despite appreciation of their strategic predicament, not because they deluded themselves into thinking that victory would be easily attained. Discrete psychological distortions may have eased the decision for war, but that decision was being driven by other forces.

Miscalculation fails to provide an adequate explanation for German behavior because elites simply were not caught off-guard by events that they could reasonably have failed to foresee. From late 1912 onward, decision makers focused more on the question of when, not if, war would begin. Germany's principal allies and adversaries had been identified well before 1914. Because of the assassination of Franz Ferdinand, war may well have broken out through a specific chain of events that no one could have foreseen. But when German elites backed the Austrians in their decision to mobilize, mobilized their own forces, and implemented the Schlieffen Plan, they were fully aware that they were

---

[132] For detailed discussion of the importance of psychological biases in shaping German behavior during the summer of 1914, see Lebow, *Between Peace and War*, pp. 119–147.

triggering a continent-wide war. Except for the fact that the Schlieffen Plan failed to rout French forces, events unfolded, for the most part, as the Germans expected.

The cognitive mechanisms delaying the adaptation of beliefs to disconfirming evidence also fail to explain German behavior. Elites initially adopted compellent strategies for sound reasons: to intimidate adversaries and fragment the opposing coalition. But, as documented above, they came to realize that their policies were not producing the intended effects. Intransigence, far from forcing the Triple Entente to back down, was strengthening the opposing coalition and only exacerbating self-encirclement. It was precisely because elites recognized that their policies were backfiring that they changed course and began to pursue an accommodationist line in 1909–1910. Incoming information should have disconfirmed, and in fact did disconfirm, the strategic suppositions that initially led to overly competitive policies. German elites did not engage in self-defeating behavior because strategic beliefs persevered in the face of discrepant information.

In the British, French, and Japanese cases, elites faced with information that should have led to a reorientation of strategy similarly failed to undertake strategic adjustment. In those cases, I argued that the strategic images deeply embedded and institutionalized within the elite community played the most important role in constraining adjustment; strategic culture affected outcomes primarily through cognitive, emotional, and organizational mechanisms. In the German case, this dynamic was clearly at work. Many of the country's top decision makers had bought into the notion of weltpolitik and, for both cognitive and emotional reasons, could not tolerate abandoning their imperial aspirations. This was one reason why key members of the elite community—Tirpitz, Moltke, the kaiser—resisted their colleagues' calls for moderation and proceeded down the path to war despite their own skepticism about the outcome. So too did the organizational interests of the army and navy become wedded to the realization of expansionist strategic conceptions.

But for two reasons, the strategic images prevailing within the elite community do not provide a fully satisfying account of German behavior. First, between 1909 and 1911, top decision makers did in fact reverse course and seek to moderate escalating tensions between Germany and the members of the Triple Entente. To be sure, Bethmann had to overcome strong opposition to his more accommodating stance; Tirpitz steadfastly resisted the chancellor's efforts to scale back the naval program. But unlike in Japan, where elite commitment to the fulfillment of imperial aspirations was so pervasive and strong that the voices of moderation were silenced, in Germany moderates were able to carry the day, if only temporarily. Scaling back the scope of imperial ambition was, as it were, thinkable. Second, compelling historical evidence suggests that decision makers were entrapped by discrete domestic pressures, not just by powerful strategic conceptions embedded in the elite community. In Britain, France, and Japan, elite-mass linkages played an important role in shaping prevailing strategic images. But these images had an impact on outcomes primarily by affecting elite thinking and defining the organizational interests of elite institutions; electoral concerns and coalitional pressures played a less important role in inducing elites to pursue inappropriate policies. As I show in the following section, in the German case mass attitudes and party politics were far more prominent elements of the entrapment process.

Domestic Considerations

Beginning in 1897, the German government resorted to a strategy of Sammlungspolitik—rallying interests or logrolling—to maintain control over the domestic polity. The battlefleet was to serve as the rallying point, as the patriotic cause around which disparate interests would unite. Industry would receive guaranteed orders for years to come. Agriculture, in return for its support of naval building, would receive tariffs to protect grain prices. And the middle classes would be carried along by improvements in the standard of living and by the rising tide of nationalism that would accompany foreign success.

This strategy worked for roughly a decade. It eventually failed for three reasons. First, the alliance between iron and rye broke down, in part over the question of how to raise tax revenues sufficient to cover the cost of armaments. Second, disputes emerged within the government itself over the pace of naval building and over the feasibility of continuing a policy of external ambition that had succeeded only in leading to self-encirclement by pitting Germany and its allies against a superior coalition of powers. Third, the Social Democrats made steady gains in successive elections, leaving the government increasingly threatened and unable to pass legislation through the Reichstag.

With logrolling no longer an option, elites were forced to rely on nationalistic appeals to unite an increasingly divided domestic polity. The problem was that the government had already implanted among the populace a brand of aggressive nationalism that it could not control. To preserve political dominance, decision makers were forced to cater to the Pan-Germans, the anti-Semites, and other extremist groups that had once been relegated to the periphery of the political arena. This domestic milieu played an important role in preventing elites from pursuing retrenchment and scaling back external ambition; political survival conflicted with strategic pragmatism, only reinforcing the ambitious strategic conceptions institutionalized in the elite community. Elites found themselves entrapped in a strategic culture of their own making. As Rohl puts it, "By allying with and encouraging the forces of rabid nationalism, the Kaiser's Government was, like the sorcerer's apprentice, raising ghosts it was unable to lay."[133] Domestic pressures are key to understanding why elites were unable to divert Germany from a head-on clash with the Entente, a clash that they were well aware could lead to the nation's military defeat.

Private Economic Interests. It is altogether plausible that powerful economic interest groups were primarily responsible for the expansionist policies adopted by Germany after 1897. At the turn of the century, the German polity was becoming increasingly cartelized.[134] A powerful industrial elite stood to gain from a policy of external ambition; a world-class navy meant secure orders for the shipbuilding industry and the many sectors that supplied it. The landed aristocracy, through the logroll with industry, also stood to benefit from naval building. The Junkers exchanged their support for the navy for protectionist grain tariffs.

Given the existence of a powerful economic elite that stood to gain from expansion, it makes sense that logrolling among different sectors within this elite could have forced a government struggling to preserve its political viability to pursue overly competitive policies.[135] As the following section shows, however, this was not the case. Sectional interests were manipulated by government elites, not vice versa. The alliance between iron and rye was conceived of and orchestrated by government and military officials, not by economic interest groups. The logroll was only one component of a broader effort to use external ambition to unite the country. Furthermore, logrolling, even though it contributed initial momentum to the adoption of expansive policies, actually played a moderating role: it allowed the government to rule without winning over the full range of parties that occupied the center and right of the political spectrum. It was when the logroll broke down that the government was forced to acquiesce to the forces of rabid nationalism and to adopt policies that would satisfy even extremist elements within the body politic. Logrolling lubricated the political

---

[133] Rohl, *Germany without Bismarck*, p. 255.
[134] Holborn, *Modern Germany*, pp. 382–389.
[135] For a detailed presentation of this argument, see Snyder, *Myths of Empire*, pp. 66–111.

system; it was its failure that left the government paralyzed and susceptible to a brand of popular nationalism that it was unable to control. Not coincidentally, the business community provided voices of reason during the years before the outbreak of war. When it became apparent that the Risikoflotte had led to a dangerous deterioration in Anglo-German relations, some businessmen began to argue that Germany had to start accommodating Britain.[136] Economic elites might have wanted a battlefleet, but they did not want war with Britain.

Domestic Politics. Sammlungspolitik emerged in 1897 as a strategy for preserving the political dominance of the traditional elite. It was the brainchild of the minister of finance, Johannes von Miquel. He believed that by focusing the attention of legislators on Germany's external policies, the government could contain political chaos and end bitter disputes over domestic issues: "We . . . have to introduce questions of foreign policy into the Reichstag, for in foreign affairs the sentiments of the nation could usually be united. Our undeniable successes in foreign policy would make a good impression in the Reichstag debates, and political divisions would thus be moderated." Bulow agreed that "the patriotic aspect must be propagated relentlessly through [the creation of] national tasks so that the idea of nationality will never cease to move the political parties, to bind then together." "Only a successful foreign policy," he asserted, could "help, reconcile, calm, rally and unite."[137]

Miquel and Bulow found a willing accomplice in Tirpitz. The navy had been pushing for an expansion of the fleet since the mid-1890s. The battlefleet would serve perfectly as a rallying point for disparate sectional interests, as "the catalyst," in Berghahn's words, "which was supposed to facilitate a *Sammlung.*"[138] The idea of building a world-class navy did not emerge solely for domestic consumption; the navy's organizational interests and the kaiser's growing preoccupation with the notion of weltpolitik created momentum of their own. The government's domestic goals, the navy's organizational interests, and the kaiser's own desire to project German influence thus intersected on the issue of the battlefleet.[139]

[136] Eckart Kehr, *Battleship Building and Party Politics in Germany, 1894–1901: A Cross-Section of the Political, Social, and Ideological Preconditions of German Imperialism,* trans. Pauline Anderson and Eugene Anderson (Chicago: University of Chicago Press, 1973), p. 465.
[137] Miquel cited in Rohl, *Germany without Bismarck,* p. 252; Bulow cited in Berghahn, *Germany and the Approach of War,* p. 30; and in Wehler, *German Empire,* p. 177.
[138] Berghahn, *Germany and the Approach of War,* p. 24.
[139] In contrast to Eckart Kehr, Geoff Eley argues that initial support for the battlefleet within the navy, the government, and the business community was not related to the

The construction of a battlefleet served the government's domestic interests in two important respects. First, it renewed the alliance between industry and agriculture which Bismarck had originally orchestrated in 1879. In this version of the logroll, industry was ensured the fixed, long-term orders that accompanied a major naval building program. In return for supporting the naval bills, the landed aristocracy secured protective tariffs. Both partners in the deal also benefited from a consolidation of the right in the face of a rising threat from the Social Democrats. These payoffs did not mean, however, that the parties to the deal were not making significant sacrifices. On the contrary, the Junkers were fundamentally opposed to the navy because its rising stature challenged the position of the army, a Junker stronghold. Furthermore, the landed elite were loath to accept the increase in taxation needed to pay for a navy and were not pleased that a major building program would further Germany's industrialization. Industry had its own objections to the deal: a new tariff bill would limit export opportunities, especially to Russia, and drive up wages. Iron and rye thus did not impose their overlapping interests on the government.[140] On the contrary, decision makers maneuvered around incompatible interests in order to find common ground between two key constituencies on the right.

The second way in which the battlefleet was to consolidate the position of the ruling elite was by winning over the middle class through foreign successes. Tirpitz explicitly packaged for mass consumption his campaign to gain support for the naval laws. He billed the navy as the service of the rising bourgeoisie, hoping to capitalize on popular resentment of the aristocratic aura of the army.[141] The secretary of the Navy League, a lobby organization formed to assist Tirpitz, acknowledged that a primary aim of the body was to create a mass movement that would be "at His Majesty's disposal at all times."[142] As Rohl describes the government's strategy, "On a scale previously unknown in Germany . . . the Government became preoccupied after 1897 with the political attitudes of the man in the street. . . . The object was to rally all those elements not irrevocably committed to the two successful mass movements of the day—Catholicism and Socialism—behind the throne."[143]

---

fleet's potential role as an instrument of domestic politics. Elites later came to appreciate the domestic role that the fleet could play. See Eley, "*Sammlungspolitik,* Social Imperialism, and the Navy Law of 1898," in *From Unification to Nazism,* pp. 110–153.

[140] Smith, *German Colonial Empire,* pp. 173–174; and Eley, *From Unification to Nazism,* pp. 130–142.

[141] Smith, *German Colonial Empire,* p. 172.

[142] Rohl, *Germany without Bismarck,* p. 254.

[143] Ibid., p. 258.

Tirpitz erected a massive propaganda machine to spread his gospel. In June 1897, the navy established the Bureau for Information and General Parliamentary Affairs. Its function was to prepare propaganda that would be used to win support for the battlefleet in the Reichstag and among the public. Groups in the private sector readily assisted Tirpitz with his mission. The German Colonial Society and the Pan-German League played a particularly active role in the propaganda campaign. During a seven-month period preceding approval of the first naval bill, the Colonial Society organized 173 lectures, printed 140,000 pamphlets, and distributed 2,000 copies of Alfred Mahan's *The Influence of Sea Power on History*.[144] The German Navy League was founded in 1898, and its membership quickly grew to 80,000.[145] The Navy League had firm backing in the business community; Friedreich Alfred von Krupp was one of its founders. Tirpitz was also successful in enlisting the support of university professors. Some of the country's most famous faculty went on lecture tours to win public support for the navy.[146] The message conveyed through this propaganda blitz was not restricted to naval matters. The navy and its supporters were selling weltpolitik and expansionist ideologies to the German people. "The imperial state," according to Eley, was seeking "to equip itself with a patriotic public tradition which was distinct from the existing paraphernalia of princely ceremonial."[147]

These efforts on the part of Germany's ruling elite to manipulate the public had a profound effect on party politics and mass attitudes. During the late 1890s and early 1900s, antimilitary sentiment among the public virtually disappeared. After the 1907 elections, even the Social Democrats publicly acknowledged the need to devote resources to national defense.[148] Germany's setback in the Morocco crisis of 1905–1906 intensified currents of militant patriotism among the public, strengthening support for the growing number of extremist right-wing groups that were vying for the allegiance of the middle class.[149]

The absence of opinion polls makes it impossible to quantify this shift in public attitudes. The consensus among historians, however, speaks for itself. Hajo Holborn observes that "the great majority of the

---

[144] Ibid., p. 254.

[145] Wehler, *German Empire*, p. 87.

[146] Rohl, *Germany without Bismarck*, p. 253. For general discussion of the navy's propaganda efforts, see Kehr, *Battleship Building and Party Politics*, pp. 95–109.

[147] Eley, *From Unification to Nazism*, p. 77.

[148] Ibid., pp. 91–92. Differing opinions about foreign policy among the socialists in fact led to divisive disputes and the formation of a splinter party, the Independent Socialists. See Hajo Holborn, "Introduction," in Fischer, *Germany's Aims in the First World War*, p. xii.

[149] Townsend, *Rise and Fall of Germany's Colonial Empire*, p. 325; Moses, *Politics of Illusion*, p. 51; and Eley, *From Unification to Nazism*, pp. 246–247.

German people, led by its ruling classes, indulged in wild dreams about the overwhelming strength that Germany had to acquire." David Calleo argues that naval propaganda was initially crafted to divert the attention of the populace away from domestic troubles, but that "what began as a diversion gradually grew into a national obsession." For John Moses, Germany's need for a battlefleet and for an ambitious external policy "had been hammered home in the minds of the public with enormous effect." Eckart Kehr notes that the German people readily accepted the notion that "armed power is everything in international competition."[150]

Because of the success of the propaganda program and the logroll between industry and agriculture, elites operated in a political environment that was conducive to the pursuit of ambitious external policies. Industry's enthusiasm for the battlefleet in fact outpaced even Tirpitz's zeal. In December 1898, Tirpitz had to counter heavy industry's effort to accelerate the naval program. The Reich Naval Office considered industry's proposals to be excessive and impractical.[151] The Navy League itself came to overstep its original mandate, often charging that the government's foreign policy was not sufficiently bold and aggressive.[152] For the most part, however, elite beliefs and domestic political trends were in synch. As mentioned above, the first Morocco crisis simultaneously fueled nationalistic sentiment among the public and emboldened elites. The kaiser, Bulow, Holstein, and Tirpitz all agreed that only an ambitious naval policy and a compellent stance in dealing with foreign powers would allow the government to cope with threats both at home and abroad.

By the end of the decade, however, the domestic political environment which elites had molded to strengthen their hand was coming to constrain their room for maneuver. Two developments led to this shift in the nature of elite-mass linkages. First, as already noted, elites began to appreciate the need to scale back the scope of German ambition and accommodate adversaries. Second, the alliance between iron and rye dissolved, threatening the conservative coalition that enabled the government to rule. Challenges to the government's ability to maintain the support of the center and right emerged over two issues: colonies and taxes.

Despite the kaiser's efforts after 1897 to pursue a more ambitious policy in the periphery, the parties and the public remained largely

[150] Holborn, "Introduction," in Fischer, *Germany's Aims in the First World War*, p. xii; Calleo, *German Problem Reconsidered*, p. 21; Moses, *Politics of Illusion*, p. 26; Kehr, *Battleship Building and Party Politics*, pp. 426–427.
[151] Kehr, *Economic Interest, Militarism, and Foreign Policy*, pp. 88–89.
[152] Fischer, *Germany's Aims in the First World War*, p. 18.

disinterested in overseas colonies. The government sought to assume from private companies principal responsibility for economic development in the colonies. The Reichstag, however, was opposed to using state funds for colonial development.[153] Part of the problem was that the anticolonial lobby effectively communicated the message that formal empire simply did not pay. The evidence that the anticolonialists marshaled was incontrovertible. In 1904, Germany's trade with its colonies was 0.5 percent of total foreign trade. Togoland was the only colony that was self-supporting; in all the others, colonial costs outstripped revenues. In 1905, 204,291,000 marks were spent on the colonies, while colonial revenues stood at 15,636,000 marks. Groups opposed to colonialism also debunked the argument that overseas empire was needed for emigration. In 1903, only 5,125 Germans were living in the colonies. Of these, 1,567 were government officials and military personnel.[154] In combination with stories of widespread corruption and abuse in the colonies, this information dampened what little enthusiasm for overseas empire existed among the populace.

Specific sectors of society continued to support peripheral empire, but, as during the 1880s, they did so largely for instrumental reasons: to unite the domestic polity through foreign ambition, to rally support for the navy, and to gain leverage over other colonial powers. Elites during the 1880s had never bothered to sell overseas empire to the public, nor did they attempt to do so after 1897. Accordingly, the periphery never entered the political mainstream. As Smith notes, "The colonial empire was a peripheral aspect of German life."[155] The political backlash over the first Morocco crisis resulted from the public's perception that Germany had been humiliated, not because the country had failed to enlarge its African empire. Even after the Algeciras Conference, the Reichstag refused to approve emergency funds to deal with uprisings in Southwest Africa. Bulow dissolved the Reichstag and succeeded in coaxing the bill through a reconstituted house. But to do so, he had to rely on nationalist rhetoric to disarm the left. The socialists indeed suffered in the elections of January 1907. Yet the center and right were also becoming increasingly infused with militant nationalism.[156] The German government initially found it easier to maneuver in a domestic milieu charged with nationalist fervor. The problem was that this fervor and the foreign policies associated with it were leaving Germany in an increasingly perilous international environment.

[153] Smith, *German Colonial Empire*, pp. 130–132.
[154] Townsend, *Rise and Fall of Germany's Colonial Empire*, pp. 238–240.
[155] Smith, *German Colonial Empire*, p. 233.
[156] Townsend, *Rise and Fall of Germany's Colonial Empire*, pp. 241–243; and Smith, *German Colonial Empire*, pp. 183–193.

Far more intractable for Bulow than colonial issues was the problem of taxation. The costs of external ambition—the battlefleet, the operations in Kiaochow and Southwest Africa, colonial administration—forced the government to increase its revenues. During 1905–1906, the Centre party tried to use disputes over tax reform and the budget deficit to undermine Bulow's position. The conservative coalition came to his rescue.[157] By the end of the decade, however, financial questions were to split the alliance between iron and rye and force Bulow's resignation. The chancellor wanted to institute an inheritance tax to cover the government's dramatic increases in military spending. The propertied classes successfully resisted Bulow on this issue, persuading him to turn to indirect taxation. This move, however, alienated the commercial and industrial sectors and led, in 1909, to a decisive rift between agriculture and industry.[158] The logroll that had produced compromise turned into a logjam that produced stalemate. The state "could be manoeuvred only through short-lived compromises between rival centres of power into an increasing ossification."[159]

When Bethmann replaced Bulow in 1909, he faced a domestic crisis that grew progressively worse. His repeated efforts to reconstitute a conservative coalition failed.[160] Bethmann suffered two votes of no confidence in the Reichstag. And the Social Democrats made gains in the by-elections of 1910. Furthermore, Tirpitz and Bethmann began to feud over the pace of naval building and over whether to make concessions to Britain. Not only was the Reichstag pitted against the government and agriculture against industry, but divisions were sprouting among top decision makers themselves. As Wehler comments, the emerging camps "remained in a strange state of paralysis amid an atmosphere of gloomy fear and complete mutual mistrust."[161]

Unable to manage the domestic situation through coalition building, the government again sought to use nationalism to unite a fragmented polity. The second Morocco crisis was inspired, at least in part, by efforts to ease the domestic stalemate. Kiderlen in May 1911 explicitly noted that his desire to intervene was partially motivated by domestic considerations: "We may assume without a doubt that tangible results [in Morocco] will change the views of many dissatisfied voters and will have a not inconsiderable effect on the outcome of the pending Reichstag elections."[162] As in 1905, this strategy backfired. The public outcry

---

[157] Craig, *Germany*, pp. 277–283.
[158] Berghahn, *Germany and the Approach of War*, p. 84.
[159] Wehler, *German Empire*, p. 64.
[160] Fischer, *War of Illusions*, p. 72.
[161] Wehler, *German Empire*, p. 99.
[162] Cited in Fischer, *War of Illusions*, p. 73.

in response to Germany's failure was far more shrill than in 1905–1906, intensifying already strong currents of popular nationalism. In 1912, both the Defense Association *(Wehrverein)* and the Army League were founded to lobby for armaments and increases in the size of Germany's ground forces. Within one year, the Army League had attracted 78,000 individual members and 200,000 corporate members.[163] These groups fueled nationalist sentiment and strengthened the extreme right wing. The feud between Tirpitz and Bethmann escalated as the chancellor tried to restrain naval building and salvage Germany's relationship with Britain. He was facing a public, however, that blamed Britain for Germany's humiliation in Morocco and that was unwilling to countenance conceding further ground to the British.[164] In addition, the Social Democrats won a crushing victory in the 1912 elections. A coalition of the socialists and the Progressive People's party made the left the dominant bloc in the Reichstag.[165] The conservative elite could no longer resist the political changes that were a natural outgrowth of German industrialization and its impact on the composition and attitudes of the domestic populace. In 1870, the working class had represented one-fifth of the population; by 1907, this proportion had grown to over one-third.[166]

By 1912, the government had no choice but to rely almost exclusively on nationalism to establish some degree of control over a deeply divided country. As Fischer puts it, "After the defeat at the polls in 1912 imperialist agitation was increasingly used to ensure that the bourgeois parties were united against social democracy."[167] The problem was that "a radical nationalist politics to the right of the government had definitely taken shape."[168] Among the middle classes, nationalism was being replaced by militant patriotism and warmongering. The public's reaction to the second Morocco crisis speaks for itself. Fischer notes that "it was not only the right-wing press but also the normally progovernment papers of the bloc parties, the Conservatives and the Centre Party, which called upon the government to hold on to Morocco. The Foreign Ministry could not banish the spirits which it had conjured up."[169] The following commentary from the press was by no means outside mainstream opinion: "The attitude of the German government is becoming increasingly incomprehensible to most patri-

---

[163] Ibid., pp. 105–107.
[164] Ibid., p. 135.
[165] Wehler, *German Empire*, p. 196.
[166] Herwig, *"Luxury" Fleet*, p. 2.
[167] Fischer, *War of Illusions*, p. 230.
[168] Eley, *From Unification to Nazism*, p. 79.
[169] Fischer, *War of Illusions*, p. 80.

German elites swept along
in tide of nationalism

ots. . . . For the nation the tension is almost unbearable; it longs, if
our neighbours do not allow us to enjoy in peace what is ours, for the
great test so that there can be a redistribution of the places in the
European order. . . . Nothing else interests the public and the only
question is: do we march?"[170] In a state of virtual paralysis, ruling
elites were swept along by this tide of rabid nationalism. Retrenchment
was simply not politically viable. The government was forced to cater
to the formerly extremist views that now represented the political center of gravity among the middle classes. By 1912, Germany's decision
makers were besieged at home and abroad.

My argument is not that domestic political pressure was solely responsible for Germany's self-defeating behavior—that is, that popular
opinion was the only constraint on elite behavior. As mentioned above,
some members of the elite community were as wedded to imperial
strategic conceptions as were extremist elements within the populace
at large. Although Tirpitz's hand was at times forced by the extreme
right, he clearly bought into the strategic conceptions that had been
concocted for instrumental purposes. He sincerely believed in weltpolitik and was willing to go to war to stake Germany's claim as a world
power. But it is also clear that other top decision makers—Bethmann
in particular—were acutely aware that domestic forces were spinning
out of control and forcing the government to pursue an extremely
dangerous foreign policy. Accordingly, he began to wage a campaign
among his colleagues and the public to gain support for a more moderate course. After the end of the Agadir crisis, he expressed concern
about the intensity of the public outcry and the mounting clamor for
war.[171] He warned the government of the dangers of excessive propaganda, arguing that "to inflame national passions to the boiling point
for the sake of utopian schemes of conquest or party purposes is to
compromise patriotism and to waste a valuable asset."[172] Berghahn
notes that "the thrust of public opinion increasingly imposed restrictions on the flexibility of German policy. In fact, this latter problem
became so serious that the Chancellor decided to utter a warning in
the Reichstag that wars had not always been planned and executed by
governments but that 'nations have often been driven into war by
noisy and fanatical minorities.' Today this danger, he added, was
greater than ever."[173]

During the course of 1913, Bethmann appears to have given up ef-

---

[170] *Allgemeine Evangelish-Lutherische Kirchenzeitung,* cited in Ibid., p. 87.
[171] Moses, *Politics of Illusion,* p. 79.
[172] Cited in Fischer, *War of Illusions,* p. 91.
[173] Cited in Berghahn, *Germany and the Approach of War,* pp. 173–174.

[414]

forts to divert the building nationalist fervor and agreed to prepare the country for war. By that point, militant patriotism was raging and the military balance was shifting decidedly against Germany. The government was entrapped by domestic political forces and powerful strategic images at home and encircled by superior military force abroad. It is for this reason that elites saw no choice but to go to war despite awareness that Germany might well not survive a military clash with the Entente. Not surprisingly, Germany's decision makers moved toward war with an increasing sense of resignation and desperation.

Military Services. The German military establishment clearly served as one of the key vehicles through which overly ambitious strategic conceptions became institutionalized and routinized. The navy's organizational interests became wedded to its procurement program which, in turn, revolved around challenging Britain's naval supremacy in Europe. An Anglo-German agreement to limit naval building would have threatened the navy's principal objective and diminished its political power and budget. Naval officials played a key role in resisting efforts to slow the pace of fleet construction and reach an accord with Britain. In so doing, they fueled Anglo-German antagonism, solidified the Entente, and contributed to self-encirclement. In addition, the navy took charge of the propaganda campaign organized to sell weltpolitik to the public. The army played a less direct role in domestic and foreign policy until 1912. After that point, the General Staff's concern about adverse shifts in the military balance, its organizational commitment to the Schlieffen Plan and an offensive strategy, and its rigid mobilization plans clearly pushed elites toward a decision for war.

The organizational interests of the military services were, however, a symptom, not a cause, of the pathologies that drove Germany to pursue self-defeating behavior. The services were only one piece of the puzzle, one component of an elite community infused with notions of weltpolitik and struggling to preserve its control over an increasingly fragmented domestic polity. Military officials were by no means the only members of the top decision-making community intent on using foreign ambition to export Germany's domestic conflicts. Rather, the military conspired with civilian leaders in using nationalism as a means of unifying the right and disarming the left. And, after being subjected to elite lobbying for a decade, the public had outpaced even the services in its support for an expansionist foreign policy and its unwillingness to countenance accommodation. The 1908 naval bill was far more ambitious than Tirpitz had intended; the extreme right forced his hand.[174] In short, the military services were willing accomplices, but they are not the key culprits responsible for the predicament in which Germany found itself in 1914. The services joined civilian elites in using aggressive nationalism to preserve the traditional political order and gain support for external ambition. But this was a domestic strategy that entailed high costs. The services and the government alike became entrapped in a strategic culture that led Germany into a self-destructive war.

Conclusions

Like Japan, Germany fell prey to excessive ambition during its ascendance as a great power. Also like Japan, Germany in its early period of ascendance, between 1870 and the late 1890s, sought to expand its power and influence in an opportunistic yet cautious fashion. Only in 1897 did Germany embark on the same type of self-destructive path that Japan followed beginning in 1937. So too was it vulnerability—working through elite beliefs and strategic culture—that induced both Japanese and German elites to pursue overly competitive, self-defeating policies.

Yet there are also marked differences between the experiences of Japan and Germany. Domestic developments did induce Japanese elites to adopt competitive foreign policies in 1931, but Japan's excessive international ambition was triggered principally by the economic vulnerability that emerged after 1937 because of the war in China. German elites, on the other hand, began to pursue overly competitive foreign policies primarily because of the government's domestic vulnerability. It was not until 1906 that military vulnerability became a key factor fueling excessive external ambition. The public also played a far more important role in Germany than in Japan. By the late 1930s, the Japanese military had so much political power that it essentially controlled domestic and foreign policy. Japanese decision makers were entrapped more by the strategic conceptions that infused the elite community than by domestic political currents. The Reichstag, unlike the Diet, was not eviscerated by the government; German elites could not ignore the legislature and had to pay close attention to election results and shifts in party alignments. In addition, deep splits emerged within Germany's traditional ruling elite. Especially after the erosion of the alliance between agriculture and industry, fragmentation and division, not centralized authority, characterized the German government. Though many German elites bought into the strategic con-

[174] Ibid., p. 65.

ceptions originally crafted for domestic purposes, the strong currents of nationalism stirred up within the broader body politic played a crucial role in strengthening hard-liners, weakening moderates, and pushing the nation toward war. Unlike in Japan, elites in Germany never sold overseas empire to the public, the bureaucracy, or the military services. Accordingly, they did not fall prey to overextension in the periphery. But they did propagate grandiose strategic conceptions and a brand of popular nationalism that led to excessive ambition and self-encirclement in Europe itself.

Germany's self-defeating behavior was the product of acute domestic as well as international vulnerability. Elites sought to disarm domestic threats by focusing the public's attention on external ambition and establishing Germany as one of the world's dominant powers. But in doing so, they precipitated the formation of an opposing coalition of superior military force. Efforts to fragment this coalition only served to increase its cohesion while simultaneously spreading ambitious strategic concepts among elites, wedding the organizational interests of the military to expansionist policies, and fueling nationalistic fervor among the German populace. By the time elites realized the predicament into which they were directing the country, it was too late. They were entrapped in a strategic culture that was rapidly pushing the country into a war that it did not have the resources to win.

[7]

The United States

After Japan's surrender brought World War II to a close, U.S. decision makers faced the daunting task of adjusting American grand strategy to a radically altered international distribution of power. American military capability and industrial capacity had reached unprecedented heights. Western Europe and Japan had been devastated by war. Only the Soviet Union was left with a military establishment that could rival that of the United States. Accordingly, shaping U.S.-Soviet relations was the central task facing American elites during the early postwar years.

Between 1945 and 1950, American thinking about U.S.-Soviet relations underwent two key transformations. At the outset of the postwar period, elites hoped to turn wartime collaboration into peacetime cooperation. Yet the initial optimism of U.S. decision makers was short-lived. During the course of 1946 and early 1947, the Kremlin's recalcitrant behavior gradually induced the Truman administration to back away from the accommodationist stance toward the Soviet Union that had been the legacy of wartime alliance. Rather than viewing the Soviet Union as an ally with whom to share responsibility for building a postwar order, American elites came to see the Soviet Union as their principal adversary. Cooperative policies had to give way to competitive ones. The administration adopted containment of Soviet expansion as the overriding objective of U.S. policy. Containment involved deterring Soviet aggression and ensuring that Eurasia's main centers of industrial capability not fall under the control of the Kremlin. Because the administration viewed the prospect of deliberate Soviet aggression as remote, preventing the spread of Soviet control was to be achieved mainly by assisting Western Europe and Japan with the task of political and economic recovery. A major military buildup was unnecessary. Moreover, by heightening Soviet perceptions of vulnerability, rearmament might only fuel U.S.-Soviet rivalry. The Truman administration also sought to contain Soviet influence by exacerbating splits within the communist bloc and by seeking to stem, on a selective basis, the

[418]

spread of communist movements in the periphery. The Marshall Plan and Truman Doctrine were the main policy initiatives through which the administration pursued these objectives. The containment of communism thus entailed the expansion of American overseas commitments. But such expansion occurred only selectively; U.S. decision makers explicitly avoided overly competitive policies that could have provoked hostilities with the Soviet Union or mired the United States in costly conflicts in the periphery.

The second critical shift in postwar U.S. foreign policy took place in late 1949 and early 1950 and was encapsulated in NSC 68, the broad reexamination of objectives and programs forwarded from the National Security Council (NSC) to President Truman in April 1950.[1] While containment of the Soviet Union remained the Truman administration's principal objective, implementing containment became a far more formidable and costly task. It was no longer sufficient to restore the confidence and stability of Western Europe and Japan; a major buildup of conventional and nuclear forces was now needed to deter Soviet expansion. Geographic priorities were also redefined. Soviet influence had to be resisted in all areas of the globe, not only those that contained substantial military and industrial potential. This expansion in the scope of U.S. defense commitments occurred in large part because the Truman administration came to view international communism in more monolithic terms. Rather than seeking to foster splits within the communist bloc by offering left-leaning states an alternative to alignment with the Soviet Union, the United States began to focus containment on all communist regimes, regardless of the nature of their ties with Moscow. The militarization and globalization of containment involved a dramatic increase in the U.S. defense budget.

---

[1] Melvyn Leffler argues that 1947 was the key turning point in American foreign policy during the early post–World War II years: in 1947 long-term geopolitical and strategic concerns became fully integrated into America's peacetime foreign policy. American willingness to assume new international obligations manifested itself through the Truman Doctrine and through growing support for a massive aid program to Western Europe. See Melvyn Leffler, "Was 1947 a Turning Point in American Foreign Policy?" in *Centerstage: American Diplomacy since World War II*, ed. Carl Brown (New York: Holmes and Meier, 1990), pp. 19–42. My focus on 1946–1947 and 1949–1950 as two equally important turning points is based on two considerations. First, although a discrete set of policy initiatives associated with containing the Soviets did not emerge until 1947, it was in 1946 that the United States began to adopt a competitive as opposed to cooperative stance toward the Soviet Union. As I acknowledge below, top officials had by no means abandoned hope of returning to cordial relations with the Soviets, and, during the course of 1946, they did not pursue a consistent set of policies toward the Soviet Union. From this perspective, the policies adopted in 1947 constitute the culmination of a gradual process of change in policy, not a sharp turning point. Second, as becomes apparent below, the brand of containment implemented between 1946–1947 and 1949 differed in several crucial respects from that implemented from 1950 onward. Given my concern

Beginning in 1950, American overseas commitments expanded in indiscriminate fashion. The overly competitive policies associated with NSC 68 had adverse consequences for the long-term security of the United States in three key respects. First, the militarization of containment intensified U.S.-Soviet rivalry and fueled a conventional and nuclear arms race between the United States and the Soviet Union which might have otherwise been avoided or at least more moderate in scope and pace.[2] Second, the strategic logic that informed NSC 68 fostered the blurring of strategic priorities and, consequently, led to overextension in the periphery. Instead of basing policy on a set of clearly defined geographic priorities and bounding American commitments accordingly, U.S. elites committed themselves to resisting communism in all quarters of the globe. With their credibility at stake whenever and wherever the status quo was threatened, decision makers found themselves dragged into costly and unnecessary wars in the Third World.[3] Third, because they mistakenly equated indigenous leftist movements with Soviet expansionism, U.S. elites sought to resist and defeat popularly based indigenous political movements in the Third World. American policy, by pushing leftist regimes toward the Soviet Union, helped secure the very outcome—the formation of a network of Soviet client states—that it was intended to prevent.[4]

These interpretations are indeed contestable. Some scholars argue that the hard-line policies adopted in the wake of NSC 68, far from having the adverse consequences just enumerated, played a critical role in eventually inducing the Soviets to undertake the set of reforms that led to the end of the Cold War. The high cost of sustaining a confrontational relationship with the United States, they argue, persuaded the Soviets to scale back dramatically the scope of their external ambition. It is not the purpose of this chapter to pursue this debate, nor is the debate directly relevant to my primary concern with under-

---

with distinguishing between competitive and overly competitive policies, 1946–1947 and 1949–1950 serve as the most illuminating turning points.

[2] George Kennan, one of the main architects of U.S. foreign policy during the early postwar years, was himself critical of the decision to build the hydrogen bomb and establish a network of anti-Soviet military alliances because he feared that these moves would unnecessarily threaten the Soviets and, therefore, make them more aggressive. See, for example, "Considerations Affecting the Conclusion of a North Atlantic Security Pact," Policy Planning Staff (PPS) 43, 23 Nov. 1948, in *Containment: Documents on American Policy and Strategy, 1945–1950*, ed. Thomas Etzold and John Lewis Gaddis (New York: Columbia University Press, 1978), pp. 153–158; and John Lewis Gaddis, *Strategies of Containment* (Oxford: Oxford University Press, 1982), pp. 71–74.

[3] See, for example, Robert Johnson, "Exaggerating America's Stakes in Third World Conflicts," *International Security*, 10 (Winter 1985–86), 32–68.

[4] For an application of this argument to the Middle East, see Charles Kupchan, "American Globalism in the Middle East: The Roots of Regional Security Policy," *Political Science Quarterly*, 103 (Winter 1988–89), 585–611.

standing the sources of the policy change that occurred in 1949–1950.[5] That this debate still rages, however, suggests that the suppositions behind NSC 68, even if they did lead to unambiguously adverse consequences, were at least arguably consistent with available information about Soviet intentions and capabilities. It is with the advantage of hindsight that one can detect the overly competitive nature of NSC 68 and its contribution to America's Cold War excesses—its "overkill" nuclear arsenal and the Vietnam War, to name two. In this sense, I am concerned with explaining the emergence of a set of policies that won out over another set of policies, both of which were based on reasonable strategic assumptions given available information.

This characteristic of the empirical inquiry has important analytic implications and distinguishes this historical chapter from the four that precede it.[6] In the other historical cases, I have sought to explain behavior that was manifestly and unambiguously *un*reasonable. I found that sufficient information was available to indicate to elites that they should have pursued policies other than those that they did and that elite beliefs, to varying degrees, were responsive to information suggesting that such a reorientation was needed. It was, in large part, this finding that made the constraints associated with strategic culture—working through domestic political pressures as well as through national self-images and strategic conceptions deeply embedded and institutionalized within the elite community—crucial to a compelling explanation of adjustment failure. In the American case, because I am concerned with explaining policies that were arguably reasonable and consistent with available information, I can rely more comfortably on elite beliefs

[5] On this debate, see Thomas Risse-Kappen, "Did 'Peace through Strength' End the Cold War? Lessons from INF," *International Security*, 16 (Summer 1991), 162–188.

[6] My argument should not be interpreted as an endorsement of American exceptionalism—that U.S. elites were less extreme in their behavior than the elites of the other countries I examine. Rather, the unique aspects of my argument in this chapter stem from my case selection and periodization of the historical record. Because of my concern with understanding the causes of the switch from competitive to overly competitive policies, I focus primarily on the initial effect of high vulnerability on strategic beliefs and strategic culture. Unlike in the other cases, I do not extend the historical analysis to cover periods in which elite beliefs changed but policies did not change accordingly. In other words, I concentrate on stages 1 and 2 of my model and not on stage 3, the period in which strategic beliefs are disconfirmed by incoming information but elites are unable to reverse course because of the strategic culture they molded to gain support for their policies. This chapter's design stems from the fact that the dynamics that fueled overly competitive behavior can be adequately studied by focusing on the 1945–1950 period. Were I to extend the analysis to cover the Vietnam War, the U.S. case would more closely resemble the other historical cases in the book. U.S. elites prosecuted the war in Vietnam despite information that discredited the suppositions on which policy was initially based. They did so largely because they became entrapped in the strategic images and domestic political forces that they had earlier created.

[421]

alone to explain outcomes. Strategic culture may still be an important variable affecting decisions, but I no longer need to rely on it (or some other variable, for that matter) to solve the empirical puzzle.

Accordingly, the argument of this chapter takes the following form. Soviet acquisition of atomic weaponry—and the resultant metropolitan vulnerability perceived by American elites—was the key cause of the reorientation of U.S. policy that took place in 1949–1950. Soviet acquisition of atomic capability had such a large impact on American perceptions of vulnerability because of the prominent role that the nuclear monopoly had played in U.S. war planning between 1946 and 1949. During those years, American planners saw little likelihood of deliberate Soviet attack but believed that Soviet conventional superiority would enable the Kremlin's forces to overrun most of Western Europe and Northeast Asia should war break out. Even if such initial setbacks occurred, however, U.S. atomic attacks on the Soviet Union would eventually allow the United States to prevail in a protracted conflict. The Soviet Union's successful atomic test of August 1949 not only raised the possibility of devastating attacks against the U.S. mainland, but also cast doubt on the assessment that the United States would be able to defeat the Soviets in a protracted war. American perceptions of vulnerability were exacerbated by the prospect of "piecemeal" communist aggression in the periphery, fueled by the communist victory in China.

Perceptions of high vulnerability had a telling effect on strategic beliefs. Deliberate Soviet aggression was now much more likely. The United States therefore had to redouble efforts to deter the Soviets and contain Soviet expansionism. But deterrence was no longer enough. The United States had to force Soviet elites to scale back the scope of their imperial ambition. Even if the Soviets did not initiate war, they would be emboldened by possession of nuclear weapons. Furthermore, the nuclear stand-off transformed the nature of the Cold War; U.S. elites now had to be as concerned about the balance of resolve as about the balance of material power. Compellent strategies were therefore necessary to demonstrate U.S. resolve. Efforts to demonstrate resolve in turn fueled concern about reputation, dominoes, and bandwagoning, leading to a blurring of geographic priorities and reinforcing belief in the need for a compellent stance, especially in the Third World. Accordingly, it was no longer sufficient to keep only major industrial areas from the Kremlin's control; the battle against communism had to be waged wherever Soviet ideology threatened to take root. North Korea's attack on South Korea furthered the expansion of American overseas commitments in both the core and periphery.

The Korean War served to translate into policy the militarization and globalization of containment recommended by NSC 68.

Of secondary importance, but by no means insignificant, in producing this critical shift in U.S. policy was elite manipulation of strategic culture. When Harry S. Truman took office in April 1945, he faced an American public that had been led by Franklin Roosevelt to believe in the potential for postwar cooperation with the Soviet Union and that was clamoring for rapid demobilization and cuts in defense spending and foreign aid. It soon became apparent to the Truman administration, however, that relations with the Soviets were going to be characterized by competition, not cooperation, and that the United States had to provide economic assistance to Western Europe to foster political stability and stem the spread of communism. The Truman Doctrine and an accompanying education campaign were unfurled in 1947 primarily to mobilize Congress and the public behind a more ambitious foreign policy and a more competitive stance toward the Soviet Union. In combination with increasingly frequent accusations of Soviet espionage in the United States, the administration's lobbying of the public set in motion a powerful wave of anticommunist sentiment that culminated in the infamous trials and purges sponsored by Senator Joseph McCarthy.

This shift in public attitudes affected policy in two ways. First, it effectively silenced those members of the policy community who favored a less competitive stance toward the Soviet Union. Those who argued against the hard-line policies advocated by NSC 68 were often branded "un-American." Those who harbored reservations about such policies kept silent for fear of being so branded. Second, the domestic anticommunist consensus forced the Truman administration into adopting policies that it considered ill-conceived. The administration, for example, explicitly decided not to intervene militarily to prevent a communist victory in China; the costs were too high and the likelihood of success too low. A domestic backlash was, however, forthcoming. If resisting communist influence was vital to American security, then why, critics asked, should containment not be implemented in the Far East? These domestic pressures soon contributed to a new level of U.S. military commitment in East Asia. The administration found itself entrapped in the strategic images that it had earlier propagated among the public to gain support for its policies. Thereafter, the economic interests of the defense sector and the organizational interests of the military also became wedded to a globalized and militarized version of containment.

This interpretation is not meant to challenge the assertion that a new U.S. posture in the Far East was directly affected by a hardening of elite attitudes. Indeed, by the beginning of 1950, elite beliefs and public attitudes were running on parallel tracks; both were tilting toward an increasingly hard-line stance toward the Soviet Union. Moreover, the policies that resulted were appropriate in their basic orientation: the Kremlin had indeed demonstrated aggressive intent, and competitive policies were needed to contain the Soviets. But the synergistic relationship between strategic beliefs and domestic politics meant that U.S. policy, while on target in general terms, was misguided in its emphases and texture. A new policy toward the Far East was warranted, but not one that starkly viewed all regional conflict as the product of a struggle between communism and democracy. Missing from the brand of containment implemented after 1949 were the flexibility, the focus on political and economic as opposed to military instruments, and the clear sense of strategic priorities that had guided policy during the first four postwar years. Beginning in 1950, images of a pervasive East-West conflict infused the elite community and the public alike, shaping mass attitudes, institutionalizing militarized and globalized strategic conceptions, and anchoring the organizational interests of the military and the economic interests of the defense industry to unnecessarily demanding roles and missions. America's Cold War strategic culture had taken shape. Vulnerability, acting through elite beliefs and strategic culture, brought the Cold War to a new level of animosity and, arguably, set the stage for some of the key failings of American foreign policy during the postwar era.

1946–1949: The Formulation and Implementation of Containment

Roosevelt's Legacy

It was during 1944 and 1945 that planners began to contemplate the possibility that the Soviet Union, though still an ally, might one day be the United States's most formidable foe.[7] Even though military plans for the postwar era identified the Soviets as a potential enemy, the planning community showed little concern about either the immediacy or the seriousness of the Soviet threat. Such complacency was based on the assessment that Soviet war-making capability—both manpower and industry—had suffered enormous damage during the war. Even if

---

[7] Until 1945, planners were uncertain as to which country should serve as the focus of war plans for the future. In addition to the Soviet Union, Japan and Germany were identified as prime candidates. See Michael Sherry, *Preparing for the Next War: American Plans for Postwar Defense, 1941–1945* (New Haven: Yale University Press, 1977), pp. 159–168, 213–214.

the Soviets entertained aggressive intentions, exhaustion and depleted resources would severely restrict their ability to wage war.[8] A consensus also emerged among American elites that Soviet behavior was motivated by legitimate security concerns, not by expansionist aspirations.[9] This reading of Soviet behavior had won a host of new supporters in May 1943, when Moscow announced that it was dissolving the Communist International, the organization founded in 1919 through which the Soviets had hoped to export communism.[10] From this perspective, Soviet insistence on maintaining a sphere of influence in Eastern Europe was not cause for alarm. On the contrary, given the suffering inflicted on the Soviets during the war, their desire to secure friendly neighbors was quite understandable.[11]

Regardless of who the eventual enemy might be, a guiding principle informed thinking within the Roosevelt administration about postwar grand strategy: no single power should be allowed to dominate Eurasia. Several considerations shaped this overarching objective. First, any power that came to dominate the Eurasian landmass would eventually have resources under its control sufficient to threaten American security. Eurasia's raw materials and industrial capability therefore had to be distributed among independent centers of power.[12] Second, the administration was concerned about the effects of postwar demobilization on the American economy. Access to at least some of Eurasia's raw materials and markets was deemed essential to the country's economic vitality.[13] Third, policy makers believed that economic nationalism and trade barriers had been primary causes of World War II. Building a peaceful postwar environment meant erecting a liberal, multilateral trading order. This order, in turn, depended on preventing a single power from organizing a closed Eurasian trading bloc.[14] Finally, defense planners were concerned about maintaining bases on the Eurasian landmass and its periphery. The advent of strategic bombers meant that U.S. territory could now be attacked by a distant adversary. Protecting U.S. territory therefore entailed building a forward line of defense in areas far from U.S. borders. According to the concept of "defense in depth," bases in Western Europe, the Middle East, and

---

[8] For an analysis of war plans, see Sherry, *Preparing for the Next War*, esp. pp. 213–215.

[9] Melvyn Leffler, "The American Conception of National Security and the Beginnings of the Cold War, 1945–48," *American Historical Review*, 89 (April 1984), 349.

[10] John Lewis Gaddis, *The United States and the Origins of the Cold War, 1941–1947* (New York: Columbia University Press, 1972), pp. 47–56.

[11] Sherry, *Preparing for the Next War*, pp. 178–182.

[12] Leffler, "American Conception of National Security," pp. 356–357.

[13] Gaddis, *United States and the Origins of the Cold War*, p. 189.

[14] Ibid., p. 20.

East Asia would be needed to attack the industrial centers of potential enemies in Eurasia as well as to control the major sea lanes.[15]

Even though assessments indicated that the Soviets had no intention of attacking Western Europe, the Soviet Union did emerge from the war as the dominant military power in Eurasia. Shaping the postwar order therefore meant, first and foremost, translating the U.S.-Soviet military alliance into peacetime cooperation. Roosevelt envisaged a great-power condominium to manage international relations. He initially put forward the concept of the "Four Policemen": that Great Britain, China, the United States, and the Soviet Union should collectively assume responsibility for enforcing a postwar international order.[16] Roosevelt later worked hard to establish the United Nations as a collective security organization whose mandate was to preserve peace on a global basis. As part of this cooperative arrangement, Roosevelt, Stalin, and Churchill, at their meeting in Yalta in February 1945, agreed that the Soviets would enjoy a sphere of influence in Eastern Europe, allowing them to ensure that hostile powers did not emerge along their borders. Roosevelt's willingness to give Stalin a relatively free hand in Eastern Europe was based at least in part on his belief that Soviet hostility stemmed from insecurity and vulnerability, not from aggressive intent.[17] Accordingly, the United States should seek to draw the Soviets into a cooperative relationship, not to isolate or encircle them. In sum, Roosevelt was confident that the United States and Soviet Union could together forge a peaceful postwar order that would meet the security needs of both parties.

In shaping the post–World War II order, Roosevelt drew an important lesson from President Woodrow Wilson's experience at the close of World War I. While Wilson had enjoyed considerable success in selling a collective security organization—the League of Nations—to his allies in Europe, he had neglected to garner sufficient support at home. Congress refused to endorse U.S. participation in the league; Wilson and his design for a postwar order suffered a serious setback. Roosevelt would not repeat this mistake. During the closing years of the war, he orchestrated an ambitious information campaign to rally the American public behind the United Nations and convince the electorate that long-term cooperation with the Soviets was not only desirable but also attainable.[18] Americans could not, Roosevelt told the public, retreat into

---

[15] Leffler, "American Conception of National Security," pp. 350–351.

[16] Gaddis, *Strategies of Containment*, p. 10.

[17] Ibid., p. 9.

[18] For details of the campaign, see Richard Freeland, *The Truman Doctrine and the Origins of McCarthyism: Foreign Policy, Domestic Politics, and Internal Security, 1946–1948* (New York: Schocken Books, 1974), pp. 41–47; Daniel Yergin, *Shattered Peace: The Origins of the*

isolationism as soon as the fighting stopped. Public attitudes shifted accordingly. While Americans were opposed to peacetime international obligations at the close of World War I, by May 1943 74 percent of the public supported American participation in a postwar international police force.[19] During the closing years of the war, only one in five Americans distrusted the Soviets and saw little prospect of postwar U.S.-Soviet cooperation.[20]

While the Roosevelt administration succeeded in garnering public support for its conception of a postwar order, these efforts to shape public attitudes did not come without costs. The vision of a liberal order set forth before the public differed significantly from the concrete arrangements agreed upon by Roosevelt and Stalin. While attacking spheres of influence at home, Roosevelt was signing off on them at Yalta. In fact, fear of alienating voters of East European origin kept the administration from revealing the full extent of the agreements reached at Yalta.[21] Because of his untimely death in April 1945, Roosevelt never fully confronted the domestic political difficulties associated with the widening gap between the substance of his foreign policies and the expectations emerging among the American public. Through the spring of 1945, U.S.-Soviet relations were still on a favorable trajectory. Roosevelt did, however, saddle his successor with problematic domestic constraints. For it was in early 1946 that the United States and the Soviet Union began to drift apart, leaving the U.S. public disillusioned and the Truman administration faced with the formidable task of explaining and justifying the hostility mounting between the two powers that were to have cooperatively forged a liberal postwar order.

Strategic Assessments

From 1945 until mid-1949, U.S. intelligence assessments indicated a favorable military balance between the United States and the Soviet Union. Perceptions of strategic sufficiency persisted despite awareness of the Soviet Union's conventional superiority. In fact, war planners admitted that the Soviets had the conventional capability to overrun much of Western Europe and the Far East in a matter of months. The key factor offsetting Soviet conventional superiority was the United States's nuclear monopoly. Assessments indicated that the United

---

Cold War and the National Security State (Boston: Houghton Mifflin, 1977), pp. 44–46; Gaddis, *Strategies of Containment*, pp. 12–13.

[19] Yergin, *Shattered Peace*, p. 46.
[20] Gaddis, *United States and the Origins of the Cold War*, p. 46.
[21] Ibid., pp. 133–149.

States could win a protracted conflict against the Soviets by using long-range bombers with atomic weapons to attack military, industrial, and, potentially, civilian targets within the Soviet Union. Policy makers thus believed that the nuclear monopoly provided the United States the wherewithal to defeat the Soviet Union should war break out.

During the first five postwar years, civilian and military analysts also agreed that war between the United States and the Soviet Union was a remote possibility. Deliberate Soviet aaggression, while not out of the question, was deemed extremely unlikely. Michael Sherry has summarized the military's view during 1945–1946: "The Soviet Union presented no immediate threat, the services acknowledged. Its economy and manpower were exhausted by the war, its technology was primitive by American standards, and its immediate goals were being achieved through occupation and wartime agreements. Consequently, the USSR would concentrate on internal reconstruction and limited diplomatic objectives for the next several years."[22] Exactly how long this period of low threat would last was a question on which there was considerably less agreement. In mid-1945, the director of the Office of Strategic Services (OSS) asserted that the services could assume, for planning purposes, that the Soviets would avoid war for at least ten to fifteen years.[23] By late 1947, this assessment had been revised. As the Joint Strategic Plans Committee of the Joint Chiefs of Staff (JCS) put it, "Theoretically, the U.S.S.R. should not, in the short term, commence any planned war. Considering the internal industrial and scientific tasks confronting the Soviet Union in her program of war preparation, and her politico-economic problems in recently subjugated territories, this short term should be at least five, and probably ten, years."[24] NSC 20/4, which served as a definitive statement of the administration's policies as of late 1948, concluded that Soviet "policies are today probably motivated in large measure by defensive considerations," and postulated that the Soviets would likely be sufficiently prepared to initiate conflict by no later than 1955.[25]

This widespread belief that deliberate Soviet aggression was unlikely was based on two suppositions. First, both military and civilian analysts agreed that with the securing of Soviet domination of Eastern Europe, the Soviets would calculate that their remaining objectives in

[22] Sherry, *Preparing for the Next War*, p. 214.

[23] Melvyn Leffler, *A Preponderance of Power: National Security, the Truman Administration, and the Cold War, 1945–52* (Stanford: Stanford University Press, 1992), p. 61.

[24] JSPC 814/3, "Estimate of Probable Developments in the World Political Situation up to 1957," 11 Dec. 1947, in *Containment*, ed. Etzold and Gaddis, p. 288.

[25] NSC 20/4, "U.S. Objectives with Respect to the USSR to Counter Soviet Threats to U.S. Security," 23 Nov. 1948, in *Containment*, ed. Etzold and Gaddis, pp. 205–206.

Europe could be achieved without the use of force. As a study by the JCS put it in late 1945, "The immediate objectives of the U.S.S.R. in Europe are already largely accomplished. What remains to be done either does not require or does not warrant resort to international hostilities."[26] This view still held in late 1948. According to NSC 20/4, the Soviet Union "is still seeking to achieve its aims primarily by political means, accompanied by military intimidation."[27] Second, planners believed that the Soviet Union would not initiate hostilities unless the Soviet military calculated that it would have a reasonable chance of attaining victory.[28] U.S. analysts posited that Soviet confidence about victory depended on two factors: the acquisition of atomic weapons and the renewal of the Soviet Union's industrial infrastructure. This logic was set forth by the JCS as follows: "It seems reasonable to assume that planned premeditated major warfare will not occur until our most probable opponent has developed and attained a stockpile of atomic or other weapons capable of comparable effect if used against the war making capacity of the United States, and until he has developed an industrial capacity capable of supporting a long major war without industrial assistance from outside Eurasia."[29]

These assessments did not mean that the policy community was certain that war would not occur before these two conditions were fulfilled. Though unlikely, hostilities could still occur as a result of accident or misperception. NSC 20/4, for example, asserted that while deliberate war was a remote possibility, "war might arise through miscalculation, through failure of either side to estimate accurately how far the other can be pushed."[30] Plans for major war with the Soviet Union therefore had to be drawn up and updated regularly, given the changes in weapons technology and force levels occurring on both sides. These war plans reveal a great deal about how U.S. analysts viewed the military balance during the early postwar years.

Intelligence estimates indicated that the Soviets enjoyed massive conventional superiority over the United States and West European countries.[31] Had the Soviets chosen to initiate hostilities on either their western or eastern frontier, opposing ground forces would not have been able to block the Red Army's advance. NSC 20/4 left little doubt

[26] JCS document of 29 Nov. 1945, cited in Harry Borowski, *A Hollow Threat: Strategic Air Power and Containment before Korea* (Westport, Conn.: Greenwood Press, 1982), p. 94.

[27] NSC 20/4, in *Containment*, ed. Etzold and Gaddis, p. 207.

[28] See Gregg Herken, *The Winning Weapon: The Atomic Bomb in the Cold War, 1945–1950* (New York: Knopf, 1980), p. 277.

[29] JCS 626/3, "Formula for the Determination of a National Stockpile," 3 Feb. 1948, in *Containment*, ed. Etzold and Gaddis, p. 313.

[30] NSC 20/4, in *Containment*, ed. Etzold and Gaddis, p. 207.

[31] Borowski, *Hollow Threat*, pp. 92–93.

about the scope of Soviet conventional superiority: "Present intelligence estimates attribute to Soviet armed forces the capability of overrunning in about six months all of Continental Europe and the Near East as far as Cairo, while simultaneously occupying important continental points in the Far East."[32] Rather than attempting to block the initial Soviet advance, U.S. troops would evacuate Western Europe, seeking to hold the British Isles as a potential staging ground for a counteroffensive. At least as important as holding Britain was the defense of the Middle East/North Africa region. While planners debated whether preserving access to Middle East oil should be a primary objective of U.S. operations, there was no question that defense of the Cairo/Suez base area was critical to allied operations. It was primarily from bases in Egypt that American bombers could reach key industrial targets in the Soviet Union. And from 1947 onward, atomic attacks on Soviet war-making capacity became the central feature of American plans for war with the Soviet Union.[33]

Though some quarters—the navy in particular—voiced skepticism about the ability of atomic attacks to devastate Soviet war-making capability, a consensus emerged among both military and civilian leaders that the United States's nuclear arsenal would allow it to prevail in a war with the Soviet Union.[34] Nuclear attack would either end the war

[32] NSC 20/4, in *Containment*, ed. Etzold and Gaddis, p. 206.

[33] See JCS 1844/13, "Brief of Short Range Emergency War Plan (HALFMOON)," 21 July 1948; JSPC 877/59, "Brief of Joint Outline Emergency War Plan (OFFTACKLE)," 26 May 1949; and JCS 1725/1, "Strategic Guidance for Industrial Mobilization Planning," 1 May 1947 (all reprinted in *Containment*, ed. Etzold and Gaddis). See also David Alan Rosenberg, "The Origins of Overkill: Nuclear Weapons and American Strategy, 1945–1960," in *Strategy and Nuclear Deterrence*, ed. Steven Miller (Princeton: Princeton University Press, 1984), pp. 122 ff.; and Robert Art, "The United States: Nuclear Weapons and Grand Strategy," in *Security with Nuclear Weapons?* ed. Regina Karp (Oxford: Oxford University Press, 1991). For discussion of earlier war plans, see Herken, *Winning Weapon*, pp. 219–230.

[34] The navy, fearful that its mission was being undermined by the growing reliance on air power, challenged the assertion that atomic attacks would ensure a U.S. victory in the event of war with the Soviet Union. The navy doubted that atomic attacks on Soviet cities would play a decisive role in the conflict and made public its concerns. In response to this public criticism, the administration purged the navy's high command during 1949. See David Alan Rosenberg, "American Atomic Strategy and the Hydrogen Bomb Decision," *Journal of American History*, 66 (June 1979), 70–78. Criticism of the nuclear component of war plans came not only from the navy. The Harmon report, a study headed by Lt. General Harmon of the air force and released in May 1949, concluded that atomic attacks would reduce Soviet industrial capacity by 30 to 40%, rather than by 50%, as had previously been predicted by the air force. The report did not reject reliance on nuclear weapons but cautioned against excessive optimism about the effectiveness of atomic attacks. Interestingly, this report was withheld from President Truman. See Borowski, *Hollow Threat*, pp. 182–183 n. 12; Rosenberg, "Origins of Overkill," p. 126; Rosenberg, "American Atomic Strategy," pp. 72–78; and Herken, *Winning Weapon*, pp. 293–295. Other critics of reliance on nuclear attack were concerned that the United States

directly or, at the least, so reduce Soviet capability that victory could be achieved "by employment of forces on a scale which would not jeopardize the national economy."[35] In Gregg Herken's word, the incorporation of nuclear retaliation into war plans bred "a new complacency founded upon the assumption that atomic bombs, even in small numbers, could be an effective counterbalance to Russia's conventional strength, and a decisive weapon in the event of war."[36]

Several pieces of evidence confirm the critical reliance of American war plans on nuclear weapons. In early 1948, President Truman, concerned that nuclear weapons might be banned through international agreement, requested that war plans for the conventional defense of Europe be drafted. The JCS began work on the project but soon abandoned it in favor of plans that relied on atomic retaliation to defeat the Soviets.[37] The war scare in the spring of 1948 similarly confirmed the reliance of U.S. war plans on atomic attack. The Soviet-sponsored coup in Czechoslovakia in February and the Berlin blockade in June led elites to conclude that war could no longer be seen as a remote possibility. In March, General Lucius Clay sent a telegram from Berlin to Washington warning that war might be imminent. The CIA circulated an assessment that conflict was not likely for sixty days but that hostilities could begin thereafter.[38] The Berlin blockade intensified these fears. The Truman administration responded principally by flexing its nuclear muscles. American bombers were dispatched to bases in Britain.[39] The air force embarked on an ambitious procurement program to increase its fleet of B-29s. Technological breakthroughs also allowed a rapid expan-

---

simply did not have sufficient bombers or bombs to carry out raids against designated targets. Indeed, between 1946 and 1948, American capabilities did fall considerably short of the number of delivery systems and weapons deemed necessary to damage severely Soviet war-making capability. Gregg Herken estimates that there may have been only a dozen operational bombs in the spring of 1947. The Joint Strategic Survey Committee reported to the JCS in October that the air force needed four hundred bombs to carry out an effective attack on Soviet war-making capabilities. Information about the size of the nuclear arsenal was, however, tightly guarded; few individuals knew of the magnitude of the shortfall. See Herken, *Winning Weapon*, pp. 196–198; Rosenberg, "American Atomic Strategy," p. 67; and Borowski, *Hollow Threat*, pp. 103–107. There was also some concern within the government that atomic attacks, especially those directed against Soviet cities, were immoral. See Herken, *Winning Weapon*, p. 290.

[35] JSPC 877/59, in Etzold and Gaddis, *Containment*, p. 331.

[36] Herken, *Winning Weapon*, p. 219. For discussion of specific war plans and assessments indicating that atomic attack would lead to a U.S. victory, see pp. 227–233.

[37] Rosenberg, "Origins of Overkill," pp. 122–123; Rosenberg, "American Atomic Strategy," pp. 68–69; and Herken, *Winning Weapon*, pp. 264–266.

[38] Yergin, *Shattered Peace*, pp. 351–353.

[39] These aircraft were not equipped to deliver nuclear weapons. See Borowski, *Hollow Threat*, pp. 125–126; and Herken, *Winning Weapon*, p. 259.

sion of the nuclear arsenal.[40] The fact that the Soviets backed down in Berlin increased U.S. confidence in the bargaining leverage associated with America's nuclear monopoly.[41]

In short, it was the U.S. nuclear monopoly that led to perceptions of strategic sufficiency and low metropolitan vulnerability during the early postwar years. The supposition that a deliberate Soviet attack was unlikely was based on the deterrent effect of nuclear weapons as well as on the exhausted state of the Soviet army and economy. The supposition that the United States would prevail over the Soviet Union should war break out was entirely dependent on projections about the ability of U.S. atomic attacks to knock out Soviet war-making capability. It follows that projections of how long the United States would retain exclusive access to nuclear weapons played a key role in shaping assessments of the balance.

Throughout the second half of the 1940s, the planning community remained quite divided about when the Soviets were likely to acquire the capability to produce nuclear weapons. General Leslie Groves, the head of the U.S. nuclear program, was highly skeptical of the Soviet weapons program. In 1945–1946, he forecast that it would take the Soviets as long as twenty years to develop nuclear weapons. Even if the Soviets were able to steal blueprints for atomic weapons from the United States, Groves argued, they would not be able to produce weapons until 1955 because of technological backwardness.[42] Many civilian scientists and some military analysts were more sober in their assessment of the Soviet nuclear program. The most cautious projections posited that the Soviets would have nuclear weapons by the early 1950s.[43] A consensus emerged by 1947–1948 that the Soviets would likely have the capability to carry out a nuclear attack against the United States by 1955 or 1956. As NSC 20/4 put it in November 1948, "Present estimates indicate that the current Soviet capabilities . . . will progressively increase and that by no later than 1955 the USSR will probably be capable of serious air attacks against the United States with atomic, biological and chemical weapons."[44]

Planners predicted, however, that even after 1955, the United States would likely retain a substantial edge in nuclear capability, largely because of constraints on Soviet access to uranium ore and, consequently, on bomb production. War plans drafted in early 1949, code-named

---

[40] Herken, *Winning Weapon*, p. 241; Yergin, *Shattered Peace*, pp. 358–362; and Art, "Nuclear Weapons and Grand Strategy," pp. 63–65.

[41] Herken, *Winning Weapon*, p. 274.

[42] Ibid., pp. 110, 125–126.

[43] Ibid., pp. 128, 230.

[44] NSC 20/4, in Etzold and Gaddis, *Containment*, p. 206.

Dropshot, projected that in 1957 the United States would enjoy a numerical edge in atomic weapons of roughly ten to one.[45] Through early 1949, then, U.S. planners believed that the United States would maintain marked military superiority well into the next decade.[46]

Dealing with the Adversary

From Roosevelt's death until early 1946, civilian and military leaders within the Truman administration shared a cautious optimism about U.S.-Soviet relations. They believed that the Soviets were neither intent on world domination nor interested in initiating hostilities any time in the near future. Differences of opinion did emerge, however, as to how best to deal with Soviet leaders. Was the Soviet Union a revolutionary state whose expansionist tendencies had to be contained through competitive policies? Or did the Soviets have legitimate security concerns that could best be satisfied through cooperative American policies?[47] Opinions about this issue by no means split along bureaucratic lines. Competing conceptions of the Soviet Union circulated within the Department of State itself. As Robert Messer notes, in late 1945 "there was in the department no single mainstream of thought regarding Soviet policy."[48]

The absence of a shared interpretive framework translated into inconsistencies in policy.[49] Truman came into office intent on taking a more hard-line stance toward the Soviet Union than had Roosevelt. Soon after Roosevelt's death in April 1945, the United States stepped up efforts to prevent communist gains in Indochina. The administration also took a firm stand on preventing Yugoslavia from occupying Trieste and the Venezia Giuilia hinterland, viewing the Yugoslavs as

[45] Herken, *Winning Weapon*, p. 284. U.S. planners assumed that by 1957, the Soviets' "known uranium sources would be exhausted." See Declassified Documents Reference System (DDRS) (Washington, D.C.: Carrollton Press, 1979), 18B, OSI/SR-10/49 (CIA), 1 July 1949, "Status of the USSR Atomic Energy Project."

[46] For assessments indicating that the military would be able to carry out successfully its plans for war with the Soviet Union, see DDRS (78) 373A, 12 May 1949, JCS 1953/1.

[47] Gaddis, *United States and the Origins of the Cold War*, pp. 273–274; and Leffler, *Preponderance of Power*, pp. 46–47.

[48] Robert Messer, "Paths not Taken: The United States Department of State and Alternatives to Containment, 1945–1946," *Diplomatic History*, 1 (Fall 1977), 304.

[49] For an excellent analysis of the oscillations in U.S. policy, see Deborah Larson, *Origins of Containment: A Psychological Explanation* (Princeton: Princeton University Press, 1985), pp. 150–249.

acting at the behest of the Soviets.[50] In May, the United States temporarily ended its lend-lease program with the Soviet Union (the program
was then resumed until the end of fighting in the Pacific), hoping to
gain leverage over the Soviets by making further economic aid contingent on cooperative Soviet behavior.

By the summer of 1945, Truman sensed that building tensions between Moscow and Washington were threatening to cause a serious
breakdown in U.S.-Soviet relations. He began to back away from the
more competitive policies adopted after April. At meetings with Soviet
elites during the later half of the year, U.S. officials made efforts to
repair relations.[51] The most intractable problem proved to be reaching
an agreement on the degree of latitude the Soviet Union would have
in its sphere of influence in Eastern Europe, especially in the Balkans.
While the U.S. government had initially demanded that free elections
be held in Romania and Bulgaria, Secretary of State James Byrnes went
to Moscow in December and reached a compromise with the Soviets
that left them considerable influence over the composition of governments in both countries. Byrnes did, however, meet a chorus of opposition on his return to the United States. Many within the administration
felt that he had been far too accommodating. American acquiescence,
they argued, would only encourage Soviet intransigence. Byrnes's dis-
appointing welcome home was only symptomatic of the absence of a
consensus within the administration over how to deal with the Soviet Union.[52]

During 1946, American elites swung back toward a more competitive
stance. The voice of the accommodationist camp grew considerably
weaker as a consensus emerged within the administration that it was
time to end making concessions to the Soviets. Truman had not abandoned hope of ultimately persuading the Soviets to cooperate with the
United States in preserving peace, but he was convinced that Washington could no longer afford to adopt a conciliatory stance toward Moscow.[53] Views began to congeal around the need for more competitive
policies for several reasons. First, the administration had effectively

[50] Yergin, *Shattered Peace*, pp. 72–73, 88–90.
[51] Ibid., pp. 100–132.
[52] Ibid., pp. 151–158.
[53] In *United States and the Origins of the Cold War*, John Gaddis argues that it was during
the first three months of 1946 that the administration forged a new framework on which
to base U.S.-Soviet relations (pp. 304–306, 312–315). In *Origins of Containment*, however,
Deborah Larson provides convincing evidence that "throughout 1946, Truman impro-
vised, following no consistent policy toward the Soviet Union" (p. 250). Top officials,
including Truman, had not abandoned hope of returning to cooperative relations with
the Soviets. It was not until 1947 that a clear consensus emerged on the need to adopt
firm, competitive policies to contain the Soviet Union (pp. 251–301).

[434]

established Soviet behavior in Eastern Europe as a litmus test for judg-
ing the intentions of the Soviet leadership.[54] Soviet interference in the
domestic affairs of East European countries as well as repeated demonstrations of Soviet disdain for the protection of civil liberties and human rights left American officials increasingly wary of Soviet leaders.
Second, the Truman administration feared that Britain's scaling down
of its military commitments and its gradual withdrawal from empire
might whet the Soviet appetitie for expansion. American officials were
particularly concerned about the Near East. In mid-1945, the Soviets,
through bilateral negotiations with the Turks, began to seek changes
in arrangements for control of the Dardanelles.[55] The following year,
the Soviet Union proposed that its troops be deployed in joint fortifications that the Black Sea powers would erect to control passage through
the straits.[56] American concern about Soviet designs in the Near East
was exacerbated by Stalin's decision to leave Soviet troops in northern
Iran past the 2 March 1946 deadline that the allies had agreed on for
the withdrawal of occupation forces. Although the crisis was resolved
the following month through negotiations between Moscow and Teh-
ran, the episode fueled American fears about Soviet expansionism,
thereby giving added impetus to the hard-line consensus that was
taking shape within the Truman administration.[57] It was Britain's decision early in 1947 to reduce the scope of its commitments in the eastern
Mediterranean which prompted the administration to come forward
with a more coherent set of initiatives to contain the Soviets.[58] The
decision to set forth the Truman Doctrine and to take active steps
to prevent the spread of communism in Greece and Turkey was the
culmination of a gradual hardening of attitudes that took place during
1946 and early 1947.

George Kennan's famous "Long Telegram," which began to circulate
within the administration in February 1946, played an important role
in facilitating the reorientation of Washington's policy toward the Soviet
Union. Given the fact that Soviet behavior had already cultivated growing wariness in Washington, Kennan's call for an end to U.S. accommodation of the Soviets fell on receptive ears. More important, the
telegram provided an interpretive framework for understanding the
Soviets, a framework that had heretofore been missing. Kennan identified the "traditional and instinctive Russian sense of insecurity" as the
root of the "Kremlin's neurotic view of world affairs." Marxism was

[54] Yergin, *Shattered Peace*, p. 85; Leffler, *Preponderance of Power*, p. 34.
[55] Leffler, *Preponderance of Power*, p. 78.
[56] Yergin, *Shattered Peace*, pp. 233–235.
[57] Ibid., pp. 179–192.
[58] See Larson, *Origins of Containment*, p. 303.

[435]

more of a "fig leaf of their moral and intellectual respectability" than a critical ideological principle guiding Soviet leaders. The Soviets would try to expand their power whenever "timely and promising" opportunities emerged. But Soviet power "does not take unnecessary risks." On the contrary, "it is highly sensitive to [the] logic of force. For this reason it can easily withdraw—and usually does—when strong resistance is encountered at any point. Thus, if the adversary has sufficient force and makes clear his readiness to use it, he rarely has to do so." Kennan concluded that containing the Soviets would depend on the "degree of cohesion, firmness and vigor which [the] Western world can muster." In providing the conceptual underpinning for a switch from cooperation to competition, Kennan helped consolidate the consensus that took shape during 1946 and early 1947.[59]

How was this framework implemented in terms of policy? What steps did the United States take to contain Soviet expansionism? The brand of containment that emerged in 1946 and 1947 was based on three principal suppositions. First, U.S. elites believed that the main threat posed by the Soviets was political, not military, in nature. It was widespread economic and political dislocation in Western Europe and the Far East that left these areas susceptible to Soviet influence and ideology. The main task facing the United States was therefore to restore economic vitality and political stability to the main power centers in Europe and East Asia.[60] As a memorandum on Europe written by the Policy Planning Staff put it, American efforts "should be directed not to the combatting of communism as such but to the restoration of the economic health and vigor of European society."[61] This view was by no means restricted to civilian elites. Even the military recognized that economic aid had to take priority over rearmament.[62]

The Marshall Plan, a program of large-scale economic assistance, served as the vehicle through which the United States was to contribute to the recovery of Europe. While administration officials had, by 1947, become convinced of the need for a massive aid program—the harsh winter of 1946–1947 had left Europe in increasingly dire straits—a war-weary Congress was hesitant to appropriate yet again funds for foreign assistance. Soviet behavior, however, helped garner congressional support for the Marshall Plan. Soviet efforts in February 1948 to ensure a communist government in Czechoslovakia left Congress

[59] "Moscow Embassy Telegram #511," 22 Feb. 1946, in *Containment*, ed. Etzold and Gaddis, pp. 50–63.

[60] Leffler, "American Conception of National Security," pp. 363–371.

[61] "Policy with Respect to American Aid to Western Europe," 23 May 1947, in *Containment*, ed. Etzold and Gaddis, p. 103.

[62] See Melvyn Leffler, "Reply," *American Historical Review*, 89 (April 1984), 392–393.

far more willing to open its coffers to contain the Soviets.[63] So too did the blockade of Berlin four months later. While the so-called Spring Crisis loosened budgetary constraints that had previously hampered the administration, the U.S. reaction also demonstrated the degree to which American officials were committed to an economic, as opposed to military, brand of containment. Despite the war scare that followed the Czech coup, no dramatic shift in U.S. military posture took place. Rather, there was a temporary surge in support for the militarization of containment, embodied in NSC 7, followed soon thereafter by a return to primary reliance on economic initiatives, embodied in NSC 20/1.

NSC 7, drafted in March 1948, called for a "world-wide counter-offensive against Soviet-directed world communism." Defensive containment was no longer sufficient; the United States now had to focus on the "defeat of the forces of Soviet-directed world communism." Compellent strategies were to supplement, if not replace, deterrent ones. To this end, the country's conventional and nuclear capability had to be substantially increased.[64] It was also during March and April that initial discussions took place on the formation of NATO. Although the idea of a defense pact for Western Europe by no means emerged exclusively from the Czech coup, events in Czechoslovakia and Berlin helped win support within Congress for the extension of U.S. defense obligations during peacetime. In addition, the NSC began to lay the groundwork for supplementing economic aid to Western Europe with direct arms transfers.[65] So too did U.S. planners begin to focus on the possibility of defending Western Europe at the Rhine, as opposed to evacuating much of the Continent in the early stages of a conflict with the Soviet Union, as called for in existing war plans.[66]

This new concern about meeting the Soviet military challenge did lead to a considerable expansion of U.S. airpower. In the atmosphere of crisis that pervaded during March, all the military services sought to increase their budgets; the air force and naval aviation reaped the most benefits.[67] Yet Truman remained adamant that the military budget not be allowed to balloon. He feared increases in military spending would have adverse effects on the performance of the U.S. economy.[68] Fur-

---

[63] Yergin, *Shattered Peace*, pp. 350–357. Congress approved the legislation and appropriations for the Marshall Plan in April and June 1948, respectively.

[64] "The Position of the United States with Respect to Soviet-Directed World Communism," NSC 7, 30 March 1948, in *Containment*, ed. Etzold and Gaddis, pp. 164–169.

[65] See "The Position of the United States with Respect to Providing Military Assistance to Nations of the Non-Soviet World," NSC 14/1, 1 July 1948, in *Containment*, ed. Etzold and Gaddis, pp. 128–130.

[66] Leffler, *Preponderance of Power*, p. 216.

[67] Yergin, *Shattered Peace*, pp. 357–362.

[68] Ibid., p. 398.

thermore, the sense of urgency that had initially focused attention on military preparedness quickly began to dissipate. During the second half of 1948, support for compellent strategies and the militarization of containment all but disappeared.

NSC 7 was superseded by NSC 20/1, a broad review of U.S. policy toward the Soviets drafted in August 1948. NSC 20/1 explicitly backed away from the notion of an offensive against Soviet-directed communism. On the contrary, the United States had to seek to moderate Soviet leaders, not to overthrow them or compel them into submission. This could be done through nonmilitary means, by creating situations that would help the Soviet government "recognize the practical undesirability of acting on the basis of its present concepts." The United States had to take measures to be prepared for war, but the NSC regarded them as "only subsidiary and precautionary rather than as the primary element of policy."[69] Though efforts to finalize the North Atlantic Treaty went forward, many in the administration viewed the main function of NATO as one of providing reassurance to the West Europeans, not deterring the Soviets. Since the United States wanted to rebuild and rearm the western portion of Germany and integrate it into Western Europe, French fears about a resurgence of German power first had to be allayed by the prospect of a firm American commitment to the Continent.[70] The State Department also argued that the North Atlantic Pact would further economic recovery in Europe because of the "sense of increased security which the Pact will promote among these countries."[71] But, the Policy Planning Staff warned, the militarization of containment would be counterproductive: "Intensive rearmament constitutes an uneconomic and regrettable diversion of effort." The "best and most hopeful course of action [for Western Europe] . . . remains the struggle for economic recovery and for internal political stability."[72] Well into 1949, American elites still viewed the economic recovery of major power centers as the main instrument for containing the Soviet Union.

The second key supposition informing the brand of containment implemented through 1949 was that, although U.S. elites believed in the need to take an increasingly competitive tack from 1946 onward,

[69] "U.S. Objectives with Respect to Russia," NSC 20/1, 18 Aug. 1948, in *Containment*, ed. Etzold and Gaddis, pp. 173–203. NSC 20/1 was Kennan's draft of NSC 20/4, which was adopted as the official policy paper for U.S. policy toward the Soviet Union in 1948.
[70] Leffler, *Preponderance of Power*, p. 235.
[71] "The North Atlantic Pact: Collective Defense and the Preservation of Peace, Security, and Freedom in the North Atlantic Community," Department of State, 20 March 1949, in *Containment*, ed. Etzold and Gaddis, pp. 158–160.
[72] "Considerations Affecting the Conclusion of a North Atlantic Security Pact," PPS 43, 23 Nov. 1948, in *Containment*, ed. Etzold and Gaddis, pp. 153–158.

the Truman administration appreciated the importance of shaping Soviet behavior through inducements as well as through threats. Policy was based on the notion that the United States had to stop making concessions to the Soviets and that the Kremlin's recalcitrant behavior had to entail costs. But taking a firm stance with Moscow did not preclude rewarding cooperative behavior on the part of the Soviets. As a memo from Clark Clifford, special counsel to the president, to Truman put it, "Action contrary to our conception of a decent world order will redound to the disadvantage of the Soviet regime whereas friendly and cooperative action will pay dividends."[73] It follows that diplomacy and negotiation with the Soviets had an important role to play in implementing containment. The United States could not afford simply to box in the Soviets and wait for them to change. As the Policy Planning Staff noted in early 1948, "Natural force, independent of our policies, may go far to absorb and eventually defeat the efforts of this group. But we cannot depend upon this. Our own diplomacy has a decisive part to play in this connection."[74]

This reluctance to confront the Soviets with countervailing power in the core and simply shut the door to diplomacy was based in part on the assessment that the expansionist strain in Moscow's foreign policy was rooted in Soviet insecurity. To exacerbate Soviet perceptions of vulnerability was therefore likely to fuel, not to moderate, the Kremlin's expansionist tendencies.[75] Kennan also argued that the militarization of containment would play into the hands of Soviet leaders, who tended to rely on the presence of an external threat to justify domestic repression and legitimate their rule.[76] Kennan thus warned that the United States should avoid "threats or blustering or superfluous gestures of outward 'toughness.'" On the contrary, "demands on Russian policy should be put forward in such a manner as to leave the way open for a compliance not too detrimental to Russian prestige."[77] It

---

[73] "American Relations with the Soviet Union: A Report to the President by the Special Counsel to the President," 24 Sept. 1946, in *Containment*, ed. Etzold and Gaddis, p. 69.

[74] "Review of Current Trends: U.S. Foreign Policy," PPS 23, 24 Feb. 1948, in *Containment*, ed. Etzold and Gaddis, p. 164. It should be noted that Kennan, who directed the Policy Planning Staff during this period, was more optimistic about the potential payoffs of negotiating with the Soviets than many others in the policy community. Especially after 1947, Kennan's views on the possibilities for negotiation were shared by few others in the administration. As Etzold and Gaddis note, "In the relative importance he attached to negotiations Kennan parted company with other top Washington policy makers, most of whom harbored greater skepticism than he about what diplomatic contacts with Moscow could accomplish, and tended to emphasize instead the need to build up alliances against Soviet power" (p. 162).

[75] Leffler, "American Conception of National Security," p. 374.

[76] Gaddis, *Strategies of Containment*, p. 20.

[77] George Kennan, "The Sources of Soviet Conduct," July 1947, originally published in *Foreign Affairs*, reprinted in *Containment*, ed. Etzold and Gaddis, p. 87.

was largely because of his fear that Soviet perceptions of encirclement would make the Kremlin more intractable that Kennan opposed the formation of NATO.[78] Although his position did not carry the day on the specific issue of the North Atlantic Pact, his concern about not backing the Soviets into a vulnerable corner was reflected in the broad tenor of U.S. policy. Through mid-1949, the Truman administration's strategy in the core consisted of "a long-term, patient but firm and vigilant containment of Russian expansive tendencies," not a militarized and overly competitive effort to threaten the Soviets into submission.[79] The United States adopted a hard line with the Soviets, but one that relied primarily on deterrence rather than compellence, and that left open the possibility of constructive diplomacy.

The third key supposition shaping the brand of containment that emerged during 1946 and 1947 was that containing the Soviet Union did not entail defending all regions of the globe against communism or Soviet forces, but only those regions that possessed significant industrial and military might. In both the core and periphery, U.S. policy was based on a clear set of geographic priorities.[80] Planning documents reflected the efforts of the policy community to set strategic priorities and determine accordingly the scope of U.S. commitments in specific regions. Western Europe was viewed as the top priority, with Britain and France at the head of the list, followed by Germany and then the smaller and less developed European countries. During peacetime, assistance to the Middle East was of secondary importance.[81] In wartime, however, its air bases would be crucial for carrying out attacks on Soviet territory. In the Far East, planners identified the top priority as defending key offshore islands: Japan and the Philippines. This strategy would keep the main industrial center of the region from falling under Soviet dominance and would offer the United States control of the main lines of communication in the western Pacific. Involvement in the Asian mainland was to be avoided. It was too vast and contained insufficient military-industrial capability to warrant a major commitment of U.S. resources.[82]

---

[78] See "Conclusion of a North Atlantic Security Pact"; and Yergin, *Shattered Peace*, pp. 388–389.

[79] Kennan, "Sources of Soviet Conduct," p. 87.

[80] Kennan was principally responsible for defining vital regions as those that contained robust industrial-military capacity. Gaddis notes that the Truman administration did not explicitly endorse Kennan's criterion for differentiating between vital and peripheral interests, but that its policies reflected adoption of his thinking. See Gaddis, *Strategies of Containment*, p. 60.

[81] See "United States Assistance to Other Countries from the Standpoint of National Security," JCS 1769/1, 29 April 1947, in *Containment*, ed. Etzold and Gaddis, pp. 72–79.

[82] See, for example, "Review of Current Trends: U.S. Foreign Policy," PPS 23, 24 Feb. 1948, in *Containment*, ed. Etzold and Gaddis, pp. 226–228; and "Conversation between

Concern about identifying geographic priorities and bounding the scope of U.S. overseas commitments stemmed from the belief that industrial potential was the foundation of national strength, but also from two other suppositions. First, the Truman administration, especially the president himself, believed that strict limits had to be placed on defense spending. Defense expenditure, by leading to inflation and, possibly, domestic economic controls, would likely have ill effects on an American economy that already faced the strain of adjusting to postwar conditions.[83] The United States had limited resources to allocate to national security, and, as mentioned above, policy makers believed that economic assistance to Europe would do more to restrict Soviet power than the rearmament of the West. Secretary of Defense James Forrestal explicitly recognized that defense preparedness was being sacrificed "to increase our expenditures to assist in European recovery. In other words, we are taking a calculated risk in order to follow a course which offers a prospect of eventually achieving national security and also long-term stability."[84] The administration also hoped that funds allocated to the economic recovery of Europe would stimulate U.S.-European trade and therefore have beneficial effects on the American economy.

Second, U.S. elites believed that communism and Soviet domination would face indigenous sources of resistance, obviating the need for the West to combat Soviet influence on a global basis. Nationalism would act as a barrier against Soviet influence in many regions of the world.[85] Splits were also likely to emerge within the communist bloc, splits that the United States could help to foster by offering support for communist regimes drifting from the Soviet orbit. There was disagreement within the administration over whether the United States could, over the long term, tolerate communist governments as long as they were not aligned with Moscow. But a consensus did exist that weaning communist regimes from the Soviet orbit was, at the least, a first step toward defending liberal democracy.[86]

U.S. strategy in the periphery, particularly Washington's approach toward East Asia, provides an excellent illustration of how these suppositions shaped policy. Military authorities affirmed "that the US strate-

General of the Army MacArthur and Mr. George F. Kennan," PPS 28/2, 5 March 1948, in *Containment*, ed. Etzold and Gaddis, pp. 228–230.

[83] Gaddis, *Strategies of Containment*, p. 58.

[84] Forrestal memo of 8 Dec. 1947, cited in Gaddis, *Strategies of Containment*, pp. 61–62.

[85] Gaddis, *Strategies of Containment*, p. 71.

[86] "United States Policy toward the Soviet Satellite States in Eastern Europe," NSC 58, 14 Sept. 1949, in *Containment*, ed. Etzold and Gaddis, pp. 211–223; and Gaddis, *Strategies of Containment*, pp. 65–71.

gic position in the Far East is based in the first instance on the off-shore islands, i.e. Japan, Okinawa, and the Philippines; accordingly our position is not directly jeopardized by the loss of China as long as the security of the islands continues to be maintained."[87] As far as China was concerned, Washington sided with the Nationalists against the Chinese Communist Party (CCP). But the Truman administration was simply not willing to expend considerable effort—in the form of either direct intervention or economic and military assistance—to prevent a CCP victory. Although the United States did not completely disengage from China, Washington played only a limited role in the civil war, despite recognition by early 1949 that a communist victory was imminent.[88] Indicative of the administration's complacency about events in China was its decision in mid-1949 to reduce military spending from roughly $15 to $13 billion.[89] Even after the Nationalists had been effectively chased off the mainland to Taiwan, the administration maintained that the Nationalist stronghold was not worth defending with American forces.[90] Truman himself publicly stated that Taiwan lay outside the perimeter of U.S. defense commitments in the Far East. The administration favored recognition of the communist government and feared that an overt commitment to defend the Nationalists in Taiwan would preclude cordial relations between the United States and China.[91]

Similar guidelines shaped American policy toward Korea. The Truman administration did see its credibility at stake in the preservation of a noncommunist regime in the south, and "most decision makers rejected total U.S. withdrawal from . . . Korea."[92] Nevertheless, the roughly 45,000 U.S. troops stationed on the peninsula in 1947 were withdrawn by 1949, and the administration declared publicly that Korea was outside the U.S. defense perimeter. So too was the administration opposed to defending Indochina with American troops. Be-

[87] "Outline of Far Eastern and Asian Policy for Review with the President," 14 Nov. 1949, Foreign Relations of the United States (FRUS), 1949, vol. 7, part 2 (Washington, D.C.: U.S. GPO, 1976), pp. 1211–1212. The quotation represents a summary of the military's views as expressed in mid-1949.

[88] Nancy Tucker, *Patterns in the Dust: Chinese-American Relations and the Recognition Controversy, 1949–1950* (New York: Columbia University Press, 1983), p. 1.

[89] Leffler, *Preponderance of Power*, p. 308.

[90] See NSC 37/7, 22 Aug. 1949, quoted in "The Position of the United States with Respect to Asia," NSC 48/2, 30 Dec. 1949, FRUS, 1949, vol. 7, part 2, p. 1219.

[91] Tucker, *Patterns in the Dust*, pp. 186–190.

[92] William Stueck, Jr., *The Road to Confrontation: American Policy toward China and Korea, 1947–1950* (Chapel Hill: University of North Carolina Press, 1981), pp. 28–30; and John Lewis Gaddis, "Drawing Lines: The Defensive Perimeter in East Asia, 1947–1951," in *The Long Peace: Inquiries into the History of the Cold War* (New York: Oxford University Press, 1987), p. 94.

cause of concern about Ho Chi Minh's ties to the Soviets, the reserves of food and raw materials in Indochina, and the potential for communism to spread throughout Southeast Asia, U.S. elites were willing to help the French and their local allies resist the spread of communist control in Vietnam.[93] But the administration was not prepared to "put itself in a forward position in the Indochina problem."[94]

Several considerations informed this policy of selective engagement in the Far East. First, most of East Asia did not contain sufficient industrial or military capability to warrant consideration as a vital interest. A communist victory in China and alignment with the Soviet Union, for example, simply would not fundamentally alter the international balance of power.[95] A Defense Department study released in the fall of 1949 expressed little alarm about communist successes in China, noting that in the event of war, China "could contribute principally unskilled labor and certain important raw materials to the Soviet Union."[96] Second, American decision makers realized that even if they wanted to intervene in China on a large scale, the capability needed to secure a favorable outcome far outstripped available American resources. As NSC 34 described the situation, a firm commitment to support the Nationalist regime was a course of action "of huge, indefinite and hazardous proportions. The American Government cannot rightly gamble thus with American prestige and resources."[97] Internal debate over U.S. policy reflected a sober appreciation of the limited options facing the administration: "In China there is not much we can do, in present circumstances but to sweat it out and to try to prevent the military situation from changing too drastically to the advantage of the communist forces."[98] In Indochina as well, part of the motivation for avoiding direct involvement was that "there appeared to be nothing we could do to alter the very discouraging prospects."[99]

Finally, U.S. decision makers believed that, in the long run, American interests would best be served by avoiding direct military intervention

[93] Gaddis, "Drawing Lines," pp. 89–91.

[94] "Memorandum of Conversation, by Mr. Charlton Ogburn, Jr., of the Division of Southeast Asian Affairs," 17 May 1949, FRUS, 1949, vol. 7, part 1 (Washington, D.C.: U.S. GPO, 1975), p. 27.

[95] "United States Policy toward China," NSC 34, 13 Oct. 1948, in *Containment*, ed. Etzold and Gaddis, pp. 240–247; Tucker, *Patterns in the Dust*, p. 14; and Leffler, "Reply," p. 392.

[96] DDRS (79) 34A, 13 Oct. 1949, "Staff Study by the U.S. Delegation to Military Committee of the Five Powers," p. 3.

[97] NSC 34, p. 245.

[98] "Resume of World Situation," PPS 13, 6 Nov. 1947, in *Containment*, ed. Etzold and Gaddis, p. 95. See also Thomas Paterson, *Meeting the Communist Threat: Truman to Reagan* (New York: Oxford University Press, 1988), pp. 65–68.

[99] "Memorandum of Conversation, by Mr. Charlton Ogburn, Jr.," p. 27.

in the Far East. The most powerful political force in East Asia was nationalism. It was therefore important to cultivate among local actors the view that the United States was supportive of nationalist aspirations: "In order to minimize suggestions of American imperialist intervention, we should encourage the Indians, Filipinos and other Asian states to take the public lead in political matters. Our role should be the offering of discreet support and guidance."[100] Direct intervention might well undermine U.S. objectives by fueling nationalist resistance and anti-American sentiment. In the words of NSC 34, "Overt intervention multiplies resistance to the intervener."[101] In addition, a more forward U.S. posture could well force regional powers to seek aid from the Kremlin. Officials were thus careful not to offset the natural political forces that would cause the Chinese leadership to resist the Kremlin's control. Fostering a Sino-Soviet split was in fact one of the key motivations behind the administration's initial willingness to accommodate and recognize the communist government in China.[102] A memo from the U.S. embassy in China to the secretary of state spelled out these concerns:

> Simply stated . . . [our] policy should be to prevent China from becoming reinforcement to Soviet power. To achieve this end, we must wait for development of Chinese form "Titoism," meanwhile doing nothing to encourage growth of strong Communist China. Policy of outright hostility toward rulers of China and overt support of subversive activity against them, while it undoubtedly would hinder consolidation of CCP power, would be unlikely to contribute toward detachment of China from USSR because it would conflict with, rather than make use of, Chinese chauvinism.[103]

Although not the preferred outcome, a communist China could be lived with comfortably, especially if it was not a Soviet client state.[104]

Recognition of the potential for nationalism to work against the spread of communism also informed thinking about Indochina. U.S. elites in fact pressed their French counterparts to grant increasing autonomy to local leaders in Indochina, lest the rising tide of nationalism provide inroads for communism. Stability in Southeast Asia would be better served not by the perpetuation of French colonial rule, but by

---

[100] "Policy Planning Staff Paper on United States Policy toward Southeast Asia," PPS 51, 29 March 1949, FRUS, 1949, vol. 7, part 2, p. 1130.
[101] NSC 34, p. 244.
[102] Tucker, *Patterns in the Dust*, pp. 17, 29–31.
[103] "The Counselor of Embassy in China (Jones) to the Secretary of State," 3 Sept. 1949, FRUS, 1949, vol. 8 (Washington, D.C.: U.S. GPO, 1978), p. 520.
[104] See NSC 34, pp. 240–247.

the emergence of indigenous noncommunist governments enjoying popular support.[105] As the Department of State informed the French Foreign Office, "The United States Government is of the opinion that it must prove difficult to save this situation and to preserve Indochina from a foreign tyranny unless the French Government offers the Vietnamese the attainment of those nationalist goals which they would continue to fight for rather than forego."[106] If the Western powers stayed out of Southeast Asia, the desire for national independence would lead free states to balance against the threat of foreign-controlled communism. A confederation of Southeast Asian states, though unlikely, might even emerge. As the U.S. ambassador to China, J. Leighton Stuart, informed the secretary of state, "The situation created by the existence of a Communist colossus in the North may possibly prove sufficiently dynamic to bring about a change in their attitude [toward confederation] very much in the same manner as the Western European States which are so intensely nationalist have come together in similar circumstances."[107]

Between 1946 and 1949, U.S. elites perceived low levels of metropolitan vulnerability. Assessments indicated that the Soviets had neither the intention nor the capability to engage the United States in a protracted war. Nevertheless, a firm stance was needed to contain Soviet expansionism. While the administration decided that cooperative policies had to give way to competitive ones, U.S. policy makers did not adopt compellent policies intended to threaten the Soviets into submission. Elites feared that vulnerability would exacerbate, not moderate, Soviet expansionism. Accordingly, the best way to contain the spread of communism in both the core and periphery was not through rearmament, but through aiding the recovery of major power centers in Europe and East Asia. American elites expanded U.S. overseas commitments to a degree unprecedented in peacetime, but they did so in a paced and measured manner. In both Europe and the periphery, the Truman administration relied primarily on deterrent strategies and an approach to the Soviet Union characterized by caution and restraint.

American policy was informed by a clear sense of strategic priorities and by rigorous assessment of which regions of the world warranted

---

[105] Stueck, *Road to Confrontation*, p. 130.

[106] "Memorandum by the Department of State to the French Foreign Office," undated, included in transmission from the "Acting Secretary of State to the Embassy in France," 6 June 1949, FRUS, 1949, vol. 7, part 1, p. 42.

[107] "Memorandum Submitted by the Ambassador in China (Stuart)," undated, submitted to the secretary of state on 8 March 1949. Drafted jointly by the Indian, Australian, British, and American ambassadors to China, FRUS, 1949, vol. 7, part 2, p. 1122.

a major American commitment. Top priority was assigned to areas of significant military and industrial capability. Other areas were deemed to be worth defending only if they were needed to project air power into the Eurasian heartland or to guard the sea lanes along the Eurasian rimland. Because elites operated under conditions of strategic sufficiency, reputational concerns ran low and commitments were generally not viewed as being interdependent. U.S. commitments were extended to areas primarily on the basis of their intrinsic value, not because of concern about falling dominoes or a loss of American credibility. [108] In much of the periphery, natural forces of resistance—balanc-

[108] As mentioned in note 1 above, Melvyn Leffler argues that 1947 was a key turning point in U.S. policy and that NSC 68 represented a continuation of policies that took shape well before 1950. In *Preponderance of Power* (see primarily chaps. 4–7), Leffler elaborates on this argument. He seeks to show that U.S. grand strategy from 1947 onward was predicated on the supposition that core and periphery were integrally wedded in strategic terms. His analysis calls into question the claim that U.S. planners set clear strategic priorities on the basis of military-industrial potential and were accordingly quite hesitant to undertake peripheral commitments. Leffler builds support for his position by arguing that the Truman administration sought to hold all noncommunist portions of the periphery in the Western orbit. He claims that the administration generally supported the maintenance of European colonies and was willing to take on new responsibilites in the periphery when the Europeans withdrew from overseas commitments. Leffler asserts that three main motivations lay behind this globalist approach. First, because decision makers believed in falling dominoes, even areas of little intrinsic strategic importance had to be defended to stem the spread of communism. Second, many areas of the periphery had to be defended because they served as forward bases from which to project power against the Soviet Union. Third, the periphery's markets and raw materials were to help fuel recovery in core areas—namely, Western Europe and Japan.

This interpretation of the historical record is unsatisfying for the following reasons. Granted, the Truman administration did not want to lose any portion of the periphery to communism. Elites of course hoped to preserve the status quo and, if possible, to make gains. The key question, however, was not what U.S. policy makers preferred, but how far they were willing to go to attain their preferences. There is a critical difference between a willingness to provide economic and military aid to a specific region and a willingness to put American lives at stake to defend what are perceived of as vital interests. If U.S. policy is examined in the light of this distinction—that is, in terms of where decision makers viewed vital U.S. interests to be at stake—the Truman administration until 1950 pursued a much more discriminating approach than Leffler suggests. Even if American officials voiced concern about the need to defend vast portions of the periphery, their actions indicate other intentions. The size of U.S. armed forces remained quite limited through 1949. The Truman administration simply was not maintaining forces capable of simultaneously intervening in different portions of the periphery. No U.S. combat forces were introduced to prevent a communist victory in China, nor were the levels of aid given to the Nationalists commensurate with what was realistically needed to preserve the regime. The Truman administration proceeded, albeit with hesitation, to pull out U.S. forces from the Korean peninsula. Given the U.S. role in establishing a noncommunist regime in the south, American decision makers understandably saw the preservation of that regime as important to the credibility of U.S. commitments. This concern did prevent the Truman administration from completely disengaging from South Korea, but it did not halt the final withdrawal of U.S. combat troops in 1949 (see Stueck, *Road to Confrontation*, pp. 7–32). In Southeast Asia, the United States was not prepared to intervene with its own forces to stem the spread of communism. In fact,

ing behavior and nationalism—would be sufficient to contain the spread of Soviet-backed communism. Well-defined geographic priorities contributed to the ability of decision makers to extend American commitments in a selective and discriminating fashion.

Domestic Considerations ~~Clerom~~

Private Economic Interests. Economic considerations indeed affected the evolution of U.S. security policy during the early postwar years. Largely because American elites viewed trade barriers and economic nationalism as important causes of World War II, free trade and liberal multilateralism became key components of the prevailing vision of a desirable postwar order.[109] In addition, both the Roosevelt and Truman administrations believed that increasing trade with Europe was necessary to offset the potentially harmful effects of demobilization on the U.S. economy. Exports of finished products and imports of raw materials were needed to sustain rapid growth in the manufacturing sector.[110]

While these suppositions led to the adoption of policies that benefited American firms, such beliefs were sincerely held by the civilian leadership, not pressed on decision makers by a self-interested business community.[111] Both Roosevelt and Truman in fact found them-

---

the Truman administration put pressure on the French and Dutch to devolve more responsibility to local leaders in Indochina and Indonesia. The Truman administration did prepare forces for potential intervention in Greece and, possibly, Turkey. But these countries were arguably integral to plans for defense of core areas. They provided strategic access to the Middle East and the air bases from which atomic attacks against the Soviet Union would be carried out in the event of war. So too was Europe increasingly reliant on oil from the Middle East.

With respect to American thinking about dominoes, the key question is not whether specific individuals expressed concern about the contagion of communism, but whether such thinking won out over competing strategic conceptions. Top decision makers were indeed worried about the possibility that a given communist victory could spark a chain reaction. But such concern was not sufficiently intense or pervasive to impel the administration to find any and all communist gains intolerable and worth preventing at the expense of American lives. This strategic outlook was clearly exemplified in the Far East. Despite some concern about American credibility and the potential for communist gains to snowball, the U.S. government focused its attention on defending Japan and key offshore islands, effectively disengaged from China, removed its troops from Korea, was not prepared to defend Taiwan against attack from the mainland, and strictly limited the scope of its involvement in Southeast Asia.

[109] Officials believed that tariffs had contributed to the Great Depression and that the emergence of trading blocs had fostered antagonism among competing power centers. See Gaddis, *United States and the Origins of the Cold War*, p. 20; Freeland, *Truman Doctrine*, pp. 16–20; Leffler, *Preponderance of Power*, pp. 19–24; and Larson, *Origins of Containment*, pp. 143–144.

[110] Paterson, *Meeting the Communist Threat*, pp. 24–26; Freeland, *Truman Doctrine*, p. 17.

[111] See Henry Nau, *The Myth of America's Decline: Leading the World Economy into the 1990s* (New York: Oxford University Press, 1990), pp. 79–80, 99–128.

[447]

selves having to garner support for their policies among an obstinate business elite. When Roosevelt wanted to suspend reconstruction loans to the Soviets in early 1945, he met opposition from business leaders who held high expectations about the future of U.S.-Soviet trade.[112] Truman's decision to take a hard line with the Soviets and use the Marshall Plan to rebuild Western Europe—which effectively cordoned off the Soviet Union and Eastern Europe in economic terms—similarly ran up against resistance from industrialists and financiers.[113] Not only would U.S. trade with the Soviet sphere of influence be cut off, but the American economy was being taxed with the huge burden of rebuilding Western Europe. To win approval for its aid programs, the Truman administration was forced to launch an ambitious domestic campaign; the business community was one of its primary targets.[114] The American-led bloc that emerged during the early postwar years, far from being the creation of a self-interested business community, was shaped primarily by the reigning set of strategic and economic beliefs held by top decision makers. The business community had to be convinced that the domestic economy should bear the burden of the Truman administration's ambitious plans for the postwar order.

A corporatist interpretation of the 1946–1949 period would focus less on the behavior of self-interested economic interest groups and more on the extent to which the structure of the domestic political economy shaped U.S. foreign policy. Michael Hogan argues that the Marshall Plan was essentially an effort "to restructure the world economy along lines similar to the corporative order that was emerging in the United States."[115] The U.S. political economy was "corporatist" in that it was based on a coalition of capital-intensive firms, investment houses, labor, and agriculture. A mix of private enterprise, institutional mechanisms, and market forces was to guide cooperation between public and private elites and foster growth that could be shared by all sectors.[116] The purpose of the Marshall Plan, according to Hogan, was to replicate this domestic order abroad. A partnership of public and private elites and "institutional regulating, coordinating, and planning

---

[112] Gaddis, *United States and the Origins of the Cold War*, pp. 185–189.

[113] The United States did originally offer to include Eastern Europe and the Soviet Union in the Marshall Plan.

[114] Freeland, *Truman Doctrine*, pp. 61–62.

[115] See Michael Hogan, *The Marshall Plan: America, Britain, and the Reconstruction of Western Europe, 1947–1952* (New York: Cambridge University Press, 1987), p. 3; see also pp. 19–20.

[116] For discussion of how to define corporatism and of its analytic strengths and weaknesses, see John Lewis Gaddis, "The Corporatist Synthesis: A Skeptical View," in *Diplomatic History*, 10 (Fall 1986), 357–362; and Michael Hogan, "Corporatism: A Positive Approach," ibid., pp. 363–372.

mechanisms" which would administer world trade and development were, in the guise of the Marshall Plan, to bring prosperity to Europe in a way that would simultaneously benefit the American economy as well as private U.S. firms. From the corporatist perspective, the narrow economic self-interest of specific groups by no means disappears as a force shaping policy, but it becomes part of a broader enterprise "to refashion Western Europe in the image of the United States."[117]

The contribution of corporatist interpretations is difficult to evaluate for two reasons. First, the notion of corporatism remains vague and underspecified. In his book on the Marshall Plan, Hogan defines corporatism as a "political economy founded on self-governing economic groups, integrated by institutional coordinators and normal market mechanisms, led by cooperating public and private elites, nourished by limited but positive government power, and geared to an economic growth in which all could share."[118] This definition is so broad in scope that it becomes uncontestable—but also somewhat uninteresting—to view U.S. foreign policy as the product of corporatist forces. Given the U.S. commitment to private enterprise and capitalism, it is difficult to imagine an aid program that the United States could have conceivably formulated to facilitate European recovery which would not be based on "self-governing economic groups, integrated by institutional coordinators and normal market mechanisms, led by cooperating public and private elites." Who would contest the notion that the basic economic principles used to guide domestic economic policy would inform foreign economic policy?

A second, and related, reason is that the nature of the claim Hogan is setting forth remains ambiguous. At times, he seems to be arguing that American policy toward Western Europe during the early postwar years can be understood almost exclusively in terms of its corporatist roots. Hogan writes that "*the goal* was to refashion Western Europe in the image of the United States" and that the key factor shaping the postwar order was "the kind of political economy they [American elites] had in mind."[119] At other times, however, corporatism is only one of several forces shaping policy: "The Truman administration and its supporters intended the measure [the European Recovery Program] to do more than revive the European economies. Their goal, in part, was to reconstruct the components of a balance of power on the Continent."[120]

---

[117] Hogan, *Marshall Plan*, p. 87.
[118] Ibid., p. 3.
[119] Ibid., pp. 89, 93. Emphasis added.
[120] Ibid., p. 89.

The appeal of Hogan's corporatist interpretation depends on how one reads the nature of his claim. If his argument is that the principal motivation behind U.S. policy was to export the structure of the domestic political economy to Europe, to remake Western Europe in the American image, then his interpretation is far too ambitious. As the analysis above has demonstrated, strategic considerations were paramount. If Hogan is claiming that U.S. policy was fundamentally shaped by the strategic environment but that the structure of the domestic economy and prevailing economic philosophies affected the specific instruments that U.S. elites chose to use to respond to the Soviet threat and instability in Western Europe, then his argument is far more compelling. He in fact provides convincing evidence that a partnership between public and private elites and institutionalized coordination among different sectors of the economy played important roles in determining the specific programs incorporated in the Marshall Plan and how they were implemented.[121] The Marshall Plan indeed reflected the nature of the U.S. political economy and, it was hoped, would contribute to prosperity at home as well as in Europe. But U.S. efforts to foster economic recovery in Europe, and containment more generally, were first and foremost the product of strategic imperatives, not of pressure from self-seeking interest groups or of explicit attempts to export America's political economy to Europe.

Domestic Politics. The Truman administration carefully monitored public opinion and domestic political trends during the early postwar years. This is not to suggest that, between 1946 and 1949, public attitudes had a direct and significant impact on policy. Rather, principal policy initiatives were generated within the elite community, but the Truman administration then had to spend considerable effort garnering congressional and public support. The administration had to mold popular attitudes on two crucial dimensions. First, it had to disabuse the public of its favorable image of the Soviet Union and of the notion that the United States and the Soviet Union could cooperatively forge a postwar order. Second, the administration had to convince the American people that the Soviets posed a threat to U.S. interests and that sacrifices were therefore needed to contain them; the end of the war did not mean the end of American responsibilities abroad. As I show below, the administration's efforts, in combination with recalcitrant Soviet behavior, were largely successful in altering public opinion and winning congressional support for containment and the Marshall Plan. As a result, elite beliefs and public opinion were running on parallel tracks by 1947. But elite efforts to shape public

[121] Ibid., pp. 136–151. See also Nau, *Myth of America's Decline*, pp. 104–106.

attitudes eventually came to constrain the administration by creating domestic political forces that pressed elites to pursue overly competitive policies after 1949.

Throughout 1945, the American public was generally optimistic about the prospects for U.S.-Soviet cooperation after the war. Polls indicated that well over 50 percent of the public felt that the Soviet leadership could be trusted.[122] At the time of the San Francisco conference convened to establish the United Nations, 81 percent of those polled supported U.S. participation in an international organization.[123] Roosevelt had succeeded in convincing the populace that great-power cooperation under the auspices of an international body would preserve peace and do away with competition for spheres of influence.[124]

The Truman administration paid close attention to these trends in public attitudes. The State Department carefully monitored public opinion and prepared both weekly surveys and daily "Summaries of Opinion Developments."[125] Indeed, public opinion came to figure prominently in policy debates in late 1945 and early 1946, as the administration began to edge toward a more competitive relationship with the Soviets. The administration was reluctant to sign off on a Soviet sphere of influence in Eastern Europe, fearful of a domestic backlash among both East Europeans living in the United States and many other Americans who had come to believe that such spheres were now historical artifacts.[126] Truman ran up against similar problems in January 1946 when he submitted to Congress a request for a loan of $3.75 billion to Britain. Although some opposition came from isolationist voices intent on cutting back U.S. foreign assistance, the loan request was also criticized on principle: it was a bilateral arrangement that, in revealing special ties between London and Washington, might undermine the multilateralism on which the UN and the notion of collective security were supposedly based.[127]

As support gathered within the decision-making community for a more firm stance toward the Soviet Union, administration officials became increasingly aware of the need to bring public attitudes into closer alignment with elite beliefs. Just after the end of fighting in the Pacific, Secretary of State Henry Stimson told Truman that public

[122] See Gaddis, *United States and the Origins of the Cold War*, p. 289; Freeland, *Truman Doctrine*, p. 44.

[123] Freeland, *Truman Doctrine*, p. 44.

[124] Yergin, *Shattered Peace*, pp. 66–68; Gaddis, *United States and the Origins of the Cold War*, pp. 30–31.

[125] See Leffler, *Preponderance of Power*, pp. 106–107.

[126] Yergin, *Shattered Peace*, pp. 127–129; Gaddis, *United States and the Origins of the Cold War*, p. 170.

[127] Freeland, *Truman Doctrine*, pp. 62–64.

resistance to postwar aid programs was a "chief danger" for the country and that "a great effort of education" was needed to overcome such resistance.[128] At the end of his "Long Telegram," Kennan similarly stressed the need to educate the public and update its opinions about the Soviet Union:

> We must see that our public is educated to realities of Russian situation. I cannot over-emphasize importance of this. Press cannot do this alone. It must be done mainly by Government, which is necessarily more experienced and better informed on practical problems involved. . . . Our only stake [in the Soviet Union] lies in what we hope rather than what we have; and I am convinced we have a better chance of realizing those hopes if our public is enlightened and if our dealings with Russians are placed entirely on realistic and matter-of-fact basis.[129]

In September 1946, Clifford reiterated this message to Truman: "Only a well-informed public will support the stern policies which Soviet activities make imperative and which the United States Government must adopt. The American people should be fully informed about the difficulties in getting along with the Soviet Union."[130] These concerns were only exacerbated by the congressional elections of 1946, in which the Republicans gained control of both the House and the Senate. While conservative Republicans were generally more willing than Democrats to support the adoption of competitive policies toward the Soviets, they were not ready to authorize the funds needed to carry out such policies. A member of the State Department's Office of Public Affairs expressed his concerns to the assistant secretary of state in a memo written several months after the election: "I think we must admit the conclusion that Congress and the people of this country are not sufficiently aware of the character and dimensions of the crisis that impends, and of the measures that must be taken."[131]

Informal and unofficial efforts to carry out public education began even before hard-line attitudes had crystallized within Washington. Early in 1946, Senator Arthur Vandenberg began to make speeches aimed at rallying public support for a more firm Soviet policy.[132] In March, Winston Churchill delivered his famous "Iron Curtain" speech in Missouri, coining the phrase that was used to refer to the Eastern Bloc throughout the Cold War.[133] In June, John Foster Dulles, one of

---

[128] Cited in ibid., p. 35.
[129] "Moscow Embassy Telegram #511," pp. 62–63.
[130] "American Relations with the Soviet Union," p. 70.
[131] Joseph Jones cited in Gaddis, *United States and the Origins of the Cold War*, p. 346.
[132] See Yergin, *Shattered Peace*, p. 173.
[133] Ibid., p. 176.

the leading Republican voices on foreign affairs, published an article in *Life* magazine in which he described the Soviet threat in bold and alarming terms.[134] These repeated appeals to the public, along with the Iran crisis, had a considerable impact on popular attitudes. Throughout 1946, polls revealed a steady shift toward an anti-Soviet consensus and growing support for a stiffening of U.S. policy. In March, some 70 percent of the public disapproved of Soviet behavior and 60 percent believed that American policy was too conciliatory. By late 1946, two of every three Americans viewed the Soviets as an expansionist power intent on world domination.[135]

This marked shift in public attitudes did not, however, succeed in solving the Truman administration's problem; the American people and Congress had come to accept the need to end cooperation with Soviets, but this hardening of views did not translate into a new willingness to appropriate the funds and accept the international responsibilities that a policy of containment entailed. To accomplish this task, a more ambitious and centralized education effort was needed. The Truman Doctrine was the first step. Presented to the American people in a presidential speech in March 1947, the Truman Doctrine set forth the administration's commitment to prevent the spread of communism in Greece and Turkey. Britain had made clear that it was reducing the scope of its commitments in the eastern Mediterranean, and communist factions were gaining ground in both Greece and Turkey. Despite its intention to resist the spread of communism only in these two countries, the administration deliberately decided to cast Truman's speech in more universalistic terms. All nations of the world, Truman told the American public, face a stark choice between communism and democracy. It is the responsibility of the United States, he asserted, "to support free peoples who are resisting attempted subjugation by armed minorities or by outside pressure."[136]

The decision to package the aid request in these bold terms stemmed from a desire to galvanize the public and Congress and to garner their support for foreign aid by overstating the nature of the threat. This interpretation has been confirmed by those involved in formulating the Truman Doctrine. As Clark Clifford put it, the Truman speech was "the opening gun in a campaign to bring people up to [the] realization that the war isn't over by any means."[137] Dean Acheson, who played a leading role in drafting the speech, believed in the need to use "sym-

---

[134] "Thoughts on Soviet Foreign Policy and What to Do about It," *Life*, 3 June 1946, pp. 113–126, and 10 June 1946, pp. 118–130.

[135] Gaddis, *United States and the Origins of the Cold War*, pp. 315, 321.

[136] Quotation from Yergin, *Shattered Peace*, p. 283.

[137] Clifford cited in Gaddis, *United States and the Origins of the Cold War*, p. 350.

bols," not "facts," to educate the public. The president, according to Acheson, had to present an image of international relations compatible with his policies.[138] Another administration official who was involved in drafting the speech noted that "the only way we can sell the public on our new policy is by emphasizing the necessity of holding the line: communism vs. democracy should be the major theme."[139] Truman told his advisers that winning support for the more ambitious foreign policy that they envisaged would entail the "greatest selling job ever facing a President."[140] His response to criticism that his address had gone too far was that "from all his contacts with the Senate, it was clear that this was the only way in which the measure could be passed."[141] Historians of the period agree that the Truman Doctrine was "a deliberate effort to create a public consensus for the private beliefs within the Administration."[142] Gaddis labels the Truman Doctrine "a form of shock therapy: it was a last-ditch effort by the Administration to prod Congress and the American people into accepting the responsibilities of . . . world leadership."[143]

Truman's efforts to alter popular attitudes were backed up by several more permanent programs. The administration established an Office of Education to prepare pamphlets and coordinate instruction on foreign affairs in schools. The Freedom Train was created to tour the country and encourage "rededication" to democracy and patriotism.[144] Just over a week after the Truman Doctrine was unfurled, the administration created a loyalty board to examine the background and activities of all federal employees, hoping to track down subversives. The loyalty program, in combination with the spy scares of 1947 and 1948, drove home the point that the battle against communism had to be waged at home as well as abroad.

The administration enjoyed the unwitting assistance of the Soviets in shaping public attitudes. The Spring Crisis of 1948, in particular, helped mobilize Congress and the public to support competitive policies and the costs they entailed; the Marshall Plan passed with little opposition.[145] But even before the war scare, the Truman Doctrine,

---

[138] Larson, *Origins of Containment*, p. 309.

[139] Joseph Jones cited in Gaddis, *United States and the Origins of the Cold War*, pp. 350–351.

[140] Truman quoted in Howard Jones, *"A New Kind of War": America's Global Strategy and the Truman Doctrine in Greece* (New York: Oxford University Press, 1989), p. 43.

[141] Freeland, *Truman Doctrine*, pp. 100–101.

[142] Yergin, *Shattered Peace*, p. 283.

[143] Gaddis, *United States and the Origins of the Cold War*, p. 351.

[144] Freeland, *Truman Doctrine*, pp. 230–233.

[145] There is evidence that the administration in fact exaggerated the gravity of the crisis and the likelihood of conflict with the Soviets in order to mobilize the public. See Yergin, *Shattered Peace*, pp. 350–353.

loyalty campaign, and education program had a major impact on the public. Polls reflected a considerable increase in anti-Soviet sentiment.[146] At the end of 1947, Acheson noted: "We are in a period now I think of the formulation of a mood. The country is getting serious. It is getting impressed by the fact that the business of dealing with the Russians is a long, long job . . . [which] can only be done by the United States getting itself together, determining that we cannot maintain a counter-balance to the communistic power without strengthening all those other parts of the world which belong in the system with us."[147]

While Truman succeeded in achieving his domestic goals in the short term, some in the administration voiced concern that the president may have gone too far, that the brand of anticommunism taking root among the public might come to constrain policy makers in their dealings with Moscow.[148] The Policy Planning Staff, under Kennan's direction, in fact drafted a memo warning of this possibility. PPS 1, dated 23 May 1947, warned that popular misconceptions resulting from the Truman Doctrine needed to be corrected. The document urged that the public be told that economic recovery in Europe was important independent of the seriousness of the communist threat; the need for foreign assitance should not be linked to ideological confrontation. Kennan and his colleagues also objected to the universalistic flavor of the Truman Doctrine and were critical of the public's understanding of policy as "a blank check to give economic and military aid to any area in the world where the communists show signs of being successful." "It must be made clear," PPS 1 asserted, "that in the case of Greece and Turkey, we are dealing with a critical area where the failure to take action would have had particularly serious consequences, where a successful action would promise particularly far-reaching results, and where the overall cost was relatively small; and that in other areas we should have to apply similar criteria."[149] Such warnings proved to be prophetic. As I show shortly, by 1949 the administration found itself entrapped by the attitudes that it had gone to such pains to instill among the American public.

Military Services. The military services played a relatively passive role in the formulation of policy during the early postwar years. Unlike during later periods, the services did not impose on civilian leaders strategic assumptions or programs that smacked of efforts to increase

[146] Ibid., pp. 284–285; and Freeland, *Truman Doctrine*, p. 114.

[147] Acheson cited in Yergin, *Shattered Peace*, p. 5.

[148] For examples of such critiques, see Freeland, *Truman Doctrine*, pp. 100–101.

[149] "Policy with Respect to American Aid to Western Europe," PPS 1, 23 May 1947, in *Containment*, ed. Etzold and Gaddis, pp. 106–107.

their political clout or their share of the budget; there is little evidence of threat inflation or manipulation of information. During the second half of the 1940s, the JCS was one of the most outspoken proponents of the view that the chances of deliberate Soviet aggression were remote.[150] The services, for the most part, supported the notion that a Soviet attack, if it occurred, could be dealt with largely through nuclear retaliation. These war plans, which effectively called for the evacuation of much of Western Europe, undercut the need for robust conventional forces. Defense officials also admitted openly that economic recovery in Europe had to be given priority over rearmament.[151] Both defense budgets and manpower were slashed by a president convinced of the ill effects of defense spending on the economy. During the two years following the end of the war, defense spending fell from $81 to $13 billion, and troop levels from 12.1 to 1.6 million.[152] The policies adopted by the administration certainly did not bear the mark of a self-interested military bureaucracy.

I am arguing not that service interests and interservice rivalry were completely eliminated from the policy process, but only that the influence of these factors was relatively minor and effectively contained by the civilian leadership. When the navy began to criticize openly war plans that relied on airborne nuclear retaliation to blunt a Soviet attack, the administration quickly silenced the debate and removed high navy officials from their posts. All three services attempted to reap benefits from the war scare associated with the Spring Crisis. Interservice rivalries did flare and the defense budget rose, but Truman managed to keep tight rein on military spending and refused to let the budget rise above $15 billion for fiscal year 1950.[153] As mentioned above, the Spring Crisis led to a substantial increase in aircraft production but did not fundamentally alter U.S. military posture. The bottom line is that the civilian leadership dominated policy making between 1946 and 1949. The competitive policies that emerged came largely from the State Department and the White House, not from the military services.

Conclusions

During the course of 1946 and early 1947, the Truman administration adopted with increasing consistency competitive policies toward the Soviet Union. Fearful that cooperative policies would only be exploited

[150] Leffler, "American Conception of National Security," p. 359.
[151] Leffler, "Reply," pp. 392–393.
[152] See John Gaddis, "Comments," *American Historical Review*, 89 (April 1984), 383.
[153] Yergin, *Shattered Peace*, pp. 398–400.

by the Soviets, the administration decided that firm measures were needed to contain the spread of communism. In a manner consistent with my central argument, perceptions of low vulnerability and conditions of strategic sufficiency led to policies of selective expansion. Deterrent and, in some cases, compellent policies were needed to contain the Soviets in both the core and periphery. But the expansion of U.S. overseas commitments occurred in a discriminating fashion. Decision makers exercised caution and restraint; they explicitly avoided policies that threatened to provoke hostilities with the Soviet Union or mire the United States in the periphery.

The brand of containment implemented between 1946 and 1949 was informed by three main suppositions. First, elites believed that the economic recovery of important industrial centers would be the most effective means of containing Soviet expansion and influence. Economic assistance took priority over rearmament. Second, although the Truman administration had decided to take a firm stance in dealing with the Soviets, policy makers believed in the need to keep open the possibility of constructive diplomacy and were careful to avoid making the Soviets feel highly vulnerable in military terms. Third, elites set geographic priorities on the basis of strategic and economic, as opposed to reputational, considerations. Accordingly, well-defined strategic priorities guided the establishment of defense commitments and the allocation of resources.

Despite the successful efforts of elites to limit the scope of U.S. foreign commitments, the Truman administration had to gain domestic support for the sacrifices entailed in pursuing a more competitive policy. The administration therefore embarked on an ambitious program to persuade the American people and their elected representatives to accept the costs associated with containing the Soviets. Elites weaned the electorate from the more conciliatory attitudes propagated by the Roosevelt administration and effectively garnered congressional support for the Marshall Plan and a general stiffening of policy toward the Soviets. Elite manipulation of the public succeeded in empowering the administration.

1949–1950: The Militarization and Globalization of Containment

The Soviet atomic test of August 1949 had a profound impact on U.S. perceptions of vulnerability.[154] Before August, U.S. elites believed

---

[154] My argument is not intended to suggest that the Soviet atomic test was the only development that caused a dramatic change in U.S. perceptions of vulnerability and a

that the Soviets were unlikely to initiate war and that if they did, the United States would be able to prevail in a protracted conflict. After Soviet acquisition of the bomb, U.S. decision makers believed that the Soviets were far more likely to initiate war and began to doubt the ability of American forces to attain victory should war break out. In this section, I examine the strategic calculations that produced this assessment and argue that U.S. perceptions of high metropolitan vulnerability fueled a fundamental change in U.S. policy toward the Soviet Union. High vulnerability induced elites to believe in the need to adopt compellent strategies to demonstrate American resolve. Rearmament now had to take priority over the economic recovery of Eurasia's power centers. The clear ordering of strategic priorities that prevailed from 1946 to 1949 was blurred by a strategic logic infused with notions of bandwagoning and falling dominoes. As a result of these changes in strategic beliefs, competitive policies of selective expansion gave way to overly competitive policies of indiscriminate expansion. I also show that the efforts of the Truman administration to alter public attitudes came, by 1950, to entrap elites in a domestic political milieu that contributed to the formulation of a new and overly competitive brand of containment. American policies came to fuel U.S.-Soviet rivalry and mired the United States in peripheral conflicts that both drained metropolitan resources and drove leftist regimes into alignment with Moscow. By 1950, the intellectual paradigms, organizational interests, and domestic political forces that constituted U.S. Cold War strategic culture were in place.

Strategic Assessments

During the early postwar years, the U.S. planning community based its assessment that the likelihood of Soviet aggression was very low on the supposition that the Soviets would not attack Western Europe unless they believed they had a good chance of attaining victory. Planners reasoned that the Soviets would not have this level of confidence until they had achieved the capability to carry out nuclear attacks against the United States. U.S. assessments of the Soviet nuclear program indicated that the Soviets would not have an operational arsenal until the second half of the 1950s. During the late 1940s, this reasoning

consequent shift in U.S. policy. The sterling crisis, the difficulties entailed in integrating Germany into Western Europe, the communist victory in China, and the Korean War all contributed to increases in American perceptions of vulnerability. As I show below, however, it was the effect of the Soviet acquisition of atomic weapons on U.S. assessments of the military balance that was the central force behind NSC 68 and the major changes in U.S. policy that were in place by the middle of 1950.

led the policy community to conclude both that the likelihood of war would remain remote well into the next decade and that should war break out, America's nuclear monopoly would allow the United States to prevail.

The realization in September 1949 that the Soviets had successfully tested an atomic device during the second half of August radically altered these assessments. Soviet nuclear weapons and the prospect of new long-range delivery systems made the U.S. homeland vulnerable to attack in a way that it had never been before. The nature of the U.S. response was colored not just by Soviet possession of nuclear capability but also by the extent to which the planning community had misjudged the state of the Soviet weapons program. Perceptions of low vulnerability gave way to perceptions of high vulnerability. The United States had the resources necessary to build a far superior nuclear arsenal, but conditions of strategic deficiency prevailed inasmuch as elites could do nothing to redress the vulnerability of the metropole to Soviet nuclear attack and consequently began to doubt the ability of the United States to prevail against the Soviet Union in a protracted conflict.

Planning documents drafted in late 1949 and early 1950 reveal, in operational terms, the sources of this heightened sense of vulnerability. Analysts revised their assessments of when the Soviets might be prepared to initiate conflict. NSC 68, drafted in February and March 1950 by an ad hoc committee put together by Paul Nitze, the new director of Policy Planning,[155] predicted that the Soviets would, by 1954, have a nuclear arsenal large enough to make them reasonably confident of their chances of successfully invading Europe.[156] Other analyses indi-

---

[155] Nitze replaced Kennan as director of Policy Planning in January 1950. Although this change in personnel had a significant impact on the positions taken by Policy Planning, it would be unjustified to see it as a major cause of the shifts in policy that occurred at roughly the same time. Mainstream thinking within the administration had diverged from Kennan's views before his departure from Policy Planning. Kennan resisted the hardening of policy that was occurring around him and dissented from the majority on several critical issues; he opposed the formation of NATO and the development of the hydrogen bomb. As Yergin puts it, "Kennan's own role within the State Department was changing, from that of savant and seer to grumbler and irritant" (*Shattered Peace*, p. 390). Kennan's replacement by Nitze was thus more a reflection than a cause of the changing policy paradigm.

[156] The following calculations led planners to focus on 1954 as the year in which a Soviet offensive would become feasible. One hundred atomic bombs were deemed the minimum necessary to do serious damage to the United States. Given the fact that the Soviets could deliver between 40 and 60% of their weapons on target, an arsenal of two hundred bombs would give the Soviets robust offensive capability. The U.S. planning community calculated that the Soviets would have roughly two hundred bombs by 1954. See "United States Objectives and Programs for National Security," NSC 68, 14 April 1950, in *Containment*, ed. Etzold and Gaddis, p. 400.

cated that the growing Soviet nuclear arsenal might encourage the Kremlin to initiate hostilities as early as 1951–1952.[157] The CIA asserted that the likelihood of war would rise markedly when the Soviets acquired the capability to deliver a crippling atomic attack against their adversary. In November 1950, the CIA warned that the Soviets could attain that capability "at any time and the situation may become critical at any time within the next two years." Planners also lost, virtually overnight, their confidence about the ability of the United States to maintain a nuclear arsenal larger and more sophisticated than that of the Soviet Union.[158] If the intelligence community had so misjudged when the Soviets would acquire nuclear capability, they reasoned, it could easily underestimate the size and sophistication of the Soviet arsenal. The Military Liaison Committee alarmingly concluded in 1950 that Soviet "stockpile and current production capacity are equal or actually superior to our own, both as to yields and number." The director of air force intelligence, noting the uncertainties plaguing U.S. assessments of the Soviet nuclear program, asserted in July 1950 that "it is possible that an H-bomb could be available to the Soviets today."[159]

U.S. planners also began to express doubts about the adequacy of existing war plans. Soviet acquisition of atomic capability meant that the U.S. target set had to be expanded to cover both nuclear storage and production sites, leaving fewer warheads for hitting industrial infrastructure. In addition, planners worried that the Soviets might supply their war machine by relying on industrial plant in occupied Western Europe, thereby preventing the United States from using nuclear attack to destroy their war-making infrastructure.[160] As a result of these considerations, the JCS began to revise its assessment that the United States would be able to prevail in a protracted conflict with the Soviet Union. A JCS report from February 1950 expressed concern that "logistical deficiencies and expected bomber attrition rates preclude an offensive on the scale currently contemplated" in the war plans.[161] Another JCS report from early 1950 concluded that, should war break out, the Soviets stood a reasonable chance of attaining victory.[162]

---

[157] Herken, *Winning Weapon*, p. 314.

[158] DDRS (80) 226A, NIE-3, 15 Nov. 1950, "Soviet Capabilities and Intentions," p. 5, Rosenberg, "American Atomic Strategy," p. 85.

[159] Committee report cited in Herken, *Winning Weapon*, p. 326; DDRS (79) 20A, CIA/SCI-2/50, 4 July 1950, "Joint Atomic Energy Intelligence Committee: Status of the Soviet Atomic Energy Program," p. 3.

[160] Herken, *Winning Weapon*, p. 313.

[161] DDRS (76) 159A, JCS 1952/11, 10 Feb. 1950, "Weapons Systems Evaluation Group—Report No. 1," p. 158. See also DDRS (76) 242A/B, 11 April 1950, "USAF Capabilities in Event of War in 1950," memo from Major General S. E. Anderson, Director of Plans and Operations, to Mr. Symington.

[162] Herken, *Winning Weapon*, p. 324.

These dramatic shifts in strategic assessments had profound implications. NSC 68, the document drafted in answer to Truman's request for a study of how the United States should respond to Soviet possession of atomic weaponry, laid the groundwork for the largest peacetime buildup in American history. Its conclusions were unequivocal: the country had to devote itself to the militarization of containment. Not long after the detection of the Soviet atomic test, Truman authorized research on the hydrogen bomb to proceed.[163] An increased arsenal of atomic weapons and the development of the H-bomb were needed to strengthen deterrence, to demonstrate American resolve, and to use in wartime if necessary.[164] Not only did more targets now exist in the Soviet Union, but the United States had to develop an arsenal robust enough to retaliate even after a Soviet first strike.[165] Finally, conventional forces had to be considerably strengthened. A conventional buildup was needed to bolster deterrence and to hamper and delay Soviet forces should they try to invade Western Europe.[166] In sum, NSC 68 categorically rejected the notion that containment could be implemented primarily by restoring the economic vitality and self-confidence of power centers in Western Europe and North Asia. On the contrary, the Soviets could now be stopped only if confronted with superior opposing force. As the Policy Planning Staff wrote, "Without superior aggregate military strength, in being and readily mobilizable, a policy of 'containment'—which is in effect a policy of calculated and gradual coercion—is no more than a policy of bluff."[167]

Dealing with the Adversary

A new template for the formulation of U.S. foreign policy crystallized during late 1949 and early 1950. As NSC 68 made clear, deterrent policies had to give way to compellent ones, to "calculated and gradual coercion." As during the reorientation of policy that occurred during 1946–47, the ideas that led to a new course were not entirely new; they were already circulating within the elite community but had not yet become central principles guiding the formulation of policy. NSC 68 similarly represented not a bolt from the blue, but a crystallization and

---

[163] See DDRS (86) 3299, "Recommendations," approved by President Truman on 31 Jan. 1950.

[164] NSC 68, pp. 417–418; and Herken, *Winning Weapon*, pp. 306, 316, 326. On the need to accelerate the production of atomic bombs, see DDRS (77) 189C, JCS 1823/16, 28 Oct. 1949, "Note by the Secretaries of the JCS on Implications of the Accelerated Atomic Energy Program," p. 112; and Rosenberg, "Origins of Overkill," pp. 132–133.

[165] NSC 68, pp. 415–416; and Leffler, *Preponderance of Power*, pp. 323–327.

[166] NSC 68, pp. 411–412.

[167] Ibid., p. 402.

rise to prominence of hard-line views that had heretofore existed only on the fringes of the policy community. As argued below, the new policies adopted in 1950 were largely the product of the set of strategic beliefs that emerged from the vulnerability associated with Soviet acquisition of atomic weapons. A policy community that had based its diplomatic and military strategies on the U.S. nuclear monopoly and long-term military superiority found itself confronted with the prospect of an entrenched adversary soon to possess the ability to carry out nuclear attacks against the U.S. homeland and, potentially, to defeat the United States in a protracted conflict.

American perceptions of vulnerability were made more acute by the communist victory in China (proclamation of the People's Republic virtually coincided with detection of the Soviet test) and by North Korea's invasion of South Korea. But Soviet acquisition of nuclear weapons was the critical development triggering a major reorientation of U.S. policy. The changes in thinking occurred well after officials recognized that the CCP would defeat the Nationalists and well before the invasion of South Korea. U.S. officials recognized by early 1949 that a communist victory in China was essentially inevitable. In January, the director of the Office of Far Eastern Affairs informed the acting secretary of state that "generally speaking, Nationalist units are surrounded, isolated, or so badly weakened that they can do little more than temporarily delay the winning of any Communist military objective. The Communists enjoy a marked numerical superiority in both north and central China."[168] U.S. officials admitted that they could do little but watch as CCP forces gradually took control of the country.[169] China was effectively "lost" well before September, yet it was not until after the Soviet atomic test that U.S. policy in the Far East began to undergo fundamental change.[170] Furthermore, the key changes in

[168] "Memorandum by the Director of the Office of Far Eastern Affairs (Butterworth) to the Acting Secretary of State," 7 Jan. 1949, FRUS, 1949, vol. 8, pp. 14–15.

[169] See, for example, "The Ambassador in China (Stuart) to the Secretary of State," 14 Feb. 1949, FRUS, 1949, vol. 8, pp. 136–139; and "Memorandum by the Director of the Office of Far Eastern Affairs (Butterworth) to the Secretary of State," 18 March 1949, FRUS, 1949, vol. 8, pp. 187–188.

[170] I am not suggesting that U.S. policy changed immediately after detection of the Soviet test. On the contrary, many of the planning papers drafted in November and December 1949 reaffirmed some of the key suppositions that had come to inform policy during 1946–1947. NSC 48/2, for example, reiterated the need to "exploit, through appropriate political, psychological and economic means, any rifts between the Chinese Communists and the USSR and between the Stalinists and other elements in China" ("The Position of the United States with Respect to Asia," FRUS, Dec. 1949, vol. 7, part 2, p. 1219). The State Department cautioned that the United States had to contain communism in the Far East "by means other than arms," and that "we are more apt to consolidate their position [communist regimes] by attempting openly to overthrow them than by dealing with them in order to exert our influence directly on them" ("Outline of Far

Defense spending

thinking that led to a major shift in policy occurred during the winter and spring of 1950—before the invasion of South Korea in June. Events in Korea indeed played an important role in ensuring that the recommendations set forth in NSC 68 were translated into policy; North Korean aggression helped convince Truman that Congress would support vast increases in defense spending. But, as detailed below, the key changes in strategic thinking took place before the Korean War started.[171]

In response to the successful Soviet atomic test, President Truman requested an overall review of U.S. defense policy. The product—NSC 68—was drafted during the early months of 1950 and accepted by the National Security Council in April. NSC 68 reflected three critical changes in strategic thinking that were to alter for decades to come how U.S. elites sought to contain Soviet expansion. To begin, NSC 68 rejected the notion that economic recovery had to be given priority over rearmament. On the contrary, checking Soviet expansion now required the militarization of containment. As NSC 68 put it, "A building up of the military capabilities of the United States and the free world is a precondition . . . to the protection of the United States against disaster."[172] Pushed forward by U.S. involvement in the Korean War, the Truman administration acted on the advice of Nitze and his committee. Between 1950 and 1953, defense spending rose from roughly $15 to $50 billion. While some of this increase was related to the war in Korea, much of it was the result of a general buildup, including the stationing of five U.S. divisions in Western Europe.[173] Of the $54 billion that the administration in the fall of 1950 sought for 1951, only $13 billion was earmarked for operations in Korea.[174] In Richard Freeland's words, "From 1950 onward, rearmament through N.A.T.O. rather than economic aid through E.R.P. [European Recovery

---

Eastern and Asian Policy for Review with the President," 14 Nov. 1949, FRUS, 1949, vol. 7, part 2, pp. 1211–1212). As I demonstrate below, these policy positions changed during the first half of 1950. It took time for new attitudes to percolate through the bureaucracy. NSC 68, like Kennan's "Long Telegram," provided a conceptual framework that facilitated the crystallization of policy around a specific set of suppositions. In addition, as discussed below, domestic political pressures played a role in inducing the administration to pursue a far more ambitious policy in the Far East.

[171] Nancy Tucker argues that the key changes in U.S. policy toward the Far East did not occur until the Korean War (*Patterns in the Dust*, pp. 57–58). The following analysis demonstrates, however, that the weight of opinion within the administration moved decidedly toward a more hard-line stance before hostilities broke out in Korea; those arguing in favor of militarizing and globalizing containment had already gained the upper hand. For an interpretation similar to my own, see Leffler, "Was 1947 a Turning Point?" pp. 37–38.

[172] NSC 68, p. 427.

[173] Yergin, *Shattered Peace*, p. 408.

[174] Leffler, *Preponderance of Power*, p. 374.

Program] was the mechanism for the organization of the Western bloc."[175] NATO was being transformed from an institution aimed primarily at reassuring Western Europe to one focused on confronting the Soviets with preponderant military power.

This military buildup did not signal that the administration had abandoned efforts to contain the Soviets through political, economic, and psychological means. On the contrary, especially in Western Europe and Japan, the United States continued to view economic recovery and political stabilization as central to stemming the spread of communism. Restoring confidence to the power centers of Europe and Asia was, however, no longer enough; containment now entailed confronting the Soviets with countervailing military force.

The move toward a substantial military buildup was predicated on two suppositions. First, planners believed that as the Soviet arsenal grew in size and technical sophistication, the Soviets would become increasingly optimistic about their ability to attain victory in an all-out war. A Soviet attack was no longer a remote possibility; the United States therefore needed to strengthen its war-fighting capabilities. As mentioned above, planners believed that the United States could sustain overall military superiority only by dramatically expanding its arsenal of nuclear weapons and substantially increasing its conventional forces-in-being. And even if these steps were taken, elites believed, they could by no means be confident that the United States would prevail in a protracted conflict, especially as the Soviet nuclear arsenal expanded.[176]

Second, a major buildup was needed to demonstrate U.S. resolve, to bolster the reputation of U.S. decision makers and broadcast their intention to stand firm in what was emerging as a battle of wills between Washington and Moscow. Growing reputational concerns were in part related to efforts to strengthen nuclear deterrence. Officials argued that the best way to prevent a Soviet nuclear attack on the United States was to make it clear to the Soviets that American elites had the capability and will to retaliate with nuclear forces. As Stuart Symington, secretary of the air force, wrote to Defense Secretary Louis Johnson only a month after detection of the Soviet test, "The only

[175] Freeland, *Truman Doctrine*, p. 324.

[176] In 1953–1954, top U.S. decision makers, concerned that the United States would not be able to maintain military superiority after Soviet acquisition of the hydrogen bomb, discussed the possibility of waging preventive war against the Soviet Union. President Dwight Eisenhower effectively ruled out preventive war but approved planning documents that left open the possibility of preemption should a Soviet attack appear imminent. See Rosenberg, "Origins of Overkill," pp. 143–145.

consideration which could keep the Soviet Union from making this attempt is the fear of a retaliatory atomic attack."[177]

But U.S. concern about demonstrating resolve and bolstering reputation went beyond the question of how to erect a credible deterrent. American officials feared that Soviet acquisition of the bomb would embolden the Kremlin on all fronts. The problem was not that analysts feared a shift in Soviet intentions. The U.S. ambassador in Moscow made this clear in a cable to the secretary of state on 29 September: "Feel no reason alter basic Embassy estimate Soviet intentions even if Soviets have now produced their first satisfactory bomb."[178] U.S. officials did fear, however, that the Kremlin would be more forceful and aggressive in pursuing its basic objectives. The ambassador's telegram from Moscow also informed the secretary of state that the administration would be justified in speculating "that in field current Soviet foreign tactical policy they will consider their hand strengthened and will tend toward increased firmness, less disposition to 'concessions' and endeavor to exploit fears of popular masses everywhere."[179] Nitze was also more concerned about the "diplomatic shadows" cast by Soviet nuclear weapons than by the war-making capability itself.[180] The CIA agreed that "the USSR in the near future will make political and diplomatic rather than military use of its atomic weapon."[181] A few months later, the CIA reported that Soviet behavior had in fact changed as expected: "Soviet behavior at nearly every point of contact with the non-Soviet world suggests the USSR is mounting a new 'offensive' in the cold war."[182] These assessments were predicated on the supposition that the bomb had convinced the Soviets that they had gained the upper hand in psychological terms; they were therefore more willing to challenge the United States and to take risks in order to test the balance of resolve.[183]

These considerations played a prominent role in shaping NSC 68 and its insistence that the administration not forgo development of the hydrogen bomb or issue a declaration of no-first-use. American decision makers, the Policy Planning Staff argued, could not afford to appear weak or indecisive at this critical juncture in U.S.-Soviet rela-

---

[177] "Memorandum for Secretary Johnson," 8 Nov. 1949, in *Containment*, ed. Etzold and Gaddis, p. 367.

[178] "The Ambassador in the Soviet Union (Kirk) to the Secretary of State," 29 Sept. 1949, FRUS, 1949, vol. 5 (Washington, D.C.: U.S. GPO), p. 658.

[179] Ibid.

[180] Leffler, "Was 1947 a Turning Point?" p. 39.

[181] DDRS (77) 282D, CIA 11–49, 16 Nov. 1949, p. 2. Unless otherwise noted, all citations to DDRS (77) refer to CIA World Situation Reports.

[182] DDRS (77) 283B, CIA 2–50, 15 Feb. 1950, p. 2.

[183] See Leffler, *Preponderance of Power*, pp. 331–332, 356.

tions.[184] On the contrary, only by taking unambiguous steps that would impress on Soviet elites U.S. determination to meet any and all challenges could a reputational setback of this sort be avoided. The major military buildup advocated by NSC 68 was based on these considerations as much as on specific military objectives. In fact, the effort to build military capabilities sufficient to demonstrate U.S. resolve played an important role in driving the acquisition of America's overkill nuclear arsenal. Even if nuclear weapons were not needed to fulfill specific military missions, nuclear superiority was needed to demonstrate U.S. determination.[185]

As I have argued, vulnerability tends to increase the extent to which concern about resolve and reputation shapes policy decisions. Elites seek to compensate for an adverse shift in the material balance of power through an advantageous shift in the balance of resolve. Strategic deficiency is to be offset by convincing potential adversaries of an indomitable will to stand firm. This logic clearly played an important role in shaping the U.S. response to Soviet acquisition of atomic capability. Yet reputational concerns were exacerbated by the very nature of nuclear weapons, as well as by these shifts in the distribution of capability per se. Because of their destructive potential, nuclear weapons automatically turn confrontational interactions into tests of will and games of brinkmanship. The dynamics of nuclear risk-taking reinforced elite concern about resolve and reputation, and shed considerable light on why U.S. elites embarked on a massive military buildup in 1950 and why other key components of containment strategy shifted as well.

This line of argument is not intended to imply that there was unanimity within the administration about the impact of Soviet acquisition of atomic weapons on the likelihood of war or on Soviet behavior. In April 1950, for example, the CIA circulated a draft estimate arguing that acquisition of nuclear capability was likely to lead to little change in Soviet behavior. The paper noted that "possession of the atomic bomb has not yet produced any apparent change in Soviet policy or tactics, and probably will not do so at least through 1950." It also stated that "the primary aggressive instrument of Soviet foreign policy is the international Communist apparatus, acting through subversion and revolution, rather than military conquest by the Soviet armed

---

[184] See NSC 68, pp. 417–418.
[185] See ibid.; and note 196 below. For an excellent analysis of how strategic thinking and organizational pressures interacted in shaping the size of the U.S. nuclear arsenal, see Rosenberg, "Origins of Overkill."

forces."[186] The draft met vehement opposition from other agencies. The Department of State dismissed the paper's assertion that nuclear weapons would not make the Soviets more likely to initiate war.[187] The army stated that "the differences of opinion are considered to be so divergent that it is impractical to consider resolving them on the basis of the present paper. . . . The threat of Soviet aggression is minimized to the point where dissemination of the paper and its use for planning purposes could seriously affect the security of the United States." The air force charged that the CIA paper "failed to point out the full and true character of the Soviet threat. . . . There is ample reason to believe that the Kremlin regards its growing atomic capability to be the major force which will eventually place them in position to liquidate the center of hard-core opposition—the United States—utilizing all means at their disposal, including military action."[188]

These criticisms had a powerful impact on the final draft of the CIA report. Two of its conclusions are particularly noteworthy: "Soviet possession of atomic weapons increases the possibility that the USSR will be able to weaken seriously the power position of the United States without resorting to direct military action." The report went on to state that "the possibility of direct military conflict between the Soviet Union and the United States is increased as a result of Soviet possession of atomic weapons."[189] The evolution of this document illustrates the existence of competing views within the administration but also demonstrates that hard-line strategic conceptions were prevailing. The United States *had* to take steps to redress the adverse impact of Soviet acquisition of atomic weapons on the balance of resolve as well as on the balance of war-fighting capabilities.

The second key change in the orientation of U.S. policy had to do with thinking about how best to moderate Soviet behavior. By early 1946, the Truman administration had already backed away from accommodating Soviet demands; the implementation of a competitive policy meant no more concessions. The administration, however, left the door open for negotiation and recognized the need to promise reward for Soviet cooperation at the same time that it threatened punishment for Soviet intransigence. Many officials were wary of taking too threaten-

---

[186] DDRS (79) 19A, ORE 91-49 (CIA), 6 April 1950, "Estimate of the Effects of the Soviet Possession of the Atomic Bomb upon the Security of the United States and upon the Probabilities of Direct Soviet Miliary Action," pp. 7, 14.

[187] Ibid., pp. 29–30.

[188] Ibid., pp. 31, 35–36.

[189] DDRS (81) 420B, ORE 32-50 (CIA), 9 June 1950, "The Effect of the Soviet Possession of Atomic Bombs on the Security of the United States," pp. 2, 3.

ing a posture, lest heightened vulnerability make the Soviets only more intractable.

NSC 68 signaled a marked change in the emphasis of U.S. policy, a rethinking of what diplomatic stance would best serve the goals of containment. Concern about fueling Soviet fears of encirclement was replaced by conviction that the Kremlin had to be confronted with superior military force; the United States and its allies had to intimidate the Soviets and compel them to moderate their behavior.[190] NSC 68 did note that "it is essential . . . that we always leave open the possibility of negotiation with the U.S.S.R." But the document later clarified that the administration's notion of negotiation had taken on new meaning: "Ultimately, it is our objective to negotiate a settlement with the Soviet Union (or a successor state or states) on which the world can place reliance as an enforceable instrument of peace. But it is important to emphasize that such a settlement *can only record* the progress which the free world will have made in creating a political and economic system in the world so successful that the frustration of the Kremlin's design for world domination will be complete."[191] In short, negotiation was not "a possible separate course of action," but merely a means of codifying the Kremlin's retreat.[192] Diplomacy was to begin only after the Soviets had abandoned their international designs—an outcome that was to be brought about by convincing the Kremlin that it could neither surpass nor even match the power and resolve of the West.

This reorientation was not based on a perceived shift in Soviet behavior. Rather, like the militarization of containment, it was primarily a product of the perceptions of high vulnerability that accompanied Soviet acquisition of atomic capability. U.S. decision makers believed that atomic weapons would embolden the Kremlin and that they therefore needed to demonstrate resolve to the Soviets.[193] Elites were taking yet another step to ensure that the balance of resolve did not shift in the Soviets' favor, as the balance of material power had. Vulnerability produced a hardening of attitudes and fostered the belief that the United States could not appear to be conciliatory on either the military or diplomatic front.

The third key shift in policy stemmed from a reassessment of geographic priorities. Between 1946 and 1949, decision makers recognized the need to set priorities and limit the scope of U.S. commitments

[190] NSC 68, p. 437.
[191] Ibid., pp. 402, 426. Emphasis added.
[192] Ibid.
[193] Herken, *Winning Weapon*, p. 305; and Gaddis, *Strategies of Containment*, p. 85.

accordingly. Several considerations guided U.S. elites in their allocation of economic and military assistance. American interests were deemed vital only in areas of substantial military-industrial capacity and in those parts of the Eurasian rimland needed to project U.S. military power against the Soviet Union. Soviet expansion would also meet natural forces of resistance, including rivalry among communist regimes, indigenous nationalism, and balancing behavior against aggressors. So too did military spending have to be severely limited because of its harmful effects on national economic performance. As a matter of both necessity and opportunity, the United States could be selective in its implementation of containment.

The Soviet atomic bomb, in combination with the communist victory in China, led to a blurring of geographic priorities that gradually drew the United States into costly commitments in the periphery. After the events of late 1949, top priority was still assigned to major power centers, but U.S. elites believed that they could no longer afford to pursue a policy of selective engagement in less developed areas. The problem was not that these areas had suddenly become of more economic and military importance, but that confrontation with the Soviets had become as much a battle over resolve and reputation as over power resources themselves.[194] And resolve and reputation, unlike resources, were not geographically bounded. As NSC 68 put it, "At the ideological or psychological level, in the struggle for men's minds, the conflict is world-wide."[195] Communist victories, regardless of their location, might do little to strengthen Soviet industry or military power, but they could tip the balance of resolve in favor of the Kremlin. Furthermore, the Soviets might well exploit the perceived gains associated with their acquisition of atomic weapons to challenge the United States precisely in areas where nonvital U.S. interests were at stake. The CIA expressed concern that "the USSR may interpret the current uneasiness in the US over a potential H-bomb armaments race, added to the present atomic weapons contest, as an indication of wavering US determination to oppose Soviet expansion in areas where definite US commitments would not be challenged."[196]

Two serious consequences could result should the United States not adopt a more ambitious strategy in the periphery and fail to defend areas even if of little intrinsic importance. First, the Soviets might be emboldened and encouraged to engage in further acts of aggression. The problem with allowing "piecemeal aggression against others" was

---

[194] Gaddis, *Strategies of Containment*, pp. 91–92.
[195] NSC 68, p. 391.
[196] DDRS (77) 283C, CIA 3-50, 15 March 1950, p. 2.

that "we will have to make gradual withdrawals under pressure until we discover one day that we have sacrificed positions of vital interest."[197] Second, communist victories might demoralize U.S. allies and sap their determination to resist the extension of Soviet ideology and influence.[198] In March 1950, the CIA interpreted the drift toward neutrality in some European countries as the result of Soviet atomic weapons and their ability to undermine European confidence in the merits of alliance with the United States.[199] Rather than joining the United States in balancing against the Soviets, countries would likely bandwagon with the Soviets. The combination of steady Soviet efforts to expand and the demoralization of free nations, NSC 68 warned, created the risk that "a descending spiral of too little and too late, of doubt and recrimination, may present us with ever narrower and more desperate alternatives."[200] This logic naturally led to skepticism of the notion that communism would eventually be defeated by natural forces of resistance. Rather than basing policy on the supposition that nationalism would contain the spread of communism, elites worried that communist ideology might spread uncontrollably among demoralized states in the periphery. Policy debates became infused with concern about dominoes—that a communist victory in one location would spill over into neighboring regions and, possibly, reverberate in distant areas as well. U.S. elites thus began to see communism in more monolithic terms. Communist regimes, even if not closely aligned with Moscow, presented a threat to the West.[201] The spread of communism, regardless of whether military-industrial capacity was at stake, had to be resisted. In contrast to previous reviews of policy, NSC 68 made little mention of the need to foster splits within the communist bloc. American preoccupation with the balance of resolve and the need to counter any appearance of weakness left little room for a more selective and discriminating approach to dealing with the adversary.

NSC 68 also categorically rejected the notion that U.S. defense spending had to be severely limited in order to protect the health of the U.S. economy. On the contrary, the size of the military budget could be at least tripled without ill effects on the economy or a decline in the standard of living. Through expanding the economy and increasing total output, the administration could obtain the resources necessary for national defense "by siphoning off a part of the annual

[197] NSC 68, pp. 414, 441.
[198] Ibid., p. 414.
[199] DDRS (77) 283C, CIA 3-50, 15 March 1950, p. 2.
[200] NSC 68, p. 414.
[201] Paterson, *Meeting the Communist Threat*, pp. 74–75.

increment in the gross national product."[202] The implications of this analysis were clear: the U.S. economy could sustain—and indeed would benefit from—the militarization and globalization of containment necessitated by the Soviet threat.

These generalizations about how and why U.S. elites shifted from pursuing competitive to overly competitive policies are clearly borne out by the changes that occurred in U.S. policy toward the Far East during early 1950. In his study of American relations with China and Korea during the early Cold War, William Stueck accurately recognizes the main causes of the shifts in policy that took place in 1950:

> Growing fears about the situation in Europe actually encouraged Washington officialdom to stand firm against Communism in Asia. . . . Each potential Communist gain assumed a global cast, with American credibility in Europe and the Mediterranean the most important prospective loser. The "free" peoples in those regions looked to the United States for leadership, but in the face of recent events in China and the Soviet acquisition of the atomic bomb, further Communist victories might have a snowballing effect that ultimately would destroy their faith in America's will. Whereas in 1947 concern about Europe had discouraged the diplomats from insisting on deeper involvement in the Chinese civil war, now such concern encouraged a more assertive policy in Asia.[203]

The communist victory in China was no longer a development with which the United States could comfortably live, one that did not fundamentally alter the international balance of power. On the contrary, "the loss of China to Communists," wrote Dean Rusk, assistant secretary of state for far eastern affairs, in a memo to Acheson, "has marked a shift in the balance of power in favor of Soviet Russia and to the disfavor of the United States."[204] While the United States could do little to reverse what had happened in China, it could do a great deal to prevent events in China from being repeated elsewhere in East Asia. As the deputy assistant secretary of state for far eastern affairs wrote to the assistant secretary, "The Department's policy with respect to Southeast Asia is to stop Communism at the southern border of China . . . by all feasible and appropriate political, economic and *military* measures."[205]

[202] NSC 68, pp. 405–408; quotation from *Containment*, ed. Etzold and Gaddis, p. 384.
[203] Stueck, *Road to Confrontation*, p. 152.
[204] "Extract from a Draft Memorandum by the Assistant Secretary of State for Far Eastern Affairs (Rusk) to the Secretary of State," 30 May 1950, FRUS, 1950, vol. 6 (Washington, D.C.: U.S. GPO, 1976), p. 349.
[205] "Memorandum by the Deputy Assistant Secretary of State for Far Eastern Affairs (Merchant) to the Assistant Secretary (Butterworth)," 7 March 1950, FRUS, 1950, vol. 6, p. 750. Emphasis added.

The perceived need to stop the spread of communism with American equipment and, if necessary, manpower was predicated on the assumption that natural forces of resistance—splits within the communist bloc, nationalism, and balancing behavior—were no longer adequate to do the job. Far from believing that Beijing and Moscow would inevitably part ways, U.S. policy makers became increasingly convinced that Soviet and Chinese leaders were conspiring to spread communism throughout the region: "Developments in Asia confirm that there is a comprehensive program, in which the Soviet and Chinese communists are cooperating, designed as a present phase to eliminate all Western influence on the Asiatic mainland, and probably also in relation to the islands of Japan, Formosa, the Philippines, and Indonesia. . . . What has happened shows that our policies have been sound in so far as they have recognized the impossibility of separating the Chinese and Soviet communists, at least for the predictable future."[206] Furthermore, the notion that a growing threat from the Soviet Union or China would cause the states of the region to balance against communism all but disappeared. On the contrary, the states of the region were more likely to bandwagon and fall like dominoes. As the final report of a State Department mission to Southeast Asia put it in late 1950, the "loss of any one of the countries to the enemy would almost certainly result in the loss of all the other countries, with the possible exception of the Philippines." The CIA noted in February 1950 that "the total defeat of the French and Bao Dai would cause Western influence to sink to a new low throughout the Far East. . . . If Indochina fell into Communist hands, the way would be paved for Communist control over Thailand and Burma. . . . Even Indonesia will be vulnerable."[207] John Foster Dulles argued that the implications of the advance of communism in East Asia would be even more far-reaching. Further losses to communist aggressors, he maintained, "would have grave psychological repercussions upon the Japanese nation and the countries and islands of South East Asia. The repercussions will not be limited to Asia, but will extend to Western Europe and the British Commonwealth."[208]

It was primarily these considerations that led to the extension of new U.S. defense commitments in East Asia. In justifying a new stance in the Far East, NSC 48/1, approved in December 1949, asserted that "the extension of communist authority in China represents a grievous

---

[206] Paper prepared by Mr. John Foster Dulles, consultant to the secretary of state, "Estimate of Situation," 30 Nov. 1950, FRUS, 1950, vol. 6, p. 162.

[207] "Final Report of the Joint MDAP Survey Mission to Southeast Asia," 6 Dec. 1950, FRUS, 1950, vol. 6, p. 166; DDRS (77) 283B, CIA 2-50, 15 Feb. 1950, p. 4.

[208] "Estimate of Situation," p. 162.

political defeat for us; if southeast Asia also is swept by communism we shall have suffered a major political rout the repercussions of which will be felt throughout the rest of the world."[209] In March, the State and Defense departments joined forces to persuade President Truman that "a program of military assistance for Thailand and Indochina should be undertaken for the purpose of providing military equipment to assist in maintaining the security and independence of these countries against communist aggression from without and subversive activities from within."[210] The JCS took a firm and unequivocal stance on the issue: "The mainland states of Southeast Asia also are at present of critical strategic importance to the United States because . . . Southeast Asia is a vital segment in the line of containment of communism stretching from Japan southward and around to the Indian Peninsula. . . . The fall of Indochina would undoubtedly lead to the fall of the other mainland states of Southeast Asia."[211] In May, the administration decided to give military and economic aid to the French to bolster their position in Indochina.[212] The suppositions that had guided policy through 1949 were falling by the wayside; the United States was being drawn onto the Asian mainland.

A similar transformation in thinking occurred on the question of Taiwan. Although a commitment to defend Taiwan with the Seventh Fleet was not formally announced until two days after the invasion of South Korea, pressure to extend that commitment had been building throughout the first half of the year. During the winter and spring, both military and diplomatic quarters urged Acheson to alter his stance on Taiwan.[213] In April military attachés in Hong Kong and Taipei requested immediate military assistance for Nationalist forces in Taiwan, arguing that "the Nationalists are now absorbing the major attention and efforts of the Communists' military forces, which if Taiwan falls may be expected to exert full pressure on Southeast Asia."[214] Assistant Secretary Rusk proved to be one of the strongest proponents of de-

[209] "The Position of the United States with Respect to Asia," NSC 48/1, 23 Dec. 1949, in *Containment*, ed. Etzold and Gaddis, p. 259. See also Leffler, *Preponderance of Power*, pp. 354–355.

[210] "Memorandum by the Secretary of State to the President," 9 March 1950, FRUS, 1950, vol. 6, pp. 40–41. See also problem paper prepared by a working group in the Department of State, "Military Aid for Indochina," 1 Feb. 1950, FRUS, 1950, vol. 6, pp. 711–715.

[211] "The Secretary of Defense (Johnson) to the Secretary of State," 14 April 1950, FRUS, 1950, vol. 6, p. 781.

[212] Stueck, *Road to Confrontation*, p. 148.

[213] Ibid., pp. 149–151; and Gaddis, "Drawing Lines," pp. 85–86.

[214] Views of the attachés as reported in "Memorandum by the Assistant Secretary of State for Far Eastern Affairs (Rusk) to the Secretary of State," 26 April 1950, FRUS, 1950, vol. 6, pp. 333–334.

fending Taiwan against a communist attack. The island, he argued in May, is "important politically if not strategically, for what it represents in continued Communist expansion."[215] Rusk also maintained that the United States could not afford to send the message that it was willing to defend only the NATO area. "If our conduct seems to confirm that conclusion," he wrote, "then we can expect an accelerated deterioration of our influence in the Mediterranean, Near East, Asia and the Pacific." Accordingly, the United States needed to defend Taiwan "to keep the national prestige required if we are to play our indispensable part in sustaining a free world."[216] The Joint Chiefs of Staff, who in 1949 were still excluding Taiwan from the list of key offshore islands worth defending, wrote in July 1950 that they "strongly recommend that, irrespective of the situation in Korea, the United States plan to continue the present policy of denying Formosa to communist forces." The JCS also called for a more offensive posture in the Far East: "The continuation of a policy of solely defensive measures of a passive nature cannot halt communist aggression. There must come a time, if the expansion of communism under Kremlin domination is to be halted, when adequate forces in being must be provided and placed in a position to counter that expansion even though the risk of war be increased."[217] Compellent policies were needed to make clear American determination to thwart the spread of communism. Concern about bolstering resolve and maintaining credibility similarly contributed to the nature of the U.S. reaction to the outbreak of hostilities in Korea. According to the CIA, "a failure to draw this line [in Korea] would have seriously discredited the whole US policy of containment, gravely handicapping US efforts to maintain alliances and build political influence with the Western European powers and with other nations closely aligned with the US."[218]

These shifts in strategic beliefs and the accompanying changes in policy did not reflect a temporary alteration of course. The Korean War ensured that many of the recommendations set forth in NSC 68 and the other planning documents drafted during the first half of 1950 were translated into policy. NSC 141, drafted during 1951–1953, reaf-

---

[215] Rusk as paraphrased in "Memorandum by the Deputy Special Assistant for Intelligence (Howe) to Mr. W. Park Armstrong, Special Assistant to the Secretary of State for Intelligence and Research," 31 May 1950, FRUS, 1950, vol. 6, p. 347.
[216] "Extract from a Draft Memorandum by the Assistant Secretary of State for Far Eastern Affairs (Rusk) to the Secretary of State," 30 May 1950, FRUS, 1950, vol. 6, pp. 350–351.
[217] "Memorandum by the Joint Chiefs of Staff to the Secretary of Defense (Johnson)," 27 July 1950, FRUS, 1950, vol. 6, pp. 392–393.
[218] DDRS (77) 284B, CIA 7-50, 19 July 1950, p. 1.

firmed the basic tenets of NSC 68.[219] In this sense, NSC 68 marked a key turning point in the trajectory of U.S. foreign policy during the postwar era. It also set the stage for the Vietnam War, perhaps the most notable manifestation of America's Cold War excesses in the periphery.

NSC 68 encapsulated key shifts in the thinking of American elites about how to deal with the Soviet Union. These shifts in beliefs were brought about principally by the high vulnerability associated with Soviet acquisition of the atomic bomb. It was now insufficient to contain the Soviets by restoring economic vitality and self-confidence to independent power centers in Europe and Asia. The Soviets had to be confronted with a massive conventional and nuclear buildup. The Truman administration no longer feared that the militarization of containment would only make the Soviets more aggressive. On the contrary, formidable military forces and the determination to use them were needed to intimidate the Soviets, force them to abandon their international objectives, and, if necessary, confront them on the battlefield. Deterrent strategies had to give way to compellent ones. Only by offsetting an adverse shift in the balance of material power with a favorable shift in the balance of resolve could the United States contain Soviet expansionism. Negotiation with the Kremlin would lead nowhere. Diplomacy's only function was to record the Kremlin's submission to Western power and resolve.

Preoccupation with bolstering resolve also led to a blurring of strategic priorities. During the early postwar years, areas of vital interest were defined as those that contained significant military-industrial capacity or were key to the projection of power. In addition, natural forces of resistance would contain the spread of Soviet-controlled communism in many areas of the periphery. After 1949, concern about dominoes and bandwagoning meant that geographic priorities could no longer be defined in terms of intrinsic strategic value. Natural political forces in the Third World, far from containing the Soviets, would now work to the Kremlin's advantage. The view from Washington was becoming increasingly zero-sum. In a world in which resolve and reputation were more important than the material components of power, U.S. defense commitments were growing increasingly interdependent and geographic priorities increasingly blurred. As a result, policies of selective expansion gave way to policies of indiscriminate expansion.

As stated at the outset of this chapter, this critique is not meant to suggest that the Truman administration should have done nothing in response to the events of 1949–1950. On the contrary, given the degree

---

[219] Gaddis, *Strategies of Containment*, pp. 124–125.

of hostility between the United States and the Soviet Union, Soviet acquisition of atomic weapons, and communist gains in the Far East, efforts to strengthen containment and demonstrate U.S. resolve were indeed warranted. Prudence justified an increase in nuclear and conventional capabilities and a reassessment of peripheral strategy. But the United States did not need to build an overkill nuclear arsenal, to undertake a massive conventional buildup, or to defend against communism in all areas of the globe. My argument is that high vulnerability was the most important factor in creating excessive concern about resolve and in inducing elites to adopt compellent strategies and blur strategic priorities. It was these shifts in elite thinking that set foreign policy on an extremist course which arguably led to the most serious setbacks for the United States during the postwar era. It is no coincidence that some of those involved in decision making during 1950 had clear reservations about the new orientation of policy:

> I would like to point out that the demands on the U.S. for Indochina are increasing almost daily and that, sometimes imperceptibly, by one step after another, we are gradually increasing our stake in the outcome of the struggle there. We are, moreover, slowly (and not too slowly) getting ourselves into a position where our responsibilities tend to supplant rather than complement those of the French, and where failures are attributed to us as though we were the primary party at fault and in interest. We may be on the road to being a scapegoat, and we are certainly dangerously close to the point of being so deeply committed that we may find ourselves completely committed even to direct intervention. These situations, unfortunately, have a way of snowballing.[220]

Domestic Considerations

The impact of vulnerability on strategic beliefs provides a sufficient explanation of the changes in U.S. policy that occurred in 1949–1950. The evidence offered in this section, however, suggests that domestic considerations—in particular, the political pressures resulting from the shifts in public attitudes that the administration set in motion in 1947–1948—shed further light on the nature of the reorientation of policy associated with NSC 68.

Private Economic Interests. Given the fact that the massive buildup of the armed forces recommended by NSC 68 meant huge profits for the so-called military-industrial complex, it is entirely plausible that private

---

[220] "Memorandum by the Deputy Director of the Mutual Defense Assistance Program (Ohly) to the Secretary of State," 20 Nov. 1950, FRUS, 1950, vol. 6, pp. 929–930.

economic interests played a key role in bringing about the militarization of containment. Manufacturers in the military sector indeed had good reason to encourage a military buildup and to propagate the claim so prominently set forth in NSC 68 that a sizable expansion of the economy would allow major increases in defense spending without a decrease in the standard of living. It is also plausible that industrialists and financiers, fearful of losing their overseas markets to Soviet expansionism, pressed decision makers to redouble efforts to resist the spread of communism. Some historians have in fact given considerable weight to such economic interpretations of U.S. behavior.[221]

Economic interpretations of U.S. policy, however, simply lack empirical support. As discussed above, decision makers were indeed motivated by the desire to build a liberal trading order. They believed that open trade would help the U.S. economy weather the transition to peacetime production and would prevent the reemergence of international rivalries associated with protected trading blocs. But there is essentially no sound evidence to support the claim that a self-interested economic elite had a major impact on policy debates during the 1949–1950 period.[222] Although the business community, like the American public more generally, was warming to the notion that the United States had to sustain a growing range of costly overseas commitments, neither industrialists nor financiers were key players driving forward the expansion of those commitments. In the Far East, for example, self-interest induced the business community to support, not to oppose, accommodation of the CCP. As Nancy Tucker writes, businessmen "made clear their desire to buy and sell in China. Not merely potential supporters for future dealings with the CCP, businessmen indicated that they would willingly participate in America's efforts to entice Mao and his cohorts to cooperate with the United States and

---

[221] See, for example, Joyce Kolko and Gabriel Kolko, *The Limits of American Power: The World and U.S. Foreign Policy, 1945–54* (New York: Harper and Row, 1972); William Appleman Williams, *The Tragedy of American Diplomacy* (New York: Dell, 1962); and David Horowitz, *The Free World Colossus: A Critique of American Foreign Policy in the Cold War* (New York: Hill and Wang, 1965). The thrust of this so-called revisionist literature is that concern about protecting and enlarging capitalist markets was the principal force behind the expansion of U.S. overseas commitments after World War II. These authors differ as to whether it was the wider elite community or a more narrow sector of self-interested industrialists and financiers that was responsible for establishing the preservation of an international capitalist system as the country's main foreign policy objective.

[222] Critiques of the revisionist literature include Gaddis, *United States and the Origins of the Cold War*, esp. pp. 357–361; Robert Maddox, *The New Left and the Origins of the Cold War* (Princeton: Princeton University Press, 1973); and Lisle Rose, *After Yalta: America and the Origins of the Cold War* (New York: Charles Scribner's, 1973). For a review of the revisionist literature and its critics, see Geoffrey Smith, "Harry We Hardly Know You," *American Political Science Review*, 70 (June 1976), 560–582.

establish mutually beneficial diplomatic relations."[223] The main actors behind the formulation of a new brand of containment were civilian elites worried about U.S. national security, not corporate executives worried about maximizing their profits.[224]

To be sure, corporate interests began to play a more prominent role in policy debates after 1950. The military buildup associated with NSC 68 stimulated the growth of a defense industry whose political power was rooted in the regional economic benefits of major defense contracts and in the steady flow of personnel between high government positions and top corporate jobs. A powerful military-industrial complex became a feature of the political landscape and a key component of the United States's Cold War strategic culture. But the growing impact of private economic interests on policy was the product, not the cause, of the ambitious policies that decision makers began to pursue in 1950.

Domestic Politics. After 1947, the Truman administration's campaign to mobilize the public behind anticommunism took on a life of its own. By 1950, anticommunism had reached quite formidable proportions. It was fueled abroad by the behavior and new nuclear capability of the Soviet Union as well as by the communist victory in China. At home, the education and loyalty campaigns and successive spy scares heightened concern about subversives. In February 1950, Senator Joseph McCarthy made his infamous speech in West Virginia in which he claimed to have a long list of communists working in the federal government. At the same time that NSC 68 was being drafted, an atmosphere of suspicion and almost frenzied anticommunism was building among the public.[225]

These domestic forces appear to have had both an enabling and a constraining effect on decision makers. On the one hand, the administration did not have to battle Congress and the public to win support for a major military buildup. In March 1950, the State Department carried out a survey of public opinion and found not only that most Americans supported a more hard-line policy toward the Soviet Union, but also that there might well be "increasing public pressure, which could become dangerous, for some sort of bold action."[226] Despite these assessments, Truman procrastinated several months before approving NSC 68 because he was concerned that the recommended

[223] Tucker, *Patterns in the Dust,* p. 133.

[224] One could also construct a corporatist interpretation of the roots of NSC 68. This interpretation—and its weaknesses—would essentially parallel the treatment of corporatism presented above (pp. 448–450).

[225] Yergin, *Shattered Peace,* p. 407.

[226] Survey cited in Herken, *Winning Weapon,* p. 327.

measures might not pass Congress.[227] The Korean War, however, removed any lingering doubts he had about public willingness to support major increases in defense spending.

On the other hand, it appears that public attitudes pushed the administration further than it might have otherwise gone on the issue of defense commitments in the periphery. Beginning with the Truman Doctrine, the administration, against the advice of Kennan and others, portrayed the battle against communism as global in scope. The communist victory in China thus left the administration open to criticism that indeed resonated with the public: How could the United States stand idly by as communists took charge of the largest country in the Far East? Republicans sought to fuel this critique and to use it as ammunition against the administration, charging that Truman was being too soft on communism.[228] These domestic forces made it increasingly difficult for the administration to seek good relations with a communist China or to continue to pursue a policy of selective engagement in the Far East. Under pressure both from an increasingly powerful lobby supporting the Nationalists in Taiwan and from a public charged with anticommunism, the Truman administration found itself pushed toward a new and demanding set of defense commitments in the Far East.[229] As Freeland puts it, the administration "had

---

[227] Yergin, *Shattered Peace*, pp. 407–408.

[228] Leffler, *Preponderance of Power*, pp. 341–344.

[229] Jack Snyder presents a somewhat different interpretation of how domestic political forces affected policy. He contends that the expansion of U.S. defense commitments was fueled by a logroll between "Europe-first internationalists" in the Democratic party and "Asia-first nationalists" in the Republican party: in order to gain congressional support for aid to Europe, the administration needed to co-opt the Asia-first nationalists by taking a firmer stand against communism in the Far East (*Myths of Empire: Domestic Politics and International Ambition* [Ithaca: Cornell University Press, 1991], p. 256). The problem with this argument is that in the late 1940s, the Asia-first wing did not dominate the Republican party; the Truman administration did not need to logroll the Asia-first nationalists to garner sufficient congressional support for its foreign policies. Especially after the Democrats gained ground in the 1948 elections, "bipartisan collaboration between the administration and the moderate, internationalist wing of the Republican party . . . set the stage for Truman's notable legislative triumphs in the field of foreign affairs" (Hogan, *Marshall Plan*, p. 381). Supporters of Chiang Kai-shek did threaten to obstruct the approval of European aid in order to secure increased assistance to the Chinese Nationalists, but authorization for the Marshall Plan passed "virtually on schedule, and without a major reorientation of American China policy" (Stueck, *Road to Confrontation*, p. 59). In addition, "pro-Chiang forces in Congress did not prevent a total withdrawal from China" (ibid., p. 56). In 1950, the United States markedly expanded the scope of its military commitments in the Far East, but not to protect its aid program for Europe. By 1950, Democratic control of Congress and growing bipartisan support for economic and military aid to allies in Europe meant that "despite the growth of the China bloc in size and vocalness, its threat to administration programs in Western Europe had declined" (ibid., p. 131). I am indebted to Peter Trubowitz for drawing my attention to these arguments.

been led, against its will and policy, but according to the logic of its rhetoric and politics, to a full application of the Truman Doctrine in Asia."[230]

Since strategic logic and concern about resolve and reputation were also driving the reformulation of U.S. policy in the Far East, it is difficult to assign relative weights to the importance of public attitudes and discrete domestic pressures as opposed to sincerely held elite beliefs. Two arguments, however, do strengthen the case that domestic political pressure played a significant role in inducing elites to pursue overly competitive policies in the periphery.

First, administration officials were clearly aware that their handling of developments in the Far East had important implications for domestic politics. Political pressure on the administration mounted well before China had been completely taken over by the communists. In February 1949, fifty-one Republican members of Congress sent a letter to Truman expressing their concern about communist gains in China and urging the administration to commit more economic and military aid.[231] In July, John Davies, a member of the Policy Planning Staff, circulated a memo calling on the administration to pursue some widely publicized measures to clarify its commitment to stemming the spread of communism in East Asia. His recommendations were motivated in large part by concern that "in the American public mind our policy toward Asia is suffering from an acute sense of negativism. That the objective situation in East and South Asia does not permit a wide range of solid action on our part is not adequately understood and, even if it were, would not satisfy the demand in the American nature for 'positive action.'"[232] In the debate over how to deal with a new communist government in China, policy makers shied away from an accommodationist stance toward the CCP in part because conciliation would "be opposed by [a] large portion of [the] American public."[233] So too did domestic pressure color debate over Taiwan. In a conversation that took place in January 1950, Secretary Acheson described one senator's response to his statement that Taiwan was not a vital U.S. interest: "At this point Senator Knowland stated that in all respect to me he must reiterate that he felt the State Department was pursuing a policy of

---

[230] Freeland, *Truman Doctrine*, p. 358.

[231] See "The Ambassador in China (Stuart) to the Secretary of State," 19 Feb. 1949, FRUS, vol. 8, pp. 136–139.

[232] "Suggested Course of Action in East and South Asia," paper drafted by Mr. John P. Davies, Jr., of the Policy Planning Staff, 7 July 1949, FRUS, 1949, vol. 7, part 2, pp. 1148–1151.

[233] "The Counselor of Embassy in China (Jones) to the Secretary of State," 3 Sept. 1949, FRUS, 1949, vol. 8, pp. 519–521.

grave danger to the American people and that he considered the issue to be one of paramount importance. He said he felt it his conscientious duty to endeavor to acquaint the American people with what he regarded to be a fatal policy I was espousing which we would live to rue and regret."[234] Decision makers recognized that their popularity at home was linked to the policies they adopted in the Far East.

The second argument supporting the claim that domestic politics had a consequential impact on policy stems from the timing of the shifts that took place in the administration's thinking about the Far East. In late 1949 and early 1950, months after the Soviet atomic test and the communist victory in China, the balance of opinion within the administration still sided against taking on new commitments in the Far East. Although NSC 48/1, dated 23 December 1949, expressed concern about preventing the spread of communism in the Far East, it also recognized that "if it is not to lose the advantages of the initiative . . . the United States for its part must be able to apply pressure on fronts at times of its own choosing rather than spreading itself thin in reacting to every threat posed by the Soviets." In addition, the United States should seek to avoid intervention in the region to preserve "the U.S. traditional reputation as a non-imperialistic champion of freedom and independence for all nations." In terms of military planning, NSC 48/1 encouraged continued focus on protecting island strongpoints and avoiding commitments on the mainland. In January 1950, Secretary Acheson stated unequivocally that "the retention of Formosa has been defined to be not of *vital* importance to our security" and that he "did not believe it was in the interest of the American people to hazard a war over Formosa."[235] At roughly the same time, the U.S. consulate general in Shanghai cabled to Acheson an impassioned plea not to defend Taiwan, arguing that such action would only push the Chinese government toward closer alignment with the Kremlin.[236] At this point, U.S. officials were still actively concerned about fostering splits between the Soviet and Chinese leadership.[237]

That these main tenets of policy fell by the wayside in relatively short order—and, importantly, before the Korean War—strengthens the case for the consequential role played by domestic constraints. The

---

[234] Memorandum of conversation, by the Secretary of State (Acheson), 5 Jan. 1950, FRUS, 1950, vol. 6, p. 263.

[235] NSC 48/1, pp. 261–267; Memorandum of conversation, by the Secretary of State (Acheson), 5 Jan. 1950, p. 260.

[236] "The Consul General at Shanghai (McConaughy) to the Secretary of State," 5 Jan. 1950, FRUS, 1950, vol. 6, pp. 264–269.

[237] See, for example, "The Position of the United States with Respect to Asia," NSC 48/2, 30 Dec. 1949, p. 1219.

timing of shifts in thinking may have been the product of a lag between receipt of information and the adaptation of reigning beliefs, or of the time needed for a new conceptual framework to percolate through the bureaucracy. But given the existence of powerful domestic pressures, it is likely that policy was driven at least in part by domestic political considerations. The most compelling interpretation of this historical episode is that strategic logic and domestic pressure worked together to push the administration into a new range of commitments in the periphery. Overextension occurred both because of the effects of vulnerability on strategic beliefs and because elites found themselves entrapped in the political imperatives they had created. Thereafter, through their own rhetoric and behavior, elites also came to internalize the strategic conceptions initially propagated to gain support for their policies. Beginning in 1950—and for roughly two decades thereafter—the notion of a global struggle between communism and democracy infused both public attitudes and the intellectual paradigms and values of top decision makers. As John Gaddis writes, "Washington officials encouraged a simplistic view of the Cold War which was, in time, to imprison American diplomacy in an ideological straitjacket. . . . [They were] trapped in their own rhetoric."[238]

Military Services. The shifts in defense policy associated with the new course adopted in 1950 indeed furthered the interests of the military services. NSC 68 and the Korean War stimulated an across-the-board buildup. The administration ordered more capability for the air force, expanded conventional forces and permanently deployed a sizable contingent in Europe, and laid the groundwork for global naval deployments during peacetime. There is little evidence, however, to support the claim that the military played an important role in bringing about these changes. Although military analysts carried out many of the analyses and projections that fueled recommendations for a substantial buildup, as during the 1946–1947 period, it was civilian elites who were driving the reorientation of policy and arguing that rearmament now had to be given priority over economic aid. The military, if anything, served as a restraining force because of its fear that the administration would take on a range of commitments that exceeded available resources. In January 1950, the Joint Chiefs made it clear that they were "becoming concerned as to the increased military liability which

---

[238] Gaddis, *United States and the Origins of the Cold War,* p. 352.

apparently is developing in the Far East." Even as late as October 1950, Rusk noted that "it is recognized that the JCS may not wish to enter into military commitments more specific than those implied in the general position of a defense line through Japan, Okinawa and the Philippines."[239] Furthermore, even after NSC 68, the civilian leadership maintained tight reins over defense policy. The militarization and globalization of containment were simply not the product of self-interested services acting against the wishes of the civilian leadership.

Although the services did not play a major role in devising the new policies adopted in 1950, they did play a key role in institutionalizing and perpetuating the new course. The military establishment came to define its organizational interests in terms of the roles and missions specified in NSC 68. The dramatic increase in defense spending and force levels, the permanent deployment of ground troops to Europe, and the building of a vast nuclear arsenal and new delivery systems were developments that came to symbolize the intensity of the East-West conflict and to deepen the extent to which Cold War images infused both elite thinking and public attitudes. But as in most of the other cases I have examined, the military's behavior was a symptom, not a cause, of the pathologies that fueled overly competitive behavior. The organizational interests of the military, the economic interests of the defense industry, the intellectual paradigms of decisions makers, and the attitudes of the populace—these were all components of the strategic culture that shaped U.S. policy from 1950 until the Vietnam War shattered America's Cold War consensus nearly two decades later.

Conclusions

In the British, French, Japanese, and German case studies, elites made crucial decisions that were clearly at odds with incoming strategic information. They pursued policies that jeopardized core security interests despite the availability of strategic assessments that, by standards of reasonable judgment, should have produced different policy choices. In the U.S. case study, the historical record is somewhat more ambiguous. Given the information available to U.S. decision makers, their behavior was not manifestly unreasonable; they did not pursue policies that directly contradicted incoming information. Elites did, however, adopt overly competitive policies after 1949, policies that both

---

[239] "Memorandum by the Joints Chiefs of Staff to the Secretary of Defense (Johnson)," 20 Jan. 1950, FRUS, 1950, vol. 6, p. 6; "Memorandum by the Assistant Secretary of State for Far Eastern Affairs (Rusk) to the Deputy Under Secretary of State for Political Affairs (Matthews)," 9 Oct. 1950, FRUS, 1950, vol. 6, p. 148.

fueled the arms race between the United States and the Soviet Union and drew the United States into costly and counterproductive commitments in the periphery. Had my analysis focused on the Vietnam War itself, the U.S. case would have more closely resembled the other historical cases. Beginning in the mid-1960s, U.S. elites pursued a protracted and futile war in Southeast Asia despite incoming information that challenged the basic tenets on which U.S. policy was based. Decision makers found themselves entrapped in the strategic images and domestic political forces that they had created during the early Cold War years.

The causes of overly competitive American policies clearly resonate with the forces that produced adjustment failure in the other case studies. Between 1946 and 1949, elites perceived low levels of metropolitan vulnerability. Conditions of strategic sufficiency led to policies of selective expansion in both the core and periphery. After 1949, elites perceived high levels of metropolitan vulnerability because of Soviet acquisition of nuclear weapons. Conditions of strategic deficiency led to policies of indiscriminate expansion in both the core and periphery. High vulnerability fueled excessive external ambition by producing a set of strategic beliefs that induced elites to adopt compellent strategies. As in other rising powers, vulnerability led to a preoccupation with demonstrating resolve and bolstering reputation as a means of intimidating the adversary. Accommodation, officials believed, would only fuel Soviet expansionism and allow the contagion of communism to spread. The character of nuclear weapons reinforced concern about resolve; nuclear deterrence and brinkmanship served to increase the extent to which American elites viewed the Cold War as a confrontation of will and determination rather than of material power. So too did perceptions of high vulnerability lead to a blurring of strategic priorities. Belief in bandwagoning and falling dominoes lured the United States into new commitments in the periphery.

Elite manipulation of popular attitudes also played an important role in shaping U.S. policy. The Truman administration initially succeeded in convincing the public that effective containment of the Soviets would entail massive economic aid. But elites later paid a price for manipulating public attitudes and overselling anticommunism. In 1950, they found themselves entrapped in domestic pressures of their own making, forced by political considerations to extend the militarization of containment to the Far East. A new level of American involvement in the periphery would have been forthcoming even in the absence of these domestic pressures. Yet the historical evidence suggests that strategic beliefs and domestic politics acted synergistically to expand the scope of America's overseas commitments.

From 1950 onward, the economic interests associated with lucrative defense contracts and the organizational interests of the military services became prominent features of the domestic political landscape, adding momentum behind the policies and deepening the mindset associated with NSC 68. The ingredients of America's Cold War strategic culture were in place: an elite community infused with images of a pervasive and hostile East-West struggle; a domestic polity galvanized by anticommunism and fear of the Soviet Union; an industrial sector basking in the benefits of high defense spending; and a military establishment wedded to demanding nuclear and conventional missions. This strategic culture sustained a set of policies that fueled the intensity of the Cold War and deeply mired the United States in costly conflicts in the Third World.

[8]

Grand Strategy and Peaceful Change: Avoiding the Vulnerability of Empire

THE MAIN ARGUMENT

Both rising and declining powers are able to adjust their grand strategies to rapid shifts in the international distribution of power. Britain and France before World War I, Japan between 1931 and 1937, Germany between 1870 and 1897, and the United States between 1945 and 1949 all were major powers that successfully reoriented their grand strategies to respond to major upheavals in the constellation of international power. In these cases, perceptions of metropolitan vulnerability were relatively low; elites believed that if war broke out, their country and its allies would be able to prevail against the likely adversary. Elites operated under conditions of strategic sufficiency and were thus able to respond readily to the constraints and opportunities arising from shifts in the distribution of power. In declining states, elites balanced in a timely fashion against emerging threats. In rising states, they took advantage of opportunities to increase the state's power and influence but were quick to rein in external ambition when it threatened to provoke a preponderant opposing coalition or to mire the state in protracted peripheral wars. In general terms, elites behaved in a reasonable and prudent manner. During other historical periods, each of these powers reacted to international change in a very different manner. Elites pursued overly cooperative and overly competitive policies that jeopardized core security interests; their behavior was questionable, if not unreasonable, given available information. The perception of high metropolitan vulnerability was the key variable producing this very different response to international change. In all the cases of adjustment failure examined in this book, national elites operated under conditions of strategic deficiency and faced quite gloomy assessments of the likely outcome of war.

Perceptions of high metropolitan vulnerability led to self-defeating behavior through a three-stage process. At time 1, perceptions of high vulnerability under uncertainty about if, when, and where threats would come due, about what motivated the adversary, and about how the adversary would react to specific initiatives produced strategic beliefs that induced elites to pursue extraordinary policies. In declining powers, elites adopted overly cooperative policies in the core and overly competitive policies in the periphery. In rising powers, elites adopted overly competitive policies in both core and periphery. These policies emerged as a logical response to systemic constraints and conditions of strategic deficiency. Overly cooperative policies were pursued to avoid or, at least, to delay war. Overly competitive policies were pursued to demonstrate resolve, extract resources from empire, and bolster domestic legitimacy. At time 2, elites sought to garner domestic support for their extraordinary policies by propagating throughout the polity specific conceptions and images of empire. Not only did public attitudes change, but the central roles and missions of the elite community and its institutions did so as well. Accordingly, elite beliefs and strategic culture were running on parallel tracks. At time 3, as the strategic landscape crystallized and uncertainty diminished, elites became aware of the gap emerging between their beliefs and strategic reality; they realized that extremist policies were not producing their intended effects but were leading to strategic exposure, self-encirclement, and/or overextension. Elite beliefs adapted to incoming information, even though vulnerability often induced elites to cling far too long to outmoded strategic suppositions. Only when confronted with overwhelming contradictory evidence did decision makers fully adapt their belief systems. Yet even after beliefs had been brought into line with strategic realities, successful adjustment of grand strategy was rarely forthcoming. The reason was that elites found themselves entrapped in the strategic culture that they had earlier molded to gain support for their extremist policies. Such entrapment occurred because domestic political pressures prevented decision makers from pursuing their preferred policies and/or because the arguments and rhetoric used to garner domestic support so infused the elite community—its intellectual paradigms, fundamental values, and organizational interests—that deeply embedded strategic images contradicted, and in fact overrode, strategic logic. Domestic political pressures appear to have been more pronounced in the German and U.S. case studies, whereas the conflict of institutionalized strategic images with strategic logic applies most readily to the British, French, and Japanese cases. This three-stage dynamic explains why great powers are so frequently unable to adjust their grand strategies to international change.

In two important respects, this general argument needs to be quali-

[487]

fied in order to explain certain variations across the historical cases. In the British, French, Japanese, and U.S. case studies, it was primarily strategic vulnerability that drove the dynamic producing self-defeating behavior. Domestic vulnerability and the instability of ruling elites were of secondary importance. In the German case study, and to a lesser extent in the Japanese case study, domestic political forces played a more prominent role. In the German case, domestic vulnerability—the threat posed to top elites by the rising strength of the Social Democrats—in fact provided the initial impetus behind overly competitive policies and efforts to use external success to unite a fragmented polity. It was only after domestic chaos induced decision makers to pursue excessive external ambition that Germany was confronted with strategic vulnerability. As in the other cases, perceptions of strategic vulnerability then fueled the pursuit of extremist policies. In the Japanese case, the emergence of domestic political chaos triggered the initial adoption of competitive policies in the early 1930s. But in Japan, domestic developments led only to selective expansion and efforts to sell contained visions of empire to the polity. It was only after the China war produced strategic vulnerability that Japanese elites began to pursue overly competitive policies and engage in self-defeating aggression. These findings confirm the supposition of other scholars that domestic and strategic vulnerability tend to have very similar effects on decision making.[1] The causal mechanism at work is clear: elites see external ambition as a way of disarming domestic opposition, whether arising from political chaos at home or strategic threats from abroad.

The other key variation has to do with how adjustment failure manifested itself in each of the cases. Unique geographic and historically contingent factors are of critical importance in explaining outcomes. The experiences of World War I played a powerful role in shaping both British and French behavior during the interwar period. The reluctance of British decision makers during the 1930s to reequip the Expeditionary Force for operations on the Continent can only be understood within the context of the "never again" syndrome and the visceral aversion to continental entanglement that spread among elites and masses alike. In France, the participation of indigenous colonial troops in the defense of the metropole during World War I had a telling impact on interwar planning. During the 1930s, French elites placed excessive reliance on the ability of the colonies to provide the metropole with the wherewithal to stave off the German onslaught. The colonial orien-

---

[1] See, for example, Richard Ned Lebow, *Between Peace and War: The Nature of International Crisis* (Baltimore: Johns Hopkins University Press, 1981), pp. 66–70.

[488]

tation of the military and this widespread exaggeration of the strategic benefits of empire contributed substantially to the plight of the metropolitan army in 1940.

In Japan, the political power of the military services played a much more important role in determining outcomes than in any of the other case studies. The autonomy of the military and the self-interested behavior of both the army and navy are central to understanding how the Japanese found themselves simultaneously mired in a costly land war on the Asian mainland and engaged in a maritime conflict against a vastly superior adversary. Unlike in the other cases, the military itself—and not top civilian leaders—was primarily responsible for propagating the strategic conceptions that shaped how decision makers defined Japanese security and how the services conceived of their central mission.

Germany's unique geographic location, sandwiched between two major land powers, sheds considerable light on why the Germans fell prey to self-encirclement in the core but not also to overextension in the periphery. With France on its western front and Russia on its eastern front, Germany could little afford to allocate military resources to peripheral missions. Geography explains, in large part, why German leaders made few attempts to sell peripheral empire to the polity. Accordingly, the public, the bureaucracy, and the military never bought into overseas empire. The lack of a strategic culture wedded to peripheral empire in turn helps explain why Germany did not fall prey to overextension. German behavior in fact provides strong support for my argument about the central importance of strategic culture in producing adjustment failure. The one case in which top decision makers did not sell peripheral empire to the public or reorient the bureaucracy and military toward overseas missions—even though they did acquire overseas possessions—is the one case in which overextension did not come about.

In the U.S. case, the advent of nuclear weapons helped determine the allocation of resources between peripheral and core missions. Nuclear weapons drew the United States into peripheral commitments by heightening American concern about demonstrating resolve, but they also enabled U.S. decision makers to tolerate in Europe what they perceived as marked Soviet superiority in conventional forces. It is interesting to speculate about how U.S. elites, had they not had nuclear weapons at their disposal, would have coped with perceived Soviet conventional superiority in Europe. These unique features of each case study by no means undercut my central argument about the causes of adjustment failure. Rather, they help illuminate how vulnerability, strategic beliefs, and strategic culture interact with geographic and historically contingent factors to produce the range of outcomes described in the case studies.

THEORETICAL IMPLICATIONS

This study represents a call for theoretical eclecticism. The conceptual and empirical puzzles raised at the outset have been solved only by examining variables at all three levels of analysis: international structure, domestic politics, and the belief systems of decision makers. The underlying theoretical agenda of the book has not been to argue that any single level of analysis or analytic approach should have primacy. Rather, my aim has been to show how different variables interact with one another and to identify what feedback mechanisms affect the relationship among systemic, domestic, and cognitive forces. The explanation of self-defeating behavior put forth above is complex: adjustment failure results from shifts in the international distribution of power. When such shifts produce perceptions of high metropolitan vulnerability, elites beliefs about how to deal with adversaries and about geographic priorities lead to overly cooperative and overly competitive behavior. Elites then seek to gain support for their extremist policies within the domestic polity, and the resultant shifts in strategic culture in turn constrain the policy-making process. This complexity and eclecticism are needed to explain adequately the key dynamics driving an important and recurring historical phenomenon.

In building on several different theoretical traditions, this book points to two variables that are in much need of more scholarly attention: elite belief systems and strategic culture. Both of these variables are sorely understudied, at least in part because they are nonmaterial in nature and therefore difficult to measure. Methodological obstacles all too often divert attention from ideational variables. Nevertheless, this study demonstrates the critical importance of taking beliefs seriously, of treating beliefs as variables that shape how elites interpret events and formulate policy, not just as the cognitive medium through which incoming information is assimilated. What elites believe about the relative merits of deterring or accommodating adversaries, about the likelihood of balancing as opposed to bandwagoning behavior, and about the importance of reputation in shaping the behavior of other states has a major impact on how they deal with threats and formulate grand strategy. Similarly, the conceptions and images that constitute strategic culture, by shaping the boundaries of domestic legitimacy and serving as organizing principles for the elite community and its institutions, play a key role in the formulation and implementation of national strategy.

My analysis points to four main conclusions that, in effect, serve as departure points for further work on elite beliefs. First, the case studies confirm the analytic utility of the notion of the operational code or belief system. Elites do hold coherent beliefs about the dynamics of international relations, and they do base their policy choices on these beliefs. Although the cases by no means suggest that top elites all hold the same suppositions, there is usually sufficient agreement among decision makers to justify the use of historical analysis to specify a set of reigning strategic beliefs. By identifying key dimensions of these beliefs and how to measure them, it is possible to "get inside" the mind of decision makers and understand the key causal inferences that shape policy. Accordingly, more research should focus on the content of elite beliefs and the historical trajectory of the ideas and suppositions that shape policy.

Second, the cases suggest that the notion of bounded rationality accurately captures the nature of the beliefs held by elites. For the most part, decision makers acted on the basis of beliefs that were grounded in reality and logically consistent. Although there was a significant time lag between receipt of disconfirming information and change in beliefs, such adaptation was forthcoming. As far as the realm of beliefs is concerned—that is, excluding the effects of elite-mass linkages and strategic culture on decisions—elites processed information and drew inferences in a reasoned and reasonable manner. This conclusion does not indicate, however, that beliefs should be treated as mere reflections of reality, as nothing more than the medium through which observations are conceptualized. Bounded rationality indicates only a *range* of reasonable beliefs, the actual content of which depends on numerous variables.

Third, vivid events and the drawing of lessons from those events play a key role in shaping elite beliefs. World War I, for example, was a watershed for all major powers in terms of strategic thinking. Elites came to appreciate that economic planning was central to the formulation of national strategy. This lesson had a decisive influence on the scope and pace of rearmament programs during the 1930s. So too was the cult of the offensive discredited by the static nature of trench warfare on the European battlefield. The consequent emphasis on defense affected procurement programs, doctrine, and even alliance strategies during the interwar period. At the same time, however, elites in different countries drew very different lessons from the war depending on their unique experiences in the conflict. For British elites, the war demonstrated the importance of building up economic strength and financial stability, even at a clear cost to military preparedness. For French elites, it revealed the strategic value of overseas empire. Japanese decision makers observed the battle from afar but nevertheless drew a lesson with ominous implications: the country needed to strive for economic autarky. Vivid events indeed shape elite beliefs, but the content of lessons draw is dependent on the nature of a country's participation in those events.

Fourth, this book suggests that elite beliefs are affected by structural variables as well as by formative experiences and the lessons drawn from discrete events. Elites held a different set of beliefs under conditions of low vulnerability than they did under high vulnerability. The beliefs of elites in declining states differed significantly from those of elites in rising states. This finding suggests that the content of beliefs may also correlate with other structural features, such as a state's position in the international hierarchy, its geographic attributes, or its endowment of human and natural resources. Accordingly, it would make sense to organize a research agenda around the notion of the "first image reversed": that ideational variables, while they shape a state's behavior in the international arena, are also shaped by the structure of the international system.[2]

My analysis also shows that the scholarly community needs to develop a better understanding of strategic culture and elite-mass linkages. Elite efforts to garner domestic support for their extremist policies and the eventual constraints placed on the decision-making community by shifts in popular attitudes and national self-images had a telling impact on policy outcomes. I introduced the notion of strategic culture because it encompasses the more ephemeral attitudes associated with public opinion as well as more deeply embedded images that affect how the body politic defines itself in both geographic and behavioral terms. Strategic culture can shape policy by determining the bounds of domestic political legitimacy and forcing decision makers to choose between political survival and strategic pragmatism. Alternatively, it can infuse the elite community—both individual decision makers and bureaucratic structures—with images that contradict, and sometimes override, strategic conceptions informed by logic alone. Individual decision makers come to believe in the strategic conceptions they have articulated and become emotionally committed to their fulfillment. So too do the organizational interests of bureaucratic struc-

[2]The use of the term *first image reversed* draws on Peter Gourevitch's use of the term *second image reversed* to refer to the effects of the international system on domestic politics. See Peter Gourevitch, "The Second Image Reversed," *International Organization*, 32 (Autumn 1978), 881–912.

tures become wedded to the realization of these strategic conceptions. In this respect, it is especially important to study when and how image-based notions of security propagate within the elite community, altering the intellectual paradigms and values of top elites, reshaping how the bureaucracy and the military services define their roles and missions, and leading to the pursuit of policies inconsistent with inference-based strategic pragmatism. Again, the conceptual and methodological difficulties involved in measuring strategic culture and probing elite-mass linkages should not stand as obstacles to further research on these issues.

This study points to some surprising conclusions about the relationship between domestic structure and the process through which elites become entrapped in strategic culture. One might expect elite-mass linkages and elite lobbying to produce more pronounced cases of adjustment failure in democracies than in nondemocracies. Leaders in democratic polities, after all, are more beholden to domestic political forces than are leaders in autocratic ones. The case studies reveal, however, that nondemocratic states suffer far more acute bouts of self-defeating behavior than do democratic states. British, French, and American decision makers indeed pursued policies that jeopardized core security interests. But they did not, like their counterparts in Wilhelmine Germany and interwar Japan, initiate wars against a preponderant opposing coalition. Self-evaluation and self-correcting mechanisms appear to have been far more robust in democratic states than in autocratic ones. British elites did eventually build a continental army in the 1930s, though the decision to do so came exceedingly late. Likewise, French decision makers in 1939 finally began to update their strategy for metropolitan defense and recalled many troops from the periphery. Although U.S. elites engaged in overly competitive behavior after 1949, they too eventually reined in the scope of international ambition. Losing the battle for Vietnam served to expose dangerous strategic conceptions, not to fuel increasingly ambitious external policies.

Several factors account for the more moderate and self-limiting behavior of democratic states. First, democratically elected elites do not need to rely on external ambition to legitimate their rule. They turn to foreign success to bolster domestic support only under unique circumstances. In the British, French, and American cases, elites sought to mold public attitudes primarily in response to external threats and international crises. In the German and Japanese cases, decision makers initially adopted ambitious external policies and propagated ambitious strategic conceptions primarily in response to internal threats and domestic crises; Germany in 1897 and Japan in 1931 faced no

use
this

serious external threats. Autocratic rulers do not enjoy the legitimacy that accompanies representative government and therefore need to rely more heavily on external ambition, nationalism, and imperialistic ideologies to sustain domestic support. Not only are autocrats more likely to use external ambition as an instrument of domestic politics; they also work harder to manipulate public attitudes to maintain domestic legitimacy. The propaganda machines that developed in Wilhelmine Germany and interwar Japan were far more ambitious and influential than their counterparts in Britain, France, and the United States. The imperial strategic images that infuse the public and the elite community are far more grandiose and more deeply embedded in autocracies than in democratic states.

Second, the free exchange of ideas that takes place in democratic polities is likely to expose and undermine fallacious strategic concepts. In interwar Britain, for example, the public turned against appeasement far earlier than did the cabinet, virtually forcing elites to end their accommodation of Hitler's demands. In both France and the United States, public protests played an important role in persuading elites to withdraw from their respective quagmires in Vietnam. In autocratic polities, because of secrecy and the absence of public debate, dangerous strategic concepts are less likely to be exposed. Few challenged the notion of weltpolitik in Germany or that of the Greater East Asia Co-Prosperity Sphere in Japan. And those who did were viewed as traitors and effectively silenced.

Third, because democratic societies are less monolithic in political and ideological terms than autocratic ones, opposition parties and interest groups are almost always ready and willing to take the lead in pushing alternate policies whenever setbacks or incoming information discredits reigning strategic concepts. In Britain during the 1930s, for example, critics of government policy were patiently waiting to take advantage of opportunities to further their own programs. They played a critical role in providing alternatives to policies that were proving to be counterproductive. This feature of democratic society helps explain why British elites—albeit far too late—eventually reoriented grand strategy. In autocratic societies, there is little tolerance for opposition groups or opposing points of view. As a result, even when incoming information discredits prevailing strategic assumptions, there is no locus of political will or intellectual capital available to push forward alternatives. In both Germany and Japan, incoming information clearly indicated that elites were leading the country down a very dangerous path. This realization led only to a period of paralysis, however, not to a serious reconsideration of policy. Not without trepidation, decision makers soon found themselves swept along by the domestic political

[494]

currents and institutionalized strategic images that they had created. A monolithic political and ideological environment left elites entrapped in a strategic culture of their own making.

Fourth, democratic forms of governance, because they provide for the regular turnover of leaders, moderate processes of entrapment. A new leadership may bring a different strategic outlook to high-level decision-making bodies. Furthermore, a change in personnel may lower the political costs incurred in attempting to reverse the course of policy. It is risky in political terms for an incumbent leader who has been championing empire for years suddenly to advocate retrenchment and withdrawal. A new leader, while still having to face opposition from colleagues, the bureaucracy, and the public, could pursue such policies without discrediting his previous behavior. Autocratic polities favor continuity of leadership. This attribute makes it less likely both that leaders with a new strategic outlook will come to power and that those in power will find it politically feasible to reverse course. These four points not only explain why democracies suffer less severe forms of adjustment failure than autocracies, but also lend credence to the claim made by other authors that democracies are more pacific than nondemocracies.[3]

EXPLAINING THE END OF THE COLD WAR

The end of the Cold War represents a remarkable instance of successful and peaceful strategic adjustment. The Soviet leadership presided over a retrenchment in foreign policy that ended Soviet hegemony in Eastern Europe and dramatically reduced East-West tensions. The Soviet Union itself then disintegrated into the Commonwealth of Independent States (CIS) with surprisingly little bloodshed. The United States and its allies responded by scaling back and, in some cases, dismantling the web of military and economic instruments that had been erected to contain Soviet expansion. A definitive account of how and why this dramatic shift in superpower relations came about awaits years of historical research and access to Soviet archives. Nevertheless, this study, in two important respects, sheds light on the forces that brought the Cold War to an end. First, the behavior of both the Soviet Union and the United States confirms one of the major propositions of the book: that successful adjustment occurs under conditions of low vulnerability. Second, the manner in which the Cold War ended reinforces the claim that elite beliefs and elite-mass linkages play a

[3] See note 15 below.

central role in determining when and how states adjust to international change.

It is clear that Soviet retrenchment during the second half of the 1980s occurred during a period of relatively low strategic vulnerability. The Soviet Union had reached effective nuclear parity with the United States, and the Warsaw Pact, at least in numerical terms, enjoyed conventional superiority over NATO. Soviet behavior indicates that the leadership did not perceive NATO to pose a pressing threat to Soviet security.[4] Had Soviet leaders perceived a high level of metropolitan vulnerability, they would not have unilaterally withdrawn forces from Eastern Europe.[5] Furthermore, the precise timing of the shift in Soviet policy toward a more accommodationist stance corresponds well with a shift in Soviet threat perceptions. During the early 1980s, the Soviet Union faced a series of threatening developments: the Reagan military buildup and its accompanying anti-Soviet rhetoric, NATO's deployment of intermediate-range nuclear forces in Western Europe, the increase in the lethality of conventional weapons due to the development of emerging technologies, and growing momentum in the United States for the deployment of a space-based missile shield—the Strategic Defense Initiative—that threatened to undermine mutual deterrence. Soviet elites responded by pursuing a panoply of hard-line policies during 1983–1984. They publicly declared their determination to counter America's new crusade against socialism.[6] In 1983, they shot down a Korean airliner and, amid the international tension that followed, went on alert status because of concern about a U.S. attack. Soviet leaders stepped up their activities in the Third World. Their "response to the deployment of Euromissiles was to withdraw from the negotiations on intermediate-range nuclear forces (INF) and to make offsetting deployments on their own. They also reduced Soviet-American contacts and business to a trickle."[7]

Soviet perceptions of vulnerability began to change after Mikhail Gorbachev came to power in 1985. Perceptions changed not because of a shift in the disposition of NATO forces, but because of a reinterpretation of the requirements of Soviet security which was part and parcel of "new thinking." Soviet defense policy now had to be focused on

[4] For an incisive discussion of the factors informing Soviet perceptions of a relatively low external threat, see Daniel Deudney and G. John Ikenberry, "The International Sources of Soviet Change," *International Security*, 16 (Winter 1991–92), 82–97.

[5] As mentioned in Chapter 1, nuclear weapons counteract the tendency for declining powers facing high vulnerability to adopt overly cooperative policies in the core. Nuclear-capable states can deter adversaries of even vastly superior military strength.

[6] See Michael MccGwire, *Perestroika and Soviet National Security* (Washington, D.C.: Brookings Institution, 1991), pp. 116–117.

[7] Ibid., p. 122.

averting war rather than on winning war; notions of peaceful coexis-
tence and mutual advantage prevailed over a more competitive, zero-
sum view of international relations. This new thinking informed a set
of policies and assessments that led to a steady decline in Soviet perceptions of vulnerability.[8] Direct meetings between Reagan and Gorbachev eased tensions and put arms control back on the agenda. Soviet
analysts began to see NATO's deployment of Euromissiles not as an
effort to build a first-strike capability, but as a response to the Soviet
SS-20. From this new perspective, the Soviets' unilateral efforts to improve their security had only intensified the external threat. Contacts
between the Soviet and American military establishments also helped
convince the Soviet military that the West did not pose an offensive
threat to Soviet security. These changes in Soviet perceptions of vulnerability set the stage for the policies of unilateral retrenchment that
were implemented from 1988 onward. Soviet elites began to pursue
cooperative policies not because they felt overwhelmed by Western
superiority, but because they realized both that the West did not pose
a military threat to the Soviet Union and that cooperation offered a
safer and more effective way for them to attain their security goals.
Although Gorbachev's domestic agenda and his conviction that a cooperative and peaceful international environment would further economic and political reform at home indeed played an important role
in driving the reorientation of Soviet defense policy, lower perceptions
of vulnerability served as a key enabling condition for Soviet retrenchment.

Similarly, the United States and its NATO allies undertook a major
reorientation of their defense policies only after changes in Soviet force
levels and force postures had reduced the threat that the Warsaw Pact
posed to Western Europe. Not until it was clear that the Soviet Union
had neither the intention nor the capability to mount in short order
offensive operations against Western Europe did NATO members begin to remove troops from Germany and agree to revise NATO strategy.
Perceptions of low vulnerability appear to have been a necessary condition for successful adjustment by both sides. From this perspective,
the hard-line policies of the Reagan administration may have facilitated
Soviet reform, but not because they forced Soviet leaders to back down
under pressure. By intensifying U.S.-Soviet rivalry and the arms race,
the Reagan administration provided momentum for the spread of new
thinking in the Soviet Union. A new set of elite beliefs then led to a
radical reappraisal of threat perceptions. Soviet elites retrenched not
because they felt encircled by a superior coalition, but because they

---

[8] Ibid., esp. chaps. 6–8.

came to appreciate that the West did not pose a threat to Soviet security.

While perceptions of low vulnerability *enabled* the superpowers to retrench, both Soviet and American grand strategy was no doubt *driven* by shifts in the global balance of power. With the economic and military capabilities of countries in Western Europe and the Far East growing steadily, the relative strength of both superpowers had declined since the early postwar decades. The dire condition of the Soviet economy drove home the need for cutbacks in military spending. So too did American preoccupation with relative decline and concern about a ballooning budget deficit create domestic pressures for retrenchment.

But the long-term decline of the Soviet economy began in the 1960s, not the 1980s. The timing of economic decline in the Soviet Union suggests that ideational change—shifts in elite beliefs—was at least as important as material considerations in precipitating the developments that brought the Cold War to a close. If any single factor best explains the dramatic change of course in Soviet foreign policy, it is the emergence of Soviet new thinking. Elite beliefs about how to deal with the West, about Soviet geographic priorities, and about how to stimulate economic growth underwent dramatic change during the 1980s. These shifts in beliefs were no doubt influenced by the poor performance of the Soviet economy as well as by Soviet setbacks in the realm of foreign policy. But contact with Western elites and the exposure of Soviet society to foreign media and ideas also played a key role in discrediting reigning beliefs.[9] Shifts in the distribution of material power are only a piece of the puzzle. Systemic change necessitated a change in elite beliefs, but the actual content of new thinking was determined by the lessons drawn from discrete events, the socialization of Soviet elites into Western norms and values, and the unique historical trajectory of Soviet ideology.[10] The way in which the Cold War came to an end reaffirms that elite beliefs must be viewed as a critical variable shaping policy outcomes.

This book's focus on elite-mass linkages and strategic culture also sheds light on the dynamics that led to the dismantling of the Soviet empire. Soviet leaders had long used the notion of an ideological struggle between capitalism and communism and the specter of an imminent and grave external threat to Soviet security to legitimate their rule

---

[9] See Vladimir Shlapentokh, *Soviet Intellectuals and Political Power: The Post-Stalin Era* (Princeton: Princeton University Press, 1990).

[10] On the issue of socialization within the international community, see John Ikenberry and Charles Kupchan, "Socialization and Hegemonic Power," *International Organization*, 44 (Summer 1990), 283–315.

and justify domestic repression.[11] The power and interests of the Communist Party and the military establishment were wedded to the image of a grave struggle between East and West. *Perestroika* and *glasnost* entailed a restructuring of the relationship between the ruling elite and the public. Legitimacy was to be built through political and economic liberalization, not through ideological mobilization or threat inflation. Gorbachev's efforts to alter public attitudes both at home and across the Soviet bloc, however, went far further than originally intended. Initiatives that were meant to lead to paced liberalization throughout the Soviet empire triggered a series of revolutions that swept through East European countries and successively toppled their communist regimes. *Perestroika* and *glasnost* could no longer be managed from above; elites were being pulled along by domestic political forces that they could not control. The failure of the hard-line coup in August 1991 and Gorbachev's eventual resignation in the wake of the breakup of the Soviet Union further demonstrated the extent to which a new set of attitudes had permeated the military and the bureaucracy as well as the public.

As in the historical cases examined in this book, elite efforts to garner domestic support for their policies ended up constraining the leadership. New ideas and images, once implanted among the public, the bureaucracy, and the military, again took on a life of their own. The arguments and analytic tools used to understand past cases of strategic adjustment shed considerable light on the forces leading to the dismantling of the Soviet empire and the end of the Cold War.

IMPLICATIONS FOR POLICY

The analysis presented above speaks to two important policy issues: how decision makers should deal with potential adversaries and what steps elites can take to facilitate their ability to adjust to shifts in the constellation of international power. Whether to cooperate or compete with potential adversaries is a thorny, long-standing problem in the study of international relations. Like many such questions, the only reliable answer is that the appropriate stance depends on the nature of the adversary and the characteristics of the specific interaction in question. This study indeed confirms the contingent nature of such choices. My analysis has shown that threats and the vulnerability they produce are Janus-faced in their impact on potential adversaries. On

[11] John Lewis Gaddis, *Strategies of Containment* (Oxford: Oxford University Press, 1982), p. 20.

[499]

the one hand, vulnerability fuels the pathologies that produce strategic exposure, self-encirclement, and overextension. It alters elite beliefs in ways that induce leaders to pursue overly cooperative and overly competitive policies, and it sets in motion domestic forces that can push the polity, almost inevitably, to pursue self-defeating initiatives. On the other hand, preponderant opposing force—and the vulnerability that accompanies it—is precisely what is needed to deter enemies and to convince them that going to war will not serve their interests. Accordingly, policy prescriptions must be broken into two categories: those that apply when an aggressor state is not present and those that apply when an aggressor state exists.[12]

In an international setting without aggressors, elites should seek to satisfy the security needs of other states, to reassure rather than to threaten. Put differently, they should take steps to ameliorate the security dilemma. When states are secure, they are less likely to fall prey to the self-defeating pathologies associated with high levels of vulnerability. As my analysis has shown, it is when elites perceive high vulnerability that they engage in extremist behavior and pursue policies that precipitate international conflict. It follows that accommodationist strategies are more likely to preserve peace than deterrent or compellent ones. In addition, when prudence requires the adoption of competitive policies, elites should rely primarily on defensive rather than offensive initiatives. Offensive actions and capabilities unnecessarily heighten vulnerability, exacerbate the security dilemma, and increase the chances that even deterrent initiatives will threaten states and fuel extreme responses.

From this perspective, the end of the Cold War augurs well for Europe. Perceptions of vulnerability among NATO and former Warsaw Pact members have declined dramatically. Both the United States and Russia have reduced the offensive components of their nuclear and conventional forces. Perceptions of low vulnerability in many European states should help elites adjust successfully to ongoing changes

[12] Although aggressor states and rising states both seek to alter the international status quo to further their interests, they differ as to the nature of their objectives and the means they use to attain them. Rising states attempt to change the international order to increase their prosperity and security. They rely primarily on economic and diplomatic initiatives to achieve their objectives and turn to territorial expansion and military conquest as a last resort. Aggressor states are driven primarily by the desire to accumulate power, not security. They seek power in absolute terms, regardless of the implications of expansionist policies for their relative prosperity and security. They are predators who rely primarily on the use of force to attain their objectives. For aggressor states, military conquest and territorial expansion are the preferred means of altering the status quo. For discussion of differing definitions of the term *aggressor state*, see Stephen Van Evera, "Primed for Peace: Europe after the Cold War," *International Security*, 15 (Winter 1990–91), 32, n.65.

in the strategic landscape. In this respect, it is essential to incorporate East European countries and the independent states of the former Soviet Union into a meaningful European security structure. Helping these countries to meet their security needs, inasmuch as it will moderate vulnerability, will decrease the chances that one or more of them will pursue an aggressive foreign policy. So too does it make sense to ensure that a unified Germany stays deeply integrated into multinational economic and security structures. Given Germany's preponderance of resources, a return to national rivalries among Europe's major powers would no doubt leave both Germany and its neighbors increasingly insecure.

This study shows, however, that overly competitive behavior is not caused by international conditions alone. On the contrary, domestic forces played a far more important role than external threats in transforming rising powers into aggressor states. The three major aggressor states of this century—Wilhelmine Germany, Nazi Germany, and interwar Japan—emerged in the midst of relatively peaceful and nonthreatening international environments. The overly competitive policies pursued by Wilhelmine Germany were triggered by the domestic political crisis of the 1890s. The new course of foreign policy adopted in 1897–1898, including the inculcation of aggressive nationalism among the public, was in large part intended to restore domestic order. The critical turning point during the interwar period was the worldwide depression that began in the late 1920s. Before the depression, both Germany and Japan were experimenting with parliamentary democracy and pursuing foreign policies that did not threaten the status quo. Economic crisis in the early 1930s triggered a return to autocracy, the spread of nationalism, and the pursuit of increasingly ambitious external policies.

Two policy prescriptions follow. First, especially during the current period, when so many countries are experimenting with democratic institutions and market economies, it is crucial to buffer these states against economic shock. As the early 1930s demonstrated, economic duress can destroy fledgling democratic institutions and create social and political conditions conducive to the rise of militaristic and belligerent governments. Policy makers in the West should therefore provide economic and technical assistance to ease the transition to market economies. The depression revealed not only the sensitivity of new democracies to economic conditions, but also the degree to which unforeseen economic disturbances can spread quickly throughout an integrated international economy. Given the fragility of the economies of Eastern Europe and the CIS, it is important to develop international institutions to prevent isolated shocks from reverberating throughout the international system.

Second, the international community should focus on ways to suppress, if not eliminate, the domestic pathologies that lead to aggressive behavior.[13] Promoting the spread of democratic government would be an important first step in this direction. As noted above, the nondemocratic polities examined in this book suffered much more acute bouts of overexpansion than did the democratic ones. It is no coincidence that the three principal aggressor states of the twentieth century were ruled by essentially autocratic governments. Autocratic rule exacerbates the pathologies that produce overexpansion. Democratic rule counteracts many of these pathologies. In addition, the historical record suggests that democracies tend not to go to war with one another.[14] The deductive case for the claim that the spread of democracy should lead to a more peaceful international setting is also quite compelling.[15]

Steps should also be taken to prevent the resurgence of aggressive nationalism. History provides ample evidence of the disastrous consequences of unchecked nationalism. Especially in the current period, when the end of the Cold War has unleashed long-suppressed ethnic

[13] For a more detailed analysis of this issue, see Charles Kupchan and Clifford Kupchan, "Concerts, Collective Security, and the Future of Europe," *International Security*, 16 (Summer 1991), 114–161.

[14] Michael Doyle, "Liberalism and World Politics," *American Political Science Review*, 80 (December 1986), 1151–1169. John Mearsheimer justifiably argues that the empirical evidence supporting this claim is somewhat scanty. In Mearsheimer's words, "Democracies have been few in number over the past two centuries, and thus there have not been many cases where two democracies were in a position to fight each other." For those cases that do exist, the presence of a common external threat provides at least as compelling an explanation for harmony as does common domestic structure. See "Back to the Future: Instability in Europe after the Cold War," *International Security*, 15 (Summer 1990), 50–51. Mearsheimer's arguments do not, however, call into question the strong deductive case for the proposition.

[15] This case rests on six main points. First, leaders that are democratically elected do not need to turn to external ambition as a means of legitimating their rule. Second, democratic debate exposes policy to the marketplace of ideas, thereby allowing unsound strategic concepts to be critically evaluated and challenged. See Van Evera, "Primed for Peace," p. 27. Third, the mass public—the sector that stands to suffer most from war—can use the electoral process to prevent elites from engaging the state in war. Fourth, citizens in one democratic state will respect the political structure of other democratic states and therefore be hesitant to engage in hostilities against them. See Doyle, "Liberalism and World Politics," pp. 1160–1161. Fifth, the electoral process tends to produce elites that are risk-averse and policies that are centrist. Both attributes militate against decisions for war. See Jack Snyder, "Averting Anarchy in the New Europe," *International Security*, 14 (Spring 1990), 18–19. Sixth, states willing to submit to the rule of law and civil society at the domestic level are more likely to submit to their analogues at the international level. See Gregory Flynn and David Scheffer, "Limited Collective Security," *Foreign Policy*, 80 (Fall 1990), 83.

tensions, it is crucial to pursue efforts to dampen exclusionist and expansionist ideologies. Chaos in Yugoslavia and in the former Soviet Union has already given rise to the use of aggressive nationalism by elites seeking to further their political ambitions. Ongoing instability in these areas suggests that leaders are likely to continue to use nationalistic ideologies as a way to secure their rule.

An international body could contribute to the suppression of expansionist ideologies through three principal mechanisms. First, it could watch carefully to ensure that elites do not use nationalist propaganda as a domestic tool. It could expose those caught doing so, single them out for censure, and press them to cease by widely circulating a "blacklist" of irresponsible leaders. Second, efforts to protect the rights of foreign journalists would play an important role in making local elites more accountable for their actions and rhetoric. At the same time, the body could take steps to ensure that a free domestic press thrives in all states. An international body could also become involved in local radio and television programming, in terms of both monitoring broadcasts and countering nationalistic propaganda through its own broadcasts. Third, the body could monitor national education systems. It is critical that the textbooks used in primary and secondary education present an accurate account of national history.[16] All scholars, both foreign and national, should have full access to government archives. Guidelines could be set forth in each of these three areas, and access to international development funds could be made contingent on compliance with these guidelines.

The preceding discussion has been predicated on the assumption of an international setting without aggressor states. Should an aggressor state exist, an entirely different set of considerations and policy prescriptions apply. To begin, elites in status quo powers must adopt competitive rather than cooperative policies. The potential aggressor must be confronted with the prospect of opposing preponderant force. But deterrent policies may not be enough. The historical analysis presented above suggests that aggressor states, once they have emerged, are difficult to deter. After Wilhelmine Germany embarked on its naval buildup, Britain, France, and Russia joined forces to deter Germany; they kept pace with German military power every step of the way. Germany, however, was not persuaded to moderate its foreign policy. During the interwar period, initial Japanese expansion went virtually

---

[16] See Van Evera, "Primed for Peace," pp. 52–53; Holger Herwig, "Clio Deceived: Patriotic Self-Censorship in Germany after the Great War," *International Security*, 12 (Fall 1987), 5–44; and Paul Kennedy, "The Decline of Nationalistic History in the West, 1900–1970," *Journal of Contemporary History*, 8 (January 1973), 77–100.

unchallenged. But such accommodation did not quench Japan's thirst for acquisition; Japanese elites soon engaged in far more extreme bouts of imperial conquest. Neither timely balancing nor accommodation was able to stop Germany and Japan. Furthermore, both countries went to war despite the fact that elites were pessimistic about the likelihood of victory. Saddam Hussein similarly failed to withdraw from Kuwait in January 1991, despite being confronted with overwhelming force and a clear deadline. In all three cases, aggression was the most preferred outcome, regardless of the costs.

The lesson for the future is clear: status quo powers must be on the guard for rising aggressors, pursue measures to prevent them from emerging, and be prepared to take early and decisive action should an aggressor state appear. Given the difficulties involved in stopping fully developed aggressors from engaging in expansionist behavior, it is important to consider how to identify potential aggressor states before they reach the stage at which they embark on a program of territorial conquest. My analysis suggests that polities pass through three stages in the transition to becoming aggressor states. During the first stage, economic and political instability provides fertile ground for opportunistic elites to attack existing forms of government and whip up mass nationalism. During the second stage, domestic forms of governance become increasingly autocratic and the state's foreign policy takes on belligerent tones. During the third stage, the state engages in repeated acts of territorial aggression. I now consider how to identify polities that are passing through these stages and what steps can be taken to prevent them from developing into full-blown aggressor states. The following discussion is particularly relevant for the states of Eastern Europe and the former Soviet Union, inasmuch as many of them are now in the first stage, that of economic hardship and political turmoil.

The first stage is characterized by growing disillusionment among elites and masses alike, often brought on by adverse economic conditions.[17] Incumbent politicians face growing disaffection and mounting threats to their rule. Ruling elites and their opponents seek to improve their political fortunes by taking advantage of this disillusionment to attack publicly and further discredit existing forms of governance. These attacks often include appeals to nationalism, to a return to traditional values through cleansing society of unwanted elements, and the need to counter external threats through internal mobilization. At the

---

[17] For discussion of the onset of disillusionment during transitions to democracy, see Samuel Huntington, *The Third Wave: Democratization in the Late Twentieth Century* (Norman: University of Oklahoma Press, 1991).

same time, lobby groups reflecting a partnership between public and private elites often emerge to spread propaganda and garner mass support for leaders promising to solve the country's domestic problems and thwart foreign challengers.

During this first stage, third parties should seek to address the sources of disillusionment: they should provide financial and technical assistance in an effort to ease economic hardship and foster political stability. The cases of Japan and Germany during the 1930s suggest that there is a window of opportunity between the onset of economic turmoil and adverse political change. In both cases, several years separated the depression and the consolidation of authoritarian, militaristic regimes. Accordingly, timely and ambitious aid programs are needed during this phase of disillusionment. It is also during this first stage that efforts to promote democracy and dampen nationalism would be most effective. Elites seeking to consolidate power through nationalistic appeals could be discredited by international reproof. Lobby groups hoping to monpolize the flow of information and propagate dangerous strategic concepts could be thwarted by the spread of personal computers, fax machines, and photocopiers and by international efforts to protect the freedom of the press. Attempts to impede free elections and undermine democratic institutions could be deterred or prevented by the presence of monitoring bodies. These measures could help block states entering the phase of disillusionment from continuing down the path to aggression.

The second stage is characterized by a transition to autocracy. Those seeking to subvert existing forms of government succeed in doing so. Even if elected, elites undermine representative government by curbing opposition activities and the press. Appeals to nationalism and the need to cleanse society of its ills strengthen in intensity. Those opposed to such developments are silenced or driven from the political arena. In the realm of foreign affairs, external threats are viewed as more acute, in part to justify domestic centralization and repression. Hard-line foreign policies prevail and are likely accompanied by a military buildup, if not isolated acts of aggression. Relations with outside powers become strained.

During this second phase, more interventionist steps are needed to interrupt the process of transformation. In order to prevent further adverse developments in both domestic and foreign policy, third parties should threaten and, if necessary, implement economic and diplomatic sanctions. Economic and logistical support to democratic opponents of the regime should be provided. Efforts should continue to ensure that the domestic populace is exposed to the free flow of ideas and is not sealed off from the international community. Such external pressure on the regime should, however, be economic and political, not military, in nature. If precautionary military measures are needed, they should be overtly defensive in orientation. As this study has shown, during this crucial transition phrase, high levels of strategic vulnerability are more likely to exacerbate them than to moderate the domestic pathologies fueling increasingly aggressive behavior.

If a state enters the third stage and begins to engage in repeated acts of territorial aggression, third parties must consider taking military action before the aggressor develops robust military capabilities. This does not mean that any state that repeatedly engages in territorial expansion should automatically be attacked by a coalition of status quo powers. Military action becomes extremely dangerous if the aggressor possesses nuclear weapons. Furthermore, not all states that engage in repeated acts of expansion are powerful enough to warrant intervention by the major powers. Only if an aggressor possesses or has the potential to develop war-making capability strong enough to pose a threat to entire regions, not just to its neighbors, should major powers view military intervention as a necessity. If an aggressor does begin to develop such robust capability, it is better for status quo powers to act against it sooner rather than later. Status quo powers cannot afford a repeat performance of the 1930s, when two autocratic aggressor states conquered their neighbors and prepared for major war while the Western democracies stood idly by.

In this respect, those powers with the capability to do so should maintain the ability to take early action against a rising aggressor before it acquires preponderant military power. As the British and French cases revealed, after the military balance has shifted decidedly in the challenger's favor, status quo powers face strong incentives to adopt accommodationist policies and tolerate aggression. Accordingly, even if political and economic transition in Eastern Europe and the CIS continues to proceed peacefully, the United States should retain the capability to bring significant force to bear on the European continent. A sizable presence of U.S. troops and equipment should remain in Europe in order to strengthen deterrence against would-be aggressors. Britain, as well, should maintain a firm continental commitment—in terms of both capability and resolve—and not allow itself to slip into the illusory belief of the 1930s that its security can best be preserved by avoiding the engagement of its troops on the European continent.

Finally, this book points to three lessons that should guide elites in their efforts to facilitate peaceful change and respond appropriately to shifts in the constellation of international power. First, elites should seek to avoid responding to conditions of high vulnerability by adopting extremist policies. Even if such policies make sense in the short term, decision makers should resist pursuing overly cooperative and overly competitive initiatives. When faced with rising threats and high vulnerability in the core, elites in declining states should seek to balance as best they can through mobilization and alliance. If fearful of provoking a spiral, they can still accommodate the adversary, though at the same time prepare robust defensive capabilities in case accommodation should fail to satisfy the adversary. Elites in rising states should similarly realize that attempts to fragment an opposing coalition in the core are far more likely to consolidate than to split the opposition. During the 1930s, Germany's military buildup and aggressive behavior indeed intimidated France and Britain and temporarily stymied the formation of a robust opposing coalition. But the Nazis were soon defeated by a blocking alliance of preponderant military and economic power. Similarly, when facing commitments in the periphery that undermine metropolitan security, elites in both declining and rising powers should view retrenchment as a viable and desirable option. The historical cases reveal that decision makers all too often respond to high vulnerability by pursuing high-risk policies, assuming that they can reverse course should these policies prove counterproductive. But they simultaneously set in motion powerful domestic forces that soon entrap them and lead to self-defeating behavior.

Second, when operating under conditions of high vulnerability, elites should doggedly guard against buying into specific strategic conceptions that fuel overly cooperative and overly competitive behavior. They should be particularly wary of reputational arguments. Reputation does matter in international relations, but demonstrating resolve should not be viewed as a valid motivation for defending peripheral interests at a cost to metropolitan security or for challenging an opposing coalition and risking self-encirclement. Nor should the notions of bandwagoning and dominoes—unless specific historical circumstances provide good reason to believe in them—serve as justification for globalizing defense commitments. Similarly, peripheral empire can provide needed resources for the metropole, but the cases suggest that elites tend to exaggerate vastly the strategic benefits offered by overseas possessions. So too must decision makers be wary of the notion that external ambition can bolster domestic legitimacy without leading to costly side effects. Especially during periods of high vulnerability, elites must be particularly deliberate and hard-headed in defining geographic priorities. They must be aware of and explicitly resist the different strands of strategic logic that fuel self-defeating behavior.

Finally, elites should exercise foresight in the management of elite-mass linkages. In both democracies and nondemocracies, decision makers must be concerned about garnering domestic support for their policies. But they should be careful to educate the public, not to manipulate it. If public attitudes were shaped more by discrete causal suppositions, rather than by deeply embedded images, they would be more responsive to changes in the international environment. Elites would face fewer difficulties in convincing the electorate of the need for a reorientation of strategy. In addition, decision makers should consider the policies for which they might need electoral support several years hence, not just in the immediate future. They should therefore be careful not to "oversell" strategic conceptions. So too should elites be aware of the potential for strategic conceptions to so infuse the broader decision-making community and its institutions that important policy options are effectively removed from the agenda. The propagation of strategic images affects not only public attitudes, but also how the elite community defines its core values and central roles and missions. Once these images have become institutionalized, embedded intellectual paradigms and entrenched bureaucratic interests will make it far more difficult for elites to reverse course. The case studies also demonstrate that strategic images, once implanted among the public and within the wider elite community, tend to take on a life of their own. All too often, elites initially succeed in winning support for their policies, only to find themselves shortly thereafter entrapped in a strategic culture that has changed in content and intensity in ways unintended by top decision makers. Awareness of these dangers might enable elites to be somewhat more forward-looking and circumspect in their efforts to manage domestic politics and gain support for their policies.

Especially in the aftermath of the Cold War, elites should devote particular attention to leading public opinion and reshaping the missions and organizational interests of elite institutions. The images that fueled East-West hostility have been shattered, but new strategic conceptions have yet to take their place. In Britain and the United States, elites should make it clear to the electorate that the dissolution of the Soviet Union does not mean the end of strategic responsibilities on the European continent. In addition, decision making structures should be adapted to incorporate economic considerations more fully into policy and to ensure that the military is willing and able to take on new peacekeeping and peacemaking functions. In Russia, political leaders must spread the message to the public, the bureaucracy, and the military that national renewal entails improving the quality of life at home, not rebuilding empire or reasserting Russia's domination of its neighboring states. German elites should communicate to their populace that full integration into European structures and institutions will reinforce, not conflict with, Germany's self-interest. And throughout much of Eastern Europe and the former Soviet Union, political leaders should stress among the public the importance of ethnic and religious tolerance, minority rights, and political and social values that will strengthen civil society.

The Cold War has given way to more peaceful and cooperative relations among the major powers. Nevertheless, shifts in the international distribution of power will continue to occur, leaving some states stronger and others weaker. The key question is whether such transformations can be managed peacefully. Can rising states satisfy their quest for power without becoming aggressor states? Can declining powers make room for newcomers without falling prey to the pathologies that impair adjustment? The manner in which the Cold War ended suggests that successful adjustment and peaceful change are indeed possible. Perhaps great powers have begun to pay attention to the lessons of history and are becoming increasingly able to avoid the vulnerability of empire.

Index

Abyssinia, 160, 174–175, 179, 227
Accommodation: Britain's interwar pursuit of, in core, 11, 130, 136, 144, 151–153, 160–172, 176, 179–180, 183, 494; Britain's pre–World War I pursuit of, in periphery, 115–25, 129, 153; declining states' use of, 79, 80, 487; definition of, 67–68; France's interwar pursuit of, in core, 11, 186, 187, 213, 220–267; Germany's Wilhelmine pursuit of, 393–394, 414; Japan's pursuit of, 304–305. *See also* Deterrence; Diplomacy
Acheson, Dean, 453–455, 471, 473, 480–481
Adamthwaite, Anthony, 226–227, 248
Afghanistan, 107, 108, 173
Ageron, Charles-Robert, 260
Aggressor states, 500n, 501, 503–507
Air power, 105, 139–140, 218–219, 228. *See also* British Royal Air Force
Albert (King of Belgium), 397
Algeciras Conference, 391, 394, 411
Algeria, 188, 196, 200, 214, 233, 272, 292
Alliances. *See* Bandwagoning, Diplomacy; *specific alliances*
Alsace, 185, 189, 190, 193, 195, 198, 200, 363
Amery, Leo, 134
Andrew, Christopher, 195, 251
Angola, 368, 391
Anschluss, 150, 153, 161, 162, 166, 170, 171, 179, 228, 242, 256
Anti-Comintern Pact, 311, 313, 326, 331
Antilles, 223
Antiwar sentiments: in Britain, 133–134, 169, 178–79; in France, 291–292, 494; in U.S., 494
Appeasement. *See* Accommodation
Armée d'Afrique, 231, 233, 237, 241

Asada Sadao, 347
Asquith, H. H., 120, 135–136
Assessment. *See* Adversaries; Information
Atomic bomb. *See* Nuclear weapons
Auriol, Vincent, 270, 276, 278, 280
Australia, 144, 332
Austria, 395–398; Bismarck Germany's victory against, 362, 376; as Germany's ally, 363, 366, 389, 392, 394, 403; navy of, 205, 209–210. *See also* Anschluss; Austria-Hungary; Triple Alliance
Austria-Hungary, 108, 109, 366
Autocratic governments: adjustment failure and, 54–55, 57n, 88–89, 493–494; in aggressor states, 316–318, 493–494, 501, 502, 504, 505–506
Autorité, L', 199
Axelrod, Robert, 45, 97

Balkan countries, 388, 389, 392, 394–396, 400, 434. *See also particular countries*
Bandwagoning, 18n, 77, 78; French concerns about Indochinese, 278–279, 283, 294; recommendations about, 507–508; U.S. concerns about, 422, 458, 470, 472, 475, 484
Bao Dai, 472
Barnhart, Michael, 326–327, 334n, 350
Barrès, Maurice, 256
B.E.F. *See* British Expeditionary Force
Belgium, 194, 220, 224–227, 239, 396–398, 400
Bem, Darly, 93n
Berger, Gordon, 317, 320
Berghahn, Volker Rolf, 401, 407, 414–415
Berlin blockade, 431–432, 437
Berlin Conference (1884), 370
Berstein, Serge, 293
Bessières, M., 189

Scalapino, Robert, 348
Schlieffen Plan, 396–399, 403–404, 415
Schumann, Robert, 283
Scott, William, 101n
Seiyukai party (Japan), 318–320
Selborne, Lord, 115, 122
Self-encirclement: as form of adjustment failure, 3, 4, 7, 15, 16, 21, 23–24, 33, 48–49, 104, 487; in Germany, 12, 26, 360, 385–417; Japanese avoidance of, 298, 315; in Japanese case, 12, 299, 325, 346, 350, 358, 489; Snyder on causes of, 55–64; Soviet fears about, 439–440, 468
Self-interest. *See* Economic interests; Military interests
Senegal, 188, 236
Serbia, 395, 396–397, 400
Shanghai, 224, 328
Sherry, Michael, 428
Shidehara Kujuro, 304–305, 307, 316–320, 351
Shimada Toshihiko, 310
Shirer, William, 245, 246
Siam, 194, 210, 211. *See also* Thailand
Singapore, 105, 144, 146, 147, 153, 156, 158, 161, 174, 181
Smith, M. Brewster, 97
Smith, Tony, 259, 293
Smith, Woodruff, 377, 411
Snyder, Jack, 18n, 28, 55–64, 93n, 316n, 355, 379n, 396, 479n
Social Democratic party (Germany), 361, 376, 378–380, 382, 383, 385, 386, 405, 408, 409, 412, 413, 488
Somaliland, 369
South Africa, 120, 368. *See also* Boer War
South America, 390
Southwest Africa, 368–369, 411, 412
Soviet Union, 9n, 429; break-up of, 2, 495–496; Britain's relations with, 152; France's relations with, 187, 228–230, 240, 241, 243, 244, 253–254, 262, 267–269, 278; Japan's relations with, 301–302, 308, 310, 312, 313, 321–323, 325–326, 329, 331, 332, 356; Nazi Germany's attacks on, 334–335; "new thinking" in, 496–499; nuclear capability of, 269, 422, 429, 432–433, 457–471, 475, 478, 484, 496; postwar conventional superiority over U.S., 427, 429–430; as postwar "policeman," 426; speculations about motivations of, 426, 435–436, 439; as U.S. adversary, 13, 418–485. *See also* Commonwealth of Independent States; Cold War; De-

tente; Eastern Europe; Nazi-Soviet Nonaggression Pact; Russia
Spanish Civil War, 225, 228, 235, 239
Spring Crisis (1948), 437, 454, 456
Stalin, Joseph, 426, 427, 435
States. *See* Declining states; Rising states; Vulnerability: effects of, on decision making
Stimson, Henry, 451–452
Storry, Richard, 305
Strategic assumptions, 66n
Strategic beliefs, 490–495; in adjustment success or failure, 13, 14, 21, 24, 33, 42–45, 48–49, 487, 495–496; of American elites, 421–424, 462, 484; of British elites, 128, 130, 154–155, 167; as decision makers' guide, 7, 8; definition of, 40–41, 66n; differentiated from strategic culture, 21–22, 28, 89; effects of vulnerability on, 68–87; of French elites, 186–187, 264–266, 277–284, 294; of German elites, 388–405; of Japanese elites, 298, 300–315, 324, 342–345, 351; Snyder on, 61–64; of Soviet "new thinkers," 496–499; testing and measuring of, 46–47, 66–68, 490; unthinkability of some, 92–95, 102, 114, 168, 300, 345–350, 358, 494; about value of empire during strategic deficiency, 19, 79–82, 94, 155–156. *See also* Cognitive variables; Lag time; Leaders
Strategic conceptions, 66n
Strategic culture, 490–495, 508–509; changes in, in France, 204; colonies not a part of Germany's, 361, 368, 381, 417, 489; definition of, 5–6, 21, 26–30, 66n; effects of vivid events on, 23, 43, 62, 89, 99–101, 491–494; elite entrapment by, 15, 21–24, 30, 59–61, 87–103, 487, 493, 495, 500; elite entrapment by, in Britain, 132, 154, 160, 168–171, 174, 182–184, 404–405, 487; elite entrapment by, in France, 187, 243, 246–248, 252, 258–260, 265–267, 285–296, 404–405, 487; elite entrapment by, in Germany, 362, 382, 385, 386, 404–406, 415–417; elite entrapment by, in Japan, 299–300, 324, 325, 346–354, 358, 404–405, 416, 487; elite entrapment and role of leaders in, 50, 60, 61, 181, 292, 383, 406; elite entrapment by, in Soviet Union, 499; elite entrapment by, in U.S., 423, 451, 455, 458, 482–485; elite propagation of, 15, 23, 90–93, 95, 101, 487, 493, 500; elite propagation of, in Britain, 89n, 90n, 131–132, 136–137, 154,

Cornell Studies in Security Affairs

edited by Robert J. Art, Robert Jervis,
and Stephen M. Walt